# WHO'S IN,
# WHO'S OUT

# WHO'S IN, WHO'S OUT

## THE

# JOURNALS

## OF

# KENNETH ROSE

### VOLUME ONE
*1944–1979*

## EDITED BY D.R. THORPE

WEIDENFELD & NICOLSON

First published in Great Britain in 2018 by Weidenfeld & Nicolson
This paperback edition published in 2022 by Weidenfeld & Nicolson
an imprint of The Orion Publishing Group Ltd
Carmelite House, 50 Victoria Embankment
London EC4Y 0DZ

An Hachette UK Company

1 3 5 7 9 10 8 6 4 2

A CIP catalogue record for this book is available from the British Library.

ISBN (Trade Paperback) 978 1 4746 0155 9
ISBN (eBook) 978 1 4746 0156 6
ISBN (Audio) 978 1 4091 8934 3

Typeset by Input Data Services Ltd, Somerset

Printed and bound in Great Britain by Clays Ltd, Elcograf S.p.A.

MIX
Paper from
responsible sources
FSC® C104740

www.weidenfeldandnicolson.co.uk
www.orionbooks.co.uk

*In memory of*
*Graham C. Greene*

# CONTENTS

*[S]o we'll live,*
*And pray, and sing, and tell old tales, and laugh*
*At gilded butterflies, and hear poor rogues*
*Talk of court news, and we'll talk with them too –*
*Who loses and who wins, who's in, who's out[.]*

*King Lear,* Act 5, Scene 3

# PREFACE

'What sort of diary should I like mine to be?' pondered Virginia Woolf. 'I should like it to resemble some deep old desk, or capacious hold-all, in which one flings a mass of odds and ends without looking them through.'[*] Such was the approach adopted by Kenneth Rose for seventy years, after he began recording the events of his life in 1944. The six million words that followed are kept in 350 boxes in the Bodleian Library, Oxford, to which institution he bequeathed the bulk of his estate. 'After the writer's death,' observed Jean Cocteau, 'reading his journal is like receiving a long letter.'[†] This 'long letter' took me two years to read and to photostat relevant material, followed by a further two years of selecting the text and supplying footnotes and linking passages.

Unlike Kenneth's early mentor Harold Nicolson, who observed ruefully, as the three volumes of his diaries were such a success when published by his son Nigel between 1966 and 1968 that he was now famous for a book that he did not realise he had written, Kenneth always intended that his journals would one day be his legacy.[‡] Of one thing he was absolutely clear: no entry should be rewritten in the light of later developments. 'A diary', wrote Tony Benn, 'is not trying to establish a reputation, but to give people an idea of what you thought at the time.'[§]

It was owing to Tony Benn – then Anthony Wedgwood Benn, later 2nd Viscount Stansgate, before campaigning successfully for the right to disclaim his peerage, and a compulsive diarist from the age of fourteen – that Kenneth began recording his experiences. The two were contemporaries in the 1940s at New College, on the same staircase in the Garden Quad. After

---

[*] Diary, 20 Apr. 1919.

[†] Diary, 7 June 1953.

[‡] Nigel Nicolson allowed K.R. to read the complete Harold Nicolson diaries from 1948 to 1952 when Nicolson was writing his life of George V. 'Reading the unpublished diaries shows me how skilful Nigel has been in separating his nuggets of gold from a considerable amount of dross.' K.R., Journal, 14 June 1976.

[§] *Daily Telegraph*, 30 Sept. 1995. Benn's published diaries eventually ran to eight volumes.

Hall one evening the pair, in customary undergraduate style, were putting the world to rights in Benn's room. The next day Kenneth visited Benn and noticed that his friend was colouring in a large sheet divided into twenty-four squares, representing hours. It was clear that this was a generalised record of the previous day. Kenneth asked Benn what the colours meant. Benn explained that black was when he was asleep, red was when he was working, and blue was when he was enjoying himself. Kenneth could not help noticing that the hours from 9 p.m. to midnight were at that moment being coloured in yellow. He asked what that colour represented. 'Oh that', replied Benn frankly, 'was a waste of time!' However, it was not a waste of time for Kenneth, who that very day resolved also to discipline himself to write up the events of his life, a task he maintained thereafter until a few days before his death on 28 January 2014. Bernard Donoughue, sometime Labour minister, a regular and accomplished diarist himself, acknowledged that 'the itch and urge to record life's events, however trivial, can never be fully suppressed'.[*] So it was with Kenneth.

Despite the many prize-winning histories that he wrote, Kenneth, like Sir Walter Scott, left as his posthumous *magnum opus* a journal. The editor of Scott's journal, Eric Anderson, wrote of Scott: 'he numbered among his friends almost all the great men of his day; his public was the entire civilized world'.[†] It is an apt description too of Kenneth at the height of his powers. William Shawcross described his journal as 'the most detailed, amusing and accurate account ever of the post-war world of the English Establishment'.[‡] His close friend, Lord Carrington, was able to read much of the journal in its original form. He recorded his impressions:

> During his long and distinguished journalistic career, Kenneth Rose had the opportunities to meet, formally and informally, most of the interesting and influential figures of the time. All welcomed and trusted him, for he was the most discreet of men. The diaries, chronicling the events of previous generations, give a unique glimpse of the personalities and preoccupations of the statesmen of that time. Harold Macmillan and Rab Butler, among other figures, are shown in a different and more informal way than their biographers have done and the differences in their approach to politics and each other are amusingly revealed. The cast of characters is long and varied: the arts, politics, business and many powerful Americans

---

[*] *Westminster Diary* (I.B. Tauris, 2016), p. ix.
[†] *The Journal of Sir Walter Scott* (Canongate Classics, 1998), p. xxiii.
[‡] *Sunday Telegraph*, 2 Feb. 2014.

and Europeans. They are a fascinating insight into the concerns of their time and those most involved. They are entertaining and funny, and, to those of us engaged in public affairs, offer a glimpse of that aspect of the people and events of the time, of which we know very little.

•

Hints are given as to the content of the journals in the thirty-six years of the 'Albany' column. Such a distinctive achievement attracted admiration, envy and parody. When Duff Hart-Davis was Literary Editor of the *Sunday Telegraph*, he organised a competition in which readers were invited to submit parodies of the paper's regular features. Cod versions of 'Albany' far outnumbered any others. The winning entry included the memorable line, 'Few other junior liberals, I imagine, ride a dromedary before breakfast.'*

In retrospect, the most interesting diarists, from Samuel Pepys to Jock Colville and later, are those who are not in high executive office themselves, but are on what Colville described as 'the fringes of power', which also applied to three of Kenneth's contemporary diarists, Harold Nicolson, Chips Channon and James Lees-Milne. It is a fitting description of Kenneth. The abiding interest of his life was in what that observer of statecraft F.S. Oliver described as 'the endless adventure of ruling men'. The unique quality of Kenneth's journals lies in the sheer range of those ruling men and women. It includes major political figures, eminent academics, fellow historians and biographers, the aristocracy and the Royal Family, opera singers and conductors, bishops and public-school headmasters. The worlds of science, medicine, commerce, industry and business are less well represented and he had no acquaintances among sportsmen, 'personalities' and people famous for being famous.

His friendships with members of the Royal Family were wide-ranging. After the war, when still in his twenties, he was a frequent guest of Princess Marina, the widowed Duchess of Kent, at her home Coppins in Iver, Buckinghamshire, and through her he came to know the young Duke of Kent, with whom he was to enjoy a lifetime of musical visits, including three trips to the Wagner Festival at Bayreuth. Princess Margaret was a figure for whom he felt much sympathy through her many difficulties. She particularly enjoyed his capacity for making people laugh.

The two royal figures whom he knew best, a unique combination, were the Duke of Windsor (he attended the last dinner party the Duke gave in January 1972 in Paris) and the Queen Mother, who was to give him so many

---

* *The Times*, 6 Feb. 2014.

insights into the character of King George V when Kenneth was researching his life of the monarch. From both figures he received intimate details of primary historical importance about the Abdication Crisis and its aftermath, duly recorded in his journals.

He was also well known and trusted in the world of the royal courtiers over the years. His many friendships also extended to foreign royalty, so much so that when he once asked his secretary at the *Sunday Telegraph*, 'Get me the King,' she had to ask, 'Which King?'[*]

Kenneth knew particularly well the political giants in the Conservative, Labour and Liberal parties, conversing intimately with the Churchill and Eden families, and all the prime ministers from Harold Macmillan onwards. When Hugh Gaitskell died unexpectedly in January 1963, his widow Dora advised his successor as Leader of the Opposition, Harold Wilson, to get to know Kenneth, as then he would find out so much of what was going on in the political world. Their friendship struck a spark from the beginning, partly owing to their respective West Yorkshire backgrounds of Huddersfield and Bradford, the latter described by J.B. Priestley as 'the right sort of town'.

Kenneth never asserted his Jewishness, and there were some close friends who did not know he was Jewish until the address given at his memorial service by Lord Waldegrave in the Chapel of the Most Excellent Order of the British Empire in St Paul's Cathedral. Though not a religious figure, he was drawn to the Anglican Church and its place in the nation's history. He noted the dates of major festivals in his diary, and attended many at St Mary Abbot's Church, Kensington.[†] Kenneth counted many of the higher clergy as friends: archbishops such as his fellow Reptonian, Michael Ramsey; Donald Coggan, at one stage Bishop of his home city of Bradford, before archiepiscopates at York and Canterbury; and Robert Runcie, with their joint links in Guards regiments. He had, though, no belief in an afterlife. In his letter to Harold Nicolson on the death of his wife Vita, he wrote: 'I wish I could write words of comfort to ease your pain. But to those of us denied a bright and tidy image of immortality there is no real consolation.'[‡]

Oxford and Cambridge loom large in the journals, with acute observations of the activities of so many of the key figures of post-war academic life: Noel Annan, Isaiah Berlin, Robert Blake, Asa Briggs, Alan Bullock (Kenneth contributed financially to the foundation of Bullock's St Catherine's College,

---

[*]  Charlotte Hofton to the editor, 2 June 2015.
[†]  The lady vicar of St Mary Abbot's conducted his funeral at Kensal Green. He had wanted no one to attend, as a memorial service would follow later. Nevertheless, Lord and Lady Waldegrave, Graham C. Greene, Sir John Nutting and D.R. Thorpe did attend.
[‡]  3 June 1962.

Oxford), F.R. Leavis, Jack Plumb, A.L. Rowse, John Sparrow, A.J.P. Taylor and Hugh Trevor-Roper, recording their achievements and feuds in the enclosed world of the Senior Common Room and High Table. Of All Souls he observed that though the Fellows changed, the guests remained the same.

The world of the public schools, in a transitional and sometimes difficult age for those institutions, also features strongly in the journals. There are uninhibited accounts of the difficulties they faced, both politically and financially. After returning from war service, Kenneth initially taught at Eton when Kenneth Wickham, a housemaster and history beak, was unexpectedly indisposed for eighteen months after an operation. Claude Elliott, the Head Master, moved quickly to secure Kenneth's services, though the latter never saw this as a long-term career. He could be sharp with the sophisticated and independent-minded boys. 'You boys, you boys, I don't know why I bother to teach you,' he once told his division in exasperation. 'Sir, you need the money,' came the reply. 'The money I get here doesn't keep me in cigars,' was his response, an episode of which Claude Elliott disapproved when he heard of it, though it rather impressed the pupils.[*] Of one of his students, Antony Armstrong-Jones, Kenneth wrote in a report, 'Armstrong-Jones may be good at something but it is nothing that we teach at Eton.'[†]

As with bishoprics, deaneries and ambassadorships, Kenneth always seemed to have advance notice of forthcoming headships; sometimes, it was said, even before governing bodies had finally made up their minds. There are perceptive portraits of Sir Robert Birley and his successor as Head Master of Eton, Anthony Chenevix-Trench, who departed the Cloisters prematurely. Kenneth asked that devoted son of Eton, Harold Macmillan, his views on the sort of man to succeed Chenevix-Trench as Head Master. 'Preferably someone in Holy Orders,' replied Macmillan, 'so that if he does not do very well at Eton he can always be made a Bishop.'[‡]

Eton became in many respects a substitute alma mater for Kenneth: not just annual fixtures such as the Fourth of June celebrations and cricket versus Harrow at Lord's, but the whole ambience of the lotus years of that enchanted valley, as he described it. Many of his closest friends, such as the Hon. Giles St Aubyn, a fellow Bayreuth pilgrim, Wilfrid Blunt, Hubert Hartley and Hubert's formidable wife, Grizel Hartley, were part of the fabric of the College over many years, and of Kenneth's life. Grizel Hartley's observant humour

---

[*] The late Hon. Giles St Aubyn to the editor, 27 Sept. 2014.

[†] Ibid.

[‡] Journal, 17 Aug. 1969. Interestingly, a question he put to the former Prime Minister whilst Chenevix-Trench was still in office.

particularly pleased him. When a haughty mother told Grizel that she hoped her daughter would marry a Moor, Grizel replied, 'What, like Desdemona?' He agreed with Grizel Hartley when she wrote, 'At Eton, the very stones cry out names.'*

Kenneth was not unaware of the idiosyncracies of Eton's ways, and when some years later he received a letter from the College offering him the very rare opportunity to become an honorary Old Etonian (an accolade he shared with the Queen Mother), his initial reaction was that it must be a practical joke. Only when he examined the envelope and saw that it bore a second-class stamp did he accept that the offer was genuine.†

He numbered among his close associates the leading diplomats and ambassadors of the day; a small number of businessmen, especially Lord King, who transformed British Airways, and Victor Rothschild, who spanned many worlds and who was Kenneth's last biographical subject; banking titans, especially those at Coutts; military figures from Field Marshal Bernard Montgomery, who later wrote to him after the war saying he did not recall him then as the two of them were on somewhat different levels; his fellow colleagues in the Welsh Guards during the war; artistic figures such as Salvador Dalí and Lucian Freud; broadcasting moguls and his fellow journalists; many of the greatest composers and musicians of his time, including Benjamin Britten, Sir Malcolm Sargent, Sir Georg Solti, Wagner's grandsons, Wieland and Wolfgang, and Sir William Walton; literary and publishing figures of note, especially his own mentor, Lord Weidenfeld, John Betjeman, Norman Douglas of *South Wind* fame, Lady Antonia Fraser, Anthony Powell and C.P. Snow. Like Harold Macmillan, he considered Snow's novel *The Masters* to convey acute insights into human nature. His journals and letters are punctuated with shrewd assessments. He much admired Arnold Bennett, noting that 'other novelists had written about industrial life – Dickens, Disraeli, Mrs Gaskell. For them it was something new and terrifying. For Bennett it was home.'‡ Of Henry James, he noted that nothing <u>important</u> ever happens, but he holds the attention of the reader for 500 pages.§ He thought that H.G. Wells's *The New Machiavelli* 'quite his best novel'.¶

London clubland – he was a member of the Beefsteak and Pratt's – mattered

---

* Ibid., 12 May 2010. P.S.H. Lawrence (ed.), *Grizel: Grizel Hartley Remembered* (Michael Russell, 1991), p. 110.
† K.R. to the editor, 11 Jan. 2011.
‡ Journal, 28 June 1984.
§ Letter to Sir Philip Magnus, later Magnus-Allcroft, 4 Feb. 1964.
¶ Journal, 8 Oct. 1949.

greatly to him. He called the Beefsteak 'the sixth form of the Garrick'.* In the legal world, two of his longest-standing friendships were with Lord Goddard, the Lord Chief Justice (though, unlike Goddard, Kenneth was always resolutely opposed to capital punishment), and Lord Shawcross, who was the leading British prosecution counsel in the post-war Nuremberg Trials. He was with Sir Brian Horrocks when Horrocks received the surrender of Heligoland in 1945.

He had an eye for quirky details, recording that whenever Lord King, Chairman of the Belvoir Hunt, saw a fox he shouted out, 'Charles James'! At a Gentleman versus Players match at Lord's Kenneth noted that a bishop was asked to remove his pectoral cross, as it was dazzling a batsman. He had close links to many of the oldest families in the land, and friendships with prominent Americans and Europeans. His interests were legion and in many cases unexpected. He was fascinated by astronomy and eclipses and was a regular at the Hastings Chess Congress. His *Times* obituary recalled that 'it was not a party unless Kenneth Rose was there'.†

J.M. Keynes wrote of Edwin Montagu, the Liberal politician: 'I never knew a male person of big mind who was more addicted to gossip than Edwin Montagu. He could not bear to be out of things.'‡ The same applied to Kenneth, who once confessed: 'I find it difficult to let a good story pass me by.'§ When an acquaintance once disparaged 'gossip' to Kenneth, he responded: 'The cobbler must not criticise leather.'¶

Kenneth was not a mere fair-weather friend, but was especially supportive to those who fell into difficulties, notably Jeremy Thorpe and Jonathan Aitken. Sarah, Duchess of York, to whom he wrote his last letter, was also someone for whom he made much time. He was very good with children and observant of their ways, noting how Sarah's daughters said grace before their nursery tea, though when they called him 'Ken' he commented that the only person to do likewise was Sybil, Marchioness of Cholmondeley.

Without family commitments and with no dependants as a lifelong bachelor, Kenneth was immensely generous to institutions that he loved – Repton, New College, the Welsh Guards, Eton College, the London Library, his two clubs and the Bodleian Library. When by chance he heard from a headmaster of Repton that a promising pupil would not be able to stay on after O-levels

---

\* Journal, 7 Oct. 1990.

† 31 Jan. 2014.

‡ *The Collected Writings of John Maynard Keynes* vol. X, *Essays in Biography*, 1933 (Macmillan/CUP for the Royal Economic Society, 1972), p. 42.

§ Journal, 4 Sept. 1966.

¶ Ibid., 12 Dec. 1965.

owing to his parents' financial difficulties, he privately undertook to pay the school fees himself, anonymous philanthropy he repeated on more than one occasion over the years. Many of his friends who fell on hard times he helped with thousands of pounds, never wanting repayment. Politically he was a Whig, not a Tory, always preferring Gladstone to Disraeli. He never drove a car, owned a computer or a mobile phone. As an author of highly regarded books, his main characteristic was his thoroughness. His famous book on Lord Curzon and his circle was published in 1969, but he had begun researching it in the late 1940s.

•

Kenneth Vivian Rose was born on 15 November 1924 (a birthday, as he noted, that he shared with Nye Bevan, who was born in 1897), the second son of Dr Jacob Rosenwige, a distinguished surgeon of 348 Wakefield Road, Bradford and his wife Ada, née Silverstein. His mother trained as a pharmacologist and served in the Voluntary Aid Detachment in both world wars. His parents 'anglicised' their names to Jack and Ada Rose, a practice not uncommon at the time of covert, and at times not so covert, anti-Semitism. Kenneth's elder brother, Toby, who died of cancer in his early thirties in April 1953, also followed his father into the medical profession after wartime service in the Royal Navy, becoming an expert on the treatment of infantile paralysis. Kenneth endowed a medical prize at St Catherine's College, Oxford, for biological sciences in memory of his brother. This family background led Kenneth to publish a monograph on William Harvey, the discoverer of the circulation of the blood, in 1978.

Kenneth went to Repton School in September 1939. 'I remain grateful to all those who taught me so well and for the friendship and laughter of those days,' he later wrote of his schooldays. A precursor of his later career came in the form of his editorship of The Reptonian. A stalwart of the debating society, in February 1941 he proposed the motion that 'In the opinion of this House, communism is the only solution to the present social and economic chaos in Europe.' Not surprisingly, the motion was lost by eighty votes to fifteen. Unlike many of his contemporaries, he was never a 'professional' old boy and later declined offers to become President of the Old Reptonian Association. When his research into Lord Curzon's life took him to nearby Kedleston, he strained for a glimpse from the train of the needle-sharp spire in whose shadow Reptonians have lived for centuries. 'On the platform of Derby Station, too, at certain times of the year were piles of trunks labelled "Repton via Willington". Sometimes I have felt a little glow of nostalgia for my schooldays, but have generally preferred them to remain a distant prospect.'*

Though Kenneth had enjoyed Repton, his scholarship to read Modern History at New College in 1942 introduced him to a world that broadened his horizons. His time there fell into two phases, as he went away on war service with the Welsh Guards before returning to complete his degree. The contemporaries he met became lifelong friends – Lord Altrincham, later John Grigg; Tony Benn; Sir David Butler, the pre-eminent psephologist; Richard Ollard, historian and author; Sir John Smith, later MP for the Cities of London and Westminster, an eminent diarist himself;† and the distinguished biographer and author Philip Ziegler. Kenneth learned much from these friendships. Tony Benn and John Grigg, in that order, were the first two hereditary peers to disclaim their titles on 31 July 1963 following the passage that day of the Peerage Act that was eventually the means by which the Earl of Home became Prime Minister as Sir Alec Douglas-Home in October that year. It happened that Kenneth dined with John Grigg and Tony Benn on the evening they both disclaimed, an arrangement made some days before, none knowing what an historic day it would be. Oxford remained an important part of the rest of his life and he delighted in recording details of the university.

Kenneth remained immensely proud that he was able to experience action in the later stages of the war in the Welsh Guards, though his preliminary spell at Staff College saw him suffer bullying and anti-Semitic prejudice. He never forgot the support he was given at this time by Matthew Ridley, the 4th Viscount.

Kenneth was a latter-day Thomas Creevey (1768–1838), an observer of the doings of others rather than a participant. Creevey's fame derived from the extensive letters he wrote to his stepdaughter, Elizabeth Ord. No contemporary was a more important historical source on the appearance, looks and activities of royal personages and the most important political figures of his age. Kenneth was greatly influenced by this example. He also derived intense pleasure from the political diary of Sir Edward Hamilton (1847–1908), Gladstone's Private Secretary, which he kept from 1880, when he joined the secretariat in Downing Street, until 1906. The work comprises fifty-four volumes, now in the British Library. Creevey and Hamilton were, in their

---

* K.R., *One Boy's War, 1939–1942* (printed privately, 2006). *The Reptonian*, Mar. 1941 (no. 462, vol. LXII).

† The John Smith diaries, kept in Eton Coll. Library, contain many insightful references to K.R. over the years. The author is grateful to Sir John Smith's widow for privileged access to these closed volumes.

different ways, model influences on Kenneth. Dudley Bahlman's notice of Sir Edward Hamilton in the *Oxford Dictionary of National Biography* describes him as possessing 'diligence, accuracy, discretion, tact, and above all an ability to write clear summaries of complex questions',[*] attributes that were echoed in Kenneth's style and practice, something he had gleaned from his work, including intelligence matters, for the British Council in Rome and Naples from 1948 to 1951.

Kenneth's last years were blighted by recurrent cancer, though he died following a serious fall at home. The last person to visit him in hospital was the Duke of Kent, who was to read the lesson at his memorial service on 8 May 2014, a few weeks after he had gone to Paradise 'by way of Kensal Green'.[†] Lord Carrington reminded the congregation of Kenneth's lucid, elegant prose by reading a passage from his masterpiece, the life of King George V, which characteristically illuminated his careful scholarship.

---

[*] Vol. 24 (OUP, 2004), p. 785.
[†] G.K. Chesterton, 'The Rolling English Road'.

# ACKNOWLEDGEMENTS

My greatest debt is to Kenneth, who entrusted me some years ago with the task of editing his journals and letters. We had spoken a lot about what this would entail and he had been hoping to work with me, at least initially, on the vast project. Sadly, his sudden and unexpected death at the age of eighty-nine in January 2014 prevented this. However, much preliminary work had been done.

I am indebted to many people for their help and advice on so many aspects, particularly his executor, Lord Waldegrave of North Hill, who has supported me constantly throughout the process of selecting material from the 350 boxes in the Bodleian Library. My publisher at Weidenfeld & Nicolson, Alan Samson, and his team, Celia Hayley, Linden Lawson and Simon Wright, have been a mine of information and valued advice regarding editing the text, the publishing house being not only Kenneth's, but also a specialist in publishing some of the most important diaries of the twentieth century. The late Graham C. Greene, who has been a mentor to me for over thirty years, has again been a valuable source of encouragement. I am very grateful to Sir Eric Anderson for reading the complete text in typescript and for his valuable comments.

My work would not have been possible without the skilful assistance of Richard Ovenden, Librarian of the Bodleian, and his dedicated team: Theodora Boorman, Dr Chris Fletcher, Michael Hughes and Oliver House.

I value greatly the support given to me by His Royal Highness the Duke of Kent, a friend of Kenneth's for over sixty years.

Other friends, colleagues, godchildren, secretaries, authors and publishers whose support has been invaluable include:

Tomás Almeida, Lady Anderson, Christopher Arnold, Jane Birkett, the late Tony Benn, Michael Bloch, Sir David Butler, Peter Catterall, Hannah Cox, Professor David Dilks, Christopher Everett, Helen Ewing, David Faber, Lady Antonia Fraser, Cary Gilbart-Smith, Dean Godson, Field Marshal Lord Guthrie of Craigiebank, Marie-Louise Hamilton, Duff Hart-Davis, Charles Hastings, Louise Hayman, Dr Simon Heffer, Lord Hennessy of Nympsfield,

Charlotte Hofton, Robert Holroyd, Graham and Vanessa Jones, Robert Lacey, Nicolas Marden, Michael Meredith, Charles Moore, Ferdinand Mount, the late John Julius Norwich, Sir John Nutting, Daniel Poole, Lady Prudence Penn, Angela Reed, the late Brian Rees, Natasha Rees, Viscount Ridley, Professor Jane Ridley, Professor Dr Andrew Roberts, the late Hon. Giles St Aubyn, Nicholas Shakespeare, the Hon. William Shawcross, Anthony Shone, Stephen Shuttleworth, Anton Smith, Lady Christian Smith, Rachel Smyth, Christopher Spence, Paul Stevens, the Hon. James Stourton, Joanna Taylor, Robert Tyerman, David Twiston Davies, Hugo Vickers, Professor Geoffrey Warner, the late Lord Weidenfeld, Tom Wheare, Nicholas Winston, the Revd John Witheridge, Ruth Winstone and Philip Ziegler.

The Betjeman estate has given permission to use John Betjeman's drawing of Huddersfield Station.

The Carrington estate has given permission for the inclusion of Lord Carrington's description of Kenneth Rose.

# The 1940s

*The defining moment of Kenneth's war came on Sunday 18 June 1944 when a V1 flying bomb, known as a doodlebug, destroyed the Guards' Chapel at Wellington Barracks during the Sunday-morning service just as the choir was starting the Sung Eucharist; 121 soldiers and civilians were killed and 141 others seriously injured in the most serious V1 attack on London of the war. Hours later, the altar candles in the six silver candlesticks given to the Guards' Chapel by King George VI in 1938 were seen still to be alight. Kenneth was only nineteen at this time, his studies at New College interrupted by war service. Only by the chance of the Guards weekend rotas was he not in the chapel itself when it was destroyed.*

*Like other newly commissioned young officers in the Brigade of Guards, Kenneth had been posted to Wellington Barracks as an Ensign of the King's Guard before joining an active service battalion. The Westminster Garrison Battalion, as it was called, contained detachments from each of the five regiments of Foot Guards, Grenadiers, Coldstream, Scots, Irish and Welsh. The Commanding Officer of the composite battalion, Lieutenant-Colonel Lord Edward Hay, had drawn up weekend leave lists for which Kenneth was overdue. The twelve days since the D-Day landings had been ones of intense pressure. By chance, Kenneth and John Grigg were not at the service. Their unwitting saviour was killed just as he had finished reading the lesson. Later Kenneth, still engaged in rescue work, witnessed Churchill weeping as he stood on a heap of rubble, gazing at the ruins of the chapel.*

*The next day Kenneth sent his parents in Bradford an account of the happenings, omitting some of the dreadful scenes he had witnessed as a member of the rescue party. Only to others did he later recall some of the grimmer details. Every 18 June thereafter, up to his last in 2013, he put at the head of the page of his journal, not the fact that it was the anniversary of the Battle of Waterloo, but 'Guards' Chapel Day'.*

## 19 June 1944, letter to parents

When I heard that Wellington Barracks had been bombed, I left immediately and found an appalling state of affairs. I should have preferred not to tell you anything about this, except that if I do not tell you what has really happened, you might pick up an exaggerated version of the incident. Shortly after eleven o'clock on Sunday morning one of the fiendish German pilotless planes crashed onto the Guards' Chapel here a few minutes after the morning service had begun. Casualties are horrible – practically nobody escaped without being seriously injured, and most people were killed outright. We lost many officers, and the Battalion is heartbroken about it. Those who were killed include our dear old Commanding Officer, Lord Edward Hay* and Colonel Ivan Cobbold,† a delightful Lt-Col on General Eisenhower's staff. There were many others killed whom you would not know.

As soon as I had arrived, I was asked to lead a company of guardsmen in rescue and clearing work. We worked all through the night with the help of arc-lamps, but managed to get nobody out alive.‡ The civil defence workers were splendid, and did an immense amount. Several high officers, including the GOC Brigade of Guards, came to help.

I cannot tell you how much I hate giving you this sad news on your Silver Wedding but that is how things seem to happen nowadays. It is not only the lost lives which we miss so much; the Guards' Chapel, a memorial known to guardsmen in every corner of the world, is now completely destroyed.

*As one who passed 'with a high grading' in his training at Staff College, Kenneth was soon attached to the company of Sir Brian Horrocks when he experienced the German surrender at Heligoland. Much of his job in the late 1940s with the British Council in Rome and Naples included sensitive intelligence work with the Italian navy after the peace treaty of 1947, and so he did not include details in his journals.*

## 10 May 1945

During the past few days the Division has been busy with its last war operation. It consisted of an advance of about fifty miles up to a North German

---

* (1888–1944); served at the Paris Peace Conference 1918–19; Staff Capt. to Gen. Sir Edmund Ironside 1921; Military Secretary to Sir Herbert Samuel 1921–3.

† (1897–1944), brewer; founder of Ipswich Town football club; m. Lady Blanche Cavendish, dau. of 9th Duke of Devonshire, in the Guards' Chapel in 1919.

‡ Astonishingly, after this letter was sent some survivors were found under the rubble.

port to accept the surrender of the 7th German Paratroop Division. It was an extraordinary sight to see this broken army pouring into the area to lay down their arms – most of them sitting with their few miserable possessions on horse-drawn transport, the officers travelling in high-powered Mercedes looking very Prussian and sour. They hardly looked the cream of the German army, and gave no trouble at all about the surrender. As a precaution we surrounded the area with tanks.

### 13 May 1945
The Prime Minister has just finished speaking on the wireless – it was a good speech, although I doubt if he will ever again reach his 1940 standard of oratory.

### 10 November 1945
I have spent this week mostly listening to debates in the House of Commons – Anthony Eden got me tickets for a seat under the Gallery. I especially enjoyed a debate on education, the speakers including Eden, R.A. Butler,[*] Kenneth Lindsay[†] and Ellen Wilkinson.[‡] I thought the speeches of backbenchers to be of a far higher standard generally than in the last Parliament.

### 3 November 1946
To a party given by Julian Faber[§] at his flat. Found myself in a corner next to Harold Macmillan the politician. He told me all about the new Conservative Party, 'a party of youth', as he put it. I had drunk enough to remark to him that the singular fact about youth parties was that they were organised entirely by the middle-aged. Collapse of stout party.

---

* Richard Austen Butler, Baron Butler of Saffron Walden (1902–82), Conservative politician. President of the Board of Education 1941–4; Minister of Education 1944–5; Chancellor of the Exchequer 1951–5; Leader of the House of Commons 1955–61; Home Secretary 1957–62; Foreign Secretary 1963–4.
† (1897–1991); National Independent MP for Kilmarnock 1933–45; Independent MP for the Combined English Universities 1945–50; Parliamentary Secretary to the Board of Education 1937–40.
‡ (1891–1947); entered the House of Commons in 1924 as MP for Middlesbrough East, the only woman Labour MP in that Parliament. Winifred Holtby's headmistress Sarah Burton in the novel *South Riding* is partly based on her. In 1945, by then MP for Jarrow, she became Minister of Education in Attlee's government.
§ (1917–2002); Commanding Officer in the Welsh Guards, where K.R. served under him.

## 13 November 1948

I have been reading *Eyeless in Gaza*, which reads exactly like a brilliant parody of an Aldous Huxley novel.[*]

---

[*] Aldous Huxley (1894–1963) published *Eyeless in Gaza* in 1936. Its title is taken from Milton's *Samson Agonistes*. The novel contains a scene in which a dog falls from an aeroplane on to a couple making love on a flat roof, splattering them with blood.

# The Early 1950s

*When Kenneth worked for the British Council in Rome and Naples between 1949 and 1951 he struck up a friendship with Sir Max Beerbohm (1872 –1956), the caricaturist and writer. He was a wry observer of the foibles of his time, a factor that made him of particular fascination for Kenneth.*

*On his return from intelligence work in Italy, of which he was justly proud, Kenneth settled into what would be his principal occupation as a journalist, joining the* Daily Telegraph. *He was on the 'Peterborough' column for nine years. 'It is great fun,' he wrote on 16 June 1952. Alongside this he continued with his detailed research for his biography of Lord Curzon.*

## 26 March 1950

I visited Sir Max and Lady Beerbohm at the Villa Chiaro, Rapallo. First impression of Max – small, apple-cheeks, beautiful eyes, long white hair at back, full white moustache – gives impression of Lloyd George. Wore spats, double-breasted waistcoat, shirt with tiny buttons on collar. Voice not at all like the delicate affectation of wireless; but frequent use of 'don't ye know'. When sitting, looks small & neat & vivacious. We have excellent tea. M.B. takes wine instead of tea. We talk about conversation & oratory. M.B. says Wilde is best conversationalist he ever knew – had nice manners and was not a monologuist. George Bernard Shaw was best for debating, and Linky Cecil[*] for public oratory. M.B. then gave imitations of Haldane, Rosebery & Asquith making speeches. We talk about Curzon.[†] M.B. says he had vulgar side – wanted to be made a Duke; drew up complete plan for funeral, lists of guests etc. on death bed. M.B. says that Asquith behaved weakly to dismiss

---

[*] Lord Hugh Cecil, Baron Quickswood (1869–1956), one of the subjects of K.R.'s *The Later Cecils* (Weidenfeld & Nicolson, 1975).
[†] George Nathaniel Curzon, Marquess Curzon of Kedleston (1859–1925). Viceroy of India 1898–1905; Foreign Secretary 1919–24; one of the few men born as a commoner to ascend all the steps of the peerage except a dukedom.

Haldane in World War I – one of his few mean actions.[*] Spoke highly of Joseph Chamberlain, who said that he would make things hum if he were at the Foreign Office. M.B. shows me interesting frescoes done by him of leading political & literary figures in early twentieth century – Asquith, Arthur James Balfour, Lytton Strachey, etc. Says that Edward VII was too coarse to appreciate any of them. I ask him where his cartoons are now of Edward VII. He says in Royal Library at Windsor, but this is to be kept secret. We talk of George V & Harold Nicolson's forthcoming biography.[†] M.B. says George V was a kind man.

We talk of the Kaiser: his first words on arriving in exile to stay with the Bentincks: 'Now can I have a nice cup of tea.' Max says the Kaiser had great presence and personal charm, and that everybody who met him was impressed.

We talk about Churchill and painting – 'His work is very professional, but uninteresting,' says Max. He points to the drawing table – 'I have done most of my cartoons there. This inoffensive table has given much offence.'

We talk about Oxford and *Zuleika Dobson*, but we cannot decide exactly where Judas College is. Max says Oxford is now totally ruined, and that he advises people not to send sons there, but to Cambridge.

## 13 July 1950

Conversation with Count Sforza[‡] at Palazzo Chigi, Rome. I asked Sforza for an estimate of Curzon's character and work. 'I liked and respected Curzon, but I have never known a man of such blue blood who was so great a snob. Curzon worshipped titles, orders and decorations.'

I asked Sforza whether he had ever spoken to Curzon on subjects other than politics. 'Generally I enjoy talking to British statesmen on outside subjects. I have talked to Bonar Law[§] of the Canadian temperament, and to Ernest Bevin[¶] on religion. But Curzon was a monument, and one cannot speak informally to a monument!'

---

[*] Richard, Viscount Haldane (1856–1928), dismissed as Lord Chancellor by Asquith in May 1915 and at once made a Member of the Order of Merit by George V, according to K.R., 'to solace an ill-used Lord Chancellor'. K.R., *King George V* (Weidenfeld & Nicolson, 1983), p. 260.
[†] *King George V: His Life and Reign* (Constable, 1952). K.R. had access to all Harold Nicolson's research notes for his own, later biography of George V.
[‡] Count Carlo Sforza (1872–1952), Italian diplomat and anti-Fascist politician. Minister for Foreign Affairs 1947–51.
[§] Andrew Bonar Law (1858–1923), Conservative Party statesman and Prime Minister 1922–3.
[¶] (1881–1951), trade unionist and Labour politician; a key figure in the founding of the Transport and General Workers' Union (TGWU), Jan. 1922. Minister of Labour 1940–45; Foreign Secretary 1945–51.

I asked Sforza how far one should take L.G.'s constant interference into consideration. 'It is impossible to judge Curzon alone, because L.G. constantly opposed him. I know of no parallel case in which a PM so attacked his Foreign Minister. There was an immense difference in temperament. L.G. was an adventurer and loved confidential talks and secret agents. L.G. wanted his revenge on the upper classes.'

We discussed the conference at Lausanne, 1923. 'To achieve success, a conference with a beaten enemy must be quick. But Curzon was very verbose, and while he talked, the Turks grew stronger.'

### 1 May 1951

Conversation with Leo Amery* in Eaton Square about Curzon. Amery saw little of him before World War I when the university was appealing for a large fund. Curzon was Chairman of the committee, and asked all its members to write begging letters to friends. Two or three weeks later he summoned them again, and like a schoolmaster asked each person in turn how many they had written. One replied three, another two, etc. And Amery was proud at having sent twenty (dictated) letters. Curzon looked round the committee in scorn. 'I have written 3,000 letters,' he said, 'and all in my own hand!'

Curzon played a great part in bringing about conscription, but by the time he became Foreign Secretary in October 1919 he had lost his grip, and could only argue or write memoranda, never taking bold and immediate action.

Amery was a Secretary to Cabinet Committees. First Cabinet he ever attended was in December 1916. Curzon cleared his throat and began, 'You may not be aware—'. At this point he was interrupted by Balfour. 'It's all right, George, we all know you have written a monumental work on Persia!'†

In the Conservative Party, Curzon was mistrusted, e.g. House of Lords reform. Amery wanted Asquith to make extra peers and so be forced to reform compositions of the second chamber. But Curzon wanted exclusive H of Lords. In coalition from 1919 to 1922, the government was really in the

---

* Leopold Amery (1873–1955), Conservative politician. Colonial Secretary 1924–9; a crucial figure in the appointment of Stanley Baldwin in 1923 and Winston Churchill in 1940.

† *Persia and the Persian Question*, 2 vols (Longmans, Green & Co., 1892). In his journal for 5 Mar. 1955 K.R. noted: 'At Forbes and Francis, booksellers by Windsor Bridge, buy Curzon's *Persia and the Persian Question* in 2 volumes. I have had my eye on them for some time.' K.R. ensured that friends had something of his to remember him by: he gave these two volumes to the current editor.

hands of four men – Winston, Lloyd George, F.E. Smith[*] and Austen Chamberlain.[†] Curzon was rather out of it, and so felt no doubts about leaving coalition in 1922.

Amery related the important part he played in choice of Baldwin as PM in 1923. Amery had gone skiing and met Bonar Law passing through Paris on his return. Amery was told by Bonar Law that he must shortly resign premiership [owing to ill health]. Back in London as First Lord of the Admiralty, Amery was visited by Bridgeman,[‡] who had just seen Salisbury. Bridgman told Amery that Curzon was definitely to be PM. This was not unexpected as Curzon had been presiding over Cabinets in absence of B.L. (although B.L. would have preferred Cave[§] to do so). Amery did not think Curzon suitable on personal grounds as PM. He went round to see Salisbury, who confessed that he had not previously thought that any alternative to Curzon was possible. But eventually he agreed to accepting Baldwin. Amery and Bridgeman immediately went round to Stamfordham's[¶] house: he was already on way to Palace. They caught up with him in St James's Park. There, standing for about twenty minutes, they convinced Stamfordham, and Curzon's fate was sealed. Later that day Balfour arrived and suggested that Curzon being a peer should be offered as reason for choice of Baldwin: real reason was Curzon's domineering temperament. Unfortunately, Stamfordham sent a clumsily worded telegram to Curzon, which caused him much unnecessary distress. Curzon was wonderfully magnanimous to Baldwin. Also to Amery, who had thought it his duty to deny Curzon's greatest ambition.

---

[*] (1872–1930), 1st Earl of Birkenhead, lawyer and Conservative politician. Lord Chancellor 1919–22, most renowned for his part in the Irish Treaty of 1921.

[†] Sir Austen Chamberlain (1863–1937). Chancellor of the Exchequer 1903–5 and 1919–21, leader of the Conservative Party in the House of Commons 1921–2, Foreign Secretary 1924–9. Awarded the Nobel Peace Prize after the Treaty of Locarno in 1925.

[‡] William, 1st Viscount Bridgeman (1846–1935), Conservative politician. Home Secretary 1922–4. A key figure in the break-up of the Lloyd George coalition in 1922, and in Baldwin's succession to the premiership in 1923. Balfour had been summoned to London from his sick bed in Sheringham to advise Stamfordham. On his return to the house party in Norfolk one of the ladies, agog for news, asked, 'And will dear George be chosen?' 'No, dear George will not,' replied Balfour. 'Oh, I am so sorry,' said the lady. 'He will be terribly disappointed.' 'I don't know,' said Balfour, remembering the wealth of Curzon's second wife. 'After all, even if he has lost his hope of glory, he still possesses the means of Grace.' D.R. Thorpe, *The Uncrowned Prime Ministers* (Darkhorse Publishing, 1980), p. 149.

[§] George, Viscount Cave (1856–1928), lawyer and Conservative politician. Home Secretary 1917–19, Lord Chancellor 1922–8.

[¶] Arthur Bigge, Baron Stamfordham (1849–1931), courtier. PS to Queen Victoria 1895–1901 and to George V 1910–31. His grandson, Michael Adeane, was PS to Elizabeth II 1954–72.

## 8 June 1951

Conversation with Philip Swinton.[*] Lloyd George conducted a foreign policy separate from that of Curzon. L.G. used to consult Swinton over foreign affairs without informing Curzon. L.G. knew Curzon would never resign.

Break up of coalition in 1922. Did Curzon ever tell L.G. he would vote against him at the Carlton Club? Perhaps the last straw for Curzon was when an important telegram to Australia was drafted at Chequers without Curzon being present. Chanak[†] really brought discontent v. L.G. to a head. Austen Chamberlain was loyal to L.G. 'A.C. was the straightest man in the world. If he had found the Goat[‡] in bed with his wife, he would not have believed his eyes'! Balfour told Swinton that he could never forgive Curzon for having gone v. L.G. in 1922. Yet Curzon owed no loyalty to L.G. after way he had been treated.

Swinton was devoted to Bonar Law, and instead of leaving London on Friday nights he would stay to play bridge with Bonar Law. Once Bonar Law asked him for an election slogan. Swinton replied: 'We don't want to be buggered about!' Bonar Law commented: 'The sentiment is perfect, but the phraseology is open to improvement.'

Of Beaverbrook,[§] Swinton said: 'He is rarely trammelled by truth. Bonar Law was the only man Beaverbrook was ever loyal to.'

Swinton was recently discussing some parliamentary tactics with Winston. Swinton said that there were two good ways of leading a party – either to intervene like a Guards Division going into battle; or else to sit back and do nothing, like Baldwin. 'You don't want me to be like Baldwin, do you?' said Winston. 'Well,' replied Swinton, 'you fought him for ten years, and lost every round!' 'That is profoundly true,' observed Winston.

---

[*] Philip Cunliffe-Lister, 1st Earl of Swinton (1884–1972). Conservative MP for Hendon 1918–35; Director of Overseas Trade Dept. 1921–2; Cabinet Minister under Bonar Law, Stanley Baldwin, Ramsay MacDonald, Neville Chamberlain and Winston Churchill.

[†] The Chanak Crisis was a war scare in Sept. 1922 between Britain and Turkey. The coalition Conservatives did not want a war and the mishandling of the crisis contributed to Lloyd George's downfall in Oct. 1922.

[‡] Baldwin's nickname for Lloyd George. Baldwin said one of his main political aims was 'to dish the Goat'. Early in World War I, Kitchener said that he tried to avoid sharing military secrets with the Cabinet, as they would tell their wives, apart from Lloyd George, who would tell someone else's wife.

[§] William Maxwell Aitken, 1st Baron Beaverbrook (1879–1964), newspaper proprietor and politician. A key figure in propelling Bonar Law into the Conservative leadership in 1911, and into 10 Downing Street in 1922. Member of the War Cabinet 1940; Minister of Aircraft Production 1940–41.

## 13 March 1952

Saw the Earl of Halifax* about Curzon. Curzon was pathetic in his later years. He was often overruled by the Cabinet and that hurt him very much.

When Curzon laughed he did so from the waist and shook all over.

One day the Cabinet was discussing Oswald Mosley. Curzon expressed the hope that the Cabinet would not be deflected from its proper course by 'the conduct of my sinister son-in-law'.†

Even if Curzon had been in the House of Commons in 1923 he would still not have become Prime Minister. He was too unpopular in his own party.

Halifax agrees that Chamberlain wanted him, Halifax, to be Prime Minister in 1940 – 'but this was a stupid plan for a variety of reasons'.

The day Curzon died in 1925, Halifax met Lord Salisbury‡ in the street and said to him: 'Were you a great friend of Curzon?' Salisbury replied: 'Yes, I suppose I was, if he had any.'

Halifax once casually mentioned to Curzon that he was going to look at the châteaux on the Loire. The next day he received sheets and sheets and sheets of information about them in Curzon's own hand.

## 22 March 1952

The other day a friend took me to Harrow – quite the ugliest school I have ever seen, & such parents!

*After he had concluded his spell with the British Council Kenneth made a decisive career change when he joined the* Daily Telegraph *in June 1952. Initially he shared a room with the celebrated cricket commentator E.W. Swanton, and among his colleagues was Bill Deedes, later Editor of the paper, an important figure in his life, with whom he worked on the 'Peterborough' column. When Bill (by then Lord) Deedes died Kenneth wrote to Deedes's son Jeremy: 'So the great warrior has at last departed for Valhalla, leaving us all impoverished.'§*

---

* Edward Wood, 1st Earl of Halifax (1881–1959). Viceroy of India 1925–31; Foreign Secretary 1938–40; George VI's favoured candidate for the premiership in May 1940; Ambassador to the US 1940–46.

† Sir Oswald Mosley (1896–1980), 6th Bt of Ancoats, politician. Chancellor of the Duchy of Lancaster in the Labour government 1929–31; founder of the New Party, and later the British Union of Fascists. His first wife was Curzon's daughter, Lady Cynthia Mosley (1898–1933).

‡ James Gascoyne-Cecil, 4th Marquess of Salisbury (1861–1947).

§ K.R. letter to the Hon. Jeremy Deedes, 20 Aug. 2007. Deedes's memorial service was in the rebuilt Guards' Chapel.

## 24 August 1952

Conversation with Sir Thomas Beecham[*] at his Edinburgh hotel, after hearing him conduct the Royal Philharmonic Orchestra. He drinks iced milk, and I am given sherry and a cigar at 5 p.m.

Much talk about politicians and music. On Curzon – 'A great statesman, the last of the statesmen. Sometimes, owing to fatigue, he was reticent, restrained and brief. In congenial company, he shone. The three best conversationalists in England were Curzon, Balfour and Harry Cust.[†] Delius was good in argument. George Bernard Shaw did not shine in conversation.

Neither A.J.B. nor Curzon were good at public speaking. Lansdowne[‡] was the worst of all at it – but the most charming. Winston Churchill spoke as if with pebbles in his mouth, and had an irritating trick of letting his voice rise at the end of a sentence.

What a pity Curzon did not succeed Bonar Law as PM. Instead, there was Baldwin, who led us onto the rocks, and Neville Chamberlain, who led us into the quicksands.

No English politician except A.J.B. has ever really loved music. Neville Chamberlain? No. He loved to preside over committees for municipal musical projects in Birmingham, but he never <u>loved</u> music. A shocking old humbug.

## 27 August 1952

Bill Deedes[§] tells stories in the office about Evelyn Waugh. He wrote *Black Mischief* in Ethiopia when at coronation of Haile Selassie. Waugh covered the coronation for *The Times*, but he sent his copy by land post – it arrived weeks after the event. Deedes also describes how Winston sold documents of his wartime premiership to syndicate including Camrose[¶] for £250,000 therefore no tax payable. He then edited them free of charge!

---

[*] Sir Thomas Beecham, 2nd Bt (1879–1961), conductor, impresario and founder of the Royal Philharmonic Orchestra.

[†] (1861–1917), Conservative politician, journalist and member of the social coterie 'The Souls' (see p. 33n). He had several affairs and was the father by Violet Manners of Lady Diana Manners, later Lady Diana Cooper.

[‡] Henry Petty-Fitzmaurice, 5th Marquess of Lansdowne (1845–1927). Liberal statesman, later Conservative; Governor General of Canada 1883–8; Viceroy of India 1888–94; Secretary of State for Foreign Affairs 1900–05.

[§] William Deedes, Baron Deedes (1913–2007), Conservative politician. MP for Ashford 1950–74; Cabinet Minister under Harold Macmillan. Editor of the *Daily Telegraph* 1974–86.

[¶] William Ewert Berry, 1st Viscount Camrose (1879–1954), a key figure in the history of the *Daily Telegraph* from 1927 until his death.

## 11 September 1952

A Rugby master, discussing an essay in 1899 by the young William Temple,[*] the future Archbishop of Canterbury, asked him: 'Are you not a little out of your depth here?' 'Perhaps, sir,' was the confident reply, 'but I can swim.'

## 24 October 1952

Bill Deedes tells me that at a meeting of Labour Party at which Bevanites were defeated by 188 votes to 51, Bevan[†] turned the meeting against himself by saying: 'If you do not support me, the party will lose the next election. This will not matter for me. I am young. But you (pointing at old trade union leaders) will go on the dole again.' Great fury aroused.

## 17 November 1952

A story I heard about Lord Kemsley.[‡] When first given a peerage he was asked what title he would like to take. He replied 'Lord Farnham-Royal', the name of his estate. The Crown Office informed him that he could not have the title of 'Lord Farnham-Royal', but might take that of 'Lord Farnham-Common'.

## 4 December 1952

I heard the censure debate in the House of Commons. Winston sat with oriental impassiveness listening to debate & only showed signs of life when he got up to speak. Rather a rubbery look on his face. Still deaf – when speaking & somebody raised a point of order, Harry Crookshank[§] had to pull his coat to tell him to sit down. Commons had a crowded eighteenth-century atmosphere & sense of expectation. Best crack came from Crookshank – said that unlike rules of cricket twelfth man could be put on to bowl. Reference was to Nye Bevan, who just managed to get himself elected as twelfth man of Socialist Shadow Cabinet, & was making his first

---

[*] (1881–1944), Archbishop of York 1929–42; Archbishop of Canterbury 1942–4.

[†] Aneurin (Nye) Bevan (1897–1960), Labour MP for Ebbw Vale 1929–60. As Minister of Health and Housing 1945–51 Bevan was the architect of the National Health Service. He resigned as Minister of Labour and National Service in Apr. 1951 after the Chancellor of the Exchequer, Hugh Gaitskell, imposed prescription charges in the Budget. The subsequent ideological battle between the Bevanites and the Gaitskellites bedevilled Labour throughout the 1950s and beyond.

[‡] James Gomer Berry, 1st Viscount Kemsley (1883–1968), newspaper proprietor, was elevated to the peerage by Stanley Baldwin in 1936.

[§] Harry, 1st Viscount Crookshank (1893–1961), Conservative politician.

appearance as Opposition frontbench speaker after a long absence.*

### 26 December 1952
Bill Deedes tells story of how in the Smoking Room recently Winston & Bevan had a two-hour discussion on political life – it was so sparkling that about twenty MPs on each side gathered round to hear. At end, they warmly embraced & Winston said he had spent a delightful evening. They are, of course, the only two orators left in the House.

### 29 March 1953
To the Remembrance Service for Queen Mary at Queen's Chapel of the Savoy.† Then to Whitehall, just opposite Haig‡ statue, to see procession from Marlborough House to Westminster Hall. At first crowds not at all heavy, but fill up in last half-hour. Gusty cold wind, but dry. A little before 2.30 hear minute gun, & immediately the distant strains of 'Dead March' by Handel. Procession itself seemed to fall between simple dignity of King George VI's gun-carriage journey from King's Cross to Westminster, & his funeral a week later. Duke of Windsor looks very miserable, & as at last funeral he looks about constantly.

### 8 June 1953
Listen on wireless to Gala Performance at Covent Garden of Benjamin Britten's new opera *Gloriana*. Very dreary music, full of the old tricks, and rather harsh on the ear. Most unsuitable for such an occasion.

### 10 June 1953
Benjamin Britten's *Gloriana* rather a failure, it seems. Somebody asked Menzies, Australian Prime Minister,§ in an interval of the opera whether he was not exhausted by Coronation engagements: 'Not till tonight,' was the

---

* The censure motion was defeated by 304 votes to 280.
† Queen Mary (1867–1953) had died on 24 Mar., having left instructions that should she no longer be alive for the Coronation on 2 June on no account should the sacred ceremony be postponed for any mourning.
‡ F.M. Douglas, 1st Earl Haig (1861–1928), C.-in-C. of the British Army in the Great War. After his death Parliament paid £10,000 for an equestrian statue in Whitehall, designed by A.F. Hardiman, which was finally unveiled in 1937 following much controversy over its design. Haig's widow declined to attend the event.
§ Sir Robert Menzies (1894–1978), Prime Minister of Australia 1939–41 and 1949–66.

reply. Beverley Baxter[*] writes that they should have sung *Merrie England* instead.[†]

## 11 June 1953

To Covent Garden to see Britten's *Gloriana*. Wonderful pageant with splendid dresses, but little agreeable music. Especially poor ending like a village pageant. Peter Pears sings badly & is full of irritating tricks & postures. Britten himself appears on stage at end, but rather tepid applause.

## 2 July 1953

Group Captain Peter Townsend[‡] to leave Royal Household & to become Air Attaché in Brussels. Result of newspaper reports that he and Princess Margaret want to marry each other.

Announced that Tenzing,[§] who climbed Everest with Hillary, is to receive the George Medal, compared to Hillary's KBE.

Giles St Aubyn[¶] comes to London for day and we dine at the Epicure. Delicious meal. Begin with whitebait. Giles says: 'What a long time it must have taken to catch each fish with a hook.' He tells me that after Hector McNeil,[**] Socialist Secretary of State for Scotland, had lunched with King George VI at Balmoral, the King turned to Giles & said: 'You can never tell with ministers nowadays. He looks as if he might have come to mend the window cords.'

---

[*] Sir Beverley Baxter (1891–1964), Conservative MP and journalist.

[†] It is ironic that Baxter should have suggested *Merrie England* (1902) by Sir Edward German (1862–1936) as more suitable for the occasion. The Royal Gala Performance of Britten's opera was an ignominious debacle before an official Establishment audience to whom, as Michael Kennedy wrote in his biography of the composer, '*Merrie England* would have represented a musical experience of the most adventurous and intellectual kind.' Michael Kennedy, *Britten* (J.M. Dent, 1981), p. 65.

[‡] (1914–95), Wing Cdr RAF 1941, mentioned in despatches, DFC and bar; equerry to George VI 1944–52 and to Elizabeth II 1952–3.

[§] Sherpa Tenzing Norgay (1914–86) was a veteran of four expeditions to Everest before succeeding in climbing the mountain, making the first ascent with Sir Edmund Hillary (1919–2008) on 29 May 1953. There were some adverse comments on the disparity in the honours that Tenzing and Hillary received, but the Prime Minister of India, Jawaharlal Nehru, had not allowed Tenzing to be given a British knighthood.

[¶] The Hon. Giles St Aubyn (1925–2015), biographer of Queen Victoria and Edward VII, and long-serving housemaster at Eton. They first met when K.R. became an Eton master and kept up with one another for the rest of their lives.

[**] (1907–55), Scottish Labour politician, Secretary of State for Scotland 1950–51.

## 7 July 1953

John Betjeman comes in & we talk about the beauty of railway stations. He draws me a fine picture of Huddersfield Station, like the Parthenon.*

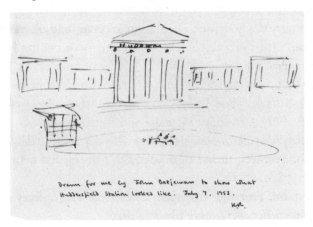

## 26 July 1953

I had a talk with Lord Chief Justice Goddard† at Sir Hartley Shaw-cross's‡ house near Lewes.

Accommodation in Law Courts a terrible problem due to (1) bombing (2) increase of litigation encouraged by free legal aid scheme.

Once on a Northern circuit he was persuaded to attend a village dance. He danced with a pretty girl, who, after staring at him, said: 'Weren't you the judge who hanged my uncle Harry?' It transpired that he was. 'He was a bad hat,' was the girl's only comment to the LCJ.

We discussed the Christie case. Goddard thought that Evans had in fact murdered his wife but had been put up to it by Christie.§

---

* Sir John Betjeman (1906–84), Poet Laureate from 1972 until his death. He described the frontage of Huddersfield Station as the most splendid in England.
† Rayner Goddard, Baron Goddard (1877–1971). Lord Chief Justice 1946–58.
‡ Hartley William Shawcross, Baron Shawcross (1902–2003), barrister, politician, business-man; leading British prosecuting counsel in the Nuremberg Trials, 1945. As his political pilgrimage drifted away from Labour in the 1950s he was dubbed 'Sir Shortly Floorcross'. Shawcross and his family were among K.R.'s longest-standing friends.
§ John Christie (1899–1953), murderer. In 1949 he was the chief prosecution witness in the trial of Timothy Evans (1924–50), alleged murderer of his own wife and daughter at 10 Rillington Place, Christie's home, where the Evans family were tenants. Three years later, six female bodies were found at the address. Christie was convicted of their murder and before his execution confessed to murdering Mrs Evans. The case was a major factor in the eventual abolition of capital punishment in Britain in 1965. In 1966 Evans was granted a posthumous pardon.

He goes on to quote the case of a convicted murderer who tried to commit suicide by cutting his throat. He failed, though his throat was badly injured. His doctors insisted that he must not be hanged, otherwise his head would part company with his body. 'It would not really have mattered,' said Goddard, 'as only the governor, chaplain, hangman and doctor would have witnessed this.'

### 1 October 1953

Dine with Sir Charles[*] and Lady Peake at the Athens Embassy. The other guests include Lady Alexandra Metcalfe and Jim Thomas.[†]

The Embassy is rather a poor building, with a grubby little garden. But it has some good pictures, including a portrait of Byron and a Turner insured for £12,000.

About 10 p.m., everyone disappears from the dining room except Jim Thomas and myself, and we have a long gossip.

He tells me that all the ministers at the moment are worn out with the exception of David Eccles,[‡] who is never ill. Rab[§] has come out in head sores as a result of overwork. There is some dissatisfaction among ministers about Winston. He tells all sorts of outsiders what he never tells his colleagues. When Jim was last at Chequers, the Prime Minister spent most of his time on the croquet lawn. Jim also thinks that the United States, with its money bags, exerts too strong an influence on the Prime Minister.

The Edens are in Greece, staying at a little house some miles away belonging to the Embassy. Eden is thin, but vigorous and full of energy.

A wonderful story about the resignation of Sam Hoare[¶] in 1935. After he

---

[*] Sir Charles Peake (1897–1958), Ambassador to Greece 1951–7.

[†] Lady Alexandra ('Baba') Metcalfe (1904–95) was Curzon's youngest daughter; awarded the CBE for her work for the Save the Children Fund. Jim Thomas, Viscount Cilcennin (1903–60), politician, was 1st Lord of the Admiralty 1951–6. K.R. noted that 'he loved gossip but was utterly without malice'. *Oxford Dictionary of National Biography* (*DNB*), vol. 54 (OUP, 2004), p. 345.

[‡] David Eccles, 1st Viscount Eccles (1904–99), businessman and Conservative politician. His nickname at Westminster was 'Smarty Boots' and Harold Macmillan observed that he was the only Old Wykehamist who could be mistaken for an Old Harrovian.

[§] R.A. Butler, Baron Butler of Saffron Walden (1902–82), Conservative politician. The uncrowned Prime Minister and the second person, after Sir John Simon, to have held the three major posts of Chancellor of the Exchequer, Home Secretary and Foreign Secretary, but never Prime Minister. James Callaghan later became the only person to have held all four offices.

[¶] Sir Samuel Hoare, 1st Viscount Templewood (1880–1959), Conservative politician. Secretary of State for India 1931–5; Foreign Secretary 7 June–18 Dec. 1935, when he was forced to resign following the Hoare–Laval Pact with the French Prime Minister; Home Secretary 1937–9; Ambassador to Spain 1940–44. In his biography of George V, K.R. was to cast doubt

had negotiated the Hoare–Laval Pact to dismember Ethiopia, he returned to the unpopularity of the Pact. He went to Buckingham Palace to be received in audience by King George V, a few weeks before his death. The King said to him: 'Well, one thing we have all learned from this. Just as one should not send coals to Newcastle so one should not send Hoares to Paris.' Later the King related this to one of his cronies at Sandringham, saying: 'I have known Sam Hoare for a very long time as a neighbour in Norfolk and as a minister. But he really has no sense of humour. He never even smiled.'

---

on the accuracy of this story. 'It is inconceivable he [George V] should have thrown so cruel a jest in Hoare's face at the nadir of his political fortunes, then mocked him for his supposed lack of humour.' K.R., *King George V*, p. 400.

# 1954

### 2 January 1954

Shocked & distressed to read of Duff Cooper's[*] death whilst on way to Jamaica. Last night in office we received message to say he was ill, but never thought it serious. What irony, writing a book called *Old Men Forget*, but really feeling young, then dying a few weeks later. Feel particularly sorry for John Julius, who missed seeing them off by going to wrong station last Wednesday. Diana[†] too will be desolate. Feel miserable about it all day.

### 4 January 1954

Read shockingly bitter *Times* obituary on Duff. Says he was not a good Ambassador to France yet does not even mention the 1947 treaty of alliance between Britain and France signed at Dunkirk. Writing in the *Financial Times*, Brendan Bracken[‡] pitches into *The Times*, with its shameful Munich record.

### 7 January 1954

John Grigg[§] dines to meet Giles. John has been this morning to Duff's memorial service at St Margaret's, Westminster. Bob Boothby,[¶] who didn't know Duff well, was asked by Diana to give an address – I suppose because she had read Bob's article in the *Evening Standard* praising Duff's anti-Munich policy. John tells me that Duff agreed with him that the tall hat at Eton should not be abolished. 'Whip up the clergy,' Duff wrote to John, 'Tell them that a threat to the tall hat is a threat to the mitre.'

---

[*] Duff Cooper, 1st Viscount Norwich (1890–1954), diplomat and Conservative politician.
[†] Lady Diana Cooper, Viscountess Norwich (1892–1986), the renowned society beauty of her day.
[‡] Brendan, 1st Viscount Bracken (1901–58), Conservative politician and publisher.
[§] 2nd Baron Altrincham (1924–2001), historian and Lloyd George liberal, latterly a Conservative politician. He disclaimed his title in 1963.
[¶] Sir Robert Boothby, Baron Boothby of Buchan and Rattray Head (1900–86), Conservative politician. The Queen Mother described him as 'a bounder but not a cad'. John Grigg wrote the notice of his life for the *DNB*.

## 8 January 1954

Go straight from office to Covent Garden, where I meet Giles St Aubyn. We hear *Madama Butterfly*. Flimsy plot & sugary music, though here & there a good theme, especially one reminiscent of Nicolai's *Merry Wives of Windsor*. Good seats in Grand Circle. Met an Eton pupil of Giles's who says to him: 'Call me any time you want any gin.'

Giles talks of his relations with the Royal Family. Says they are thoughtlessly ungrateful. He had no present or even real thanks for taking Duke of Kent[*] on summer tour. He had much conversation with Queen Mary at Sandringham, but can remember practically nothing – except her coming into his bedroom to see new decorations one morning. Giles was shaving, but she never batted an eyelid! Giles also says that King George VI told him that history should always be taught backwards.

## 26 January 1954

In evening to party given for Somerset Maugham. Talk to the great man. Am astonished to find how tiny he is, coming up only to my shoulder. Beautifully dressed, face of lined yellow parchment with tortoise mouth, easy agreeable conversation. Says he reads 'Peterborough' every day of his life, though always of course a day late when in South of France. Also meet C.P. Snow, author of *The Masters*: large, old, gentle man, who says that Christ's College didn't mind his novels.[†]

## 27 January 1954

John Grigg tells me that Diana Cooper created a sensation in Paris on way back to England with Duff's body. Lots of people turned up to pay respects, dressed in deepest mourning. Diana appeared in flaming-scarlet cloak!

## 11 February 1954

Hartley Shawcross to lunch at the Guards Club. Thinks his stock in Labour

---

[*] Prince Edward, Duke of Kent (b. 9 Oct. 1935) knew K.R. for sixty years, and read the lesson at K.R.'s memorial service. Giles St Aubyn was a tutor and mentor to the Duke of Kent in the holidays from Eton.

[†] Charles Percy, Baron Snow (1905–80), writer, civil servant, Labour politician and scientific administrator. His most famous novel, *The Masters* (1951), was the third in the eleven-volume sequence *Strangers and Brothers*, written between 1935 and 1970. *The Masters* relates the events surrounding the bitterly fought contest, a paradigm of the political process, for the vacant Mastership in a thinly disguised Christ's Coll., Cambridge. Rose much admired the writings of C.P. Snow and never approved of the condescending attitude of the literary Establishment towards him, especially by the critic F.R. Leavis after Snow's essay on 'The Two Cultures' (science and the arts) of 1956.

Party now very low & doubts if he would be offered job in a new Socialist Cabinet. 'I feel there is little to choose between left wing of Tories & Right wing of Socialists.' Would like, in political sphere: (1) Lord Chancellorship – but Jowitt* would get it. (2) Home Office – but Soskice† making political comeback & wants it. (3) Attorney-General – would accept it without much enthusiasm. (4) Foreign Office. H.S. has not spoken for about two years. Wants big constitutional issue on which to speak. Says Jowitt was always useless in Cabinet – would never commit himself. Thinks Winston in good shape physically & mentally. Winston still says he is prepared to resign over judges' salaries, which implies he would not otherwise do so.

H.S. thinks police have behaved badly in Montagu‡ case by making arrest before re-hearing of original charge. 'There is no doubt M would have been acquitted on original charge retrial had not second arrest taken place.' Both H.S. and Lord Chief Justice [Lord Goddard] think offences between adult males in private should be allowed by law. Recently when LCJ was being pestered to talk on question by Ava Waverley,§ he testily replied: 'Reason there are so many offences is that people talk about them too much!'

H.S. tells me he received one morning brief to take part of *Daily Mirror* in warmonger action brought by Winston ('Whose finger on the trigger?'). Had to accept it. In afternoon he received Winston's brief, which he would have preferred. Fortunately, case settled out of court. Winston now determined to go down in history as a peacemonger.

H.S. alarmed at extent of McCarthy influence in USA. 'Next election slogan will be "20 years of treason"'.

Long talk to Hooper¶ of Schweppes. Tell him Welsh Guards can't get tonic water in Middle East, & he sends for report & orders inquiry.

---

* Sir William Jowitt, 1st Earl Jowitt (1885–1957), Labour politician and lawyer. Lord Chancellor 1945–51.

† Sir Frank Soskice, Baron Stow Hill (1902–79). Solicitor-General in Attlee's government and Home Secretary in Harold Wilson's. He was the first Home Secretary during whose tenure no one was hanged.

‡ Edward Douglas-Scott-Montagu, 3rd Baron Montagu of Beaulieu (1926–2015). Conservative politician and founder of the National Motor Museum. Montagu was twice charged with performing gross offences. The first charge failed to achieve a conviction. He was arrested again in 1954 and this time was imprisoned for twelve months. The case led to the setting-up of the Wolfenden Committee, which recommended in 1957 the decriminalisation of homosexual activity in private between consenting adults. Parliament carried out this recommendation in 1967.

§ Viscountess Waverley (1896–1974), political and social hostess.

¶ Sir Frederic Hooper, 1st Bt (1892–1963), industrialist and MD of Schweppes from 1948 until his death. K.R., who lived in the same block of flats as Hooper at Clive House, Connaught Place, wrote the notice of his life for the *DNB*.

## 12 February 1954

Letter from Hooper of Schweppes about sending tonic water to Welsh Guards in Middle East. I pass it on to Regimental Headquarters, Welsh Guards.

Bill Deedes tells me he has lunch with Eccles, who wants to have 'Welcome Home to our Queen' in enormous letters down Mall when Queen returns from Commonwealth Tour! He has almost every quality except good taste.

Item in newspaper about some young soldiers sentenced to detention for unnatural acts: they took place at Army School of Health!

## 25 February 1954

To House of Commons where I hear part of debate on German rearmament. Attlee makes statesmanlike speech & Churchill is full of vigour, if a little too studied. Split in Socialist Party over this question. Labour MPs divided about half and half for and against rearmament of Germany. But in the Socialist constituencies, overwhelming majority opposed to German rearmament. If an election on the question, the Attlee wing might be wiped out by the Bevanites.

## 3 March 1954

Read Hensley Henson[*] letters. Am again struck by wonderful incisive clarity of his writing. He also bears out another criticism of John Grigg's against Archbishop Temple – that Temple wasted too much time on vague committees & movements within the Church.[†]

## 8 March 1954

Bill Deedes tells me how in Smoke Room of House of Commons he heard two MPs talking about a third. First MP related in turn how third MP (a) drank (b) was in money difficulties (c) abandoned his wife for another woman. To all this, second MP was non-committal. Then first MP concluded: 'And what's more, I hear he doesn't answer all his letters!' Second MP immediately came to life. 'Good God! How awful,' he said.

---

[*] The Rt Revd Hensley Henson (1863–1947), Dean of Durham 1917–20; Bishop of Hereford 1918–20 and of Durham 1920–39.

[†] 'None of his predecessors', observed Henson, who was at odds with Temple over many policies, 'appealed to so large a proportion of the Christian Society throughout the world, and none will be more sincerely and affectionately remembered.' When Churchill was asked why he had nominated a well-known Labour sympathiser to Canterbury, he replied that Temple was 'the best half-crown article in a penny bazaar'.

Talk to Lord Alanbrooke* on telephone, to ask him if he ever took Winston bird-watching. 'God forbid!' he replied.

## 27 March 1954
Read diaries of Lewis Carroll, 1855–67. Was a most unpleasant man. With an impure zest for the society of little girls. He would get into conversation with them in trains & send them copies of *Alice in Wonderland*. He seems to have had a great deal of leisure for this – & for taking photographs of them. Apparently Mrs Liddell† disapproved greatly of this. Very dull diaries with no reported conversation or wit.

## 28 March 1954
Talk about Lewis Carroll with Charles Adeane.‡ Charles quotes story of little girl who, when approached by L.C., replied: 'Mama says I wasn't to talk to anybody.' 'Oh,' said L.C., 'but I'm not anybody, I'm somebody!' He had it all worked out.

## 8 April 1954
Dine Rex Leeper.§ Good conversation over enormous brandy glasses. On Eden: a vain man. Much concerned with what sort of press he is receiving. A massive knowledge of foreign affairs. Lamentably deficient on home affairs – Baldwin always told him this would be his weakness. His real love is Parliament.

Much interesting information about Neville Chamberlain & foreign policy. Leeper once asked Lord [Bobbety] Salisbury¶ if he was a friend of

---

\* FM Sir Alan Brooke, 1st Viscount Alanbrooke (1883–1963), Chief of the Imperial General Staff 1941 and principal military adviser to Winston Churchill. 'Brookie', as he was known, was a vital figure in the conduct of the war and said he 'would not have missed working with Churchill for anything on earth'. Ornithology was one of his great passions.

† Lorina Hannah Liddell (1826–1910, mother of Alice, the model for Alice in *Alice in Wonderland*.

‡ (1930–64), journalist.

§ Sir Rex Leeper, diplomat (1888–1968). Key figure in the establishing of the British Council, for which K.R. later worked; a staunch anti-appeaser; Assistant Under-Secretary at the Foreign Office in 1940 and a close observer of the replacement of Neville Chamberlain as Prime Minister by Winston Churchill; Ambassador to Greece 1943 and to Argentina 1946–8.

¶ Robert Gascoyne-Cecil, 5th Marquess of Salisbury (1893–1972), known as Bobbety. Under-Secretary at the Foreign Office as Lord Cranborne, resigning with Anthony Eden in 1938; held important posts in Churchill's wartime administration; leader of Conservatives in the House of Lords 1942–57; Lord Privy Seal 1951–2; Commonwealth Secretary 1952; Lord President of the Council 1952–7, resigned from Macmillan's government in Mar. 1957 over the release of Archbishop Makarios from detention.

Winston's. 'No,' he replied, 'all his friends are buccaneers!'

## 2 May 1954

Colin Welch[*] tells me story of Duke of Gloucester[†] welcoming ex-King Umberto[‡] when he came to England for funeral of King George VI. D of G said to him: 'Had much rain in Rome lately?' 'Well, as a matter of fact, I don't live in Rome now.' 'Then who the hell are you?'

## 23 May 1954

John Grigg says Roger Scarbrough[§] told him that at Coronation he had to carry inkwell for Queen's signing of declaration. To his horror, when first she dipped in pen, no ink appeared. Was just about to whisper, 'Pretend to sign, ma'am,' when second dip proved more fruitful!

## 17 June 1954

Great fury among Conservatives over refusal of Sir Thomas Dugdale[¶] to censure the civil servants who misled him over the Crichel Down case.[**] Socialists are, of course, supporting him in this, as the report is a terrible indictment of state control of land. The whole episode is a vivid example of the New Despotism.

---

[*] (1924–97), *Daily Telegraph* parliamentary correspondent.

[†] Prince Henry, Duke of Gloucester (1900–74), third son of George V and Queen Mary. Regent presumptive 10 Dec. 1936–21 Apr. 1944; m. Princess Alice, Duchess of Gloucester (1901–2004).

[‡] Umberto II (1904–83), last King of Italy 9 May–12 June 1946. He lived in exile in Portugal.

[§] Roger Lumley, 11th Earl of Scarbrough (1896–1969). Conservative MP for Hull East 1922–9 and York 1931–7, civil servant, Grand Master of the United Grand Lodge of England, 1951; Lord Chamberlain to the Royal Household 1952–63.

[¶] Thomas Dugdale, 1st Baron Crathorne (1897–1977), Conservative politician. Minister of Agriculture and Fisheries 1951–4.

[**] The Crichel Down affair arose over 725 acres of agricultural land at Crichel Down, Dorset, compulsorily purchased in 1938 by the RAF for bombing practice. In 1940 the owner died on active service in the RAF and the estate passed to his daughter, Mary Stuart, who m. Cdr Marten in 1949. In 1941 Churchill promised in the House of Commons that the land would be returned to its original owners when it was no longer needed by the RAF. After the war this promise was not honoured and the land was handed to the Ministry of Agriculture. In 1949 Toby Marten and his wife campaigned for the government's promise to be kept. A public inquiry headed by Sir Oliver Franks severely criticised those acting for the government. The subsequent outcry and Commons debate led to the resignation of Sir Thomas Dugdale, who saw that ministerial responsibility for the actions of civil servants required him to do so. The case was an important stepping stone on the way to the creation of the post of the Ombudsman. A parallel case came in 1982, when Lord Carrington, a Parliamentary Secretary at the Ministry of Agriculture in 1954, resigned as Foreign Secretary on account of mistakes made by his subordinates.

## 20 July 1954

Crichel Down debate in H of C. Tommy Dugdale resigns, after promising radical reform of present iniquitous land system of state. Bill Deedes, who by his brilliant article on Crichel Down in *Daily Telegraph* has largely contributed to Dugdale's downfall, is now misty-eyed about him.

## 25 July 1954

When collecting material for my life of Lord Curzon, I wrote to Lord Beaverbrook asking whether he could give me any personal reminiscences of Curzon or lend me any letters he might have received from him. In reply he said he was going abroad shortly, but would be pleased to help me on his return. Eventually I was invited to tea at his flat in Arlington House, behind the Ritz, on 4 July 1951.

After waiting a few minutes in a room commanding a view over the Palace and Westminster Cathedral, I was shown into another room on a lower floor. Both rooms contained dictaphones. Beaverbrook was wearing a well-used blue suit. On one foot was an ordinary brown shoe, on the other a dancing pump with a little bow. This he immediately explained by saying he suffered from gout (he pronounced it 'goot').

Although I had been invited for tea, there was no tea. On a low table in front of us, however, there was whisky, soda water and ice. He asked me whether I would like some. 'Thank you,' I said, and made to help myself. He stopped me and rang a bell. A black-coated secretary entered. 'Fix Mr Rose a drink,' said Beaverbrook. About half an hour later, when my glass was empty, the same process was repeated.

It seems hardly necessary to relate all the useful information about Curzon which Beaverbrook gave me that afternoon. Sometimes he was a little difficult to follow as he referred both to George Curzon and to Lloyd George as 'George'. Several times he said, 'I hope you are not writing a eulogy of him.' He suggested that a life of Northcliffe[*] was needed more urgently. I noticed that, except for several copies of a book about Beaverbrook's time at the Ministry of Aircraft Production, almost the only book in the room was a life of Northcliffe.[†]

Beaverbrook advised me to ask Lady Curzon[‡] about her sexual relations with Curzon – 'he was impotent when he married her, and the shame and

---

[*] Alfred Harmsworth, Viscount Northcliffe (1865–1922). Newspaper proprietor known as 'the Chief'; launched the *Daily Mail* in May 1896; founded the *Daily Mirror* in Nov. 1903; bought *The Times* in Mar. 1908.

[†] A. P. Ryan, *Lord Northcliffe* (Collins Brief Lives, 1953).

[‡] Grace Duggan, later Marchioness of Curzon (1885–1958).

worry of this added to his troubles at the Foreign Office'. Also: 'At dinner Curzon was wonderful. He would take guests by the arm and make them laugh with him. But behind this gaiety was a hard and ruthless man.' Said that it was not Curzon's peerage which prevented him from becoming PM in 1923, but his personal faults. 'Had there been a normal General Election in 1915 and a Conservative victory, Lord Lansdowne would have become PM.'

When I challenged the accuracy of a paragraph in the *Evening Standard* which had appeared the day before, Beaverbrook became angry. The paragraph had stated that Lord Salisbury had not been consulted in 1923 as to who should succeed Bonar Law as Prime Minister – I suspect that Beaverbrook had put it in to see if I would comment on it when I saw him the following day. I told him that Lady Salisbury* had shown me a note she had made in 1923 of these events, and that Lord S had travelled specially to London to see Lord Stamfordham. Beaverbrook banged the table: 'Tell Lady Salisbury that Lord Beaverbrook says Lord Salisbury was NOT consulted.' He added: 'No statement in *Politicians and the War* or *Politicians and the Press* has ever been refuted.' I mentioned that I had never seen *Politicians and the Press*. He sent me a copy the next day with a nice letter, a kindness I appreciated greatly.

## 22 August 1954

Lunch with Somerset Maugham at St-Jean-Cap Ferrat. Drive out with Giles St Aubyn and Prince Eddie from Nice. On the gate of the house is the famous sign against the evil eye which appears on the front of all his books.

Maugham meets us on the door-step wearing white trousers and an old cardigan. He looks nearer sixty-five than eighty. M. treats Eddie with great deference throughout. We have cocktails in a pine-scented garden. Then a long and delicious lunch, with two white-coated servants.

On the wall is a picture of a male nude. M. says he will give us a hundred dollars if we can guess who painted it. None of us can. It is, curiously enough, by Toulouse-Lautrec. The conversation does not flag for an instant. We tell him about Bayreuth.

Then we walk round the garden. A lovely swimming pool with urns designed by himself. M. receives about 400 letters a week from strangers. A great proportion of these come from Americans, since part of the curriculum of every high school is *Of Human Bondage*. Every letter is answered. Many people write to him for advice on pursuing a literary career. He invariably advises them to 'Stick to the job you have. Only about a dozen people in England earn their living by writing novels.'

---

* Lady Cicely Alice Gore, later 4th Marchioness of Salisbury (1867–1955).

## 3 October 1954

Lunch at Coppins with Princess Marina, Prince Eddie, Princess Alexandra, Princess Alice and Lord Athlone, and Giles St Aubyn.*

Princess Marina, a little acerbic & exaggerated by gruff foreign accent. When I mention that after Bayreuth I took Eddie & Giles to lunch with Max Beerbohm and Somerset Maugham on successive days, she says: 'I thought Max Beerbohm was dead and Mr Maugham rather unsavoury.'

Dear old Princess Alice a tremendous character. When somebody mentions Churchill, she says: 'Winston? Why, at Sandhurst, Alge used to send him off parade for being late, untidy & dirty.'

Princess Alexandra says how much she hated sailing in the *Queen Mary* – 'like an hotel'.

## 4 November 1954

Dine Beefsteak with Peter Carrington,† looking thin but fit. Much talk with Harold Nicolson, with whom I walk back to Albany.‡

King George VI objected to only two bits of H.N.'s life of King George V, both trivial:

(a) Letter of Canon Dalton§ to King George V, beginning 'My own darling Georgie.' 'He was eighteen at the time' was George VI's comment.

(b) Letter of King George V's describing Battle of Jutland and saying: 'It wasn't what I had expected.'

## 30 December 1954

Dine at the Beefsteak with Harold Nicolson. After dinner he considers going

---

* Coppins, Iver, Buckinghamshire with its estate of 132 acres was the Kent home of Princess Marina, Duchess of Kent (1906–68); Alice, Princess, Countess of Athlone (1883–1981), granddaughter of Queen Victoria, wife of Alexander ('Alge') Cambridge, first Earl of Athlone (1874–1957), Governor General of South Africa 1923–31; Governor General of Canada 1940–46. Princess Alexandra (b. 1936), dau. of Princess Marina.

† Peter, 6th Baron Carrington (1919–2018), Conservative politician. Parliamentary Secretary to the Ministry of Agriculture, Fisheries and Food at the time of Crichel Down. Foreign Secretary 1979–82.

‡ Albany is an apartment complex in Piccadilly, built in 1770–74 by Sir William Chambers for the 1st Viscount Melbourne, father of the prime minister. In 1802 it was converted into sixty-nine 'sets', some of the most prestigious apartments in London. Residents have included Lord Byron and two prime ministers, Gladstone and Heath. Albany features in Charles Dickens' *Our Mutual Friend* and Oscar Wilde's *The Importance of Being Earnest*.

§ The Revd Canon John Neale Dalton (1839–1931), Canon of Windsor for forty-seven years, royal tutor. Father of Hugh Neale, Baron Dalton (1887–1962), Chancellor of the Exchequer 1945–7.

to a news-cinema[*] – 'I like to see Mr Morrison[†] being received at Cardiff.' But instead asks me to walk round to Albany for a drink. Full of most excellent stories.

When Queen Mother came to lunch at Sissinghurst, H & Vita[‡] went to great trouble – gold and silver plate, wines, liqueurs, flowers, etc. Queen Mother later told Tommy Lascelles[§] that she had enjoyed it all very much – 'What I particularly liked was that the Nicolsons had gone to no special trouble for me – it was just like a cottage meal!'

In early 1940 Harold Nicolson was a member of old [4th Marquess] Lord Salisbury's 'watching committee' of peers and MPs which met in Arlington Street. On day before the great censure debate in May, they came to the conclusion that they could no longer support Chamberlain. So Lord Salisbury said he would go and see the Prime Minister and tell him so. But before he left he went upstairs and put on frock coat to make the visit!

Harold says that Chamberlain's appeal to his 'friends' during 1940 debate was to his personal, not parliamentary friends, and created a terrible impression. When figures of vote were announced, Chamberlain went the colour of ivory – 'I thought he had fainted,' said Harold.[¶]

---

[*] Where newsreels played on hourly loops all day; a popular feature in London in the 1950s.

[†] Herbert, Baron Morrison of Lambeth (1888–1965), Labour politician. Home Secretary 1940–45, Lord President of Council and Leader of the Commons 1945–51, Foreign Secretary 1951. Of his unhappy brief spell at the Foreign Office it was said: 'Ernie Bevin didn't know how to pronounce the names of the places either, but at least he knew where they were.'

[‡] Vita Sackville-West (1892–1962), writer and gardener wife of Harold Nicolson.

[§] Sir Alan Lascelles (1887–1981), courtier. Assistant PS to George V and Edward VIII, of whom he was a harsh critic, PS to George VI 1943 and to Elizabeth II 1952–3.

[¶] On 8 May 1940 Chamberlain called on 'my friends in the House – and I have friends in the House – to support us in the Lobby tonight'. The vote after the debate on 7–8 May 1940 was 281 to 200, which left the government with a majority of only 81 instead of a possible 213, a hollow victory which made Chamberlain's position untenable.

# 1955

### 5 January 1955

Malcolm Sargent[*] asks me with whom I would spend my last (non-carnal) night on earth and why. I reply, Max Beerbohm, because one would be diverted and also be secure from any emotional scene. Malcolm horrified by this: he would spend it setting someone on the path for good – someone who would always remember it was Malcolm's last night. I say this is dishonest, and we have a spirited philosophical argument.

### 8 January 1955

With Philip de Zulueta[†] to Albert Hall to hear Malcolm conduct magnificent performance of the *Messiah*. In evening I have Malcolm, Giles St Aubyn and Prince Eddie to dine. Soup, snails, steak, fruit salad, with Macon '42.

Malcolm full of Benjamin Britten stories. When Duke of Edinburgh left Royal Box after *Gloriana* he remarked: 'Lucky I didn't marry the first Queen Elizabeth otherwise Britten would now be in the Tower awaiting execution.' When Britten got the CH it was called 'Companion of Harewood'.[‡]

### 15 January 1955

In evening dine Malcolm Sargent, Marie-Lou Hennessy and Sylvia Darley (Malcolm's secretary) at Garrick Club. Malcolm is very conscious of being Malcolm, and made rude remarks about other members who are watching TV. 'It should be banished from all civilised clubs, etc. etc.' Wonderful dinner

---

[*] Sir Harold Malcolm Watts Sargent (1895–1967), conductor.

[†] Sir Philip de Zulueta (1925–89), civil servant and businessman. K.R. was his contemporary at both New Coll. and in the Welsh Guards, and a close friend of his and his wife, Marie-Lou, née Hennessy, who both appear in the journals. He served three prime ministers and was PS for Foreign Affairs to Sir Anthony Eden, Harold Macmillan and Sir Alec Douglas-Home. His thanksgiving Mass was at the restored Guards' Chapel on 22 May 1989.

[‡] George Lascelles, 7th Earl of Harewood (1923–2011). Editor of *Opera* magazine 1950–53; Director of the Royal Opera House 1951–3 and 1969–72; Artistic Director of the Edinburgh Festival 1961–5; MD of the English National Opera 1972–85.

– delicious sticky caviar, vodka, saddle of lamb, brandy and a huge cigar which needs two hands to support it. Malcolm full of his grand stories about the Royal Family – how he refused to spoil his beautiful clothes by joining in the making of a bonfire, when staying during war with the Gloucesters in Australia. Marie-Lou says Patrick Plunket[*] told her that any member of Royal Family who made Duke of Gloucester laugh his curious laugh was instantly fined a fiver!

From Garrick Club we go to Crazy Gang show.[†] Very lewd jokes, but well staged and produced. After show, go round and drink whisky with the Crazy Gang in their dressing room. Bud Flanagan says that he has constant trouble with Lord Chamberlain's office. Norman Gwatkin[‡] really rather likes the show, but has to act if he receives complaints. Apparently the Superintendent of the Oxford Police has complained that the show, recently touring in Oxford, is immoral. When Bud saw Lord Scarbrough, latter said: 'I have to consider the morals of the undergraduates. I have a son at Oxford myself!' Another member of the cast tells story of how he sang in a duet with 'Gilly' – i.e. Gigli! Quite weak with laughter, we go to La Bohème for some soup, scampi and Chablis, about midnight. Wonderful evening. Bed about 1.30. Pity Eddie could not have come as originally intended.

## 1 February 1955

Read Humphrey Lyttelton's[§] *I Play As I Please*, a most amusing book to come from an Etonian and Grenadier. Good description of arriving to play at a ball. Stately woman looks them up and down, saying: 'I thought you were going to be black.' As H.L. adds: 'We followed her upstairs making rather weak excuses for being the wrong colour.' At Eton, his housemaster, J.C. Butterwick,[¶] would confiscate his trumpet if unsatisfactory in school. So had

---

[*] Patrick Plunket, 7th Baron Plunket (1923–75), equerry to Elizabeth II; Deputy Master of the Royal Household 1954–75.

[†] Entertainment group formed in the 1930s at the London Palladium, consisting at their peak of Bud Flanagan, Chesney Allen, Jimmy Nervo, Teddy Knox, Charlie Naughton and Jimmy Gold.

[‡] Sir Norman Gwatkin (1899–1971), royal equerry. Comptroller in the Lord Chamberlain's Office 1960–64.

[§] (1921–2008), jazz musician and broadcaster.

[¶] (1881–1966), long-standing Eton housemaster, who once acquired for twopence a first edition of Milton's *Paradise Lost* in the School Pound, where unwanted text books were stored. An epigram recorded his discovery:

O, J.C.B., too penny wise
For the pound-foolish Pound,
How dearly lost is Paradise,
And oh! How cheaply found!

a special cheap trumpet for handing in, and kept proper one to practise with!

## 5 February 1955

Read Aldous Huxley's *Eyeless in Gaza* – one admires way in which he drags into novels unexpected bits of medical or philological or philosophical knowledge he has picked up. In this one he has tiresome habit of chopping up the time sequence.

## 7 February 1955

David Eccles, now Minister of Education, lunches with me at Guards Club. Says that civil servants are getting above themselves, especially Sir Edward Bridges.[*] It was quite wrong for latter to be made a Privy Councillor – he is now able in theory to advise Queen by demanding an audience, whereas his real job is to advise ministers. At time of Crichel Down scandal, Bridges tried to protect civil servants in same way that Jim Campbell[†] looked after interests of the National Union of Rail Workers during recent threatened rail strike. Eccles says that John Maud[‡] is another political civil servant whom he dislikes. When Eccles took over from Florence Horsbrugh[§] at Education, he found that she called senior civil servants by their Christian names. Quite rightly Eccles never does this, but thinks he is in a minority among ministers.

Eccles says he has just spent a profitless morning going through Honours List recommendations for next June. If he has only one OBE, and two head-masters of equal service and merit competing for it, he sends for the election figures. It would go to the man in a marginal-seat constituency.

Is doubtful whether public schools can absorb up to half their numbers from scholarship and council-aided boys. If councils are going to pay for boys, they will want to be represented on governing body of schools. What then?

He proudly points out to me that our two best despatch-writing Ambassadors, Makins in Washington and Hayter in Moscow, are both Wykehamists.

---

[*] Edward, 1st Baron Bridges (1892–1969). Secretary to the Cabinet 1938–47, Permanent Secretary to the Treasury and Head of the Civil Service 1945–56.
[†] (1895–1957), trade unionist. General Secretary of the NUR 1953–7. Killed in a road accident in Leningrad.
[‡] Baron Redcliffe-Maud (1906–82), civil servant and diplomat. Permanent Secretary at the Ministry of Education 1945–52, and the Ministry of Fuel and Power 1952–9; High Commissioner in South Africa 1959–61; Ambassador to South Africa 1961–3.
[§] Florence, Baroness Horsbrugh (1889–1969), Conservative politician. MP for Dundee 1931–45 and for Manchester Moss Side 1950–59; Minister of Education 1951–4.

Jebb* also good, but too self-centred in his approach to events.

## 23 February 1955

Lunch with Frank Pakenham† in House of Lords. Also there are Sir Brian and Lady Horrocks.‡ I remind him how we went to Heligoland in May 1945, which brings back a flood of memories. He says that the 2nd Battalion Welsh Guards was the best under his command, which pleases me. Talks about generalship and conscience, e.g. RAF offered to wipe out Kleve for him, and he agreed; but had terrible conscience about it. Said that a general must not allow himself to think about these things – otherwise he ceases to sleep and goes to pieces.

Says he misses having had no academic education: 'I never did a hand's turn of work until I was twenty-six.' Talks a little about his duties as Black Rod. When he had to marshal procession of peers once for a lying-in-state, an elderly marquess came up to him and said: 'Watch the Barons – they are always barging in.'

Lord Beveridge§ joins us for a few minutes. Complains of Oxford traffic. Also says: 'I don't want the Welfare State, but the Welfare Society.'

Horrocks says that great fault of Eisenhower towards end of war was that he would not listen to advice, but would merely walk about perhaps swinging a golf club. If one wanted to get a point across, it had to be made in the first two minutes.

## 24 February 1955

Lunch Beefsteak. Edward Ford,¶ Assistant Private Secretary to Queen, tells

---

* Roger Makins, 1st Baron Sherfield (1904–96), Ambassador to the US 1952–6; Joint Permanent Secretary to the Treasury 1956–9. Sir William Hayter (1906–95), diplomat and college head. Ambassador to the Soviet Union 1953–7; Warden of New Coll., Oxford 1958–76. Sir Gladwyn Jebb, 1st Baron Gladwyn (1900–96), British representative at the UN 1950–54; Ambassador to France 1954–60.

† Frank Pakenham, 7th Earl of Longford, 1st Baron Pakenham (1905–2001), Labour politician and philanthropist, Leader of the House of Lords 1964–8.

‡ Sir Brian Horrocks (1895–1985), British Army officer. Lt-Gen. commanding XXX Corps during Operation Veritable, Feb.–Mar. 1945, when 90 per cent of the buildings in Kleve were destroyed by Allied bombing. Gentleman Usher of the Black Rod 1949–63.

§ William Beveridge, 1st Baron Beveridge (1879–1963), economist. Master of University Coll., Oxford 1937–45; Chairman, Inter-Departmental Committee on Social Insurance and Allied Services 1941–2, which led to the Beveridge Report of 1942.

¶ Sir Edward Ford (1910–2006), courtier. Assistant PS to George VI 1946–52, and to Elizabeth II 1952–67. In 1992 he wrote to the Queen's PS commiserating that in the fortieth year of her reign the Queen had endured an 'annus horribilis', a phrase the Queen used on 24 Nov. that year in a speech.

me that Vice-Chamberlain, an MP, sends Queen telegram from the House
every day about 8 p.m. describing first few hours of business. At beginning of
reign, Queen was asked if she wanted to continue custom. Replied, Yes: and
reads them with care. This task used to be done by PM.

Buy evening paper and see that Bank Rate has gone up one per cent to four
and a half per cent – measure of Butler's to curb inflation. Stock markets take
a tumble. Go down to House of Commons and hear Butler make a statement.

## 28 February 1955

John Grigg tells me of Winston's visit to Manchester. When his train arrived,
platform crowded with all the nobs and their wives – Lord Mayor, Lord
Lieutenant, etc. These were ignored for about two hours and train remained
sealed. Then a few of them were bidden to enter the train (but not their wives),
and were welcomed to Manchester by Winston with champagne. Eventually
he bathed, dressed and emerged, and expressed gratification at huge crowd
of people outside the barrier. But they were Mancunians still waiting for
their trains to work, having been held up by Winston. Then he was told that
his train would leave from Victoria Station that evening. 'No, no,' he said,
'I wish to leave from gallant, war-scarred London Road.' Only when it was
explained that this would mean shunting his train into Yorkshire and back,
did he agree to original plan.

## 1 March 1955

To Turf Club for drink with Peter Carrington. Tells me how he missed official dinner in Paris last week because on day he was flying across, Winston
asked him to lunch at No. 10 to meet Shah of Persia. Lunch went on so long,
Peter missed about three planes: he wanted to leave early, but Jock Colville[*]
said it would not be etiquette!

Peter also tells me how he wanted to resign with Dugdale over Crichel
Down, but that Winston would not allow him to. So he consulted Lord Salisbury, who said, 'It doesn't matter whether you resign or not, we shall give
you another job.' Peter thought this a most difficult, even unfair, position to
put him in. Finally, he did not resign, and was given present job of Under-
Secretary at Ministry of Defence during Cabinet reshuffle.

---

[*] Sir John Colville (1915–87), diplomat, civil servant and diarist. Assistant PS to Neville
Chamberlain 1939–40, to Winston Churchill 1940–41 and 1943–5, and to Clement Attlee
1945; PS to Princess Elizabeth 1947–9; joint Principal PS to Winston Churchill 1951–5.

## 2 March 1955

To House of Commons where I have a talk with Anthony Wedgwood Benn, immersed in all the possible ways in which he can try to renounce his succession to Viscountcy of Stansgate, in order to remain in House of Commons.

## 3 March 1955

See copy of Harold Nicolson's *King George V*, in which Queen Mary wrote just before her death – 'a noble record of the life and work of my husband, King George V'. This was in case other members of Royal Family should later accuse Harold of having written a caricature.

## 5 March 1955

To Eton by well-upholstered Great Western Region train. Always reminds me of Queen Victoria.

At Forbes and Francis, booksellers by Windsor Bridge, buy Curzon's *Persia and the Persian Question* in two volumes for £15. Have had my eye on them for some time. They come from Panshanger, which used to belong to Lord Cowper.*

Buy some crystallised fruit at Rowlands to take to Grizel [Hartley]. Notice how absolutely filthy are some of the boys' collars. Never saw anything like it when I was there. Find Grizel cheerful but in bed, recovering from 'flu. Hubert, she tells me, once described a parent as 'wearing fur braces, with the insides of her nostrils rouged like a rocking horse'. See Giles [St Aubyn] also recovering from 'flu. Prince Eddie comes over, full of stories about his skiing holiday in Switzerland. One particular row was when he enraged a drunk American by laughing at him – he was trying to light a cigarette at the filter tip end! Eddie gives me a lift back to London, calling at Coppins for a few minutes on the way.†

---

* Francis Cowper, 7th Earl Cowper (1834–1905), Liberal politician and landowner. Panshanger in Hertfordshire was one of the meeting places of 'The Souls', the group that included, among others, Balfour, Curzon, Margot Tennant, George Wyndham, Francis Horner, Alfred Lyttelton, Alfred Milner and St John Brodrick. When Curzon became Viceroy of India in 1898, a farewell gathering was held for him at Panshanger.

† Hubert Hartley (1896–1977), Grizel Hartley (1900–87) and Giles St Aubyn were K.R.'s closest and most long-standing friends from his days teaching at Eton, where Hubert and Giles were housemasters. Hubert Hartley stroked the Cambridge crew to victory in the Boat Race for three successive years. Giles St Aubyn wrote a lengthy account of his sixty-year friendship with K.R. for the editor.

## 9 March 1955

Dinner party in my flat in evening – Nicky Gordon Lennox[*] and Prince Eddie. Then in Eddie's car to hear Humphrey Lyttelton.

Nicky tells story of Lord Mowbray, 25th Baron, suddenly exclaiming very loudly in middle of Coronation service: 'Some bugger's pinched me coronet an' me sandwiches an' me lunch ticket!' Andrew Devonshire had hidden it under a seat. At 1937 Coronation, Nicky's father heard one peer say loudly to another: 'And I ran her four times as a two-year-old, and she never won a race.' Story at rehearsal for 1953 Coronation. Archbishop of Canterbury: 'What do I do now?' Duke of Norfolk: 'You pray.'

## 11 March 1955

To Dorchester for Foyle's Poetry Lunch. Have a few words with Lord Samuel[†] before it begins. At lunch itself, when Betjeman receives prize, Samuel makes a rather deplorable speech mocking obscurity of modern verse. He sarcastically quotes some early Dylan Thomas, and Stephen Spender walks out in disgust. Also talk with Patrick Kinross.[‡] Says that when House of Lords was in Robing Chamber during the war, conversations could easily be overheard. He once heard old Lord Salisbury [the 4th Marquess] discussing domestic chores with old Lord Fitzalan[§] – 'And should the mattress be turned over every day?'

## 13 March 1955

Dine with Philip de Zulueta at Foreign Office. See large Rolls-Royce outside No. 10 – new car for Winston on retirement? Philip de Zulueta tells me one reason why Herbert Morrison was such a bad Secretary of State at Foreign Office was that he did not read all the papers sent to him – he has only one eye and could not cope with them.

## 15 March 1955

I tell Hartley Shawcross I have tonight written paragraph for 'Peterborough' in *Telegraph* suggesting that PM's trial of private Rolls-Royce may be pointer

---

* Lord Nicholas Gordon Lennox (1931–2004), Ambassador to Spain 1984–9.
† Sir Herbert, 1st Viscount Samuel (1870–1963), Liberal politician. Home Secretary 1931–2, leader of the Liberal Party 1931–5. The first nominally practising Jew to become a Cabinet minister and leader of a major British political party. Lloyd George was a fierce critic of Samuel, remarking: 'When they circumcised Sir Herbert Samuel, they threw away the wrong bit.'
‡ Patrick Balfour, 3rd Baron Kinross (1904–76), journalist and writer.
§ Edward Fitzalan-Howard, 1st Viscount Fitzalan of Derwent (1855–1947), Conservative politician.

to his early retirement. He replies that the PM could sue me for libel, as it implies he is no longer fit for work! 'But I shall defend you – Oh no, I won't, the PM has first claim on my services. So I shall advise him not to sue you.'

## 16 March 1955
Read Winston's life of his father, Lord Randolph Churchill.[*] Latter part of book much better than former. Altogether, I find his eulogistic tone a little hard to stomach. After all Randolph Churchill was a dreadful bounder and his behaviour on any great occasion can rarely be justified.

## 19 March 1955
To Eton by train. Lunch Grizel and Hubert. Grizel has story of new Bishop of Oxford, Dr Carpenter,[†] saying to confirmation godparents in Eton Chapel that he knew of a case in which a boy who had been confirmed said his parents did not go to church – then added: 'But I can go with our cook.' Bishop told this to point moral that boy's spiritual welfare should not be in hands of a cook. As Grizel pointed out, cooks are usually delightful people, and Bishop was obviously not used to having a cook. 'No,' said Hubert, 'it shows he was not <u>aware</u> of having a cook.' How very Johnsonian.

## 22 March 1955
Talk to Anthony Benn about his attempts to remain in the House of Commons on his father's death. He has now persuaded the Bishop of Bristol to present the Bristol Corporation's Petition asking for this to the House of Lords.

Talk to Edward Boyle[‡] at Claridge's lunch. He thinks it doubtful whether the Conservatives will win next General Election – textile situation may alienate votes in Lancashire, where there are many marginal seats.

To House of Commons. Winston as always in tremendous form at Question Time. I suspect his health changes from day to day. One day he will determine to resign, but after a good dinner decide he is good for another year or two.

Philip de Zulueta and Marie-Louise[§] dine with me in flat. Malcolm Sargent

---

[*] (1849–95), Conservative politician. Chancellor of the Exchequer 1886.
[†] The Rt Revd Harry Carpenter (1901–93), Warden of Keble Coll., Oxford 1939–55, Bishop of Oxford 1955–70.
[‡] Edward, Baron Boyle of Handsworth (1923–81), Conservative politician. Minister of Education 1962–4; Vice-Chancellor of Leeds University 1971–80.
[§] Philip de Zulueta m. Marie-Louise Hennessy in 1955.

joins us after dinner, and stays very late. Good story of Michael Tippett* at an orchestral rehearsal of his new opera *The Midsummer Marriage*. He kept telling the drum player to play louder in a certain passage – 'After all, it is the main theme.' 'What!' exploded the drummer.

Malcolm also tells the good story of meeting a man in a train during the war, who said to him: 'I'm a bit of a celebrity too. You know those advertisements for venereal disease? Well, the woman is my wife. She's all right really, of course.'

## 4 April 1955

Return London by train. Ticket collector says he is not noticing the newspaper strike – he is receiving his *Manchester Guardian* as usual.

Conservatives regain control of West Riding County Council in Yorkshire. This might point to the wisdom of having an early General Election.

To House of Commons to hear Eden wind up the debate on the Turco–Iraq Pact – his last speech as Foreign Secretary, I expect. Has a bad debating manner, and often turns his back on the Speaker to address his supporters.

Excitement mounts in Downing Street, where Queen dines with Winston.

## 5 April 1955

The day of Churchill's resignation

Great political excitement, though still no newspapers owing to strike. Quick lunch at House of Commons, then into Chamber. It is extraordinarily crowded in hope that Winston will make a last appearance before resignation.

But the visitors are disappointed. Harry Crookshank answers the questions put down for Winston. Emrys Hughes† asks: 'Has the Government yet decided whether it will bury Caesar in the House of Lords, or allow him to come back to his House to worry Anthony?'

Leave office about 5 p.m. Motor past Palace, where a great crowd. A helicopter skims along Mall over trees and drops down into garden of Palace. Then it takes off again – presumably the Duke of Edinburgh

---

* Sir Michael Tippett (1905–98), composer. His first opera, *The Midsummer Marriage*, a decade in the creation, was premiered at Covent Garden on 27 Jan. 1955, with Joan Sutherland in the cast. As with Britten's *Gloriana* two years earlier, the opera had a lukewarm reception. Only after a celebrated studio performance for the BBC under Norman Del Mar in 1963 was its full lyrical magnificence recognised.

† (1894–1969), Labour politician; biographer of Keir Hardie.

returning from an engagement. About 5.15 Winston's car, with Lord Warden's flag, slowly emerges from Palace. Great cheer from crowd. As his car slowly passes I see he is wearing a tall hat and in tears. He has just resigned.

Call on P. de Z. at Foreign Office about 9.45 p.m. He tells me he is to be one of Eden's secretaries at No. 10 – a great chance of influencing events.

With Marie-Lou and her nice brother, David,[*] we go on to balcony of Foreign Office. Rather a small crowd singing and shouting for Winston. He does not appear while I am there, but butler washing up on first floor gets a tremendous cheer when he comes to window.

To bed after eventful day at 1 a.m.

## 7 April 1955

Wicked cartoon in *Punch* this week – large reproduction of Sutherland's[†] portrait of Winston in every detail – but instead of Winston's face, a cruel cartoon of Eden's. Malcolm Muggeridge[‡] obviously inspired it.

To Hughenden to visit Disraeli's house. Hughenden well kept by National Trust. Two good rooms – library and drawing room. Others equally interesting owing to cases of relics. Ugly bedroom, with good mahogany furniture badly painted white, and tiny fireplace. In study *Leaves from Our Journal of Life in the Highlands* contains affectionate inscription from V.R.I. But pages uncut. In dining room, one chair has about one inch cut from bottom of each leg. Done so that Queen Victoria could put her foot firmly on floor when lunching. Ugly little church, with memorial erected by Queen Victoria. Study contains boxes of Hughenden writing papers received from the stationer. Lovely view, but no peacocks.

## 8 April 1955

In afternoon to Malcolm's box in Albert Hall, to hear him conduct whole of *Messiah*. In Malcolm's flat, where we drink champagne afterwards, Prince Eddie points to photograph of Mountbattens[§] and says to me: 'They and Malcolm have much in common.'

---

* David Hennessy, 3rd Baron Windlesham (1932–2010), Conservative politician. Lord Privy Seal and Leader of the House of Lords 1973–4; Principal of Brasenose Coll., Oxford 1989–2002.
† Graham Sutherland (1903–1980). His portrait of Winston Churchill was commissioned by the House of Commons on the occasion of Churchill's eightieth birthday.
‡ (1903–90), journalist and media personality.
§ Louis, 1st Earl Mountbatten of Burma (1900–79), naval officer and final Viceroy of India, 1947. Dame Edwina Mountbatten, Countess Mountbatten of Burma (1901–60), director of emergency relief services 1945–7 and Vicereine of India, 1947.

Eddie has to return to Coppins for dinner, but Malcolm and I dine magnificently at Gore Hotel, few hundred yards away. I feel slightly uneasy doing this on Good Friday, but Malcolm says it doesn't count after 3 p.m. So we eat caviar with hot buttered toast and vodka, duck and a fine cheese surrounded by grapes. Then a huge and succulent Havana from a box given him by Lord Horder.

In flat again, Malcolm and I talk for another hour or two over 1904 brandy. Malcolm talks of dearth of good young conductors – 'Had I been ill this morning, there is not a young conductor who could have done *Messiah* in my place.' Real trouble, says M, is that aspiring young conductors are conceited, and lack tact necessary to handle old-established choirs, especially in North.[*] Home about 1.30 a.m.

## 26 April 1955
To House of Lords for debate on the Wedgwood Benn case. Anthony tells me he has received a letter of support from Winston which he cannot use until the old man retires.

## 3 May 1955
Call on David Eccles at the Ministry of Education. I ask him what difference he notices between Winston and Eden as PM. He replies, 'At Cabinet meetings one notices how much the room lacks pictures, for there is nothing else to look at. In Winston's day one always looked at him.'

## 10 May 1955
Harold Nicolson talks of the three men in the House of Commons who were all once marked as future PMs. They were Walter Elliot,[†] Oliver Stanley[‡] and W.S. Morrison the present Speaker.[§]

## 12 May 1955
Chips Channon[¶] once complained to James Stuart,[**] the Chief Whip: 'Why

---

[*] Sir Malcolm Sargent was principal conductor of the Huddersfield Choral Society 1932–67.
[†] (1888–1958), Scottish Unionist politician.
[‡] (1896–1950). Sir Charles Petrie wrote of Stanley, 'He was one of the most gifted men of the century, and would have made a very great Prime Minister.'
[§] William Morrison, 1st Viscount Dunrossil (1893–1961), Conservative politician. Speaker of the House of Commons 1951–9. Owing to his deep knowledge of Shakespeare he acquired the nickname 'Shakes', Bernard Shaw's abbreviation of Shakespeare's name.
[¶] Sir Henry Channon (1897–1958), diarist and Conservative politician. MP for Southend-on-Sea 1935–50 and Southend-on-Sea West 1950–58.
[**] James Stuart, 1st Viscount Stuart of Findhorn (1897–1971), Conservative politician. MP

are you always so rude to me? I never miss a division or cause trouble.' Stuart replied: 'My dislike of you is purely personal.'

## 24 May 1955

Conversation with the Aga Khan[*] at the Ritz Hotel. Charming and delightfully friendly reception in sitting room of his suite. Excellent tea with chicken sandwiches. He told me Curzon was a wonderful host. Would mark with his own hand the names of guests on table-cards. All notes to friends and others were written in his own hand, never dictated.

Though he was genial, he made few close friends. He quarrelled with his lifelong friend Brodrick[†] over India. 'I tried to reconcile them at lunch here. They <u>had</u> to behave, but talked only about such innocuous subjects as the fog of Calcutta. He had a terrible gift of cutting people the wrong way. His staff called him the Imperial Bounder, and nothing caused so much pleasure in the Foreign Office as when his lift stuck. Like Northcliffe, he thought he had a Napoleonic look – hence his collection of Napoleonic relics.

Curzon thought that for Indians to rule India was as absurdly remote as if he said today that the Martians will rule the earth. Real reason for Curzon's fall in India was his anti-Afghan policy which Cabinet disapproved of. Curzon was always afraid of self-government for India. Walter Lawrence[‡] advised him to make declaration of it as an eventual aim at time of Durbar. After World War I Curzon had 'self-government' changed to 'responsible government' in declaration of Montagu–Chelmsford reforms.[§] This meant parliamentary government, which was not suitable for Eastern countries.

## 26 May 1955

General Election Day. Vote for Commander Noble,[¶] Chelsea Conservative candidate, before going to the office.

---

for Murray and Nairn 1923–59; Chief Whip 1941–8; Secretary of State for Scotland 1951–7.

[*] Aga Khan III (1885–1957), first President of the All-India Muslim League.

[†] Hon. St John Brodrick, later 1st Earl of, and 9th Viscount, Midleton (1856–1942), Conservative and Irish Unionist Alliance politician. Secretary of State for India 1903–5, a time blighted by his rows with his former schoolfriend Lord Curzon, which led to Curzon's resignation as Viceroy in Nov. 1905.

[‡] Sir Walter Lawrence (1857–1940), administrator in India.

[§] The basis of the Government of India Act, 1919; named after Edwin Montagu (1879–1924), Secretary of State for India 1917–22, and Frederic Thesiger, 1st Viscount Chelmsford (1868–1933), Viceroy of India 1916–21.

[¶] Cdr Sir Allan Noble (1908–62), Conservative politician. PPS to Anthony Eden 1947–51.

Rather a day of anti-climax after the election campaign. To the Camrose[*] election party at the Savoy. An extraordinary collection of people there. My supper table includes Malcolm Sargent, and Gerald Kelly[†] with whom I have a lot of talk. He tells me he never believed the Elgin Velasquez to be genuine, as it seemed to lack the anatomical poise he would expect to find in it. He praises the writing of Max Beerbohm. We have a great deal of champagne as each result is announced. I share a cab home at 4 a.m. through heavy rain with Malcolm Sargent.

### 27 May 1955

Spend practically the whole day tied to my desk writing about the election results as they come in. It is clear very early in the morning that the Conservatives will have a majority, in fact it turns out to be about sixty. I am sorry to see John Grigg has been beaten at Oldham, but most other friends are returned as expected. David Butler[‡] is admirable as television commentator. Woolton's[§] appearance is no less impressive in a music-hall way.

### 18 June 1955

Take Malcolm Sargent and Prince Eddie to *The Boy Friend*[¶] at Wyndham's Theatre. We are much pestered by photographers which puts Eddie in a temper. Malcolm minds less. During supper afterwards M. talks endlessly but very well. He describes how during the time when he went abroad to conduct in neutral countries these visits obviously had some prestige value. So he asked for a special allocation of clothing coupons to replace his very frayed evening shirts. He received an official typewritten letter of refusal, but at the bottom of the letter was written by hand, 'If you should by any chance receive a further document, on no account acknowledge it.' Shortly afterwards in a plain envelope came 80 clothing coupons.

---

[*] John Berry, 2nd Viscount Camrose (1909–95), Deputy Chairman of the *Daily Telegraph* at the time.

[†] Sir Gerald Kelly (1879–1972), artist. President of the Royal Academy (RA) 1949–54.

[‡] Sir David Butler (b. 1924), pioneering psephologist, famed for his television appearances on election nights; Fellow of Nuffield Coll. and main author of the Nuffield Election Studies. A New Coll. friend of K.R.

[§] Frederick Marquis, 1st Earl of Woolton (1883–1964), businessman and statesman. Conservative Party Chairman 1946–55. He became a public figure as Minister of Food 1940–43.

[¶] Celebrated musical by Sandy Wilson which opened in London in 1953 and ran for five years and 2,082 performances.

He describes his relations with Adrian Boult:* 'He disapproved of everything I ever did.' At some jolly party one night Malcolm once asked Adrian Boult, 'Have you ever kissed a woman!' A.B. replied, 'I hope I have always behaved like a gentleman.'

Curious story of how the Duchess [of Kent] was once going to the play *A Streetcar Named Desire*. Queen Mary heard of this, told Duchess it was unsuitable, and persuaded her against her will to cancel. So Duchess instead went to *The Vortex*.† Queen Mary furious.

### 15 August 1955
Read *The Longest Journey* by E.M. Forster. Fills me with a deeper revulsion than even *Howards End*. The style is too contrived and spinsterish, the situations absurd and the characters tiresome beyond belief. Oh, for a little red-hot sex in his books!

### 25 September 1955, letter to parents
Malcolm Sargent tells me an amusing story. He once complained to Gustav Holst that a triangle-player in the orchestra had been playing the triangle for fifty years & still made the same mistakes. 'I could do it better myself,' added Malcolm. To which Holst replied: 'Yes, that is why you are a conductor and he is only a triangle-player after fifty years.'

The Burgess–Maclean affair‡ has shocked everyone deeply & there will be a massive row when Parliament reassembles. On Monday when it all blew up, both Macmillan and Reading§ happened to be lunching at the Beefsteak where I was too. They seemed singularly ignorant of the effect it will have.

### 26 September 1955
Lunch Bill Deedes off oysters and Chablis at Wheeler's. We walk down to Lancaster House, where I listen to round-table conference on Malta. On way we argue loudly about Burgess–Maclean scandal. Suddenly we notice a man is walking past us, staring very hard. It is Hector McNeil, former Socialist

---

* Sir Adrian Boult (1889–1983), chief conductor of the BBC Symphony Orchestra 1930–50. He was renowned for his championing of English music, especially Elgar, Holst and Vaughan Williams, whose 4th and 6th symphonies he premiered.
† Tennessee Williams' play *A Streetcar Named Desire* (1947) examined controversial social issues. Noël Coward's *The Vortex* (1924) dealt with issues such as sexual vanity and drug abuse.
‡ Guy Burgess (1911–63) and Donald Maclean (1913–83), spies who defected to Russia in 1951.
§ Gerald, 2nd Marquess of Reading (1889–1960), Liberal then Conservative politician. Minister of State for Foreign Affairs 1953–7.

Minister of State at FO, who introduced Burgess into FO as his Secretary!

## 29 September 1955

Interesting talk with Frank Pakenham about present state of Labour Party. Thinks Gaitskell will be next Socialist PM and a subdued Wilson his Chancellor of the Exchequer. He says that Wilson, tinted with Bevanism, is working his way back to orthodoxy, just as Rab Butler, tainted with Chamberlainism, is working his way back to Edenite orthodoxy.

## 5 October 1955

Leave for Conservative Conference at Bournemouth by 6.30 train. Share carriage with Anthony Wedgwood Benn, who is covering it for BBC. Much good political gossip. He relates his conversation with Attlee on subject of dismissals from Government. For instance, 'Feather-Bed' Evans[*] refused to resign after tactless speech and so Attlee dismissed him after a friendly half-hour talk. Simonds,[†] when Lord Chancellor, received two letters at hand of messenger. First said he was dismissed; second was his to Winston, thanking him for honour of serving in his administration. He was required to sign it, and return it to PM by hand of waiting messenger. 'At least I always <u>saw</u> the people I dismissed,' was Attlee's comment. Arrive Bournemouth in pouring rain. See Edward Boyle, stranded like a vast whale on platform, and mournfully clutching a red box.

## 6 October 1955

A pleasant day, with nice gardens and woods going down to sea, and long vista of coast. To Pavilion, Bournemouth, picking my way through a well-nigh impenetrable wall of Bentleys. Usual dreary oratory from Young Conservatives, and a dispirited address from Butler.

Have Bill Deedes and Tom Driberg[‡] to lunch at hotel. Tom tells good story of pre-war election in Bournemouth, and a young girl going to polling booth with question: 'Where do servants vote for Sir Henry Page-Croft!'[$]

After lunch Tom shows us St Stephen's Church, Bournemouth, a very fine

---

[*] Stanley Evans (1898–1970), Labour politician. Parliamentary Secretary at the Ministry of Food 1950. He was forced to resign after a speech at Manchester on 14 Apr. 1950 saying that farmers were 'feather-bedded', hence his nickname.

[†] Gavin, 1st Viscount Simonds (1881–1971), judge and politician. Lord Chancellor 1951–4.

[‡] Thomas Driberg, Baron Bradwell (1905–76), journalist and Labour politician.

[$] Sir Henry Page-Croft, 1st Baron Croft (1881–1947), Conservative politician. MP for Bournemouth 1918–40.

example of Gothic-revival – Betjemanism at its finest, not the monstrosity which he is often and wrongly thought to favour.

See Edward Boyle, still clutching a red box, driven away for economic visit to India! More conference.

## 7 October 1955

Geoffrey Lloyd,[*] again taking me down to conference, surprises me by saying that he visited Jung in Zurich on his 80th birthday, or thereabouts. How odd to find a British minister who has even heard of Jung – unless they have been to psychiatric treatment!

Talk to Randolph Churchill about his book on Lord Derby,[†] due to appear next year. Also talk to Nigel Birch,[‡] Minister of Works, about the historic buildings he is restoring. He promises me an early visit to Dover House in Whitehall, which the Scottish office are soon to reoccupy. It is refreshing to find how fond of beautiful things he is. He is also smoking a cigar in the morning, a good sign.

Hear Macmillan. An able speech, though he looks very tired. As I leave Pavilion, Selwyn Lloyd, Minister of Defence,[§] sweeps up steps followed by retinue of menials bearing red boxes. How the crowd loves it!

## 8 October 1955

How primly Lord Woolton looks, when a speaker casts the faintest shadow of criticism across the Government's policy. Hear farewell speeches to Lord Woolton, as Tory Chairman. Mine is the only dry eye. Lady Eden[¶] looks very sour, though bares her fangs and smiles at appropriate moments.

In afternoon, PM himself, showing all those film-star teeth. Quite a good speech, but oh, how one misses Winston. PM's gestures are also too lamentable for words.

To station for special train for London. As I wait on platform, a small,

---

[*] Geoffrey Lloyd, Baron Geoffrey-Lloyd (1902–84), Conservative politician. MP for Birmingham Ladywood 1931–45, Birmingham King's Norton 1950–55 and Sutton Coldfield 1955–74; Minister of Fuel and Power 1951–5 and Minister of Education 1957–9.

[†] His life of Edward Stanley, 14th Earl of Derby (1799–1869), *Lord Derby, King of Lancashire*, a 300,000-word biography of 618 pages (Heinemann, 1959) was motivated by his desire to prove that he was capable of eventually writing the official life of his father, Sir Winston Churchill, a task Churchill promised him in May 1960. The first two volumes of the official life of Churchill were written by Randolph before his death in 1968.

[‡] Baron Rhyl (1906–81), economist and Conservative politician.

[§] Baron Selwyn-Lloyd (1904–78), Conservative politician. Foreign Secretary 1955–60; Chancellor of the Exchequer 1960–62; Speaker of the House of Commons 1971–6.

[¶] Clarissa Eden, Countess of Avon (b. 1920).

shabby, rather Italian figure stumbles along, carrying a suitcase. It is Lord Kilmuir,[*] Lord Chancellor.

In my carriage are the Birches[†] and Thorneycrofts,[‡] all chattering like magpies.

## 9 October 1955

Read Robert Blake's *The Unknown Prime Minister – Bonar Law*, for review in *National Review*.[§] Admirably done, though not untinged by the spirit of Beaverbrook.

## 11 October 1955

John Grigg to dine. Shows me statement he and Linton Andrews,[¶] Editor of *Yorkshire Post*, have prepared for Home Secretary, in attempt to have inquiry into Evans-Christie case reopened. It is a formal document, and I advise John to remove all cracks about Maxwell Fyfe and rhetorical phrases – the arguments are strong enough. John describes his visit to Rillington Place – very squalid. A woman married to a negro now lives there. She described how Christie had once tried to assault her in the house which he shared with Evans – 'but I told him I wasn't having any'. At this, Linton Andrews' face shone with admiration of virtue triumphant. But she went on – 'No, I should want someone a good deal better-looking than him, and want to be paid for it!' Collapse of Linton Andrews.

Before Parliament meets, John and Linton Andrews will see Home Secretary in person. If Evans can be proved innocent of murder for which he was hanged, it means end of capital punishment in England.

---

[*] David Maxwell Fyfe, Earl of Kilmuir (1900–67), Conservative politician and lawyer. Deputy to Sir Hartley Shawcross as Nuremberg prosecutor 1945. Minister of State for Wales 1951–4, where he was nicknamed 'Dai Banana', and Home Secretary 1951–4 (the two posts then being coterminous); Lord Chancellor 1954–62. When he was dismissed as Lord Chancellor by Harold Macmillan on 13 July 1962 in the Night of the Long Knives, he complained that one's cook would have had more notice, to which Macmillan replied that it was easier to find Lord Chancellors than cooks.

[†] Nigel Birch's wife was the Hon. Esme Glyn, dau. of 4th Baron Wolverton.

[‡] Peter, Baron Thorneycroft (1909–94), politician. President of the Board of Trade 1951–7; Chancellor of the Exchequer 1957–8; Conservative Party Chairman 1975–81. Thorneycroft's (second) wife was Countess Carla Roberti (1914–2007), a founder member of the Venice in Peril Fund. Peter Thorneycroft and Enoch Powell resigned together as the Treasury team on 6 Jan. 1958 over Macmillan's economic policy.

[§] Robert, Baron Blake (1916–2003), historian and college head. His biography of Disraeli (Eyre & Spottiswoode, 1966) was described by the American scholar Clarence Cline as 'the best biography of anyone in any language'.

[¶] Sir Linton Andrews (1886–1972), Editor of the *Yorkshire Post* 1939–60.

## 16 October 1955

To office after lunch. All papers have long articles and stories about Princess Margaret and Peter Townsend. Fantastically detailed accounts of their first encounter, secret meetings at Dunnet in August, interview with Queen Mother at Clarence House on Thursday, etc. etc. Hardly any facts, much imagination and some downright lies. All papers except *The People* say marriage is almost certain.

## 16 October 1955, letter to parents

Yesterday I went down to lunch with the Hartleys at Eton – very quiet and pleasant in the mild October weather.

Otherwise I have done little except write a 3,000-word review for John Grigg's paper on the new life of Bonar Law. John is very busy at the moment – with Linton Andrews he is pressing the Home Secretary to reopen an inquiry into the trial of Evans for murder. Many people believe that it was committed in fact by Christie, who was afterwards hanged for other murders. The two men lived in the same house. John has shown me his evidence to be sent to the Home Office. It seems formidable. If he manages to prove that Evans was hanged for a murder he did not commit, it will probably lead to the abolition of capital punishment in England – and that is really John's purpose.

Of course the Townsend business is the main topic of thought in Fleet Street. As you will have seen, we had some sharp comment on the way the Palace has handled it all. In spite of the last statement it seems likely that the Princess will marry him. I think it is a pity, but it is difficult for any outside person to know what is going on.

## 20 October 1955

Dine with Jack Wheeler-Bennett.[*] He is immersed in writing biography of George VI. I ask him what the King used to read. He replies: 'Nothing at all,' and wonders how he can say so. I suggest he uses method of Sydney Lee[†] in writing of Edward VII's foibles – when describing his greed he wrote: 'The King was not a man to toy with his food.' So with George VI's lack of literary interest I suggest – 'His harshest critic could not accuse him of being a bookish pedant.'

---

[*] Sir John Wheeler-Bennett (1902–75), historian; official biographer of George VI.
[†] Sir Sidney Lee (1859–1926), literary scholar; biographer of Edward VII.

## 21 October 1955

To unveiling of Memorial in Mall to King George VI by the Queen. It pours
so heavily with rain that it is hard to see who of the Royal Family are present
– but I do not see Eddie there. I wonder if a snub was intended to Princess Margaret in the Queen's Speech – she talked of 'my mother and other
members of my family'. It would surely have been better to include Princess
Margaret's name as well – she was probably closer than all the others to her
father.

## 23 October 1955

To lunch at Kensington Palace with the Kents. Their apartments have been
decorated most beautifully. Eddie and Princess Alexandra, David Loram
and Charles Johnston (in Foreign Office)* also lunch. I sit next to Princess
Alexandra and have much talk. She tells me that she reads the *DT* leaders,
and I offer my congratulations on her courage. Wants to come and dine at
my flat, and we fix a date. She makes a lovely lemon-juice dressing for the
salad. Not a great deal of talk with the Duchess. As usual she seems restless
and preoccupied, but brightens up when I mention plays, and writes down
their titles.

David Loram, very charming naval equerry to the Queen, insists on
driving me down to the *DT*. We begin to talk about the Princess Margaret-
Townsend affair. I suggest to him that two things at least might have been
done by the Palace. (1) A meeting between the Queen's Private Secretary
and editors, asking them to say nothing until an official announcement was
made – and promising that it would be made. (2) Townsend should have
been invited to do his present courting of the Princess at Balmoral, where
reporters could not have spied on the two of them. As it is, there has been
the present most undignified series of meetings at Clarence House, with the
Queen Mother popping in and out so as not to meet Townsend when he
drives up in his conspicuous motor-car every few hours.

## 24 October 1955

Albert Richardson, President of the Royal Academy, gives me good material
on proposed Chapel of the Order of the British Empire in St Paul's Cathedral.†

Dine John Grigg at Buck's. John thinks there will be great attack on Royal

---

* Vice-Adm. Sir David Loram (1924–2011), Gentleman Usher to the Queen 1982–94. Sir
Charles Johnston (1912–86), High Commissioner in Australia 1965–71.
† Sir Albert Richardson (1880–1964), architect. President of the RA 1954–6. K.R.'s memorial
service took place in this chapel on 8 May 2014.

Family and Church by *Daily Mirror* if Princess M. does not now marry Townsend. The paper will accuse them of 'breaking up a happy romance', etc. etc. He has heard that the night Burgess disappeared with Maclean, he was due to dine with Michael and Pam Berry![*]

Aldrich, the American Ambassador, says that Harriman may get the Presidential nomination instead of Stevenson. 'If so,' he added, 'he will be the worst President in American history since F.D.R.'[†]

### 31 October 1955, letter to parents

You can imagine what a week it has been with the Budget & the Princess Margaret affair still hanging ominously in the background. I heard Butler's speech, rather boring, & a feeble Budget which has annoyed everybody without really grappling with the economic situation. But it did not justify Gaitskell's venomous attack.

This afternoon I am going to the House to hear the vote of censure debate – it will be Morrison's turn to have a go, and I expect he will relish it.

What a row of exhausted volcanoes our ministers look today – except for Eden, with his cinema organist's smile and film-star teeth.

### 31 October 1955

H of C for vote of censure debate on Government. So bad is Herbert Morrison that his election as leader of the Socialists in succession to Attlee is now very remote indeed.

Dine quietly at home. While doing so, wireless programme interrupted to broadcast a Clarence House statement that Princess Margaret does not now intend to marry Group Capt. Townsend. A great relief, and a dignified statement. I suspect she would have been most reluctant to have given up all the comfort and position of Royalty: perhaps this was as influential a factor as her expressed desire not to offend Churchmen by marrying a divorced man.

### 1 November 1955

Lunch Beefsteak. John Grigg tells me he and his deputation of other editors had an hour and a quarter with Gwilym Lloyd-George[‡] at Home Office,

---

* Lady Pamela Berry (1915–82), political hostess.
† Winthrop Aldrich (1885–1974), US Ambassador to the UK 1953–7. Averell Harriman (1891–1985), US Ambassador to the UK 1941–3 and Apr.–Oct. 1946. Adlai Stevenson (1900–65), American Democratic politician and diplomat.
‡ (1894–1967), 1st Viscount Tenby, Liberal and Conservatice politician. Home Secretary and Minister of Welsh Affairs 1954–7.

unsuccessfully trying to persuade him to reopen inquiry of Evans murder trial. Ll. G. did not seem to know much about the case, and had frequently to be prompted by Sir Frank Newsam,[*] Permanent Secretary.

' Walk up Whitehall with Robin Turton,[†] Under-Secretary at FO. Tells me that he often has to say who shall be asked to official lunches given by HMG to distinguished foreign visitors. Some Socialists are usually included, say the Leader and Deputy Leader of the Opposition. But as there are now three men waiting to step into Attlee's shoes – Morrison, Gaitskell and Bevan – all three have sometimes to be asked!

### 3 November 1955

Matthew and Anne Ridley[‡] to dine, and a most agreeable evening. Anne describes visit to Comptroller's office in President's House, Delhi. It was all as in the time of the Viceroys, with photographs of former Comptrollers on the wall and English furniture. Behind the desk sat the present holder of the office – a venerable Indian dressed entirely in snowy white. On the desk was one book only – Mrs Beeton.[§]

### 7 November 1955

To Commons for debate on Burgess and Maclean. Macmillan wounded and hurt by their conduct. Morrison again makes a feeble speech. Best one of all comes from Dick Crossman[¶] – a good rough and tumble on subject of FO complacency about security. Of course, real question is not that they were spies, but that they behaved so badly yet were never sacked.

### 8 November 1955

To Conservative book launch where Robert Blake talks about his life of Bonar Law. Have a few words with Lord Davidson.[**] He tells me he never wrote his famous minute which damned Curzon's chances of premiership

---

[*] (1893–1964), Permanent Under-Secretary of State in the Home Office.

[†] (1903–1994), Baron Tranmire, Conservative politician. Minister of Health 1955–7.

[‡] Matthew, 4th Viscount Ridley (1925–2012) and Lady Anne Ridley (1928–2006) were long-standing friends of K.R., who often spent Christmas at their home, Blagdon Hall, Northumberland.

[§] *Mrs Beeton's Book of Household Management* (1861) by Isabella Beeton (1836–1865) was a guide to running a Victorian household.

[¶] Richard Crossman (1907–74), Labour politician. MP for Coventry 1945–74; his three-volume *Diaries of a Cabinet Minister* was published posthumously following a failed legal attempt by the government to block publication.

[**] J.C.C. Davidson, 1st Viscount Davidson (1889–1970), civil servant and Conservative politician. PS to Bonar Law 1915–20 and 1922–3.

with that intention. He did not know that Ronald Waterhouse[*] would show it to King George V's Secretary, Lord Stamfordham.

Dine Beefsteak with Peter Carrington. On serious ground when discussing the Middle East. Peter insists that Egypt <u>must</u> be supported against Israel if GB is to safeguard supplies of oil.[†]

### 9 November 1955

John Grigg sends me card he has received from Oliver van Oss at Eton praising my article in the *National Review*. As John remarks, Van Oss[‡] is not a man to distribute bouquets lavishly.

To House of Commons where Col. Lipton makes no expected statement withdrawing charge he made recently that a Mr Philby of the FO, now resigned, had helped Burgess and Maclean to escape. Macmillan said on Monday that he had no evidence to bear this out, and Philby himself has challenged Lipton to withdraw or repeat it outside the H of C.[§]

### 10 November 1955

To H of C in afternoon to hear Col. Lipton withdraw his accusations against Philby in a short personal statement. It is heard in hostile silence, and of course cannot be debated. I hear he is now quite the most unpopular MP, even among his own party.

Read *Salvidge of Liverpool* by Stanley Salvidge.[¶] Biography of the Conserv-

---

\* Col. Sir Ronald Waterhouse (1878–1942), PS to Bonar Law. Waterhouse delivered Bonar Law's official resignation letter to George V at the Royal Pavilion, Aldershot, together with J.C. Davidson's memorandum, a well-argued case for Stanley Baldwin to be appointed Prime Minister. Stamfordham gained the impression from Waterhouse that this memorandum 'practically expressed the views of Mr Bonar Law, who was too ill to see the King in person'. Thorpe, *The Uncrowned Prime Ministers*, p. 148.

† Ironic in the light of future events in Oct. 1956 during the Suez Crisis when the British government colluded with Israel to invade Egypt so that Britain and France could intervene to 'separate the combatants' and secure the Suez Canal.

‡ (1909–92), schoolmaster at Eton 1930–59, Lower Master 1959–64, Acting Head Master 1963; Headmaster of Charterhouse 1965–73. A civilised and cultured force in independent education, he was instrumental in commissioning John Piper to design stained-glass windows for Eton Coll. Chapel.

§ Col. Marcus Lipton (1900–78), Labour politician noted for asking difficult questions of the Executive. Despite his denials, Kim Philby (1912–88) was unmasked as a member of the Cambridge Five spy ring in 1963.

¶ Sir Archibald Salvidge (1863–1928), Conservative political organiser, was known as 'the king of Liverpool'. His son Stanley completed *Salvidge of Liverpool*, essentially an edition of Sir Archibald's memoir notes, for publication. It was published in 1934, the year after Stanley's death (Hodder & Stoughton).

ative Party boss who really made F.E. Smith and helped Winston to return to the Conservatives in 1924.

## 13 November 1955

John Grigg to dine. Tremendous indictment of present Government. On home affairs Budget will not solve our economic plight. All the odium of a second Budget, with irritating little purchase tax increases, yet none of the advantages. Trade unions will use this Budget as excuse for pressing more wage claims. Government stupid not to have a strong, unpopular Budget, which could be relaxed in year or two. All Governments can afford to make themselves unpopular during first year of office.

Timidity over capital punishment abolition. Gwilym Lloyd George in hands of Home Office civil servants, e.g. could not deal with delegation about Evans case with confidence.

On foreign affairs absurd to insist that Germany must be reunited; it has ruined Geneva talks. Macmillan was also foolishly optimistic at Alamein reunion – said we had only to lean up against Russia and she would give way again, as she had over Austria. Government will not give self-determination to Cyprus though insisting on it for East Germany. And why not self-determination for Poland for whom ostensibly we went to war in 1939.

## 15 November 1955

My birthday. Nice pigskin cigar-case from Prince Eddie.

Walk along Embankment in sun to H of C. Sydney Silverman* gets leave to bring in his Bill to abolish hanging. It is carried unanimously after his fairly restrained speech under 10-minute rule. This is surprising, and may show change of public opinion in attitude to hanging.

## 16 November 1955

To *DT* for lunch with Michael Berry on 5th floor. I sit near Colin Coote† and we have much gossip. Is very bitter about the whole of the Munich crowd, particularly Neville Chamberlain. Of his editor at *The Times*, Geoffrey

---

* (1895–1968), Labour politician. In 1965 he successfully piloted the Murder (Abolition of Death Penalty) Bill through Parliament for a spell of five years with provision for extension. The necessary resolutions were carried in 1969.

† Sir Colin Coote (1893–1979), journalist and Liberal politician. Editor of the *Daily Telegraph* 1950–64. A fierce opponent of appeasement, which led to him leaving *The Times* in 1942 over their policy on the issue. He then joined the *Daily Telegraph*.

Dawson,[*] he says: 'In his diary he writes that he ordered me to write a leader: he doesn't say that I refused.' When 'The Establishment' is mentioned, Coote refers to me as its Secretary-General.

## 17 November 1955

Train from Oxford to London. Share carriage with Lord and Lady Beveridge, full of chatter the whole journey. He says how poor he is – illustrated by the most frayed tie I have ever seen. They look at Wrench's[†] life of Geoffrey Dawson which I have with me, and Lady B.[‡] comments: 'I said to Harold Nicolson in 1938 that instead of taking a gamp to Munich, Chamberlain would have done better to take Mrs Gamp[§] herself.'

From Paddington go straight to Trocadero for memorable lunch given by the St Emilion wine growers. Also there are John Betjeman, very giggly, and Sir John Hunt,[¶] leader of Everest expedition, with a most impressively tough yet sensitive face.

To House of Commons where Crookshank rather frightful as usual in discussing next week's business. Even the nauseating Gaitskell scores some effective points.

## 18 November 1955

To House of Commons at noon. Talk to Crookshank, who questions me closely about when precisely I begin to write political part of 'Peterborough'. He has obviously noticed its hostile tone towards him during past year or so.

In evening annual dinner of Welsh Guards Comrades Association.

## 19 November 1955

Read Evelyn Wrench's biography of Geoffrey Dawson. It is obviously intended as a corrective to the chapters in *The History of The Times*. But it fails in its purpose. Wrench is not clever enough to select just those passages from Dawson's diaries which would throw his actions into an acceptable pattern. Instead there are tremendous give-away passages, e.g. on hearing Winston

---

[*] (1874–1944), Editor of *The Times* 1912–19 and 1923–41. Harold Macmillan said that *The Times* was always wrong and every twenty years published the next volume of its official history to demonstrate the fact.

[†] Sir Evelyn Wrench (1882–1966), promoter of the British Empire and author of *Geoffrey Dawson and our Times* (Hutchinson, 1955).

[‡] Lady (Jesse) Beveridge (1876–1959), journalist and writer.

[§] Drunken old nurse and midwife in Dickens' novel *Martin Chuzzlewit*.

[¶] (1910–98) Baron Hunt of Llanfair Waterdine, mountaineer and public servant.

make his blood, toil, tears and sweat speech of May 1940 – 'a good little warlike speech'. His appeasement policy appears in all its murkiness, and will only do harm to Dawson's reputation.

### 23 November 1955

Lady Milner[*] talks of the pathos of Curzon's funeral. He had gone to great trouble even about procession from Carlton House Terrace to Westminster Abbey. But hardly anybody in streets noticed it.

### 26 November 1955

Morning train to Ashford to spend weekend with Bill Deedes. Much political talk. Duncan Sandys[†] was apparently disappointed not to be made Minister of Defence when Macmillan[‡] went to FO. Job given instead to Selwyn Lloyd. Bill thinks Rab Butler is utterly knocked out by death of wife, and will leave Treasury to become Leader of House.

### 27 November 1955

More political talk. Bill points out tyranny of trade unions today. Miners will not produce enough coal, even in mild winter, to enable nation to build up a reserve – they are afraid we might have a showdown with them about wage increases. Similarly, London Transport is in a state of mutiny. All this leading to crushing out of existence of middle class.

Bill's work at Ministry of Housing has also revealed some seamy things to him, e.g. Coventry and similar cities are interested only in prestige and wealth of factories, and allow terrible modern slums to develop, with resulting crime wave, immorality, etc.

Also the corruption which money can cause – at Lynmouth[§] there has been so much compensation paid that the whole town is given up to commercialising itself. He spent a day composing mercenary quarrels there. As he drove away he said to civil servant with him: 'Don't look back or you will be turned into a pillar of salt!'

---

* Violet Milner, Viscountess Milner (1872–1958), Editor of the monthly *National Review*.

† Baron Duncan-Sandys (1908–87), Conservative politician and government minister in the 1950s and 1960s; son-in-law of Sir Winston Churchill.

‡ An accurate prediction. Rab Butler became Leader of the House, and Lord Privy Seal, on 29 Dec. 1955. His wife Sydney (1902–54) had died after a prolonged battle with cancer on 9 Dec. 1954, Rab's fifty-second birthday.

§ On 15–16 Aug. 1952 floods devastated the seaside town of Lynmouth in Devon. The final death toll was thirty-four.

## 29 November 1955

Anthony Benn again very helpful in giving me material about peerage law.

Lunch Beefsteak – very full table, including Foreign Secretary, Harold Macmillan. Sit next to Harold Nicolson. He describes scene in Beefsteak before war when Geoffrey Dawson was defending Munich settlement. Robert Byron* suddenly hissed across the table at him: 'Are you in German pay?'

## 30 November 1955

To Eton for St Andrew's Day. Lunch at Grizel Hartley's. A nice-mannered Eton boy also there called Nicholas Ullswater. He succeeded his great-grandfather, the Speaker of the House of Commons, as the 2nd Viscount in 1949: must be a unique succession.† See a little of the unexciting Wall Game, a word with Giles, a glimpse of photographic exhibition.

## 2 December 1955

Dine at Pratt's. Randolph Churchill also here, and talks incessantly till about 1 a.m.

Tells me in great detail how Pamela Berry and Clarissa Eden came to quarrel. When Eden, then For. Sec., was ill, Pamela told a visiting American journalist that he would now never become PM, but was finished. This journalist told Duff Cooper, who wrote to Clarissa from ship in which he died a few hours later, on New Year's Eve 1954, saying that Pamela was out to make mischief.

Whole of Randolph's conversation punctuated by hatred of the PM – 'jerk Eden', he calls him. He is in pugnacious mood, and we have a ding-dong over *DT* policy. He is rather savage in accusing me of having written something offensive about him. Then I discover that he thinks I am Bill Deedes. When I tell him I am not, he apologises, and gives me 'the largest beaker of ducal port' as a gesture of peace.

He is very amusing describing Evelyn Waugh in Yugoslavia. He once accused R.C. of cowardice because R.C. had told him to take off an absurd white duffel coat when a German plane was overhead.

## 8 December 1955

Attlee to take an Earldom after his retirement as Labour leader. To House

---

* (1905–41), travel writer.

† Nicholas Lowther, 2nd Viscount Ullswater (b. 1942), a Lord-in-Waiting. Whip in 1989, Parliamentary Under-Secretary at the Dept. of Employment 1990–03; PS to Princess Margaret 1998–2002. James Lowther, 1st Viscount Ullswater (1855–1949), Conservative politician. Speaker of the House of Commons 1905–21.

of Commons for funereal tributes to him. Eden rather feeble, though it is in his favour that he uses no notes. Winston makes a rare appearance – rather tottery on his legs. Sits in corner seat below the gangway and laughs at Silverman's newly grown beard across the House. He remains alone with his memories for about fifteen minutes of drab committee stage of Finance Bill, then makes a slow and unsteady way out.

Dine with Hartley Shawcross at Savoy Grill. Says that Gaitskell's election as leader of the Socialists almost a certainty. 'I shall vote for Morrison. Would be cruel to oppose him after such service.' Says that Dalton is actively canvassing for Gaitskell, and Shinwell* for Morrison. In both cases, God save them from their friends.

We talk of forthcoming debate on capital punishment. H.S. says he is an anti-hanger. 'If I thought it was a deterrent, I should be in favour of hanging.' On Evans case question, he says he is uneasy – doesn't know whether he did murder or not, but is certain he would not have been convicted had jury known of existence of all Christie's victims. I persuade him to speak against hanging when subject comes up – he had not before intended to. But he may unhappily be doing a case in Singapore when debate takes place. I tell him (a) it is his duty to speak against hanging as the leading advocate in the country, (b) it will do him a lot of good in his party.

## 13 December 1955

Up early to be at Marble Arch for preview of film *Richard III*. Enjoy film enormously, though battle scenes not as effective as they might be. Too few men. Brilliant touch – close up of dead Richard's armour, showing Garter on leg of armour, with *Honi soit qui mal y pense*. Then to Claridge's for most excellent buffet lunch. Talk to Olivier† – he is rather small and entirely unaggressive in conversation.

## 15 December 1955

*DT* has a good story forecasting changes in the Government – Rab to be Leader of the House, Macmillan to Treasury and Selwyn Lloyd to Foreign Office.

To H of C. Gaitskell appears as leader of Socialists for first time. Great ovation. Mrs Gaitskell‡ sits smugly in Speaker's Gallery. Winston in House, very tottery.

---

* Emanuel ('Manny'), Baron Shinwell (1884–1986), trade union official and Labour politician. Minister of Fuel and Power 1945–7, War Secretary 1947–50, Minister of Defence 1950–51.
† Sir Laurence Olivier, Baron Olivier (1907–89), actor; Director of the Chichester Festival Theatre 1961–5, Director of the National Theatre 1963–73.
‡ Dora, Baroness Gaitskell (1901–89), Labour politician.

## 19 December 1955

To House of Lords – dull committee stage of copyright Bill. Then to H of C. Cheese and wine party in Members' Dining Room. Somebody asks Reginald Maudling,* Minister of Supply, if he is a gourmet. 'No,' he replies, 'I just like food.'

## 21 December 1955

Tepid reception to Cabinet changes. Butler from Treasury to be Leader of the House; Macmillan from FO to Treasury; Selwyn Lloyd from Defence to FO; Monckton from Labour to Defence; Macleod to Labour; Turton to Health; Birch to Air; Boyd-Carpenter† from Transport to Pensions, now not to have a seat in Cabinet; Jim Thomas still Admiralty, and a peer; Geoffrey Lloyd leaves Fuel, and no peerage.

## 25 December 1955

Hear Queen's Christmas broadcast. So platitudinous that Anthony Eden must surely have taken a hand in its composition.

## 28 December 1955

Charming little letter from Marie-Lou, sent from Chequers where she and Philip have been staying for Christmas. Postal address is 'Butler's Cross'!

Lunch Donald McLachlan‡ at Brooks's to discuss devastating article to appear in *DT* on Tuesday, attacking policy, or rather lack of it, of Eden Government. I am inclined to be even more severe than he.

Much general talk about the *DT*. He describes lunch at Barton Street with Michael and Pam Berry – far too much petty malice about Eden, without getting at the real failure of his policy.

## 30 December 1955

To Covent Garden as Malcolm Sargent's guest to watch him conducting Walton's *Troilus and Cressida* – I heard it for first time a year ago. It does not

---

* (1917–79), Conservative politician. Chancellor of the Exchequer 1962–4, Home Secretary 1970–72.

† John Boyd-Carpenter, Baron Boyd-Carpenter (1908–98), Conservative politician. Minister under Churchill, Eden, Macmillan and Douglas-Home.

‡ (1908–71), author and journalist. Deputy Editor of the *Daily Telegraph* 1954–60. Founding Editor of the *Sunday Telegraph* 1961–6. In his article 'The Firm Smack of Government' in the *Daily Telegraph* on 3 Jan. 1956, McLachlan wrote: 'There is a favourite gesture with the Prime Minister. To emphasise a point he will clash one fist to smash the open palm of the other hand but the smash is seldom heard.' He claimed that people were waiting in vain for 'the smack of firm government'. Eden was deeply wounded by this criticism and unwisely responded to it.

seem to have improved in the interval – still too many Brittenish discords, and no longer such a good Pandarus as Peter Pears. Gossip with Malcolm in his dressing room. He is going to Broadlands to stay with the Mountbattens for New Year. How he loves it all. When someone once taunted him with staying with Mountbattens, he replied: 'Yes, they are climbers, aren't they?'

# 1956

*The year 1956 ushered in a pivotal phase in the post-war history of Britain. The Cold War dominated foreign policy considerations during this period and for many years afterwards. Late in 1956, the Suez Crisis divided the nation and Kenneth was highly critical of the role of the British government.*

### 1 January 1956
Another Bloody Year, as Sir William Eden[*] would say.

To office, where spend most of the afternoon writing about the Honours List. Extraordinary that Osbert Sitwell[†] should have been given only a CBE. Even more extraordinary he has accepted it.

Anthony Benn most helpful in advising me on archiepiscopal peerages; as he rightly says, they are not so much <u>honours</u> as conveniences to allow archbishops to remain in Lords.

McLachlan shows me proof of his article on the Eden Government. I suggest that he should not kill Eden to make Butler king – as Ch. of Ex. he has been disastrous.

John Altrincham [Grigg][‡] to dine. Doubts whether Aubrey Jones,[§] new Minister of Fuel, will appeal strongly to the miners. Quotes penetrating remark made by Lord Salisbury – 'The trouble about Jones is that he makes me feel so common.'

### 3 January 1956
In morning to Ministry of Education for talk with David Eccles. Good political gossip. Is delighted that Rab Butler has at last left the Treasury. 'I used to come out of Cabinet meetings in summer almost in tears. Butler made the mistake of thinking that when our economic position improved it

---

[*] Sir William Eden, 7th Bt (1849–1915), sportsman and artist. He was renowned for his rages. Father of Anthony Eden.
[†] Sir Osbert Sitwell, 5th Bt (1892–1969), writer.
[‡] 2nd Baron Altrincham (b. 1934).
[§] (1911–2003), Conservative politician and industrialist. Minister of Fuel and Power 1955–7.

was due to his handling of it; in fact it was due to economic factors. When these began to turn against us, Butler became a spent force.' As Lord Privy Seal he will have no real power: this has now passed to Macmillan – 'the man who has the money has the power'. Eccles has great faith in Macmillan. He agrees that Donald McLachlan's article on the Government in today's *DT* is justified. Is very sorry Bobbety Salisbury has not been given job, if not FO, at least should have been Minister of Defence. Selwyn Lloyd not a strong character – 'Eden will write his despatches.' Also mentions that there might be divorce between Selwyn and wife, which would be bad for Government.

He then shows me his pictures which line walls of his office. Mostly Paul Nash, including one just acquired of hilly landscape, with bright touches of unexpected colour. Another of some toadstools. Believes there are only three modern painters worth buying – Nash, Augustus John and Walter Sickert.

Later John Altrincham turns up with Sir Linton Andrews for much good talk. L.A. says: 'I was disturbed to read today's attack on the Government by the *Daily Telegraph* (long pause) because I could not think of an answer to it.' Says that Eden used to send his speeches to Arthur Mann, Editor of the *Yorkshire Post*, to be 'improved'.

Talks of *Yorkshire Post* and Abdication Crisis. When L.A. saw afternoon report of Bishop of Bradford's[*] speech, he at once decided it was signal for general release of comment on situation. But he did not realise that the rest of the press might not regard it as such. Arthur Mann[†] was in London, but agreed with Andrews. Poor Bishop of Bradford had not, of course, intended to precipitate the crisis. He did not even know who Mrs Simpson was when asked. On night that *Yorkshire Post* was preparing to break press silence, a reporter asked L.A. if he should telephone Blunt to check what he had said. 'For God's sake no!' he replied. Dr Blunt was very angry about it all – he never got his expected preferment.

Andrews likes Bishop Winnington-Ingram of London,[‡] but found him a bit of a humbug. He once met him in a club and mentioned that he had confirmed him. 'Of course I remember,' said W.I., 'it was at Harrow.' But it

---

[*] Dr The Rt Revd Alfred Blunt (1879–1957), Bishop of Bradford 1931–55. On 1 Dec. 1936, addressing his Diocesan Conference, Dr Blunt said that the King needed to give more positive signs of awareness of his need for God's grace. Dubbed the blow from a blunt instrument, Edward VIII said that the Bishop's statement was 'the spark that caused the explosion'.

[†] (1876–1972), Editor of the *Yorkshire Post* 1919–39. He helped to precipitate the Abdication of Edward VIII by publishing Bishop Blunt's comments on the King.

[‡] Arthur Winnington-Ingram (1858–1946), Bishop of London 1901–39.

wasn't! 'And have you kept all your promises?' continued the Bishop. 'No' replied Andrews.

Stories of the Princess Royal[*] in Yorkshire. One Lord Mayor of Bradford asked her for the fat she had left on her plate, and a Lady Mayoress at some ceremony went up to her every fifteen minutes to ask her if she wanted to go to the loo.

At the Beefsteak have some amusing talk with James Pope-Hennessy[†] who is writing the official life of Queen Mary. He is shortly going to Scandinavia to talk to all Royals who can give him information. Then he will go down the Rhine on similar quests. Has already discovered the Duke of Teck's[‡] valet – is over ninety and lives in Battersea. James is most amusing about little Prince Charles. Says he may well turn out to be another Edward II, as he hates boxing and other rough games!

### 5 January 1956

Lunch Beefsteak. Philip de Zulueta dismisses *DT* article on Eden Government as a typical piece of Lady Pamela Berry's spite. I try earnestly to convince him that it isn't – but of course Lady P.'s vendetta does blunt the point of our attack when we have a really strong case to make.

Malcolm Sargent tells me about his re-scoring of the organ parts of the *Messiah* for brass instruments. Also at the lunch Harold Nicolson repeats to Malcolm the remark of his secretary – 'You go to the best tailors and the best shirt-makers, but you never look as smart as Sir Malcolm Sargent!'

Harold describes how when the Burgess and Maclean scandal was at its height, a man came to call on him at Albany, implying he was a friend of Burgess wanting news. So Harold told him all he knew of him. Then the man revealed for the first time that he was from the *Daily Express*. Next morning the whole thing appeared as an interview. How stupid of H.N. to be so incautious. He added that he often read of officials being paid to reveal secrets 'but I never knew any secret that was worth anything while at the Foreign Office, except the ciphers. Diplomats are not given military secrets.' He doubts whether either Burgess or Maclean were of any use to the Russians.

### 6 January 1956

In office John Betjeman wandering dismally round the passages looking for

---

[*] Mary, Princess Royal and Countess of Harewood (1897–1965), wife of Henry Lascelles, 6th Earl of Harewood (1882–1947).

[†] (1916–74), biographer and travel writer.

[‡] Francis, Duke of Teck (1837–1900), father of Queen Mary.

a telephone. I lead him to my room, where he telephones Slough! Apparently a doctor there gave shelter to his wife, stranded in the fog. 'Come friendly bombs, and fall on Slough . . .'!

Get a note from Michael Berry soon after 4.30 to say that Jim Thomas's new title is Lord Cilcennin. I ring Admiralty but find he has left for Paddington. Telephone stationmaster's office, and manage to get on to Jim a couple of minutes before his 4.45 train leaves. He gives me correct pronunciation of Cilcennin.

### 7 January 1956

*Messiah* at the Albert Hall, Malcolm conducting. Usual good performance, though the new brass parts do not compensate for loss of the organ. Then to Malcolm's flat for tea and champers. Malcolm has put away all his Christmas cards except the Royal ones! He also shows me a by now much-thumbed letter from the Queen, saying she has enjoyed him on TV, and a charming little letter from one of the Gloucester boys. Apparently Malcolm sends them all very good presents every Christmas.

### 8 January 1956

*Sunday Express* has a leader supporting the PM and attacking the *DT* for its petticoat government by Lady Pamela Berry. Eden again gets a bad press. Worst folly of all, No. 10 has denied that Eden is going to resign. He really has reached a nadir of popularity.

Malcolm Sargent, Marie-Lou and John Altrincham to dine – Philip is with the PM at Chequers. As usual Malcolm Sargent dominates the conversation. Tells story of how Danny Kaye[*] once addressed Princess Margaret as honey. There was a hush, broken by Princess Margaret saying: 'Oh well, honey soit qui mal y pense!'

Malcolm is delighted with the remark of my butcher when I ask him if he has any brains: 'No, if I had I should be writing for the *Observer!*'

### 9 January 1956

Play Malcolm's recording of the *Messiah*. Such a stroke of genius to have it made by Huddersfield Choral Society, with their broad vowels – 'oontoo oos a soon is given'.

### 10 January 1956

David Loram to dine. Much amusing talk about his work as equerry to the

---

[*] (1911–87), American actor, singer, dancer and comedian.

Queen ... We discuss whether it is justified to criticise Queen on grounds that she does not carry out enough engagements. He says she has between one and two hours with Private Secretary, even at Balmoral. When in London she also has an hour or so of reading State papers after dinner. Then she has her family and the running of her household. David says: 'She takes a most minute interest in these matters. One cannot move a cushion from one chair to another without her permission. She knows everybody's name, arranges table seating plans, introduces all guests to others herself, makes sure a guest sits next to her at dinner the night before he leaves. But above all she feels a great responsibility as head of the Commonwealth.' Is most amusing about way palaces are run. At Balmoral picnics even the butter is made into pats, each bearing the Royal cipher. One night David dined alone in equerries' room. There were twenty-five pieces of cutlery on the table, and he was given five large chops, of which he ate only one.

## 11 January 1956
Lunch Beefsteak. Lord Sherwood[*] says, 'My New Year resolution is to try and think better in future of Lord Beaverbrook and all those other colonials.'

## 12 January 1956
Meet Bill Deedes for a drink at the Junior Carlton Club, then take him to dine at the Beefsteak. Michael Adeane[†] there – amiable, but I don't really think he is up to the immense responsibility of being the Queen's Private Secretary.[‡] But he talks well on the niceties of official correspondence – when to use the prefix 'dear' and when 'my dear'. Bill also makes the point that the word Cabinet should never have a prefix, i.e. 'Cabinet decided today', not 'The Cabinet'.

Bill and I return to my flat for a couple of hours of good political talk. He likes being at the Home Office, where he was appointed an Under-Secretary on 20 December. Gwilym Lloyd George will take two minutes to discuss a problem where Duncan Sandys at Ministry of Housing would take two hours. Bill's problems are mainly civil defence, aliens and fire brigades.

Takes a gloomy view of the Government's prospects. 'All the vitamins have gone out of them. I have a hunch that in a year's time we shall be in Opposition. Eden will not fall alone – we shall all be out together. The Conservative

---

* Hugh Seely, 1st Baron Sherwood (1898–1970), Liberal politician.
† Michael Edward Adeane, Baron (1910–84), courtier. Principal PS to Elizabeth II 1954–72.
‡ 'I was utterly wrong.' Note added by K.R., 1 Aug. 2004.

Party is impressive only in adversity, e.g. in 1947. There is now no intellectual support for it.

Main reason why Conservatives have lost faith of their supporters is that the Government has not fought for the middle class. Since 1951 the middle class has declined faster than during Socialist Government. Monckton must bear much of the blame for this – he has never stood up to the tyranny of the unions. How ridiculous to promote him, yet sack Geoffrey Lloyd, who appeased the miners under orders just as Monckton appeased the unions.

The Conservatives must break through this conspiracy of silence about the tyranny of the unions. It is wrong to imagine the unions will break off their outrageous demands if they are not openly criticised. What we need is a Lord Randolph Churchill group to fight the Government on the issue of the middle class. They must demand better pensions, better officers' pay. Trouble is that about 150 Conservative MPs are immobilised through their being in the Government, PPSs or officers of committees. But Bill Deedes has hopes that some of the younger MPs will take up the cause.

As far as Eden himself is concerned, Bill thinks it was a very great mistake to issue an official denial that he was going to resign. George Christ,[*] who should have been PM's PRO, would never have made that mistake. When making speeches Eden should remember advice for Lloyd George – if you use your hands when speaking, use them from the shoulder.

Doubtful if Macmillan has the health to inaugurate the reform of the Treasury which is needed. Macmillan is the sort of man who is at his best when letting his mind play over problems. But at Treasury most of his time spent presiding over routine work and committees of ministers. Financial Secretary to the Treasury and Economic Secretary to the Treasury could quite easily remove this burden from him, but protocol will not allow it. It must be reformed by a strong man. Burden of work on ministers today is so great that there is increasing habit of following the Churchillian habit of working for an hour or two in bed in the morning.

Says Crookshank will be a loss to Government – was quite brilliant and very shrewd in committees. Ted Heath may not be as good a Whip as Buchan-Hepburn.[†]

---

[*] (1904–72), Conservative Party Liaison Officer 1946–65. Speech-writer for Harold Macmillan.

[†] Patrick Buchan-Hepburn, Baron Hailes (1901–74), politician. Governor General of the Federation of the West Indies, 1957–62; Conservative Party Chief Whip 1948–55; Minister of Works 1955–7.

## 13 January 1956

In *The Times* Robert Blake answers rather weakly the letter sent by Violet Bonham Carter* in which she denied Blake's story in his life of Bonar Law, told him by Beaverbrook, that on Whit Monday morning, 1916, Asquith was playing bridge with three women and would not interrupt it to see Bonar Law.†

See that Walton's *Troilus and Cressida* has been rather a flop at La Scala, Milan. Apparently it pleased neither the Verdi school nor the extreme modernists – 'Too much borrowed music,' was the verdict.‡

## 19 January 1956

Beefsteak. Have a long talk with Sir Michael Adeane. We discuss whether it was wise of Alec Hardinge§ to publish in *The Times* recently his account of the pre-Abdication episode when he wrote King Edward VIII a letter about his relations with Mrs Simpson. He was provoked into doing so by Beaverbrook's review of Wrench's new life of Geoffrey Dawson, to whom Hardinge showed draft of letter before sending it to Edward VIII. Adeane would not have attempted to vindicate himself in this way.

Real trouble was that Edward VIII inherited Hardinge. Although he had no confidence in him, he decided to keep him to ensure continuity. Mistake King made was in thinking he could lead two quite different lives, public and private. He thought nobody would care about his private life – in fact, as recent events regarding Princess Margaret show, they care more about private than public lives. Adeane adds: 'Edward VIII had no real sense of duty. The late King and King George VI did what was asked of them.'

---

* Helen Violet Bonham Carter, Baroness Asquith of Yarnbury (1887–1969), British Liberal politician and diarist. Randolph Churchill wrote to her to say that the ensuing angry correspondence on the matter was the only thing worth reading in *The Times* for many months.

† Robert Blake's revelation regarding Asquith playing bridge on a Monday morning at a crucial time during the Battle of the Somme angered the Asquith relatives, though it was true. Ironically, Bonar Law's hostile reaction was dominated by the belief that it could not have been a serious bridge game as it was with three women. Others more realistically regarded it as a dereliction of duty by the Prime Minister at a crucial time in the war.

‡ The failure of *Troilus and Cressida*, both in its original version and in its revised version of 1971, performed like the original at Covent Garden, was the greatest disappointment of Walton's career, following the triumphs of Britten's *Peter Grimes* (1945) and *Billy Budd* (1951), and the impact of Tippett's *Midsummer Marriage* (1955). Both Britten and Tippett were now regarded by the musical world as the leading British composers, displacing Walton from his 1930s pre-eminence.

§ Sir Alexander Hardinge, 2nd Baron Hardinge of Penshurst (1894–1960), PS to Edward VIII and George V.

## 20 January 1956

Giles St Aubyn and Wilfrid Blunt* dine with me. Robert Birley† is making himself rather unpopular at Eton. Apparently a member of Pop was caught cribbing in school, and Birley put great pressure on President of Pop to de-Pop him, which was done. Birley had also forced Watkin Williams to give up his house – it had gone completely to pieces. Birley discovered all this by grilling members of the house.

## 2 February 1956

To House of Commons. I see a danger that Gaitskell might become a sort of Socialist Walter Monckton,‡ invariably cheered by the Conservatives whenever he speaks. This he could achieve by being reasonable in public yet evolutionary in private, as is the wont of public-school Socialists.

Dine at the Fishmongers' Hall. Annigoni portrait of the Queen a most distinguished piece of work.§ Filthy food, including cod which is brought in literally to a fanfare of trumpets, but has no taste and no sauce. The wines too are served in the wrong order – a sweet dessert wine with the fish, and Chablis with the pudding. Sit next to a Fleetwood trawler owner, who loudly complains about it all with great justice. He also gets rather plastered, and when Heathcoat-Amory,¶ Minister of Agriculture, says how nice it all is, he shouts out: 'Blurry orful.'

## 4 February 1956

Read Evelyn Waugh's *The Loved One* – it still provokes a smile.

## 9 February 1956

Lunch Beefsteak. Sit next to Harold Nicolson. Today is election for Oxford Professorship of Poetry, but Harold says he has heard from John Sparrow**

---

\* (1901–87), art teacher. Curator of the Watts Gallery, Compton.

† Sir Robert Birley (1903–82), headmaster and educational administrator. Headmaster of Charterhouse 1935–47; educational adviser to the military governor, Allied Control Commission, Germany 1947–9; Head Master of Eton 1949–63; Professor of Education at the Universiy of Witwatersrand, South Africa 1964–7, where he campaigned against apartheid.

‡ 1st Viscount Monckton of Brenchley (1891–1965), Conservative politician and adviser to Edward VIII. Minister of Labour 1951–5; Minister of Defence 1955–6; Paymaster General 1956–7; Chairman, Midland Bank 1957–64.

§ Pietro Annigoni (1910–88), Italian portrait painter. His 1955 portrait of the Queen was commissioned by the Worshipful Company of Fishmongers.

¶ Derick Heathcoat-Amory, 1st Viscount Amory (1899–1981), Conservative politician. Minister of Agriculture, Fisheries and Food 1954–8; Chancellor of the Exchequer 1958–60.

** (1906–92), academic. Warden of All Souls Coll., Oxford 1952–77.

that the vote will go against him. Pretends to be philosophic, but is really very sad.

To Church Assembly, where for once they are not talking about sex, but about education.

Hear result of Oxford election. W.H. Auden elected with 216 votes, Nicolson has 192 and Wilson Knight 91. Disappointing for Harold to miss it by so little, but I suppose he has little to say about poetry, whereas Auden might be quite exciting.

John Altrincham telephones. Is going off to lecture in Germany. Says he has been talking to Alan Bullock about his life of Ernest Bevin. Among papers he has discovered some evidence that in 1942 Beaverbrook wanted Bevin to help him to overthrow Churchill. Bevin refused, and said he would tell Churchill what Beaverbrook was up to. 'Do so,' replied Beaverbrook, 'he won't believe you.' So Bevin went to Churchill, and Churchill didn't believe him!

Also tells story of Arthur Deakin* being stopped one evening by three tough dockers, who threatened him and accused him of having sold them to the employers in some dispute. 'And how much do you think I would get for three miserable buggers like you?' said Deakin.

## 10 February 1956

Lunch Hartley Shawcross at the Savoy. Judicial appointments. Lord Chief Justice Goddard likely to retire on eightieth birthday. Probably succeeded by Manningham-Buller.†

Hartley Shawcross himself still anxious for a City job. At the moment he can save little, partly due to taxation, partly to his own extravagant tastes – yacht, motor cars, etc. Of his big case in Singapore soon, he will make £75 for every £1,000 marked on brief – i.e. several weeks' work for about £250. Cannot refuse briefs – once one does that, practice declines.

Hartley Shawcross also tells me of a case before the Lord Chief Justice where he had pleaded that his client had been ruined. 'Ruined?' said Goddard, with a leer at Hartley Shawcross, 'He doesn't seem to have exercised any particular economy in his choice of counsel.'

---

* (1890–1955), General Secretary of the Transport and General Workers' Union 1945–55.
† Sir Reginald Manningham-Buller, 1st Viscount Dilhorne (1905–80), lawyer and Conservative politician. Solicitor-General 1951–4; Attorney-General 1954–62; Lord Chancellor 1962–4. Nicknamed 'Bullying Manner'. A sounder of opinions in the Oct. 1963 Conservative leadership contest, he fulfilled his task, in Rab Butler's words, 'like a large Clumber spaniel sniffing the bottoms of the hedgerows'.

## 14 February 1956

David Eccles sends me a Valentine he has received from some disgruntled teachers.

With Marie-Lou de Zulueta and Malcolm Sargent for Walton's *Troilus and Cressida*. I still don't like the opera very much – rather a jumble of styles, with a most disagreeable character in Pandarus. In interval talk to Christopher Hassall[*] in foyer. He wrote libretto, and went out to Milan recently for first night at La Scala. Says it had a mixed cast but superb scenery. Reception of it ruined by a small claque, one with a small whistle.

As we leave Covent Garden, a rather shy-looking boy who has been hovering for some time approaches Malcolm. He holds out an autograph book with the words: 'You are Sir Thomas Beecham,[†] aren't you?' Without batting an eyelid, Malcolm signs his book. Outside, we ask him what he signed. 'Thomas Beecham,' he replied.

## 15 February 1956

Dine Beefsteak. Much talk with Lord Somervell.[‡] He is still consumed by dislike of Winston. Tells me story of wartime debate on whether MPs could remain so when holding offices of profit under the Crown abroad, as did Duff Cooper and Louis Spears.[§] Somervell was to speak early in debate, and Winston was to wind up. 'Don't steal my thunder,' said Winston to Somervell before Somervell rose!

Much talk on how culpable Baldwin was over failure to rearm. Somervell says: 'You don't know what it was like to fight a marginal seat when Bob Cecil[¶] and the League of Nations Union posted up pictures of babies wearing gas masks.' In any case, he adds, Winston was to blame for not keeping armaments at a proper level when Chancellor in 1924. We never caught up

---

[*] (1912–63), dramatist and librettist.

[†] Sir Thomas Beecham, 2nd Bt (1879–1961), conductor and impresario. He founded the London Philharmonic Orchestra with Sir Malcolm Sargent in 1932. Beecham was a great champion of the music of Frederick Delius. Originally buried at Brookwood Cemetery, Surrey, his remains were exhumed in 1961 and reburied in St Peter's Church, Limpsfield, Surrey, next to the grave of Delius.

[‡] Sir Donald Somervell, Baron Somervell of Harrow (1889–1960), barrister, judge and Conservative politician. Attorney-General 1936–45; Home Secretary 25 May–26 July 1945.

[§] Maj.-Gen. Sir Edward Spears, 1st Bt (1886–1974). Senior British Army officer and National Liberal, later National Conservative, MP for Loughborough 1922–4 and Carlisle 1931–45; Liaison Officer between British and French forces in both world wars.

[¶] Lord Robert Cecil, 1st Viscount Cecil of Chelwood (1864–1958), lawyer, Conservative politician and diplomat. He was an architect of the League of Nations and was awarded the Nobel Prize for Peace 1937.

once we began to be unprepared.

Story of Quickswood[*] bidding farewell to Fellows of Eton: 'Most Provosts leave Eton for Heaven, but I leave for Bournemouth.'

## 16 February 1956

Hear the result of Commons debate on capital punishment. It is to be abolished by a majority of thirty-one.

## 21 February 1956

To National Book League for the opening of the book sale by Rab Butler. Have some talk with him. Is worn out. In a little speech he goes out of his way to say he has not accepted this invitation to publicise himself, but because he loves books. Until he said his, nobody would have suspected that it was otherwise.

## 22 February 1956

In evening to Londonderry House for party given by George Weidenfeld[†] and Nigel Nicolson[‡] to celebrate Tom Driberg's life of Beaverbrook. Tom himself stands at top of stairs, magnificently gracious in receiving guests.

Bob Boothby tells me he has just come from the House, where he had an hour's talk with Winston. The old man had admitted to Bob that he felt he had deteriorated since leaving office. A word with Sydney Silverman, very modest about the success of his anti-hanging campaign.

## 24 February 1956

See that the Government have ratted over hanging. Instead of introducing a Bill to abolish hanging themselves, they are merely allowing Silverman time to bring in his Bill.

## 28 February 1956

Oliver Franks[§] has described the United States President as 'George III for

---

[*] Lord Hugh Cecil ('Linky'), Baron Quickswood (1869–1956), Conservative politician. Provost of Eton 1936–44. Nicknamed Linky by his brothers, who saw a resemblance to the Missing Link between ape and man.

[†] (1919–2016), Baron Weidenfeld, publisher and philanthropist. He founded the publishing firm Weidenfeld & Nicolson with Nigel Nicolson in 1948. He published all K.R.'s books and was instrumental in securing Rose's journals for the firm.

[‡] (1917–2004), publisher and Conservative politician.

[§] Sir Oliver Franks, Baron Franks of Headington (1905–92), civil servant, diplomat and college head. Provost of Queen's Coll., Oxford 1946–8; Ambassador to the US 1948–52; Provost of Worcester Coll., Oxford 1962–76; Chairman, Inquiry into the Falklands War 1982.

four years' – i.e. complete powers during that period. President Truman once told him that before breakfast he had to sign 500 papers with his own hand. What if he is too ill? The signature is forged with tacit understanding that its legality will not be challenged in the courts. To legislate for the reform of this clumsy system might mean altering the Constitution of the United States.

## 29 February 1956

Meet Bill Deedes in House of Commons. Says that Silverman's anti-hanging Bill is going to be a protracted struggle in committee – many amendments put down by its opponents to qualify its effects will have to be debated.

## 3 March 1956

To Eton to lunch with Hubert Hartley and Grizel. Grizel shows me a collection of Eton beaks' photographs about thirty years ago – very much more full of character than the present lot. Hubert makes typical remark about Alan Barker and his wife:* 'You must see their new house in the High Street. Everything has been beautifully done – her father was an upholsterer.' Grizel explains that Hubert really means her mother was an interior decorator.

## 5 March 1956

Donald McLachlan is writing to Geoffrey Harrison,† an Assistant Under-Secretary at the Foreign Office, to suggest that we tell the Russians that unless they sign an agreement on subversive activities and propaganda, we shall publish a White Paper setting out all the damaging information we have collected about them on the subject. I believe that McClachlan got the idea from Curzon's attitude to the Russians.‡

Stories from Jim Thomas [Cilcennin] of how appalling Randolph Churchill can be. One day Jim took Admiral Eccles,§ Commander-in-Chief Home Fleet, to White's. Randolph Churchill lurched up rather drunk. When Jim introduced the Admiral, Randolph merely said: 'What is it like to have a First Sea Lord who is a Communist spy?' Randolph has also been making similar remarks to Senators while in the USA. In fact, says Jim, Dickie Mountbatten

---

* Alan Barker (1923–88), cavalry officer, wounded in Normandy 16 June 1944. Schoolmaster at Eton 1947–53 and 1955–8; Fellow of Queens' Coll., Cambridge 1953–5; Headmaster of the Leys School, Cambridge 1958–75; Headmaster of University School, Hampstead 1975–82. Jean Barker, Baroness Trumpington (b. 1922), Conservative member of the House of Lords.
† Sir Geoffrey Harrison (1908–90), Ambassador to the Soviet Union 1965–8.
‡ In 1921 Curzon, as Foreign Secretary, had rebuked the Bolsheviks for their intrigues, which he declared were 'more than usually repugnant to normal international law'.
§ Adm. Sir John Eccles (1898–1966), C.-in-C. Home Fleet 1955–8.

is the best First Sea Lord he has ever worked with.

We discuss stormy waters in which the Government has found itself lately. Jim says there is a hoodoo on it! Also Jim says that Eden needs soothing during his rages by those who understand him and do not carry out instructions given in a rage and regretted in later moments of calmness.

## 6 March 1956

Take Andrew Bruce[*] to dine at Beefsteak. Harold Nicolson and James Pope-Hennessy coo at each other, separated only by Peter Quennell.[†] Also there are Lord Somervell and Sir Basil Bartlett,[‡] who was at Repton under Fisher as a boy. It has left him with a deep hatred of the Archbishop! Basil Bartlett tells me that *Mr Norris Changes Trains* was written as a joke against Arthur Norris,[§] the Drawing Master at Repton. Nobody knew what sort of private life he led, so Isherwood wrote this fantasy, and gave the central character the name of Norris, who was rather flattered by it all.

## 7 March 1956

Many years ago Tommy Beecham was asked whether Malcolm Sargent had been knighted. 'No,' replied Beecham, 'only doctored.'

## 9 March 1956

Government arrests and deports Archbishop Makarios of Cyprus. First strong thing it has done in a long time – and probably an unwise move.

## 11 March 1956

Lunch at Kensington Palace, alone with Prince Eddie. Princess Alexandra in the Royal Yacht with the Queen, and the Duchess has gone to Eton to take Michael[¶] out to lunch.

As usual admirable food – eggy dish, roast chicken, salad, fruit salad, cheese and Moselle. After lunch we sit in Alexandra's room, with blue walls and a piano. Then Eddie takes me on a tour of the whole house. Dining room,

---

[*] 11th Earl of Elgin (b. 1924). Chief of the Clan Bruce; Lord Lieutenant of Fife 1987–99.

[†] Sir Peter Quennell (1905–93), biographer and literary historian.

[‡] 2nd Bt Bartlett of Hardington Mandeville (1905–85). Captain at Dunkirk 1940; actor and screenwriter; head of the BBC's script dept. in the 1950s.

[§] (1889–1962), artist and schoolmaster. Drawing Master at Repton 1922–52, where he was nicknamed 'Arty' by Repton boys, and with his bow tie, trilby and grey curls was the antithesis of the sporting hero. He was a mentor to Roald Dahl, among others. Geoffrey Fisher, Baron Fisher of Lambeth (1887–1972), Headmaster of Repton School 1914–32; Bishop of Chester 1932–9; Bishop of London 1939–45; Archbishop of Canterbury 1945–61.

[¶] Prince Michael of Kent (b. 1942).

of course very fine. The Duchess's little sitting room lined with books – a great number of them about the various Royal families of Europe. Also some Philip de Laszlo* portraits. Eddie's study full of his father's books in splendid bindings – one feels sad that all that good taste of his should have perished.

On staircase, for instance, one of four Gobelin tapestries bought by Prince George, and, says Eddie, the most valuable things in the house. Upstairs see Eddie's large bedroom, with sweet clock given him by Queen Mary. Duchess's bedroom large and pink, with bathroom carpeted and arm-chaired like a drawing room. A vast bed, with a telephone on either side. Princess Alexandra's bedroom nice, but hardly palatial.

Then to attics where Michael has a huge playroom with model railways. Also a Ministry of Works model of Kensington Palace, built in sections so that the Duchess could decide how to plan the house before moving in. Most windows look out onto a courtyard or onto Kensington Gardens. The garden belonging to the house is rather bleak, but will not be used in the summer. They move to Coppins in about a month's time. All inside is being redecorated. Eddie now has a new car and drops me at the *Telegraph*.

### 12 March 1956

Good talk at lunch with Sir Henry d'Avigdor-Goldsmid,† who entered Commons as Conservative MP for Walsall last year. Has a dry, engaging wit. Is an anti-hanger and is voting for Silverman's Bill. Describes how, when he was High Sheriff of Kent, his duty was to pay the hangman for an execution – it was fifteen guineas. The hangman's assistant was not only unpaid, but had to pay the hangman for the privilege of being there. His profession was a schoolmaster.

He is a complete anti-Baldwinite: 'If the term Albion perfide means anything, it means Stanley Baldwin.'

To Commons, where great row on Government's arrest of Archbishop Makarios in Cyprus.

### 13 March 1956

Dine Bill Deedes at House of Commons. Bill still looks thin, but in good spirits. Says that to work in the Home Office after the Ministry of Housing is like leaving an efficient line regiment for a rather smart regiment which

---

* (1869–1937), Hungarian painter. Among his commissions was a portrait of Prince George, Duke of Kent (1902–42), killed on military service in an air crash, and Princess Marina, Duchess of Kent (1906–1968), the parents of Prince Edward.

† Maj.-Gen. Sir Henry d'Avigdor-Goldsmid, 2nd Bt (1909–76), British Army officer and Conservative MP for Walsall South 1955–74.

has gone to seed. In Housing, all his work on speeches etc. was carefully prepared for him, and he had a choice of two secretaries. In Home Office, they are much more casual even in briefing him for parliamentary debates, and he has to share two secretaries.

Much talk about the hopelessness of the PM still. Bill has heard that Eden is thinking of giving a lunch for newspaper editors – would be a great mistake.

Bill shows me his room in the House, conveniently near the Chamber, one floor up from the rooms of the PM and the Chancellor of the Exchequer. After House has risen we walk through the Chamber, with its business-like mess of paper on benches and floor. All looks very small. I believe it is the first time I have ever been through it.

### 20 March 1956

John Altrincham gives me proofs of longish pamphlet he and Ian Gilmour[*] have written on the Timothy Evans murder case. It seems convincing, but I urge John to tone down any strongly written passages against the police and Home Secretary.

Lunch Beefsteak. Tell Michael Adeane to try and avoid photographs being taken of Bulganin and Khrushchev[†] with the Queen during Russian leaders' visit to Windsor next month. He says he agrees with me that they would be used for propaganda purposes by the Russians, and would dishearten people in Soviet-occupied countries. But Queen has no option if Foreign Office want them taken. He thinks, however, that none may be taken – usually they are only taken when Heads of State visit the Queen.

On deportation of Archbishop Makarios from Cyprus, Harold Nicolson says that Makarios begged Francis Noel-Baker,[‡] who was acting as mediator out there, to get Government to deport him, as the situation was getting out of hand and beyond his control.

---

[*] Sir Ian Gilmour, Baron Gilmour of Craigmillar, 3rd Bt (1926–2007), Conservative politician. Defence Secretary Jan.–Mar. 1974; Lord Privy Seal 1979–81.

[†] Soviet politicians. Nikolai Bulganin (1895–1975), Minister of Defence 1953–5; Premier of the Soviet Union 1955–8. Nikita Khrushchev (1894–1971), First Secretary of the Communist Party of the Soviet Union 1953–64. B. and K., as they were known, visited Great Britain 18–27 Apr. 1956.

[‡] (1920–2005), youngest Labour MP in the landslide of July 1945. In 1971 he left the party because of its opposition to British membership of the EEC. Later he joined the Social Democratic Party, and later still the Conservative Party. Owing to his Greek connections, in 1955–7 Noel-Baker mediated between the Governor of Cyprus, FM Sir John Harding, 1st Baron Harding of Petherton (1896–1989), and Archbishop Makarios.

## 21 March 1956

Julian Amery* has recently returned from Egypt, and is very disturbed by eagerness of Government there to remove all British influence from the Middle East. But does not think they will attack Israel until they have done so.

## 24 March 1956

To Boat Race party given at Hammersmith by Alan Herbert.† An extraordinary crowd of people – Lord Montgomery,‡ Gwilym Lloyd-George, Charlie Chaplin, Douglas Fairbanks and Gerald Kelly. See little of the actual race as it passes (won by Cambridge by one and a quarter lengths) but some pleasant talk. See Malcolm Muggeridge for the first time for many months. I say to him: 'Whatever we think of the feeble policy of the Prime Minister, we should not leave him alone to try and do better. He is punch-drunk, and there is no suitable successor, unless we want the Socialists.' To which M.M. rather feebly replies, 'That is no concern of mine. I am merely editing a paper.' It bears out what an irresponsible fellow he is, an utter anarchist.

Gwilym Lloyd-George as charming as ever. He tells me that as Home Secretary he must be accompanied everywhere he goes by a detective. His bodyguards particularly like going shooting with him – one of them is a keen ornithologist, and tells him the names of passing birds between drives. He also deplores absence of rowing men in the Government. Was at Jesus, Cambridge, a great rowing college, himself. Last rowing minister was John Maclay, former Minister of Transport, who was in the Cambridge crew that beat Oxford in 1927.

Wonderful sight during the race of Monty and Charlie Chaplin framed in the same window.

---

* Julian Amery, Baron Amery of Lustleigh (1919–96), Conservative politician who served in Parliament for thirty-nine years. Son-in-law of Harold Macmillan. Secretary of State for Air 1960–62; Minister of Aviation 1962–4, in which he played an important role in the development of Concorde. He held three ministerial posts during the government of Edward Heath, 1970–74.

† Sir Alan Herbert (1890–1971), humourist, writer and law reform activist. Independent MP for Oxford University 1935–50, when university seats were abolished.

‡ FM Sir Bernard, 1st Viscount Montgomery of Alamein (1887–1976), victor of the second Battle of El Alamein Oct.–Nov. 1942. Cdr of the Eighth Army during the Allied invasion of Sicily and Italy; Cdr of Allied ground forces during Operation Overlord until after the Battle of Normandy, 1944; Cdr of the 2nd Army Group, N-W Europe; received the German surrender at Lüneburg Heath 4 May 1945; Chief of the Imperial General Staff 1946–8. Churchill said to George VI: 'Monty would like my job,' to which the King replied, 'That's a relief, I thought he wanted mine.'

On way to Hammersmith by Tube notice that by far the greatest influx of Boat Race spectators is at Gloucester Road Tube Station, Kensington. Sociologists could no doubt deduce quite a lot from this.

Lunch Beefsteak, to see Giles St Aubyn. Is now going to get a house at Eton earlier than he expected – in 1961.

On advice given me last week by Gay Kindersley,* back horse called E.S.B. for the Grand National. It wins and I make over £20. But it is a lucky win – the Queen Mother's Devon Loch ought to have won but slips when in the lead fifty yards from the winning post.

In evening to BBC studios to hear Malcolm Sargent conduct Brahms's Symphony No. 3, followed by Vaughan Williams' Cantata, *Dona Nobis Pacem*. Rather pretentious stuff, with loud and uninteresting musical setting of bits from the Bible, Walt Whitman and John Bright's[†] speech about the Angel of Death.

Then to supper with Malcolm, and Mr and Mrs Lanning Roper.[‡] He is a very charming Bostonian. A most jolly evening, with Malcolm in tremendous form and full of good jokes. Perhaps this due to the quarter-bottle of champers he drank during concert interval! Several new stories – during recent visit to Moscow, Ernest Thesiger[§] wrote on a lavatory wall: 'Burgess loves Maclean.'

Great fun during supper, with Malcolm teasing the head waiter – 'I want plenty of cucumber with my salmon, not to eat, but just to look at.' He also orders his mixture of brandy and Benedictine, insisting on mixing it himself. One sees the waiters all shrugging their shoulders and rolling their eyes at 'Ce fou, Sir Sargent'.

### 26 March 1956
Tube to the office, sitting next to Lord Beveridge. He talks wistfully of his *Morning Post* days as leader writer, and threatens to return if we are not kinder to Eden.

---

* (1930–2011), champion amateur jockey who often advised K.R. on racing odds.

† (1811–89), Liberal politician and famous parliamentary orator. His greatest speech on 'the Angel of Death' was delivered on 23 Apr. 1855 and was subsequently the first parliamentary speech to be set to music, in Vaughan Williams' cantata *Dona nobis pacem*.

‡ Lanning Roper (1912–83), American landscape architect and gardener, m. 1952 Primrose Harley (1908–78).

§ (1879–1961), actor; George Bernard Shaw wrote the part of the Dauphin in *Saint Joan* for him.

## 27 March 1956

Dine Beefsteak, and have much talk with Lord Somervell. We touch on capital punishment. He is an abolitionist, but not because an innocent man may sometimes be hanged under old system. Real objection to hanging is that it does not deter murderers. In any case, he says, the sanctity of human life means very little when 5,000 people a year are killed on the roads, and millions more in periodic wars. In the Evans case, he says, a jury found him guilty largely because he committed perjury.

One cannot safeguard a man against the consequences of his own lying.

We go over the whole Munich story again. Somervell says: 'I am a convinced Nevillite, though I recognise that there is a strong case against him – he alienated the Opposition with taunts at a time when he should, like Baldwin, have tried to unite the country.'

As usual, Somervell has strong words to say about Winston. He gives an example of Winston's opposition to the India Bill – an impassioned speech on the offence of champerty, which was not to be included in Indian law. In fact, says Somervell, Winston did not care at all either about the merits of the case or even about India.

We discuss the Marconi case.* Somervell says that Asquith had doubts about appointing Reading to be Lord Chief Justice. This, however, was not because of his conduct over Marconi shares, but because Reading had confessed to Asquith that he had once committed perjury by putting a false age in his declaration to become a member of the Stock Exchange.

## 28 March 1956

To House of Commons where Malenkov† is in Gallery. Have a word with Lord Attlee, then to House of Lords. I ask Attlee what the Russian visitor had said to him. 'Oh, merely how much he had enjoyed our show.' Outside of the House thick with policemen, uniformed and plain-clothed. As Malenkov drives off, a woman waves rather mildly and sheepishly with a giggle. Malenkov returns a tremendous wave.

---

* A British political scandal in 1912, concerning allegations that members of the Liberal government under Asquith had profited by insider information about the government's intention to issue a lucrative contract to the British Marconi Company.
† Georgy Malenkov (1902–88), Soviet politician. Premier of the Soviet Union 1953–5; Deputy Chairman, Council of Ministers 1955–7.

## 29 March 1956

Read A.W. Baldwin's life of Stanley Baldwin, the first real vindication to appear. Most impressive in its loyalty, and devastating on G.M. Young's life of Baldwin.

## 2 April 1956

Read *The Flowers of the Forest* by David Garnett.[*] Is the second of his volumes of autobiography, and deals with the Bloomsbury set during World War I. In spite of trying not to be blimpish, I am deeply irritated by the book, particularly the smugness which most conscientious objectors seem to breed. All the trivialities of Lytton Strachey and Clive Bell[†] and Duncan Grant[‡] appear almost obscene against the carnage going on across the Channel. I must talk to Clive Bell about it. Perhaps he will put it in a more generous light. Most irritating of all I found some of the author's remarks about Rupert Brooke, because he despised those who did not enlist – though the evidence for thinking that Brooke really abandoned his old friends for this reason is scanty.

## 5 April 1956

*The Times* has a leading article on Eden. It mentions how the Budget[§] 'can set a new climate of opinion' and ends with the Delphic utterance that 'Sir Anthony Eden's future depends on his remaining true to himself.' Letter from John Betjeman about some architectural conference. As always, it begins: 'My dear boy'.

Dine Beefsteak. Long talk with Lord Bridgeman, which we continue at his club, the In and Out.[¶]

Bridgeman, I notice, illustrates the growing tendency of politicians to blame Winston's delayed resignation for many of our present troubles. Thus he says Winston should have faced up to a railway strike four years ago – it would have prevented much later trouble.

He is particularly interesting on the railways. This industry has the greatest proportion of low-grade labour. By spending a great deal of capital gain

---

[*] (1892–1981), writer and publisher; prominent member of the Bloomsbury Group. His autobiography *The Flowers of the Forest* was published in 1955 (Chatto & Windus). A further volume, *The Familiar Faces*, appeared in 1962.

[†] (1881–1964), art critic and member of the Bloomsbury Group.

[‡] (1885–1978), painter and member of the Bloomsbury Group.

[§] Rab Butler's last Budget on 26 Oct.

[¶] Robin Bridgeman, 3rd Viscount Bridgeman (b. 1930), Conservative politician. The Naval and Military Club, founded in 1862, took its name from its second clubhouse from 1866–1999, Cambridge House overlooking Green Park, which had In and Out clearly marked on its two gates.

on, say, carriage-washing machinery, thousands of low-grade workers could be released and given jobs elsewhere. Pay of rest could be raised. If the union objects to this obvious move, 'we must then think of a strike'.

Also much talk on House of Lords reform – Bridgeman thinks that 400 is a suitable size, and would cover every peer one ever wanted to hear.

## 6 April 1956

Attlee made a Knight of the Garter.[*]

Andrew Devonshire[†] is to give Hardwick Hall to the nation as part of his father's death duties – also some valuable pictures from Chatsworth which would be suitable in the house. It is all rather complicated by the fact that he must negotiate with his uncle, the Chancellor, Harold Macmillan. Andrew Devonshire hopes it may be possible one day to live in Chatsworth, perhaps in about ten years.

## 10 April 1956

Lunch with Frank Pakenham at Guards Club. He likes Harold Macmillan as Chancellor – he will maintain closer links with the bankers.

I raise point of why Gaitskell and Jay[‡] never served in forces – after all, Frank did, though released owing to ill health. He replies that the Services did not take kindly to the Socialists and that in any case many Conservative intellectuals never joined forces.

## 12 April 1956

By a superb Foreign Office bog, the programme issued in the Press for the visit of Bulganin and Khrushchev next week has been sent out with detailed times. These were supposed to be secret for security purposes.

Lunch Kenneth Harris[§] of the *Observer* at the Savile Club. Full of much scurrilous and amusing gossip. Says that Clemmie[¶] no longer

---

[*]  On 8 Apr. 1956 Attlee sent his brother Tom 'a little verse I made for the occasion':
  Few thought he was even a starter
  There were many who thought themselves smarter
  But he ended PM
  CH and OM
  An earl and a knight of the garter.
[†]  Andrew Cavendish, 11th Duke of Devonshire (1920–2004), Conservative, later Social Democrat and later crossbencher in the House of Lords.
[‡]  Douglas Jay, Baron Jay (1907–96), Labour MP and Minister.
[§]  (1919 –2005), official biographer of Clement Attlee.
[¶]  Clementine Spencer-Churchill, Baroness Spencer-Churchill (1885–1977), wife of Sir Winston Churchill and life peeress in her own right.

lives with Winston – he has become very tiresome since going to retirement: 'He does everything except pee on the carpet.' K.H also thinks his book may be a flop – *History of the English-Speaking Peoples*, to be published later this month. Was paid about £20,000 for it before the war by Cassells when he was broke. It was useless, but he has since touched it up.

Says that Eden annoys his fellow ministers by commenting on their parliamentary answers. Thus the other day Henry Brooke[*] said he had not yet made up his mind on the proposed demolition of the Imperial Institute. 'I have,' exclaimed the PM in an audible voice.

Gaitskell unpopular on the *Observer*. He promised to do them a review of second volume of President Truman's memoirs – then told them he couldn't the day before they were ready to receive it.

## 17 April 1956

To House of Commons to hear Macmillan's first Budget. As usual, I find a note saying *Daily Worker* on my seat. So I sit on it.

Great comings and goings. Clarissa Eden in a smart hat, Winston tottering in and out, those two clowns, Nabarro and Thornton-Kemsley,[†] in tall hats, and Butler with a ghastly smile on his face.

Macmillan's opening five minutes barely hold the attention of the House – an elaborate compliment to Winston, whose Budget was the first he ever heard, followed by an Oxford Union sustained comparison between a Budget day and a prize day at school. Much of the speech is contrived – presumably to provide a little luxurious literary allusion as well as a Gobi Desert of economics. Many quotations from Dickens and Macaulay.

As a Budget, it is fairly harmless. His proposal to encourage savings by a bond lottery scheme will meet with much opposition.[‡] A pity he also tried to appease the Socialists by putting yet more tax on company profits, both

---

[*] (1903–84), Baron Brooke of Cumnor, Conservative politician. Financial Secretary to the Treasury 1954–7; Minister of Housing 1957–61; Chief Secretary to the Treasury 1961–2; Home Secretary 1962–4.

[†] Sir Gerald Nabarro (1913–73), businessman and Conservative politician. MP for Kidderminster 1950–64. Sponsored the Peerage Act 1963 with Anthony Wedgwood Benn. Sir Colin Thornton-Kemsley (1903–77), Conservative and National Liberal politician. MP for Kincardine and Western Aberdeenshire 1939–50 and for North Angus and Mearns 1950–64.

[‡] Premium Bonds, as they were known, with a top prize of £1,000, proved popular with the public and continue to this day. When the first draw was made on 1 June 1957, £82 million had been invested. Premium Bonds were denounced by the Archbishop of Canterbury in apocalyptic terms, and by Harold Wilson, the Shadow Chancellor, as 'a squalid lottery'. When Wilson became Prime Minister he increased the value of the top prize to £25,000.

distributed and undistributed. Small increase in tobacco tax probably not enough.

## 18 April 1956

Watch arrival in London of Bulganin and Khrushchev. Dick Stokes[*] says that he is refusing all invitations to meet B. & K. And when Russians write to ask if they can buy machinery from his firm, he replies: 'Yes, when you let your fifteen million slaves out of forced-labour camps.'

## 19 April 1956

To Badminton for the day, to watch Olympic Horse Trials. Lunch of cold chicken in train, arriving Badminton about one o'clock.

Vast crowds of people, mostly upper-middle-class, the women with the sort of voices one supposes breeds Communism. Badminton itself looks very picturesque, with a huge Royal Standard flying over it.

Queen, Queen Mother, Princess Margaret, Princess Royal with Duke of Beaufort[†] hovering in attendance, watch jumps from farm wagon. The Gloucesters, with their two nice little boys,[‡] watch independently and unhampered by crowds. Returned to London by train, having enjoyed a leisurely day in the open air.

## 20 April 1956

Police and magistrates are being high-handed with the few people demonstrating against the visit of B. and K. Huge fines imposed.

Lunch Beefsteak. John Altrincham has been asked to meet B. and K. at Claridge's party on Tuesday. The inscription which the Russians attached to their wreath laid at the Cenotaph implies for the first time that Russia now recognises that she and GB were allies in World War I as well as II.

## 21 April 1956

Bill Deedes says that abolition of hanging Bill will probably go through, but

---

[*]  Maj. Richard Stokes, MC and bar (1897–1957), soldier and Labour MP for Ipswich 1938–57; Lord Privy Seal Apr.–Oct. 1951.

[†]  Henry FitzRoy Somerset, 10th Duke of Beaufort (1900–84), leading figure in the equestrian world; founded the Badminton Horse Trials in 1949.

[‡]  Prince William of Gloucester (1941–72), eldest son of the Duke and Duchess of Gloucester; after his death in an air crash Giles St Aubyn, his housemaster at Eton, collated a book in tribute to his memory. Prince Richard, Duke of Gloucester (b. 1944); read Architecture at Magdalene Coll., Cambridge, and intended to practise as an architect. The death of his elder brother meant that, on his father's death in 1974, he assumed the duties of the Dukedom of Gloucester.

they are worried about possible increase in attempts to resist arrest by using firearms. For a man cannot physically be kept in prison for more than fifteen years. So penalty for murder and for armed robbery will not be very different. Bill describes how B. and K. came to Home Office to lay wreath at the Cenotaph, but arrived ten minutes too soon. While Bill and Gwilym Lloyd-George were being fetched, the head doorkeeper put the visitors into a little cubby-hole where aliens wait for their passports. Bill, who had promised his constituents not to fawn on B. and K., was gratified when K. bowed deeply on being introduced to him.

## 22 April 1956

Bill Deedes says how for the first time in his life he is now regretting he never went to university. 'I spend much of my time trying to convince clever civil servants they are wrong, and I could do it far more quickly had I been to a university.' It is in fact this arguing against civil servants, who have probably prepared a plan of campaign together beforehand, which he finds most exhausting in the Home Office. He thinks the Government is recovering its reputation. But *Daily Telegraph* now hated in the Conservative Party.

Good story of Sir Henry Marten,* when tutoring the then Princess Elizabeth. Every lesson he would begin by sitting down at the table, opening the book, and saying: 'Page 96, gentlemen.'

## 23 April 1956

People who have been to lunch today to celebrate the publication of Winston's new *History of the English-Speaking Peoples* say he is rapidly breaking up.

John Altrincham tells me has been to stay with Col. Astor of *The Times*, now Lord Astor of Hever. This title causes great confusion with that of his nephew, but he could not bear to drop the name Astor.† Lord Reith‡ was also staying there – rather rude yet consumed by a massive inferiority complex

---

* (1872–1948), Provost of Eton 1945–8 and private tutor to Princess Elizabeth. After his funeral in Eton Coll. Chapel his predecessor as Provost, Lord Hugh Cecil, observed: 'Such a mistake to have that lesson. There is nothing Marten would less like to see than "a new Heaven and a new Earth".'

† John Jacob Astor, 1st Baron Astor of Hever (1886–1971), newspaper proprietor and Conservative politician. His nephew with whom there was confusion was William, 3rd Viscount Astor (1907–66), businessman and Conservative politician whose Cliveden estate in Buckinghamshire was connected with the Profumo scandal of 1963.

‡ John, 1st Baron Reith (1889–1971), Dir.-Gen., BBC. He introduced the former King Edward VIII as 'Prince Edward', before standing aside to allow Edward to make his Abdication broadcast. He served in the wartime governments of Neville Chamberlain and Winston Churchill. The BBC's Reith Lectures were instituted in 1948 in his honour.

– e.g. he came timidly to John before he left, and asked how much he should tip the servants.

John tells me that Alan Pryce-Jones[*] has 'ghosted' for Winston's *Great Contemporaries*. For Winston likes a framework, a chronological or other sequence to be provided, on which he moulds his own ideas and words.

## 24 April 1956

To the party the Soviet Ambassador is giving at Claridge's for B. and K. Great queues outside Claridge's and hundreds of police. Guests have to enter the ballroom in single file through a barrier, with obvious Special Branch men scrutinising everybody.

Long tables with every sort of Russian wine and vodka, caviar in mounds, smoked sturgeon, smoked salmon, chicken etc., as well as all the usual nasty little hotel bits and pieces of glazed toast. Not many people when I arrive but it soon fills, and people tear each other to pieces to get at the food and drink.

Meet Peter Carrington, who says: 'I have a nose for caviar like a truffle hound.' He describes dinner to B. and K. Peter sat next to a man whose name card, he thought, was Brimelov. So he talked to him in slow and courteous phrases, asking him about Russia. The man was very angry and said he was called Brimelow,[†] and was in the Foreign Office.

I talk to Lord Fraser of North Cape,[‡] the Admiral. He tells me that one of the waiters who served under him during the war and recognised him has just brought him a huge plate of caviar. 'I seem to have done even better than a Prime Minister,' he says, pointing to Attlee, who is gloomily munching a patty.

Attlee in rather good form. He has just been to the Palace to be invested as a Knight of the Garter. Tells me has been reading *Little Arthur's History of England*,[§] brought up to date and revised by Winston Churchill. He adds: 'This *History of the English-Speaking Peoples* contains about as much history as I knew at my private school!'

---

[*] (1908–2000), author, journalist and Liberal politician.

[†] Thomas, Baron Brimelow of Tyldesley (1915–95), Vice-Consul in Moscow 1942–5; Minister, British Embassy in Moscow 1951–4 and 1963–6; Ambassador to Poland 1966–9; Permanent Under-Secretary at the Foreign Office 1973–5. He was renowned for his knowledge of the Russian character and language.

[‡] Adm. of the Fleet Bruce, 1st Baron Fraser of North Cape (1888–1981), senior naval officer. Served at Gallipoli in World War I; Cdr of the Home Fleet May 1943–Aug. 1944, leading the force that destroyed the German battleship *Scharnhorst* in the Battle of North Cape on 26 Dec. 1943; First Sea Lord and Chief of the Naval Staff 1948–51.

[§] (1835), a children's history of England by Maria Callcott (1785–1842), written as though she were telling a series of stories to a young boy called 'Little Arthur'.

Almost everyone one has ever met is at the party. The three Socialist figures of Bevan, Gaitskell and Shawcross can be seen in three corners of the room, each holding court. While I am talking to Shawcross we are suddenly pushed violently apart. It is the security men making a passage for B. and K. They pass within a couple of feet, at the trot. B. has a pleasant complexion and well-trimmed white beard and hair. K. rather small, fat and sinister. Talk to Harry Hylton-Foster, Solicitor-General and MP for York. He will be there tomorrow for Archbishop Ramsey's enthronement. Has to leave London at 7 a.m. to lunch officially before the service. 'Vodka is a poor foundation for such a journey,' he says.*

### 25 April 1956
Catch early train to York to attend enthronement in the Minster of Dr Ramsey as Archbishop of York.

Service in the Minster very colourful and impressive. Procession of mayors and mace-bearers rather comic, all in a variety of extraordinary hats, and carrying exotic baubles. Many stout, Jorrocks-like figures among them.

A wonderful moment like something out of *Richard III* when the Archbishop comes to the Great West Door to ask for admittance, and the Dean and Chapter form an anxious semi-circle to await him. The doors are flung open, and the medieval figure of the Archbishop is seen silhouetted against the light, with mitre, cope and staff – and a great jutting jaw.

York very lovely with beds of flowers, and the ramparts covered with daffodils. Have a word or two with Lord Halifax, whose father gave a gift of a cope to the Chapter.

### 26 April 1956
Dine at the Beefsteak. Sit next to the actor Nicholas Hannen, who played the Archbishop in the recent film of *Richard III*.† I tell him how all the Chapter of York so resembled him.

### 27 April 1956
Hear Eden make a very colourless broadcast on the Russian visit, with what

* Michael Ramsey, Baron Ramsey of Canterbury (1904–88); Bishop of Durham 1952–6; Archbishop of York 1956–61; 100th Archbishop of Canterbury 1961–74. Sir Harry Hylton-Foster (1905–65), Conservative politician. Solicitor-General 1954–9; Speaker of the House of Commons 1959–65.
† Nicholas Hannen (1881–1972) appeared in Olivier's film of *Henry V* as the Duke of Exeter and in his *Richard III* as the Archbishop of York.

I suspect will be a vain appeal to the Communist-tinged engineering union to increase output.

## 30 April 1956

To evening party at Kensington Palace Gardens given by the Japanese Ambassador to celebrate the Emperor's birthday. Delicious little bits of food, and hundreds of very polite bowing Japs, their women in enchanting coloured kimonos. Talk to Herbert Morrison about the Webbs[*] – he says that when he visited them towards the end of their lives, Beatrice had become very much the country lady, with servants in Victorian slavery and lots of silver on the tea table.

## 2 May 1956

To Press view of Royal Academy, neither better nor worse than other years, in spite of Munnings'[†] diatribe on the modern pictures. Particularly notice Ruskin Spear's poster-like picture of Olivier as Macbeth.

In Commons George Christ tells that the Archbishop of Canterbury's recent controversial speeches have led the Dean of Canterbury[‡] to go about saying: 'I find it so embarrassing abroad to be mistaken for the Archbishop of Canterbury.'

Giles St Aubyn telephones to say that he has taken a box for the second cycle of *The Ring*, and will I be his guest for all four operas. It is most kind of him.

Try to find out whether ministers who received presents from B. and K. are allowed to keep them. David says he has been given a painting in nineteenth-century style and about seventy records, presumably as the British Minister of Culture. He does not know yet whether they are to be his personal property. I also ask Jim Cilcennin, who says that he too has been given a picture, which will hang in the Admiralty, also some vodka, which has now all been consumed without asking Prime Ministerial permission.

Dick Stokes tells me that B. and K. arrived at Chequers without any luggage, and declined all offers of pyjamas, even of a razor – 'We shaved yesterday, thank you.'

---

[*] Sidney Webb, 1st Baron Passfield (1859–1947), socialist co-founder of the London School of Economics, m. 1892 Beatrice Potter (1858–1943), socialist and economist.

[†] Sir Alfred Munnings (1878–1959), artist renowned for his paintings of horses. President of the RA 1944–9. In his valedictory speech, broadcast on radio, he delivered an outspoken attack on modern art.

[‡] Hewlett Johnson (1874–1966), Dean of Manchester 1924–31 and of Canterbury 1931–63. Known as the 'Red Dean' because of his political views.

## 7 May 1956

Lunch House of Commons to mark the diamond jubilee of Wycombe Abbey School. Peter Carrington in the chair. A few minutes' conversation with the Archbishop of Canterbury after lunch. Tells me he is unrepentant about his controversial speeches on Cyprus and on the Government schemes for a bond lottery. 'I am attacked when I speak, but attacked by a different set of critics when I don't. Most of the criticism is not about the substance of what I have said, but on the point that I have said anything at all.' He also says that both he and Michael Ramsey, the Archbishop of York, will be at Repton for the Quatercentenary celebrations. The Queen will visit the school later – she does not come for the main ceremonies.

## 9 May 1956

To Commons. Where PM answers questions – or rather refuses to do so – on how a British frogman came to lose his life while apparently making an underwater examination of the Soviet cruiser which brought B. and K. to Portsmouth. His exploit was not authorised by the Admiralty, but probably by a branch of the Secret Service, and has caused Government great embarrassment. Gaitskell very foolishly tries to make party capital out of it, presumably to counteract Socialist discomfiture at the failure of their dinner to B. and K.*

## 10 May 1956

House of Commons. Arrive at same time as PM in Speaker's Court. Eden gives one of those dazzling film-star smiles and a lordly wave of a cigar. Later makes a good and reasonable statement on the introduction of automation in industry.

To Londonderry House for *New Statesman & Nation*. Incredible assortment of Socialists who assemble. Talk to the charming C.P. Snow. I wish I

---

* Cdr Lionel Crabb (1909–56) was killed during a secret surveillance of the hull and propeller of the Soviet cruiser *Ordzhonikidze* in Portsmouth harbour authorised by MI5 and the Secret Intelligence Service, unknown to Eden, who was understandably furious that such an episode might undo all his diplomatic efforts with B. and K. In fact, Anglo-Soviet relations had already been dealt a severe blow by the famous row a few days earlier at the Labour Party dinner for B. and K. when George Brown, Shadow Defence spokesman, attacked the Russian guests over the 1939 Molotov–Ribbentrop Pact. Khrushchev declared that if he lived in Britain he would vote Conservative. When Selwyn Lloyd, then Foreign Secretary, visited Moscow in 1959 with Harold Macmillan he asked Khrushchev if he would still vote Conservative. 'Of course,' replied Khrushchev, 'it was Bulganin who was Labour and look where he is now!'

could have had a photograph taken of John Rothenstein[*] talking to Father
Trevor Huddleston, with the caption 'Set my people free.'

## 11 May 1956

Catch early train to Oxford. Share cab from station to All Souls with John
Sparrow, whom I cannot really like, try as I do.

Call on Harry Bell,[†] who is delighted to see me, and asks me to dine on
High Table with him tonight. Has rooms overlooking Garden Quad.

To lunch with Anthony Grigg[‡] at his rooms in the High. Anthony has
also asked John Bayley,[§] already an unmistakable don, with great charm and
wit, and John Buchanan Riddell.[¶] The conversation has a touch of inspired
frivolity which I enjoy. At one moment John Buchanan Riddell says that
he once offended all his sisters by saying that he couldn't understand what
people saw in incest.

John Bayley is most interesting on the psychology of John Sparrow,
saying that he has a philosophy of living dangerously which shows itself
in his support for hanging. For capital punishment, like the laws against
homosexuality, are rather exciting obstacles to be avoided during life; their
existence makes life more interesting, Sparrow claims. I point out that Sparrow had plenty of opportunity for excitement during the war, but remained
in London and Washington.

Also story of a scout coming to tell Warden Fisher[**] of New College that
one of the Fellows had hanged himself. 'Don't tell me,' the Warden replied,
'let me guess.'

To party in Wyatt Library of New College, to look at a small exhibition of stained glass by modern artists. David Cecil[††] there in a beautiful
checked suit. I tell him how dated and vulgar is Nancy Mitford's theme
about U and non-U, and that John Ormsby-Gore[‡‡] was already draw-

---

[*] Sir John Rothenstein (1901–92), art historian and arts administrator. Director of the Tate
Gallery 1938–64. Father Trevor Huddleston (1913–98), Anglican bishop, best known for his
anti-apartheid activism.
[†] (1913–64), Sub-Warden of New Coll.
[‡] 3rd Baron Altrincham (b. 1934).
[§] Prof. John Bayley (1925–2015), literary critic and writer. Professor of English at Oxford
University 1974–92.
[¶] Sir John Buchanan Riddell, 13th Bt Riddell (1934–2010), PS to the Prince of Wales 1985–90;
Lord Lieutenant of Northumberland 2000–03.
[**] H.A.L. Fisher (1865–1940), historian, educator and Liberal politician. Warden of New Coll.,
Oxford 1926–40.
[††] Lord David Cecil (1902–86), biographer, historian and academic.
[‡‡] Capt. the Hon. John Ormsby-Gore (1925–2008), Coldstream Guards.

ing attention to fish knives when Nancy Mitford was still talking about notepaper.

Also meet John Piper* and his wife, Myfanwy, and John Betjeman. Piper asks me not to mention his name directly as the successor to Evie Hone† for the Eton Chapel windows. It seems that the Provost may choose him, but that publicity may cause him to change his mind.

Dine High Table. Sit next to the Warden, Halford Smith,‡ leaner and madder than ever.

Catch late-evening train back to London, after a most rewarding visit to this lovely town. I have felt more Oxford tugs on the heartstrings than for several years.

### 16 May 1956

Lunch Beefsteak with Michael Adeane and walk back to Buckingham Palace with him. He says: 'The Royal Family is not a Government department – and if it should ever become one it would cease to exist.' He says advice is not always taken by members of the Royal Family – especially when given in an emotional state.

Dine John Grigg in Brompton Road restaurant. Hear result of committee-stage vote of capital punishment Bill. Hanging to be retained when murderer does it for second time, which last occurred in early nineteenth century.

### 17 May 1956

Small dinner party in my flat – Giles St Aubyn, Martin Gilliat§ and Jim Thomas. Martin says that since he was a POW he has hardly slept more than three hours a night. He has some amusing gossip about the Queen Mother – how she hates being asked to take a decision and will dig in her toes the more she is pressed; how perfectly poised she always is at public occasions; how she spends many of her evenings watching TV; and how she would love to live in Marlborough House.

Jim thinks that Quintin Hogg is likely to succeed him fairly soon as First

---

* (1903–92), artist, printmaker and designer of stained-glass windows, m. 1937 Mary Myfanwy Evans (1911–97), art critic and opera librettist, particularly for Benjamin Britten.
† (1894–1955), stained-glass artist; designed the East Window in Eton Coll. Chapel. After her death John Piper was commissioned to design the flanking windows. Sir Claude Elliott did much to restore the fabric of the College after World War II.
‡ Alic Halford Smith (1883–1958), Warden of New Coll. 1944–58.
§ Sir Martin Gilliat (1913–93), PS to the Queen Mother for thirty-seven years.

Lord of the Admiralty.* 'The only qualification for the job is to look well in a yachting cap.'

In Cabinet, apparently, Winston frequently opposed Jim's naval policy, saying: 'I have been First Lord twice.' And, as Jim adds, Winston put a ten-year ban on armaments when he was Chancellor of the Exchequer, so his record in defence matters is not impeccable.

Jim describes the embarrassment the frogman's body having been found near the Russian warship which brought Bulganin and Khrushchev to Portsmouth. At the banquet which was given to B. and K. in the painted hall at Greenwich, K. made an angry speech about it. But Bulganin whispered to Jim: 'When you come to Russia you will not be insulted in my country house!'

A great admiration for Prince Philip, but Jim thinks he needs somebody far better than Boy Browning† as a confidant. It broke Philip's heart to leave the Navy, which provided an anchor to his life. As he once complained rather pathetically to Jim: 'I never really had a country.' Jim tells me he was about to retire as First Lord when the Commander Crabb affair blew up. He has now had to postpone his retirement in case he is thought to have been dismissed.

### 10 June 1956, letter to parents

Yesterday I was down at Cowes, sailing in the Household Brigade yacht, *Gladeye*. It was quite delightful to sail along the coast of the Isle of Wight under a stiff breeze. There were six or seven of us aboard, most of whom I knew from the war.

One night last week I dined with Philip de Zulueta at the Beefsteak. Afterwards I went with him to 10 Downing Street, where he had to pick up some papers. While waiting there, I was most interested in the books in the Cabinet Room at No. 10. Each has been presented by a Cabinet minister – so one has a complete record of the political history of England by looking at the signed inscriptions which each minister puts inside the book he presents. Jowitt, I notice, has given the letters of Keats; Cripps‡ – some volumes of William Morris; Archie Sinclair§ – *The Compleat Angler*;¶ Winston – his

---

* The prediction was accurate. Viscount Hailsham became 1st Lord of the Admiralty on 2 Sept. 1956.

† Lt-Gen. Sir Frederick Browning (1896–1965), senior British Army officer.

‡ Sir Stafford Cripps (1889–1952), Labour politician. Chancellor of the Exchequer 1947–50. K.R. was to ask Cabinet ministers later which books they had presented to the Downing Street library on entering the Cabinet and published regular details in 'Albany'.

§ Archibald Sinclair, 1st Viscount Thurso (1890–1970), leader of the Liberal Party 1935–45.

¶ By Izaak Walton (1594–1683), first published in 1653.

own books; Hartley Shawcross – the poems of Coleridge.

Finally, an amusing remark by one of David Cecil's little boys. He was once asked what he wanted to be when he grew up. To which he answered, 'A neurotic, like Father.'

### 21 June 1956

John Altrincham wrote to Archbishop of Canterbury urging ordination of women. Archbishop replied that whatever the rights and wrongs of the case, he could not risk the unity of the Church, which John answered by pointing out that A of C should <u>always</u> consider the rights and wrongs of a case. John adds to me: 'We shall never have a vigorous Church of England until its High Church element has gone over to Rome.'

### 4 July 1956

Take Bill Deedes to dine at La Bohème. Almost entirely political talk. Bill has been consulted by Eden on public relations side of Government. Part of trouble is that the stock of the Lobby correspondents has fallen – few are now trusted. Instead, same news is given to twenty of them, which cuts its news value by one-twentieth. Ministers afraid to use journalists as Sam Hoare, for instance, used to use Bill. PM needs a second PPS to give Press all information it wants – William Clark[*] hasn't the knowledge or the ability to manage this.

Bill rather gloomy about future of HMG. Anti-Eden revolt growing in party – will probably come to a head by the autumn. But Socialists in little better position – 'Gaitskell is the white trash of our party' one of them said to Bill.

### 15 July 1956

Read Sławomir Rawicz's *The Long Walk*.[†] Some think this account of an escape from a Soviet prison across the Gobi Desert and the Himalayas is a fake. More likely, he was a bit unhinged, and unconsciously invented parts of it afterwards. Curious he never asked wife of Soviet officer who helped him to escape for a map – practically nothing is said about their successful navigation. Nor, apparently, do any Indians now remember his arrival there.

---

[*] (1916–85), economist and public servant. Press Secretary to Sir Anthony Eden 1955–6, when he resigned over Suez; senior executive at the World Bank 1968–80.
[†] Published with considerable impact in 1956 and translated into twenty-five languages. Rawicz (1915–2004) describes his arrest, torture and imprisonment in a Siberian prison after the Soviet invasion of Poland in 1939, and his subsequent escape with a group of fellow prisoners. Four of them make it to British India. Controversy has always surrounded its veracity.

## 17 July 1956

Lunch Beefsteak. Sit next to Harold Nicolson. He tells me he was lunching at Wellington recently. The Chaplain told him he had recently heard a visitor saying to his wife, as he pointed to a window, 'It was from there that I planned to throw myself when a boy, I was so unhappy.' The man was not, added the Chaplain, a persecuted aesthete, but Sir Gerald Templer,* Chief of the Imperial General Staff.

*On 26 July 1956 Colonel Gamal Abdel Nasser, President of Egypt 1956–1970, nationalised the Suez Canal Company, following the withdrawal of Anglo-American funding for the Aswan High Dam. Two-thirds of the oil supplies of Western Europe (sixty million tons annually) passed through the Suez Canal. At the time of the nationalisation of the Canal Britain's oil reserves were enough for only six weeks. The subsequent Suez Crisis divided opinion like the Munich Crisis of 1938 and dominated political life for months. Sir Anthony Eden's health gave way and he resigned as Prime Minister in January 1957. The entries in Kenneth's journals reflect the bitter divisions the Suez Crisis caused.*

## 29 July 1956

Talk on the telephone with Philip de Zulueta. He tells me that in spite of the nationalisation of the Suez Canal, the PM is at Broad Chalke.† This shocks me.

Telephone Jim Cilcennin and ask if I can come round to Admiralty House to see him. Spend from 11.45 until 1 p.m. there. Jim tells me that owing to the crisis he is staying in London the whole weekend, and having meetings with the Sea Lords. Mountbatten, who is entertaining the Queen at Broadlands, came up this morning. At present there are warships at either end of the Canal and we could easily block it but Jim fears that the PM has cold feet.

He tells me he is anxious to leave the Admiralty. In the old days the First Lord got a £1,000 a year less than his colleagues because of the house. This deduction no longer operates but the servants have to be paid for by the First Lord, and this is a considerable drain. He receives hardly any hospitality allowance, yet cannot properly do his job without considerable entertainment.

---

* FM Sir Gerald Templer (1898–1979), senior British Army officer. British High Commissioner in Malaya 1952–4; Chief of the Imperial General Staff 1955–8 and chief military adviser to Sir Anthony Eden during the Suez Crisis.
† The Edens' home in Wiltshire.

## 2 August 1956

To House of Commons at noon – last day of parliamentary session – to hear Eden make speech on Nasser's nationalisation of the Suez Canal Company. Probably the best he has made since becoming PM, though he is hampered by having no final decision to give the House of Commons until Three-Power talks are concluded. Rather marred by his habit (less frequent lately) of turning his back on the Speaker to address his own supporters; also by beginning almost every sentence with the words, 'Now, sir'. Attlee crouches in front row of peers' gallery, both elbows and chin resting on the rail. Winston slumped in his seat below.

In office, Donald McLachlan tells me he has just breakfasted with John Altrincham – a very Lloyd-Georgian habit. This month's new *National Review* includes some very bad-tempered and foolish comments on rejection of Silverman's abolition Bill by House of Lords. John implies it was the work of the backwoodsmen, who will thus bring about their own exclusion from the House of Lords, if not its complete destruction. What he doesn't mention are the number of backwoodsmen who supported Silverman's Bill in the House of Lords. In any case, whatever one's views on abolition of capital punishment, the peers have as much right to follow their consciences as the House of Commons.

Read Evelyn Waugh's *Men at Arms* and *Officers and Gentlemen*. How good he is at painting a world he never knew except as a chance observer – that of the old English Catholic families. Rather good on the Brigade, though of course tinged with spite.

## 14 August 1956

Malcolm Sargent tells me that Sibelius[*] is going to burn all his unpublished works.

## 21 August 1956

Talk Donald McLachlan about political situation. He thinks we may have to use force in Egypt. He has also been infected by the Foreign Office line of thought – indeed bases his argument on it – that Nasser will be provoked into some act of aggression, upon which we, too, shall use force with a clear conscience.

---

[*] Jean Sibelius (1865–1957), Finnish composer. Sibelius did indeed do so, notably destroying the sketches for his unfinished 8th Symphony in the stove in his home Ainola, north of Helsinki. Sargent was on tour in Finland when Sibelius died while he was listening to a live broadcast of one of the performances on 20 Sept. 1957. One newspaper headline read, 'Sibelius dies listening to Malcolm Sargent conducting his 5th Symphony'.

Nasser's position, he adds, is (a) Canal pilots are giving trouble, and could bring traffic to a standstill, (b) more than half Canal dues are being paid to the old Suez Canal Company, not to Nasser, (c) Egyptian assets frozen in London and New York.

## 22 August 1956

Talk to Speaker on telephone, and discuss possible recall of Parliament.

In afternoon, talk to General Martin[*] about Suez Crisis. He produces large-scale map of Egypt, and points out how almost our only satisfactory landing place would be Bay of Tina – but even here, Cyprus is too far away to provide fighter cover. This would have to come from carriers, and Egyptians have MiG fighters. He also mentions Eden's vanity. Pug Ismay[†] told Martin: 'I could always tell Winston where he was going wrong, but Eden will not listen to criticism.'

## 25 August 1956

Worried generally by Suez situation – Prime Minister has rattled his sabre, but cannot really want war with Egypt in face of world opinion.

Immersed in Angus Wilson's[‡] *Anglo-Saxon Attitudes*, splendidly complex novel about the world of archaeologists and historical associations, with undertones of low life and overlapping social levels.

## 31 August 1956

Lunch Beefsteak. Sit next to Lord Reading. He has just had a visit at the Foreign Office from a member of the Russian Embassy. The Soviet athletic team, due to compete at the White City tomorrow, is being withdrawn because the woman discus thrower[§] was arrested yesterday by London police for shoplifting. She did not surrender to her bail this morning. Russians, says Lord Reading, cannot realise that once a charge has been preferred, Government have no power to halt proceedings. All rather curious – woman stole five hats, valued at £1 12s and 11d. As Lord Reading commented: 'Discus

---

[*] Maj.-Gen. James Martin (1902–86), senior British Army officer. Brig. General Staff 1943–4.

[†] Gen. Hastings Lionel Ismay, 1st Baron Ismay (1887–1965), wartime military adviser to and confidant of Winston Churchill. First Secretary-General of NATO 1952–7.

[‡] Novelist (1913–91); *Anglo-Saxon Attitudes* (1956) was his most popular novel and many consider it his best.

[§] Nona Ponomaryova (1929–2016), known as 'Nina of the Five Hats' and 'Miss Muscles' after the alleged shoplifting episode at C&A in Oxford Street, London; gold-medal winner at the Rome Olympics 1960. The diplomatic incident caused much embarrassment to the British and the Russians.

throwers of the world unite – you have nothing to lose except your hats.'

### 1 September 1956

Have a drink at Admiralty House with Jim Cilcennin. A great deal of talk about the nationalisation of the Suez Canal. Jim tells me that on the Friday morning there was to have been a meeting of the Defence Committee of the Cabinet to discuss why so many expensive ships were necessary in the Mediterranean. Late on the Thursday night the news of Nasser's nationalisation arrived so the meeting was instantly cancelled.

An amusing story about somebody who telephoned Jim at the Admiralty the other day, and asked for the First Lord. The telephone operator replied: 'I am afraid the First Lord has gone abroad with Lady Mountbatten and will not be back for several weeks.'

Also an anecdote of Fred Woolton at Conservative Central Office, remarking to poor Jim with a spacious gesture: 'Of course, people like you and me do not need salaries.'

### 20 September 1956

Give Bill Deedes lunch at Wheeler's – we each eat a dozen oysters, a perfectly grilled plain sole, some brie and drink a bottle of Chablis.

Bill still disgruntled with the Government, and so very bored but at the moment there is no suitable moment for resigning. 'I find it so hard to be loyal to the Prime Minister, but that is what I am paid for.'

Amusing about the stuffiness of the Home Office. His Private Secretary comes to him when Bill has turned up after an absence of several days, and says: 'Sir Frank Newsam was asking for you yesterday' in a voice of deep reproach. Bill then becomes breezy and jaunty and Palmerstonian.*

### 18 October 1956

Somehow I had not the stomach to travel all the way up to Llandudno for the Prime Minister's speech;† instead I went to Covent Garden to watch that incomparably more skilful ballerina, Ulanova,‡ dance *Giselle*. It was an

---

* Henry John Temple, 3rd Viscount Palmerston (1784–1865), Prime Minister 1855–8 and 1859–65; popularly known for his 'gunboat diplomacy', conspicuous displays of naval power.
† In his keynote speech to the Conservative Party Conference on 13 Oct. Eden declared: 'We have refused to say that in no circumstances would we ever use force. No responsible government could ever give such a pledge.' This was received with scenes of great enthusiasm.
‡ Galina Ulanova (1909–98), Russian ballerina, one of the greatest of the twentieth century. Her appearance in Great Britain in 1956 was the first time she had been allowed to perform abroad.

enchanting performance, such beauty of grace and movement as I have never seen before. The Royal Family have been there practically every night, and poor Ava Waverley has had to relinquish the Royal Box – which she has come to regard as her own private property.

Walter Monckton is expected to leave the Ministry of Defence within a few days to be succeeded, it seems, by Antony Head.* This is only rumour, but strongly supported. At Llandudno the other day, one of my colleagues asked Rab Butler whether there was any truth in the rumour. Rab replied: 'No. It is absolute rubbish.' Of course he may not have been told by the PM, or he may even have been lying. But it does seem surprising. One wouldn't put it past the PM to change the Minister of Defence in the middle of the present muddle. But neither Selwyn Lloyd nor Macmillan had many months there before being moved to other posts. The whole Middle East Crisis has been handled with such clumsiness that one would be surprised by nothing.

Somebody who was at Llandudno told me that both Rab and Macmillan received about the same amount of applause after their respective speeches. But the applause which greeted Eden's references to Rab was far greater and more sustained than that for the PM's reference to Macmillan. I should personally regard the return of Rab to power and influence as a most melancholy spectacle.

I had tea with Somerset Maugham two days ago. Astonishing energy for a man of 83, though he looked frailer than when I last saw him a year or so ago. He has had a strenuous year, first in Egypt and the Sudan, then a Grand Tour of Italy followed by a protracted house party at his villa near Nice. This was apparently the most exhausting period of all – they were left limp and bewildered by Gerald Kelly, who for weeks on end NEVER stopped talking.

### 1 November 1956

To House of Commons for further debate on Suez. On the question of whether prisoners captured by the Egyptians are entitled to be treated as prisoners of war, the Opposition becomes noisy. Neither Selwyn Lloyd nor Eden can cope with the situation, and eventually the Speaker suspends the sitting for thirty minutes.

Dine Beefsteak with Martin Gilliat after having a drink with him at the Travellers' Club. Talk is almost wholly about Suez. I bet Martin two pounds that Eden will not be Prime Minister on 1 May 1957. We send for the Betting

---

* An accurate prediction. Antony Head, 1st Viscount Head (1906–83), soldier, Conservative politician and diplomat. War Secretary 1951–6; Minister of Defence 18 Oct. 1956–9 Jan. 1957; High Commissioner to Nigeria 1960–63 and High Commissioner to Malaysia 1963–6.

Book and ask Sir Roderick Meiklejohn,[*] who was Asquith's Private Secretary, to witness the bet. Also notice in the Betting Book that Prince Francis of Teck,[†] one of Queen Mary's brothers, was a great bettor in the early years of the century. It was he, of course, who lost £10,000 backing a horse in Ireland at 10–1 on.

Walk back to Clarence house with Martin, past the George VI statue which makes extraordinary shadows on the walls of nearby buildings. The Queen Mother, the Ministry of Works and Martin have taken endless trouble before finding an effective way of illuminating the statue. The Queen Mother has made several visits to see the result at night.

## 2 November 1956

To House of Commons for 11 a.m. sitting. My stomach turned by Rab Butler replying to an Opposition request that the House should sit on Sunday: 'Some of us have conscientious objections to doing this.'

See Bill Deedes, who describes at length and dramatically the emergence of Bevan as the one man of stature in the Socialist Party.

Lunch Hartley Shawcross at the Carlton Grill. He tells me that Manningham-Buller has been having a troubled few days over Suez. What caused the disturbance on Wednesday was the Prime Minister did not know whether in fact we were at war or not with Egypt. Manningham-Buller was sent to the library to find out. His popularity at the Bar is not great. On the question of Crown privilege for documents, he became extremely angry with Simon[‡] at a recent meeting of the Bar Council and found himself in a minority of one.

Gay Kindersley to dine. Gay on his own at the moment while Margaret recovers from her baby. He, of course, supports the Government over Suez, though thankfully we have little parliamentary conversation.

## 3 November 1956

To House of Commons for special noon sitting. On the steps of the entrance in Speaker's Court I bump into David Eccles. He tells me how 'disappointed' he is in John Altrincham's attitude towards the Government – 'I thought we should get his support on this.' How little he knows John.

---

* (1876–1962), first Civil Service Commissioner 1927–39.
† (1870–1910), second son of the Duke of Teck. Because of his gambling debts he was sent to pursue a military career in India.
‡ Jocelyn Simon, Baron Simon of Glaisdale (1911–2006), Law Lord, Conservative politician and later judge. Financial Secretary to the Treasury 1958–9; Solicitor-General 1959–62; President of the Probate, Divorce and Admiralty 1962–71.

While I am talking to Eccles there is a blaring of horns and the Prime Minister arrives in Speaker's Court. Philip de Zulueta gets out of the car behind the Prime Minister, and when he sees me waves and shouts, 'Good morning, Kenneth.' I am in the middle of a sentence so merely wave back. At this moment the Prime Minister turns his head, assumes I am a loyal supporter offering encouragement and gives me the full Douglas Fairbanks smile. This makes me feel rather ill.

On the whole not as stormy a debate as the previous day's, though I hear it deteriorates later, after I have left. Shinwell very grave and silent, Gaitskell reproving, and Anthony Benn like a startled Boy Scout.

## 4 November 1956

Anthony Nutting's resignation announced.* How fantastic that he alone of all the ministers has resigned.

On way to office in afternoon see huge crowds in Trafalgar Square being addressed by Anthony Greenwood.† It is a much-advertised protest meeting against the Government's Suez policy. Find huge crowds in Whitehall and Downing Street.

## 5 November 1956

To House of Commons. Another strong scene, with Selwyn Lloyd under heavy fire. Then Eden intervenes to announce surrender of Port Said to our troops – great storm of cheering.

## 5 November 1956, letter to parents

What an appalling week it has been. You can imagine what a strain it has all been particularly the House of Commons each day. I am sorry you think the Government are justified. Personally I think they have not a moral leg to stand on – as world opinion seems to show. Eden has committed an undoubted act of aggression; broken our relations with the Commonwealth and the USA; shattered the unity of the United Nations at a time when its authority is most needed to prevent the terrible massacres in Hungary;‡ and blocked

---

* Sir Anthony Nutting, 3rd Bt (1920–99), diplomat and Conservative politician. PS to Anthony Eden 1944. In 1954 he negotiated the treaty with Nasser under which British troops withdrew from the Suez Canal Base in 1956; Minister of State for Foreign Affairs 1954–6. His book *No End of a Lesson*, published in 1967, was the first to disclose many of the details of Suez, including the secret negotiations with the French and Israelis in Paris.

† Baron Greenwood of Rossendale (1911–82), Labour politician; he held various offices in the first and second Wilson governments.

‡ A large Soviet force had entered Budapest on 4 Nov. to crush Hungarian resistance against

the Suez Canal. Whatever one may think of Gaitskell or Egypt is quite irrelevant. Either nations live by the rule of law or by self-interest. And in invading Egypt, we have abandoned our entire moral foundation. I suspect you might agree with me had not Eden's action indirectly helped Israel. You certainly would, had the Government sent an impossible ultimatum to Israel & then bombed Israeli territory. Do you remember who else used to adopt that sort of action? There is a great deal of anxiety even in the Conservative Party at Eden's tactics. I have spoken to many MPs and ministers about this. But of course, now we are committed they, like me, must support the Government. To withdraw now would really be fatal.[*]

### 6 November 1956

Queen opens Parliament. In afternoon to House of Commons where Bill Deedes defends use of mounted police during Sunday's riots.

About 6 p.m. Eden announces the final ceasefire in Suez. He seems more confident than at any other time during the crisis. Gaitskell gives a poor impression as a strategist. Have a drink with Peter Thorne[†] who tells me that the band this morning outside Buckingham Palace was playing a march from *Aida*, written to celebrate the opening of the Suez Canal in 1869![‡]

Dine Beefsteak. Sit between Harold Nicolson and Sir Percy Loraine.[§] Sir James Marshall-Cornwall also there.[¶] Harold takes the seat at the head of the table, and deliberately picks quarrels over Suez – he and I against the rest. I tell Harold I am waiting for a letter to the newspapers from John Sparrow supporting the Government's action over Suez. I shall then know that I have been right from the beginning in opposing the Government over this. Harold replies, 'You will not have long to wait – there will be one in the papers tomorrow.'

Walk back to Albany with Harold where we hear 11. p.m. news about Port Said ceasefire. He tells me that Nigel wrote to the Chief Whip to resign his

the Communist government and its Soviet-imposed policies.

[*] This is what happened the next day.

[†] Sir Peter Thorne (1914–2004), Serjeant-at-Arms 1976–82 after many years' service in the House of Commons.

[‡] Though commissioned by the Khedive of Egypt in 1869, *Aida* was in fact written to celebrate the opening of the Khedivial Opera House in Cairo, delayed until 1871.

[§] 12th Bt (1880–1961), participant in the Paris Peace Conference 1919; British High Commissioner to Egypt 1929–33; Ambassador to Turkey 1933–9 and to Italy 1939–40.

[¶] Gen. Sir James Marshall-Cornwall, MC (1887–1985), senior British Army officer and linguist. Worked with Harold Nicolson at the Paris Peace Conference on new European boundaries; Lt-Gen. in charge of the air defences of Great Britain 1940.

seat a few days ago, but was persuaded to tear up the letter. Nigel Nicolson and Lionel Heald[*] sat whilst others cheered the PM yesterday.

### 7 November 1956

To Parliament Square, where I watch Speaker Morrison unveil the Epstein[†] memorial statue to Smuts.[‡] General impression of it unfavourable, especially from those who knew Smuts.

In afternoon to House of Commons where Aubrey Jones makes rather a grim statement on our oil prospects.

William Clark resigns as Press Secretary to the PM. It was unavoidable that this should break up. Clark expected to be consulted on policy – Eden expected a good press. Both were disappointed.

### 8 November 1956

To House of Commons at 11 a.m. for unveiling by the Speaker of the memorial to parliamentary journalists killed in World War II. One of the most moving and eloquent short addresses I have ever heard.

After lunch to the House of Commons. Winston very tottery indeed. At one moment I think he is going to stagger and fall on the way from the Bar of the House to his seat below the gangway.

In late afternoon John Altrincham telephones me to say that Edward Boyle is about to resign from the Government.

Bill Deedes to dine at flat alone. I try to convince him of the Government's folly in going into Suez at all at this moment – not only folly but dishonour. He replies with one of his ranging philosophical surveys of world affairs and their slight impact upon politicians. He refuses to resign.

After dinner we go to House of Commons together, passing the open side door of Buckingham Palace on the way. There is an evening party and powdered footmen are standing on the steps. It all seems very remote from Suez.

I am in time to hear the end of Thorneycroft's speech – a histrionic effort which I find distasteful. He ends the speech by declaring his faith in the Government and flinging down his notes on the Despatch Box, but the effect of this is slightly spoiled when a moment later he rises from his seat to retrieve them. His vindication of the Government on the count that they have

---

[*] Sir Lionel Heald (1897–1981), barrister and Conservative politician. MP for Chertsey 1950–70; Attorney-General 1951–4; prosecuted John Christie on charges of murder.
[†] Jacob Epstein (1880–1959).
[‡] FM Jan Christian Smuts (1870–1950), South African statesman. Prime Minister of the Union of South Africa 1919–24 and 1939–48; served in the Imperial War Cabinet of Winston Churchill; the only man to have signed the peace treaties of both world wars.

frustrated the Russian plot in the Middle East I find unconvincing.

Rumours are going round the House that so many Conservative MPs are going to abstain that the Government will fall. I meet David Llewellyn[*] in the Lobby and say, 'Are you sound, David?' He replies: 'I have been sounder.'

Few MPs in fact abstain and the Government has a firm majority. During division I talk to Edward Boyle in one of the side galleries. He seems bewildered at what he has done and says, 'After dining with John Altrincham I had to do it.'

Soon after the division, Bill and I go down to the Harcourt Room for a drink. At the next table are Anthony Benn and his wife[†] and David Butler, who is now returned from Washington. To our consternation they are joined by Edward Boyle, who is still with them when we leave twenty minutes later. In spite of some House of Commons traditions it is very odd of Edward so openly to consort with Socialists on the very evening he has resigned. Anthony Benn certainly relishes the situation.

I walk back as far as Sloane Square with Bill. On the way he gives me an amusing account of Colonel Wigg and Leslie Thomas, now MP for Canterbury, having a fight in the House over Suez.[‡] Both had to apologise to the Speaker.

## 11 November 1956

Recent remark of John Sparrow's – 'One should not rock the boat, particularly when it is a landing craft.' Those who know John Sparrow may perhaps raise an eyebrow at his new-found familiarity with landing craft!

Wilfrid Blunt comes in for a drink before dinner. Wilfrid tells me of a letter written, protesting against the Government's Suez policy, by a large group of Eton beaks, but was not in fact sent to the Prime Minister, after intervention by Robert Birley.

Philip de Zulueta and I dine alone. I detect a great sense of failure over the PM's policy. What worries me is that the PM is still only thinking in terms of overturning Nasser. I ask Philip why no attack on Egypt was made when the Canal was first nationalised. He replied that all our forces were deployed in readiness against Russia. It seems to be quite extraordinary that in spite

---

* Sir David Llewellyn (1916–92). Capt., Welsh Guards. Conservative MP for Cardiff North 1950–9; journalist.
† Caroline Benn (1926–2000), educationalist and advocate of comprehensive schools.
‡ George Wigg, Baron Wigg of Dudley (1900–83), Labour politician. Paymaster General 1964–7; Chairman, Horserace Betting Levy Board 1967–72. Sir Leslie Thomas (1906–71), Conservative MP for Canterbury 1953–66; son of James ('Jimmy') Henry Thomas (1874–1949), Labour Cabinet minister 1924, 1931 and 1935–6.

of spending £1,500 million a year on defence we were so caught unprepared to meet the nationalisation of the Suez Canal – always granted of course that force is to be used.

Philip speaks very gravely of the PM's health, which is privately giving them a great deal of anxiety.

### 11 November 1956, letter to parents

Another very strained week, as you can imagine, with Parliament still in a ferment each day. The Prime Minister seems to flourish on crises & looked remarkably well! I was at the Smuts memorial unveiling in Parliament Square – one of the worst Epstein statues I have ever seen. Such a pity.

I was not surprised by Edward Boyle's resignation from the Government. He is an old Oxford friend – and a particularly close friend of John Altrincham. Bill Deedes dined with me one night. He had hoped to resign from the Government soon to come back to Fleet Street and earn some money – he used to make quite a lot with the BBC too. But now he feels that if he resigned, it would be put down to disagreement with Eden!

### 12 November 1956

Talk to John Altrincham on telephone. He says that William Haley,* editor of *The Times*, was told some of the facts about Suez in confidence. What he was told so shocked him that he at once turned the policy of the paper against the Government. He cannot, of course, publish what he was told. It suggests there may have been collusion between HMG, the French and Israel.

### 18 November 1956

A quiet day in the office, in the course of which I watch a perfectly dreadful man called Liberace on television. He is a sort of musical David Eccles.

### 20 November 1956

Aubrey Jones announces rationing of petrol.

Dine Buck's with John Altrincham. While waiting for dinner we look at today's *Manchester Guardian*, which has a headline about French intervention in Suez, suggesting that French planes directly helped with Napalm precision bombing. I say I do not believe it, and that both the *Observer* and the *Manchester Guardian* are doing us all a disservice by attacking Government policy on Suez in such immoderate terms. If one is to convince

---

* Sir William Haley (1901–87), Dir.-Gen. BBC 1944–52; Editor of *The Times* 1952–66. It was said that he was 'Halier than thou' over the Profumo Affair in 1963.

reasonable men that Government policy has been foolish and dishonourable, one must state one's case in the language of reason. John disagrees and wants an all-out propaganda campaign.

## 21 November 1956
At 7 p.m. to House of Commons. Though the House is empty for a dreary debate on rents, the Speaker is still in the Chair. It brings home how much bad oratory he must endure.

Have a drink with Bill Deedes in the Harcourt Room, then bring him back to my flat to dine. He mentions how little junior ministers are told. They hear neither Cabinet secrets nor generally do they attend the ministerial briefings, nor the 1922 Committee.[*]

## 23 November 1956
Lunch Beefsteak with Harold Nicolson. He talks to me at lunch about the difficulties Nigel is having in Bournemouth, obviously not the constituency for a sensitive Conservative.[†]

Tea with Marie-Lou de Zulueta. Philip has gone to London Airport to see the PM leave for Jamaica. A curious time to be taking a holiday.[‡]

## 24 November 1956
To Eton for the day. Lunch Hubert and Grizel Hartley.

Colin Wilson[§] has been down to talk to the Literary Society and went out to startle and shock. Grizel, who met him in Wilfrid Blunt's rooms afterwards, refused to be impressed. When Wilson casually mentioned that nine-tenths of the people he knew were homosexuals, Grizel replied: 'That should solve the housing problem.'

After lunch, walk round the Drawing Schools with Grizel. See little Michael of Kent drawing a road traffic sign of all things. He is still very shy indeed.

In the evening, Giles St Aubyn takes half a dozen of his pupils to London to see Bernard Shaw's *The Doctor's Dilemma*. We travel up in a bus, which

---

[*] A pressure group of the Conservative backbenchers in Parliament.

[†] After Weidenfeld & Nicolson published Vladimir Nabokov's novel *Lolita* in 1959, the constituency voted against Nigel Nicolson and he was forced to step down at the Oct. 1959 general election.

[‡] On medical advice Eden recuperated at Goldeneye, the writer Ian Fleming's property on the northern coast of Jamaica, from 22 Nov. On their return on 14 Dec. Clarissa Eden wrote in her diary, 'Everyone looking at us with thoughtful eyes.'

[§] (1931–2013), writer and philosopher. One of the 'Angry Young Men' of British literature, his most famous book *The Outsider* was published by Gollancz in 1956.

Giles has hired for the occasion. He says it is cheaper than two cars. The play is admirably performed and has lost none of its wit.

## 25 November 1956, letter to parents

With the Prime Minister out of the way in Jamaica, things may perhaps improve a little – though the situation still looks very grave. The oil cut is going to have quite appalling effects on our economy if it lasts many weeks, and the Government really <u>must</u> leave Port Said as soon as possible.

At the American Thanksgiving Day dinner at the Dorchester on Friday I felt how very strained the atmosphere had become, & the Ambassador, Aldrich, skated over a great deal of thin ice in his speech.

Bill Deedes dined with me one night. He says that all the Government are now in pretty bad health. It is not only the heavy office and parliamentary work, but also the need to attend so many official lunches & dinners, followed by long speeches. 'There is not a sound digestion in the Cabinet,' says Bill, and I am not surprised. It has, of course, been Winston's great asset in public life that he has the stomach of an ox.

## 27 November 1956

Reports that Anthony Eden is having extra telephones installed in his Jamaica bungalow, Goldeneye, fill me with gloom. It would be terrible if he started to interfere from a distance.

Lunch Beefsteak. Harold Nicolson says that when people complain to him that Eden is being stabbed in the back, 'I tell them that he should not present so much of it to view.'

Malcolm Sargent is also there. He says he is doubtful whether Bob Boothby should have been elected to the club, particularly after his old affairs with the wife of Harold Macmillan,* one of the club's trustees. I reply: 'The committee of the Beefsteak is not a court of morals.'

Catch afternoon train to Westbury to lecture to the School of Infantry. As usual receive a delightfully warm welcome. The lecture goes well, with many intelligent questions. A delicious dinner, but the Guest Night lacks the usual band. There is no petrol to bring it over to Warminster.

## 29 November 1956

To House of Commons. Selwyn Lloyd's statement on our withdrawal from

---

* Lady Dorothy Macmillan (1900–66), dau. of the 9th Duke of Devonshire; m. Harold Macmillan 1920. Her long-standing affair with Bob Boothby was common knowledge in the Westminster village, but was not then known to the wider public.

Suez not very informative, but more to follow on Monday. Nye Bevan speaks little but well: 'Don't be so schoolboyish,' he says, leaning across the Despatch Box to the Government benches.

In the evening hear Beethoven's Mass in D conducted by Malcolm at the Albert Hall. Delicious supper in Malcolm's flat after the music. He tells me the story of Randolph Churchill saying to Hailsham in White's: 'Did you hear my broadcast last night?' 'Yes,' replied Hailsham, 'how did it end?'

### 30 November 1956

See David Eccles at Ministry of Education at 11 a.m. I so disapprove of the line he has taken over Suez and he so disapproves of what John Altrincham has written to him that our relations are far from easy this morning. He talks slightingly of 'the long-haired boys who want us to become a third-rate power'. When I ask him point-blank why the PM lied to the House of Commons, he replies: 'That is a short-term view.' But later adds, 'The Prime Minister bounced us into it.' He admits he was surprised that there were not more resignations from the Government, which is in itself an admission of how shabby the Government and all its supporters have been.

He does not think Eden will last long as PM. I ask him who will succeed. He replies, 'Macmillan, I am a Macmillan man.' He mentions that Monckton still wants to be Lord Chief Justice, but is very doubtful whether he will achieve this. After thirty minutes' sparring I leave the Ministry with a greater contempt of Eccles than I have ever had before.

Lunch Beefsteak and sit next to Maurice Macmillan. He says the rumours that his father wishes to retire from politics are nonsense – in fact he would be quite happy to become PM if asked. Rab Butler much hated in the North, he says.

### 1 December 1956

Lunch John Altrincham at excellent French restaurant in Sloane Street. Several readers of the *National Review* have cancelled their subscriptions. He shows me some of their angry letters. David Eccles has sent a furious letter. He and John are not now on speaking terms.

John says Ted Heath does not emerge from the Suez Crisis with particular credit. He suggested to William Clark that Nutting's resignation should be quietly attributed to pressure from his American mistress.

John also tells me that shortly before the *Daily Mirror* was to have a full-scale article on the rival claims of Butler and Macmillan, eventually to succeed Eden, Macmillan's secretary telephoned to say that Macmillan 'gave his voice to the Suez ceasefire'.

Prince Eddie and Giles St Aubyn dine with me before the opera. Eddie tells me it was originally intended that he should go into the RAF and so follow in his father's career. When he saw the maths papers which had to be passed he changed his mind. He expects to be in the Army till he is twenty-five, but may do public engagements before the end. He hopes to take his seat in the Lords some time in January. It will depend whether he can have some leave then. Says that Michael saw me at Eton in the Drawing Schools the other day, but was too shy to speak to me. Eddie tells me that his father had great shopping manias. Would think nothing of suddenly buying three little antique jewelled boxes at several hundred pounds each. Malcolm Sargent apparently lunched at Kensington Palace the other day, and shocked Princess Alice with his improper stories. We discuss what is the right pattern of coronet for Eddie's crest. He will ask Mountbatten, the greatest authority on all these matters. Mountbatten has apparently produced family tree for the Royal Family in several volumes.

## 2 December 1956, letter to parents

The political situation is as melancholy as ever, and I should like to see the PM resign. I wrote a paragraph to this effect, saying how disquieting it was that the PM was installing extra telephones in Jamaica. This appeared on Wednesday. On Thursday the *Daily Mirror* reproduced it, & on Friday the *Daily Worker* did the same! So I will not be popular at No. 10.

## 3 December 1956

I met Bill Deedes on my way to the House, grimacing furiously. Lord Attlee shuffles by, with his pipe.

The main business of the day is Selwyn Lloyd's statement on Suez. He irritates the Socialists by a long historical disquisition. Nye Bevan in splendid form: 'I sympathise with the Right Honourable gentleman for having to sound the bugles of advance to cover his retreat . . .' and he ends, 'Having regard to the obvious embarrassment of the Government, I feel I should be a bully if I continued further.'

Sir Ian Horobin* intervenes with one of the most disagreeable questions I have ever heard in the House – asking, 'Whether American consent will be forthcoming in due course for bringing back our Prime Minister from Jamaica?'

---

* (1899–1976), Conservative politician. MP for Southwark Central 1931–5 and Oldham East 1951–9.

## 5 December 1956

House of Commons for the debate on Suez. Nye Bevan makes the best parliamentary speech I have heard since Winston's last speech on defence. He
compares Rab Butler's speeches to the life of Madame Bovary, 'a long story
of moral decline'. Most of his speech is devoted to covering one by one the
half-dozen reasons put forward by the Government for its intervention in
Suez. He shows how they are all contradictory, and all untenable. Then he
ends with a statesmanlike appraisal of the foolishness of attempting to solve
world problems by the use of force.

John Altrincham tells me that Alan Bullock has been asked to prepare a
dispassionate analysis of the evidence that there was collusion between Great
Britain, France and Israel on the Suez venture. Bullock is aware, however, of
the difficulties in this. The evidence simply may not exist, and in any case
he does not want to quarrel with the Foreign Office, who have allowed him
access to their secret files in order to write his life of Ernest Bevin.

## 6 December 1956

Lunch Beefsteak. Malcolm Sargent and Robert Speaight* have a fascinating
discussion on the value to be given to words in music and on the stage.
'Shakespeare's rhythm', says Speaight, 'cannot be improved upon, though
many actors try, just to produce something new.'

To House of Commons. As I approach the entrance in Speaker's Court,
Winston drives up in his car. He descends very slowly, mounts the three or
four steps leading to the door, then stands there blocking it. He remains deep
in thought for at least half a minute, while I wait patiently a short distance
away. He suddenly turns round and sees me. A vast grin spreads over his
face. 'Well,' he says, 'why don't you come in?'

Little of importance in the Commons. Rab Butler rather slimy. Gerald
Nabarro asks me to have tea with him. He shows me a list of sixteen Conservatives who will abstain from supporting the Government's Suez policy.
He says he could raise at least thirty names but, (a) he does not want to see
the pound slump abroad, (b) there is not yet agreement on who will be PM if
Eden goes. So they do not yet wish to bring down the Government, they wish
merely to make a demonstration.

## 11 December 1956

A charming story of Ernie Bevin's modesty – on arriving each morning at

---

* (1904–76), Shakespearean actor; he was the first Becket in T.S. Eliot's *Murder in the
Cathedral*.

the Foreign Office, he would say to the lift man, 'Second floor please.'

## 12 December 1956

Meet Edward Boyle in the House of Commons – portly and gracious. Says: 'The day I resigned I felt the years slide off me. I am now rediscovering the delights of being a backbench MP.' Rather good at thirty-three.

Good talk with Harold Nicolson. Much talk of Winston, who sent him birthday telegram. He saw Winston the other day at presentation of Duff Cooper Memorial prize to Alan Moorehead,[*] for his book on Gallipoli. When Harold asked: 'How are you?' Winston replied: 'I am a broken figure.'

Nigel Nicolson still having trouble in his constituency, Bournemouth, owing to his opposition to Government's Suez policy. But his Chairman, Quickswood, has supported him – in fact his last act before dying was to dictate letter of support to be read out publicly.[†]

## 17 December 1956

To House of Commons. Every gallery crowded with ghouls awaiting the return of Eden from Jamaica. Eden receives a very tepid welcome. After-wards in the Lobby Henry Kerby[‡] tells me that if the *Daily Telegraph* now turns against Eden, he will not last five days in office.

## 18 December 1956

Lunch with Peter Thorne at House of Commons. Eden looks very washed out in spite of a heavy sunburn. Harold Wilson most rude and disagreeable.

Dine at the Beefsteak. Arthur Onslow[§] says how at a Buckingham Palace banquet one night he noticed that the food on the hot plates was tepid, so he suggested that a hot cupboard should be bought. This was done at a cost of only £18. Nobody had ever thought of it before.

## 22 December 1956

Read C.P. Snow's *The New Men* about Whitehall and the atomic research scientists during the war. Behind a very moving story is the fundamental decency of men, even when tempted by power.

---

[*] (1910–83), war correspondent and historian. The Duff Cooper Prize was first awarded in 1956 and was presented to Moorehead by Sir Winston Churchill.
[†] Lord Quickswood died on 10 Dec. 1956.
[‡] Capt. Henry Kerby (1914–71), Conservative MP for West Sussex 1954–71.
[§] Arthur, 6th Earl of Onslow (1913–71), Capt. of HM Bodyguard of the Yeoman of the Guard 1951–60; Asst Chief Conservative Whip in House of Lords 1951–60.

## 26 December 1956

Give John Altrincham dinner at the Bohème. He has been abused like a footpad on the platform of Badminton Station by the Duchess of Beaufort* for his attitude on Suez. He says that James Ramsden† has now come round against the Government over Suez. John claims this is a symptom that the present Government will not last. I doubt, however, whether Ramsden, or indeed any of the Conservative MPs with very few exceptions will ever dare to vote against the Government.

## 31 December 1956

Receive advance copy of Honours List. The only items which particularly please me are the knighthoods for Edward Hulton‡ and C.P. Snow.

---

* Mary Somerset, Duchess of Beaufort (1897–1987).
† (b. 1923), Conservative MP for Harrogate 1954–74; the last holder of the post of War Secretary 1963–4.
‡ (1906–88), magazine publisher and writer.

# 1957

**3 January 1957**

Drink with Harold Nicolson at Albany in the evening. Nigel, he tells me, has made an anti-Eden speech at the 1922 Committee. Eden began by thanking MPs for 'their loyalty'. Nigel began his speech by saying: 'As one of the disloyal ones . . .' He also applied the word 'dishonourable' to Government policy.

**5 January 1957**

To Albert Hall to hear Malcolm conduct *The Messiah*. Bob Boothby is also there, and we spend a whole interval in political talk. Macmillan, he says, will succeed Eden as PM before Parliament assembles. He expects to be taken into the Cabinet as Secretary of State for Scotland or Special Minister for European Affairs. All who opposed the Government's Suez policy may also expect jobs – Edward Boyle and Nigel Nicolson; [Antony] Head and Selwyn Lloyd will go. But Bob does not expect the change to take place immediately. He leaves tonight for a week at Monte Carlo.

**6 January 1957**

Read Tom Driberg's *Guy Burgess*. It is an extremely naïve production, betraying all the innumerable chips which Tom has on his shoulder. He also thinks in terms of labels such as 'reactionaries' and 'progressives'. It is astonishing that someone as intelligent as Tom could so easily swallow the Burgess line. He has, however, dug up some amusing little sidelights, such as Robert Birley's Eton reports on Burgess.

**7 January 1957**

Hartley Shawcross is alarmed when I tell him that I do not think Eden, or indeed the Government, will last very long for he has a £100 bet with somebody that the Government will not fall in the immediate future.

## 9 January 1957

I spend part of the morning writing a paragraph suggesting that Eden must have had urgent political business to submit to the Queen during his visit to Sandringham yesterday and today. No sooner have written this than the news comes through that the Queen is returning to London. In the evening Eden resigns.

I discuss the situation with Colin Coote who thinks Rab will succeed. No appointment of new PM expected until tomorrow. I have won my bet with Martin Gilliat that Eden will not continue to be PM. Nick Gordon Lennox tells me that the Foreign Office are not sad to see Eden go.

## 10 January 1957

During the morning Winston and Salisbury are summoned to the Palace.

Marie-Lou tells me that Philip went down to Chequers last evening and had one of the gloomiest dinners of his life.

Lunch at the Beefsteak. Boofy Gore[*] describes a children's party at Chartwell where Randolph dressed up as Father Christmas. Although he looked the part, he spoilt the effect by giving the children a political harangue on the iniquities of the Eden Government.

In the afternoon Harold Macmillan appointed PM and I write about him. The first King's Scholar at Eton since Walpole,[†] and first regimental officer of the Brigade to become PM. Will Robert Boothby now come rushing home? On the wireless I hear a plummy little speech from Macmillan.

## 11 January 1957

Martin Gilliat writes and sends me his cheque in settlement of the Eden bet.

Hear a programme on wireless about change of PM. Jo Grimond[‡] very polished and sincere, and Fred Woolton as cagey as ever.

## 13 January 1957

In the office we wait all day long for Macmillan to announce his new Cabinet. At last I speculate on what the main appointments will be. I score three bull's-eyes: Sandys to Defence, Eccles to Board of Trade and Thorneycroft to Treasury. But there are surprises when the list is telephoned to me about 9 p.m. Butler to the Home Office, Selwyn Lloyd remains at the Foreign Office.

---

[*] Arthur Gore, 8th Earl of Arran (1910–83), Conservative Whip in the House of Lords.

[†] Sir Robert Walpole, 1st Earl of Orford (1676–1741), Prime Minister of Great Britain 1721–42.

[‡] Baron Grimond (1913–93), leader of the Liberal Party 1956–67, and briefly, as an interim, 1976.

Heathcoat Amory not promoted, Hailsham to Education, and Sir Percy Mills* brought in from Industry to be Minister of Power.

## 16 January 1957
Receive a message from the office that the second list of ministerial appointments is due about 7 p.m. The list does not in fact appear until 7.45 p.m. The new Government has much to learn about its relations with the Press. We do some frantic writing of paragraphs.

There are two unexpected demotions – Maudling goes from Ministry of Supply to be Paymaster General, answering for the Ministry of Power in the Commons; Nigel Birch leaves Air Ministry to become Economic Secretary to the Treasury. An absurd promotion is that of David Ormsby-Gore† to be Minister of State at the Foreign Office after only two months' ministerial experience.

## 17 January 1957
Story of David Ormsby-Gore. Apparently a boy committed suicide at his house. The housemaster called together the whole house and asked if anybody could give any reason for this. There was complete silence until David, then the lowest of Lower Boys, said, 'Please sir, could it have been the food?'

## 18 January 1957
Macmillan's last list of appointments – the junior ministerial jobs. Bill leaves the Home Office, but Mancroft‡ becomes Under-Secretary for Defence. There are two big surprises: Julian Amery goes to the War Office, and Edward Boyle is to be Parliamentary Secretary to the Ministry of Education under Hailsham. I telephone John Altrincham, who is very disappointed by Edward's decision to join the Government. We discuss Edward's return at some length, and are agreed that it is both politically and morally wrong. He has thrown away his entire moral position over Suez, and must not be surprised if people in future think of him as 'just another politician'. John reproaches himself for not having gone personally to talk him out of it. I say to John, 'If Edward needed to be talked out of it at the last minute he was not worth persuading.'

---

* 1st Viscount Mills (1890–1968), industrialist and politician.
† Sir David Ormsby-Gore, 5th Baron Harlech (1918–85), diplomat and Conservative politician. Ambassador to the US 1961–5.
‡ Stormont, 2nd Baron Mancroft (1914–87), Conservative politician. Minister without Portfolio 1957–8.

## 20 January 1957

Diana Westmorland* to lunch. She tells me Winston's main pastime nowadays is conducting music on long-playing gramophone records, and will not be satisfied until he has a symphony orchestra under his control. We also discuss Winston's painting. It is the custom of the Royal Academy to hang two pictures by a recently dead Academician in the annual exhibition following his death. When Sir John Lavery† died two Academicians went to his studio to select the two pictures. One which they chose was a self-portrait of Lavery. The housekeeper, however, told them that this portrait had not been painted by Lavery, but by one of his pupils, Winston Churchill.

## 22 January 1957

Parliament assembles. A not very enthusiastic welcome for Macmillan.

## 23 January 1957

To House of Commons. Have a drink with Bill Deedes in the Harcourt Room. He has recently lunched alone with Rab Butler, who gave him a great deal of information about the recent change of PM. Eden recommended Rab to the Queen, but the weight of other opinion was against this.

Rab had an unfortunate conversation with Winston, who was about to leave for the South of France just after the change. Rab telephoned him to wish him a pleasant journey and holiday. But Winston thought he was being questioned about his advice to the Queen, and all he would say was, 'I voted for the older man.' It was not one of Winston's clearest days.

It was originally intended that Marples should become Minister of Power, but they discovered, however, that his business included the making of generators, so this was impossible. Maudling was offered the Ministry of Health, but turned it down because it did not carry a seat in the Cabinet; but was later persuaded to speak for Lord Mancroft, the Minister of Power, in the Commons with the sinecure office of Paymaster General. Bill looks most relieved to be out of office at last. Macmillan was in fact most charming over his resignation. He pressed Bill to accept another job, but quite understood his reasons for refusing. At Bill's request there was no public exchange of letters, though Macmillan had written him a delightful letter beginning, 'I am so sorry I was unable to persuade you ...' He added that he hoped Bill would one day return to the Government when his children had been

---

* Diana, Countess of Westmorland (1893–1983).
† (1856–1941), Irish painter.

educated. He also said to Bill, 'I know you are not the sort of man who wants to go out with a baronetcy.'

Dine Beefsteak. Bob Boothby sits next to me. Bob is disappointed at being given no office in the Government. He gives a number of reasons for this, though among them he does not mention his personal relations with Lady Dorothy, or about the affair of Czech gold.[*] He says that Lord Salisbury has never forgiven him for divorcing his wife, a sister of Betty Salisbury.[†] But the strongest reason he gives is that no Government can afford to have a television star in the Cabinet, who could become PM overnight with popular acclaim.

The Scottish Unionists, he says, are furious that not one of their members is now in the Government. This may well lead to the growth both of Liberalism, north of the border, and of Scottish Nationalism.

He criticises the Foreign Office team as being particularly weak. Today in the House he has been talking to Selwyn Lloyd, who was much impressed by his recent visit to the Pope:[‡] 'The Vatican treated me much above my station.' On this Bob comments, 'He forgets he is the British Secretary of State for Foreign Affairs.'

Bob tells a good story about Lady Salisbury and Dot Head meeting at the hairdressers. Lady Salisbury said to Dot Head:[§] 'I am sorry Antony is not in the Cabinet, but then it is a very middle-class Cabinet.'

We all have much sympathy with Eden at the moment – no home, no money, no friends.

Bob says that Nye Bevan does not give the Government more than a year's life.

Talking of income tax, Bob says he claims two suits a year as a business expense – for his TV appearances! He also put in a colossal claim for booze, used for entertaining. The tax people asked for the bills, and returned them with the comment: 'We should never have thought it possible.'

## 26 January 1957

Morning train to Bentley to stay with Donald McLachlan. Squiff Ellis,[¶] who

---

[*] Boothby had to resign on 21 Jan. 1941 from his post as Parliamentary Secretary to the Ministry of Food for not declaring an interest when asking a parliamentary question about blocked Czechoslovakian assets.

[†] Elizabeth Vere Cavendish (1897–1982), wife of the 5th Marquess of Salisbury. Lady Diana Cavendish (1909–92), first wife of Robert Boothby 1935–7.

[‡] Pope Pius XII (1875–1958), r. 1939–58.

[§] Lady Dorothy Ashley-Cooper (1907–87), wife of Antony Head.

[¶] Maj. Lionel Ellis (1885–1970), official war historian.

was second in command of the training battalion at Sandown Park when I joined the Welsh Guards, comes to dine. Appears far younger and less terrifying than he seemed in 1944. As one of the Official War Historians he is now at work on the history of the Normandy Landings. He has discovered that Monty used to give detailed orders for each operation, which used to turn out to be only about a quarter successful. Yet he would always declare himself quite satisfied, and wrote that the operation had gone entirely as planned. He could never admit that anything he had ordered had failed even partially. Monty also, he says, extracted many documents from the War Office official files when he was CIGS. They were mainly letters he had written to Alanbrooke.

Local opinion near Bentley is not apparently entirely pro-Monty – he lives a mile or two away in Isington. The vicar gets very annoyed with him. Monty evidently believes in the nutritional value of herrings, and gives barrels of them to the vicar to distribute in his car.

Ellis is a neighbour of Attlee in Buckinghamshire. One day he came to London by train with him. Attlee was working on some papers and explained to Ellis: 'This afternoon I must make the official Opposition speech in the Commons on the death of George VI. I am looking up the speech I made on the death of George V in 1936 to see how much alteration it needs.'

Also story of Winston and Attlee travelling by train to North during the war. At Carlisle a slightly drunken sailor tried to enter reserved carriage. Detective stopped him, but Winston said: 'Let him sit down, the train is very crowded.' He encouraged the sailor to talk at length about the war. After half an hour Winston disappeared down the corridor. Sailor turned to Attlee, a thought having struck him, and said: 'That's Winston Churchill, isn't it?' 'Yes,' replied Attlee. 'Fancy him talking so friendly like to a couple of twerps like you and me,' said the sailor.

Ellis also tells the story of how Frank Pick,* a high official of London Transport, was sent to Ministry of Information during the war. Here he opposed a plan of Winston's on the grounds that it was political and immoral, and that his conscience would not allow him to carry it out. Winston commented: 'Never let me see or hear again this impeccable bus conductor.'

## 27 January 1957, letter to parents

One feels so sorry for Eden – without health, money, reputation, home or friends. He even had the disappointment of having his advice – that Butler

---

* (1878–1941), transport administrator. Chief Executive and Vice-Chairman, London Passenger Transport Board 1933–40.

should succeed him as PM – rejected by the Queen.

### 27 January 1957

Long walk in cold sunny weather to gather moss for the bowls of tulips which the McLachlans sell from their small nursery garden.

We touch on Suez again, and Donald insists that the intelligence reports we had about Russian intervention in the Middle East were so grave as to justify our Suez intervention. But of course such reports cannot even be made available to the public. He is most interesting on our intelligence services. Trouble during war was not so much to find out what the Germans were going to do next – we had wonderful service of intercepting conversations between top commanders – but in ensuring that Germans did not know how much we knew about them by loosely worded messages between our own commanders.

Drive up to London along empty roads – petrol rationing has cleared all traffic. Donald mentions how bad the social side of the US Embassy is. They invite only the socially eminent, not the informed semi-official or professional people.

### 28 January 1957

At 3 p.m. to Claridge's to see Mrs Anna Rosenberg,* ex-Assistant Secretary for Defense in the United States. A smart, shrewd, attractive woman. She tells me she reads the *Manchester Guardian* and the *Economist* regularly. Her view on Suez coincides with that of the State Department, but she feels a deep friendship for England. We have several minutes' conversation off the record during which she wants to know how Aldrich did as Ambassador. Dulles,† she thinks, will soon leave office. He cannot bear being under fire, and this will break him. The next Secretary of State will be a great improvement.

### 29 January 1957

Dine P. de Z. and M.-L. Philip finds Macmillan easier to work for than Eden. We spend most of dinner going over Suez. Philip sums up the problem by saying that Eden should have decided in September whether: (a) we should negotiate with Egypt and secretly agreed with the United States eventually to bring down Nasser by economic sanctions, or, (b) use force. The temptation

---

* (1902–83), American public official and businesswoman.
† John Foster Dulles (1888–1959), Secretary of State under Eisenhower 1951–9; architect of the South-East Asia Treaty Organisation (SEATO) in 1954. Churchill said that Dulles was the only bull he knew who carried around his own china shop.

came when Israel invaded Egypt. We had so much at stake, says Philip, in oil and in the use of the Suez Canal that we should have been prepared to fight for it. He refuses to see Suez as in any way a moral problem. We disagree at some length over his mystic regard for official sources of information and reports: 'Do you think you know better than the Chiefs of Staff of the Suez operation?' I reply: 'In view of its utter failure, yes.'

Philip tells me that R.A. Butler is making a great joke of going to the Home Office. It is, he tells people, positively Victorian. 'I sign warrants for two minutes every day. I am told that it took the last Secretary all day. They are written out in copperplate, and I am not sure that the 's's are not written like 'f's. Whenever I ask for blotting paper I expect them to bring sand.'

## 31 January 1957

To House of Commons. Harold Wilson as disagreeable as ever. Enoch Powell* very good as Financial Secretary to the Treasury, but must cultivate a more urbane manner.

Parliament is as quiet as I have ever known it. After the emotional weeks of Suez and the change of premiership the Commons seems limp and dispirited. Macmillan received a very tepid cheer from his supporters on his first day as Prime Minister.

There are rumours that Thorneycroft will bring in an 'incentive' Budget to repair some of the electoral damage done by Suez and petrol rationing

To the Albert Hall to hear Verdi's *Requiem* conducted by Malcolm. It is extraordinarily well sung by operatic singers.

## 7 February 1957

Talk with John Altrincham and Tony Benn. I had always thought that Anthony Benn was a Bevanite, but he speaks very critically of Nye's instability. Here I suspect he is revolted by Nye's addiction to booze and good living. There is still a strong Puritanical streak in Anthony.

When I call Anthony's attention to the need for fiscal reform if we are to re-equip our factories, he says the solution is nationalisation. We are both agreed that high rewards for executives do not alone ensure good management.

They talk amusingly about Attlee. At Cherry Tree Cottage apparently there are among Attlee's books rows and rows of Haileybury lists. He has also placed Nye Bevan's *In Place of Fear* next to Aesop's *Fables*.

---

* (1912–98), politician and classical scholar. Conservative MP for Wolverhampton South West 1950–74; Ulster Unionist MP for South Down 1974–87; Minister of Health 1960–63.

Anthony and John have a ding-dong over the growth and strength of the party machine. As John rightly points out, the Conservatives tolerate rebels to the right, and the Socialists tolerate rebels to the left, but neither will tolerate rebellion to the centre.

I am much interested in a small technical point raised by Anthony. When Eden was appointed to the Chiltern Hundreds[*] last month, there was in fact no Chancellor of the Exchequer to appoint him. All ministers had handed in their resignations and a new Chancellor had not yet been appointed. I should have spotted this at the time.

## 11 February 1957, letter to parents

Hear from both Grizel and Giles St Aubyn how unpopular Robert Birley has made himself with almost the entire staff at Eton. For instance, when Hubert retired after more than thirty years' teaching he received no letter of appreciation at all from Birley. He is also very mean about any form of entertaining.

The young beaks too are angry about the bad living conditions and low pay. When they complain, Birley says: 'I slept in a bath for my first half as a beak.' Grizel says this is quite untrue. He had the most expensive lodgings there were.

Giles, perhaps the most tolerant person I know, is full of mistrust and dislike. He asks me to ensure that when eventually Birley retires, Brian Young[†] is not chosen to succeed him. He would certainly be a second Birley.

## 11 February 1957

To House of Commons. An air of great tension. Israel still refuses to withdraw from the Gaza strip and from Akaba without guarantees from Egypt. Selwyn Lloyd answers questions quite well. The whole House appears to be pro-Israel from Bevan to Captain Waterhouse.[‡]

To dine at the Hyde Park Hotel with the Anglo-German Association. Frank and Elizabeth Pakenham[§] receive the guests.

Frank introduces me to Selwyn Lloyd, the Foreign Secretary, and we have

---

[*] An administrative area in Buckinghamshire. Taking the Chiltern Hundreds is a legal procedure to enable the person appointed to resign from the House of Commons.
[†] Sir Brian Young (1922–2017), Headmaster of Charterhouse 1952–64; Director of the Nuffield Foundation 1964–70; Dir.-Gen., Independent Broadcasting Authority 1970–82; Chairman, Christian Aid 1983–90.
[‡] Capt. Charles Waterhouse, MC (1893–1975), Conservative politician.
[§] Countess of Longford (1906–2002), historian, better known as Elizabeth Longford; biographer of Queen Victoria and the Duke of Wellington, among others.

some interesting talk. His first question is: 'How did you think my questions went in the House this afternoon?' I reply that I thought they went excellently. 'Yes,' he says, 'but whether we shall get any oil through the Canal is a different matter.' We touch on the Suez problem. He astonishes me by saying that if he could live those weeks over again, he would still have taken the decision he did, but he adds: 'We should have waited longer before sending the ultimatum to Egypt.' I ask him how he manages to look so fit when nearly all his colleagues are physical wrecks. He replies: 'I make it a rule never to worry about anything. I even gained weight during the week of the Suez Crisis.'

On less serious topics, I ask him why Reading was retired from being Minister of State at the Foreign Office, and why he received only a KCMG as his farewell reward. Selwyn replies that Reading went only on account of age – he is sixty-eight. As for the KCMG, it was considered that for a politician to receive this Order was in itself a very great, if not unique, honour. I reply that while I appreciate this, I still think he should have been given a Grand Cross. Selwyn adds, 'Yes, I should have gone into it at the time, but he may yet get a Grand Cross.'

After dinner I have some talk with Herwarth,* the German Ambassador. I tell him how much I enjoyed the Wagner Festival at Bayreuth. He makes an interesting observation: 'Much as I love the beauty of Wagner's music, I do not listen to it often. It arouses in one all those passions one should try to subdue. Sometimes when I listen to Wagner, I seem to imagine that we are back in the brutal years of 1933 and 1934.'

### 13 February 1957

John Wheeler-Bennett tells me that when he lunched with the Kaiser† just before World War II he noticed how the Kaiser drank rather a bad sparkling burgundy instead of the good Moselle which was also on the table. The Kaiser explained that he always drank sparkling burgundy because he had never been allowed it as a child.

To Covent Garden with Giles St Aubyn at 6 p.m for *Die Meistersinger*. It is sung in English, which always depresses me. Peter Pears good as David.

### 14 February 1957

To the Dorchester for the Foyle's lunch given to Field Marshal Lord

---

* Hans von Herwarth (1904–99), the Federal Republic of Germany's Ambassador to Britain 1955–61.
† Kaiser Wilhelm II (1859–1941), last German Emperor, eldest grandchild of Queen Victoria.

Alanbrooke. He is an impressive figure with rather rounded shoulders, and a throaty voice.

I walk from the Dorchester with Lord Strang,* the retired permanent head of the Foreign Office. He says that Selwyn Lloyd is 'not one of the greatest Foreign Secretaries, but a good advocate. He puts a case well.'

## 16 February 1957

At the Beefsteak Malcolm Sargent talks about the work he is conducting tonight for BBC – Rossini's *Petite Messe Solennelle*, 1863. An old red-faced man called Roundell,† sitting opposite him, says: 'I will tell my housekeeper to listen.' Before Malcolm can answer with a suitable retort, he adds in the same matter-of-fact tones: 'As a matter of fact she doesn't think much of you – she says you conduct Gilbert and Sullivan too fast.' Malcolm, for once, is speechless.

## 18 February 1957

Dine Martin Gilliat at Prunier's. We start at once arguing about relations between the Press and the Palace, which lasts us the whole evening. He says he is shocked that I should write an attack on the Palace Press Office for publication, and tells me I should have worked for improvement quietly and behind the scenes. To which I reply that I have already done my best with Michael Adeane, but to no purpose. Martin goes on to say that even if I do write an article, it would carry much more weight with my own name rather than anonymously. I agree, but point out that I cannot claim to represent the *DT*, or reveal in any way my own experiences with the Palace whilst writing 'Peterborough'.

On the general question of relations between Royalty and the Press, he puts forward the view, though it is not exactly his own view, that once one starts to explain and justify every move of the Royal Family, all the magic goes out of it. This may be, I reply, but if explanations are not given at all there will be no monarchy to preserve in fifty years' time.

I suspect that although Martin puts up a stubborn defence of the Palace, he is privately worried about the Press side. I have given him quite a lot of examples to think about.

## 19 February 1957

Reports from New Zealand that Anthony Eden has had two bouts of fever on

---

* William Strang, 1st Baron Strang (1893–1978), Permanent Under-Secretary at the Foreign Office 1949–53.
† Christopher Roundell (1876–1958), civil servant.

the ship taking him there. It doesn't sound at all good.

Adrian Boult talks about Toscanini, who died recently, on the wireless: 'He had nothing else but music to think of.' Like Eden and politics.

### 21 February 1957
Some conversation with Marshal of the RAF, Lord Portal.[*] He strikes me as having the same sharp yet calm intellect as Alanbrooke, whose war memoirs we discuss. I ask Portal jokingly when we can expect to read the Portal diaries. He replies: 'There ain't no such things.' What surprises him is not so much that Alanbrooke should have kept a diary and later allowed extracts from it to be published, but that he should have had the energy to write up about 1,000 words each night after exhausting meetings. 'We tried to tell Brookie that it was too early to publish them, and that his criticisms of Winston would be taken out of their context and magnified.' Portal personally was never insulted to the same extent as the generals, whose courage Winston used to doubt – or pretend to.

Portal existed during the war on about five hours' sleep. But had the gift of not worrying (cf. what Selwyn Lloyd told me the other day). During the war he never had a pipe out of his mouth. Then he decided he was literally burning too much money, so took to snuff.

### 22 February 1957
Drink in the St James's Club with Hugh Lawson.[†] Tells me a remark by Winston during the Suez Crisis: 'None of this would have happened if my old friend Eisenhower had still been alive.'

### 23 February 1957
A drink with Jim Cilcennin. Jim looks very brown and well after going round the world with the Duke of Edinburgh. Every Commonwealth Government thought that Eden had gone mad. Sid Holland,[‡] PM of New Zealand, told Jim: 'We will always come to the aid of England. But this is the last time we shall do so until we are told what is happening.'

Jim says how distressed the Duke was by the Press rumours of a Royal 'rift'.[§] As I suspected, the plans for his stay in Gibraltar after the return of the

---

[*] Sir Charles Portal, 1st Viscount Portal of Hungerford; Chief of the Air Staff 1940–46.
[†] 6th Baron Burnham (1931–2005). General Manager and Deputy Managing Director, *Daily Telegraph* 1955–86, Deputy MD 1984–6; a Deputy Speaker of the House of Lords 1995–2001.
[‡] Sir Sidney Holland (1893–1961), Prime Minister of New Zealand 1949–57.
[§] There was speculation in some parts of the press that the marriage of the Queen and Prince Philip was in difficulties.

Royal Yacht *Britannia* were made a long time ago, and were influenced by the shortage of petrol. Jim absolutely agrees with me that the rumour could have been killed at once if the Palace had issued explanations and plans beforehand. Jim told the Queen this when he saw her the day he flew back from Gibraltar. In one of the Household offices there he heard one of the courtiers say: 'We tried to feed the petrol story to the Press, but they would not take it.' This makes me very angry, and I tell Jim my recent experience. He suggests I write a letter to him which he can show to the Duke. I shall do so, outlining some of the shortcomings of the Palace Press Office.

### 27 February 1957

Hartley Shawcross to dine at the flat. He nearly decided to retire permanently the other day as he thinks the practice of collecting outstanding fees tax-free on retirement will soon be abolished. Certainly he will not stand for Parliament at the next General Election. Should the Socialists be returned he thinks he is certain to be offered the Lord Chancellorship, but does not yet know whether he would accept it – the difficulty of defending measures in which one does not believe. As far as the future of the Lord Chief Justiceship is concerned, he would like it, but has no chance of receiving it from the present Government.

Andrew Bruce turns up, and we have some excellent talk with Hartley. In Sussex Hartley is a neighbour of Dr John Bodkin Adams,* the Eastbourne doctor accused of poisoning patients, though Hartley has rarely met him. But he does describe their first meeting, when both were lunching at the house of a friend. Adams constantly boasted of his possessions – watches, cameras, cars, so that Hartley said jocularly to him: 'You seem to have everything. I have obviously chosen the wrong profession. I cannot kill off my patients!'

In fact Adams may well get off, as the medical evidence is so conflicting. His defending counsel actually thinks he is innocent of murder.

### 28 February 1957

Lunch Beefsteak. Walk back as far as the Palace with Michael Adeane. We have a few words about the Royal 'rift' rumour, and restore our harmonious relations. He says what a wonderful success the Royal visit to Portugal was. 'The only good thing about the rumour is that it focused world attention on its success.'

---

* (1899–1983) suspected serial killer; 132 of his patients left him money in their wills. He was committed for trial on 14 Jan. 1957 at Lewes on the charge of murdering one patient, but was acquitted.

To House of Commons, where Macmillan is strongly pressed by Socialists about an alleged indiscretion by David Eccles about the forthcoming Budget. Macmillan rather unwisely loses his temper, and stands at the box white and trembly. Admittedly Harold Wilson is at his nastiest, not to mention Gaitskell.

## 6 March 1957

Dine alone with Jim Cilcennin, then settle down to a great deal of gossip over brandy and cigars. I read him extracts from my journal over the Suez episode, which of course he heard about from the other side of the world. He agrees that the only justifiable time for armed intervention against Egypt was as early as possible. We recall that Sunday at Admiralty House when Eden was ready to do so. It would have been when Nasser nationalised the Canal in July.

He tells me that during his last year of office his relations with Eden were difficult – the PM would abuse him on the phone like a madman. He did not particularly want to become a peer, but having done so he was furious when almost at once Bobbety Salisbury wanted him to leave the Admiralty so that the job could be given to an hereditary peer – either Carrington or Hailsham. Jim insisted on staying at least until the Naval Estimates of March 1956 – he had been made a peer a few weeks before. He was ready to go in May when the Commander Crabb affair blew up, the frogman inspecting the Russian cruiser which brought B. and K. to England for official visit. It would, however, have looked as though he were being dismissed. So he stayed on. Then came the Nasser nationalisation of the Canal. Eventually he did go in September.

Prince Philip asked him to go round the world with him in *Britannia* several months before he left the Admiralty. He not only wanted a friend and experienced politician, but knew that Jim would be able to have daily treatment for his arthritis in the sick bay of the Royal Yacht.

The voyage itself was splendid, and he has nothing but the highest and most genuine admiration for the Duke. He writes all his own speeches entirely, says Jim, but shows them to friends for advice and criticism. He also did some painting on the tour.

## 13 March 1957

I sound John Altrincham on reform of the House of Lords. John thinks reform of its composition essential, since its influence will rest on the respect for it of the public. Prestige rather than the veto is its real weapon. He is in fact in favour of abolishing the veto altogether, since the Commons in the long run has its way; to use the veto at all merely inflames opinion.

## 14 March 1957

Go with Frederic Hooper to see John Osborne's *Look Back in Anger* at the
Royal Court Theatre, Sloane Square, and stay only for two acts. Malcolm
Muggeridge sits next to us, and he stays only for one act! The theme is the
bloody-minded young man with an unhappy childhood and a grudge against
the 'respectable' world, living in calculated squalor though not poverty. The
play is all the rage now. As a case from a psychiatrist's notebook it would
have a certain ephemeral interest, but as justification of squalid behaviour its
philosophy is simply half-baked. I read a parody of it in *Punch* with immense
relish when I return.

## 20 March 1957

John Altrincham lends me copies of *Encounter* containing the verbatim
texts of the broadcasts given by P.G. Wodehouse from Berlin when a civilian
interned in Germany. He was much attacked for them, and practically tried
for treason. In fact, they are most witty and ironical attacks on the Germans,
who were too stupid to realise this.

## 8 April 1957

Jim Cilcennin to dine at flat. Tells me he has decided not to show Prince
Philip my letter about Press relations at the Palace, although he will talk to
him about the subject. Jim, curiously enough, maintains he is doing this to
protect me. In fact, he does not wish to offend his friends among the courtiers.

   In private, however, he advocates some fairly radical reforms in the Royal
Family. He thinks they will have to reside more and more in Commonwealth
countries. The Queen Mother would make an admirable Governor General
in Canada or Australia, provided she was prepared to take on the job for a
minimum of two years. As Jim discovered in Australia, the Americans are
perpetually sending high-powered missions there. He also thinks the Royal
Family should cut the length of their holidays.

## 1 May 1957

Dine Beefsteak. Talk to Sir Arthur Willert.* After Curzon had been very
kind and polite to him in the FO one day, W. said: 'I suppose that now you
have been kind to me today, we shall have a great deal of friction tomorrow.'
C. replied: 'My dear Willert, it may be that after praising the butler for the
way he has cleaned the silver, one finds the next day he has scratched a valuable salver; or after complimenting a housemaid on her dusting of china

* (1882–1973), journalist and civil servant.

she breaks a piece of Sèvres. But let us leave such superstitions to the servant class.'

Clive Bell tells me story of Tennyson who, lunching with Jowett at Balliol, met an undergraduate who could recite *Maud* by heart and showed great knowledge of its meaning. Tennyson was flattered, and asked the undergraduate to go for a walk after lunch. At which Jowett said: 'I will come too.' This was not at all what Tennyson wanted. So on way to gate he told two indecent stories. At gate, Jowett embarrassed, 'remembered' some letters he had to write, and returned to the Master's Lodge. Tennyson turned with satisfaction: 'I thought I'd stink the old bugger out,' he said.[*]

### 21 May 1957

Osbert Lancaster[†] tells me Max Beerbohm had a great love of Charterhouse. He would not speak to Robert Graves[‡] for six years after he had been struck off the OC list for writing *Goodbye to All That*.

Max Beerbohm did only one indecent drawing. At the Café Royal one night, while discussing homosexuality, Frank Harris[§] said he could never imagine himself taking part in such activities – 'though if Shakespeare had asked me, I might not have been able to refuse'. On the spot, Max drew cartoon of F.H. in bed, being approached by an effeminate Shakespeare!

### 7 June 1957

John Altrincham was unexpectedly asked to dine with Robert Birley at Eton on 4 June,[¶] & found him agreeable, but conscious of not having happy relations with his staff.

---

[*] Alfred, Lord Tennyson (1809–92), Poet Laureate 1850–92. *Maud* (1855) is a lengthy narrative poem in three parts. Dr Benjamin Jowett (1817–93), Master of Balliol Coll., Oxford 1870–93. A legendary figure of whom one Balliol verse read:

My heart leaps up when I behold
A rainbow over Balliol Hall,
As though the Cosmos was controlled,
By Dr Jowett after all.

[†] Sir Osbert Lancaster (1908–86), cartoonist. Like Beerbohm and Graves, he was educated at Charterhouse.

[‡] (1895–1985), novelist, poet, critic and classicist. His memoir of his early life, *Goodbye to All That* (Jonathan Cape, 1929), gave a frank account of the deficiencies, as he saw them, of Charterhouse, and one of the most vivid portraits of the horrors of World War I.

[§] (1855–1931), writer and publisher, best known for his four-volume autobiography *My Life and Loves* (privately published, 1922–7), a graphic account of his sexual adventures.

[¶] The birth date of George III and the College's principal festival.

John also tells me that Henry Fairlie[*] recently wrote to Gaitskell, saying that he was disappointed in his leadership. Instead of sending back a curt line at most, as Attlee would have done, Gaitskell replied at length in his own hand, & telling Fairlie to consult Douglas Jay[†] and Roy Jenkins[‡] as impartial referees on how much progress he had made, in leading the Labour Party. So it seems he is as sensitive to criticism as Eden – not the stuff of which great leaders are made.

John is preparing a whole number of the *National Review* on the Royal Family. Some months ago he suggested I did an article on the Queen's programme; now he wants me to do one on Royal Family's finances. I decline both – it would be embarrassing to write familiarly of people whose hospitality one has enjoyed, and I should hate the process of spying and delving.

### 8 June 1957
When Noël Coward, at any social gathering, wants to go to the loo, he always says, 'I must telephone the Vatican.'

### 9 June 1957, letter to parents
Dinner at Coppins last night with the Duchess of Kent was most amusing. Noël Coward very kindly took me down & drove me back in the large car he had hired. He is staying at the Dorchester in the very expensive penthouse suite designed by Oliver Messel.[§] We had a great deal of most interesting talk, & he came in for a drink when we arrived back in London, staying until two o'clock this morning. So I think I could quite easily write a biography of him on the spot!

He was most interesting about his finances. The stories put about by the gutter papers that he fled from England because he owed the Inland Revenue £25,000 are quite untrue. He went to live in Jamaica only to avoid paying

---

[*] (1924–90), journalist, principally on the *Observer* and *The Times*, though later freelance. He described prominent social figures as the Establishment, explaining: 'By the "Establishment", I do not mean the centres of official power – though they are certainly part of it – but rather the whole matrix of official and social relations within which power is exercised. The exercise of power in Britain (more specifically, in England) cannot be understood unless it is recognised that it is exercised socially.'

[†] Douglas Jay, Baron Jay (1907–96), prominent Labour politician in the Attlee and Wilson governments. President of the Board of Trade 1964–7.

[‡] Baron Jenkins of Hillhead (1920–2003), Labour Party, SDP and Liberal Democrat politician and biographer. Minister of Aviation 1964–5; Home Secretary 1965–7; Chancellor of the Exchequer 1967–70; President of the European Commission 1977–81; Chancellor of the University of Oxford 1987–2003.

[§] (1904–78), artist and stage designer.

surtax in the future, & in fact is now, he tells me, managing to save money for the first time in his life. He was fascinating talking about the hostility he has had to put up with from critics of all kinds – 'If I had worked my way up from the gutter, they would have been delighted. But I came from the suburbs, and they will never forgive me for that.'

He is, of course, one of the Duchess of Kent's closest friends and it was charming to see the affectionate courtliness of his manner towards her. He used to be a close friend of the late Duke of Kent. We were a small party last night – the Duchess, Prince Eddie, Noël, Giles St Aubyn and myself. The usual admirably cooked yet simple dinner – an egg dish, Wiener Schnitzel with asparagus, and strawberries, with white wine, followed by port or brandy. No cigars – there never are, I fear, at Coppins.

But much amusing talk all about Jamaica & the stage world. The Duchess much the same as ever, still extraordinarily beautiful, but never terribly interested in what goes on around her – and certainly never hesitating to yawn even in the middle of Noël's best stories! Prince Eddie very well indeed, having a week's leave from the Army & busy training a retriever puppy.

The first night this week of *The Trojans* at Covent Garden. This massive opera by Berlioz (6 p.m.–11 p.m.) has some good dramatic episodes, but musically it had little of the thrilling grandeur of Wagner. I suspect I should like it better after hearing it once or twice more.

Martin Gilliat tells me that whenever he goes to a big race with the Queen Mother he always feels he must back the Royal horse, if any. Otherwise, he says, 'One cannot raise a genuine cheer if it wins!' So he must have had a good day at Epsom on Friday at the Oaks.⁵

### 13 June 1957

Queen's official birthday. Mall packed with crowds.

Welsh Guards Club dinner at the Dorchester. Highlight of the evening is when Prince Philip auctions old regimental drums in order to raise funds to buy new ones. He does it superbly, waving a wooden hammer, with his Garter ribbon slightly disarranged. He points to an old, old officer with a purple tweed face and says: 'Now then, Mr Onassis, open up the bidding.' When somebody bids £20, Prince Philip looks hard at him and says: 'Are you sure you have that in the bank?' By the end of the auction, he has sold the three drums for the handsome sum of £206. People with large houses like to have them as paper-baskets. He signs each of them, too, adding to one man – 'I shall sign yours in port.'

---

⁵ The Oaks in 1957 was won by Elizabeth II's horse, Carrozza, ridden by Lester Piggott.

## 29 June 1957

Up early and to Brompton Road Station en route for London Airport and plane to Dunkirk. Office thick with bemedalled veterans all going for ceremony of unveiling BEF memorial by the Queen Mother.

At the airport the wonderful apparition slowly comes into view up the moving staircase of Field Marshal Alexander,* in blue ceremonial dress, sword and Garter ribbon. We have some interesting talk. His first visit to Dunkirk since evacuation when he was last British officer to be taken off. Shows me his lovely sword, presented to him by the City of London, and bearing arms of London, Order of Bath, Order of St Michael and St George, his own, and crossed Field Marshal's batons – all in beautifully painted enamel. Throughout the day no special arrangements are made for him, which I think a pity. Yet never a trace of irritation shows. What an admirable man he is.

Land at Belgium airfield about one o'clock, and by bus to Dunkirk cemetery, across the frontier. Large crowd of people. Gladwyn Jebb, his morning coat covered with stars; Monty, rather rudely dressed in lightweight service-dress instead of blue, like Alex, Templer and Duke of Gloucester. Queen Mother, as always, looks enchanting in white. A most moving service, and a finely delivered address by Queen Mother. Afterwards I have a few words with Martin Gilliat, in his Green Jacket uniform. We were both very touched by the service. He gives me a copy of the Queen Mother's speech, which is a great kindness.

## 5 August 1957, letter to parents

You will have seen all the fuss about John Altrincham's attack on the Queen. I warned him not to do so – it spoils the genuine and legitimate case which can be made against some of the courtiers. His judgement on these things is surprisingly unsteady, not only on this occasion, but when writing on political matters too.†

---

* FM Sir Harold Alexander, 1st Earl Alexander of Tunis (1891–1969), served with distinction in both world wars. C.-in-C. of Middle East Command 1942–3; C.-in-C. of the 18th Army Group, North Africa 1943 and of Allied Armies in Italy 1943–4, Supreme Allied Cdr of the Mediterranean Theatre 1944–5; Governor General of Canada 1946–52; Minister of Defence 1952–4.

† In the Aug. edition of the *National Review* John Altrincham wrote that the Queen's court was too 'tweedy' and 'upper-class', and that the Queen's style of speaking was 'a pain in the neck'. He added: 'The personality conveyed by the utterances which are put into her mouth is that of a priggish schoolgirl, captain of the hockey team, a prefect, and a recent candidate for Confirmation.' His article caused a furore and he was physically attacked outside the studios of ITV by a member of the League of Empire Loyalists, Philip Burbidge.

### 23 August 1957

Harold Nicolson tells me that one of the books which King George V most enjoyed was his own *Some People*, published in 1927. It contained some disobliging vignettes of fellow members of the Diplomatic Service and much upset the Foreign Secretary, Austen Chamberlain, especially when Lord Stamfordham told Chamberlain that the King had never laughed so much over a book.

### 3 November 1957, letter to parents

Somerset Maugham and John Altrincham came to lunch with me yesterday at the flat. The old man was in very good form, and liked John very much. He eats and drinks very well for a man of his age – he will be eighty-four in January – and could easily be twenty years younger. He told me how delighted he was to discover a pub in Wales called *The Moon and Sixpence*!

### 8 November 1957, letter to parents

What a fuss about the Russian satellites – the final touch of lunacy was an appeal for a silent minute in honour of the dog!

### 16 November 1957

John Altrincham shows me appalling anonymous letters sent him (one signed 'Four Old Etonians') threatening him with violence after his article on the monarchy.

### 17 November, letter to parents

I have been to the House of Lords, where Lord Hailsham was very bouncy and rather silly – he does not inspire me with much confidence.

### 23 November 1957, letter to parents

I had an amusing lunch with Michael Adeane, the Queen's Private Secretary, the other day. He told me that when he first joined the Royal Household, he noticed George VI eyeing his wardrobe with disfavour, so he decided to buy a new overcoat. He found out from the King's valet who his tailor was & had a new coat made. The bill was enormous, but he felt very proud of himself when he wore it for the first time. All the King said was: 'What a most extraordinary coat. I suppose you inherited it.'

### 29 November 1957

Jim Cilcennin to dine at the flat. He tells me how in 1937 he was appointed

PPS to Eden at the Foreign Office through the influence of Horace Wilson.*
When first approached, Jim refused to accept the appointment unless Eden
actually said he wanted Jim as PPS. To which Wilson replied: 'We have
changed all that.' John did accept the appointment, having made it quite
clear to Wilson that he would not be a Downing Street spy.

He talks of his years as PPS to J.H. Thomas. In the final resignation speech,
Thomas pointed dramatically to the sky, saying: 'There is one up there that
knows all!' He was, however, referring not to the Almighty, but to his wife
who was sitting in the Gallery.

## 8 December 1957, letter to parents

Nearly every day I have spent an hour or so at the tribunal investigating the
Bank Rate leak. It is a most fascinating procedure. There is hardly any action
at all which cannot be construed to one's disadvantage under clever cross-
examination. One result of it all, I think, is that ministers in future will be
less willing to talk privately to journalists in case it all comes out later. This
will be particularly irritating for people like myself who rely to a great extent
on confidential sources of information.

---

* Sir Horace Wilson (1882–1972), civil servant with a key role in Neville Chamberlain's
appeasement ministry.

# 1958

## 8 January 1958

Some talk with Commander Grenfell,* who speaks scathingly about apartheid. The South African Government accepts an Ambassador from Ghana, but latter has the greatest difficulty in getting his hair cut as he cannot use shops frequented by Europeans.

Tommy Lascelles would like John Betjeman to be the next Poet Laureate.† Tommy says the late King had to pay £4,000 for Max Beerbohm's drawings of Edward VII – 'The Seven Ages of Man'. T.L. thinks Max the greatest English essayist since Addison.

He also tells me he has prepared a long paper on ministerial changes – audiences of the Queen, seals of office, kissing hands, etc., which is now in the Royal Archives. When in Treasury during the war, Tommy was put to providing Winston with analysis of time spent on committees by civil servants. Discovered that 2,000 man years spent on them – had often become largely a matter of prestige for a man to be a chairman of a committee, whatever it did.

## 12 January 1958, letter to parents

Thorneycroft's resignation as Chancellor of the Exchequer was a great surprise, and I cannot really think that Macmillan was right to dismiss it so lightly. In the public mind Thorneycroft now stands for economy & the Cabinet for inflation – though the truth is not at all as simple as that. With the percentage of old people needing pensions rising each year, the whole problem of paying for such social services will have to be faced sooner or later.

---

* Cdr William Grenfell (1920–2013), joined the Royal Navy in World War II as a torpedo man; radar operator on the Murmansk convoys; also served in Norway and Malta; naval attaché in Bonn 1961; led the campaign to award medals to survivors of the Arctic convoys, and in the 2005 general election stood against Geoff Hoon, former Defence Secretary, to draw attention to the campaign. At the age of eighty-six he was the oldest parliamentary candidate.
† Betjeman was the next Poet Laureate but one in 1972.

## 24 January 1958

Sir John Ferguson, Chief Constable of Kent,[*] tells me that each year he makes a courtesy call on Winston at Chartwell. Usually he finds him in bed. This year, however, he was very smartly dressed, drinking whisky & soda. When Ferguson was offered the same drink, but refused as it was too early in the day, Winston said: 'Good God! Are you ill?' Winston, he says, is of course very deaf & has a disconcerting habit of reverting to a remark made several minutes before. Ferguson was apparently wearing the tie of his regiment at Chartwell, the Durham Light Infantry. Winston asked him what regiment it was, & at once commented: 'I played against them at polo in 189–'. Later in the conversation he suddenly said: 'And their names were ----, ----, ----, and ----,' a quite extraordinary feat of memory.

## 26 January 1958

Dine with John Altrincham. First time I have seen him since his return from India & Kenya. He is disturbed by the political situation there. Still far too much colour bar & no attempt to accept the educated Africans as equals or even potential equals. The Government files for invitations to Government House consist of several thickly packed trays of Europeans & about one-third of a tray of Africans and Asians. HMG stupid not to give the Africans even more power than they ask for – they would be entirely dependent on our Government, & would work well with it. As it is, the Mau Mau[†] seems to be emerging again in various forms.

## 30 January 1958

Some pleasant talk at the Beefsteak with Jonah,[‡] delighted at the reception of his third volume of memoirs, *Georgian Afternoon*, but annoyed by *Financial Times* which sneers at Balliol.

We discuss Harold Macmillan. As a young man, says Jonah, he was shy & diffident with a very weak handshake. His American mother[§] must have been a very difficult person – she had duplicates made of Daniel Macmillan's keys to read all the letters in his desk.[¶] Jonah thinks that HM once proposed a motion at the Union in favour of Socialism.

---

[*] Maj. Sir John Ferguson (1891–1975), senior police officer, Chief Constable of Kent 1946–58.
[†] The Mau Mau movement was an uprising in the British Kenya Colony, 1952–64.
[‡] Sir Lawrence Evelyn Jones (1885–1969), barrister and writer.
[§] Helen ('Nellie') Artie Tarleton Belles (1856–1937).
[¶] Daniel Macmillan (1886–1965), Harold's brother, Chairman, Macmillan & Co., publishers 1936–65.

## 2 February 1958, letter to parents

In the Lords I heard the third reading of the Life Peerages Bill. At one point Lord Winterton* referred to 'responsible papers like *The Times* and the *Telegraph*'. At once little Lord Stansgate† was on his feet. 'Why', he asked, 'does the noble Earl call *The Times* a responsible newspaper?' There was a great gale of laughter at this.

I saw Martin Gilliat at Clarence House, on the eve of the six-week Commonwealth tour with the Queen Mother. Martin, cool & calm as ever, produced a complete programme of the tour for me. He also showed me a most interesting document he had prepared for the Queen Mother. It was divided into two columns. One showed the engagements to be done in each town on the tour. By the side of this, in the second column, were shown the engagements she did thirty-one years ago in the same towns when Duchess of York. It explains why the famous 'Royal memory' is so often admired.

## 8 February 1958, letter to parents

I heard a story about Hilaire Belloc‡ this week. When Winston became PM he offered the Companionship of Honour to Belloc. Belloc went to Debrett, looked up the Companions of Honour, and found that the list began 'Lady Astor, Lord Attlee, Miss Margaret Bondfield . . .'§ He read no further, but at once wrote declining the decoration!

## 16 February 1958, letter to parents

Harold Nicolson is back from a long cruise with his wife to South America, and looks very well. It is really extraordinary, but he has such a hatred of the Franco¶ government that he would not even go ashore when the ship called

---

* Edward Turnour, 6th Earl Winterton (1883–1962), Irish peer and British Conservative politician. Elected MP for Horsham in a by-election in 1904 at the age of twenty-one, the youngest MP and 'Baby of the House'. He served for forty-seven years, by which time he was the Father of the House, a unique double to have achieved; Chancellor of the Duchy of Lancaster 1937–9, in Neville Chamberlain's government.

† William Wedgwood Benn, 1st Viscount Stansgate (1877–1960), Liberal politician. Secretary of State for India 1929–31; Secretary of State for Air 1945–6; father of Tony Benn, who fought a long campaign to disclaim the title of 2nd Viscount Stansgate so that he could remain in the Commons.

‡ (1870–1953), Anglo-French writer and historian. Liberal MP for Salford South 1906–10.

§ Nancy Astor (1879–1964), Unionist politician; first woman MP to take her seat, for Plymouth Sutton 1919–45. Margaret Bondfield (1873–1953), Labour politician; first woman Privy Councillor; first woman Cabinet Minister, Minister of Labour 1929–31.

¶ General Francisco Franco (1892–1975), Spanish dictator; Caudillo of Spain 1939–75.

at Spanish ports. It is fantastic, but then Harold has never been considered a serious politician!

## 12 March 1958

Read Peter Wildeblood* – *A Way of Life*. All about homosexuals and their problems. One remark made by a male prostitute – he doesn't mind going to bed, but hates it when his employers try to educate him & take him to the ballet!

## 21 March 1958

While shopping in the King's Road I meet Peter Thorneycroft, in orange corduroy trousers, a British warm [overcoat], no hat, & a poodle!

## 22 March 1958

To film of Orson Welles in *Othello* – superb photography as well as startlingly good acting.

Jim Cilcennin told me a story of a woman dining out who was introduced to her neighbour at the table. He was Reid Dick, the sculptor, but she thought he was Dick-Read, the gynaecologist.† So the following conversation ensued:

She: 'You must meet all sorts of eminent people who need your services. Who was the most famous?'

He: 'President Roosevelt.'

(long pause)

She: (trying again) 'I suppose you are always trying out new techniques with instruments?'

He: 'Oh no, I stick to my old hammer and chisel.'

## 27 March 1958

Carol‡ and Julian Faber to dine, Macmillan's daughter and son-in-law. Carol says her father was on point of resigning from the Government when Eden's illness made him PM. Reason was over Cabinet's attitude towards his estimates – as Thorneycroft was to find a year later.

Carol very anti-Shawcross. They both dislike Julian Amery, their

---

* (1923–99), writer and civil rights campaigner. In 1954 he was sentenced to jail along with Lord Montagu and Michael Pitt-Rivers for conspiracy to incite acts of gross indecency.

† Sir William Reid Dick (1879–1961), Scottish sculptor. Designer of many war memorials, notably that in Bushey, Hertfordshire; sculptor of the statue of President Roosevelt, Grosvenor Square. Grantly Dick-Read (1890–1959), gynaecologist.

‡ Lady Caroline Faber (1923–2016), eldest daughter of Harold Macmillan.

brother-in-law – very pushing and dishonest they say. And they tell me he has a Napoleon cult & collects relics.

Talk to Malcolm Sargent on telephone about Vaughan Williams' new 9th Symphony. He tells me his wireless talk on the work yesterday was done from a few notes scribbled in the cab, not from a text. I tell him how very good I thought it.[*]

## 2 April 1958

At the Beefsteak talk with John Altrincham of the implications of the Torrington by-election result[†] – that Young Conservatives are leaving the party in great numbers. As a typical Conservative toady who is enough to drive anybody out of the party, we mention Humphry Berkeley[‡] – at which moment he walks in to dine accompanied by Peregrine Worsthorne![§] In a half-friendly, half-serious few moments of conversation, Perry tells John he is doing great harm in the party by his attacks on its leaders. John rightly insists that it is only by the efforts of people who think as he does that the utter decay of the party can be stopped.

The other day John met Martin Charteris,[¶] an Assistant Private Secretary to the Queen. They discussed the whole Commonwealth and Crown problem. John was horrified when Charteris insisted that the Queen could not spend too much time on tour 'as she is a landowner'. How can any courtier – least of all one who is supposed to be the most enlightened of his circle – weigh a few acres in Norfolk and Balmoral against the boundless opportunities of the Commonwealth? I really despair of our remaining a monarchy for fifty years.

---

[*] Malcolm Sargent gave the first performance of Vaughan Williams' 9th Symphony on 12 Apr. 1958 with the Royal Philharmonic Orchestra. Vaughan Williams was due to attend the recording of the symphony under Sir Adrian Boult on 26 Aug. 1958, but died that morning.

[†] On 27 Mar. Mark Bonham Carter won by 219 votes, the first gain by the Liberal Party at a by-election since 1929. He lost the seat at the 1959 general election and failed to regain it in 1964.

[‡] (1926–94), socially liberal politician. Conservative MP for Lancaster 1959–66; joined the Labour Party in 1970, and the Social Democratic Party in 1981; introduced a Private Member's Bill in 1965 to legalise homosexual relations in line with the Wolfenden Report. The Bill was given a second reading by 164 votes to 107 in Feb. 1966, but fell when Parliament was dissolved for the March general election.

[§] Sir Peregrine 'Perry' Worsthorne (b. 1923), journalist, writer and broadcaster. Editor of the *Sunday Telegraph* 1986–91.

[¶] Sir Martin Charteris, Baron Charteris of Amisfield (1913–99), PS to Elizabeth II 1972–7; Provost of Eton 1978–91.

John also gives me an account of a dinner with George Lyttelton.* John has the greatest admiration for G.W.L – he encouraged the talent of pupils such as John Bayley. John also quotes a remark by G.W.L. during the evening – 'No man can be a good schoolmaster unless he has a strain of homosexuality.'

## 10 April 1958

Harold Nicolson tells me that Nigel has now given up hope of winning the Bournemouth seat back from the Association. But is having talks with Central Office, and hopes they will find him another seat. I am sorry he is not making more of a fight of it.

At Clarence House with Martin Gilliat. As Martin ushers me into a cab, he says to the driver, 'Wormwood Scrubs', which amuses the driver all the way to Draycott Place. As I pay the cab driver, he says, 'Fancy 'im coming out of Clarence House and saying that!'

## 1 May 1958

Harold Nicolson and the C.P. Snows to dine with me. Harold talks of Robert Vansittart's memoirs, & absurdity of his calling his life a failure – because he failed to persuade Stanley Baldwin on rearmament. Snow says he was a vain man. 'No,' says Harold, 'conceited.'†

## 14 June 1958, letter to parents

Anthony Eden has now, I hear, almost completed his memoirs. *The Times* is reputed to have offered him £400,000 for them, in the hope of recouping by selling them to America, but the response from there has so far been tepid. The memoirs, I am told, reflect harshly and unjustly on Eden's colleagues, and Selwyn Lloyd was not even consulted on the chapters dealing with Suez.‡

The bus strike continues its dreary way, but appears to be wavering as I write. It has made one's daily life rather tiring – cabs have not been easy to find at any particular moment.

---

* The Hon. George Lyttelton (1883–1962), renowned teacher of classics and English literature at Eton 1908–45. He taught Aldous Huxley, George Orwell and Cyril Connolly. The six volumes of his correspondence in retirement with his former pupil Sir Rupert Hart-Davis, published 1978–84, were described by K.R. as 'one of the most urbane, civilised and entertaining correspondences of our time'.

† Sir Robert Vansittart, 1st Baron Vansittart (1881–1957), senior diplomat. Permanent Under-Secretary at the Foreign Office 1930–38; opponent of appeasement policy.

‡ This was a common misapprehension at the time. 'When Eden returned to Wiltshire and an uncertain financial retirement he often invited Selwyn over to Broad Chalke to discuss details of his own volume of memoirs, *Full Circle*.' D.R. Thorpe, *Selwyn Lloyd* (Jonathan Cape, 1989), p. 259.

Glyndebourne was charming in the sunshine one evening. We heard Gluck's *Alceste*, rather a boring opera. It was like a novel by Henry James: great technical perfection, but nothing ever happens.

Such a good story about A.L. Rowse* told me by one of his colleagues. He subscribes to a Press-cutting agency, and one day noticed a short review of his latest book in a Portsmouth evening paper. It did not think highly of the book. Most historians would have ignored it, but not A.L.R. He at once sent off an angry letter to the editor, complaining of 'your third-rate reviewer'. The reviewer was stung to reply. 'I am sorry,' he wrote in a letter printed immediately under A.L. Rowse's protest, 'I am sorry that I am only a third-rate reviewer. But I am working hard, and I hope that one day I may become, like Mr Rowse, a second-rate reviewer.'

From America I hear they are saying that Vice-President Nixon has gone grey in the service of himself.

### 21 June 1958

Dine Philip de Zulueta and Marie-Lou. Philip talks of ecclesiastical appointments made for Eden by Sir Anthony Bevir.† One day Bevir sent Eden a minute about a vacant bishopric, in which he rejected the Bishop of Exeter's‡ being 'addicted to extreme practices'. Eden was very upset by this – he thought it meant unnatural vice, not merely an excessive wearing of chasubles.

When Archbishop Fisher, in an attempt to bring about a start to reunion of the Churches, asked the Pope to preside over a sort of inter-Church committee, Macmillan commented: 'I suppose Fisher added that there would be tea and possibly Princess Margaret, & was rather hurt when the Pope turned it down.'

### 31 July 1958

Philip Goodhart§ says Gaitskell wanted Hartley Shawcross to be Chancellor of the Exchequer in next Socialist Government – but Hartley Shawcross stuck out against nationalisation.

### 7 August 1958

Gave Noël Coward lunch at the Savoy Grill. He amuses me by asking for bangers & bacon – the dish he can get neither in New York nor the South

---

* (1903–97), historian and Shakespearean scholar.
† (1895–1977), Secretary for Appointments to the Prime Minister 1947–56. PS (from 1940) successively to Neville Chamberlain, Winston Churchill, Clement Attlee and Anthony Eden.
‡ The Rt Revd Robert Mortimer (1902–76), leader of the Anglo-Catholic wing of the C of E.
§ Sir Philip Goodhart (1925–2015), Conservative MP for Beckenham 1957–92.

of France! He has a Betjeman-like love of the suburbs. He tells me story of
Marlene Dietrich very proud of having received Legion of Honour, & wearing it on all her clothes. A fellow actress met her one day & said: 'Forgive me
darling, but you have a laundry mark on your coat!'

### 8 August 1958

To Cambridge by 10.45 train. Station announcement warns passengers on
Newmarket trains not to play cards with strangers – a curiously nineteenth-
century warning.

A nasty drizzle over Cambridge, whose traffic is as thick and disagreeable
as in Oxford. Stay at University Arms.

Spend an hour or so with Professor N.F. Mott,* Cavendish Professor of
Physics. Much talk with this slightly uneasy, donnish man, about Churchill
College, and difficulty of finding tutors among scientists – who of course
prefer research work. Good description of how executive committee met
at Winston's house in Hyde Park Gate, beneath picture of the Battle of
Blenheim. He gives me a great deal of valuable information on Churchill
College.

Mott also tells me of his fear that the work of the university radio telescope
will be rendered useless if a third TV channel swallows up the bit of the
wavelength they need. There is much difficulty about this, and he may need
my help in 'Peterborough'. 'At the moment we are receiving information
about collisions between heavenly bodies which collided before the creation
of the earth – so far away were they. Yet we are threatened with being denied
this information because of a new TV channel.'

### 10 August 1958

There is a controversy over whether Churchill College should have a chapel.
C.P. Snow tells me that Winston apparently commented: 'Were not the disci-
ples content with an Upper Room?'

### 16 August 1958

Catch 9.20 train to Rugby to lunch with Halford Reddish.† On way to his
house we stop to look at Rugby School, his alma mater, extraordinarily ugly
Edwardian architecture, and even the older parts in nasty yellowish brick.
Now I know why so many Rugbeians run away. Make second stop to look at

---

* Prof. Sir Neville Francis Mott (1905–96), theoretical physicist. Master of Gonville and Caius
Coll., Cambridge 1959–66.
† Sir Halford Reddish (1898–1978), MD of Rugby Portland Cement.

Ashby St Ledgers, where Guy Fawkes's plot was hatched. Nice little tumble-down church.

### 20 September 1958

John Wilson[*] tells of a startling difference between Selwyn Lloyd and Eden. Eden used to minute all his papers carefully, so that after a short time one knew how his mind worked & what his aims were. But Selwyn Lloyd hardly ever marks a paper; only when he is at the United Nations & sends telegrams home does one know what he is thinking, what conclusions he had reached & what course he intended to take. Eden had no real <u>chums</u> therefore his Private Secretaries, e.g. Guy Millard,[†] had to read to him, walk with him in St James's Park, & generally be guide, philosopher & friend. Eden felt that he had been so long in politics as to dwell on a different plane from all his colleagues.

Eden behaved with an extraordinary sense of his own infallibility. Instead of circulating Cabinet papers, he would have his proposals sent to a few members of Cabinet. These would send their comments, Macmillan and Salisbury being the most discerning. Yet Eden would not take their views into account: instead a curt note telling them what conclusion he had reached.

John's father, Lord Moran,[‡] Churchill's doctor, now does not practise except for Winston, but constantly engaged as a referee for increases in Health Service grants to specialists. And so he has to travel to drab towns in bad weather & be interrogated.

### 21 September 1958, letter to parents

I have managed to read the whole 900 pages of John Wheeler-Bennett's life of George VI. It is not as great a book as Harold Nicolson's life of George V, either in style (which is often banal) or in content. There is not enough about the King himself, particularly his private life, and far too much about the politics and foreign affairs of his reign, much of which I found pretty stale stuff. I would like to have known more about who were the King's personal friends; whether he ever read a book; what he liked to eat and drink. John Wheeler-Bennett is a friend of mine, and so I am glad I shall not be reviewing the book.

---

[*] 2nd Baron Moran (1924–2014), Ambassador to Hungary 1973–6 and to Portugal 1976–81; High Commissioner in Canada 1981–4: biographer of Sir Henry Campbell-Bannerman 1973.
[†] Sir Guy Millard (1917–2013), diplomat. PS to Eden for Foreign Affairs 1955.
[‡] Sir Charles Wilson, 1st Baron Moran (1882–1977), won the MC at the Battle of the Somme 1916; Churchill's personal doctor from May 1940.

## 26 September 1958

Dine with Philip de Zulueta and Marie-Lou. Good story of how John Wyndham[*] was annoyed with Gaitskell at interrupting PM's Scottish holiday with
public letter on Quemoy dispute.[†] So he sent PM's reply round to him about
11.30 p.m., then arranged for the Press to be told, so that Gaitskell would be
questioned by telephone all night!

## 28 September 1958, letter to parents

One interesting afternoon I spent watching the film of the climbing of Everest – it is not new, but I had never seen it before. The photographer, Tom
Stobart,[‡] was there with Sir John Hunt, and the others of the expedition.
It is a superb piece of photography, particularly as little oxygen could be
spared for anyone so useless as a photographer – so he suffered. I had just
read Stobart's book *Adventurer's Eye: The Autobiography of the Everest Film
Man* – hardly a wild & remote place in the world he has not filmed. Rather
an exciting book.

Dinner at the Beefsteak. As all had read Wheeler-Bennett's life of George
VI, the talk turned almost entirely on the book. The general opinion is that
W.-B. is an admirable historian but a poor biographer – not really very interested in a man's personal character. Arthur Mann, who saw a lot of the King,
said how sorry he was to find so few examples of the King's rather dry wit.
He gave us one story I had never heard. When showing Mann his collection
of foreign orders and decorations at Windsor one day, the Queen picked up a
German Cross, weighed it in her hand, and remarked how light it was. 'Yes,'
replied the King, 'they had to be – as they never took them off!'

## 5 October 1958

Wheeler-Bennett's life of King George VI discloses that the King was full
of misgivings about competence of new Socialist Government in 1945. This
could legitimately be used as anti-monarchical propaganda by the Socialists.
Far too early to reveal King's private diaries on these matters – it is one instance where the fifty-year embargo on State papers should apply.

Read final extract of Field Marshal Monty's memoirs in *Sunday Times* –
superbly good and effective.

---

[*] 1st Baron Egremont (1920–72), PS to Harold Macmillan 1955 and 1957–63. Macmillan
wrote the notice of his life for the *DNB*, comparing his services to those of Montagu Corry
for Disraeli.

[†] The Quemoy dispute, also known as the Second Taiwan Strait Crisis, erupted on 23 Aug.
1958 when the People's Republic of China's Liberation Army bombarded Quemoy.

[‡] (1914–80), cinematographer for the 1953 Everest expedition.

## 13 October 1958

Watch the funeral of Pope Pius XII on TV – the usual shambles round his body. There are reports of the embalming being a failure, & of the body having begun to decompose. Obviously very hot, with crowd & candles, & no time after his death to do a proper embalming job.

## 26 October 1958, letter to parents

Sitting in a gallery in the Lords next to a Socialist MP, as some of the new life peers made their maiden speeches, who remarked during Lady Wootton's Godless declaration: 'Bang go another half million Socialist votes!' Talking of life peers, I had a letter from Bob Boothby the other day absolutely covered with coronets. He has lost little time!*

## 31 October 1958

Trenchard Cox,† Director of the Victoria and Albert Museum, talks to me; 'When I say St Mark's, I mean Venice; when John Betjeman says it, he means Swindon.'‡

He adds: 'Queen Mary's possessions contain much rubbish – the sort of thing one brings one's charwoman from a holiday.'

## 20 November 1958

Ian Harvey, Under-Secretary at the Foreign Office, arrested last night in St James's Park on charge of indecency with a guardsman.§

## 21 November 1958

*Daily Worker* reports Harvey's arrest with great glee, & adds that he is the author of several works on advertising, including *The Technique of Persuasion*!

## 4 December 1958

David Eccles tells me that the Archbishop of Canterbury is ex-officio a

---

* Barbara Wootton, Baroness Wootton of Abinger (1897–1988), university professor. First lady life peeress, cr. 8 Aug. 1958. Lord Boothby was created a life peer on 22 Aug.

† Sir Trenchard Cox (1905–95), Director of the V&A 1955–66.

‡ St Mark's, Swindon, in the decorated Gothic style, was designed by George Gilbert Scott, 1843–5. In *First and Last Loves* (John Murray, 1952), Betjeman wrote: 'If ever I feel England is Pagan, and that the poor old Church of England is tottering to its grave, I revisit St Mark's, Swindon.'

§ (1914–87), businessman and Conservative MP for Harrow East 1950–59. Harvey and the guardsman were both fined £5, a fine Harvey also paid for the guardsman. When Churchill heard of the incident he remarked: 'And on the coldest night of the year too; makes one proud to be British.'

member of the Board of Trade – 'Very suitable,' he says, 'the Church has large holdings of industrial shares, and the Archbishop is always ringing up for advice on them!'

# 1959

## 1 January 1959

Evening drink at Albany with Harold Nicolson. Amusing story of Gerald Berners,[*] who amassed an imposing collection of pornography when at the Embassy in Rome. Difficulty in getting it past English customs. So he inscribed the name of Bishop Winnington-Ingram[†] in each volume.

Nigel Nicolson also there and we discuss the whole Bournemouth situation. An ex-mayor of Christchurch is likely to be adopted in his place. What Nigel will not face is that his row with Bournemouth Conservative Association is not really constitutional, but personal. It is simply not a suitable constituency for him.

## 16 January 1959

Call on Lord Chandos[‡] at head offices of AEI overlooking garden of Buckingham Palace. Much good talk on Curzon. 'He was the finest company in the world. Like Winston, he would try out a speech or a chapter of a book on the person he was talking to. He talked rather as Macaulay did – a rather florid and sumptuous style.'

Chandos tells me that his father was appointed both by Brodrick and Curzon to patch up their quarrel. He was given a silver inkstand for his pains.

Chandos talks at length about the power of the Sovereign at a time when a new Prime Minister has to be chosen: 'It is generally supposed that all power has departed from the Crown. This is not so. The power is still there,

---

[*] Gerald Tyrwhitt-Wilson, 14th Baron Berners (1883–1950), composer. Attaché in Rome 1911–19; at his home, Faringdon House, he built the last folly in England, a 100-foot tower, at the base of which he put a notice: 'Members of the public committing suicide from this tower do so entirely at their own risk.'

[†] Arthur Winnington-Ingram (1858–1946), Bishop of London 1901–39. He was noted for the moderation and simplicity of his life.

[‡] Oliver Lyttelton, 1st Viscount Chandos (1893–1972), businessman and Conservative politician. Colonial Secretary 1951–4; Chairman, Associated Electrical Industries 1945–51 and 1954–63; first Chairman, National Theatre 1962–71; its Lyttelton Theatre is named after him.

but is rarely used. When it is used, moreover, it can alter the whole course of history. The choice before George V in 1923 was Curzon or Baldwin. Curzon had an immense knowledge of foreign affairs and approached politics on the grand scale. Baldwin's entire political value lay in adroitness. He had no knowledge of Europe at all. Flandin once came and asked Baldwin for help at the time of the Ruhr Crisis.[*] Baldwin's only response to his request was: 'Do you know I haven't seen the apple blossom in Worcestershire for three years.' The choice of Stanley Baldwin changed the whole conception of British foreign policy.

Chandos claims that when Macmillan went to the Treasury, he (Chandos) told Michael Adeane that he would be PM after Eden. On Eden's resignation, Adeane consulted Salisbury (who was against Macmillan), Chandos, Waverley[†] and Winston (the latter just a formality – decision really made by then). Rab Butler might have become PM but for his 'double-cross' over Suez – to right-wing Tories he claimed he was keeping Eden to a firm policy, while to left-wing Tories he claimed he was acting as a brake on Eden.

### 9 February 1959

Spend morning at work on my biography of Curzon – his pre-Parliament period as Private Secretary to Lord Salisbury.[‡]

Then lunch with Donald McLachlan at Brooks's. He tells me that Field Marshal Montgomery came to dine with him at Christmas, and said he was not surprised that President Ike had not sent him a Christmas card this year – 'I have destroyed the Eisenhower legend of generalship in my memoirs. He is already destroyed as President.'

### 10 February 1959

In evening to Richard Strauss's *Salome* at Covent Garden. Strauss's music very good, but absurd that all the leading characters should sing in broken English instead of the original German. Final scene, of Salome making love to a severed head, very macabre.

---

[*] Pierre Flandin (1889–1958), Prime Minister of France 1934–5; Minister for Foreign Affairs 1936. The Ruhr Crisis (1923–5) was the period of military occupation of the German Ruhr Valley by France and Belgium owing to the Weimar Republic's failure to continue reparation payments.
[†] Sir John Anderson, 1st Viscount Waverley (1882–1958), civil servant and independent politician. Home Secretary 1931–40; Chancellor of the Exchequer 1943–5.
[‡] Robert Gascoyne-Cecil, 3rd Marquess of Salisbury (1830–1903). Conservative Prime Minister 1885–6, 1886–92, 1895–1902; leader of the Conservative Party in the House of Lords 1881–5; leader of the Conservative Party 1885–1902.

## 12 February 1959

Take Philip de Zulueta to dine at L'Epicure to celebrate the birth of his son. An evening full of good talk. He tells me Marlborough House is to become a Commonwealth HQ for use of PM's meetings. There are now so many Commonwealth PMs they have outgrown Downing Street.

Amusing story of a Downing Street party for Vice-President Nixon of USA. Among the guests was Edward Hulton, whom PM whimsically introduced to Nixon as 'one of the most influential of all Englishmen'. Nixon was very puzzled at finding so shy and tongue-tied a man.

## 16 February 1959

Dine with David Metcalfe,* Curzon's grandson. He says that whenever he goes into Pratt's, somebody is defending Suez!

## 22 February 1959

Hear good short BBC programme on Bradford, my home town. But how genteelly they all talk nowadays.

## 28 February 1959

C.P. Snow says he is annoyed by American intellectuals such as Lionel Trilling† saying that he was a blunt Northcountryman, with monosyllabic prejudices. He objects to being made into a Dostoyevsky character.

He tells me that Mott's recent election as Master of Gonville and Caius was hotly disputed. 'It will take years to heal the breach,' says C.P.S. Echoes of *The Masters*!

## 6 March 1959, letter to parents

I leave shortly for Cambridge. I shall see Noel Annan, Provost of King's, and Mott, the new Master of Caius. The latter has just been elected after a fight that will be long remembered in Cambridge. The voting was very close indeed. As Charles Snow said to me the other day, not without relish, 'It will be twenty years before the Fellows will be on speaking terms with one another again!'

I dined with Violet Bonham Carter among others the other evening. There is such a gulf between Lady Violet's opinionated and prickly public personality and her very intelligent and amusing private conversation. I took to her immensely. She told such a good story about St John Brodrick, the Tory

---

* (1927–2012), insurance broker and society figure.
† Prof. Lionel Trilling (1905–75), American literary critic.

minister of fifty years ago, who was reputed to be the most tactless man of his day. At Westminster one day he said to the old Duke of Northumberland:[*] 'I am so pleased your boy is doing well in the Commons. What a pity his career there must soon be cut short when he succeeds you in the House of Lords.' Lord Lansdowne, who was also standing with the Duke, was horrified by Brodrick's gaffe, and although many years younger than the Duke said to Brodrick, 'I suppose you feel the same about my son Kerry in the Commons.' 'Oh, no,' replied Brodrick, 'I only meant brilliant elder sons.'[†]

### 21 March 1959, letter to parents

Last night Oscar Gross[‡] took me and the Hartleys to the American musical *West Side Story* by Leonard Bernstein about juvenile gang warfare in New York. Technically it was extremely well produced, but it is not really my sort of show. I didn't care much for the music. I hear that Princess Margaret has already been three times.

### 5 April 1959, letter to parents

The Zuluetas dined with me last night, and I heard a great deal of interesting gossip about the PM's recent visit to Moscow. It was all rather a strain because they did not stay in the Embassy, where they could have relaxed. Instead they were the guest of the Soviets, and suspected that all the guest rooms had hidden microphones and even cameras. All documents had to be read in great secrecy, and the only place where the British delegation could safely talk among themselves was in the garden! What a nightmare country.[§]

Nicky Ridley,[¶] Matthew's brother, has at last been adopted for a Conservative seat. He will succeed the present Speaker at Cirencester. Being an MP nowadays is a dog's life. I once rather fancied the idea – before I knew

---

[*] Algernon Percy, 6th Duke of Northumberland (1810–99), Conservative politician. His son, Henry Percy, 7th Duke of Northumberland (1846–1918), had been MP for Northumberland North.

[†] Lord Lansdowne's eldest son was Lt-Col. Henry Petty-FitzMaurice, 6th Marquess of Lansdowne, styled Earl of Kerry; Liberal Unionist MP for West Derbyshire.

[‡] (1923–2010), American theatre historian.

[§] Macmillan and Selwyn Lloyd visited Moscow 21 Feb.–3 Mar. 1959. As host Khrushchev proved difficult and unpredictable. On 26 Feb. he declined to go with Macmillan and Lloyd to Kiev owing to what became known as the 'toothache insult', saying he had to have a new filling. Selwyn Lloyd said that the previous dentist must have used a British drill. At this, Khrushchev broke into broad smiles, almost like a naughty schoolboy who has been caught out but who is determined to pretend otherwise. D.R. Thorpe, *Supermac: The Life of Harold Macmillan* (Chatto & Windus, 2010), p. 427

[¶] Baron Ridley of Liddesdale (1929–93), Conservative politician and government minister; MP for Cirencester and Tewkesbury 1959–92.

the place. Nothing would now induce me ever to stand. Extraordinary how intelligent people such as Nigel Nicolson break their hearts on leaving the House of Commons. Even Harold Nicolson always looks back with longing to his years as an MP.

## 7 April 1959

Some good talk with Maurice Macmillan. He wants a Budget in which every man is allowed to keep a quarter of what he earns, i.e. no surtax above 15/- in the pound. I ask him whether he thought his father would be such a good PM before he got the office. M. replies: 'Doing the work of a PM, yes. But not in his appeal to the country.'

## 29 June 1959

Story of Hugh Fraser,* head of House of Fraser, who is bidding for Harrods – a deal involving many millions. He had to make an urgent telephone call to an associate about it, but failed to do so. Came on the phone later & explained he was sorry he was late, but he had to speak from a public call-box to maintain secrecy, & hadn't four pennies! 'Could you not have used a sixpence?' he was asked. 'I'm not doing that sort of thing,' he replied!

## 1 July 1959

Read Michael Innes'† *Death at the President's Lodging*. A brilliant & witty murder story about Oxford. Quite in a class of its own for intellectual brilliance.

## 8 July 1959

Take Alan Bullock to lunch at Simpson's. He is recognised by the waiter from his television appearances, so we are looked after well. He tells me how not long ago a man came up to him in the rain, told him he had enjoyed his television performances, and added: 'What I really like is that you are not one of those clever fellows.'

He tells me how fond he is of Isaiah Berlin,‡ but admires his character rather than his intellect. Alan tried to persuade Isaiah to become head of Nuffield College, but Isaiah valued his freedom more.

Alan himself is intensely happy at St Catherine's, Oxford. He would not

---

* 1st Baron Fraser of Allander (1903–66), department-store owner and businessman.

† The pseudonym of J.I.M. Stewart (1906–94), Scottish novelist and academic. Student (Fellow) of Christ Church, Oxford 1949–73.

‡ Sir Isaiah Berlin (1909–97), philosopher and historian of ideas. Founder President of Wolfson Coll., Oxford 1966–75.

have enjoyed so institutional a place as New College. He talks at length about other friends we have in common. On John Altrincham, he comments on the enormous gulf between the harshness of his public utterances and the affection of his private character. He thinks C.P. Snow is not first-rate either as a novelist or as a scientist, but finds him a good and kind man.

## 8 July 1959

Hugh Astor* tells me that *The Times* will use a portable press for producing their newspaper should there be a complete national stoppage, as seems likely.

He tells me that the episode of the frogman, Commander Crabb, during B. and K.'s visit in 1956, was due entirely to the Secret Service acting without the knowledge of the Prime Minister. This might have led to an ugly parliamentary situation, but Eden quashed the whole debate.

Mentions that he was offered the appointment of High Commissioner in Australia, but refused.

## 12 July 1959, letter to parents

I managed to lunch at the Beefsteak one day this week and I found I had the Prime Minister as my neighbour. He is quite extraordinarily charming in conversation, and with a very quick wit. We were talking about the Cassandra† libel case, and I said I thought he was a brilliant journalist who was generally right on important issues. 'Yes,' said Harold Nicolson, 'he is a patriot.' To which the PM replied: 'I suppose he is a patriot – if you consider as I do that the *Daily Mirror* is the last refuge of a scoundrel!'

## 14 July 1959

Letter from Isaiah Berlin, to whom I wrote to ask when he was going to lecture again on Boris Pasternak's‡ *Dr Zhivago*. He replies that the Pasternak family had asked him not to give publicity to him, for his own sake, though,

---

* (1920–79), publisher.

† The pseudonym of journalist Sir William Connor (1909–67), who was sued in 1956 by the American entertainer Liberace (1919–87) for implying that he was homosexual. After a six-day hearing the jury found for Liberace and he was awarded then-record £8,000 in damages.

‡ (1890–1960), Russian novelist; awarded the Nobel Prize in Literature in 1958, the year after the publication of his novel *Dr Zhivago*. The Communist Party of the Soviet Union would not allow him to accept the prize, though it was eventually accepted on his behalf by his family in 1988.

as Isaiah adds, to keep Pasternak's name out of the papers nowadays is like keeping out that of Frank Cousins[*] of the TUC.

## 21 July 1959

Lunch with Nicky Gordon Lennox at Buck's. Nicky full of stories. The Duke and Duchess of Windsor recently came to stay at the Washington Embassy for first time. She now speaks in modulated tones of an ancient university, he with a broad American accent! He is still conscious of having been King, e.g. 'Pierson Dixon[†] had some silver which was made during my reign.'

One day Nicky, the Duke & the Embassy butler descended to the cellars to examine some wine he had left there many years ago. First they went to look at brandy, which appeared to have been broken open. But the Duke knew all about it – 'It was when Oliver Franks was Ambassador, & Winston came to stay. Franks suddenly found he had no brandy, & I was asked if they could use some of mine.' Then they went to look at wine. It was Chilean and in an awful state, with bubbling corks & much decay. 'That doesn't look as if it is much good,' said the Duke. 'If I may say so, your Royal Highness,' commented the butler, 'I don't think it ever <u>was</u> much good!'

At the Beefsteak in the evening, someone asks John Wyndham whether pictures on the wall are by Whistler. He calls for a magnifying glass (how like the Beefsteak to have one) & spends about five minutes minutely examining them. Then he announces with conviction: 'No f------ butterflies.'[‡]

I walk as far as Piccadilly with him. He tells me that his gardener, who used to do flowers for the first Lady Curzon, refused a rise in wages 'as it would upset my surtax.'[§]

## 25 July 1959

Robert Corbett[¶] to lunch. Amusing on the appointment of his father, Lord

---

[*] (1904–86), trade union official and Labour politician. General Secretary of the Transport and General Workers' Union 1956–69; Minister of Technology 1964–6.

[†] Sir Pierson Dixon (1904–65), diplomat and writer. Principal PS to the Foreign Secretary 1943–7; Ambassador to Czechoslovakia 1948–50; Deputy Under-Secretary of State at the Foreign Office 1950–54; Permanent Representative of the UK to the UN 1954–60; Ambassador to France 1960–64.

[‡] James Whistler (1834–1903), American artist based in the UK. His signature on his paintings was a stylised butterfly.

[§] Mary Curzon, Baroness Curzon of Kedleston (1870–1906). As Vicereine of India she held a uniquely high office for an American woman. Nigel Nicolson published her biography in 1977 (Weidenfeld & Nicolson).

[¶] 'Bobby' Corbett (1940–91), fifth son of the 2nd Baron Rowallan, art connoisseur; member of the Curatorial Committee, National Trust for Scotland.

Rowallan,* to be Governor of Tasmania. Lady R.† very displeased – 'I would rather go to Holloway.' Like wife of a former Governor who kept a large calendar in her sitting room on which she crossed off days like a private schoolboy waiting for the holidays!

Also very good on Scouts. To succeed his father as Chief Scout, Sir Charles Maclean‡ has been appointed. But he says – and I find it hard to believe – that Field Marshal Montgomery asked to be appointed & was turned down.

In evening to first night of new season's Proms at Albert Hall. At supper afterwards in Malcolm's flat, Jock Balfour§ says that the best example of repartee he knows was when F.E. Smith was in Washington & about to address a meeting – although very drunk. Cecil Spring-Rice¶ looked very anxious, but F.E. reassured him: 'I'm very good at tightrope-walking.' 'Yes,' replied S.-R., 'when only the rope is tight.'

Jock Balfour also tells me that when anybody rang Curzon at Carlton House Terrace, Curzon answered the telephone himself and said: 'His Lordship has left for the country.'

### 26 July 1959

James Pope-Hennessy is coming at 8 p.m. to give me dinner, & to talk about his Queen Mary book and my own Curzon. He telephones about 7 p.m. to ask if he can bring his new friend, a New Zealand ballet dancer! He does so, quite a pleasant young man, but little to say.

James rather drunk – he has been down to Sissinghurst for the day & got very sunburnt – so a boiled-lobster face. Also very indiscreet about his private life, which I had long suspected. I do hope he does not one day fall into serious trouble.**

James says Lady Crewe†† is likely to lend me her Curzon letters if I produce proof of Jewish blood!

---

* Thomas Corbett, 2nd Baron Rowallan (1895–1977), distinguished soldier in both world wars. Chief Scout of the British Empire and Commonwealth 1945–59; Governor of Tasmania 1959–63.

† Lady (Gwyn) Rowallan, née Grimond (1899–1971), sister of Jo Grimond, Liberal Party leader.

‡ Sir Charles Fitzroy Maclean, Baron Maclean of Duart and Morven (1916–90), 27th Chief of the Clan Maclean 1936–90. Chief Scout of the Scout Association 1959–71.

§ Sir John Balfour (1894–1983), Ambassador to the Argentine Republic 1948–51 and to Spain 1951–4.

¶ Sir Cecil Spring-Rice (1859–1918), Ambassador to the US 1912–18; author of the patriotic hymn 'I Vow to Thee, My Country'.

** Sadly, K.R.'s fears were justified. See entry for 25 Jan. 1974.

†† Lady Margaret Primrose, Marchioness of Crewe (1881–1967), political hostess; younger dau. of 5th Earl of Rosebery, second wife of the Marquess of Crewe. Lady Crewe's mother was a Rothschild.

### 2 August 1959, letter to parents
Rab Butler came to the Beefsteak the other night. Unlike the PM, he is a very rare visitor indeed. But as he sat between a very deaf man and a timid guest, neither of whom had any conversation, I expect it will be a very long time before he comes again! I rather enjoy his company, but he is considered untrustworthy by his fellow politicians.

### 3 August 1959
Grey Gowrie[*] told me how amusing he found Vladimir Nabokov's *Lolita* – though Harold Nicolson said it was obscene & revolting, & was really aimed at making one want to go to bed with little girls of twelve. Harold also feels that Weidenfeld & Nicolson's association with the novel really lost Nigel Nicolson the Bournemouth constituency poll.

### 17 September 1959
Jim Cilcennin and Harold Nicolson to dine at the flat.

Jim describes a Privy Council at Windsor. When it was over Jim and Antony Head were invited to stay overnight. Woolton was not, and this annoyed him. A little later Lady Woolton[†] wrote urgently to Jim to ask whether he could dine at forty-eight hours' notice to meet somebody. But as it happened Jim was staying at Windsor for Ascot week and so had to reply on Castle writing paper. This annoyed Woolton even more.

At the end of a Privy Council meeting which passed Orders in Council for Guernsey, the Queen asked Antony Head how his Guernsey herd was doing. Head replied: 'Not at all well. The artificial insemination people sent me a Red Poll bull instead of a Guernsey by mistake.' Woolton was furious at this flippancy, but the Queen was enchanted by it.

A story too of how Jim was lunching at Clarence House one day. That afternoon he had a board meeting of his insurance company at which he would be paid a fee for every document he signed. Much as he enjoyed the Royal lunch he was terrified at missing such a valuable addition to his income. So he watched the clock anxiously as the minutes ticked away and really had rather a miserable time. Eventually, he managed to escape just in time to take his place at the boardroom table.

---

[*] Alexander Ruthven, 2nd Earl of Gowrie (b. 1939), Scottish hereditary peer and Conservative politician. Chancellor of the Duchy of Lancaster 1984–5.
[†] Maud Smith, Baroness Woolton (1912–61).

## 23 September 1959

Dine with Robert Wade-Gery* in Resident Clerk's rooms at the Foreign Office. We spend much of the evening listening to broadcast of *Die Walküre* from Covent Garden.

As always he is a charming & attentive host. Points to a beer barrel – 'One of my colleagues bought it for a party, but it was not drunk. So daily we have Brueghel-like scenes here.'

We argue about the forthcoming General Election. Robert inclines to the Socialists, but feels that a Foreign Office official should not vote at all. 'I don't accuse you of hypocrisy, only of cowardice,' I find myself saying in a good-natured way in the course of our discussion! But he is very forgiving, & we both agree that Suez is an appalling stain on the Conservative record. He tells me that when we attacked Suez he was in Germany. Just the sort of Germans he most hated congratulated him, and those he admired accused us of hypocrisy.

## 2 October 1959, letter to parents

I fear that there will be a Socialist majority in the General Election on 8 October – though not a large one. It is difficult to forecast, but that is what I think, having weighed up all the factors. You will be interested to hear that Bob Boothby, to whom I spoke this morning, agrees with me. Frederic Hooper is also far from confident that the Tories will be returned. After all, we cannot expect to go on having a Conservative Government for ever – though I fear the Socialists will do a lot of harm to the country.

One night I dined with Harold Nicolson at the Beefsteak and afterwards went back to Albany to have a drink with him. His son Nigel was there, rather unhappy at not having a parliamentary seat to fight. But he will soon be in the midst of another fight – he and Weidenfeld are writing to ask the Director of Public Prosecutions† if they can publish *Lolita*. If he says yes, they will do so. If he says no, they will sell six copies in order technically to have published it, and then invite the Director of Public Prosecutions to prosecute them for obscenity. I have not read the book, but in general I am against literary censorship.

---

* Sir Robert Wade-Gery (1929–2015), High Commissioner in India 1982–7.
† Sir Theobald Mathew (1898–1964), the longest-serving DPP (1944–64). Weidenfeld & Nicolson had no response, so published the book on 6 Nov. 1959. During the launch party, news came from the DPP that he did not intend to prosecute. In 1960, however, Mathew was responsible for prosecuting Penguin Books for publishing D.H. Lawrence's *Lady Chatterley's Lover* – unsuccessfully.

*Kenneth was abroad throughout the general election period so there are no first-hand accounts of Harold Macmillan's landslide victory by 100 seats, but he did make a brief reference to the result in a letter to his parents from Porto.*

### 9 October 1959, letter to parents
We listened until 2 a.m. this morning to the election results. It came as a great surprise to see that the Conservatives should have been returned with so thumping a majority – I expected a small Socialist majority. It was so odd to be sitting there, miles from anywhere, listening to the BBC programme.

### 13 October 1959
Patrick Gordon Walker tells story of Nye Bevan prancing out of Cabinet. As he opened the door, Attlee turned & in a small voice said: 'Minister of Health, shut the door & sit down' – and Nye did!

### 20 November 1959
Evelyn Waugh refused the CBE in 1957 because it was offered to Anthony Powell[*] the previous year!

### 29 November 1959
At All Souls I lunched with A.L. Rowse. He was agreeable, but is a mass of most odd complexes, and full of hatreds – Harold Nicolson, in particular, he loathes. He constantly refers to 'conspiracies among the third-rate intellectuals against me', and other such nonsense. In spite of the quality of his history, I think he is a little mad, and has one of the most marked persecution manias I have ever come across. As a result of this he failed to be elected either Warden of All Souls or Regius Professor of History (Trevor-Roper[†] was appointed) – indeed, he went out of his way to make an enemy of anyone who could possibly be of help to him. These disappointments have left him even more unhappy and embittered. But he also shows great kindness, too. For instance he told me that whenever I want to do a few days' research in All Souls Library or the Bodleian, I am to stay as his guest in the college.

There has been a great deal of reconstruction to the Warden's Lodgings in New College. William Hayter showed me a silver groat found between some

---

[*] (1905–2000), novelist.

[†] Hugh Trevor-Roper, Baron Dacre of Glanton (1914–2003), Regius Professor of Modern History at the University of Oxford 1957–80.

ancient floorboards. It bore the head of Henry VIII – exactly like Charles Laughton.*

### 9 December 1959
Geoffrey Lloyd speaks highly of Macmillan – 'the breadth and imagination of Baldwin, together with the great power of administration which Baldwin never had'.

David Eccles says how sad it is for Gaitskell to be pitted against so supremely skilful a politician as Macmillan. He also tells me he forecast result of General Election in first week of campaign – 'I found that everyone who had voted for me in 1955 was likely to do so again in 1959 – thus I should probably attract a few more who hadn't. Over the whole country this looked to me an indication we would have a majority of about eighty-five.'

### 13 December 1959, letter to parents
I must get out my Christmas cards – such a very convenient way of thanking people for being kind and helpful throughout the year.

One occasion I enjoyed recently was to lunch with John Betjeman and his publisher, Jock Murray.† I like Betjeman more and more, and admire his work increasingly. Over lunch (he characteristically took us to the Victorian comfort of Broad Street Station Hotel, full of coal fires and green painted walls!) he read some of his memoirs of Marlborough and Oxford in blank verse. It is tremendous stuff, as good as anything he has previously written, and it will make a deep impression when eventually he publishes it.

### 28 December 1959
Dine with Ava Waverley at her little house in Lord North Street. She talks a great deal about John, particularly the drama of his having received the Order of Merit on his deathbed. He not only cared to have it, but wished it to be known that he had had it. After his death, it was decided that the memorial service should be held at Westminster Abbey. But the then Dean, Dr Don,‡ would not allow Ava to have the hymns she wanted. So she threatened to have the memorial service transferred to St Paul's Cathedral. Archbishop Fisher was sympathetic with her over this, but asked her not to make the row public. Fisher invited her to a special early-morning Communion service

---

* Stage and film actor (1899–1962); star of the 1933 film *The Private Life of Henry VIII*.

† (1908–93), publisher; editor of the letters and journals of Lord Byron. Betjeman's *Summoned by Bells*, his blank-verse autobiography, was published in 1960.

‡ Dr Alan Don (1885–1966), Dean of Westminster 1946–59, a period which included the Queen's Coronation, in which he took a prominent role.

on the morning of the memorial service, which was kind and thoughtful of him. He said to her: 'Why are you still suffering from such a sense of shock?' Ava replied: 'Because I expected a miracle. I expected John to recover.' But Fisher said: 'But you have had your miracle. You were able to carry on and support John during all those last anxious months.'

Ava has now almost forgiven Gaitskell for opposing John's appointment as Chairman on the Royal Commission on Income Tax, which John resented to the end of his days. She describes how kind Gaitskell was at a Buckingham Palace party when John felt very faint. The only drinks available were champagne and orange juice, but Gaitskell disappeared and came back in triumph with a glass of brandy.

# 1960

### 10 January 1960

I had to talk to Attlee one day last week about some lectures he is to give at Oxford. I never fail to be impressed by his utter lack of pomposity and his very forthright helpfulness. Were it not for his age, I should like him to be the next Chancellor of Oxford University in succession to Halifax. If they nominate the PM I shall go down in person to vote against him!*

### 11 January 1960

Rupert Hart-Davis has told me that the two best-sellers at present are Nabokov's *Lolita* and James Pope-Hennessy's *Queen Mary*. They are known in the trade as 'Blest Pair of Sirens'!

### 24 January 1960

I am glad Nye Bevan is holding his own. But I doubt if he will last long.† Certainly he will never be a force in public life again. I shall always be glad that I heard him and Winston at their best in the Commons, for there are no comparable orators left there today. The Lords is better, not least Lord Samuel in his ninetieth year.

### 26 January 1960

*The Times* is publishing Eden's memoirs. They bear every mark of having been written by him alone, without any sort of literary help. No, that is not quite fair. I expect Selwyn Lloyd helped a little.

An amusing comment from an Eton boy on sermon in College Chapel by Birley: 'It began quite well about the East Window, but turned out to be a commercial for Early Service.'

Donald McLachlan sends for me suddenly in middle of morning. He

---

* 'They' did, and so did K.R.
† Bevan died on 6 July 1960.

has Lord Burnham* with him, raising every possible objection to name of Albany – won't the present Duke mind (he is a German & his peerage is in suspension). Lord B. says that Albany has nothing to do with writing or Fleet Street. At which point Donald mentions all the writers who live in Albany, of every shade of social & political opinion. So Lord B. is routed!

### 13 February 1960

Great difficulty getting down to the Foreign Office to dine with Robert Wade-Gery. France has just exploded its first atomic bomb in the Sahara & anti-nuclear-test people were demonstrating. Downing Street sealed off by cordon of police, but my bowler hat & umbrella act as an automatic passport!

Robert tells me of All Souls elections for Warden. First, when Sumner died, there was deadlock between Isaiah Berlin & Sir Eric Beckett.† So Hubert Henderson‡ was brought in as a compromise candidate & elected. But he died a few months later, & college faced by appalling prospect of another election. Neither Berlin nor Beckett would stand, so it became a contest between A.L. Rowse and John Sparrow. In spite of his great scholarship, Rowse was considered unreliable – even mad. Sparrow was considered a rather dim but safe candidate.

### 17 February 1960

Philip de Zulueta telephones me from No. 10 to tell me that Harold Macmillan will fight election of the Chancellorship of Oxford versus Oliver Franks.

The reason a politician is generally chosen as Chancellor of Oxford is that he is the unofficial link between the university & the Government. As such, a politician can usually get what the university needs far more smoothly than a mere scholar!

### 18 February 1960

Nigel Nicolson gives me an example of Winston's punctilio & lack of grandeur in the House of Commons. During divisions he always gives his name to tellers – 'Churchill, W.S.' He doesn't expect to be recognised!

---

* Edward Lawson, 4th Baron Burnham (1890–1963), newspaper executive. MD of the *Daily Telegraph* 1945–61.
† (1896–1966), legal adviser to the Foreign Office 1943–58. His career was ended when he fell under a train at Putney Station and was paralysed.
‡ Sir Hubert Henderson (1890–1952), economist. Professor of Political Economy 1945–51; elected Warden of All Souls 1951, but never took up the appointment.

## 19 February 1960

We are all awaiting the birth of the Queen's baby with some impatience. I
hope it is born at a reasonable hour during the day – otherwise the whole of
the paper has to be remade at night. Queen Mary, I remember, most incon-
siderately died at 10 p.m., and caused endless difficulties.

I have been reading a proof copy of C.P. Snow's latest novel, *The Affair*,
to be published in a month or two. It is about the Cambridge college of
*The Masters* some twenty years later, i.e. about 1963, and concerns a Fellow
who has been dismissed by the college for scientific fraud. As always, an
enthralling story, and with rather more wit than in his previous novels.

His account of donnish malice and intrigue appears generous compared
to what has been happening over the election for a new Chancellor. Oliver
Franks has been nominated by most heads of houses, and now to everybody's surprise Macmillan has announced that he will stand against him. I
hope Franks will not stand down – Oxford deserves the spectacle of a public
fight. Macmillan, I think, will win, especially as his Wind of Change speech[*]
in South Africa has disarmed so many Socialists. I had great fun two days
ago when I discovered that Kilmuir and David Eccles had never bothered to
proceed from their BA to their MA, and so would not be able to vote for the
PM.[†]

The decision of the Queen that certain of her family shall in future years
bear the name of Mountbatten-Windsor has been received without enthusiasm. It recalls the remark of Winston's father, Lord Randolph Churchill,
about Sclater-Booth:[‡] 'How often do we find mediocrity dowered with a
double-barrelled name.' I suppose we must now refer to Brown Mountbatten-
Windsor soup.

## 26 February 1960

Press Agency reports official engagement of Princess Margaret to Antony
Armstrong-Jones. Staggering. I have always found him agreeable on the few
occasions I have met him since teaching him at Eton. But he seems to belong
to a world of dress designers, photographers & interior decorators. Seems to

---

[*] On 3 Feb. 1960 Macmillan made a speech to the Parliament of South Africa in Cape Town
in which he said: 'The wind of change is blowing through this continent. Whether we like it or
not, this growth of national consciousness is a political fact.'

[†] Oxford graduates had to be MAs to vote. The university reaped a windfall of £1,500 as some
300 people, among them a marquess, three barons and fifty knights, including David Eccles
from the Cabinet, upgraded their BA degrees. The fee for taking an MA degree was £5.

[‡] George Sclater-Booth, 1st Baron Basing (1826–94), Conservative politician. President of the
Local Government Board under Disraeli 1874–80.

mark a tremendous revolution in development of Royal Family. Odd that the news should be announced during court mourning for Lady Mountbatten.[*]

### 4 March 1960
An undergraduate at Magdalene – in love with a girl called Mary – collected cornflake coupons & got six spoons with 'M' engraved on them. When the engagement was broken he presented them to Magdalene and is invited each year to a feast as a college benefactor.

### 10 March 1960
The poor Queen and her baby[†] have been overshadowed by the death of Edwina Mountbatten and now the engagement of Princess Margaret. I know Tony Armstrong-Jones a little. I taught him as a small boy at Eton twelve years ago and found him intelligent and agreeable. At the end of one half he gave me some not very good photographs which he had secretly taken of me in school as I held forth: I thought it a good joke. Since then I have seen him from time to time. The last occasion was at the Institute of Directors' carnival, when he asked a well-nourished director to put out his cigar as the blue smoke would ruin the colour photographs. But of course he has a past which needs living down. The popular Press has so far been very malicious in a guarded sort of way. But what if the *Sunday Express* announces a series of articles by his former 'friends'?

I went down to Oxford to vote in the Chancellorship election. The result was expected, but the small majority must have come as a sobering shock to the Prime Minister.[‡] It is generally believed that the governessy leader in *The Times* telling everyone to vote for Oliver Franks did a great deal of good to the Macmillan cause. There were some interesting cross-currents to be discerned in the voting, quite apart from college or personal loyalties. Thus the Roman Catholics voted for Franks because Macmillan's chief supporter in the university was the anti-clerical Trevor-Roper; and some Socialists obviously hated Franks the banker more than Macmillan the Conservative. I voted for Franks.

Last weekend I spent in Cambridge, looking enchanting in the pale sunshine, with seas of crocuses everywhere. I lunched at Trinity with Kitson Clark.[§] He was much upset by a savage attack in the *Oxford Magazine* that

---

[*] Edwina Mountbatten had died on 21 Feb.; she was buried at sea on 25 Feb. off Portsmouth.

[†] Prince Andrew had been born on 19 Feb.

[‡] The vote, announced in Latin in the Gothic Divinity School, was Haroldus Macmillanus 1,976, Oliverus Frankus 1,697.

[§] George Kitson Clark (1900–75), historian specialising in the nineteenth century.

morning on the Ford Lectures he has been giving by invitation at Oxford this term. But I fear he received little comfort from his fellow dons at Trinity. He showed the article to two of them while I was there. One, Gow,* replied: 'They had no right to print such a malicious attack however bad your lectures were.' The other, Simpson, historian of the Second Empire, replied: 'The first two lines of the article seemed friendly enough.'

I also dined with Mott, the new Master of Caius. It surprised me to see one of the Fellows dined with a row of pencils, pens and even one of those little inspection lamps sticking out of his jacket pocket – exactly like a caricature of brash young scientist in a novel by C.P. Snow. Perhaps it was to be able to see exactly what he was eating and drinking – so very difficult with all that old-fashioned candlelight.

Harold Nicolson is back from his South African cruise looking ten years younger. He was horrified by what he saw of apartheid, and as a protest queued up for railway tickets at the window marked for Africans. It merely meant that he was politely directed to the one for whites. But what a Harold-ish thing to do. I heard him the other day advising a friend that there was really only one way of losing weight, and that was to live on oysters.

I am rather hard-worked at the moment. There has been an eternal succession of official lunches and dinners lately – and I go to one for Selwyn Lloyd and the Foreign Minister of Portugal† tomorrow. The one gleam of humour in all this mummery was at the Gala Performance for the President of Peru‡ at Covent Garden (where Margot Fonteyn danced supremely well in *Giselle*). They played the Peruvian National Anthem, and everyone thought it was the overture!

### 3 April 1960
Read Randolph Churchill's life of Lord Derby. Rather too big a volume, & one gets tired of same old political history being repeated. But some good stories told him, & also extensive use of Royal Archives. Too much about Beaverbrook, as is usual in books written by journalists. But I think R.C. has used his evidence fairly.

### 15 April 1960
Talk with Robert Wade-Gery about Gladwyn Jebb's peerage – he is calling himself Lord Gladwyn. A few weeks ago, when Robert was dining with him,

---

* Andrew Gow (1886–1978), historian and biographer of A.E. Housman.
† Marcello Mathias (1903–99), Foreign Minister of Portugal 1958–61.
‡ Manuel Prado y Ugarteche (1889–1967), President of Peru 1956–62.

he said he would choose this title so that he could sign his letters 'Gladwyn' – & nobody would know whether he was being particularly amicable or not!

Wade-Gery also said that during the Cyprus discussions, Archbishop Makarios came near to signing agreement, but at last minute withdrew saying: 'I do not want to become a Michael Collins.'[*]

## 20 April 1960

Tommy Lascelles tells me that Princess Helena Victoria[†] was a very kind and good-natured woman. She was staying with rest of Royal Family at Balmoral during the Munich Crisis, & everyone was very glum & silent. So she told them story of an old profligate who had gone to live in Ireland. His family in England heard he was ill, so one son went over to visit him. The old man died, & son sent a telegram back to England: 'Father has gone. Safe in the arms of Jesus.' Unfortunately, this telegram was badly transmitted. Son received reply: 'Where has he gone to, and who is Jessie?' This cheered up everybody at Balmoral!

Dine Sir Frederic Hooper. H. is in a cross mood. Reason soon emerges – he was not told beforehand by Harold Watkinson,[‡] Minister of Defence, about decision to abandon the nuclear missile 'Blue Streak'. There was naturally a storm in the Press at writing off £65 million & Sir F. had no opportunity of helping minister to present the best answer to the attacks on him & his Ministry. Yet it is on just such occasions, Sir F. rightly claims, that his advice to the minister could be most valuable. Though called by the innocuous title of 'Adviser to the Minister of Defence on Recruiting', his real job is to present minister in best light on all defence matters – which in fact will of course help recruiting. We draft a rather cross letter to minister to tell him this, together with suggested line to be taken by him during parliamentary debate. What makes F. particularly cross is that he saw Watkinson the day before the 'Blue Streak' announcement, but was told nothing. The Ministry claim (a) they did not want to bother Sir F. when he had been in the job so

---

[*] (1890–1922), leading figure in the struggle for Irish independence. Delegate to the Anglo-Irish Treaty talks in London Oct. 1921; when he signed the Treaty on behalf of the British government, Lord Birkenhead said: 'I may have signed my political death warrant.' Collins on the Irish side replied: 'I may have signed my actual death warrant.' He was sadly right in his foreboding. He was assassinated on 22 Aug. 1922 by anti-Treaty ambushers.

[†] Princess Victoria Helena of Schleswig-Holstein, known as Princess Helena Victoria (1870–1948), a granddaughter of Queen Victoria.

[‡] 1st Viscount Watkinson (1910–95), British businessman and Conservative politician. Minister of Defence 1959–62, when he was sacked in Harold Macmillan's Night of the Long Knives; Chairman, Cadbury Schweppes 1969–74; President of the Confederation of British Industry 1976–7.

short a time (b) the PM had specially asked that the list of those knowing of the decision in advance should be kept very small.

## 3 May 1960

Leave for Dublin. To Ministry of External Affairs to see Conor Cruise O'Brien,[*] who has arranged my audience with President Éamon de Valera[†] later today. We discuss IRA. O'Brien says that there are about 500 active members, aged eighteen to twenty-two. They receive money from the USA. Irish Government naturally doesn't approve of their border raids, but it is essential not to make martyrs of them, therefore no extradition to Ulster.

Also discuss de Valera. 'He has inherited Anglo-Irish history, and does not pretend it never existed.' Has now little to do as President – 'but he was author of the Constitution which now imprisons him'.

From Ministry of External Affairs I go to call on Sir Ian MacLennan,[‡] our Ambassador, most charming and friendly. He says he is not a frequent visitor to Trinity College, Dublin.

(a) TCD doesn't want to identify itself too much with the English.

(b) If he lectures there, there is possibility of being drawn into acrimonious debates on partition.

He gives no party on Queen's birthday – there would be too many people to offend by omission.

Finds Dev personally charming. Dev has courted unpopularity by attending rugby matches (he used to play the game very well). It is considered by many to be too English a game.

Take taxi to Phoenix Park. Stopped at gate by guards, who know my name and are expecting me. Met by an ADC, elderly officer in khaki. Asks me to sign the President's book, and apologises for the 'Civil Service pen'. I am a little early, and wait in a handsome drawing room looking out onto lawns, white-painted balustrade, geraniums in white urns – can have changed little for a century. Even the old-fashioned lamp standards still have little crowns on the top.

Shown into Dev's study. He rises to meet me, and puts me in a wooden armchair by his side at a desk. Charming smile and very bright eyes behind his thick, gold-rimmed spectacles, though of course he is almost totally

---

[*] (1917–2008), Irish politician, writer and academic.

[†] (1882–1975), prominent Irish politician. Participant in the Easter Rising, 24 Apr. 1916; President of the Irish Republic 1921–2, accrediting delegates to the talks establishing the Anglo-Irish Treaty of 1922; Taoiseach 1937–48, 1951–4, 1957–9; President of Ireland 1959–73.

[‡] (1909–86), Ambassador to the Republic of Ireland 1960–63; High Commissioner in New Zealand 1964–9.

blind. Wears a black suit with a red ring about size of halfpenny in lapel (later I discover that this is badge of a society for encouraging the speaking of Irish). Also wears black sandals. Plain desk with two white telephones and nothing more than a pad of paper. Shelves of books behind him include the *Encyclopaedia Britannica*, the *Catholic Encyclopaedia*, *Who's Who*, and some Loeb volumes.

As his views on such subjects as partition are well known and on record, I try to draw him out on personal reminiscence. He tells me that Randolph Churchill sent him the proofs of his book on Lord Derby after he had supplied R.C. with information about Derby's role of intermediary between Lloyd George and himself. 'But the book is so full of minor inaccuracies that I simply did not have the time to start correcting them.' I ask if he has more leisure than when PM. 'No, I get up earlier and go to bed later. I have little time for exercise, and only twice have I been for a long walk round the garden. People are always asking me to perform more duties.'

I ask him about the honorary DSc he is to receive from Trinity College, Dublin. He says he is delighted by it – 'My only regret is that I did not earn it by examination.' He has much to say about maths, still his favourite recreation. In spite of blindness he has trained his secretary to help him continue his mathematical studies, 'general theorems rather than the writing out of examples'. He draws symbols on a blackboard, and she follows the textbooks.

When he was in prison at Lewes after the Easter Rising he was allowed maths textbooks, but no pencil, in case he worked out a code. So one day he stole the point of a pencil from a fellow prisoner checking washing, and recorded the results of his mathematical between the lines of sums printed in the book. This allowed him to use the slate he was given for working out problems instead of using up its valuable space recording results.

A long talk on the Irish language. Quite apart from its national aspect, he thinks it gives the learner the same disciplined training as Latin or Greek. He rings for an Irish–English dictionary, and shows me that it contains <u>all</u> the words one needs – so it is not merely a curious survival. He tells me it must be learned as a living language – 'not as I learned French, merely as a book language, so that I can hardly <u>speak</u> a sentence'. Tells me he has never really learned German – 'I tried with German maths books, but was more interested in maths than German.' He deeply regrets that the Cornish language is no more. Tries to explain the link between various Celtic languages by drawing phonetic symbols on a pad with a thick blue pencil, but it is all rather beyond me.

Describes how a letter planning his escape from Lincoln Prison was written in three languages – harmless English beginning, boasting of learning

Latin, with which was mingled the instructions for escape in Irish! Letter was sent out to order wine – 'I think it was a typical English regulation going back to the days of Napoleonic prisoners of war!' – and he took advantage of it.

Dev recommends me to read *The Irish Republic* by Dorothy Macardle[*] for the best account of his public life.

As so often during the time we spend together, he laughs delightedly. As I am seen out by the ADC he tells me that Dev has kept me longer than most of his visitors.

## 6 May 1960

Princess Margaret's wedding. A lovely sunny day for the Royal wedding. Decide to wear black rather than grey tall hat. Have to be in Abbey by 10.45 – I arrive about an hour early, largely owing to utter absence of traffic. With special label on windscreen of cab, it takes only five minutes. Go through privileged Constitution Arch, <u>and</u> through the only slightly less privileged Horse Guards Arch.

Superb seat in Abbey, in front of a stand looking across to the altar. See John Betjeman wandering about gazing up at details of architecture. Dr Mervyn Stockwood,[†] Bishop of Southwark, clad in purple like a prince of the Church (unlike Dean of St Paul's & other prelates in decent black!). Friends of Princess Margaret and Armstrong-Jones mixed up with official guests in seating, including the PM, Eden (thin & sunburnt), Attlee and Winston in grey (he sits for most of service), David Cecil, Salisbury and Alex. A.-J. seems to have aged very much in last few weeks, & a bad colour.

Then the Royal Family. Queen like a Reynolds portrait in the curiously long dresses worn on such occasions by Royal ladies. But a sulking Queen Victoria face throughout the entire service – not a ghost of a smile. Queen Mother, on the other hand, like a great golden pussycat, full of sad little smiles. Prince Philip full of funny jokes & a great pink flower in coat. Duchess of Kent elegant in yellow. Eddie getting so Hanoverian – chin falling, eyes more prominent & hair, I suspect, going a little thin. His brother Michael now tall & darkly handsome. Duke of Gloucester true to type – mops his face vigorously, & taps his hand impatiently during playing of enchanting Schubert anthem. Lady Harewood a charming figure with tiny gold hat.

---

[*] (1889–1958), Irish writer. *The Irish Republic*, published in 1937 (Gollancz), covers the existence of the Irish Republic, the Irish War of Independence, the Anglo-Irish Treaty and the Irish Civil War.
[†] The Rt Revd Mervyn Stockwood (1913 –95), Bishop of Southwark 1959–80.

Princess Royal in gold, & Princess Alice like a kingfisher.

The curious thing is that Mountbatten alone wears service uniform among family guests – Eddie, for instance, in morning coat. The German in M. seems to come out very strongly.

Princess Margaret looks charming, in very simple white dress. Dean's diction admirable. Notice how all other Royal ladies curtsey as Q. & Q.M. pass on way to & from the vestry.

Manage to get away from Abbey very quickly. Service over at 12.30, & am in Beefsteak at 12.55.

Later watch sailing of Royal Yacht *Britannia* on honeymoon. But almost best joke of whole wedding is article by Dermot Morrah[*] in Official Souvenir Programme. He writes with utmost seriousness: 'The beauty & vigour of the many pictures in these pages which are the product of the bridegroom's own camera justify the thought that today's ceremony involves the symbolic recognition that photography as one of the Fine Arts has come of age.'

### 7 May 1960

Martin Gilliat tells me about the dinner party at Clarence House last night with the Queen. They saw film of Princess Margaret's wedding – & Queen looking so sulky. So everybody said: 'How <u>unkind</u> the cameras are,' 'most unfair,' etc. etc.

10.45 train to Oxford. Brilliant sunny weather. Spend most of afternoon in a deckchair in back garden of All Souls talking to Leslie Rowse. He is very excited by his honorary degree at Exeter this week, and so curious to see young men on roof of Queen's sunbathing!

Later A.L.R.'s other guests arrive – Raleigh Trevelyan, very agreeable, with a touch of gravity I like; Arthur Bryant, who always gives me an impression of being amiably second-rate; and Felix Kelley, a rather smart painter.[†]

Bedroom in one of the Hawksmoor towers & a superb view of Radcliffe Camera, Bodleian and St Mary's, magnificent at any hour of the day or night.

Dine well off plates with the All Souls mallards. Other people include

---

[*] (1896–1974), Arundel Herald Extraordinary 1953–74. He always explained that 'Extraordinary' meant 'Unpaid'.

[†] Raleigh Trevelyan (1923–2014), author, editor and publisher; biographer of Walter Raleigh, 2002. Sir Arthur Bryant (1899–1985), historian; Andrew Roberts in *Eminent Churchillians* (Weidenfeld & Nicolson, 1994) gave a scathing portrait of Bryant, describing him as 'a supreme toady, fraudulent scholar and humbug'. Felix Kelly (1914–94), New Zealand artist, noted for the four murals he painted at Castle Howard.

Kodály,* neat & bearded Hungarian composer, and Lord Salter,† whom I sit next to at dessert. Much enjoy talk of Salter. He tells me how Asquith's beautiful tributes to his colleagues, e.g. on Alfred Lyttelton, were carefully prepared well in advance. Augustine Birrell‡ once remarked that Asquith would compose them when bored at Cabinet meetings – 'and would look at one with that obituary eye'.

Salter says that there are few professional administrators who have become ministers. Sir John Anderson was the most successful. Difficult task – 'An administrator selects arguments in real order of their importance, a politician selects arguments to achieve a certain end.'

### 10 May 1960
Sad to see that Beethoven's birthplace in Bonn has been destroyed by fire. It moved me deeply in 1945.

### 13 May 1960
Talk to Philip de Zulueta. He is off to the summit meeting in Paris tomorrow with Macmillan – PM Khrushchev, Eisenhower and de Gaulle. Tense situation: they do not want K. to sign peace treaty with East Germany. Philip believes not too much importance should be attached to K.'s anti-American outburst over US spy planes over Russia – it was to appease the Russian 'reactionaries', for internal consumption, not to influence world opinion.§

### 18 May 1960
Summit talks in Paris end before they have begun – Khrushchev demands impossibly humiliating apology from Eisenhower for recent flight of U-2 spy plane over Russia.

### 6 June 1960
Dine alone with Sir Halford Reddish in his room at the Dorchester. He is worried by increasing difficulty of getting skilled labour. Every establishment

---

* Zoltán Kodály (1882–1967), Hungarian composer.
† Arthur Salter, 1st Baron Salter (1881–1975), Conservative politician and academic. Gladstone Professor of Political Theory in 1943 and Fellow of All Souls; MP for Oxford University 1937–50 and for Ormskirk 1951–3; Minister for Economic Affairs 1951–2.
‡ (1850–1933), Liberal politician; Chief Secretary to Ireland 1907–18.
§ On 1 May 1960 a US U-2 spy plane, flown by Gary Powers, was shot down in Soviet airspace. Philip de Zulueta was over-optimistic about the Paris summit, the first to be attended by Western and Soviet leaders for five years. It was abandoned after just one day when Khrushchev walked out and returned to Russia when Eisenhower refused to apologise for the incident.

with which he is connected is now under-strength, & even in comparatively unskilled Rugby Cement they could do with more men. He is also appalled by the low standard of our Trade Commissioners abroad.

Tells me he much enjoyed visiting Noël Coward at his house near Montreux the other day – walls of the loos were decorated with covers of N.C.'s songs! He agrees with me that N.C. does not monopolise conversation, but is also a good listener. N.C. apparently asked Queen Ena* of Spain what she felt about Princess Margaret's marriage. She merely replied: 'I am a granddaughter of Queen Victoria.'

H.R. is apparently a great chum of Lord Reith, whose hobby is collecting special tablets of soap from aeroplanes, hotel rooms, ships, etc. Most odd. On one occasion he had a tablet in a guest room – it had been taken from a ship. The Chairman of the shipping company happened to come & stay with Reith, & occupied this room. He thought that the provision of his own soap was the last word in thoughtful hospitality!

### 3 July 1960

Dine with John Altrincham at the Hyde Park Hotel. We have a long discussion on the recommendations of the Wolfenden Report† that homosexual behaviour between consenting adults in private should no longer be a criminal offence. This was again defeated in the House of Commons last week. John angry about it. But I wonder (a) whether there are many such prosecutions – most cases one hears of seem to be caused by public behaviour; but one or two outstanding exceptions, e.g. the Montagu case (b) whether one can educate public opinion sufficiently fast to diminish the sense of public repugnance to homosexual behaviour – it is a social as well as a criminal problem (c) whether homosexuals will not go down the age scale if given freedom over the age of twenty-one.

### 5 July 1960

Jim Cilcennin to lunch at the Guards Club. He tells me that the Queen Mother's visit to Hereford passed off very well indeed, although he himself was in such pain from his arthritis at lunch that he nearly fainted. The Queen Mother was kind and sympathetic. He speaks scathingly of both David Eccles

---

* Victoria Eugenie of Battenberg (1887–1969), Queen Consort of Spain 1906–31.

† John Wolfenden, Baron Wolfenden (1906–85), educationalist best known for chairing the Wolfenden Committee that published the *Report of the Departmental Committee on Homosexual Offences and Prostitution* on 4 Sept. 1957. Owing to the presence of ladies on the committee, Wolfenden suggested that they use the terms Huntley and Palmers after the biscuit manufacturers, Huntley for homosexuals and Palmers for prostitutes.

and Duncan Sandys. Whenever he has invited either of them to Admiralty House, they have both asked what the catch is. Neither, says Jim, recognise hospitality for its own sake.

*With plans well advanced for the new* Sunday Telegraph *newspaper to be launched in February 1961, Kenneth considered for some time what name he should give to the feature that he was to write for thirty-six years.*

## 27 July 1960

To Jim Cilcennin's memorial service at St-Martin-in-the-Fields.[*] On the pavement about fifty yards above the church I see the PM in a tall hat tapping impatiently on the pavement & surrounded by an awed little crowd – he has lost Lady Dorothy!

Not a very moving service, except for the naval prayers at the end. The Bishop of Chester[†] gives the address. Makes Jim into a paragon of Christian virtues, but does not say what a jolly man he was.

Huge congregation, including almost all the Cabinet & Sir Anthony Eden, looking haggard & sunburnt, a dreadful combination. Also Mountbatten, white & thinner. Peter Carrington reads lesson in a forthright way which the Navy will love.

I walk away with Harold Nicolson. He teases me about the *DT* – this morning we have a picture of a woman in evening dress, with a caption referring to her as Major ------. Harold didn't know that women in the Services have men's ranks. I tell him that anyone who had served in the Armed Forces in either war would understand it. At which, in mock indignation, he replied: 'I may not have fought in either war, but I did declare war in 1914!' And that, of course, is perfectly true.[‡]

A glass of sherry in Albany, where there is a solemn man sitting in the entrance hall of Harold's rooms. I ask if he is a bailiff (H.N. has just told me he is £600 overdrawn) but Harold insists it is only a messenger from the National Trust with some deeds to sign!

Very curious, pink loo paper. I tell Harold that when, in fifty years, a young American comes to ask me what I know of H.N. for a thesis, I shall reply: 'He was the kind of man who had pink loo paper!'

Walk with him to Cook's, where he enquires about a winter cruise. The

---

[*] Jim Cilcennin had died unexpectedly on 13 July. K.R. had lunched with him only eight days beforehand.

[†] Gerald Ellison (1910–92), Bishop of Chester 1955–73; Bishop of London 1973–81.

[‡] As the Foreign Office's junior Second Secretary in 1914, Nicolson was despatched to hand Britain's declaration of war to the German Ambassador in London.

rather disagreeable clerk smirks twice – once when Harold says he won't go to South Africa because of apartheid & again when he gives his address as a castle!

### 3 August 1960, letter to Donald McLachlan

Here are some thoughts on the new venture, with particular reference to my own feature.

We must not imitate 'Peterborough'. Nevertheless, 'Peterborough' has played a far from negligible part in raising the circulation of the paper and has become almost a household word among the educated public.

It depends for its success on:

(a) News, and above all news about people who matter.

(b) A distinct approach which is not predictable.

(c) A sense of erudition and an appeal to minority tastes – whether clavichords, Zanzibar liqueurs, pelota or Siamese Orders of Chivalry.

(d) Gentle snobbery. Most of our readers have not been to public schools or ancient universities, served in smart regiments, become members of London clubs, owned yachts or racehorses. But they like to read of such things when presented to them in a tone of confiding intimacy.

All these elements should find their place in the new feature. In addition I should like to have more emphasis on the following:

(a) The activities of women.

(b) Books.

(c) Distinguished visitors to London from the Commonwealth overseas and from the Colonies.

(d) Universities. I hope to have the advice and help of C.P. Snow in this, particularly for Churchill College and the red-brick universities.

(e) Senior civil servants – first, because they have such power, and secondly, because they hate being mentioned.

(f) Scotland and its extraordinary institutions – Holyrood, the General Assembly of the Church of Scotland and the Scottish universities.

(g) The City.

(h) The Bar.

(i) The world of entertainment.

During the autumn I hope to do a certain amount of travelling in the British Isles to renew old contacts and make fresh ones.

### 5 August 1960

After much thought & research, I decide that the best name under which to write my new column in the *Sunday Telegraph* is 'Albany' – a beautiful word, simple, easily pronounced, connected with London & has a flavour of a peerage about it – Dukedom of Albany[*] is in fact held by some German whose family were stripped of it in 1919.

Lunch Beefsteak. A nice little exchange of schoolboy chaff – Malcolm Sargent comes in & says to John Wyndham: 'Why are you not busy working at No. 10?' Without lifting his head from his plate, John replies: 'Go and look after your band.'

## 6 August 1960

Hear an extraordinary story about Sir Claude Elliott's[†] son, Nicholas,[‡] when he was at Eton where his father was Head Master. The boy was lazy and used to ask clever young Julian Amery to write his essays for him. One week the subject was Sir Roger Casement.[§] Julian Amery wrote the essay & gave it to Nicholas, who merely glanced at the first two scholarly pages, dealing with the background history of Ireland, & approved. The next day in school it was Elliott's turn to read out his essay. He began confidently, reached the bottom of the two pages he had seen, & turned over. All the rest of the essay was devoted to Casement's health & sexual habits in great detail! Amery had guessed that Elliott would not have read as far as that the previous evening.

## 21 August 1960

Talk to Lord James,[¶] High Master of Manchester Grammar School. He is scathing on the intellectual quality of provincial universities in Arts subjects compared to Oxford & Cambridge.

## 22 August 1960

Dine Beefsteak with the publisher Daniel Macmillan, a gentle old man, brother of the PM. Tells me that PM had described to him a meeting in Paris between Macmillan, de Gaulle, Adenauer & Eisenhower. The conversation was in French, which Ike didn't understand. De Gaulle, with Gallic precision,

---

[*] The dukedom was first granted in 1398 by King Robert III of Scotland (1337–1406). The last holder of the title was Charles Edward, Duke of Saxe-Coburg and Gotha (1884–1954), forfeited on 14 Nov. 1918, instrumental 1919. The Duke of Albany in Shakespeare's *King Lear* was Goneril's kind-hearted husband.

[†] (1888–1973), Head Master of Eton 1933–49; Provost of Eton 1949–65.

[‡] (1916–94), MI6 intelligence officer.

[§] (1854–1916), British diplomat of Irish extraction; seeking German support for an armed Irish rebellion against British rule, he was arrested, convicted, stripped of his knighthood and executed. His *Black Diaries* revealed his homosexual lifestyle.

[¶] Eric James, Baron James of Rusholme (1909–92), prominent educationalist. High Master of Manchester Grammar School 1945–62; first Vice-Chancellor of York University 1962–73.

was describing a certain train of events which could only lead to war.

Ike: 'What did he say?'

Macmillan: 'He said we would all be blown up.'

Ike: 'Oh my, how awful.'

Then de Gaulle continued with an alternative chain of events which could end in peace and happiness.

Ike: 'What did he say?'

Macmillan: 'He said it's going to be all right.'

Ike: 'Oh, I'm so glad.'

Daniel describes how he was defrauded of £9,000 by a Captain Maxwell.[*] One of his earlier rackets, when in Control Commission of Germany after the war, was to get the job of having wartime German learned periodicals printed for distribution to important libraries of the world. Maxwell sold these for huge sums to the libraries, particularly in America.

Gladwyn Jebb comes in to dine. An agreeable companion but extraordinarily conceited. We talk of his son Miles.[†] 'He got an inferiority complex at Eton which even getting into Pop did not cure. Then he got a Third at Magdalen – I, of course, got a First – and failed the Foreign Service exam. It may be that he was handicapped by having a famous father, but others have survived it,' etc. etc. He spoke without a spark of sympathetic understanding. I astonished to hear him praise the scheme for a Channel Tunnel: I thought all informed opinion was against it.

He is very bitter about Beaverbrook Press. Tells me he made them print an apology & was told he could have got £15,000 damages. 'The paper said I was hated by the French, but it wasn't true. They gave a wonderful party before I left Paris.'

### 23 August 1960

I hear that Patricia Brabourne[‡] has decided to send one of her sons to Gordonstoun. Can this mean that Prince Charles will also be going there?

### 4 October 1960, letter to William Berry, Editor-in-Chief of the *Daily Telegraph*

I have given much thought to a pen-name for the new feature in the *Sunday Telegraph*.

---

[*] Robert Maxwell (1923–91), media proprietor and Labour MP for Buckingham 1964–70. He died in mysterious circumstances after falling from his yacht in the Atlantic Ocean.

[†] Miles Jebb, 2nd Baron Gladwyn (b. 1930), businessman.

[‡] Patricia Brabourne, 2nd Countess Mountbatten of Burma (b. 1924), godmother to Prince Charles. K.R.'s prediction was correct.

Here are some possibilities which I have rejected: Ajax; Apollo; Ariel (a rebel angel); Cerberus (all the secrets of the underworld, but a dog); Clio (Addison used it in the original *Spectator*); Coningsby; Creevey; Ivanhoe; Ludgate; Nestor; Orlando; Scipio; Tristram; Vanburgh.

The drawback of many classical names is that they are not easy to pronounce and that most of them have obscene episodes in their lives.

Crispin, with its flavour of Henry V, is a possibility; though there seems no apparent connection between the new paper and the patron saint of shoemaking.*

ALBANY is my best suggestion. It has the following points in its favour:

1.  It is euphonious and easy to pronounce.
2.  It has associations with London – and that part of London which is reputed to house the civilised and well informed.
3.  Like 'Peterborough', it has a faint flavour of peerage about it. Until 1919 there was a Dukedom of Albany. One of Queen Victoria's sons had the title (he was the father of Princess Alice). But as the family took up arms against us in 1914, George V stripped them of the Dukedom. It is unlikely to be revived.

I hope you will approve this name. If necessary I am prepared to go and live in Albany.

## 18 October 1960

Sir Duncan Swann[†] makes a rare appearance at the Garrick. Harold Nicolson leans across the table & says: 'I suppose you were at the Labour Party Conference. Do you support Mr Gaitskell or Mr Cousins?' Sir Donald rather annoyed at this.

Later Sir Duncan says of Gaitskell: 'He lacks the popular appeal of a political leader.' H.N.: 'Do you mean that all political leaders should have a streak of vulgarity?' – and turning to Maurice Macmillan, sitting next to Sir Duncan – 'You must tell your father that.' Maurice replies: 'I am sure my father has nothing to learn in that direction!'

## 27 October 1960

Read D.H. Lawrence's *Lady Chatterley's Lover*. Very good on the Derbyshire

---

* In Act Three of Wagner's *Die Meistersinger von Nürnberg* the shoemakers' guild enter singing a song of praise to St Crispin.
† 2nd Bt (1879–1962), barrister and Labour MP for Hyde 1906–9.

miners and their attitude to the 'big house'. The sexy parts are very sexy indeed, but had I been a member of the jury in the recent prosecution for obscenity, I should <u>not</u> have said that it was an obscene & corrupting book.

# 1961

*This year was a great turning point for Kenneth. He was one of the principal figures on the new* Sunday Telegraph *that was launched in February. He began contributing the 'Albany at Large' column, which continued without a break for the next thirty-six years and became an essential guide to the unfolding events of contemporary history.*

### 3 January 1961

Dine with Harold Nicolson at the Beefsteak. He talks of King Edward VII. Lord Carnock,* who was a very moral man, once came back to his house just before he was due to leave on a cruise in the Royal Yacht with the King, saying: 'I am so pleased, Mrs Keppel† has agreed to come.' Harold said to his father: 'I never thought I should live to hear you rejoice that the King was taking his mistress with him on a foreign tour.' Lord Carnock laughed, and admitted that when Mrs Keppel was present the King was always in a good humour. When she was not, the King would be bad-tempered and drum his fingers on the table when dining with admirals' wives.

But Lord Carnock believed, contrary to popular opinion, that the King loved Queen Alexandra.‡ He was sitting on the deck of the Royal Yacht one day while the Queen ran about taking snapshots, and he gazed on her, according to Lord Carnock, with a look of deep feeling and affection on his face.

Harold describes how he once had to give a lecture in Leeds. On the train he met Malcolm Sargent, also going north for a concert in Huddersfield. They had luncheon together. In the middle of the meal, Malcolm saw someone approaching with an autograph album and groaned: 'Here we go again.' The person came up to the table, held out the book and said: 'Would you mind signing, please, Sir Harold?'

---

* Arthur Nicolson, 1st Baron Carnock (1849–1928), Permanent Under-Secretary for Foreign Affairs 1910–16.
† Alice Keppel (1868–1947), society hostess and long-term mistress of Edward VII.
‡ Alexandra of Denmark (1844–1925), Queen Consort of Edward VII.

## 4 January 1961

I had thought that the name 'Albany' was now settled for my new column. But this afternoon Brian Roberts* sent a note suggesting Peter Pindar. I write a strong memo against such a change. It really sounds more suitable for a greyhound tipster.

In the evening Lady Vansittart† tells me how disgracefully Robert Vansittart was treated by Neville Chamberlain. But she feels almost as strongly at Winston's refusal to give him any work during the war, particularly as Winston and Van had worked closely opposing the Munich policy. 'It got to the stage', she said, 'that even the Foreign Office messengers pitied him.'

## 5 January 1961

Lunch Bill De Lisle‡ at White's. He says of Anthony Eden: 'It was characteristic of him that in the centenary year of the Victoria Cross he should have sacked his only two VC ministers.' One was Sir John Smyth,§ the other Bill himself.

## 12 January 1961

To Buckingham Palace to discuss Queen's tour of India and Pakistan with Michael Adeane. He stressed how remarkable it was that only fourteen years after independence and civil war both India and Pakistan should have worked closely together in planning the Queen's tour. There was not the slightest jealousy or rivalry between the two governments in doing this.

It is obvious that there are many in India who disapprove of the country's membership of the Commonwealth. On the other hand the great majority no doubt have no knowledge of constitutional questions, and possibly think that Queen Victoria is still on the throne.

In Pakistan on the other hand the Government is inclined to take a Kiplingesque view of her membership of the Commonwealth. The President, General Mohammed Ayub Khan,¶ might have stepped straight out of the pages of Kipling. In conversation he talks like an English general of the old school. So there is unlikely to be any opposition to the Queen's visit.

The Queen will be able to go to church every Sunday – a programme which

---

* (1906–88), Editor of the *Sunday Telegraph* 1961–6.
† Lady (Sarita) Vansittart, née Enriqueta (1891–1985), second wife of Lord Vansittart.
‡ William Sidney, 1st Viscount De L'Isle, VC (1909–91), Conservative politician. Secretary of State for Air, 1951–5; Governor General of Australia 1961–5.
§ Brig. Sir John Smyth, VC (1893–1983), Parliamentary Secretary, Ministry of Pensions 1953–5.
¶ Gen. Mohammed Ayub Khan (1907–74), President of Pakistan 1958–69.

will be understood and approved by all religions in the Indian continent. The programme includes one or two visits to race meetings. It has become the custom of the Press to emphasise these. In fact, the Queen really only enjoys watching racing when her own horses are engaged.

Dine at Pratt's and have much talk with Ralph Anstruther,[*] who recently became Treasurer to the Queen Mother. Ralph also looks after the Castle of Mey, largely because he has a house of his own in Caithness. We discuss the whole relations between the Royal Family and the Press. Ralph epitomises the whole matter well by saying that the Royal Family simply do not think of themselves as ordinary people nor imagine why their private lives can possibly be of interest to the Press or the public.

On the subject of the appointment of equerries to Clarence House, Ralph tells me it has always been the custom for the Queen Mother to appoint young men only from her own cavalry regiments. Ralph finds the Duke of Gloucester easier to talk to than do most people. The secret is to talk to him about military history.

### 19 January 1961

Dr Ramsey, Archbishop of York, to succeed Dr Fisher as Archbishop of Canterbury – another archiepiscopal triumph for Repton.

### 20 January 1961

Lunch with Maurice Macmillan at the Beefsteak. He tells me an extraordinary story. When his small boy was at his private school at the age of ten he had a friend who was a precocious and brilliant mathematical calculator. This boy was passionately interested in aeroplanes. In one of the aeronautical magazines he saw some advance plans and drawings of the Hunter aircraft. He came to Maurice's boy one day and said: 'I have worked out that if this plane fires all its guns in the air it will come to pieces.'

Maurice's boy was alarmed by this and told his friend to put all the information in a letter, which he sent to his grandfather – at that time Minister of Defence. Harold Macmillan took the boy's letter to a meeting of the Defence Committee and read it out. There was much laughter, but it was agreed that all the mathematics of the aircraft should be recalculated. This was done and it was found that the ten-year-old boy was quite right!

Have a battle to get my 'Albany' feature set in three wide columns instead of four little columns, but eventually succeed. It will now stand out well.

---

[*] Maj. Sir Ralph Anstruther (1921–2002), royal courtier.

## 1 February 1961

Sir Frederic Hooper and Sir Gilbert Laithwaite* and Sir Ifor Evans† dine at my flat. Gilbert discusses the Queen's Indian tour at length, pointing out that so successful a visit could not have taken place before independence; there would always have been some faction making an angry demonstration. The success of the present tour could not have been lost on those Americans who constantly stress our so-called colonial policy.

An interesting story told by Gilbert of when he was Private Secretary to the Viceroy, Lord Linlithgow,‡ in Delhi. One day when Gandhi came to see the Viceroy, Gilbert had had his hand heavily bandaged after a riding fall. He said to Gandhi: 'You see, I have been converted to a policy of non-violence!' 'Ah,' replied Gandhi, 'that does not count. Your conversion was under compulsion!'

Ifor Evans tells me a story of Nancy Astor. One day when Mrs Pandit§ was complaining about the iniquities of British rule in India, Nancy rounded on her and said: 'You have no right to talk like that. But for British rule in India you would have been burnt as a widow.'

We discuss Ifor's efforts to get money for London University from the Isaac Wolfson Foundation. Wolfson¶ met Evans one day and said to him: 'What is your job?' 'I run London University,' he replied. 'Yes. Yes, I know,' said Wolfson impatiently, 'but what is your real job?'

A story about Eisenhower – he has stopped reading even Westerns because they make his lips hurt.

*The* Sunday Telegraph *was launched on 5 February 1961, a major turning point in Kenneth's life. An indication of the attention that the 'Albany' column at once attracted was that the Prime Minister, Harold Macmillan, sent him some copy that he thought he might find useful for 'Albany', as 22 February was the eighteenth anniversary of the plane crash in North Africa that nearly cost Macmillan his life.*

## 7 February 1961

John Wyndham telephones me from Downing Street. The Prime Minister

---

* Irish-British civil servant and diplomat (1894–1986). High Commissioner to Pakistan 1951–5; Permanent Under-Secretary of State for Commonwealth Relations 1955–9.
† Baron Evans of Hungershall (1899–1982), Provost of University Coll., London 1951–66.
‡ Victor Hope, 2nd Marquess of Linlithgow (1887–1952), Viceroy of India 1936–43.
§ Vijaya Pandit (1900–90), Indian diplomat and politician; she was the widow of Ranjit Pandit (1893–1944), barrister.
¶ Sir Isaac Wolfson, 1st Bt (1897–1991), Scottish businessman and philanthropist.

wonders if I would like to use this following piece in 'Albany'.

'February 22 will be the eighteenth anniversary of an event which might have given us a different Prime Minister at this moment. At about 1 a.m. on 22 February 1943, Mr Macmillan was in a bomber taking off from an airfield near Algiers. The plane crashed when taking off and burst into flames. Mr Macmillan tried to get out of a window but was stuck for several moments and received bad burns. He was taken to hospital and then continued his journey to Cairo heavily bandaged.'[*]

Mr Macmillan's comment on this is as follows: 'For lesser exertions, such as to enter Parliament, to struggle through years of political failure and frustration, other motives may serve. Ambition, patriotism, pride – all these can impel a man and bring him within the hallowed precinct of the Privy Council and the Cabinet. But to do what I did in the early hours of that Monday morning only one motive in the world is sufficient – fear (not fame) is the spur.'

## 10 February 1961

Osbert Lancaster tells me a good story about Lord Beaverbrook, concerning an occasion during World War I when Beaverbrook was at lunch with Nancy Astor. Nancy was complaining that far too many people donned uniform only in order to go out to the front and drink to excess – and here she looked hard at Beaverbrook. Beaverbrook replied: 'Yes, only the other day F.E. Smith and I were out at the front, and we were so drunk we thought we saw Waldorf[†] there!'

## 20 February 1961

Dine Brooks's with Donald McLachlan in a private room to meet Hugh Gaitskell and Patrick Gordon Walker. A snatch of conversation:

Gordon Walker: 'Now John Betjeman is what I call an eccentric.'

Gaitskell: 'But Betjeman isn't an eccentric. He now goes to the same tailor as I do.'

Gordon Walker: 'I should call that a mark of the highest eccentricity.'

---

[*] What is not repeated in this message is that Macmillan went back into the burning aircraft to rescue other passengers.

[†] Waldorf Astor, 2nd Viscount Astor (1879–1952), American-born English Unionist politician and newspaper proprietor; husband of Nancy Astor.

## 27 February 1961

To Bishopscroft, the Heaton house of the Bishop of Bradford, for tea with Dr Donald Coggan and Mrs Coggan.* It lies right up at the top of Heaton. Although the approach is down a scruffy little road the house itself is solid and attractive, with a fine view towards Baildon, my home town, and a charming garden. Dr Coggan, who is in his early fifties, looks even younger. He has a smooth unlined face with gold-rimmed spectacles. His wife looks very much the Church worker, and is full of friendly kindness. She produces a delicious tea with home-made cakes.

I discuss at some length with the Bishop the various revisions of the language of the basic documents of the Church which he has undertaken:

1. A revised catechism.
2. Revision of the Psalter. Dr Coggan is Chairman of a Commission appointed by the archbishops. Other members of the Commission include T.S. Eliot and C.S. Lewis.†
3. Revision of the Prayer Book. Dr Coggan has recently taken over the Chairmanship of this Commission.

Most of these various meetings are held at Lambeth. For the Psalter revision, however, C.S. Lewis likes it to be held in Cambridge and occasionally it is held in Oxford.

Dr Coggan thinks it wise that the Prayer Book should be revised and republished bit by bit. This will avoid the fiasco of 1928, when the revised Prayer Book was rejected wholesale by Parliament. We discuss the English of the *New English Bible* to be published on 14 March.

On more general subjects Dr Coggan tells me that he is particularly interested in the work of the Anglican Churches overseas, and hopes when he is translated to York shortly to do as much travelling as both his predecessors there.

Also on the subject of York, he tells me how much he likes Northerners, particularly their openness and vigour. The Bishop says he does not intend to lose the common touch once he has become Archbishop. This week he has taken the wedding services of two curates and hopes that this sort of thing will continue.

* The Most Revd and Rt Hon. Baron Coggan of Canterbury (1909–2000). Bishop of Bradford 1956–61; Archbishop of York 1961–74; Archbishop of Canterbury 1975–80. Lady (Jean) Coggan (1908–2005), wife of Dr Coggan, had a special concern for the wives of clergy.
† T.S. Eliot OM (1888–1965), one of the foremost twentieth-century poets. C.S. Lewis (1898–1963), academic, poet, medievalist, Christian apologist; renowned for *The Screwtape Letters* (HarperCollins, 1942) and *The Chronicles of Narnia* (1950–6).

## 1 March 1961

David Eccles to lunch at the Guards Club. We talk of public-school head-masters. He tells me that Tom Howarth,* who was recently appointed to be the new High Master of St Paul's at the end of the summer term in 1962, is a protégé of Field Marshal Montgomery. Realising that other schools would soon be looking for new headmasters (e.g. Manchester Grammar School, on the departure of Lord James to be head of the new University of York), Monty took a three-year option on Howarth as one of the governors of St Paul's. The military planner at work.

Eccles was consulted about a job for Tony Armstrong-Jones. He strongly suggested that he should work for Michael Croft's† National Youth Theatre, but the Queen thought it undignified. Eccles cannot see how the marriage will last if Tony is cut off from all his real interests.

Last night Gladwyn Jebb dined with Eccles. Freya Stark,‡ who was also there, asked Gladwyn what he was doing nowadays. Gladwyn looked down his nose and replied contemptuously: 'You can't have been reading the papers very much lately.'

## 19 March 1961

Watch huge anti-apartheid demonstration in Hyde Park from my windows. Led by Jo Grimond and a black man carrying a big 'Remember Sharpeville' banner. There are even children carrying such slogans. But nobody carrying a banner which says 'Remember Hungary' or 'Remember Tibet'. As always in politics, sympathy is selective.

## 22 March 1961

Harold Nicolson sat next to Ava Waverley at a party the other night. She told him that John Waverley advised the King not to give Sir Alexander Fleming the OM because he had failed as a scientist to develop the possibilities of penicillin. The real credit, he thought, should go to the Oxford scientists who did this.

Lunch at Beefsteak. Tommy Lascelles tells me a story of Oliver Esher, who is eighty tomorrow. Soon after the Duke of Wellington had succeeded to Stratfield Saye, Esher went to stay there and found him very pompous. On

---

* Thomas Howarth (1914–88), academic. High Master of St Paul's School 1962–73; Senior Tutor, Magdalene Coll., Cambridge 1973–80.
† (1922–86), Founder and Director of the National Youth Theatre of Great Britain from 1956.
‡ DBE (1893–1993), explorer and travel writer.

his return a friend asked him what had struck him most during his visit. He replied: 'The elevation of the host.'*

## 27 March 1961

Quite a lot of talk with both Gaitskell and Horace Evans† at dinner. Gaitskell thinks Perry Worsthorne knows nothing of the internal currents in the Labour Party. 'In fact,' he adds, 'there are no good political columnists writing today.' I am surprised to hear that the only weekly he reads is the *Economist*. Presumably he knows beforehand what the *New Statesman* is going to say.

I discuss Curzon's medical history with Horace Evans. He thinks that the injured spine was due to a tubercular infection rather than from a physical injury.

In Monte Carlo recently Evans had lunch with Winston – 'He is eating far too much.' Winston commented: 'I have ordered this meal, but it is not obligatory to finish it.'

I also have some general talk with Evans about the medical history and temperaments of politicians. He thinks that Anthony Eden had the worst temperament of all to be a politician – 'He comes from a family of artists.' Macmillan, he says, has the best temperament – nothing ruffles him.

At the end of the evening, Gaitskell offers me a lift. 'Where are you going?' he asks. 'To the Ritz, I suppose.'

## 28 March 1961

6 p.m. to the Commonwealth Relations Office to see Sir John Maud, High Commissioner in South Africa, who is in London for a week or two for consultations.

We have much talk about his life in South Africa. As High Commissioner for the Territories he has visited each of them six or seven times during the last two years. These territories cannot be administered by telegram from the seat of government as many people seem to think.

Before the Commonwealth Prime Ministers' Conference began in London he did not think that South Africa would leave the Commonwealth – although he warned the Government of South Africa that the outcome of the

---

* Oliver Brett, 3rd Viscount Esher (1881–1963), trustee of the British Museum; advocate for the preservation of historic buildings. Gerald Wellesley, 7th Duke of Wellington (1885–1972), diplomat, soldier and architect.

† 1st Baron Evans (1903–63), physician to Queen Mary, George VI and Elizabeth II.

conference would not be a mere formality designed to keep the Union within the Commonwealth.

The departure of South Africa will, Maud thinks, lead to three results:

1. The beginning of a new phase in the history of the Commonwealth based on common values.
2. A strengthening of the British position in our relations with South Africa, especially over the Territories. We are now in a better position to protect their inhabitants.
3. A worsening of the outlook for the English who have settled in Africa.

Maud has found Dr Verwoerd[*] to be a good listener and a courteous disputer. I ask Maud whether it has not been painful to live in the midst of apartheid. He replies: 'Apartheid is really greed. It is a cruel system and it made me very unhappy to see it in action. The whole country, though beautiful, is plastered with offensive notices. One also sees it acting in material ways, e.g. all the best beaches are reserved for whites and the rocky or shark-infested beaches for Africans.'

He adds that it was not the putting of apartheid on the Statute Book that caused him such distress, but the theory that three million whites are to have permanent supremacy. South Africa is essentially a Victorian country. One illustration of this is that women are kept very much in the background and segregated.

Maud says that he would have found his task impossible had he not felt that his distaste of apartheid was shared by Macmillan and the British Government.

### 29 March 1961

Martin Gilliat tells me that the Queen Mother never sees Tommy Lascelles these days. She is frightened of clever people & always suspects that they are laughing at her.

Leslie Rowse to dine in flat. He reads my early chapters of Curzon, makes one or two excellent suggestions, & leaves with barely enough time to catch the last train back to Oxford.

### 6 April 1961

At 10.30 to see Lady Alexandra Metcalfe, Curzon's daughter, at her flat in Eaton Place. Find her immobile; after driving several thousand miles from

---

[*] Dr Hendrik Verwoerd (1901–66), Prime Minister of South Africa 1958–66; assassinated.

the Far East, she arrived safely back but slipped a disc while lifting a suitcase from the back of her car.

In Delhi Lady Alexandra saw Nehru, who feels deeply that the traditions of Tibetan learning must be preserved in the face of Chinese destruction in Tibet itself. He offered Lady Alexandra 'the retreat' in Simla for the education of Tibetan children – a house which the Viceroys used to have. This was not in fact suitable, but another house has been offered by the Indian Government. It will house 100 Tibetan children, and a full staff will be provided.

## 12 April 1961
Lunch with Richard Wood[*] at his flat in Eaton Place. A good story about status symbols. When Richard's father, Lord Halifax, returned from being Viceroy of India, he was appointed President of the Board of Education. The curtains in his room at the Board were very shoddy, so he asked for some replacements. He was curtly told that the President of the Board was not a senior enough minister to warrant the sort of curtains he had demanded. This after ruling 300 million people!

Later spend an hour talking to Victor Hochhauser[†] about the arrangements for the visit to this country of the Mariinski Ballet from Leningrad. Lord Harewood has asked him to try and get Shostakovich to visit the Edinburgh Festival next year. I ask Hochhauser how much Shostakovich earns under the Soviet system. 'I can assure you', he replies, 'that Shostakovich has no money troubles.'[‡]

## 27 April 1961
Michael Adeane tells me four points about next week's State Visit of the Queen to Rome.
1. The Queen cannot possibly visit Rome without also paying a State Visit to the Pope.[§] Inevitably, there will be criticism from the extreme Protestants. But there are precedents. Edward VII and George V both visited the Vatican and no one could accuse either of these Sovereigns of being inclined towards popery. Some may maintain, in order to disarm criticism, that the Queen is visiting the Vatican as a private person. This is

---

* Baron Holderness (1920–2002), Conservative politician. MP for Bridlington 1950–79; Minister of Power 1959–63; Minister of Pensions and National Insurance 1963–4; Minister of Overseas Development 1970–74. He was the youngest son of Lord Halifax, Viceroy of India.
† (b. 1923), impresario.
‡ Dimitri Shostakovich (1906–75), celebrated Soviet composer. He was a principal guest at the 1962 Edinburgh Festival, which saw the British premieres of his 4th and 12th Symphonies.
§ Pope John XXIII (1881–1963), r. 1958–63; canonised 2014.

not so. She will be accompanied by a minister. Thus all her actions will be taking place on the advice of her government.

2. During her State Visit to the Republic of Italy she will attend two equestrian events – the International Horse Show and the Derby. This is no wish of hers, the programme having been drawn up by the Italian Government. It is like tiger-shooting in Nepal. But once she ends the State Visit and begins her private visit to Venice and Florence, there will be no more horses.

3. The Royal Yacht is being used economically for three distinct purposes – the visit of the Queen Mother to Tunisia, the visit of the Queen to Italy, and the visit of the Duke of Gloucester to war cemeteries in Greece and Turkey.

4. Owing to the outcry when the Queen rode in a German car in India, Rolls-Royces are being taken to Italy for the Queen's private visit. But this may well offend the Italians! One cannot please everybody.

## 4 May 1961

10.30 to the Ministry of Defence to see Lord Mountbatten in order to discuss his years at the Admiralty with Jim Cilcennin, the notice of whose life I am writing for the *Dictionary of National Biography*. Frequently striding up and down the L-shaped room he has as an office, Mountbatten tells me that he had known Jim since the war, though Edwina was a childhood friend.

The Navy, he says, meant more to Jim than anything else in his life. His attachment to the Navy was loyal, affectionate and understanding, and surpassed that of most naval officers. Jim was not a strong character, but he revealed great strength on matters of principle.

'Because Winston believed I had betrayed the Empire by handling Indian independence, he later opposed my appointment as First Sea Lord. Jim, however, thought that I was the one man who could pull the Navy together, and he stood up to Winston on this matter through thick and thin.'

One day Jim said to Winston: 'You surely agree that the Navy needs a strong man as First Sea Lord.' 'I don't want a strong man as First Sea Lord,' replied Winston.

Similarly, Jim stood up to Anthony Eden on several occasions. There was one rather trivial matter. Eden had asked Jim to go with him to a performance of the Royal Tournament. Unfortunately, Lord Dynevor* died suddenly and Jim had to go to the funeral. So he wrote to Eden explaining that he would

---

* Walter Rhys, 7th Baron Dynevor (1873–1956). Lord Lieutenant of Carmarthenshire 1928–48; Financial Secretary to the Admiralty 1943–5.

not be able to go to the Royal Tournament. Eden stormed at him for a long time on the telephone but Jim would not budge.

Far more important than this was the way that Jim opposed the Suez landing of October 1956. When the Canal was nationalised in July, both Mountbatten and Jim were prepared to send the Fleet, which was at Malta, to Cyprus. There they would pick up two Royal Marine commandos and land them at Port Said. They would then be able to capture the first few miles of the Canal practically unopposed and with a great measure of surprise. Eden considered this plan but eventually rejected it, since he wanted the whole of the Canal to be in our hands. Otherwise, Nasser would simply have blocked the other end of the Canal (as in fact happened later in the year).

Eden then went mad – these are Mountbatten's actual words – and mounted the operations which ended in the fiasco of November 1956. Jim repeatedly tried to dissuade him from this plan, and told Mountbatten that he would have resigned from the Admiralty had he not been due to leave in any case.

Walter Monckton, at that time Minister of Defence, also said he would resign. In fact he did not, but he found an excuse to leave the Government soon after.

To sum up this matter of Suez, no minister saw more clearly than Jim that if we were to use force against Nasser, it must be immediate, i.e. in July 1956, and not protracted, as in October–November 1956.

Mountbatten praises Jim for being a big enough man to see his limitations. When Jim came to the Admiralty, Mountbatten told him that a powerful committee should be set up to see what economies could be made without substantially reducing our naval strength. Sir John Lang[*] advised Jim that the First Lord should be Chairman. Mountbatten, however, told Jim that he himself ought to be Chairman, with the First Lord remaining outside the committee. This in fact is how the committee worked, with Mountbatten in the chair, reporting to Jim as First Lord. The committee saved £15½ million a year without taking one ship away from the sea. Lang came round to the composition of the committee in the end. The root of the matter is that no admiral is frightened of the First Lord, whom he regards merely as a politician. Admirals are only frightened of the First Sea Lord, and Jim was wise enough to realise this.

If Jim had a weakness it was that he did not prepare sufficiently for Defence Committees, and was too lazy to study his briefs. Instead, he would

---

[*] (1896–1984), Permanent Secretary to the Admiralty 1947–61.

turn the arguments over to the First Sea Lord.

Finally, we discuss Jim's intense loyalty to the Royal Family. He was really responsible for having Prince Philip made an Admiral against the wishes of the Queen's other advisers. The War Office wished him to be only a Major-General and the Air Ministry only an Air Vice-Marshal. But Mountbatten told Jim how the Admiralty had refused to make the Prince Consort* an Admiral of the Fleet. So Queen Victoria, to show her disapproval to the Admiralty, refused to allow the Prince of Wales to accept naval rank until his accession. Both Mountbatten and Jim were determined that this sort of situation should not happen again.

## 6 May 1961, letter to parents

A good story about Lord Halifax. He was asked whether he put after his name 'MFH, KG' or 'KG, MFH'. He replied: 'The former. A Master of Foxhounds comes from God, the Garter from Man.'

## 16 May 1961

To Queen's University, Belfast, to meet the Vice-Chancellor, Dr Michael Grant.† A man of charm and scholarship. He tells me that, compared to many other British universities, they have not a difficult financial problem. 'The Government dare not stint us as they depend on us so much for the graduates we produce.' The university receives a grant of about £830,000 per annum, together with a building grant of £750,000.

I ask him for his comments on the remarks I hear everywhere that Belfast is starved of culture. He agrees, but says the situation is improving, largely helped by the university. An Arts Theatre – the first one for sixty years – has recently been opened and promises to be a success. Perhaps the most difficult problem the university faces is in finding suitable staff. The best of them obviously try to go to Oxford or Cambridge. This problem is likely to affect the new universities of York and Norwich very acutely. Rather less than half of the university is given up to science. There is an annual lectureship of Fine Arts which has attracted enormous audiences. The last lecturer was John Betjeman and next year there will be Kenneth Clark.‡

---

* Prince Albert of Saxe-Coburg and Gotha (1819–61). Husband of Queen Victoria from 1840; Prince Consort 1857–61.

† (1914–2004), classical scholar. President and Vice-Chancellor, Queen's University, Belfast 1959–66.

‡ Baron Clark of Saltwood (1903–83), author, museum director and art historian, best known for his BBC TV television series *Civilisation* in 1969. Director of the National Gallery 1934–45; Surveyor of the King's Pictures 1934–44.

About 10 per cent of the students live in halls of residence but there is no attempt to turn the university into a purely residential organisation. As far as the religious problem goes, the university takes both Protestant and Catholics.

From the university drive back to Stormont to see the Prime Minister, Lord Brookeborough,[*] in his little sitting room. On the wall is a large photograph of three Field Marshals sitting in an open car – Alanbrooke, Alexander and Montgomery. I am also struck by the smallness of the Prime Minister's writing desk, about two-thirds the size of my own.

I began by asking him about the parliamentary question which has been put down for answer this afternoon. It demands that Northern Ireland should have adequate representation in the reformed House of Lords. He points out that there are in fact a number of peers who live in Northern Ireland, and he hopes that the Select Committee will include some plans to bring them to Westminster. I ask him why he never speaks himself in the House of Lords. He replies that he is reserving this in case he ever needs to raise problems of Ulster urgently. When the scheme for leave of absence for peers was introduced, he was among those who asked for this. But the Lord Chancellor begged him to leave his name on the roll and this he has done.

On the question of why there are so many Field Marshals from Ulster, he puts it down simply to chance and to the sturdy character of the Northern Irish: 'We are England's oldest colony.' Brookeborough is the nephew of Alanbrooke.

After half an hour he has to hurry away to another appointment. He says goodbye with the flattering remark, 'So nice to meet another soldier.'

After leaving the PM I am taken to see R.F.K. Dunbar,[†] the Permanent Secretary to the Ministry of Home Affairs – a quiet, shrewd, agreeable man. With him is W.F. Stout,[‡] Senior Assistant Secretary, like a stage detective but with a dry sense of humour. First we discussed crime. Most of the crime in Northern Ireland is larceny. Wage snatches are almost unheard of since it would be impossible for the thieves to go to ground in any large industrial town. Very few murders and no man has been hanged since 1942. Unlike England, where the responsibility for reprieve rests with the Home Secretary

---

[*] Basil Brooke, 1st Viscount Brookeborough (1888–1972), Ulster Unionist politician. Prime Minister of Northern Ireland 1943–63; he held government office continuously for thirty-three years, a UK record.

[†] Sir Richard Dunbar (1900–65), Head of Northern Ireland Civil Service 1961–5.

[‡] William Stout (1907–2005), civil servant. Permanent Secretary, Ministry of Home Affairs 1961–4; security adviser to the Government of Northern Ireland 1971–2.

alone, it is a Cabinet decision in Northern Ireland. Dunbar remarks: 'There is nothing like studying a table of weights and drops for a hanging to make one an abolitionist.' Discussing IRA incidents on the border, Stout admits that the Southern police have not been as helpful as they should have been. But, he adds, how could one expect them to be when the IRA has the general sympathy of most of the people in the South.

I ask about the problem of smuggling. Stout replies: 'Do you mean problem – or national industry?' In fact, there is now not much smuggling as the prices between the North and South are much the same.

### 25 May 1961

Harold Nicolson and Anthony Benn to dine. Anthony is very depressed by the attitude of the House of Commons towards his Bristol election. The Speaker has denied him the use of the House of Commons Library. This is a cruel blow as he is conducting his own case before the election court and needs access to a law library to prepare for this. He will write again to the Speaker asking for this courtesy, and if it is again refused he will ask Gaitskell to raise the matter in the House.

It seems particularly hard that the Speaker should take this line. All ex-MPs who are peers can use the library. The Speaker, however, contends that this privilege should be extended only to those peers who have taken their seats in the Lords.

Harold describes the Royal Academy banquet the other night. Going down the stairs with very great difficulty was Winston Churchill, supported by two other men. It was a pathetic sight. Harold was looking at this when Lord Attlee joined him and said: 'I don't expect we shall see that next year.' Harold was so shocked by this remark that all he could think of to reply was: 'Is Lady Attlee* driving you home?'

### 4 June 1961, letter to parents

Hugh & Dora Gaitskell asked me to a nice little cocktail party on Friday evening. The other guests were almost entirely Socialist – except for Martin Charteris, one of the Queen's Assistant Private Secretaries. The Gaitskells' house is in a semi-rural part of Hampstead, very quiet and green, but not awfully nicely furnished. I like them both so much – so very different from the public impression they used to make on me.

---

* Violet, Countess Attlee (1895–1964), wife of Clement Attlee for forty-two years and a notoriously dangerous driver.

# 4 July 1961

Lunch Beefsteak. Prime Minister at head of table. Poor Macmillan has Basil Fordham[*] as his neighbour. After a time he retreats to an armchair to read a magazine.

I ask John why Claude Elliott received a knighthood, but not Birley. John replies that Claude's honour was to mark Eton's contribution to the world, and so was given to the Provost, not to the man. We agree that Birley would make a good life peer.

# 12 July 1961

Harold Nicolson says that he once tried to heal the ill-feeling caused by Somerset Maugham's *Cakes and Ale*, with its cruel portraits of Thomas Hardy and Hugh Walpole.[†] He wrote in his review: 'Some may try to identify the characters with real writers. But Edward Driffeld is no more like Thomas Hardy than Alroy Kear is like John Drinkwater.'[‡] Only result of this was that Hugh Walpole asked H.N., 'Since when have I resembled John Drinkwater?', and that John Drinkwater cut him at a party.

I like Kenneth Clark, but modesty is entirely lacking. He starts a sentence: 'When Ramsay MacDonald[§] made me Director of the National Gallery at the age of twenty-nine ...' But he makes the point that everybody abroad assumed he had been given the job because he was 'Laboriste'.

# 13 July 1961

John Wyndham tells me two good stories of the Church of England.

The late Lord Hesketh,[¶] when he had a vacancy in a living, used to tell applicants to come to Brooks's. There they would be met by the hall porter and told that Hesketh had been delayed and offered a large glass of vintage port on his instructions. If they accepted, they were halfway to getting the job. If they refused with expressions of pious horror, they would gently be told they were wasting their time.

---

[*] (1923–2011), author.
[†] Sir Hugh Walpole (1884–1941), novelist.
[‡] (1882–1937), poet and playwright, particularly of Abraham Lincoln, Mary Stuart and Oliver Cromwell. When Bernard Shaw was asked why he had written *Saint Joan* he replied: 'To save her from John Drinkwater.'
[§] Ramsay MacDonald (1866–1937), first Labour Prime Minister; in office 1924, 1929–31, and of a National Government 1931–5.
[¶] Frederick Fermor-Hesketh, 2nd Baron Hesketh (1916–55), soldier.

The nineteenth-century Lord Erroll* used to take family prayers, and one day found that the lesson was about the camel going through the eye of a needle. He read it to the end, then said: 'That's all damned nonsense. Now let us pray.'

## 16 July 1961

Talk to Anthony Wedgwood Benn. His election court case, he says, is going very well, and he thinks he has a good chance of winning it. At worst, there will be another by-election: he does not think that his Conservative opponent, whom he beat at the by-election following his father's death, will be seated in his place. His opponent's counsel, Sir Andrew Clark,† is behaving very shabbily and rudely, complaining to Anthony at the end of each day's hearing: 'How long are you going to take? I have another case.' In the event of Anthony's losing altogether, costs will be heavy. Clark's brief is £1,000, with £100 a day refresher, and his junior has brief of £445.

## 18 July 1961

Spend a couple of hours listening to Anthony Wedgwood Benn arguing his case in the Law Courts. He shows amazing forensic skill, and I am deeply impressed by his command of material. The two old judges are very kind and agreeable.

## 21 July 1961

My brother Toby would have been forty today, had he lived.

At 10.30 to Cloth Fair to see John Betjeman. He has, I believe, a special key on his typewriter, a cross, for putting in front of bishops' names.

The purpose of my visit is to go to look at Euston Station, now threatened by demolition. As we walk through Smithfield he points to lovely eighteenth-century lettering on the side of a butcher's handcart – like lettering in a Gillray cartoon.

Also a story of a rich bummaree, a self-employed porter at Smithfield, who before the war used to go to the opera at Covent Garden before reporting for work as a meat porter at 3 a.m. One night he went to a party and did not turn up to Smithfield until 5 a.m. As he walked down the long nave of the market, wearing white tie and tails, all the other bummarees rang their meat hooks in derision.

We go by Underground to Euston. We both agree that although the portico

---

\* William Hay, 19th Earl of Erroll (1823–91), landowner.
† (1898–1979), barrister; conducted the Crichel Down Inquiry 1954.

is magnificent, its prospect was ruined years ago by the erection of the hotel.

But the upstairs rooms should certainly be saved, he says, as well as the Great Hall. We cannot inspect them as a meeting is going on. A messenger in the head office offends John very much by saying that as far as he is concerned, Euston can be demolished tomorrow – and as for the Doric portico, it impedes traffic.

So we go and drink in a nearby pub, where a stout barmaid advises us to put Worcester sauce on our potato crisps.

### 26 July 1961

David Eccles gives me the details of how he failed to get a knighthood for Robert Birley, Head Master of Eton. As is the custom, he received a note from the Prime Minister's office to say that in the next Honours List he could give a knighthood to one headmaster of an independent school. The choice obviously lay between Robert Birley and Desmond Lee,[*] Headmaster of Winchester. Everybody whom he consulted agreed that Birley was the obvious man. So he sent in his name. Then there began a whispering campaign in the Cabinet, and Macmillan was persuaded to nominate Lee instead. Eccles not only thought this a wrong decision but was also embarrassed because Lee was Headmaster of his old school.

### 3 August 1961

Dinner party at my flat for Peter Carrington, John Wyndham and Martin Gilliat.

We have much talk about Australia. All are knowledgeable. Peter was High Commissioner there, Martin was Military Secretary to Bill Slim[†] in Australia, and John accompanied the Prime Minister there a year or two ago.

Peter says that Menzies is very disenchanted with Macmillan. This largely began with our hostile attitude to South Africa at the last Conference of Commonwealth Prime Ministers. Menzies thinks that had the PM been firmer we could have saved the Commonwealth from such an open split.

All are agreed that Duncan Sandys made an appalling impression on the Australians during his recent visit. He is almost as unpopular there as Iain Macleod is in Africa.

Talking of the appointment of Bill de L'Isle to be Governor General of Australia, Peter says Bill was hurt not to have received any letters of

---

* Sir Desmond Lee (1908–93), classical scholar. Headmaster of Winchester Coll. 1954–68.
† FM Sir William Slim, 1st Viscount Slim (1891–1970), British Military Cdr and the thirteenth Governor General of Australia 1952–9.

congratulation from his former political colleagues. John replied: 'But Macmillan <u>appointed</u> Bill de L'Isle to Australia.' This is technically nonsense, as the appointment is in the hands of the Prime Minister of Australia.

An amusing story told by Peter. When Prince Henry, Duke of Gloucester returned from being Governor General of Australia, Queen Mary asked him: 'What was Australia like?' The Duke replied with deep feeling: 'Tewwible, Mama, tewwible.'

We have some talk about the expenditure of the Royal Family. John says that the Queen Mother sets a bad example by extravagance. Martin replies that of course she lives extravagantly but that most of the money she spends is not from the Civil List but from her private inherited fortune.

On the subject of the Royal Yacht, we are all agreed that it is far too expensive for the purpose it fulfils. It also has another disadvantage – that although the Royal Family can live aboard her in great luxury, the living quarters of the crew are far below those of most British warships. A great deal of news equipment had to be installed after the ship was completed, and ate into the living quarters of the crew.

The other day, Peter says, the Queen sent for him to talk about the Royal Yacht. She said: 'I see the ship is due for another refit. You spend the money and I get the blame.' When John and Peter had left, Martin stays behind to talk about Princess Margaret and Tony Armstrong-Jones. We agree that at the present time of economic difficulty, some gesture waiving the £50,000 to be spent on their new house in Kensington Palace is needed. Their popularity is lower at the moment than ever before. Martin says that John Griffin[*] thinks I am the only person apart from Princess Margaret who has any influence on Tony. And Martin thinks it would be wise if I talked to Tony about this before they left for Scotland in a few days' time.

### 4 August 1961

In view of widespread criticism of Princess Margaret for the huge amount – now £70,000 – to be spent on restoring 1A, Kensington Palace for her and Tony, I decide, in the light of what Martin Gilliat told me about John Griffin, to advise them to make some gesture of self-denial at the present time of economic strain. So I telephone Tony to ask to see him. 'It's nothing awful, is it?' he nervously enquires. I agree to see him before lunch at their present house in KP.

Wearing a check jacket, trousers, suede boots, no coat and huge spectacles. He is rather deaf from having been to his shooting school this morning in

---

[*] Maj. Sir John Griffin (1924–2009), Press Secretary to the Queen Mother 1956–91.

readiness for Balmoral. Leads me up to his bed-sitting room. The house is so small, he says, that 'for the first time in my life I have no room of my own except a bedroom'.

Then Princess Margaret comes in, warm in her welcome. But she tiresomely interrupts everything Tony says. I launch into my set speech on the need for them to make some gesture towards the present economic needs of the country, such as an announcement that they have asked for the postponement of renovations to the larger KP house into which they want to move. This is not at all well received. With a shrug of her shoulders she whines: 'We must have a roof over our heads.' And when, a few minutes later, I am alone again with Tony, he bursts out: 'She has given twenty years of service to the country, works very hard indeed, and deserves something in return.' I don't bother to point out that she is still only thirty, and already receives £15,000 a year from the state for a far from heavy burden of public duties.

Instead Tony takes me to see the terrible tumbledown state of 1A, which the Ministry of Works has wantonly neglected and allowed to fall into sad decay. Inside it is no more than a ruin of a house, with gaping holes in the floorboards. Tony rightly points out that Lord John Hope,[*] the minister, is trying to extricate himself from the responsibility of allowing this Wren palace to rot by implying that the entire cost of restoration is to make it habitable for the Joneses; whereas in fact it would have to be restored even if nobody intended to live there. Tony also resents Hope's patronising manner. After hostile questions about the cost of restoration had been asked in the Commons, Hope met Tony, patted him soothingly on the shoulder and said: 'All went well in the House.'

I agree with Tony that the public has no idea of the state of 1A, and, since he refuses to persuade Princess Margaret to ask for a postponement of renovation, he asks me to draft a letter for him to send to Hope. I also make the suggestion that he should ask Hope to allow journalists to see 1A. It would make a good August news story with pictures.

## 5 August 1961
I draft a letter for Tony Armstrong-Jones to send to Lord John Hope. It reads:

'Both Princess Margaret and I have been much disturbed lately at public and private criticism about 1A, Kensington Palace. The remarks made by

---

[*] 1st Baron Glendevon (1912–96), Conservative politician. Minister of Works 1959–62.

Mr William Hamilton* in the House of Commons were, as most people are aware, ill received. But it may be that at the present time of economic strain, such criticisms of our alleged extravagance will be more widely repeated. I am, therefore, writing to ask for your help in putting the true facts of the situation before the public.

'As you know, it was simultaneously announced in March (a) that the Queen had offered Princess Margaret and myself the use of 1A, Kensington Palace as a permanent home, and (b) that the restoration and adaptation of the property would cost £70,000, of which £50,000 would be charged to the Royal Palace Vote by your Ministry.

'These two statements seem to have become so confused in the public mind that nearly everybody believes that this large sum of money is being spent only to provide us with a new home. Whereas the truth is that your Ministry would have had to spend £50,000 on the building whoever went to live there; and that the only alternative to spending such a sum is to let a magnificent example of Wren architecture crumble to ruins.

'A further public criticism we have heard is that 1A, Kensington Palace is absurdly large for us – one paper mentioned that it contained twenty main rooms, as well as space for a nursery. As you know, it is in fact far smaller.

'It seems to me essential that the true facts about the house should be made known to as wide a public as possible, and I wonder whether this would not best be done by our holding a Press conference actually inside 1A, Kensington Palace.'

*This letter was sent by Antony Armstrong-Jones, and Kenneth's arguments prevailed. The issue was debated in Parliament in January 1962 and March 1962, when William Hamilton again raised objections. The work was put in hand, costing £85,000 overall, and the Snowdons moved into 1A, Kensington Palace on 4 March 1963.*

### 6 August 1961

Lord Stanley of Alderley† tells me of a Russian delegation to London some years ago. Their programme began with a visit to London docks. They were shown round by Lord Waverley. They then went to the Atomic Energy offices to hear about our progress in atomic research. In the evening they were invited to Covent Garden, and for the third time that day they were received

---

* (1917–2000), Labour MP for constituencies in Fife 1950–87, known for his strong republican views.
† Edward Stanley, 6th Baron Stanley of Alderley (1907–71).

by Lord Waverley. What a very curious picture of English life they must have taken away with them.

## 8 August 1961

Giles St Aubyn discusses the virtues and failings of Robert Birley.

On the credit side, he is one of the most hard-working of Head Masters. He often does a twenty-hour day, and as well as his normal duties has undertaken a great deal of valuable research into College Library. Outside Eton he is a much more important and respected figure. Many people at Eton feel in fact that he devotes too much time to outside activities.

His unpopularity among the masters is largely owing to the fact that he undertakes too many jobs, while not keeping a strict order of priorities. Thus he insists that all requests for boys' leave away from Eton should go through him. This is a matter which housemasters could easily deal with by themselves. But that is not all. Having laid down the rule, Birley then forgets to answer the requests from housemasters.

Giles considers Birley a poor chooser of assistant masters. He concentrates on the intellect of candidates, not on whether they have teaching ability.

## 15 August 1961

I have Sir Austin Strutt,[*] Deputy Under-Secretary at the Home Office, to lunch at the Savoy.

Small, energetic, friendly, indiscreet. He tells me that all the plans for the funeral of Winston Churchill have been drawn up to await the day of his death. Originally it was decided that the service should be at Westminster Abbey, followed by burial at Blenheim. Now the service will be at St Paul's Cathedral, from where the coffin will be taken by water to Waterloo, then by train to Chartwell. The Minister of Health has already drafted a document giving permission for burial to take place there.[†] The Queen will attend if in England – one of the rare occasions a Sovereign attends the funeral of a subject. The order of service is very Royal. Question of pall-bearers not yet fixed, but Mountbatten wants to be one. Strutt dislikes Mountbatten, who is always trying to interfere in ceremonial matters. But he met his match in the Duke of Norfolk at the time of King George VI's funeral.

Strutt also dislikes Prince Philip – 'He will bring the whole monarchy down in ruins.' He tells story of how Philip was in the Royal Yacht during Channel Islands visit with Queen and party of officials, including Strutt. It

---

[*] (1903–79), civil servant; at the Home Office 1925–61.

[†] These plans changed. When Churchill died in Jan. 1965 he was buried at Bladon.

was necessary to change plan owing to bad weather. Queen did not understand why it was necessary, and asked. At which Philip, in front of everybody,
said to her: 'Haven't you the intelligence to realise . . .'

Strutt has much contempt for the way in which the Royal decisions are
taken – though a great regard for Michael Adeane. The other day Strutt
was arranging the Remembrance Day service in Whitehall. The Queen and
Philip will be in Ghana, so he asked who would represent her. Answer came
back – her ADC-General. Strutt replied this would not do. So now Duke of
Gloucester will do it, assuming his health is all right.

### 18 September 1961

Lord Goddard talks to me about legal cases of bestiality. He tells me that
a judge had once given a man nine months for having intercourse with a
bitch. 'Only nine months?' said Goddard. 'Yes,' replied the other judge, 'but I
disqualified him from holding a dog licence for three years.'

### 25 September 1961, letter to parents

I dined at Pratt's the other night and sat next to old Lord Goddard, the retired Lord Chief Justice. He ate a huge meal, drank a lot of port, smoked a big
cigar and remarked: 'I cannot understand this Government. They won't give
me any work to do, and after all I am only eighty-four.'

### 25 September 1961

I see that the Queen has been visiting Gordonstoun and lunched with the
Chairman of the Governors.* This may well be a pointer to a decision about
Prince Charles.

### 28 September 1961

John Wyndham tells me that at the time of Suez many members of the Foreign Office wanted to resign. So Ivone Kirkparick,† at that time Permanent
Under-Secretary, called them all together and gave them a pep talk on duty.

We both agree that Warden Hayter should either have resigned at the time
or not continued to go on attacking Suez now he has left the Service. I think
this even though I disliked Suez as much as he did.

John Wyndham tells story of how, when in Tunis with Harold Macmillan

---

* Sir Iain Mark Tennant (1919–2006), Lord Lieutenant of Morayshire 1963–94; Chairman of
the Governors of Gordonstoun 1954–71.
† Sir Ivone Kirkpatrick (1897–1964), Permanent Under-Secretary of State, Foreign Office
1953–7.

during the war, he bathed near Carthage. To his alarm an American soldier began firing at him in the water, thinking it was just some old floating object. When John Wyndham told Harold Macmillan of his escape, Macmillan said: 'I expect he thought you were an empty hock bottle.'

## 29 September 1961

Perry Worsthorne tells me that Gaitskell, after having a talk with Lord Home, the Foreign Secretary, the other day about the Berlin Crisis, remarked: 'The trouble with Home is that he still thinks of appeasement.' How curious that even an intelligent man like Gaitskell still sees modern affairs through a mist of Munich sentiments. In any case, though Home certainly used to be PPS to Neville Chamberlain, he is being very firm over Berlin.

To Covent Garden for Hans Hotter's* production of *Die Walküre*. Lovely orchestra and singing in Act One. It is also an agreeable surprise to see all the characters. A pleasant mise-en-scène. Act Three, sheer delight. I have never heard Hotter sing better or move with greater dignity. Prolonged applause at the end – but Lord Drogheda† and others in the Royal Box slink away in the middle of the ovation. No doubt they had to catch the last bus.

## 6 October 1961

John Wyndham tells me the story of how, as Macmillan's Private Secretary at the Foreign Office, he was responsible for arranging a dinner given by Macmillan in Geneva for the Foreign Ministers of the Great Powers. This took place in 1955. Macmillan was anxious to impress all the other delegates, so he decided that the meal should be served off gold plate. John was ordered to ring up Gladwyn Jebb, at that time our Ambassador in Paris, to ask him to bring the Waterloo plate from the Embassy. When this request was put to him, Gladwyn said: 'But nobody eats off gold plate nowadays.' To which John replied: 'Personally I always do.' This is of course quite true, as John maintains that otherwise the servants would break all his china. After being held up for two hours at the Swiss frontier, Gladwyn arrived in Geneva with the plate, and the dinner was a great success. It so happened that Gladwyn was put next to Molotov.‡ Gladwyn said to him: 'Don't you think it is delightful to dine by candlelight?' Molotov merely replied: 'In Moscow we have electric

---

* (1909–2003), celebrated German operatic bass-baritone and director of operas.

† Garrett Moore, 11th Earl of Drogheda (1910–88). MD of the *Financial Times* 1945–70, Chairman 1971–5; Chairman, Royal Opera House 1958–74. His memoirs in 1978 were appropriately called *Double Harness* (Weidenfeld & Nicolson).

‡ Vyacheslav Molotov (1890–1986), leading figure in the Soviet government from the 1920s. Minister for Foreign Affairs 1939–49 and 1953–6.

light.' But Jebb had his comeback: 'Ah, but the Grand Dukes used to dine by candlelight.'

## 9 October 1961

Geordie Ward once told Boofy Arran that he had four trays on his desk in the Air Ministry – In, Out, Pending & Oh, Christ.

## 10 October 1961

Mervyn Stockwood, Bishop of Southwark, an impressive figure in purple, tells me: 'A psychiatrist is a man who goes to the Folies Bergère & looks at the audience.' How I hate worldly bishops. Osbert Lancaster whispers to me: 'I am told that before appearing on TV he now uses <u>two</u> shades of blue rinse on his hair.'

## 11 October 1961

As is customary, Sir Austin Strutt had a draft of the Queen's Speech prepared before the Commonwealth Party Conference in Westminster Hall on 25 September. The draft was approved by the CRO and then sent up to the Queen, who also approved it. But, coming down from Balmoral in the train on the night of 24 September, Prince Philip made several alterations to the speech. These were telephoned by Michael Adeane to Strutt in the morning. The Home Secretary was away, and was not due to reach London until shortly before the Queen's Speech. But Strutt took it on himself to reject several of Prince Philip's emendations. There remained, however, one howler. Strutt had described the Commonwealth as 'a comity of nations'. Prince Philip changed this to 'organisation of nations' – which is exactly what it is not.

Prince Eddie is to appear in uniform at the Cenotaph on Remembrance Sunday this year for the first time. This is obviously suitable, as he is both a serving officer and the son of an officer killed in the war. Originally it was suggested by the Queen that Eddie and his wife[*] should only watch the ceremony from the Home Office balcony, and wear plain clothes. Princess Marina was so annoyed at this that she made arrangements to go and stay with her sister[†] at that time.

Another point about the Cenotaph service. For several years, the Home

---

[*] Katherine, Duchess of Kent (b. 1933). Chancellor of Leeds University 1966–99, during which time K.R. helped her with many of her speeches for formal occasions.
[†] Princess Olga of Greece (1903–97), wife of Prince Paul of Yugoslavia (1893–1976), Prince Regent of Yugoslavia 1934–41.

Secretary, as the minister responsible for civil defence, has laid a wreath last of all. Last year Rab Butler complained that it was infra-dig for a minister who had often acted as Prime Minister to perform right at the end. So this year he will still lay his wreath last of all, but in a gap left specially for him by the other wreath-layers. This will save him from having to walk round three sides of the Cenotaph.

Incidentally, Strutt adds, Butler has never yet committed himself publicly on the subject of the Common Market.

Martin Gilliat has just written to Strutt asking for information about Hurstpierpoint College, a minor public school which wants a visit from the Queen Mother. Strutt has replied that in his opinion the public schools occupy too small a part of our national field of education to receive such sustained attention from the Royal Family. In the last five years alone the Queen has visited fourteen public schools. Strutt thinks there should be many more visits to grammar schools and other state schools.

On the subject of Royal money, Strutt tells me that the late Duke of Kent, killed in an air crash while on active service in 1942, inherited about £350,000 from his father's private estate. But death duties, though at a reduced rate, had to be paid when he was killed. It is all tied up in trust for the children. That is why the Duchess was so poor. Nowadays she receives £20,000 of the £50,000 which the Queen has at her disposal for members of the Royal Family with no Civil List money. Eddie gets £3,000.

On the subject of Tony Armstrong-Jones's peerage, Strutt tells me that Prince Philip was against it. Princess Margaret not only insisted, but made herself quite ill with rage when she learned that the peerage patent would not be ready in time for Tony to carry out an official engagement in Glasgow as Earl of Snowdon.* Even though special measures were taken to speed up the patent, she had to bear this disappointment.

Strutt thinks that Prince Philip is still interfering too much in official matters.

### 13 October 1961

Lunch Martin Charteris at the Savoy. The first subject we discuss is whether Prince Charles will go to school at Gordonstoun on leaving Cheam. Martin says he is almost certain that it will be. The Queen is in favour of Eton, but obviously any father must have a strong say in the education of his children. The Queen Mother is a fierce advocate of Eton and the delay in making an

---

* When Harold Macmillan heard of the title he cruelly said: 'Making a mountain out of a mole hill.'

official announcement may well be in order to postpone deciding the issue against her.

Prince Charles is of good intelligence, but an introvert. So he may not be as happy at Gordonstoun as at Eton – or indeed after he has left.

We discuss Prince Philip. Martin agrees with me that he is arrogant, largely because he is praised so much as an after-dinner speaker. Nor do his staff criticise him as they should. 'He needs an Altrincham,' says Martin.

Much talk about the Queen's visit to Ghana next month. At Buckingham Palace they have grave fears for her safety. The dictatorial policy of Dr Nkrumah[*] has aroused much internal opposition, and he has hardly dared to leave his house since returning from his visit to the Iron Curtain countries. There is the possibility that someone will try to assassinate him during the Queen's visit – and thus put the Queen herself in danger. Buckingham Palace are trying to arrange that she travels in the same car as Nkrumah as little as possible. There is also the possibility that some people may demonstrate against Nkrumah and so lead to a bloody riot. In case of serious trouble the Queen would put to sea in *Britannia*.

*Following the letter that Kenneth had drafted for Tony Armstrong-Jones to send to Lord John Hope over the restoration costs of 1A, Kensington Palace on 5 August, he was often asked for advice and their friendship grew. In October 1961 there were press criticisms and Kenneth sent the following letter of reassurance and advice:*

## 24 October 1961, letter to Tony Armstrong-Jones
It was very pleasant to hear your voice again today. I am only sorry that our conversation should so often be about the misdemeanours of the Press.

May I offer a word of general advice on the subject. Now that you have become a member of the Royal Family, you are going to be perpetually exposed to a great deal of comment in the newspapers. Indeed, if there were not an intense public interest in even the most trivial details of Royal life, we should soon have a republic.

Mostly, I think, the comment will be fair. But sometimes, as you have good cause to know, it will be nasty and malicious. But anybody who chooses to enter public life – which in a sense you have done – must accept this nagging criticism in parts of the Press as inevitable.

---

[*] Dr Kwame Nkrumah (1909–72). Prime Minister of Ghana 1957–60; first President of the Republic of Ghana 1960–66.

Harold Nicolson once told me that when he first became a Member of Parliament in 1935, Stanley Baldwin, who was then Prime Minister, gave him this advice:

(a)  Always be nice to the Opposition.

(b)  Cancel your subscription to a Press-cutting agency.

(c)  Grow another skin.

I am sure that you always follow (a). You should certainly follow (b) – John Griffin will always be able to draw your attention to anything important and you will save yourself much anger and annoyance. In any case, what the public reads one day is nearly always forgotten the next. As for (c), I expect it just grows with time.

Most of what I have written you will possibly think either obvious or impertinent. But you will also, I hope, know that it is only affection for you which has prompted me to write.

### 25 October 1961

Lunch with Charles Forte* at the Café Royal. A high office looking out towards Westminster and hung with a mixed bag of pictures, including several Lowrys.

He tells me that contrary to popular belief he is not a Socialist. In fact, he votes Conservative, but cares desperately for every kind of welfare. He insists upon the obligations of charity which fall on rich men.

A characteristic story about Prince Philip. The other day he came to the Café Royal to present awards to Regent Street shopkeepers for export-window displays, or some such thing. Among those presented to Prince Philip was Mr Rayne of the shoe firm.† The following conversation ensued:

Prince: 'What do you do, Mr Rayne?'

Rayne: 'I make shoes, sir.'

Prince: 'Are you the export manager?'

Rayne: 'No, as a matter of fact I am Chairman of the company, which has the honour to make the Queen's shoes.'

Prince: 'That's why she's always complaining about her feet, no doubt.'

Prince Philip simply cannot realise the harm that this perpetual banter does him.

In the evening to cocktail party at the Spanish Embassy. Malcolm Sargent

---

* Sir Charles Forte, Baron Forte (1908–2007), hotelier. He bought the Café Royal in 1954.

† Sir Edward Rayne (1922–92), head of H.&M. Rayne; the firm had a royal warrant for supplying shoes to the Queen and the Queen Mother.

tells me the story of a rich American being shown round somebody's house in Paris. He makes an intelligent remark about every single picture he is shown, until eventually his hostess says: 'And you must not miss this Sargent.'* 'Yes,' replies the American, 'it reveals Malcolm in every stroke of the brush.'

## 27 October 1961
At 10.45 go to Whitehall Court to talk to Lord Woolton about Jim Cilcennin for my *DNB* notice.

Jim, he says, epitomised the English idea of making a point by understatement. In politics most people do the opposite. Jim had a very easy manner. Often his sentences ended with a 'Don't you think?' and a slight giggle. This was completely disarming.

Winston always referred to him as J.P.L. Inside the Central Office, whatever they may have called him in conversation, he was universally known as Jim. The significance of all this is that it was the source of his power. He very easily won the confidence of people, so they opened out to him. They never knew when being interviewed of the shrewdness of the judgement that was being passed on them.

Woolton and I next passed to Jim's relations with other Conservative politicians. 'I would not have stood for a moment,' Woolton said, 'with the way Winston treated Service ministers. He was not a leader, he was a driver. If ever Winston had been trained for business he would have known that wasn't the way to get the best out of people. But in Winston's treatment of Jim there was a subtle difference. He was much more sympathetic. I attribute this to the fact that both of them had a deep love for the Admiralty. Both were imbued with the traditions of the Navy. When Jim went to the Admiralty I was doubtful if he would get on with Mountbatten, but they never quarrelled. One must give Jim a great deal of credit that he recognised the value of Mountbatten's work.

'When I went to Central Office, it was made clear to me by some of the staff that Jim had been sent there by Eden to look after Eden's interests. I was very sorry indeed when I later saw signs that the friendship between Jim and Eden was breaking. I thought it was due in no small measure to Eden's desire not to show favouritism.

'In connection with Eden, Jim once showed how great he was in his judgements. Early in my period as Chairman of the party I heard that Eden had been very indiscreet about me over a supper table in Liverpool. So I said to Jim: "You had better go and tell your friend Eden that it was careless of

---

* John Singer Sargent (1856–1925), American artist famous for his portraits.

him to say this in Liverpool, where I have many friends, and that if he talks of me in this way I will arrange no more meetings for him." The next day Jim came into my room with a book which he wanted me to read. It was Timothy Eden's *Tribulations of a Baronet*,* the life of Anthony's father and the key to his own life – pathetically so, adds Woolton; he would say things not meaning them and then forget he had said them.

'In 1955, when Eden succeeded Winston as Prime Minister, I was the first man to serve with him. We worked intimately together and I saw signs of his outbursts of temper. The interesting thing was that an hour or two afterwards he was quite unaware of having said anything to disturb anybody. There's a character study if you like! Emotionally I am very fond of Anthony, but if you see Eden, be careful of what he says about Jim. It is a common practice among politicians to say that everybody is a great friend of theirs. This is not true. You are fortunate indeed if you have a very small number of friends. Woolton's final judgement on Jim is that he was a good second in command, but should not be built too high.'

My final remarks with Woolton concern Winston Churchill. Not long ago he telephoned Clemmie to ask whether he should come and see Winston. Clemmie replied: 'Please don't. He is very rarely lucid nowadays.'

### 1 November 1961

12 noon. Walk in golden sunshine through the park to Kensington Palace, heavily guarded by police, for drink with Princess Margaret and Tony.

Gin and tonic served. Then Princess Margaret says that Tony & I probably want to talk alone, but that we are not to be too long. We go down to the basement room where he has his workshop and photographic equipment. Also his secretary, who is typing out a draft of a speech he will give on some photographic occasion.

I sit in the only comfortable chair and Tony sits on the edge of the table, swinging his legs. He looks rather worn and harassed. He begins: 'What are people saying about my change of name?' I reply that there has been no great enthusiasm for it. He adds, with much feeling: 'I do hope people do not think that I wanted the title myself. The Queen wished me to have it, and it would have been arrogant of me to have refused.' I mention that many of us thought that the title would have been given to Princess Margaret. 'If that had happened,' he replied, 'it would have been thought that the Queen was deliberately snubbing me.' He adds: 'In any case, the title is not really important. In a year or two it will be accepted as quite natural.'

---

* Sir Timothy Eden, 8th Bt (1893–1963), author of the life of his father, 1933.

This leads us to the general question of his popularity in the country (the secretary has meanwhile been sent out of the room). I tell him that there is still mild disapproval of the fact that – as far as the public knows – he is not doing a proper job. He replies that he does not now go regularly to his office at the Council of Industrial Design because the work is administrative and he is not cut out for it. He goes on: 'I am also completely redesigning the interior of the new Kensington Palace house. I take photographs and make films. I have designed an aviary for London Zoo, which takes a very long time to construct. And furthermore, Princess Margaret deserves the eighteen months she is taking off; if I help her to enjoy them and to run the house, I think it is an important duty. I don't care what the public thinks. I want to be a real person, not a specially designed image for public consumption. In fact, I hope to take on certain public duties, including a charity which I shall run. But I shall do so slowly and in my own time.'

He continues: 'There is another thing. I am accused of living off my wife. That is not true. I worked hard as a photographer and can now live off what I earned. The legend of me being a Cinderella is absurd. Before I married I lived in much greater luxury than I do now. At present I am living in a bed-sitter for the first time in my life! When I used to sell photographs to the *Daily Express* I was always treated with great respect as a rich dilettante who condescended to let them have some of my pictures.'

We pass on to the subject of the new house at KP. Tony thought the letter to Lord John Hope which I drafted for him very good indeed, and sent it off. But the Ministry of Works did not agree that a Press conference would do any good in revealing that the building would have to be restored in any case, whoever occupied it. So work will begin on its restoration without the public's knowing what a dilapidated state it is in. But here Tony has been very clever. He has taken about 100 photographs showing in much detail exactly how poor a state the Ministry has allowed the house to fall into. If ever there is a campaign against him and Princess Margaret for their extravagance in having £70,000 spent on the house, he will be able to produce – and if necessary publish in the Press – this pictorial record of decay.

Finally, he talks about the speeches he has to make from time to time. He shows me the one he made in Glasgow the other day – a little too lapidary for his own style, but containing some provoking ideas. He asks me if I will help him with their drafting when necessary, and of course I agree.

By now we have talked for over forty minutes and we go upstairs. Princess Margaret comes out to join us on the steps and says: 'We are besieged at both ends of Kensington. At one end are the Press, at the other end the ban-the-bomb-sit-downers!' Then some scathing remarks about John Osborne. She does not look to be at all in the last stages of pregnancy.

They have the gates leading into the park specially unlocked by a nice elderly butler so that I need not walk all the way round.

## 9 November 1961

Harold Nicolson dined last night with Louis Spears. Harold Watkinson, the Minister of Defence, a fellow guest, said that he had earlier in the day been at the Cabinet meeting which decided that in spite of bomb outrages the Queen would leave for her visit to Ghana tomorrow. He announced this to all the other guests. Whereupon, Bruce,* the American Ambassador, immediately got up and proposed a toast to her. Harold comments: 'I have never loved my countrymen more. They all looked so embarrassed at this un-English behaviour.'

In the course of dinner, Harold adds, the Ambassador questioned Oliver Chandos very closely on what exactly happens in Cabinet when a minister disagrees with the Prime Minister. Chandos replies: 'He resigns, exchanges polite letters with the Prime Minister in *The Times*, and then gets a job in industry at four times his ministerial salary.' Bruce appeared very shocked at this. So did Watkinson, who takes life seriously.†

## 16 November 1961

John Griffin to dine at the flat. He tells me that all Martin Gilliat's energies during the last week have been devoted to the Queen Mother's visit to Eton tomorrow evening. First she will attend a concert in School Hall. Then she is to visit a house – Martin has even had an annotated house list prepared for her. Quite rightly, John thinks that Martin devotes far too much attention to Eton, and that the interest in Eton which he inspires in the QM is harmful to her, to Eton and himself.

We have much discussion about Tony. The Household at Clarence House are very bored indeed with him. When drinks are being poured out he expects this to be done for him by the Household, and so on. And they are also much shocked by his extraordinary dress.

Part of the trouble, of course, is that he is neither Royal nor non-Royal, and never quite knows when to be either. It is also hard luck on him that he was never in any Service. So he had to appear on the balcony with all the

---

\* David Bruce (1898–1977), US Ambassador to the UK 1961–9; previously Ambassador to France 1949–52 and to Germany 1957–9.

† This attitude did not, however, prevent Watkinson, seven months later, after he had been sacked in the Night of the Long Knives, from taking up important roles in industry, including the Chairmanship of Cadbury Schweppes.

Royal ladies at the Cenotaph Service last Sunday. Like Princess Margaret he will not confide in his staff. Thus John Griffin had a very difficult time with the Press because he did not know that Tony had given his patronage to the National Youth Theatre – Tony did not think it necessary to tell him of the appointment. John mentions that Tony was very diffident about troubling me for help with his speech to the Royal Photographic Society, and worried about it for twenty-four hours before telephoning me on Sunday.

## 17 November 1961

At 5 p.m. to Eaton Square to see Anthony Eden to talk about Jim Cilcennin. Eden looks very brown and fit, better than I have seen him for some time. He still has that curiously vain habit of smoothing his hair as he talks.

He tells me that he first got to know Jim almost by accident. In 1937 Eden's PPS was Roger Lumley,* who in that year became Governor of Bombay. David Margesson suggested that Jim should succeed him.† Jim had had previous experience of this type of work, having already been PPS to J.H. Thomas.

'He, Bobbety and I worked very closely indeed with each other. They both resigned with me in February 1938. When I went off to the South of France, Jim came with me. We saw Stanley Baldwin there. I also saw a great deal of Jim after my resignation when we formed a group of MPs who were out of sympathy with the Government. We met either at Ronnie Tree's‡ house in Queen Anne's Gate or at Jim's own house in Little College Street. There were about thirty of us.§ I was the unofficial chairman. Jim was the unofficial secretary. Winston did not belong to this group.¶ At that time he was writing his life of Marlborough and so could not attend the House of Commons regularly. But he used to come up and make set speeches. All of us abstained from voting at the time of Munich.'

At the outbreak of the war Jim wanted to join up but was rejected because of a bad knee. From then onwards he devoted all his energies to politics. His manner belied his efficiency. There was so much underneath. He was

---

* 11th Earl of Scarbrough (1896–1969), British Army General and Conservative statesman; Governor of Bombay 1937–43.

† Capt. David Margesson, 1st Viscount (1890–1965), Conservative politician. Government Chief Whip 1931–40; War Secretary 1940–42.

‡ Ronald Tree (1897–1976), Conservative MP for Harborough 1933–45.

§ The group were known as 'The Glamour Boys'. See D.R. Thorpe, 'The Glamour Boys', *DNB*, reference themes.

¶ John Churchill, 1st Duke of Marlborough (1650–1722), victor of the Battle of Blenheim, 1704. Winston Churchill wrote his biography in four volumes, 1933–8.

politically tough and far-seeing – a very formidable mixture of Irish and Welsh blood.

He was a facile speaker who could handle the House well. He liked talking to people behind the scenes rather than making speeches. He was a great manager of men; we owed much to him for the Conservative candidates he chose.

The ambition of his life was to go to the Admiralty, but he had increasing trouble with his health. 'Shortly before his death he talked to me about his operation. I was, after all, rather a specialist in operations at that time.'

Eden is vague – I suspect deliberately so – about the part played by Jim at the Admiralty when Nasser nationalised the Suez Canal Company. But he does say: 'We simply were not ready at the time. The operation would have taken six weeks to mount. So we got ready for action.'

He was even vaguer about the actual circumstances in which Jim left the Admiralty. As Jim told me at the time, he was not unwilling to leave but felt that both Eden and Bobbety had behaved shabbily. Eden also mentions that it was hard luck on Jim that he had to clear up the mess about Commander Crabb. One final word from Eden about Jim – 'He was the best personal friend in the world.'

### 27 November 1961

Clever of Sir Alec Douglas-Home to have succeeded in his work on the Rhodesian problems – though the Labour Party will never give him any credit for it. And how like Denis Healey* to drag up the fact that Alec was Neville Chamberlain's Private Secretary at the time of Munich. I am surprised nobody on the Conservative side of the Commons reminded Healey that in 1938 he had been a member of the Communist Party.

### 2 December 1961

Dine at University College, London, where Angus Wilson has just given the first of his Northcliffe Lectures.† Angus Wilson talks perpetually at dinner. What surprises me is that he is as sensitive as Virginia Woolf used to be about reviews of her novels. When he read Raymond Mortimer's comment on his latest novel, *The Old Men at the Zoo* – 'all zoo lovers will welcome this book' – he said to himself: 'Why do I bother to go on writing?' He is perpetually annoyed at the anti-cultural conspiracy which dominates English

---

* Baron Healey (1917–2015), Labour politician. Chancellor of the Exchequer 1974–9.
† The first of four lectures in this annual literary event on the subject of 'Evil in the English Novel'.

letters. Wilson has a store of anecdotes about his years on the staff of the Reading Room at the British Museum. When he joined there was one old curator who told him: 'Don't answer readers' questions. The only people who ask questions are Bolsheviks and perverts.'

## 5 December 1961

About 2.30 Tony Armstrong-Jones telephones to ask if I would like to come round to Clarence House. He wants my help in the speech he is giving at the annual dinner next week of the Royal Photographic Society.

By cab to the Household entrance, where John Griffin takes me through to the private side. The front doors are wide open, and it is very chilly. Tony has been given a sitting room at the front of the house, looking onto the hall. It is very still and rural behind the trees. The room is full of expensive flowers sent to Princess Margaret. Also two pictures by Edward Seago* – a seascape and a conversation piece of the Queen Mother and Princess Margaret.

All the tables are strewn with drafts of the speech. Tony says he has got into a panic with it, and needs my help. So I sit down at the writing table and draft the speech according to what he wants to say. His ideas seem lively and original – tributes to photo-journalists, the need to hang photographic exhibitions in an interesting way, the importance of escaping from clichés and the lack of a good photographic centre in London. Once we have planned the speech in detail he becomes much more cheerful.

A huge tray of tea is brought in. 'Look,' says Tony, as excited as a little boy, 'a great meal, with knives and forks and buns and things.' And it is indeed a good tea, with smoked-salmon sandwiches and an iced cake. Then, an hour later, there is a tray of whisky, with Malvern water and soda.

Tony tells me that he rarely reads a book. 'It is a family thing. If I have the time for reading I prefer to spend it doing something with my hands.' Nor does he intend to go to the House of Lords – 'unless I have to make a speech attacking the Minister of Works for the way he has behaved over Kensington Palace!'.

At home I read 'John Bull's Schooldays', a series of articles published in *The Spectator*. One is particularly brilliant – by Malcolm Muggeridge, saying that the advantage of a state- over a public-school education is that it does not tie one to the past.

---

* (1910–74), celebrated artist from Norfolk. He was a great favourite of the Royal Family and gave lessons to the young Prince Charles.

## 7 December 1961

Anthony Eden is furious about Iain Macleod's biography of Neville Chamberlain. He has indeed been badly done by. He went to Winston and bellowed at him, 'Who's the author?'* When told it was Iain Macleod, he said, 'Isn't he the nasty man who was Minister of Health?'

## 9 December 1961

At the Beefsteak dear old Eddie Winterton† sits at the head of the table. He is now very blind, but his conversation has lost none of its sparkle. We talk about Anthony Eden. I mention to Winterton how much Eden must have inherited of his father's instability. Winterton thereupon tells me this story about Sir William Eden, Anthony's father. He once asked a woman to lunch with him, intending to seduce her afterwards. When she arrived, Sir William asked her how she liked his new drawing room. She replied: 'It's quite nice, but I think it could do with a few palms.' Sir William was so angry at her lack of appreciation that he had lunch served to her alone while he had his in his bedroom.

At the Other Club the other evening Winterton sat next to Winston. He sat slumped in his chair most of the evening, but revived a great deal when Winterton asked him about his recent horse-racing successes. Apparently Winston relies very much on Christopher Soames‡ nowadays and treats him like a son.

## 13 December 1961

At a dinner at the French Embassy, Christopher Soames tells me that the one thing he never got used to as Winston's PPS was the number of people begging for honours – 'Of course I don't care for these things, but the wife would like it.' He says how much is lost to history by not dictating a minute, but issuing orders verbally in the Ministry or doing a job through a Private Secretary. Winston always liked working on paper.

---

* A good question. Iain Macleod published the biography in 1961 under his name, but the book, sympathetic to Chamberlain and critical of Eden, was largely ghostwritten by Peter Goldman (1925–87), who later did much the same for Rab Butler's memoirs, *The Art of the Possible* (Hamish Hamilton, 1971).

† Edward Turnour, 6th Earl Winterton (1883–1962), served at Gallipoli in World War I, twice mentioned in despatches for service in Palestine and Arabia. Unionist politician, for the constituency of Horsham in its various guises, 1904–51; Paymaster General 1939.

‡ Baron Soames (1920–87), Conservative politician, m. 1947 Mary Churchill, dau. of Winston. MP for Bedford 1950–66; War Secretary 1958–60; Minister of Agriculture, Fisheries and Food 1960–4; British Ambassador to France 1968–72; European Commissioner for Trade 1973–7.

I also hear that the latest Scout Gang Show* is very bizarre, with the scout uniforms in brightly coloured red and blue silk, 'like an obscene floor show in Cairo!'.

---

* The Gang Shows, featuring Boy Scouts in variety and musical turns, were first started in 1932 by Ralph Reader (1903–82), theatrical producer, and became a national institution, particularly in the festive season.

# 1962

### 4 January 1962

Osbert Lancaster tells me that a judge once asked counsel, who had mentioned the London Coliseum, where it was, adding that he thought it was the place where Romans threw Christians to the lions. 'My Lord,' explained counsel, 'it is ten minutes' walk from the Trocadero, where the Lyons throw food to the Christians.'

Also a story of the present Duke of Wellington. When Nancy Mitford was staying with him at Stratfield Saye they attended an official Remembrance Day parade, and felt rather sad on the way back. But as they drove through the gates he brightened up, saying: 'Oh well, if it hadn't been for two world wars I shouldn't be here.'*

### 5 January 1962

Extraordinary news. Tony Armstrong-Jones is to join staff of *Sunday Times* as an art director, his work to help the new coloured supplement they are producing next month. He has chosen to have this controversial news announced while he is having a holiday in the West Indies.

It is a bad decision. He is throwing the weight of his Royal, rather than artistic, connections into the battle for circulation among Sunday newspapers, and cannot complain if he is savagely attacked for doing so. Of course, the Royal Family always feel that Conservative politics are no politics, but he has nevertheless joined the most Conservative of newspapers. This move also comes at a time when there is disquiet at the big sum being spent by the Government on the Wren house in Kensington Palace he and Princess Margaret are to occupy.

### 7 January 1962

Dine Pratt's and have much entertaining conversation with old Lord Goddard.

---

* Lord Gerald Wellesley became Duke because his brother Richard was killed in 1914 and his nephew Henry in 1943.

He describes how a barrister defending a man of rape pleaded that the prisoner was so short-sighted that he had an inferiority complex, and thought this had upset him emotionally. When he had been found guilty Goddard addressed him as follows: 'A psychiatrist has said that what you really need is a new pair of spectacles. I say you need four years and you will have them.'

Goddard also says: 'It is almost impossible to get a conviction for incest north of the Trent; in the West, especially Wales, it is quite easy.' He also describes the trial of a man who shot a policeman in Curzon Street. Goddard: 'I determined to give him twenty-one years, so that not even Mr Butler would be able to release him before he had served fourteen.' At this, a rather toady member of Pratt's says: 'Ah, you obviously thought the sentence would see you out.' 'No,' explodes Goddard, 'I thought the sentence would see <u>him</u> out.'

### 27 January 1962, letter to parents

I saw the new Peter Sellers film *Only Two Can Play*, based on the Kingsley Amis novel, *That Uncertain Feeling*. But it was not at all as amusing and sophisticated as the novel on which it is based.

The Duke of Devonshire,* my neighbour when lunching at the Beefsteak the other day, told me a story about his grandfather, that wooden-faced man who used to be Chancellor of Leeds University. When he was put into the Cabinet in the 1920s, somebody complained to him that there were too many peers in office. 'That's all right,' he answered, 'we have that fellow Pigge to run the Government in the Commons.' He meant Douglas Hogg,† Quintin Hailsham's father.

### 30 January 1962

I talk to Prince Bernhard of the Netherlands‡ about Suez. He is very amused when I tell him that in the muddle, the first truck to be landed was the officers' mess truck of the Household Cavalry. He believes that we should have struck at Egypt straight away and not mounted what he calls 'a Monty operation', i.e. a preparation so detailed that it lost all impetus. He dislikes Monty intensely and says that although the Field Marshal sent him his photograph after the war like all other Allied leaders, it has no affectionate or even respectful

---

* Victor Cavendish, 9th Duke of Devonshire (1868–1938). Governor General of Canada 1916–21; Colonial Secretary 1922–4. When the RAF in Amman were asked who had succeeded Churchill as Colonial Secretary in 1922, they telegraphed: 'The Duke of Devonshire, thank God a gentleman.'

† 1st Viscount Hailsham (1872–1950), lawyer and Conservative politician. Lord Chancellor 1928–9.

‡ (1911–2004), Prince Consort of the Netherlands 1948–80.

inscription. Also on the subject of Suez the Prince says: 'I told Kilmuir that you should not have mounted a military operation at all, instead you should have offered £5,000 for Nasser's head. Kilmuir was very shocked.'

Talking about the German General Staff, Bernhard says that one reason why the generals supported Hitler for so long was that he revived the custom of rewarding the victorious not only with pensions, but also with estates. They turned against him only when it became obvious that there would never be the victories by which these rewards could be earned.

While in South Africa, the Prince tells me, many South Africans drew his attention with relish to the fact that Great Britain had first introduced concentration camps. He disliked the South African officials very much. They hate the Dutch for not having joined Hitler and would not let him have a parade of ex-servicemen during his visit.

### 31 January 1962, letter to Sir Frederic Hooper

You have probably seen that Hannen Swaffer* died on 16 January. I am told that his funeral was conducted by a spiritualist 'priest' who announced at the end of the service: 'How wonderful it is to think that our dear friend is now in the arms of George Lansbury.'†

A very good remark one evening at dinner from Lady Victor Paget,‡ who used to be the Duke of Windsor's particular friend: 'I never called him David like that vulgar Mrs Simpson. Either I called him sir, or I called him darling.'

Mrs Kelley,§ that most competent Governor of Holloway Prison, where I have promised to lecture next month, tells me that the committee of 100 ban-the-bomb women are very arrogant. They annoy the criminal prisoners enormously by trying to patronise them.

### 19 February 1962

To Bishopthorpe for tea with the Archbishop of York, Donald Coggan. It is about three miles from York, and looks out over the river. To the palace through an imposing and ornate eighteenth-century gateway.

Dr Coggan is as charming as always and we talk for more than an hour over tea. First we discuss the various revisions of Church documents in which he is engaged.

1. The Catechism. After four years' work, it is being published by the SPCK

---

* (1879–1962), journalist and drama critic, a proponent of spiritualism.
† (1859–1940), Labour Party leader 1932–5.
‡ Bridget, Lady Victor Paget (1892–1975), dau. of the 1st Baron Colebrook.
§ Joanna Kelley (1910–2003), Governor of Holloway Prison 1959–66.

on 27 February. It is to be given a seven-year trial. It includes a great deal of new material not in the Prayer Book.

2. <u>The Psalter.</u> About a year ago the revisers published psalms 1–41. This spring they will publish psalms 42–106. By next year they hope to have completed the task. Meetings are held about four times a year, mostly at Lambeth. But one or two have been held at Selwyn College, Cambridge, and the Archbishop hopes to invite the revisers to Bishopthorpe.

3. <u>Liturgical Commission.</u> The Archbishop followed the Dean of Lincoln[*] into the Chairmanship of this. Matins and Evensong will soon be presented to the archbishops, followed by prayers and thanksgiving; then the Litany.

4. <u>Revision of the Bible.</u> During the revision of the New Testament work has been continuing on the Old Testament. This is likely to take another four or five years before completion.[†]

We discussed the recent television broadcast which he made with Adam Faith.[‡] He maintains that he was absolutely right to undertake this, and did so only after satisfying himself in conversation that Adam Faith would approach the subject of religion seriously. One or two said it looks as though he wants to fill the Church with teddy-boys. To which he replied that that is precisely what he wants to do.

This leads us to discuss the merits of modern English against those of the Authorised Version, and we cannot quite bridge the gap between us. The Archbishop points out that I am approaching the problem with the mind of a highly educated person and it is essential to make the meaning of the Bible clear, even at the expense of the awe engendered by seventeenth-century prose. I maintain that the English of the new translation will itself have dated in less than 100 years – so one might as well stick to the Authorised Version.[§]

On the subject of the Royal Family, he thinks that Princess Margaret does little to disarm mounting public criticism of her. One reason for this, he thinks, is that she appears to have no idea of how ordinary people live. Mervyn Stockwood, Bishop of Southwark, told him that the Princess had asked him not very long ago: 'I suppose you have a swimming bath of your

---

[*] The Rt Revd David Dunlop (1897–1968). Bishop of Jarrow 1944–9; Dean of Lincoln 1949–64.

[†] The Old Testament of the New English Bible was published in 1970.

[‡] Singer, born Terence Nelhams (1940–2003). The recorded TV interview with the Archbishop of York was broadcast on 25 Jan. 1962.

[§] T.S. Eliot, reviewing the New English Bible New Testament, was to comment that the translation 'astonishes in its combination of the vulgar, the trivial, and the pedantic', adding that, if adopted for religious services, 'the more it will become an active agent of decadence'. *Sunday Telegraph*, 16 Dec. 1962.

own.' Stockwood had replied that he used the public baths.

The Archbishop is enjoying living at Bishopthorpe enormously. He has inherited a good domestic staff and has also managed to lighten his burden by learning to sleep in a car between engagements. He has met huge numbers of people at receptions, but prefers little groups of about six.

Before I leave he shows me over the state rooms of the palace. There is a particularly charming chapel. In the dining room, looking out over the river, is a very long refectory table. It was bought by Cosmo Gordon Lang[*] for £5. Before he left York he had been offered £1,000 for it.

The dining room is hung with portraits of recent archbishops, including the famous Orpen[†] of Lang and a new portrait of Michael Ramsey.

## 20 February 1962

Travel down by the afternoon train from York in time to dine with Harold Nicolson at the Beefsteak. Harold has just returned from his cruise to the Caribbean. As one might expect, he took great enjoyment in picking little quarrels with his fellow passengers. He describes how a military-looking gentleman accosted him on the first day:

'Is that an Old Harrovian tie you are wearing?'

'No, it is an Old Wellingtonian tie.'

'Ah, Wellington, very good school.'

'You know nothing whatsoever about it, it is a very bad school.'

Again, a woman passenger boasted to him that before she sailed Anthony Eden had sent her some cigarettes. Harold replied: 'And you mean to tell me that you accepted a present from the Prime Minister who has done more to dishonour the name of his country since Lord North?' But she had never heard of Lord North.[‡]

## 25 February 1962

*Sunday Times* coloured supplement still unimpressive.

---

* 1st Baron Lang of Lambeth (1864–1945). Archbishop of York 1908–28; Archbishop of Canterbury 1928–42. In May 1937 he crowned George VI and Queen Elizabeth at Westminster Abbey.

† Sir William Orpen (1878–1931), Irish artist. His portrait of Lang dates from 1924. 'They say in that portrait I look proud, prelatical and pompous,' observed Lang, to which Hensley Henson remarked, 'And may I ask Your Grace to which of these epithets Your Grace takes exception?' The Rt Revd Hensley Henson (1863–1947), Dean of Durham 1912–18; Bishop of Hereford 1918–20; Bishop of Durham 1920–39.

‡ Frederick North, 2nd Earl of Guilford (1732–92), Prime Minister of Great Britain 1770–82; he presided over the loss of the American colonies.

Lunch with William Stormont[*] at his house near the Royal Hospital, Chelsea. We have our usual dispute – this time about whether Eton should be preserved as it is. Also most interesting information about the practice by which judges are given a list of a prisoner's previous convictions even before the trial has started. Lord Devlin, for whom William was once Marshal, used to study the list in his lodgings the night before the trial. He would pencil in the appropriate sentence and stick to it if the prisoner was found guilty. This prevented his being swayed by the horrible evidence sometimes given and so giving the man too unfair a sentence.

Anthony and Carol Wedgwood Benn come in for a drink in the evening. He has just returned from the USA, where he was shocked to find that there was no articulate opinion on the Left – the opinions of Lord Home would be thought rather radical.

He is having a splendid row with Sam Watson,[†] the Durham miners' leader. Each year the speakers at the Durham miners' gala are elected by ballot. Anthony was delighted to be invited, but shocked that Watson should have written to him: 'Dear Lord Stansgate'. In reply to Anthony's request that he should be billed as Wedgwood Benn, Watson said that it was the tradition of the gala, going back ninety years, that a speaker should be billed under the name for which the miners voted – Lord Stansgate. Anthony thereupon told him that he himself was fighting a tradition that goes back 900 years, and hoped to win. There the matter rests.

*In March 1962 Kenneth had four weeks in New York to meet American politicians such as Adlai Stevenson and important personalities, including British diplomats and artistic figures. He aimed to find out as much as he could about life in the United States and the Kennedy administration, an example of his inquisitive nature of filling gaps in his first-hand knowledge. Whilst he was away Bill Deedes wrote the 'Albany' column for him. As in the United Kingdom, the range of his contacts was extraordinary, with visits to the White House, the United Nations, the British Embassy and the Metropolitan Opera House, among many landmark places.*

---

[*] William Murray, 13th Viscount Stormont (1930–2015), developed Scone Palace, Perthshire as a tourist attraction. Minister of State in the Scottish and Northern Ireland offices 1979–83 and 1983–4.

[†] (1898–1967), General Secretary of the National Union of Mineworkers (Durham Area) 1947. Member of the Labour Party's NEC for twenty-two years. Had Labour won the 1959 general election, Gaitskell was believed to have decided to appoint Watson Foreign Secretary.

## 7 March 1962

After lunch I call on Osborn Elliott,* the Editor of *Newsweek*, who wrote a pleasant piece in his magazine about the *Sunday Telegraph*. He talks at great length on the way that the space flight of Colonel Glenn† has inspired all America.

Invited by Rudolf Bing‡ to hear Verdi's *Ballo in Maschera* at the Metropolitan Opera. In the interval I have a most pleasant talk with Bing in his office. There is an unexpected step down into his office. He turns round and says to me: 'Mind the step. I do not say that to everyone.'

After telling him how much I was enjoying the rather elaborate production of the opera I ask him why he does not exclude members of the audience who arrive late (as happens in England) instead of allowing them to distract others. He replies that the traffic problem of New York is so overwhelming that people frequently arrive late, and that there is no place where they can wait in comfort outside. When the new Opera House is built at the Lincoln Center things will be much better.

I tell him how interested I am to note that his production has been made possible by a gift from Mrs John D. Rockefeller.§ He replies that it is only by means of this private patronage that he can stage new productions. Before he came to New York, a whole season would sometimes go by without a new production. Now there are four or five new productions each year, each costing more than 100,000 dollars. Some spectacular operas, such as Puccini's *Turandot*, cost between 200,000 and 300,000 dollars.

## 9 March 1962

Call on David Ogilvy,¶ who is having such a brilliant success with his advertising agency. He is about to run a campaign to persuade Europeans to travel

---

* (1924–2008), Editor of *Newsweek* 1961–76.
† Col. John Glenn (b. 1921), American astronaut, the first to orbit the Earth on 20 Feb. 1962. US Democratic Senator 1975–98.
‡ Sir Rudolf Bing (1902–97), General Manager, Glyndebourne Opera 1935–49; Artistic Director, Edinburgh Festival 1947–9; General Manager, Metropolitan Opera, New York 1950–72. When the Swedish soprano Birgit Nilsson (1918–2005) sang the final scene from *Salome* at Bing's farewell gala, she waived her fee if she could have instead the head of Bing on the silver salver for John the Baptist's head. When she lifted the lid of the salver, a cake in the form of Bing's head was revealed.
§ Blanchette Ferry Rockefeller (1909–92), active in the world of museums and the arts.
¶ (1911–99), advertising executive, founder of Ogilvy & Mather. One of his most famous slogans was 'At sixty miles an hour the loudest noise in this new Rolls-Royce comes from the electric clock.'

to the United States and he shows me some magnificent photographs which have been taken for this purpose.

In the evening I go to the Eugene O'Neill Theatre to watch John Mills act in *Ross* by Terence Rattigan, the play about Lawrence of Arabia.

John Mills cut his hand while skating in Central Park the other day. It is heavily bandaged and is obviously giving him much pain. This disturbs me throughout the performance. I have a chat with him afterwards, and arrange to see him tomorrow morning.

Emerge from the theatre into a blizzard, but quite enjoy walking home through the fairly deserted streets.

## 10 March 1962

To the Frick Collection, charming building and wonderfully rich collection of pictures. Then to Algonquin Hotel to see John Mills. He is having bad nights from his injured hand, but of course coming on with the part of Lawrence of Arabia, his first stage appearance in USA. *Ross* opened on Boxing Day night. John Mills will stay in it until June. He is staying in Laurence Olivier's suite at the Algonquin, where actors are always welcome, and which he thinks resembles the Connaught in style. John Mills had many doubts whether *Ross* would succeed in New York, as so few Americans had heard of T.E. Lawrence. The last action of the play, when he puts on cycling clips before his fatal accident (his alias of Ross having been penetrated), does not often strike a chord with an American audience. But last night, in fact, I heard several gasps at that point. John Mills, who is doing a straight play after an interval of seven years, only once met T.E. Lawrence. At a rehearsal of *Cavalcade*, Noël Coward introduced them.

Drink with Nin Ryan[*] at her charming apartment overlooking the East River, next to United Nations HQ. She thinks Adlai Stevenson[†] a great disappointment as US Ambassador to the UN – far too soft with the Afro-Asians. She tells me that she lent her apartment to Princess Marina, who was very annoyed at the casual way shop girls treated her. Describes growth of Kennedy Royal Family image – including reluctance to pay for things they ask for, e.g. books.

---

[*] Margaret Kahn Ryan, (1901–94), fundraiser for the arts, especially the Metropolitan Opera after it moved to the Lincoln Center.
[†] Adlai Stevenson II (1900–65). Defeated Democratic Party candidate for the US Presidency 1952 and 1956; US Ambassador to the UN 1961–5.

## 14 March 1962

My impressions of America: rather absurd after only a week in NY and newly arrived in Washington – traffic problems, noise problems, absence of town planning between here and NY, newspapers, advertising, food. Walk past the White House, with lots of semi-tame squirrels.

Then to State Department for 3.30 Press conference given by President Kennedy. Much checking of names and passes before one is allowed into the theatre. We sit in very comfortable red-leather seats facing a platform. Behind it is a big curtain divided vertically into three – blue on the blanks, white in the centre. And in the middle of this white section is a brightly painted replica of the Presidential Seal. There is another smaller seal on the front of the desk at which the President is to stand. At the edge of the platform are men with pick-up microphones, like long grey guns on swivels, to be turned on the questioners once the conference has started.

A minute or two before the President enters, two or three men walk about displaying cards on which is written the number 301 – the number of correspondents present.

The President enters half a minute after 3.30. A brisk, rolling walk, and rather a heave as he mounts the step – which suggests that his back is not yet completely healed. Very sunburnt and youthful. Blue suit, white shirt, purplish tie, white handkerchief in breast pocket. Accompanied by his Press Secretary, Pierre Salinger,* and his black assistant, Andrew Hatcher,† who sit on chairs below him to his left. Very strong lights trained on the President for benefit of TV cameras.

The first question is about the President's brother, Edward Kennedy,‡ who is running as Democratic candidate for Massachusetts seat in Senate. The President, in replying, refers to him as Teddy. Then other questions on more serious topics follow – possible cuts in foreign aid programme, summit conference on disarmament, US economy, Atom-test inspections, defence contract and agricultural policy.

Kennedy never at a loss for a word, and produces his answers without a moment's hesitation. No humour about it. Is absolutely the master – indicated by the imperious way in which he points the forefinger at the journalist he chooses to ask the next question when they all leap to their feet. Again, on question of summit conference, 'I would go there if we were on the brink

---

* (1925–2004), White House Press Secretary to US Presidents John F. Kennedy and Lyndon B. Johnson (1908–73).

† (1923–90), Associate Press Secretary to President Kennedy. Founder, in 1963, of 100 Black Men of America, a civic organisation to educate African-American children and teenagers.

‡ (1932–2009), Democratic Senator from Massachusetts 1962–2009.

of war or a serous international crisis, <u>where my presence would make a significant difference.</u>'

Sparing use of gesture. The moment the conference ends he is out of the hall. The entire conference is shown on TV several times, later in the day.

## 15 March 1962

Letter from Pamela Berry. She encloses the full text from *The Spectator* of the recent attack by F.R. Leavis[*] on C.P. Snow. The last time I saw Charles Snow I asked him whether he had ever met Leavis, and whether he knew anything which could account for the savagery of Leavis' attack on him. He replied: 'No, I hardly know him at all. But he did once want to become a Fellow of Christ's, and failed. He may have mistakenly attributed this to me.'

At 11.45 to the new British Embassy to see David Ormsby-Gore, the Ambassador. An appalling modern building, in the style of a particularly ugly factory. Inside like a hospital, with soundless floors and aseptic passages.

The Ambassador's study is a large room with one wall of glass leading onto a balcony and commanding a view of the old mock-Georgian Lutyens Embassy, now used as the Ambassador's residence and to house the consular department.

We talk about the present disarmament talks at Geneva, where he was our representative for many months. 'I read the reports with particular interest and keep wondering why they didn't use this argument or that, why they didn't deal with the Russian tactics in such-and-such a way.'

I ask him what he thinks of Adlai Stevenson. He replies that although he once hoped Stevenson would be President, he no longer thinks it would be suitable. Stevenson finds it difficult to take a decision and, even more serious, was a poor negotiator at the United Nations; he would begin talks with the Russians by making concessions to the limit of US policy, so that even our own delegation, who were in general prepared to take a softer line than the Americans, became alarmed.

We discuss President Kennedy. Ormsby-Gore is naturally anxious that too much should not be made of his intimacy with Kennedy. It would annoy both the State Department and other countries. In fact, he adds, we see each other about once a week, particularly as we have many friends in common.

---

[*] (1895–1978), literary critic; based for much of his career at Downing Coll., Cambridge. In 1959 C.P. Snow had published *The Two Cultures and the Scientific Revolution* (Cambridge University Press), the Rede Lecture at Cambridge that year. On 28 Feb. 1962 Leavis gave the Richmond Lecture at Downing on Snow's thesis on the two cultures, which was published by *The Spectator* on 9 Mar. 1962. In it Leavis described Snow as 'portentously ignorant'. The subsequent controversy was widely reported and discussed.

The President is a great telephoner – just as Alan Lennox-Boyd was when a minister. The other day a call from Kennedy was put through to him in the middle of a Mardi Gras ball at New Orleans. I ask Ormsby-Gore whether the President talks to the PM by telephone very much (as Harold Macmillan likes to have it put about). Ormsby-Gore replies that he thinks it is rare.

The President's back is probably still not good, but his general health remains admirable, e.g. he does not wilt at the end of long talks like a man in pain. Kennedy generally goes to bed about 10.30. He has an extraordinary memory for all he reads, e.g. he noticed a small newspaper paragraph saying that Ormsby-Gore was having a new social secretary.

The Ambassador still takes interest in British politics and tells me that at the Orpington by-election yesterday, the Liberal, Eric Lubbock,* has won by 8,000 votes, beating Peter Goldman,† the Tory Central Office man. Conservative majority at last General Election was 15,000. A tremendous swing of 26.3 per cent. On the wall behind his desk is a solid bank of bound Hansards, which exactly match in colour the leather sofa on which we sit.

Ormsby-Gore is dissatisfied with both the Embassy building (like a tyre factory, he calls it) and its furniture (like a Mirabelle Hotel). But he is pleased that the Treasury have restored the money for the annual garden parties on the Queen's birthday. Sir Pierson Dixon in Paris sent a massive letter, and Ormsby-Gore also pointed out that it would make us look particularly silly if countries such as Mauritius had a national day while we said we could not afford it.

He tells me he is still not used to being harassed by the Press in the Washington fashion, e.g. whenever he comes out of Dean Rusk's office,‡ there are five or six reporters waiting to question him. On the first occasion, when he had been discussing answers to one of Khrushchev's letters to American and British Governments, he told reporters what the answer to it would be. This was published before Macmillan had approved, and he got a pained telegram from London.

### 16 March 1962
Have an appointment at the White House with Arthur Schlesinger.§ I am

---

* 4th Baron Avebury (1928–2016), Liberal MP for Orpington 1962–70.

† (1925–87), Director of Conservative Political Centre 1955–64; Director of the Consumers' Association 1964–87. Goldman was Rab Butler's ghostwriter for his memoirs and he also wrote Iain Macleod's biography of Neville Chamberlain.

‡ (1909–94), US Secretary of State 1961–9. Harold Macmillan, who had a penchant for nicknames, privately called him 'the biscuit man'.

§ (1917–2007), American historian. Special assistant to President Kennedy 1961–3.

shown to A.S.'s room, in great disorder, with books piled up on every chair and table. He is obviously overworked and under great pressure – and we have only been talking for a short time when he is called to the President. I ask him what chance there is of meeting Kennedy. He replies that he cannot help me in this, and that any such appointment must be arranged through Pierre Salinger, the Press Secretary. This, I fear, is the result of Cassandra of the *Daily Mirror*. Pamela Berry bullied A.S. into arranging an interview for him. It was to be strictly off the record, but Cassandra wrote about it, and apparently in an offensive way. So visiting British journalists are no longer received with open arms.

Just two other things which A.S. mentions. He is having nothing to do with the course of the Geneva disarmament talks. And he has heard that the President's Press conference on Wednesday last was not considered one of his best.

## 17 March 1962

Drive out to Mount Vernon,* now preserved as a George Washington shrine. It commands a superb view of the Potomac River. One sign of the times is that what were originally the slave quarters have now been relabelled 'Service Area'. The Queen came here during her visit to the United States, but laid a wreath on the wrong grave owing to faulty instructions.

Much enjoy the walk through the beautifully restored buildings and gardens. Also see a large spring-like robin.

It is unfortunately characteristic of American beauty spots that on a road nearby I see the notice: 'Photogenic Scenery at 1,000 feet' – as if tourists are too stupid to notice it for themselves.

At dinner I hear a story about Senator Barry Goldwater.† He applied to take part in a golf tournament, but was told that Jews were not permitted. He replied: 'May I not play nine holes? I am only half Jewish.'

There are very stringent drinking rules in Washington bars. One must sit, not stand, while drinking, and whisky is served only at tables, not at the bar. Nor is one allowed to carry a drink from table to table.

## 18 March 1962

Spend the morning going round the Capitol. It is most impressive, particularly

---

* Plantation house of George Washington (1731–99), first President of the US; designated a National Historic Landmark in 1960.

† (1909–80), Senator from Arizona 1953–64 and 1969–87; Republican Presidential candidate 1964.

the Hall of Whispers and the huge statues. By contrast, the rows of schoolboy desks in the Senate Chamber are less dignified.

Everywhere one goes in Washington today one sees people almost groaning under the weight of their *Washington Post* and *New York Times* – enormous Sunday editions. How long before we see the same in England?

Outside the White House pickets are handing out nuclear disarmament pamphlets. The cab driver who takes me home tells me that he earns 3,000 dollars a year in this trade. But his real trade is as a heating engineer in the State Department. Curiously enough, there is no limit to the number of cabs allowed in Washington.

## 20 March 1962
Spend part of the morning at the White House. One enters along an arcade overlooking the gardens, then through a long, artificially lit, vaulted passage and up a big staircase. All the rooms are splendid, but give one the impression of a museum. The exception is the Green Room, small and charming, containing a Cézanne and a bad portrait of Ike. I also like the Oval Blue Room.

Lunch with Sammy Hood,* the Minister at our Embassy. He thinks that Macmillan has a strong influence on Kennedy, equalled only by that of Adenauer.† Nixon, he believes, is unlikely to win his contest against Governor Brown.‡ In any case, he is politically finished, and the Republicans are in disarray.§ Hood thinks very highly of Hugh Foot and the work he is doing on colonial problems in the United Nations: 'The only really important question is how best to liquidate what remains of the British Empire.' I hardly think Winston would approve of this view from a senior member of the Foreign Service.

After lunch take a car down to the Courts of Justice at the back of Congress, for an appointment with Mr Justice Felix Frankfurter.¶ He is a tiny, spectacled man, sitting against a background of bound law volumes in a huge marble palace. In a very real sense he epitomises the ambitions of most Americans – short of the Presidency, there is no more revered an appointment than that of a member of the Supreme Court.

We begin by discussing the influence of the Press on American life. I

---

\* Samuel Hood, 6th Viscount Hood (1910–81), HM Minister in Washington 1957–62.

† Konrad Adenauer (1876–1967), first post-war Chancellor of West Germany 1949–63.

‡ Pat Brown (1905–96), Governor of California 1959–67.

§ A predication that was correct regarding California, but not overall. Nixon was President 1969–74.

¶ (1882–1965), lawyer. Associate Justice of the US Supreme Court 1939–62.

mention to him how much more seriously journalists are taken here than in England. He replies: 'This is a frequent innovation. One never used to meet a journalist dining out, but now no dinner at an Embassy is complete without one. They regard themselves not only as the Fourth Estate, but also as the First Estate. I was once horrified when attending a dinner at the Gridiron Club to hear a journalist who had known Eisenhower at SHAEF in Paris address the President as Ike.'

Frankfurter regrets that Kennedy has succumbed to the ordeal of the Press conference. This, he continues, has many drawbacks. The President must always appear bright and alert, he never dares refuse an answer, and no follow-up is allowed to any question on which the President has given an unsatisfactory answer. 'I know from teaching at Harvard that this is not the way to educate people.'

This leads us to talk of Oxford, where he was a visiting professor between the wars.

The Bursar of Balliol once showed him the famous letter on which Curzon had written: 'Gentlemen do not take soup at luncheon.' Many of his friends were at New College, his alma mater, and he had an affection for Harold Laski.* 'Yes,' he continues, 'I have seen much of Oxford with these eyes soon to be dimmed.'

Frankfurter asks me about the British political scene, and we discuss the swing against the Government at Orpington. He says Harold Macmillan was a great success when he addressed the Press Club, but he has a deep suspicion of Harold Wilson and hopes he will not become Foreign Secretary in the next Labour Government.

## 21 March 1962

I attend the President's Press conference at the State Department. I have rarely seen a public man more in command of himself. When asked a diffi- cult question, he gives an answer, but even before he has finished his sentence he picks out another journalist with a stabbing forefinger. This ensures that there are not too many awkward supplementaries.

## 22 March 1962

I have an appointment with Robert Kennedy,† the Attorney-General. Ken- nedy has a huge office with a nautical flavour. There is a painting of a modern

---

* (1893–1981), political theorist. Labour Party Chairman 1945–6.
† (1925–68), US Attorney-General 1961–4; Senator from New York 1965–8, the year he was assassinated.

destroyer, a model of an old rigged ship and a huge stuffed shark which he caught off Florida. Among the pictures are a Canaletto, a modern canvas of a ticker-tape parade by Bill Walton,* and some of his children's drawings. I am sitting in the comfortable waiting room when there enters what I take to be the office boy – a very young, shortish, fair and tousle-headed man in shirt-sleeves and, more surprisingly, stocking feet. It is the Attorney-General. He is extremely friendly and welcoming, and plays with a presentation gavel as he talks.

I open the conversation by asking whether he attributes the high crime statistics among Negroes to their bad housing conditions. He agrees that this is a partial explanation. But on the subject of American Negroes in general, he points out that whereas before there has never been a Negro district judge, there are now three. Similarly, there are now two Negro attorneys in Federal Districts. In the last administration there were only ten out of 900 Negro attorneys in the Department of Justice in Washington: now there are over fifty.

Kennedy is also very proud of the way he has cleaned up gangsters. 'There has been more criminal legislation than at any time since 1934, as well as co-ordination of our various investment groups.' He mentions particular cases, and promises to send me details. Most vice, he says, can be traced to gambling. He adds that recently the head of the Royal Canadian Mounted Police sent him a letter of protest, complaining that the present American persecution of gangsters was driving them all across the border to Canada. He says: 'You will be better able to judge our efforts in defeating crime in five years' time.'

I ask him politely about a headline in a newspaper over his recent round-the-world trip costing 15,000 dollars. He is undismayed by this criticism: 'I don't worry about it. I have appeared before the Foreign Relations Committee, and proved to them how very inexpensive it was. I was even offered a private plane, but refused it.' He thinks the trip had most value in Japan, particularly the helpful understanding on Okinawa. He regards his trip as a useful instrument of attack on the Communists – well-disciplined, well-organised committees, who spew out mass representation. 'We must teach foreign countries the fundamentals in this propaganda.'

As Kennedy seems in no hurry to bring our agreeable talk to an end, I ask him one or two questions about his use of leisure. He reads a great deal, on planes, at weekends and also at night. At the moment he is reading T.E. Lawrence's *Seven Pillars of Wisdom*.

---

* William Walton (1910–94), American artist; confidant of the Kennedys.

He smokes only the occasional cigar, and explains how his father[*] offered each of the brothers a thousand dollars not to smoke or drink before the age of twenty-one. His final remark is on David Ormsby-Gore: 'He is doing a great job.'

At 6.30 I go up to Georgetown for a drink with Jo Alsop.[†] I ask Alsop what part Johnson[‡] plays as Vice-President. He replies that Johnson has been emasculated. He has ceased to manage the Senate, of which he had enough, and has barely been compensated for this by being given responsibility for the Space Project. 'He has not the intellect to carry out such a task.' Johnson was also sorry not to have been given Bobby Kennedy's job as Attorney-General.

## 23 March 1962

All papers, even the *Washington Post*, are making a tremendous cult of the Kennedy family – even more than our own papers make of the Royal Family. This mixture of mush and gush overdone.

## 26 March 1962

I buy several books to take back with me – including Nixon's autobiography and Theodore White's *The Making of a President*.[§]

In the evening to the Metropolitan Opera to hear *Elektra* by Richard Strauss. It consists of a single long Wagnerian Act, and I am riveted from beginning to end. It is extraordinary how, at the end of the opera, all the smartly dressed and rather elderly audience rush out to their Cadillacs without waiting to applaud.

## 28 March 1962

I attend the 999th meeting of the Security Council. First of all I have half an hour's talk in the Delegation Lounge with Colin Crowe,[¶] a young, amusing, scholarly man. He tells me that each session of the United Nations lasts three months, during which each of the 104 delegations must give a party. They are terribly annoyed if one fails to turn up.

Notice that although the handles of the doors in the Security Council Chamber are made of wood the delegates approach them cautiously through

---

[*] Joseph Kennedy (1888–1969), American businessman. US Ambassador to the UK 1938–40.
[†] Joseph Alsop (1910–89), influential American journalist.
[‡] Lyndon B. Johnson (1908–73), Vice-President of the US 1961–3; President of the US 1963–9.
[§] Theodore H. White (1915–86), American historian and political journalist. His account of the 1960 Presidential election won the Pulitzer Prize for Non-Fiction, 1962.
[¶] Sir Colin Crowe (1913–89), Deputy Permanent Representative to the UN 1961–3; Ambassador to Saudi Arabia 1963–4.

force of habit. This is because the building, as I noticed on an earlier visit, is highly charged with static electricity. Some doors cannot be pushed, but must always be pulled. That is why one sees so many delegates gingerly grasping handles with a handkerchief, using newspapers, or trying to avoid the electricity by pushing doors with a bunch of keys. The Press are everywhere. There is no real security and up to seventy journalists may turn up for a British delegation Press conference.

The Chamber is dominated by a perfectly dreadful symbolic mural. According to the official description, 'It symbolises the hopes of mankind for the world of tomorrow.'

The eleven members of the Council take their places at a horse-shoe table. Delicately puffing a cigarette is U Thant, the Secretary-General.* To the right of this official group sits Adlai Stevenson representing the United States. He seems smaller and stouter than in his photographs, with a domed, donnish head full of epigrams.

The proceedings begin with a discussion on the agenda, accompanied by a menacing little speech from Russia. But the main business of the meeting is to hear a charge of aggression brought by Syria against Israel and Israel's counter-charges. Adlai Stevenson strongly urges the two countries 'to scrupulously maintain the ceasefire'. Even split infinitives sound elegant on his lips. Then the Russian delegation intervenes: 'I shall now put forward a serious objective evaluation of the facts.' What in fact he does put forward is none of these things, but a good half-hour of strongly anti-Israel talk.

One circumstance softens this belligerency. From the right ear of each delegate hangs a little earphone for receiving simultaneous translation of the proceedings into the variety of languages. As soon as the Russian has finished his speech, it has to be officially translated into English and French. This provides a useful pause in the proceedings, and many people drift about the Chamber chattering with each other. The President interrupts and asks for silence.

I have arranged to meet Adlai Stevenson and walk with him to a car, in which we drive to the Waldorf Towers. There he flings himself back on the cushions and pours out a dismal account of his present job. Compared to the time when Cabot Lodge† was United States representative at the United Nations, official correspondence has trebled. That is not all. He travels to Washington once or twice a week for meetings of the National Security Council, and is a member of the Cabinet – though he rarely attends its

* (1909–75), Burmese diplomat. Secretary-General of the UN 1961–71.
† Henry Cabot Lodge (1902–85), US representative to the UN 1953–60.

meetings. Then he is also called upon to testify in Congress a great deal. Fortunately, he adheres strictly to the rule that he should be bipartisan. Thus he will undertake no political engagements, not even for his closest friends, although he receives £15 a day. But even this disengagement from politics embarrasses him, for he cannot repay political debts.

The social life, too, is crushing. The night before last, for instance, he made a speech in Washington in honour of Robert Frost.* He has an official luncheon every day and a banquet every night. Then there are cocktail parties, an intolerable number of them. He is also forced to see an infinite number of visitors in his office, and every few days some new crisis in world affairs upsets his schedule. 'I sometimes wonder', he says, 'whether the job is tolerable.' Though worried, he still has enormous charm and friendliness.

Although it is true that Stevenson has not had a meal by himself – not even breakfast – for several years, his health remains remarkably good. He ranks as number four in the Cabinet after the President, Vice-President and Secretary of State. Cabot Lodge had the same position. It is useful to the President to have the benefit of Stevenson's advice on foreign affairs as a member of the Cabinet and this will not offend the Secretary of State.

He still maintains a worldwide correspondence, which is useful as an intelligence system. Stevenson also maintains links with the Arts. E.M. Forster always sends him autographed copies of his books. John Steinbeck is a close friend, and so is Alan Jay Lerner, who wrote *My Fair Lady*.

### 29 March 1962

I board the SS *France* for my return voyage to England. Heavy seas, but very little motion indeed in the ship.

In the afternoon I watch the film *King of Kings*, the story of the New Testament. In the middle of the Sermon on the Mount I hear one American woman whisper to another: 'Haven't we heard all this before?'

After dinner the film is still going on. Presumably the end of the performance I attended part of earlier.

### 16 April 1962

Pick up on my research for the *DNB* notice of Jim Cilcennin. At 12 I see Michael Parker† at his office in Conduit Street. The principal purpose of my

---

* (1874–1963), American poet.

† Lt-Cdr Michael Parker (1920–2001), courtier. PS to the Duke of Edinburgh 1947–57; Parker accompanied the Duke of Edinburgh, Jim Cilcennin and Edward Seago on the Royal visit, on

visit is to talk to him about Jim Cilcennin, particularly his journey around the world on the Royal Yacht *Britannia* with Prince Philip. Parker begins by giving me the background to the construction of the Royal Yacht for which Jim, as First Lord of the Admiralty, was largely responsible. When the late King returned from his post-war visit to South Africa it seemed obvious that he could not continue to use an enormous battleship such as the *Vanguard* for Commonwealth tours. So it was proposed that a new Royal Yacht should be built. This was before the days when the Royal Family did most of their long journeys by air. The new ship was designed to be 'Buckingham Palace afloat' – a communications centre, offices, and a means of providing hospitality at any point of the globe. Originally a much larger ship than *Britannia* was proposed, but those plans were scaled down.

A trip such as that undertaken by Prince Philip in 1956–7 could not have been done by air. Jim was invited because he had been the understanding First Lord who had given much help to the whole conception. He was friendly, warm-hearted, approachable and a magnificent Ambassador, even in rather prickly countries like Australia. He was also a very brave man, in constant pain from arthritis but never heard to utter a word of complaint. Parker tells me there was one small difficulty. Jim loved to stay up talking until about 3 a.m. As most of the staff were kept very busy indeed they devised a roster by which they took it in turns to stay up with Jim.

When we have finished our talk about Jim, Parker asks me how I think Prince Philip is getting on in the estimation of the Press and public. I mention one or two of the obvious failings – his running-down of British industry when abroad; the impression he gives of despising the Press; and his tendency to drop people, having previously taken them up with some degree of intimacy, e.g. Jim Cilcennin complained to me often about this during the last year of his life.

Parker agrees he has this tendency to pick up and drop people. Edward Seago, who also accompanied the Prince on this tour on *Britannia*, made the same complaint. The trouble is, adds Parker, that members of the Royal Family have very few friends and not many acquaintances. Part of Prince Philip's trouble actually springs from shyness. But this could be avoided by a staff of skilled advisers on public and Press relations. Parker thinks there should be a Private Secretary at the Palace on the same level as Michael Adeane, but whose sole function is to deal with the Press. Incidentally, he thinks there should also be a separate Private Secretary for Commonwealth Affairs. At present, whenever a difficult situation arises, such as the

---

*Britannia*, to the Antarctic Circle in 1956–7.

absorption of Tony Armstrong-Jones into the Royal Family, the tendency is for its members merely to bury their heads in the sand. He does not, however, think that there is the will among the present Palace secretariat to carry out such a reform.

In the evening, Martin Gilliat in for a drink. He talks of the Queen Mother's solitary evenings at Clarence House, where she hardly ever has guests in the evening or goes out to dine. She eats alone and watches TV. One of the things though she does like is gossiping about racing with friends such as Peter Cazalet.[*]

Martin has heard that Giles St Aubyn has started applying for headmasterships, after having been a housemaster at Eton. But he does not think that Giles would make a good Master of Marlborough, nor Master of Wellington, his alma mater, which he would like. He has a bad habit of sadistically teasing his boys, particularly those he likes best. They hate it.

### 21 April 1962

Catch the 3.45 train to Chippenham to stay with Lord Methuen[†] at Corsham.

When I arrive at Corsham, almost everybody is in the garden preparing for a party. But it is nice to see one of the huge cats asleep on a glass-topped display table full of GCBs and GCMGs.

An agreeable sherry party in the garden, though quite a cold wind. Among those I meet is Michael Tippett, the composer of the opera *The Midsummer Marriage*. He tells me that he is a tenant of Paul Methuen. I ask him whether he pulls his forelock to Paul in the approved fashion of tenants. 'Oh no,' he replies, 'I could quite easily afford a house of my own.'

I hear a wicked remark of Maurice Bowra on Robert Birley's Reith Lectures in 1949, which were not considered a success. 'They made no contribution to knowledge,' said Bowra. 'They did not even make a contribution to ignorance.'

### 2 May 1962

Dine Beefsteak. Delighted to see Randal Dunsany, who invites me to stay at Dunsany in Ireland for Whitsuntide. He tells me an amusing story of how Lord Middleton[‡] was given his KG, and remarked soon afterwards: 'There was a bit of excitement at first, but shortly afterwards my grandson caught

---

[*] (1907–73), racehorse trainer. K.R. was with him in the Welsh Guards during the war.

[†] Capt. Paul Methuen, 5th Baron Methuen (1891–1975), soldier and architect.

[‡] Randal Plunkett, 19th Baron of Dunsany (1906–99), British Army officer in India. Michael Willoughby, 11th Baron Middleton KG (1887–1970), Lord Lieutenant for East Riding of Yorkshire; Chancellor of Hull University 1954–70.

his first salmon, so it was soon forgotten.'

We talk about John Betjeman. Randal tells me that when John Betjeman wanted to marry Penelope[*] he used to come and stay with the Chetwodes in India. Lord Chetwode, the prospective father-in-law, was at that time Commander-in-Chief. One day he said rather impatiently to John: 'Don't keep calling me sir.' 'What should I call you then, sir?' said John. 'Why not Field Marshal?'[†]

One day Betjeman particularly shocked Lord Chetwode by appearing on a bicycle and wearing a bowler hat, tweed coat, yellow gloves and carrying a riding crop. When the Field Marshal asked him what he was doing John replied: 'Just off to early service.'

## 4 May 1962

Private view of Royal Academy. Stormont Mancroft[‡] tells me that he has been helping to design a coat of arms for Isaac Wolfson, but got no marks for suggesting as the motto 'Supra Capio' – 'I Take Over'.

When in New York, he tells me, he mentioned that he was going on to Florida. 'But', said the man he was talking to, 'you will find it full of fat middle-aged Jews.' 'Well,' replied Stormont, 'here is another come to join them.'

Maurice Macmillan comes in for a talk. He hopes he will soon get office; it may be too late if the Tories lose the next election. He talks to his father often, but never discusses financial policy.

He says that the late Duke of Devonshire sent a copy of F.A. Hayek's *The Road to Serfdom* to Winston soon after its publication in 1944.[§] This gave Winston the idea for his disastrous 'Gestapo' broadcast at the General Election of 1945.

## 9 May 1962

5.30 p.m. Visit Dean Acheson[¶] at the residence of the American Ambassador in Regent's Park. He looks remarkably well and handsome; has the Anthony Eden good looks which captivate but at the same time infuriate so many Americans.

---

[*] Penelope Chetwode, Lady Betjeman (1910–86), travel writer.

[†] FM Sir Philip Chetwode, 1st Baron Chetwode (1859–1950), senior British Army officer who was at the siege of Ladysmith in the Second Boer War; C.-in-C. in India 1930–35.

[‡] 2nd Baron Mancroft (1914–87), Conservative politician. Minister without Portfolio 1957–8.

[§] Friedrich Hayek (1899–1992), economist.

[¶] (1893–1971), American statesman and lawyer. Secretary of State 1949–53; in a speech at West Point on 5 Dec. 1962 he said: 'Great Britain has lost an empire and has not yet found a role.'

He talks about the Supreme Court of the United Sates. Acheson says: 'I like the discipline of its strictly limited arguments and of being made to decide what is strictly essential. In my early days before the Supreme Court, my daughter was aged about twelve. After dinner I would state the case I intended to use on the following day, and ask her to stop me when she was no longer able to follow it. As soon as she did this I knew that the Supreme Court would not understand it either!'

This weekend he is spending in Wiltshire with Lord Devlin. He also hopes to see Eden. He mentions with pride that he is an honorary doctor of both Oxford and Cambridge.

I ask him whether he is happy as a lawyer, or yearns to return to the political and diplomatic scene. He tells me he misses political life. He welcomes 'the value of the abrasive of other points of view'.

Kennedy offered him an Embassy, but after being Secretary of State he did not think that this was 'quite good enough'. Incidentally, he mentions his 'unbounded admiration' for Oliver Franks when Ambassador in Washington. 'The best Ambassador from any country I have ever known.' The important thing about Franks was that he had the complete confidence of <u>both</u> Governments.

*The following letter reveals clearly that Kenneth had no belief in an afterlife.*

### 3 June 1962, letter to Sir Harold Nicolson on the occasion of Vita Sackville-West's death

My dear Harold,

You must have rehearsed Vita's death a thousand times in your thoughts during the past weeks. And now that blow has fallen. The sense of loss, of perpetual separation, will be no easier to endure. Winston once said that we cannot break our hearts more than once. He was wrong. Even excluding sudden whims of fate, the humdrum processes of life and death can be almost unbearably cruel.

I wish I could write words of comfort to ease your pain. But to those of us denied a bright and tidy image of immortality there is no real consolation.

Of one thing, however, I am certain: that you will face the world with the same courage I have so often admired in your political life – 'Ergo vivia vis animi pervicit.'*

No man I have ever known has inspired more love and affection than you.

---

* Lucretius on Epicurus – 'So the vital strength of his spirit won through.'

The warmth of feeling which goes out to you cannot outweigh the grief of Vita's death, but perhaps it will help a little. I am thinking of you always and long to see you again.

As ever,

Kenneth

## 6 June 1962

Call at Albany to see Harold Nicolson. Find him there with Nigel. Harold seems subdued, but not melancholy, and talks at great length about Vita's last days and the funeral. The gardens of Sissinghurst remained open to the public on the day which is exactly what Vita would have liked. In drawing up the order of service, Harold included a piece from *The Land*.* The parson, a good Kentish man, enquired rather dubiously: 'I don't have to read it, do I?' He was glad to be reassured. What made the day of the funeral tolerable was the wonderful weather. After the church service Harold and Nigel drove to Charing for the cremation. Harold says: 'It was just like posting a letter, and there was such a nice postman.' One extraordinary story. Most of Vita's writing was done with an elegant fluted marble inkstand, in the shape of a little sarcophagus. Harold has had the inkwells removed, and the little box hollowed out. 'I think it would please Vita to be buried in her inkpot.' Next Saturday her ashes are to be buried at Withyham Church, where all the Sackvilles were buried.

It was characteristic of Harold that immediately after the funeral he changed into the gaudiest tie he could find. Nigel persuaded him to wear black, at least until after the ashes had been buried, otherwise people would gossip unkindly. Sissinghurst has been left to Nigel and he hopes to live there. He hopes that Harold will be able to live in another converted part of Sissinghurst. He would like the house and garden eventually to go to the National Trust, but they will need a big endowment.†

## 20 June 1962

Pam Berry telephones, full of a story about Princess Margaret and Tony. Apparently they tried to photograph the Chichester Festival Theatre, but were driven away by Laurence Olivier with rude cries of 'No Press, No Press!'

Drive out to Wormwood Scrubs Prison to lecture on the Press. Curiously enough the Assistant Governor only turns up halfway through my talk, and

---

* A long poem by Vita Sackville-West, published in 1926, which is a hymn to the Kent countryside.

† The National Trust took over Sissinghurst in 1967.

I am introduced by a huge man like a retired sergeant-major, who later turns out to be Frederick Emmett-Dunne,[*] convicted of murder in Germany by court martial. E.-D. says that had Curtis-Bennett,[†] his counsel, been sober during the court martial, he would have been acquitted. I will look into the case. My concern sprang from having several times seen C.-B. drunk in the Beefsteak Club.

The audience of prisoners is not as intelligent as at Holloway, and there are the usual sprinkling of hostile barrack-room lawyers trying to involve me in criticism of prison regulations. When I remark to E.-D. that there is a nice show of geraniums, he replied: 'They should spend the money on more cleaning materials.'

## 24 June 1962
Giles St Aubyn discusses with me the prospects of Robert Birley's successor as Head Master of Eton.

Brian Young, Headmaster of Charterhouse, is still the favourite. In his favour:
1. Claude Elliott has never got on well with Birley, and would now like a solid, reliable Old Etonian.
2. Many senior beaks are alarmed at the decline of the classics, and feel that Young would put an end to the rot.[‡]

Against Young, in Giles's view:
1. Far too pious. One of his first actions at Charterhouse was to request the staff to attend chapel more.
2. He lacks the human touch. What is now needed is a headmaster who cares more about people and less about problems.

## 2 July 1962
I dine with David Llewellyn at the Connaught Hotel. He talks to me about Jim Cilcennin. One of the most extraordinary sidelights on him is that apparently Jim was very devout. This I never suspected. David relates the anecdote, one told him by Jim, of how Jo Godber[§] came to be interviewed by

---

[*] Sgt Frederick Emmett-Dunne (b. 1923), served in the Royal Electrical and Mechanical Engineers in Germany and was found guilty of murdering Sgt Reginald Watters in Nov. 1953 and sentenced to death, being returned to England as the death penalty was not then operative in Germany. His sentence was later commuted to life imprisonment.
[†] Frederick Curtis-Bennett (1904–56), lawyer who took silk in 1943.
[‡] Young was a notable classical scholar, with a Double First at King's Coll., Cambridge, and a Porson Prizeman (for Greek verse composition).
[§] Baron Godber of Wellington (1914–80), Conservative politician. War Secretary June–Oct.

Jim as a Conservative candidate. Jim noticed he was wearing no socks, and asked him about this. Godber replied: 'When the Labour Government came in, I swore that until my wife could buy nylons without coupons, I would wear no socks!'

Also an extraordinary story about Edward Boyle. When invited by the Prime Minister to spend a weekend at Birch Grove, he was afraid there would not be enough to eat. So he bought a pork pie in Fortnum's and wrapped it in his pyjamas. The PM's valet unpacked it, and later told Macmillan about it.

*On Friday 13 July Harold Macmillan dismissed seven members of his Cabinet, including the Chancellor of the Exchequer, Selwyn Lloyd, in what was known as the 'Night of the Long Knives'. Lord Kilmuir, who was summarily dismissed as Lord Chancellor, complained to Macmillan that one's cook would have had more notice, to which Macmillan replied, 'It's easier nowadays to find Lord Chancellors than cooks.' The dramatic events, and the subsequent reshuffle, dominated politics for some time.*

## 16 July 1962

Maurice Macmillan tells me that he will not be included in the Government promotions and appointments which are to be announced this evening following the Night of the Long Knives. He is very disappointed at this, but grateful to me for having pleaded his case in the *Sunday Telegraph*.

Roy Harrod* lunches at the Beefsteak, but forgets to pay his bill – only to be expected from an economist!

To the House of Commons, full of nervous jokes about the impending Government appointments. See Hugh Fraser† walking across the Central Lobby with a face of such gloom that I do not dare to talk to him. Stay late in the office waiting for a list of ministerial appointments. Hugh Fraser is obviously clever at disguising his feelings. He is promoted from Under-Secretary at the Colonial Office to be Secretary for Air. Delighted that Geoffrey Rippon‡ becomes Minister of Works with increased responsibilities.

## 17 July 1962

Call on Geoffrey Lloyd at his house in Chester Square. We discuss the

---

1963; Minister of Labour 1963–4; Minister of Agriculture, Fisheries and Food 1972–4.

* Sir Roy Harrod (1900–78), economist; official biographer of John Maynard Keynes.

† Sir Hugh Fraser (1918–84), Conservative politician. In fact, Fraser was appointed Secretary of State for Air on 6 July 1962.

‡ Baron Rippon of Hexham (1924–97), Conservative politician. Held various posts in Edward Heath's Government, including Secretary of State for the Environment 1972–4.

Government changes. He says it is most unlikely that Selwyn Lloyd was offered the Woolsack – he is far too rusty in his knowledge of the law.* Lloyd is bitter against the Prime Minister, to whom he applies the word 'treacherous'.

Nice letters from David Eccles and Bill Deedes. Bill Deedes, who becomes Minister without Portfolio, states that he is the only rat in the history of British politics who ever rejoined the sinking ship.

To the House of Commons. There is still a sense of excitement in the House and Selwyn Lloyd is loudly cheered when he takes his seat.

On the ten o'clock news hear that the Conservative back benches have been threatening mutiny against Macmillan, so go down to Pratt's to hear the political news. Rather full. Hinchingbrooke† is there. He says, 'How can one prevent the British Prime Minister from behaving like a South American dictator?' He believes Macmillan is finished. William Yates,‡ Tory MP, hailed a cab today and said, 'Drive me to the abbatoir.' The cab driver took him at once to the House of Commons without any further explanation.

## 18 July 1962

11.30 a.m. to Barton Street, to discuss the recent Cabinet changes with David Eccles. He is both bitter at the way he was sacked from the Ministry of Education and relieved to have been given his liberty. He comments in particular on the dishonest letter of the Prime Minister to Selwyn saying that there would be no change of economic policy. The PM said this only to reassure the bankers. On the general question of the Cabinet changes, Eccles says: 'I did hope the Prime Minister would not announce the new actors until after he had announced a new play.'

He continues: 'Of those who have just left the Cabinet only Watkinson and I have any health left at all. Rab is little better – after his wife's last illness he made no sense at all for six months. My father-in-law, Lord Dawson of

---

* Philip de Zulueta had suggested to Macmillan that Lloyd should become Lord Chancellor, but Macmillan did not consider Lloyd a distinguished enough lawyer-ironic in the later light of several Lord Chancellors in succession in the 21st century being appointed who were not even lawyers.

† Victor Montagu, Viscount Hinchingbrooke (1906–95), Conservative politician. President of the Anti-Common Market League, 1962–4.

‡ (1921–2010), Conservative MP for the Wrekin 1955–66. On 1 Nov. 1956 he interrupted on a point of order in the Commons and said: 'I have come to the conclusion that Her Majesty's Government has been involved in an international conspiracy,' the first reference at Westminster to the secret negotiations at Sèvres between Great Britain, France and Israel.

Penn,[*] told me that 99 out of 100 public men who come to him for treatment had clung to office too long.'

I ask him whether he will return to the City. He replies that he has had a tempting offer to become a partner in a merchant bank. He was offered the High Commissionership of Canada, but turned it down. 'Healthwise,' he says, 'I am really very strong. During my eight years at the Ministry of Education, I missed only one day.'

I ask him about his taking a peerage. He replies: 'I cannot do without the smell of the Palace of Westminster. It is the same in the Lords as in the Commons – a mixture of detergents and dust. I shall be glad to hear my division bell go.'

Lunch with Pamela Berry. Also there – Mrs Joe Alsop[†] and Ronald Tree. Mrs Alsop was at Petworth at the weekend, and has brought back a number of stories about the recent Cabinet changes. Sir Charles Wheeler, RA[‡] having an appointment with Macmillan about the Leonardo appeal, was mistaken for Sir Keith Joseph,[§] and offered the Board of Trade!

Apparently, the PM sent Tim Bligh,[¶] one of his PPSs, to see Selwyn Lloyd and to tell him that the PM wanted to see him urgently. By means of gentle hints Bligh tried to tell Selwyn of his impending doom, but Selwyn simply could not believe it, and a much blunter approach became necessary. The conversation went something like this:

'The Prime Minister wants to see you as soon as possible.'

'Yes, I have several points to discuss with him.'

'It will not, I fear, be an agreeable interview.'

---

[*] Bertrand Dawson, 1st Baron Dawson of Penn (1864–1945), physician to George V and Queen Mary. It was later revealed that he had accelerated the death of George V in Jan. 1936 by giving the Monarch a lethal injection of cocaine and morphine, which added piquancy to the old rhyme:

Lord Dawson of Penn
Has killed many men,
Which is why we sing
God Save the King.

[†] Susan Mary Alsop (1918–2004), art connoisseur and hostess.

[‡] (1892–1974), sculptor. President of the RA 1956–66, the first sculptor to hold the position. Macmillan asked Wheeler to delay selling the Leonardo cartoon of the Virgin and Child to allow time for a public appeal to save it for the nation. £450,000 was donated by the public and £350,00 by the government. The cartoon is permanently in the National Gallery.

[§] Baron Joseph (1918–94), barrister and Conservative MP for Leeds North East 1956–87; Secretary of State for Industry 1979–81 and for Education and Science 1981–6. Served under four prime ministers and was a key figure in the development of Thatcherism.

[¶] Sir Timothy Bligh (1918–69), Principal PS to Harold Macmillan 1959–63 and to Sir Alec Douglas-Home 1963–4.

'Oh, I am quite used to discussing our economic difficulties,' etc. etc.

Ronald Tree says he can never forgive Rab for his conduct over Munich. At the same time he has nothing but praise for Alec Home. In any case, as I point out to him, very few people can remember the rights and wrongs of Munich, and a larger number have never even heard of it.

### 28 July 1962, letter to parents

Another crowded but rewarding week. The vote of censure debate in the Commons following the Night of the Long Knives was rather a flop. Gaitskell muffed a splendid chance by reading his speech, jokes and all, from a huge bale of closely typewritten sheets. And all the fire seems to have gone out of Macmillan. The Tory cheers which greeted his speech were determined rather than enthusiastic.

### 15 August 1962

Bill Deedes to dine at flat. Talking of 'Albany', Bill says that Whitehall speaks of it with respect, even though they are frequently attacked. At the moment, he says, I am a prisoner of my own column. He suggests that I should try to have a year abroad, preferably in Africa, before taking on an editorial job.

Nearly all his time in politics is taken up by endless committees. These he enjoys, since, unlike other ministers, he is not tied to a departmental brief. He can always tell whether Macmillan is interested or not in what he is saying. If interested, his fingers perpetually flutter his papers. If not particularly interested, he sits quite still.

After he had joined the Cabinet a week or two ago a caravan of Post Office men turned up at his home in Aldington to install his scrambler telephone – the equipment for which cost about £200. They had no idea he was a minister, and asked him: 'Are you going to need the equipment long?' Bill replied that their guess was as good as his. Eventually the equipment was installed, accompanied by many contemptuous remarks from the workmen at the existing electrical equipment in the house. Eden, Bill adds, was never happy with the scrambler as he always forgot that its valves needed about two minutes to warm up.

The Chairmanship of the Independent Television Authority will soon be coming up. He thinks several of the axed ministers may fancy themselves for this.

He thinks it may be worth my while talking to Geoffrey Rippon about the functions of the Ministry of Public Building and Works. The Ministry settles how one builds, whereas the Ministry of Housing settles where and when one builds. Between them, Rippon and Keith Joseph make a formidable team.

He stays till about 11 p.m., and I let him out of the iron gate into Edgware Road. As I slam it behind him he turns round and shouts, to the consternation of the bus queue: 'Goodbye, warden, I am going straight from now on.'

### 31 August 1962

Lunch Beefsteak. The Duke of Devonshire tells me that a few weeks ago he dined at the Other Club, and was fortunate enough to sit opposite Winston. Several times Winston asked his neighbours who the Duke was, but did not seem to take it in. In the middle of the meal the Duke remarked that he was surprised to see asparagus tongs on the table – 'Even more vulgar than sugar tongs,' he said. At this Winston suddenly woke up and said across the table: 'On the contrary, an asparagus tong is a most useful implement.' He thereupon proceeded to give a demonstration, but seven times in succession failed to get the asparagus into his mouth. The eighth time he succeeded and beamed round the table in satisfaction.

John Connell* also has a Winston story. At a small dinner given to celebrate the publication of Pug Ismay's memoirs, Winston and Auchinleck met for the first time since the war. As they shook hands before dinner, Winston merely said: 'Good evening Field Marshal. Cairo.' Throughout dinner Auchinleck saw that Winston was staring at him. Just as Winston was leaving he came up to Auchinleck and said: 'I just wanted to say goodnight and goodbye.' Auchinleck was very touched by this, although he has good reason for resenting his sacking by Winston.

*Kenneth was abroad for much of the autumn of 1962 and missed news of the Cuban Missile Crisis, 16–28 October, which brought the world to the brink of nuclear war. During the crisis he was first in Israel, then in Cyprus, where he interviewed Archbishop Makarios.*

### 15 October 1962

In Israel. To the British Embassy at 9 a.m. for a talk with the Ambassador, Patrick Hancock,† after watching a hoopoe on the grass as I breakfast outside the hotel.

First, we discuss the difficulties caused by Israeli insistence, contrary to

---

* (1909–65), author and journalist, biographer (Cassell, 1959) of FM Sir Claude Auchinleck (1884–1981).
† Sir Patrick Hancock (1914–80), Ambassador to Israel 1959–62, to Norway 1963–5 and to Italy 1969–74.

the United Nations resolution of 1948, that their capital is Jerusalem rather than Tel-Aviv. Most foreign countries have established their Embassies in Tel-Aviv, but seven countries have opted for Jerusalem. Most of these are the newer nations, but also include the Netherlands. The reason for this is that the Dutch Consul-General, with offices in Jerusalem, was appointed Minister, and so remained in Jerusalem. This has forced Hancock to travel about 50,000 miles to and from Jerusalem since he became Ambassador, as all the Government offices are in Jerusalem. Documents are addressed simply to the Ministry of Foreign Affairs without mentioning the town. Most countries, including Great Britain, would be quite prepared to move their Embassies to Jerusalem. But this would now be considered an act offensive to the Arab states.

One feature of life in Israel is that all Israelis think that their country is the centre of the universe. 'One has to get away from it all from time to time or one would burst. Sometimes I choose Tel-Aviv Airport, as it is so much quieter than an Israeli cocktail party.'

Ben-Gurion* is not an entirely democratic Prime Minister. He has a Cabinet, but the army is outside Cabinet control, really responsible only to the Prime Minister.

There are few opportunities for Hancock to follow his favourite pastime of fishing. But there is a certain amount of shooting – partridge and duck. The duck are particularly plentiful, as they come to the carp ponds during their migration.

Hancock, tall, thin and in many ways a caricature of a Wykehamist, is a dry and agreeable character. As we enter his office, there is a large cat asleep on the cushion of the armchair at his desk. 'Ah, you thought you would outwit me, did you?' But instead of tipping it off the chair, he carefully lifts the entire chair with cat to another corner of the room and perches himself on a far less comfortable one.

With Alan Goodison† in an Embassy car to Jerusalem. It is extraordinary what a jaundiced view he takes of all his colleagues in the Foreign Service. He criticises most British ambassadors and their wives, generally because of the alleged meanness of their official entertainment.

After lunch we go in a jeep for a tour of the Armistice line. From Ramat Rahel we have a splendid panorama, including Bethlehem. Then to Mount Zion with its view of Mount Scopus, which is an enclave of Jordan. Finally to

---

* David Ben-Gurion (1886–1973), first Prime Minister of Israel 1948–54 and third Prime Minister 1955–63.
† Sir Alan Goodison (1926–2006), Ambassador to the Republic of Ireland 1983–6.

the Mandel Baum gate, the only official link between Israel and Jordan. I am taken into No Man's Land, to the United Nations Armistice Headquarters and meet one or two of the officers.

We have a further tour around Jerusalem, including a brief visit to the new Hebrew University, and here they are rebuilding the Government offices. I ask to be driven through the very Orthodox Jewish quarter of Jerusalem – men with fur or hard black hats, side curls, long blacksilk coats, baggy trousers and boots.

From a roof of the Chief Rabbinate, where I am reminded to keep my hat on, we have a magnificent view of the whole city, much smaller than I had imagined. But of course most of the ancient historic buildings are on the Jordan side. It is thrilling to have a distant glimpse of the Dead Sea.

Drive with Goodison to a big new hospital on the outskirts of Jerusalem in order to see the twelve stained-glass windows designed by Chagall. Although they are too close together, they are absolutely magnificent, full of exciting imagery and stimulating colours.

We drive down a minor mountain road through picturesque scenery to Rehovat, where I have an opportunity to see Abba Eban[*] at his house in the grounds of the Weizmann Institute.[†] A pleasantly furnished modern house. He sits in a rocking chair ('But this doesn't reflect my political ambitions'), facing a large signed photograph of President Kennedy. It is curious to hear the jackals howling outside as we talk.

First of all we discuss the Orthodox Jews whom I have seen in Jerusalem today. There are only a few thousand of them, and they are considered simple-minded, he says, rather than hostile by the rest of Israel. In fact they refuse to recognise the State of Israel, believing it to be a form of blasphemy, and so will not perform the normal duties of citizens, such as military service. They live like monks on money sent from abroad, and converse with each other in Yiddish – Hebrew is reserved for their biblical studies and for the day when the Messiah comes.

I ask Eban what is his chief problem as Minister of Education and Culture. He replies that about 60 per cent of the population are part of the general trend of European humanism. The other 40 per cent are Jews who for 500 years or so have had no cultural history. These come mainly from Morocco, Iraq and the Yemen. Naturally, all the important posts in the State go to Europeans. Only about 5 per cent of the Oriental Jews go to universities.

---

[*]  (1915–2002), Israeli diplomat and politician. Minister for Foreign Affairs 1966–74.
[†]  Israel's Science Research Institute, named after Chaim Weizmann (1874–1952), first President of Israel 1949–52.

Recently, 2,000 graduated from Jerusalem University. Of these, only thirty were Oriental Jews.

### 18 October 1962

Travel to Cyprus. I have a long talk with Denis Barnett,* Administrator of the Sovereign Bases, about the current problems. He begins by stating the fundamental fact of the island – that there is not yet such a thing as a Cypriot. The vernacular Press magnifies every tiny hostile act of either the Greeks or the Turks according to whom the paper belongs. There are also a great number of articles attacking the Sovereign Bases, and quite often getting facts wrong. Thus the other day we were accused of flying in nuclear bombs whereas it was merely a simple routine exercise.

Communism is an increasingly difficult problem. Our real headache is whether we can survive in spite of the Communist Party's putting pressure on the Government.

The cutting-down of the Army establishments in the bases means that the RAF will have to take over such organisations as motor transport, fire services, education and the cinema. He complains to me that Duncan Sandys is a very slow mover indeed. Barnett is still awaiting a reply from him on what policy should be adopted in Cyprus on the question of redundant Cypriot workers. An aide-memoire was sent to him at the time of Prime Ministers' Conference last month, but no reply has yet been received.

Barnett appreciates that we should do as little as possible to offend local sentiment, or to give Cypriots the impression that we are continuing to regard Cyprus – or at any rate the Sovereign Bases – as a colony. The frontier between the Sovereign Bases and the Republic of Cyprus is marked by little white posts – but one has to look carefully for them. It was for social rather than strategic reasons that we have built the splendid two-mile piece of road called M1, to avoid running through two Cypriot villages.

### 20 October 1962

After breakfast in my hotel I change into a dark suit and take cab to Nicosia for audience with President Makarios at 2.30 p.m.

His palace, formerly Government House, is on a hill outside the city. The façade has a huge Royal Arms in carved stone, and the outside lamps have crowns on top, as at Viceregal Lodge in Phoenix Park, Dublin.

A hideous waiting room with nasty slippery sofas. I am summoned at

* Sir Denis Barnett (1906–92), Cdr of the British Forces in Cyprus and Administrator of the Sovereign Bases 1962–4.

12.45. Quite a small study. Makarios, little taller than I am, wears a blue soutane. From one pocket protrudes a gold fountain pen, from the other a bit of chain such as schoolboys sometimes wear and a tiny gold crucifix. Well-laundered cuffs and onyx links. He has a plentiful supply of dark hair. There is a distinct line across his forehead, sunburnt below, pale above, where his hat has shielded it. A well-trimmed dark beard. Rather a formidable curved nose. Eyes of much power which slope up towards the bridge of his nose. Rather white teeth, and a single gold tooth which flashes as he talks.

I begin by giving him the good wishes sent by Julian Amery, and he asks me to return them. Then, facing each other across his desk, we settle down to talk.

My first question is whether the decision of the Cyprus Government, announced yesterday, to apply to the European Economic Community for negotiations on entry into the Common Market as an associate member makes it likely that Cyprus will stay in the Commonwealth. 'We are a member of a big family,' he replies. He enjoyed his exchange of views at the last Commonwealth Prime Ministers' Conference in London, and has absolutely no intention of snapping those links.

He admits that 70 per cent of Cyprus products are bought by Great Britain, and that entry into the Common Market would make it difficult for the island's agriculture. But 'We dare not depend on bilateral agreements in a world of antagonism.' He would certainly have no hesitation in trading with Russia, and scorns the idea that Cyprus could, as a result, become the Cuba of the Mediterranean, his one oblique reference to the current crisis.

I ask him for a general economic picture of the island. He replies: 'When the country first became independent I had certain fears – that after so much shooting it would be difficult to return to a peaceful life; and that there might be a drain on foreign capital. But we are working hard at a five-year development plan, and two months ago representatives of the World Bank made a good report. But we must continue to work very hard.'

On relations with England, he says that the British Sovereign Bases provide no serious problems. He would welcome visits by members of the British Royal Family, but beyond saying how much he admires the Queen, will not commit himself to preferring any individual. 'Princess Alexandra?' I ask. 'I am sure she would be most welcome,' he replies blandly.

On the continued use of the English language in Cyprus, he says it will be many years before the Penal Code ceases to be in English. He uses the language for talking to his ministers as a bridge between those who speak only Greek or only Turkish.

He adds with a broad smile that his knowledge of the language (which he modestly and wrongly says is not good) improved during the five months' negotiations with Julian Amery which led to the establishment of the Republic.

I tell him how much I have been struck by the sight of so many Greek and Turkish flags in Cyprus, but hardly ever one of the Republic, and ask him whether there are hopes of producing Cypriots. He is very forthcoming on this: 'It will never be possible to make a nation of Cypriots – there will only be a nation of Greek Cypriots and Turkish Cypriots.' Nor can he offer any solution for uniting the two factions.

When, as an example, I mention the rifts between Greeks and Turks in the army, he dismisses these episodes as unimportant – 'They are young people who will not accept the hard discipline of soldiers. They don't feel it is a real army. There are only 300 of them, and their only purpose is ceremonial.' An additional difficulty is to decide in which language the words of command should be given. We part with cordiality.

Tomorrow is the opening of the shooting season. During the emergency, all guns were confiscated, so the birds and other game on the island had a chance to increase. When Cyprus became independent, people were naturally given back their guns. As a result of this, nearly all the game on the island is wiped out on the first day of shooting.

### 20 November 1962

To dine with old Lord Goddard in the Temple. He is annoyed he has not been put on the Vassall Tribunal.[*] 'I suppose they thought I would bugger it all up.' But he approves of the choice of Lord Radcliffe as Chairman.[†]

Goddard has now resigned from the Other Club, as he did not know many of the politicians, and Winston always used to ask him to sit next to him, calling him 'Goddam'. At one time this would have been amusing, but now Winston just eats his oysters, then dozes.

Goddard tells me that Lord Kylsant[‡] is the only man ever to have been to a Buckingham Palace garden party while on bail. He once told Winston this, who was most impressed.

Goddard is a trustee of Chequers, appointed by the PM. So much talk about its future. The last lease of its farmland was made in Neville Chamberlain's

---

[*] The public inquiry into the John Vassall affair. Vassall (1924–96) was a civil servant who had spied for the Soviet Union. When Norman Brook, the Cabinet Secretary, first told Macmillan that MI5 had discovered that an Admiralty clerk (Vassall) had been selling state secrets in clubs around Victoria, Macmillan replied: 'Nonsense, there are no clubs around Victoria.'

[†] Cyril Radcliffe, 1st Viscount Radcliffe (1899–1977), lawyer.

[‡] Owen Phillips, 1st Baron Kylsant of Carmarthen (1863–1937). Liberal MP for Pembroke and Haverfordwest 1906–10, Conservative MP for the City of Chester 1916–22.

time and is due for renewal in 1963. Its improved terms will reduce the deficit on the estate from £11,000 to £8,000 a year. Shooting rights to be retained. Present trustees have raised value of capital endowment back to old figure of £110,000. The 1957 Act enabled the trustees to put funds in equities, and they were lucky enough to catch the Stock Exchange boom. Goddard himself largely responsible for putting Chequers on a sound financial footing.

### 15 December 1962

Talked with Somerset Maugham. Lord Beaverbrook has been very kind and hospitable to him in France. One thing they share is a deep knowledge of the Bible. Beaverbrook has just finished writing a life of Christ and they have spent a great deal of time discussing its problems.

Maugham also mentions that the last time he lunched with Beaverbrook he praised the champagne. Beaverbrook had a case of it put into the back of his car before he left.

I ask whether he has seen much of Winston lately. 'He is still alive, but in a lamentable condition, attended by male nurses wherever he goes.' Very occasionally the clouds roll away and Winston is his old self. Thus one day Winston sat silently in his chair while having lunch with Maugham. Suddenly Alan mentioned Lord Cork and Orrery.* Winston suddenly woke up: 'Lord Cork and Orrery talks too much. When Lord Cork has finished Lord Orrery starts.'

About his last birthday Maugham remarked to Winston: 'I have had 500 letters of congratulations.' Winston growled in reply: 'On my birthday I have 30,000.'

---

* William Boyle, 12th Earl of Cork and Orrery (1873–1967). C.-in-C. Home Fleet 1933–5; President, Shaftesbury Homes and Arethusa Training Ship; Admiral of the Fleet 1938.

# 1963

*1963 proved to be one of the most varied years of the century in so many ways. In the Vietnam War the Viet Cong won their first major victory. In January 1963 President de Gaulle vetoed Harold Macmillan's application to join the European Economic Community. In the same week Hugh Gaitskell, the Labour leader, died unexpectedly and the following month was succeeded as Leader of the Opposition by Harold Wilson, a dominant political presence for the next thirteen years. The Beatles recorded their first album,* Please Please Me. *Dr Richard Beeching proposed vast cuts in the country's rail network. Churchill was made an honorary citizen of the United States. The James Bond film* Dr No *was released in America and worldwide. Pope John XXIII died. The Profumo scandal caused political upheaval in Britain. The United States, the United Kingdom and the Soviet Union signed the partial Test Ban Treaty. The Great Train Robbery took place in Buckinghamshire. Martin Luther King delivered his 'I have a dream' speech in Washington. In October 1963, on the eve of the Conservative Party Conference in Blackpool, Harold Macmillan unexpectedly resigned as Prime Minister and was succeeded by Sir Alec Douglas-Home, who disclaimed his title as the Earl of Home to enter the House of Commons. The following month John F. Kennedy, President of the United States, was assassinated in Dallas, Texas, and was succeeded by Lyndon B. Johnson. The authors C.S. Lewis and Aldous Huxley died on the same day, 22 November.*

### 6 January 1963

Dine at Pratt's. Old Lord Goddard there. I ask him to dine with me later this month, and he gladly accepts, 'If I am still alive.'

More talk with him about Chequers. The Prime Minister who did most for Chequers was Neville Chamberlain. Winston once told Goddard that the £15 given to a Prime Minister for each weekend he is in residence was on the whole enough to pay for the food of the guests and other such expenses. What really made Chequers expensive was food for the guests' chauffeurs.

When Eisenhower came to stay at Chequers in 1959, the United States Secret Service men were so anxious for his safety that they insisted on taking up the floorboards of his room.

## 16 January 1963
Very distressed to hear how ill Gaitskell is. Unlikely to survive.

Give lunch to Bill Deedes at Wheelers. During a recent visit to Scotland, Bill was enormously impressed by the men building the new Forth Road Bridge. The only industrial trouble was when the management one day considered it was too windy for the men to go on working. The men almost went on strike as a protest.

Bill tells me it is likely that Gaitskell caught his virus infection in Poland. But for a long time he has been suffering from strain. 'Politics is rather like cycling. One either has the wind with one or against one. Until very recently Macmillan has always had it with him. Gaitskell has always had it against him.'

Dine at the Beefsteak with General James Marshall-Cornwall.* To illustrate how anti-British de Gaulle can be, the General tells me the story of a victory march-past in Paris at which de Gaulle took the salute. At the end of the French units came the Hadfield-Spears Ambulance Units.† Each vehicle flew a little Tricolour and a little Union Jack. De Gaulle whispered to an ADC, who descended from the dais and, as each vehicle passed, took off its Union Jack. The Tricolour alone was allowed.

## 19 January 1963, letter to parents
I am very sorry indeed about poor Hugh Gaitskell. As you know I used to dislike him, but in recent years have become quite friendly with him, even to the extent of being invited to their house in Hampstead. For a non-Socialist, this was quite an honour! In fact, the last time I was there the only other guests among about sixty not to be members of the Labour Party were the Queen's Private Secretary and the First Secretary of the Soviet Embassy. The Gaitskells occasionally came to my flat, and were always very agreeable.

Gaitskell's death is a blow in so many ways. I often used to consult him, had his private telephone number, and received several important pieces of

---

* General Sir James Marshall-Cornwall (1887–1985), senior British soldier. GOC British troops in Egypt 1941; GOC Western Command 1941–2; editor of captured German archives.
† An Anglo-French medical unit.

news from him.* The last was only a fortnight or so ago, when Dora told me what he was reading in bed at the start of his illness. She even telephoned me back later in the morning to tell me she had just remembered some other books he was reading.

### 30 January 1963
Snow falls again. Talk to Iain Macleod in his room at Commons. He says: 'I thrive on adversity.' He tells me of an important change he has made as Chairman of the Conservative Party to the machinery for choosing candidates. The form containing their personal particulars no longer has a section on religious beliefs. Constituencies have every right to know if they so wish, but it is not for Central Office to interfere by forcing such knowledge on constituencies.

Dine with James Cubitt† in York Terrace to meet Asa Briggs, who is amusing on the academic robes designed by John Piper for Sussex University. They are striking in colour, but the Chancellor, Walter Monckton, jibs at a biretta in place of the conventional cap. So of course does the Scottish Presbyterian Vice-Chancellor, John Fulton.‡

George Gage,§ a fellow guest, says of *Lady Chatterley's Lover*: 'Not a book to put in the hands of one's gamekeeper!'

### 7 February 1963
See Bill Deedes in his room at the Commons. First we discuss the announcement which has just been made that on Government advice Princess Margaret is cancelling her visit to Paris next month. The ostensible reason is that she must attend to her duties as Counsellor of State. This is obviously absurd, in the wake of de Gaulle's veto on Britain's application to join the EEC. Bill recalls that it is just sixty years ago since Anglo-French relations were no less strained than now. Instead of cancelling any proposed visit, the Government encouraged Edward VII to visit Paris, which was an enormous success and the forerunner of the Entente Cordiale.

We discuss Lord Home's visit to Brussels this evening. Bill mentions that in Cabinet this morning Home left early, explaining that he had to

---

* Gaitskell also received important news from K.R., which led Dora Gaitskell in Feb. 1963 to advise his successor as Labour leader, Harold Wilson, to become friends with Kenneth as he would learn so much about what was going on, advice which opened up a new and important link for both men.
† (1914–83), architect and sculptor.
‡ Sir John Fulton, Baron Fulton (1902–86), Vice-Chancellor of Sussex University 1959–67.
§ George Gage, 7th Viscount (1932–93), landowner.

catch his plane to Brussels. With memories of the failure of the Common Market talks, Macmillan stared quizzically at him. So Home added, 'I am only going for dinner.' The Prime Minister also mentioned in the course of business that when there were MPs with university seats, their election addresses used to be written by a committee of dons. Lord Hugh Cecil received his election address one morning, and returned it to the committee, saying: 'I fear this is a very unconvincing document.' How like Linky!

Having a drink in the small Members' Bar, we hear the result of the first round of the contest for a new Labour leader:

Harold WILSON 115

George BROWN 88

James CALLAGHAN 41

Wilson and Brown[*] will now fight it out between them. As Wilson only needs eight of Callaghan's votes to win, he stands a good chance. But Bill does not think that Brown is absolutely out of it. We discuss Brown's character, particularly the massive inferiority complex, which causes him to take to the bottle before any important occasion. This surely unfits him to be Prime Minister.

### 13 February 1963, letter to Sir Frederic Hooper

Peter Carrington tells me that his ministerial colleague, Lord St Oswald,[†] who lives at that fabulous house, Nostell Priory, was asked the other day by a self-important visitor: 'I believe I am right in thinking that Chippendale was your head carpenter at one time?', to which Lord St Oswald replied: 'No, he was our second carpenter.'

Westminster talks of nothing else except the impending defeat of George Brown by Harold Wilson. What will, I think, make the issue decisive are the barely disguised blackmail and threats with which Brown has waged his campaign. Temperamentally too, he is obviously unsuited to take calm decisions at moments of crisis.

### 15 February 1963

See Bill Deedes at the Ministry of Defence. Discuss with him the present unpopularity of the Government, accompanied by rumours that Geoffrey

---

[*] George Brown, Baron George-Brown (1914–85), Labour politician. MP for Belper 1945–70; First Secretary of State 1964–6; Foreign Secretary 1966–8; deputy leader of the Labour Party 1960–70.

[†] Rowland Winn, 4th Baron St Oswald (1916–84), Conservative politician. Parliamentary Secretary, Ministry of Agriculture, Fisheries and Food 1962–4.

Lloyd may be leading a secret revolt against Macmillan's leadership. Bill discounts this. Geoffrey Lloyd rarely attends Commons nowadays, and certainly has no great following. The rumours about Macmillan's leadership, Bill thinks, are due to a number of factors – a bad Gallup Poll in the *Daily Telegraph*; a fright among all Conservative Members with majorities of less than 3,000; the Prime Minister's speech on Monday admitting the failure of his Common Market mission; the clumsy way in which the visit to Paris of Princess Margaret was cancelled; general tittle-tattle; and the bad weather.

### 18 February 1963

Katie Macmillan[*] tells me that the family is still rather strained owing to the hostility of Bobbety Salisbury. Not long ago, after Maurice Macmillan had made a speech rather critical of the Government, Katie happened to meet Bobbety and Lord Lambton[†] in the House of Lords. Bobbety said to her gleefully: 'Why doesn't Maurice form a coalition with Tony Lambton against the Prime Minister?' Katie replied: 'Because he is middle-class and loyal. Only aristocrats like us can afford to stab people in the back.'

She also reveals some of that Whig harshness. She quotes a remark of Andrew Devonshire: 'I do wish Mrs Iain Macleod would not drag herself up five flights of stairs instead of taking the lift. If only she would not be so gallant.'[‡]

### 21 February 1963

Lunch with Alan Barker at the Savoy. He tells me that when Claude Elliott was asked to be a Fellow of Jesus College, Cambridge, he said to the don who invited him that he was not qualified to undertake the necessary duties. The don replied: 'Incompetence rarely knocks in vain in Cambridge.'

Alan speaks of the shrewdness of the Queen Mother. When visiting them at the Leys School in Cambridge, she was shown a crucifix which had been in the possession of John Wesley. 'How extraordinary,' she said, then added, 'but not really so extraordinary. After all his hymns are pretty high.'

### 3 March 1963

I spend the weekend at Eton with Giles St Aubyn. He gives me a chronicle of events since he first heard that Birley was to retire as Head Master.

---

[*] Katharine Macmillan, Viscountess Macmillan of Ovenden (1921–2017).
[†] Anthony Lambton (1922–2006), briefly 6th Earl of Durham, Conservative politician, cousin of Sir Alec Douglas-Home.
[‡] Eve Macleod, Baroness Macleod of Borve (1915–99), public servant; she was crippled in her late thirties by polio.

He was told that Birley had accepted an appointment at a South African university two days before the official announcement. Giles's first act was to write a letter to Birley, saying how much he would be missed at Eton, how courageous it was of him to go to South Africa and how difficult it would be to avoid a collision with the Government over apartheid. Giles added that he thought Birley ought to know there was considerable apprehension among the assistant masters, particularly the younger ones, lest Brian Young should be appointed as the new Head Master, and he hoped that Birley would do his best to see that the field was not limited to a single candidate. Young, added Giles, would be disastrous. In fact, Birley is thought to favour Young, his protégé and a successor as Headmaster of Charterhouse.

### 4 March 1963

Giles telephones at midday to say that all masters have been summoned to a meeting at 6 p.m. this evening. It will be an announcement of the new Head Master. The news is telephoned to me just before 7. The new Head Master is to be Chenevix-Trench,[*] the most unlikely of the three fancied candidates. I should not be at all surprised if it was refused by Walter Hamilton. Giles is delighted at the result. But for him I expect that Brian Young would have been selected almost unopposed.[†]

### 8 March 1963

Giles tells me that the delay between the election of Chenevix-Trench and the announcement was due to hesitation on his part – he came down to make sure that the Head Master's house was what he wanted.

### 11 March 1963

To York to see Lord James, Vice-Chancellor of the new university. He is glad that Chenevix-Trench is going to Eton, and has heard that Brian Young was rejected owing to opposition from masters. Though he taught at Winchester

---

[*] Anthony Chenevix-Trench (1919–79), classics scholar; Head Master of Eton 1963–9.

[†] In *Eton Renewed* (John Murray, 1994) Tim Card observes: 'Only two candidates were seriously considered to succeed Robert Birley, Anthony Chenevix-Trench and Brian Young. Young was very much the choice of the Provost and Vice-Provost, but the opinion of the majority of masters, fed through the masters' representative, was that he would be too much in Birley's image' (p. 245). The news of the appointment was not universally welcomed. The Old Salopians who ran *Private Eye* and who remembered him as a housemaster at Shrewsbury School dubbed him Chauvinist-Stench and constantly ran critical articles. One in 1969 contributed to Trench's eventual removal. When Mark Peel published a favourable biography of Trench, *The Land of Lost Content* (Pentland Press, 1996), Paul Foot savaged Trench in a review in the *Sunday Times*.

for twelve years, he has never had any desire himself to become Head Master of Eton – 'It's not my sort of school at all.'

Lord James, a very youthful-looking fifty-four, then gives me a progress report on the university.

1. Temporary buildings. In spite of the delay from bad weather, accommodation and lecture rooms for 200 students will be completed by October.
2. Permanent building. Plans for the first two colleges and science centre are now complete, and will be finished by 1965. By 1972, there will be 300 students.
3. Academic staff. Nearly thirty members of the teaching staff have been recruited already.
4. Students. These are being recruited steadily. If one draws a line between the Wash and the Mersey, about half come from the North and half from the South. Thus York is in no sense a university only for the North of England.
5. Money. The initial appeal was for £2 million, of which £1½ million has been raised. The university is lucky in that York has several wealthy trusts, controlled by such families as the Rowntrees. David Brown, the engineering firm in Huddersfield, have given £30,000 for a physics laboratory. Jack Lyons[*] has given £100,000 for a concert hall.
6. Chapel. There is no chapel as the university is non-sectarian.[†]
7. Library. By the time the university opens in October this should contain about 20,000 volumes.
8. Sport. It will be a rowing university, for which the river is particularly suitable.

After lunch I go out to Bishopthorpe, looking rather lovely in the late-afternoon light. There is a rookery in full cry. Dr Coggan as warm and welcoming as ever. We discuss the possibility of his writing an Easter article for the Sunday Telegraph on the Christian approach to the care for old people. He has always felt that old people should be allowed to die among their possessions, rather than being removed to some strange and frightening hospital during their last illness.

---

[*] (1916–2008), financier and philanthropist.

[†] Ironically, York University is now the regular venue for the meetings of the General Synod of the C of E.

Following my recent visit, we compare notes on Israel and I am fascinated that he, too, thought that religion was waning there.

Our usual dispute about new translation of the Bible. He tells me how surprised he was by the bitterness with which T.S. Eliot attacked it in the *Sunday Telegraph*. Coggan never suspected that Eliot was capable of such an attitude. The Archbishop concedes to me that the new translation of the Bible is a gamble, in which it is possible to lose the beauty of seventeenth-century language without necessarily bringing Christianity to those who have not previously experienced it.

### 26 March 1963

Dine at the Beefsteak with Harry Waugh.[*] A fascinating story from Basil Bartlett. He says that the Mynors twins, Humphrey and Roger,[†] once exchanged schools for a term without anyone noticing. Humphrey was at Marlborough, and Roger at Eton. Naturally, a small circle of friends at each school were let into the secret.

Alan Barker telephones me about 11 p.m. from Cambridge. He says that Donald Crichton-Miller,[‡] Headmaster of Stowe, has had a quarrel with the governors and is likely to resign. He suggests I should look into this.

### 27 March 1963

Reginald Maudling, who succeeded Selwyn Lloyd as Chancellor after the Night of the Long Knives last July, tells me that when he delivers his first Budget on 3 April he hopes to make one small reform in not being photographed waving Mr Gladstone's Budget box. But he does intend to continue the tradition of some form of liquid refreshment at the Despatch Box – 'To

---

[*] (1904–2001), celebrated wine merchant.

[†] Sirs Humphrey and Roger Mynors (1903–89), respectively Deputy Governor of the Bank of England 1954–64 and Professor of Latin at Oxford University 1953–70.

[‡] (1906–97), Headmaster, Stowe School 1958–63; previously Headmaster, Taunton School 1936–45; Headmaster, Fettes Coll. 1945–58. A full account of this episode is contained in Brian Rees, *Stowe: The History of a Public School, 1923–1989* (Stamp Publishing, 2008). Winston Churchill once said: 'Headmasters have powers at their disposal with which Prime Ministers have never yet been invested.' The departure of Crichton-Miller from Stowe in 1963 marked a new phase in public schools in which this was increasingly untrue, as headmasters could be treated like football managers if they failed to deliver. Brian Rees (1929–2016), like Crichton-Miller, had been Headmaster of three public schools – Merchant Taylors' 1965–73; Charterhouse 1973–81; and Rugby 1981–4 – when he was dismissed. When Chenevix-Trench left Eton prematurely in 1970, Brian Rees, son-in-law of Robert Birley, was one of the possible candidates to succeed him, whom Giles St Aubyn actively campaigned against. K.R. was godfather to Rees's daughter Natasha.

drink nothing would be regarded as uncharacteristic.'*

Dinner at the Savoy. Lord Reith is the guest speaker and reveals himself as a fervent reader of the *Sunday Telegraph*, particularly 'Albany'. My neighbour is Dawn Mackay, Headmistress of Heathfield School.† She is very young and sprightly and full of jolly jokes. The other day she was introduced to somebody as the Headmistress of Heathfield. 'What?' was the reply, 'did you say the mistress of Edward Heath?'

I asked her whether she had heard about the conflict between Donald Crichton-Miller and the governors of Stowe. She has not, but tells me an amusing story about him when he was Headmaster of Fettes. A rich parent came to call on him one day in a very expensive car. The Headmaster questioned the parent closely about its merits and was assured that it was the most satisfactory he had ever had. To which Crichton-Miller replied: 'Before you leave, I should be glad if you would put your most unsatisfactory son in your most satisfactory car and drive them both away.'

## 29 March 1963

Lunch with Pamela Berry. There is a lot more about John Profumo.‡ In spite of his denial of having slept with Christine Keeler, Pamela say there is much more to come out.

## 8 April 1963

I hear that at Kempton races recently the Queen Mother was not pleased when a television was put on in the box to see a football match. Then the TV started to play the National Anthem. 'Oh do turn it off,' said the Queen Mother, 'it is so embarrassing unless one is there – like hearing the Lord's Prayer when playing canasta.'

---

* William Ewart Gladstone (1809–98), Liberal politician with a career lasting sixty years; Chancellor of the Exchequer 1852–5, 1859–66; Prime Minister 1868–74, 1880–85, 1886, and 1892–4. His tipple whilst delivering Budgets was dry sherry with beaten egg.

† Later Mrs Dawn Hargreaves (b. 1930), ballet dancer. Headmistress of Heathfield School in the early 1960s.

‡ (1915–2006), Conservative politician. War Secretary 1960–63; his political career ended after his relationship with Christine Keeler (1942–2017). Under cover of Parliamentary Privilege, the Labour MP George Wigg (1900–83) brought up the issue in the House of Commons on 21 Mar. Profumo, under pressure from Martin Redmayne, the Government Chief Whip, denied to the House of Commons the next day that he had had an affair with Keeler. However, on 4 June he wrote to Harold Macmillan admitting he had lied to the House and resigned from Parliament. For the next forty-three years he worked at Toynbee Hall in the East End of London. He was appointed CBE in 1975 for this charitable work.

## 28 April 1963

Selwyn Lloyd says that one of the joys of ceasing to be Chancellor of the Exchequer is that one no longer has to read the *Economist*. Selwyn also tells me that when he accompanied the Queen on a State Visit to Portugal as Foreign Secretary, he spent quite a long time in the Embassy helping to pin oranges on an orange tree! He is glad not to be at the big meeting of ministers at Chequers today – 'Macmillan and Quintin Hailsham will do all the talking.' He says that at the interminable Foreign Ministers' talks in Geneva, secret conclaves would resolve themselves into bridge games.

*As so often when on foreign tours, Kenneth was undertaking some work for the* Daily Telegraph.

## 4 June 1963

On my African tour, I stay at Treetops. Treetops is the place where in 1952 the Queen heard of her accession. The original hotel has since been burnt down, but there is a commemorative tablet on the roof of the new one. Built entirely of wood, supported both by wooden pillars and by trees – my little bedroom has a huge bough transecting it. It has been thoughtfully padded with sheepskin where one's head could hit it. Apart from the roof, there are two long verandas furnished with comfortable seats, presented by BOAC. A big wooden dining room and bar, rather like that of a Swiss chalet. Electric light and hot water.

Tea on the roof. We are joined by baboons, very cheeky. One steals up behind one guest and steals a slice of fresh pineapple from a fork. Another steals a cake. Several monkeys have young, which cling to their backs.

Soon afterwards the animals begin to arrive, and we have a splendid view of a large forest clearing, with a small lake in the centre. Water hogs, water bucks and bush bucks. Also an old bull buffalo who drinks deeply from a muddy pool, and finally rubs his head in the mud. By now it is raining steadily and the prospects of seeing much more are remote. But about 6 p.m. a herd of elephants, a herd of buffalo and several rhinos, with their young.

Fascinating behaviour of each group. The elephants are aloof and protect the baby ones with close attention. The rhinos are more savage. They do not touch the elephants, but several times roll slowly down on the buffalo, who mostly give ground. But occasionally the buffalo retreat only after the rhino has given it a fairly gentle butt. All the animals splash and wallow in the mud with the greatest content. After dark a big floodlight is switched on, which does not worry the animals in the least. A lot of birds, including hammerheads and cranes. Deafening noise of frogs and lots of bats.

## 6 June 1963

Fantastic news in Nairobi papers. Profumo admits that there <u>was</u> impropriety between him and the model Christine Keeler and resigns from the Government and Parliament. Pamela Berry was right all along, and I was wrong. But I could not believe that he would be either so dishonest or so stupid as to stand up and lie to the House of Commons.

## 7 July 1963, letter to parents

Robert Birley is now in his last half as Head Master of Eton, and everybody is wondering how he will get on in his new job in a university there. Some think he intends deliberately to pick a quarrel with the South African Government over apartheid. I hear that not long ago he sat next to Harold Wilson at a dinner. Wilson said to him: 'You should wait until your last few weeks before having an open breach with the South Africans. Then they will deport you, and you will have your fare paid back to England!' A nice example of Socialist economics.

## 14 July 1963

Catch a morning train to Canterbury to lunch with Canon Shirley.* We have much talk about Somerset Maugham, an old boy of the school. About five years ago, he told Shirley that he had two ambitions – to be awarded the Order of Merit and to be buried in the Precincts. Shirley replied that he could do nothing about the first, but would do what he could about the second. Apparently Maugham had already given £10,000 to the school to provide a scholarship for a working-class boy. He also gave £3,000 for a new boathouse. In return, it was understood that he should have a grave in the Precincts. Canon Shirley did not find it easy to convince the Chapter of this, but pleaded that Thomas Hardy,† also an unbeliever, had his heart buried in Westminster Abbey.

## 21 July 1963

Staying at the Leys School with Alan Barker. I hear that when Oliver Dawnay‡ was in the Royal Household, the Queen Mother suggested that he should have a grace-and-favour house in Windsor Great Park. Dawnay and his wife went to see it. It was a huge barracks of a place, so they came back and told

---

* The Revd Canon John Shirley (1890–1967). Headmaster, Worksop Coll. 1925–35; Headmaster, King's School, Canterbury 1935–62; Residentiary Canon of Canterbury Cathedral.
† In fact, Thomas Hardy's heart was buried at St Michael's Church, Stinsford, possibly with the cat that is reputed to have eaten it, and his ashes at Westminster Abbey.
‡ (1920–88), civil servant. PS to the Queen Mother 1951–6.

the Queen Mother they did not think it would be quite suitable. 'Yes,' she replied, 'I knew it would be too small.'

## 31 July 1963

Dinner party in flat. Rather an historic assembly. At 6 p.m. the Royal Assent was given to the Peerage Bill, allowing peers to renounce their peerages & sit in House of Commons. Anthony Benn was the first to do so, at 6.22 p.m., followed soon after by John Altrincham. Both are dining with me tonight. Other guests include Douglas Hurd,* soon off to our Rome Embassy, and Brian Rees.

Anthony shows me his Instrument of Disclaimer. It was in fact signed by him this morning – the law knows no part of any day. It had to be sealed. He used green wax (House of Commons colour), a bit of red ribbon made for gift parcels in the United States, and a B-seal bought at Woolworth's. 'B stands for Benn and Bristol,' he says. But as it is a memorable document to be deposited in the Victoria Tower, it is typed on cartridge paper, & signed in Indian ink.

Sir George Coldstream,† as Clerk of the Crown, received the instrument. Both Anthony & John say he was the essence of friendly dignity and courtesy. As Anthony entered the House of Lords, a badge messenger said: 'Good evening, Milord.' As he left Coldstream's room, another messenger said: 'Good night, sir.'

Anthony mentions the interesting point that his Instrument of Disclaimer does not bear a ten-shilling stamp, although this is obligatory for all renunciations of property rights, even when these are of no value.

## 20 August 1963

I hear that when the Queen Mother was inadvertently booed during the recent Greek Royal Visit she remarked to her lady-in-waiting: 'Canon Collins is in good voice tonight.'‡

## 21 August 1963

Pamela Berry tells me that when Miss Keeler was entertaining Profumo, she kept telling him how poor her brother was. Being both well dressed and a generous man, Profumo gave her several of his barely worn suits to pass on

---

* Baron Hurd of Westwell (b. 1930), Conservative politician. Diplomatic Service 1952–66; Home Secretary 1985–9; Foreign Secretary 1989–95.

† (1907–2004), barrister and civil servant. Clerk to the Crown in Chancery 1954–68.

‡ The Rev. Canon Lewis John Collins (1905–82), Anglican priest. Canon of St Paul's 1948–81; one of the founders of the Campaign for Nuclear Disarmament.

to her brother. In fact, she gave them to Lucky Gordon,[*] who is wearing them to this day.

### 26 August 1963

Lunch at the Beefsteak and sit next to John Julius Norwich.[†] He tells me that he will very shortly begin a year's unpaid leave from the Foreign Office. He intends to spend it writing a book on the medieval history of Normandy. He has a passion for reference books and is at present immersed in the *Dictionary of Christian Churches*. His father, Duff Cooper, had little use for reference books – only the *English Dictionary* and a *Dictionary of Quotations*. The latter he bought for use in solving crossword puzzles, but then decided it would be unfair to use it, so it was never opened.

After lunch Philip de Zulueta takes me down to Admiralty House, which I enter for the first time since Jim Cilcennin used to be First Lord. Harold Macmillan has been living here since August 1960 whilst 10 Downing Street has been renovated, but is shortly to move back. Philip thinks the rooms have been much improved by the removal of bookcases from the drawing room. But it still has the appearance of a makeshift residence.

The Prime Minister's study is a dingy little room looking over Whitehall, but with a magnificent and unexpected view of the Dome of St Paul's. Over the fire are photographs of the original Macmillan croft on the Isle of Arran, and of Birch Grove. Masses of books everywhere, including the inevitable Trollope. Philip tells me that quite recently the Prime Minister has been reading *The Appeasers* by Martin Gilbert and Richard Gott, recently published.[‡] Macmillan said to Philip: 'I wonder if we shall one day be called appeasers? I think not. The difference is that they could have fought the war if they had wished, whereas for us war has ceased to be an instrument.'

### 29 August 1963

At 3 p.m. call on Kay Halle[§] at the Berkeley. She has just arrived from the United States, and travelled in the same ship as George Brown. He behaved most oddly on the way over, largely due to what his steward called 'wardrobe drinking'. She tells me the latest joke in Washington – 'Bobby Kennedy has eight children – and not one of them black.'

---

[*] Aloysius Gordon (1931–2017), Jamaican jazz musician, who came to public notice during the Profumo Affair.
[†] 2nd Viscount Norwich (1929–2018), historian and travel writer.
[‡] Sir Martin Gilbert (1936–2015), historian; official biographer of Sir Winston Churchill. Richard Gott (b. 1938), journalist and historian; Literary Editor of the *Guardian* 1992–4.
[§] (1904–97), Cleveland journalist.

We discuss the American political scene. Soon after his return from negotiating the Test Ban Treaty in Moscow, Kay gave a dinner party for Averell
Harriman* in Washington. The pudding was surmounted by a huge white
sugar bird bearing in its beak the message: 'Thank you, Averell, for helping
me.'

## 30 August 1963
A good story about Montgomery's recent visit to Russia. At one moment
during his talks with Marshal Malinovsky[†] he said: 'I don't think soldiers
should meddle in politics, do you, Marshal?'

## 1 September 1963
I go to Sissinghurst for tea with Harold and Nigel Nicolson. The red-brick
castle looks very pretty with its heraldic flag, but the weather is wet and
melancholy. Whilst we are having tea, a telegram arrives over the telephone
from one of the newspapers. They want Harold to make a statement about
Guy Burgess,[‡] whose death in Moscow is announced today. Nigel says to me:
'I do wish journalists would not ask my father for this; the awful thing is that
he would really like to make a statement.'

## 2 September 1963
I discuss Lloyd George with Sir Frederic Hooper, who tells me that he
vividly remembers lunching in a headquarters officers' mess in France on
11 November 1918. The unanimous theme of conversation among all the
others was: 'Now that the war is over we must immediately get rid of Lloyd
George.'

   Harold Watkinson told Sir F. the other day that the Cabinet was mostly
in favour of Rab Butler as the next Conservative Prime Minister, while the
backbenchers prefer Maudling. Naturally young and able ministers such as
Heath are not in favour of a PM of their age.

---

* (1891–1986), American Democratic politician and diplomat. US Ambassador to the Soviet
Union 1943–6 and to the UK Apr.–Oct. 1946.
† Rodion Malinovsky (1894–1967), Soviet Military Cdr in World War II. Defence Minister of
the Soviet Union 1957–67.
‡ (1911–63), Foreign Office official; member of the Cambridge Five spy ring that passed
secrets to the Russians.

## 8 September 1963

Talk to Hartley Shawcross about Lord Denning[*] and his forthcoming report into the Profumo Affair.

Shawcross describes Denning as modest, charming, opinionated, but with the social and moral outlook of a semi-detached dweller in Haywards Heath. He is not the man who should have been appointed to undertake his present inquiry, since he is not sufficiently worldly or aware of how large sections of the community live today.

He is a tremendously hard worker – the office of Master of the Rolls demands this. The trouble is that he is a law reformer, and tends to deliver judgments which reflect not what the law is, but what he thinks it ought to be.

## 12 September 1963

Glad to escape from London with Perry Worsthorne to attend the Liberal Party Conference at Brighton. We sit in the sun on the veranda of the Grand Hotel having tea and watching all the Liberal Mandarins streaming in and out. We are joined by David Butler, who relates one good incident. On TV yesterday, Lord Ogmore,[†] the conference President, apparently said that the Liberals could form a Government if required. Then Jo Grimond appeared, and repeated the claim. Later Jo said off the record: 'I could hardly contradict my President the same day. I must wait at least a fortnight.'

## 13 September 1963

At All Souls with A.L. Rowse. He tells me that Harold Wilson's greatest Oxford friend is Professor Kenneth Wheare,[‡] Rector of Exeter College, and an authority on the machinery of Government.

Oxford looks enchanting in the sun, and the view from A.L.R.'s windows is like an inspired backcloth for a setting of a Verdi opera – *I Professiori*.

After dinner, A.L.R. tells a good story of how at some meeting he was praised for his numerous services to football. He had been confused with Sir Stanley Rous, Chairman of the Football Association, of whom A.L.R had never heard.

---

[*] Alfred Denning, Baron Denning (1899–1999), lawyer and judge.

[†] David Rees-Williams, 1st Baron Ogmore (1903–76), Liberal Party President 1963–4.

[‡] Sir Kenneth Wheare (1907–79), Rector of Exeter Coll., Oxford 1956–72; Vice-Chancellor, Oxford University 1964–6. Sir Stanley Rous (1895–1986), Secretary of the Football Association 1934–61; President, Fédération Internationale de Football Associations (FIFA), 1961–74.

## 5 October 1963

11. a.m. call on Sir Pierson Dixon at the British Embassy in Paris. He is a mild, agreeable man, who is very forthcoming in answering all the questions I put to him. He tells me that in spite of the strained relations between the French and British Governments, General de Gaulle remains quite accessible to him. The Ambassador usually sees him before or after a visit to London.

The Ambassador also gives me a vivid account of one of the General's shooting parties for the Diplomatic Corps at Rambouillet. The protocol never varies. He greets his guests at 8.45 a.m. with a cup of coffee, then disappears until the last of the four pheasant drives. He never wears country clothes. As soon as the morning's sport has ended, the guns return to the château, change and lunch with the General. In mid-afternoon they leave for Paris, each with a brace of birds.

*On 8 October Harold Macmillan was laid low by prostate trouble. He decided that he would not be able to continue as Prime Minister and his decision to retire was announced the next day at the Conservative Party Conference at Blackpool by Lord Home, the Foreign Secretary. This unexpected development transformed the conference into the equivalent of an American nominating convention, with candidates for the premiership being assessed. Lord Hailsham declared his intention to disclaim his peerage so that he could stand for the premiership. The dramatic events totally dominated politics for the next eleven days, and the controversies over the outcome for many years to come.*

## 15 October 1963

Still no immediate likelihood of a decision about who will succeed Macmillan as Prime Minister. Most of the Cabinet are visiting him individually at King Edward VII Hospital to give him their views, but so far Bill Deedes has not been.

## 16 October 1963

The *Daily Telegraph*, in its leading articles, refuses to take the plunge in putting forward the name of a new Prime Minister. Instead, it merely says day after day that Macmillan and the Queen should come to a decision very quickly. Still no definite sign of whether it will be Hailsham, Maudling, Butler or Home.

Katie Macmillan tells me it has been a terrible week, with endless intrigue. As luck would have it, Maurice has to debate at the Oxford Union tomorrow night on the motion 'That this House has no confidence in Her Majesty's Government'. He will speak to me on the phone later tonight.

At 6.30 drink with Pamela Berry at Cowley Street. She has heard that Hugh Gaitskell left all his private letters and journals to Mrs Ian Fleming.[*] If so, it was a most hurtful thing to do, and I hope for Dora's sake that it is untrue.

Pamela says that Hailsham's chance of becoming Prime Minister was wrecked at Blackpool by the fervour with which his cause was pursued by Maurice Macmillan, Ian Gilmour and particularly Randolph Churchill, who pressed 'Q' badges on all he met, including Rab Butler.

Speak to Maurice Macmillan at 9.30. He thinks that the present semi-public controversy over who should be Prime Minister is rather a good thing. It ensures that everybody's views are heard and appreciated. He thinks it unfair that people should be so angry with Hailsham. It is to Hailsham's credit that he refused to make any move until the Prime Minister had announced his retirement. He is also the only Cabinet Minister who had the guts to defend the Government on TV over the Profumo Affair. Maurice personally thinks that the new Prime Minister will be either Maudling or Home – although he himself would prefer Hailsham. He adds: 'There is a temptation to pull in a man such as Home, when the strong candidates arouse so much passion.'

The Prime Minister has taken the process of testing Party opinion into his own hands so that if the Queen asks him whom she should send for, he can give her a complete account of Party opinion, not merely a card vote. It is far better that the Prime Minister himself should do this. If he left it to the Queen and Michael Adeane, they could well come to the conclusion that in the face of deep Conservative divisions she ought to send for Mr Wilson.

## 17 October 1963

The search for a new Prime Minister in succession to Macmillan (who has not yet formally resigned) continues. I am tempted to have a heavy bet on Maudling, but my bookmaker is not accepting bets on the premiership. The odds against Maudling are 5–1.

Write to Michael Adeane, asking if he can spare me ten minutes either tomorrow or early Saturday. He is likely to be under great pressure, so I doubt whether he will have time to discuss the constitutional background to the present crisis.

Cocktail party at George Weidenfeld's house in Eaton Square. Desmond Donnelly[†] thinks that Home is certain to be invited to form a Government.

---

[*] Ann Charteris (1913–81), m. 1952 Ian Fleming; her later affair with Gaitskell was known in society circles.

[†] (1920–74), politician and journalist who was a member of four different parties: Labour in

Harold Evans,* the Prime Minister's publicity man at No. 10, this evening hinted to an American journalist that the decision had been taken and that the House of Lords should not be ruled out. Donnelly also telephoned Ian Gilmour at White's. Gilmour was in despair and said: 'They have chosen the wrong H.'

At dinner I meet Peter Goldman – he failed dismally as Conservative candidate at the Orpington by-election last year, and now works in Conservative Central Office. Goldman says that after the breakdown of the Common Market negotiations the Prime Minister offered Heath the Board of Trade, but he refused it. Apparently he also cast a shadow over his relations with the Prime Minister by talking indiscreetly to John Wyndham, when staying at Petworth, of all places!

### 18 October 1963

11 a.m. to the Ministry of Defence to see Bill Deedes. It is now obvious that the Queen is about to send for Lord Home to form a Government. Bill is rather sad that Rab Butler has been passed over yet again. 'Not many people like him, but he never did anyone any harm.'

He tells me that at this moment the Queen is visiting Macmillan at the King Edward VII Hospital. I tell him that I already know this, from having noticed the traffic lights turned off at the intersection in Oxford Street which leads to Beaumont Street.

Bill stresses the importance of modern communications during the past few days. Lord Dilhorne† undertook to sound the views of each member of the Cabinet, Martin Redmayne, the Chief Whip, was responsible for ministers outside the Cabinet and backbenchers, and Lord St Aldwyn‡ sounded the House of Lords. Many Members are still overseas, but there is nobody who has not been fully consulted and made his views known about the future of the premiership to Macmillan.

I ask Bill why he was almost alone among ministers in not having visited Macmillan in hospital. He replies that as he was seeing the Press, including foreign journalists, so frequently throughout the week, he thought it better

---

1936, the Northern Ireland Labour Party in 1946, his own party 'Our Party', later the Democratic Party in 1968, and finally the Conservative Party in 1971.

* Sir Harold Evans, 1st Bt (1911–83), Macmillan's Press Secretary 1957–63, not to be confused with Sir Harold Evans, Editor of *The Times* 1981–2.

† Reginald Manningham-Buller, 1st Viscount Dilhorne (1905–80), Conservative MP for Daventry 1945–50 and Northamptonshire South 1950–62; Lord Chancellor 1962–4.

‡ Michael Hicks-Beach, 2nd Earl St Aldwyn (1912–92), Conservative politician. Government Chief Whip in the Lords 1958–64 and 1970–74.

not either to receive or to express any opinion about the Prime Minister's successor.

He tells me that printed invitations to No. 10 Downing Street to hear in advance the Queen's Speech on 28 October are in the name of 'The Prime Minister'. He thinks that in previous years the name of the Prime Minister himself has always appeared on the cards.

Lunch at the Beefsteak and have some valuable conversation with Maurice Macmillan. He tells me that his father has insisted throughout the crisis on receiving the views of all those he has consulted in writing. And the switchboard at 10 Downing Street through which he made all his telephone calls has kept a transcript of every conversation. This is in case there is controversy about the role he has played.

I ask Maurice why Frederick Erroll,* President of the Board of Trade, was one of the few Cabinet ministers not to be called to see the Prime Minister in hospital. He replies: 'Because he would only have agreed with everything my father said. So it was not worth asking him.'

Maurice says that only one thing about Lord Home's appointment will anger him – if attacks are made on Macmillan for having chosen Home from motives of snobbery.

## 19 October 1963, letter to parents

What a heavy week it has been – particularly as I had been asked to give two lectures to the Institute of Directors weeks ago. But I managed to dash from place to place and to keep abreast of events.

A great deal of work went into my long leader-page article on the Queen's Prerogative in choosing a new PM. But I was most fortunate in having expert help from two sources – Maurice Macmillan and Michael Adeane himself. In fact, Michael even rang me up early this morning to discuss it – an act of kindness I shall long remember. One thing Maurice told me is <u>most</u> interesting. Apparently his father thinks he may well be attacked for having acted unconstitutionally or for forcing the issue. So he has insisted on all advice given to him during the past days being in writing; and where he has telephone conversations from his bed in hospital, they have all gone through the switchboard at Downing Street and transcripts made of them. A wonderful source of material for some future historian.†

---

* 1st Baron Erroll of Hale (1914–2000), Conservative politician. MP for Altrincham and Sale 1945–65; President of the Board of Trade 1961–3.

† K.R. was correct. All the material, then in its complete state, was in Macmillan's archive at Birch Grove, to which I had access when writing the official biography of Sir Alec Douglas-Home. Not all the material went to the Bodleian Library.

So now we have Lord Home, which I suppose means a certain defeat at the next General Election. Even Butler, or Maudling, I think, would have found it difficult to win. But I cannot see a middle-class floating voter being attracted by the new PM.

Did you see that Philip de Zulueta has been given a knighthood for his services as Private Secretary to Eden and to Macmillan? It is a fantastically high honour for such a job. Jock Colville, who did the same work for Winston during the war, got a CB. But, of course, Macmillan has always scattered his honours broadside and a Prime Minister is never refused his resignation honours.

### 20 October 1963

The Cabinet list is announced. Rab Butler, surprisingly, has gone to the Foreign Office. I should have thought a dignified retirement to the Lords more suitable. Bill Deedes still in Cabinet and Peter Carrington brought in as No. 2 at the FO.

### 21 October 1963

More Government appointments. At last a job for Maurice Macmillan as Economic Secretary to the Treasury.

Watch Home interviewed on TV – admirably self-possessed, and seems to relish every moment of his unexpected accession to office of PM.

### 26 October 1963

Tommy Lascelles says the Queen Mother is terribly Tory in her view. So was her father when Duke of York, who would not have J.R. Clynes, Labour Home Secretary,* in the house when Princess Margaret was about to be born at Glamis, as custom then dictated. He is reputed to have said: 'Give him a glass of wine in the housekeeper's room' when he came over officially for the birth.

### 28 October 1963

Esmond Rothermere mentions that it was not so much Winston as Clemmie who hated the Graham Sutherland portrait on his eightieth birthday. Winston's family have never regarded him as a hard man, as he has been so

---

* (1869–1949), British trade unionist and Labour politician. Leader of the Labour Party 1921–2; Home Secretary 1929–31. The last time a Home Secretary was nearby to prevent a royal baby being swapped was in 1936 at the birth of Princess Alexandra.

indulgent to all the weaknesses of his children, and they had resented the hardness in Sutherland's picture.*

## 29 October 1963
Visit Giles St Aubyn at Eton. I have a few moments' talk with Oliver van Oss, who regrets he will not be acting Head Master long enough to abolish cricket. He has presented two silver cups to his house captain and to the captain of games. On the first is inscribed 'Parcere subjectis et debellare superbos', and the second: 'Nimium ne crude colori'. I translated this as 'Don't put too much trust in colours.' But Oliver says it should be translated: 'Don't put too much trust in your complexion!'

## 13 November 1963
Talk to Maurice Macmillan. We discuss Home's speech yesterday and he tells me of the method his father used in composing speeches – section by section, so that if pressed for time one or more sections can be dropped.

## 15 November 1963
John Wyndham tells me that he is unlikely to assume his newly created title of Baron Egremont until he has left No. 10. He is afraid that if he answers the telephone with the words, 'Egremont here' he will get the reply: 'I have never heard of you from Adam, but thank God that fellow Wyndham has gone!' In fact, he wants to escape from No. 10 as soon as possible, but Alec Home has asked him to stay on for a few weeks. 'I know exactly what will happen,' he says. 'It will be Christmas Day, and Wyndham will be duty officer.' I tell him not to despair, as he will doubtless become a Viscount in Home's Resignation Honours List.

John tells me that the other day he received a request from the *Sunday Times* to take photographs of Macmillan at Birch Grove. John put this to Macmillan, who replied: 'Certainly not. Comedia finita est.'

The City is evidently contemptuous of Iain Macleod for flouncing out of Cabinet and then going into a firm like Lombards.

*On 22 November President John F. Kennedy was assassinated in Dallas, Texas, one of the defining moments of the twentieth century.*

---

* In Dec. 1977, shortly after Lady Churchill's death, her executors announced that the Sutherland portrait had been destroyed, news that caused great controversy.

### 24 November 1963, letter to parents
You can imagine what a time we had in the office yesterday after the nightmare news of President Kennedy's assassination. The whole paper inevitably had to be reshaped, and a great deal of the week's work went by the board.

It is one of the really great tragedies of our time – the new President, Lyndon Johnson, is a very second-rate fellow without any of the cool vison of his predecessor. I saw Kennedy several times when I was in Washington and twice went to his Press conferences. One was left with admiration rather than affection – he had a touch of arrogance which I did not care for, but which is quite understandable in any man who bears his responsibilities.

I also saw the White House as redecorated by Mrs Kennedy – beautiful but a little too perfect, like a museum of eighteenth-century art. Washington will be very coarse-grained under the new regime.

### 30 November 1963, letter to parents
John Wyndham tells me of Harold Macmillan's last day as Prime Minister. On the day the Queen came to the Edward VII Hospital, Macmillan had a little sleep in the evening, and woke up to find two workmen in his room. They explained that they were from the Post Office, and had been sent to remove the secret 'scrambler' telephone which all Cabinet ministers have. Macmillan later commented to John: 'Nothing gets rolled up so quickly as a red carpet.'

### 4 December 1963
To Westminster. As I walk into Speaker's Court Winston is arriving in his car. He looks incredibly pale and shrunken, but fills the air with fragrant cigar smoke. He is lifted out of the car into a wheelchair, and trundled off towards the Chamber. I at once take the lift to the Gallery, and am in time to see him wheeled to the Bar of the House, then helped by two other MPs to his seat. There is barely a whisper of cheers, which I feel is what he would prefer. He is, after all, the Member for Woodford, not a freak to be cheered at sight. The House of Commons is great enough to take even a Winston in its stride.

### 10 December 1963
Talk to Katie Macmillan, and mention how surprised I am at seeing name of Bobbety Salisbury in a letter to *The Times*, protesting against the proposed demolition of Gilbert Scott's Foreign Office block.[*] She agrees with me that

---

[*] Sir George Gilbert Scott (1811–78), Gothic revivalist architect of the St Pancras Hotel, the Albert Memorial and the Foreign Office.

it is probably family affection and a remembrance of the great days of British foreign policy when his grandfather was both PM and Foreign Secretary. She adds: 'None of the Cecils have aesthetic taste. We admire Hatfield today, but in the sixteenth century it was the sort of house that the Berrys would build today.'

## 14 December 1963

Geoffrey Keating tells me he has just been in the United States. On the evening of President Kennedy's funeral, Mrs Kennedy received Heads of State and one or two other people. During these comings and goings Éamon de Valera was introduced to Prince Philip and Alec Home. They had a few words of conversation, and liked each other so much that they made a date to meet later in the evening. They then spent half an hour in a close huddle together, never having met before.

## 15 December 1963

News is filtering through from America about the Warren Commission[*] investigating the assassination of President Kennedy. One member is worried by one point. The President was shot as the car was moving away from the assassin. Yet a bullet wound was found in the front of his throat – and nobody remembers seeing him turn round in the car or has produced a photograph of him doing so.

## 17 December 1963

Walk through the Park to breakfast with Tony Snowdon at Kensington Palace. The house has been charmingly designed, with a pervading atmosphere of discreet wealth and civilised taste.

The drawing room has white walls, rose curtains and a lovely carpet. A revolving bookcase containing bound presentation volumes.

We breakfast in the dining room. It has apricot walls and pale-blue chairs. Excellent breakfast of melon, haddock and eggs. Newspapers laid out on the table.

Then to Tony's study, a very modern yet elegant room. He tells me he has done the veneer of the doors himself. He has also made his desk and a complicated box, housing record-player, tape-recorder, projector, and a system for broadcasting over the house. He also designed his bookcases with

---

[*] Chief Justice Earl Warren (1891–1974), Chief Justice of the US 1953–69, headed the commission into the Kennedy assassination that bore his name. The commission's finding that Lee Harvey Oswald (1939–63) acted alone has been challenged over the years.

adjustable screws for altering the height of the shelves. A pleasant jumble of authors and lots of pictures including two Sidney Nolans.* Three telephones, most of which are perpetually ringing.

## 30 December 1963

Lunch Beefsteak and find myself sitting next to Harold Macmillan. First time I have seen him since his illness and resignation. He has fined down, and now looks rather like the flattering portrait of him by James Gunn.† Beautifully dressed, with a great deal of sober black cloth, white linen and a pearl in his tie. Luminous and sleek, with not a white hair out of place.

John Maude,‡ the judge, talks about crime and punishment. H.M. asks if either of us has ever seen the inside of a prison. We both have. I mention how depressing I found my lecture at Wormwood Scrubs, and H.M. asks me what questions the prisoners put to me. 'Doubts about whether their trials were fairly reported,' I reply. H.M.: 'I am not at all surprised. Newspaper reports of trials make absolutely no sense to me.' He is also disturbed by the practice by which judges have a list of a prisoner's previous convictions before trial begins, and says he was worried about this view when it came up in Parliament. 'We laugh at French justice,' he says. 'But at least they find out the truth. Here it is too much of a game.'

He talks of shooting, saying in his caricature manner, making wrinkles of self-deprecation appear at the corners of his eyes, that he has not shot properly since his operation as he found it too painful. This saddens him, as it has been a tremendous year – 'I hear they got a thousand birds one day at Hatfield.' He describes the shoot given by President de Gaulle at Rambouillet, and praises the habit of not continuing after lunch – 'You know how it is, one stops for lunch, and somebody always wants some more port, so it is never very good in the afternoon.'

Andrew Devonshire comes in – 'Hallo, Uncle Harold' – and sits on my other side. He has much charm in his nervous way. Lord Sefton,§ Andrew says, was staying recently at Chatsworth and watched the Beatles singing on TV. Suddenly he observed: 'Nobody has ever accused me of being a bugger, but I do think the third boy from the left is rather fetching!'

---

* Sir Sidney Nolan (1917–92), leading Australian artist.
† Sir James Gunn (1893–1964), Scottish landscape and portrait painter;
‡ His Hon. John Maude (1901–86), Judge, City of London Court 1954–65; Judge, Central Criminal Court 1965–8.
§ Hugh Molyneux, 7th Earl of Sefton (1898–1972), soldier. ADC to the Governor General of Canada 1919 and the Viceroy of India 1926; Lord-in-Waiting to George VI 1936–7; Constable of Lancaster Castle.

See advance copy of the Honours List. Viscountcy for David Eccles which he should have had when sacked by Macmillan in July last year, and a barony for Roy Thomson.*

## 31 December 1963

Donald Coggan enjoys telling me the story of a toastmaster who once whispered to him at a local dinner: 'Speak well into the microphone, Your Grace. The agnostics here are terrible.'

---

* 1st Baron Thomson of Fleet (1894–1976), Canadian newspaper proprietor who owned both *The Times* and the *Sunday Times* in 1996.

# 1964

*The pace of the 1960s did not slacken in 1964. In January the Federation of Rhodesia and Nyasaland was dissolved. In February Cassius Clay, later Muhammad Ali, defeated Sonny Liston to become heavyweight champion of the world. In March Constantine II, a friend of Kenneth, became King of Greece. Radio Caroline became the UK's first pirate radio station. In April Gemini 1, the first unmanned two-man spacecraft, was launched. In April the first Habitat store was opened. In May, Jawaharlal Nehru died. In June Nelson Mandela was sentenced to life imprisonment in South Africa. In July President Lyndon Johnson signed the Civil Rights Act. In September the Forth Road Bridge opened over the Firth of Forth. On 15 October the Labour Party won the general election (in which Kenneth voted Labour) and Harold Wilson became Prime Minister, ending thirteen years of Conservative rule. On 3 November Lyndon Johnson defeated the Republican challenger Barry Goldwater in the US Presidential election.*

### 16 January 1964

Bob Boothby says he has just read Iain Macleod's account of change of premiership in tomorrow's *Spectator*, but quoted tonight in the *Evening Standard*. 'After this,' he says, 'the Conservatives have absolutely no chance of winning the next election.'

### 17 January 1964

Everybody is buzzing with long review by Iain Macleod in this week's *Spectator* of Randolph Churchill's book on the change of PM in October. It gives a very different version from that believed to have been fed by Macmillan to Randolph. Macleod believes that Macmillan was moved by an overwhelming wish to keep out Butler. Much anger among Conservatives at this rift in the party front. But Macleod would never have written his article if Randolph had not given the Macmillan version.

Talk to Katie Macmillan. She says she doubts whether her father-in-law ever saw Randolph after his resignation. She thinks it unlikely she would not have known of Randolph's supposed visit to Birch Grove by helicopter in November, as alleged last week by the *Sunday Times*. Nor is Macmillan likely to have talked to Randolph on the telephone – 'he is not a chatterer on the telephone'. She is furious with Macleod for washing dirty linen in public, and observes rather bitterly: 'Bobbety was right after all. Macleod is too clever by half.'

Donald McLachlan tells me he thinks that Macleod's health is very bad – a form of arthritis which has shrunk his muscles that has affected his judgement.

I ask Pamela Berry whether, from the gossipy circle of ministerial wives, she can discover the unknown woman mentioned in Macleod's article who revealed to Mrs Macleod on 17 October that the choice of a new PM was imminent.

### 18 January 1964

Pamela telephones early to tell me she has discovered who it was who told Mrs Macleod that the decision of a new choice of Prime Minister was imminent on 17 October. It was Lady Monckton,[*] who had got it from Dorothy Macmillan.

### 19 January 1964

At Eton. Talk to Oliver van Oss about Robert Birley. Claude Elliott was surprised Birley wasn't made a life peer. Oliver says Birley has an immense bibliophilic reputation – seventy stout notebooks on Eton College Library left behind for the archives. He made learning fun at Eton. He was immensely erudite with a huge knowledge of French history. Birley was very disappointed that Brian Young was not appointed HM – he regarded him as a son. Oliver thinks Giles St Aubyn did himself harm in opposing Brian Young so shrilly. Oliver does not think Giles would be a good headmaster, which he now wants to become. 'Birley used to say that the difficulty in headmastering is not so much sacking boys of sixteen or seventeen – they have their lives in front of them, but sacking beaks of forty-two, telling them that they have chosen the wrong profession.'

### 20 January 1964

It has been noticed that in the membership book of the Beefsteak Club the

---

[*] Bridget Monckton, 11th Lady Ruthven of Freeland, later Viscountess Monckton of Brenchley (1896–1982). Wartime commander of women's services in India; Conservative member of the House of Lords.

entry chosen by Iain Macleod to describe his profession is not 'Member of Parliament', nor even 'Cabinet Minister', but 'Statesman'.

## 22 January 1964
Talk to Katie Macmillan. She tells me that she made enquiries about a helicopter coming to Birch Grove, and could find absolutely no truth in it. She has, however, heard of Randolph taking a helicopter to attend Macleod's rally. She still remains doubtful whether Macmillan fed much information to Randolph. She believes that Macmillan was against Randolph's book being written. Nor does she think he saw it until it had been written.

## 24 January 1964
Dora Gaitskell telephones me about 11 p.m. Tells me that her life peerage is gazetted tonight – Baroness Gaitskell of Egremont, in Cumberland. Gaitskells have been buried there since 1640. But as John Wyndham became Lord Egremont the other day, she wrote to ask if he had any objection. He replied that he would be delighted if she took Egremont for her designatory title. Dora asks if I know of a good book on the House of Lords, and I shall try to find one.

## 27 January 1964
Charles and Pamela Snow come in to drink and talk. They are full of affection. Their son Philip* sounds precocious. Before he went to Eton they took the twelve-year-old to tea one day with Robert Birley, and the works of Ben Jonson, of all things, were discussed. Birley asked Philip if he had read *Everyman in His Humour*. The boy replied that he had not, but that he <u>had</u> read *Every Man out of His Humour*. This floored poor Birley, as well it might!

## 1 February 1964, letter to parents
A busy week in Parliament as usual. I had some talk with Harold Wilson one day, and am to see him again on Friday. I personally find him a kind and helpful fellow, with never the faintest suggestion on his part that he is talking to an 'enemy'.

I had a moving encounter as I came down the stairs of the Commons after talking to Wilson. Winston had just arrived by car and was being wheeled along a passage to the Chamber. As he drew level with me he looked up and twisted his face into a sad grimace of a smile. But what a shrunken ghost of a figure he is. It quite wrings one's heart.

---

* Hon. Philip Snow (b. 1952), writer.

## 3 February 1964

James Pope-Hennessy tells me that the other day he had the Queen Mother to tea. She was enjoying herself so much that she lingered and he managed to get rid of her only five minutes before the Windsors arrived for drinks. That indeed would have been an encounter.

## 7 February 1964

See Maurice Macmillan at the House of Commons at 12.30. He tells me that his father is one of those old-fashioned businessmen who disapprove of expense accounts. Second, that if Maurice should be defeated at Halifax at the next General Election, he will probably not join the queue to get back into the House of Commons at a by-election. He will prefer to look after the publishing business for a year or two, after which it will almost run itself.

I also see Harold Wilson for a good chat.* He is most welcoming and friendly. He waves me to an armchair and gives me a cigar. He, too, smokes one. First we talk about his years at Oxford as a don. He had rooms in Univ. near those of John Maud. He was also a close friend of Giles Alington, the brother of Lady Douglas-Home.† Harold's younger boy is named after him.

One of his pupils was Kermit Gordon, now Director of the United States Bureau of the Budget. When Wilson met President Kennedy, the President said: 'You ought to meet Gordon.' Wilson replied: 'I have already. He was a pupil of mine.'

I ask Wilson how good his languages are. He says he can get along quite well in French, but believes that many mistakes in diplomacy can be traced to statesmen who talked in languages other than their own. He has been to Moscow eleven times and has a restaurant knowledge of Russian.

I ask him how far, when he becomes Prime Minister, he would be likely to follow the Kennedy practice of using outside organisations such as the Institute of Strategic Studies to supplement his official sources of knowledge. He replies that he would be in favour of this, although there should always be two or more organisations involved. It would be unwise to depend upon a single one.

He is also against the practice of bringing outsiders into important jobs in the established Civil Service – here, he tells me, he speaks with experience. It is unwise, he thinks, to disturb promotion prospects and to plant Rasputins

---

* This introduction was owing to Dora Gaitskell.
† Giles Alington (1914–56), Fellow of University Coll., Oxford. Elizabeth Douglas-Home, Baroness Home of the Hirsel (1909–90), wife of Sir Alec Douglas-Home; first woman to be a Fellow of Eton.

in Ministries. He points out that such civil servants as Oliver Franks and
Hugh Gaitskell all started at Principal level, even in wartime. 'I started even
lower.'

He thinks that the search for talent must be directed to the executive as
well as to the administrative class. Wilson does not rule out that some outsiders may be invited to take political office, but points out that in 1950 several
leading members of today's Government were only prospective candidates.

I ask him about his plans for future Honours Lists. He thinks that most
hereditary titles will go, and also that fewer honours will be given for rewarding civil servants and businessmen in the export field. He is very critical
of the amateurish way in which Macmillan has run his office at No. 10 – 'He
is a professional politician, but not a professional administrator. He behaved
like the Chairman of a wartime colliery, instead of being both Chairman and
Managing Director.' Wilson will have a much-enlarged Cabinet Secretariat.

Our final topic is the Queen's Household. Oddly enough, he knows neither Michael Adeane nor Martin Charteris. I suggest that he dines at my flat
one night to meet Martin, and he says he would be delighted. But how stupid
of the Palace not to have taken the initiative themselves before now.

## 8 February 1964
9.15 train to Oxford. A misty morning, but the sun soon breaks through and
the city looks enchanting. Lunch with Alan Bullock in the Senior Common
Room at the new St Catherine's College, Oxford.[*] The buildings are still
uncompleted, but when finished will form one of the most magnificent
architectural conceptions in England.[†] What I particularly like about the
scheme is the use which is to be made of trees, flowers and shrubs, forming
part of a water garden. The architect has designed not only the buildings, but
also every detail of the interior, from the furniture to the cutlery.

I am called from the Senior Common Room by a telephone message from
London. Conservative Central Office have put out the text of a letter from
Harold Macmillan to the Chairman of his constituency, in which he announces that he will not stand at the next election.

At 12 noon I spent nearly an hour talking to Bill Williams[‡] at Rhodes

---

[*] K.R. was a benefactor of the new foundation.
[†] The architect was Arne Jacobsen (1902–71). In his guide to the buildings of Oxfordshire,
Nikolaus Pevsner (1902–83), scholar of the history of art, described St Catherine's Coll.,
Oxford, as 'a perfect piece of architecture'. *The Buildings of England: Oxfordshire* (Penguin
Books, 1996 edn), p. 240.
[‡] Brig. Sir Edgar Williams (1912–95). Chief Intelligence Officer to Gen. Montgomery in the
North African Campaign; Editor of the *DNB*; Warden of Rhodes House 1952–80.

House about the *Dictionary of National Biography*. First we discuss a list of about twenty names for whom he has not yet appointed a biographer. It includes Lord Quickswood, and I am delighted to be asked to write his notice in about 1,200 words.

Bill tells me that Max Beerbohm once told him: 'I have never moved in the circles – or should I say squares – in which Virginia Woolf moves.'

Finally, we have a more general talk about the structure of the *DNB*. There is room for about 700 people, of which 500 choose themselves by their outstanding eminence. The difficulty is to decide the marginal 200. What impresses Williams is that the scientists can always agree very rapidly among themselves who should go in. But those connected with the Arts have widely differing opinions. The best unused sentence that Williams can recall of any notice is as follows: 'By his frankness in later years he endeared himself to a diminishing circle of friends.'

## 10 February 1964

Katie Macmillan comes to dine and talks a great deal about her family over the years. At Birch Grove once she saw a light at the bottom of the garden in the middle of the night and found it was Dorothy tending a rare plant, with a miner's lamp on her head and two hot-water bottles strapped around her.

She tells me that when de Gaulle came to Birch Grove, he looked about him and remarked bleakly: 'Quel joli logement.'

For Harold Macmillan she has warm affection. 'We are just like the Forsytes,' he once told her, and she thought, 'Yes, you are.' He once remarked to her, 'The Cavendishes have no imagination outside their own experience.' When he married Dorothy all the Cavendishes except the old Duke looked down their noses. Dorothy had, in the idiom of fifty years ago, married into trade. At first Dorothy was brave and rebellious in defending him, but then loneliness drove her into the arms of Bob Boothby. Harold would never divorce her because he wanted to protect her from falling into a bad set, and also because he felt he had been to blame. Katie adds that when a presentation was made to him by the servants at Birch Grove yesterday, the old nanny complained to Katie: 'Why in his speech did he keep on dragging Lady Dorothy in?' She thinks that, even having become PM, Harold must see a great part of his life as having turned to dust and ashes.

## 12 February 1964

Julian Amery sits next to me at lunch at the Beefsteak. He says that Lloyd George once came, about 1940, to visit his father [Leo Amery] in Eaton Square. He looked round the enormous drawing room with its double fireplace & said, 'So this is where you plotted my downfall in 1922.'

## 18 February 1964

To Westminster. Have a drink in the Harcourt Room with Jeremy Thorpe.[*]
In another corner sits Iain Macleod, surrounded by his associates in Lombard Banking, the hire-purchase house of which he recently became a director. The Hire-Purchase Bill is being debated today. It seems a somehow degrading scene for a former Leader of the House to be thus engaged.

## 19 February 1964

A busy and interesting day in Cambridge. I leave my bag at the Leys School, then at three o'clock to see Noel Annan, the Provost of King's. As always, he is welcoming. King's, Noel says, is very proud of its old men. E.M. Forster, who is eighty-five, still lives in the college. Noel also mentions that he is writing a biography of J.F. Roxburgh, the great Headmaster of Stowe School.

Back to the Leys School and give my talk on Politics and the Press to about sixty boys. A friendly, intelligent audience. Alan and Jean give a small dinner party for me. Among the guests is Owen Chadwick, Master of Selwyn College.[†] Alan tells me that George Brown, a governor at Repton, is at present having talks on the future of the public schools under a Labour Government with a small group of headmasters. These include Alan (The Leys), John Thorn (Repton), Walter Hamilton (Rugby) and Desmond Lee (Winchester).

At the end of the evening we listen to a recording of Benjamin Britten's *War Requiem*. It is a sombre and moving work, probably the best thing he has composed.

## 26 February 1964

Lunch at the Beefsteak and have some amusing talk with Andrew Devonshire. We discuss my *DNB* notice on Linky (Lord Quickswood). In his retirement at Bournemouth, Linky lived near a chine where the murderer Heath[‡] had hidden the body of one of his victims. It was just near a railway station, and Linky used to shout at the trains: 'All murderers change here.' But he enjoyed his retirement enormously. When somebody came to see him and asked him

---

[*] (1929–2014), Liberal MP for North Devon 1959–79; leader of the Liberal Party 1967–76.

[†] (1916–2015), Master of Selwyn Coll., Cambridge 1956–83; Dixie Professor of Ecclesiastical History 1958–68; Regius Professor of Modern History 1968–83; Vice-Chancellor of Cambridge University 1956–71; President of the British Academy 1981–5.

[‡] Neville Heath (1917–46), murderer. A few moments before his execution he was offered a glass of whisky by the Governor of Pentonville Prison. Heath replied: 'While you're about it, sir, you might make that a double.'

whether he did not find it boring, he replied: 'No, it is like sitting in the hall, waiting for the fly.'

### 15 March 1964

Read Anthony Powell's *The Valley of Bones.*[*] Wonderful stuff on the Army, particularly the devious thoughts of the Welsh other ranks. Also a glorious set-piece of a Divisional Commander's inspection. I find it more enjoyable than Waugh.

### 17 March 1964

At 11.30 to the House of Commons to talk to George Brown in his room about public schools. He tells me that reform of the public schools does not rank high on the priorities of a Labour Government once it gets back into power. 'Neither Wilson nor I have the guilt complex of Hugh Gaitskell over the public schools. Unlike him, we never went to one.' Brown favours a tax reform by which children cannot be educated privately under tax-free covenants. He also says that firms such as Rolls-Royce will no longer be able to subsidise boys at Repton.

### 18 March 1964

Walk down to Westminster with Michael Adeane. He obviously has no great liking for Harold Wilson, but thinks he will not be a difficult man to work with. At least, he says, Wilson is likely to give one a <u>thoughtful</u> reply to any question one asks him.

### 26 March 1964

Alfred Ryan[†] of *The Times* tells me that whenever the Poet Laureate[‡] sends them his latest verse on some official or Royal occasion, he always encloses a stamped addressed envelope in case they do not want to use it.

### 9 April 1964

Bill Deedes tells me that an announcement will be made this evening, saying that an election is to be held in the autumn. Thus Alec Home is challenging fate by prolonging the life of his Government to its utmost constitutional limit.

---

[*] The seventh novel (Heinemann, 1964) in the twelve-volume sequence *A Dance to the Music of Time*.

[†] A.P. Ryan (1900–72), journalist on *The Times* 1947–68.

[‡] John Masefield OM (1903–67), Poet Laureate 1930–67.

## 11 April 1964

James Pope-Hennessy tells me a story which came to him from the Queen Mother. When the King died in his sleep in 1952, the Queen Mother broke the news to little Prince Charles. She explained that when the valet had taken in the King's tea that morning he had found the King dead. Prince Charles listened gravely to the news, then enquired: 'Who drank the tea?'

## 14 April 1964

Hartley Shawcross tells me he has been reading an advance copy of Lord Kilmuir's memoirs called *Political Adventure*. He says that even the title is inaccurate, as an 'r' has been missed out from the second word of the title. Hartley says it is one of the most ungenerous, offensive and trivial volumes of its sort he has ever read.

## 24 April 1964

John Wyndham tells me a story about his uncle, the late Lord Leconfield.* One day he asked John what he thought of St Paul's epistles. John replied that he rather liked them. 'Oh,' said his uncle, 'I think St Paul wrote them after rather too good a dinner.'

## 9 May 1964

Story from Bill Williams of an undergraduate in the habit of climbing into Wadham through the Warden's Lodgings. One evening he was already inside when he heard footsteps, so went down a passage. The footsteps followed. Then into a room. Still footsteps. So under the desk. The footsteps belonged to Maurice Bowra, who came into the room, sat in the armchair for four hours, then said as he went off to bed: 'Turn off the light when you go.'

## 25 May 1964

Katie Macmillan thinks that John Wyndham was 'in some things at No. 10 always a passenger', adding, 'particularly in failing to warn Harold of what people were saying about Profumo'. An amusing story of Talleyrand,† who was once engaged in conversation by a bore. Talleyrand suddenly turned to the other end of the room, where a man was yawning. 'Look,' he said, 'we are overheard.'

---

* Charles Wyndham, 3rd Baron Leconfield (1872–1952). Lord Lieutenant of Sussex 1917–49.
† Charles Maurice de Talleyrand-Périgord (1754–1838), politician and diplomat who worked at the highest levels of French Government.

### 26 May 1964

Party at the Waldorf Hotel for the Moscow Arts Theatre Company. Lots of Russian talk. Edward Boyle quotes to me a remark which Harold Macmillan once made to him about Tolstoy's *Anna Karenina*: 'No novel reveals so clearly the perils of becoming déclassé.'

### 27 May 1964

Have a drink with Katie and Harold Macmillan at Catherine Place. I mention that I have just returned from Poland. 'Ah, the Poles,' says Harold, 'they are nature's Jacobites, they believe in the impossible. It was absurd of them to try to resist both Germany and Russia, yet they did so.'

Harold looks older than when I last saw him a month or two ago, but gives a superb stage performance of the Prime Minister in retirement. We talk of the absurd nineteen undergraduates at Merton College, Oxford, who have petitioned the Warden not to have to stand during grace before dinner in Hall. Harold says: 'Well, the other day at the lunch to the Prince in Lincoln College I was asked whether I wanted to have grace, and said that as Chancellor of the university of course I did.' I like his Victorian style of referring to the Duke of Edinburgh as 'the Prince'.

On Oxford he also comments that the university has changed enormously in the last fifty years, yet the newspapers continue to write about it as though it were still the same. 'There is not much difference nowadays between town and gown.' He says this disapprovingly, a far cry from the radical MP of the 1920s.

### 28 May 1964

See with surprise but delight that Oliver van Oss has been appointed Headmaster of Charterhouse in succession to Brian Young, now heading off to run the Nuffield Foundation.

Alan Barker tells me that he thinks Oliver van Oss must have been helped enormously in getting his job by support from Robert Birley.

### 30 May 1964

Oliver van Oss replies by return of post to thank me for my letter of congratulation. He tells me he did not put in for Charterhouse, but was asked by the Governing Body. Nor do they regard his appointment at fifty-five as a stopgap.

Boys' dinner with Brian Rees. He does not think that Oliver will be an entirely good Headmaster of Charterhouse, owing to his love of mischief.

## 31 May 1964, letter to parents

I had some talk with Harold Macmillan at the home of Katie and Maurice one evening last week. He has become rather old, but some of it, I think, is assumed as a protection against undue social activity. But he was interesting on the subject of Beaverbrook, whom he worked with at the Ministry of Aircraft Production during the war. He found the only way to maintain agreeable relations with Beaverbrook was by keeping him at arm's length on everything except business because 'socially he corrupted and seduced men as he did, in other ways, women'. So Macmillan would never attend the boozy dinners unless there was official work to be done.

## 2 June 1964

Train to Blackheath to dine with John Grigg. Other guest is Megan Lloyd George.* John, who has now embarked on writing the official life of Lloyd George, closely questions Megan about Welsh affairs. One interesting remark by Megan about her father: 'He was entirely without malice – well, except when attacking big men.'

## 5 June 1964

To Hillingdon Hospital to visit Mervyn Stockwood, who was involved in a head-on collision the other day while motoring to Oxford. We have some talk about Fisher, former Archbishop of Canterbury. At the private bishops' meetings over which he used to preside, prelates were always treated like naughty schoolboys and any criticism of the Archbishop was given a malicious motive. With Ramsey things are very different and everyone loves his gentleness. Stockwood was appalled when Fisher came to him one day and said: 'I am sure you are not a Communist, but how am I to convince my friends in the City?'

## 10 June 1964

Boofy Arran tells me an odd story of how, after the war, Winston and Macmillan wanted to lunch together. 'Let's lunch at Boodle's,' said Winston, thinking Macmillan was a member. Macmillan, thinking Winston was a member, agreed. So they lunched there. But neither was a member.

## 11 June 1964

Announced that Brian Rees has been appointed Headmaster of Merchant Taylors'.

---

* Lady Megan Lloyd George (1902–66). First female MP in Wales when she won Anglesey for the Liberals in 1929.

Talk to Allan Gwynne-Jones,* the painter, who has been commissioned some months ago to do a portrait of Rab Butler for Pembroke College, Cambridge. He has had much difficulty, however, in getting Rab to sit. Rab says that he cannot spare any time from his duties at the Foreign Office, but wrote to him some months ago: 'There will be an election in June which we shall lose, after which you may have all the sittings you want.'

## 1 July 1964

To Hodder & Stoughton who are giving a party to mark the publication of a new biography of Harold Wilson.† Stimulating conversation with Harold himself. He much regrets that nowadays there are practically no books of living people, not even long biographical essays, such as the one Macaulay wrote on Gladstone. 'What we really need', he adds, 'is a book on what makes Rab Butler tick.' I ask Harold what he is reading now. He replies that it is Hugh Sidey's‡ book on Kennedy, which illustrates that politicians in power should not leave everything to civil servants but, like the late President, master the complexity of the problems themselves.

For bedside reading he has volume two of Monypenny and Buckle's§ life of Disraeli. This was part of the £20 of books he won at Oxford for his Gladstone Memorial Prize. He tells me that he had to take the list of chosen books to Sir Charles Oman, Professor of Modern History,¶ for approval. Most of the books were respectable, but to make up the balance he had included J.B. Priestley's** *English Journey*. Oman approved all the volumes until he came to the last, then asked: 'Is this by the radical Priestley, whose house was burnt down in 1791?' 'No,' replied Wilson, 'it is the modern Yorkshire novelist.' 'I suppose it is all right,' said Oman. 'After all, it only cost five shillings.' At the same time, Harold also received a college prize, and chose the complete novels of Disraeli.

Wilson also talks about his good memory. When Wilson was doing schools at Oxford he found this particularly valuable. He answered a question on the

---

* (1892–1982).

† Leslie Smith, *Harold Wilson: The Authentic Portrait* (Hodder & Stoughton, 1964).

‡ (1927–2005), American journalist and author of *John F. Kennedy: President* (Atheneum, 1964).

§ William Flavelle Monypenny (1866–1912), joint biographer of Disraeli. George Earle Buckle (1854–1935) completed the final four volumes of Disraeli's six-volume biography after the death of Moneypenny.

¶ (1860–1946), historian. Chichele Professor of Modern History, Oxford 1905–46; Conservative MP for the University of Oxford 1919–35.

** Joseph Priestley (1733–1804), theologian and natural philosopher; Priestley's enthusiasm for the French Revolution led to riots in which his house was wrecked.

Bank of England control of the London money market by quoting a great deal from an article in the *Economist*.

While searching for a letter the other day he came across a trunk full of papers connected to the work he did with William Beveridge on the problems of unemployment. He is going to present them all to the London School of Economics.

A little talk about his years as a minister. On Stafford Cripps,* Wilson says that he had immense integrity, but was the worst type of man he had ever come across.

Wilson describes how in 1952, after being elected to the Labour Party Executive, he was approached by Philip Goodhart, who was then one of the team doing the 'Peterborough' column. He asked Wilson: 'To what do you attribute your election?' Wilson replied: 'Intrigue.' Philip asked: 'May I quote you on that?' to which Wilson replied: 'Yes, if you also add that I learned the art of intrigue in helping to get your father made Master of Univ.' Wilson added: 'Not a word of our talk ever appeared!'†

As far as current politics goes, he thinks that Home has made the mistake of stumping the country too soon. He should have worked quietly in Downing Street until nearer the time of the election.

### 6 July 1964

To Eton to meet Anthony Chenevix-Trench, our first meeting. The first thing that strikes me about Trench is how small he is – even shorter than me. But he has the powerful head of a Victorian headmaster and talks both eloquently and with conviction. He is dissatisfied with the College as it is at present. He admits that in a school where accommodation is uncomfortable – as are all non-state schools – it is comforting to cling to tradition. But he feels that at present the College suffers from a lack of moral fibre, or, as he puts it more picturesquely later in the conversation, is 'morally willowy'. So widespread and so apparently respectable have become articles and books which justify complete moral freedom, that there is no form of wrong without its defenders. Naturally the most literate and intelligent boys in any school will fasten onto this and become a focus of change and discontent. Yet there is something unstable and frivolous about their opinions. Desmond Lee remarked to Trench the other day: 'All scholars of

---

* Sir Stafford Cripps (1889–1952), Labour MP for East Bristol, later South-East Bristol 1931–50; Chancellor of the Exchequer 1947–50.
† Sir Arthur Goodhart (1891–1978), Master of University Coll., Oxford 1951–63, the first American to be the Master of an Oxford college.

Winchester are both right-wing Tories and agnostics. Either would be accept-able, but not both.' So not only do Collegers feel insecure, they also do not do as well as they should academically and are often beaten by Oppidans in trials.*

Trench would like to have many more scholarships, without a Latin re-quirement, so that no boy would be deprived of an Eton place through not having had the classical education of an expensive prep school. I ask Trench how up to seventy scholarships would be financed. He replies that College, as opposed to the school, is now very rich indeed. This is largely owing to the work of Claude Elliott and his shrewd financial advisers. He hopes that a Labour Government will not remove the charitable status of Eton. If it does, all school appeals will be badly affected. But he is in favour of abolishing covenants made by grandfathers for their grandsons – nothing more than tax evasion.

Trench is proud of having succeeded in getting Elliott to agree to changes in chapel services – a problem which defeated Birley for sixteen years. The services are now to have more of a voluntary atmosphere and to be less sixteenth-century in character. Not long ago, Trench said to a boy after chapel: 'Do you not think that was a good service?' 'Yes, sir,' replied the boy, 'it is good to hear Eton worshipping itself.'

I ask him what other impressions of Eton he has acquired in his first few months. He replies: 'I had not realised that the spectrum was so broad – that the nice Eton was so nice and the bloody so very bloody.'

## 12 July 1964

In Oxford with Leslie Rowse. We walk round some of the colleges. First we look at the Waynflete Building at Magdalen. Putting the college arms on the walls exaggerates rather than redeems the vulgarity of the building.

By contrast, St Hilda's have not only put up some charming new buildings in the traditional style, but are also remodelling a Victorian Gothic block with great elegance.

Next to look at the new building of Brasenose, put up by the brilliant firm of Powell and Moya. Although in an impossible situation, they have utilised every inch of space and given much attention to the finish of the Portland stonework.†

---

* Oppidans are Etonians who board in houses in the town, and not in College, like the Schol-ars. Trials are the internal Eton examinations.

† In 2014 the Twentieth Century Society named this extension one of the 100 influential buildings of the last century.

A committee under Lord Franks is at present investigating the administration of the university. One of its problems is whether there should be a permanent Vice-Chancellor. If so, he could be housed in All Souls.

Lunch in the charming Buttery at All Souls. John Sparrow appears. We discuss the proposed series of All Souls studies. A.L.R.: 'Yes, I might write one or two.' Sparrow (in alarm): 'Oh, we only want one.'

## 14 July 1964

To the Queen's garden party at Buckingham Palace. The best weather for it I have ever known, hot sun and cool breeze. The garden is full of Prime Ministers – Home, Macmillan, Eden and Menzies. Martin Gilliat calls me up to talk to the Queen Mother, who is dressed in blue with a parasol casting a curiously unreal light on her face. We discuss the impending appointment of Harold Caccia[*] to Provost of Eton, and she asks me why I think he has been chosen. I reply that the Fellows of Eton feel that should there be a Labour Government, the Provost ought to be ... At this moment she interrupts me and says: 'Yes, what we need is someone who will be firmish with them.' I note her use of the words 'we' and 'them', no nonsense about being politically impartial. She also asks me if I have met Chenevix-Trench. When I tell her that I liked him very much at our first meeting recently, she says: 'I hear the boys like him, too, which has not always been so.' I take this to be a clear reference to the radical Birley.

Go on this evening to a party given by Charles Snow. Harold Wilson is there and calls out: 'Ah, there's my Albany.' As always with me he is warm and friendly. Paul Johnson,[†] another guest, shares my liking for Wilson. What particularly pleases him are the robust Yorkshire phrases Wilson uses. He is also certain that when Wilson comes to power he will use the Press in a far more intelligent way than do the Tories – more on American lines.

Maurice Edelman[‡] tells me of a remark made by Godfrey Winn[§] at the end of an earnest discussion on the nature of existence: 'Say what you like, but God has always been very good to me.'

## 27 July 1964

Peter Carrington tells me he is tremendously relieved not to have been asked

---

[*] Sir Harold Caccia, Baron Caccia (1905–90), Ambassador to the US 1956–61; Permanent Under-Secretary of State at the Foreign Office 1962–5; Provost of Eton 1965–77.

[†] (b. 1928), author and journalist. Editor of the *New Statesman* 1965–70.

[‡] (1911–75), Labour MP for Coventry West 1945–50 and Coventry North 1950–74.

[§] (1908–71), author and broadcaster.

by Bob Menzies during his recent visit to the Prime Ministers' Conference to become the next Governor General of Australia. Nor have Hughie Northumberland* or Andrew Devonshire, both of whom turned it down before it was offered to Bill on the last occasion. The story is that Menzies went to King's Cross Station to meet Hughie off the night train from Alnwick, so determined was he to secure his acceptance. All that Hughie said was: 'I am so sorry, Prime Minister, but I have just accepted the Presidency of the Alnwick Agricultural Society.'

### 5 August 1964

Catch the 12.34 train to Hatfield to lunch with Bobbety Salisbury and his wife. To my agreeable surprise he is waiting for me on the platform and drives me up to the house – a characteristic act of courtesy – but his driving is as frightening as that of David Cecil.

I had not realised before what an immense Tudor palace Hatfield is. The rooms in which the family live – together with a private garden – are entirely separate from that part of the house open to the public.

After lunch to Bobbety's own small set of rooms, which used to be those occupied by Linky. What apparently used to impress the family when young was the enormous size and weight of the great Lord Salisbury when Prime Minister. He was six foot three inches high and more than broad in proportion. Towards the end of his life the only exercise he could take was on a tricycle, and little asphalt paths were made for him all over the wing. Bobbety's own rooms reflect his charm and modesty. They are not exactly Spartan, but utterly un-luxurious and rather untidy. It was to these very rooms that Linky, each night after dinner, used to go to meditate, read and write.

Linky was born and buried at Hatfield, and I see the private instructions he left about his funeral for the guidance of his executors. This stresses that a man should never be concerned with his own funeral except in so far as it may give comfort or otherwise to his family. Then he points out that the main importance of a grave is horticultural rather than spiritual. He says that reverence should certainly be given to mortal remains because the body is the temple of the soul. But, he says, one should not carry this argument too far. For instance, one should not reverence the telephone, even though it carried the voices of those whom one loved.

One box of papers contains notes written by Linky for his articles

---

* Hugh Percy, 10th Duke of Northumberland (1914–88), soldier. Lord Lieutenant of Northumberland 1956–84.

and Eton sermons. One sermon is headed 'The Existence of Angels – not Essential.'

When we have finished talking about Linky, there is still half an hour before my train back to London. So we go out into the garden. On the way we pass a small but delightful chapel and Bobbety tells me that there is a morning service each day – 'with a chaplain and organist,' he adds triumphantly.

We have a little talk about the resignations of Eden and himself at the beginning of 1938, and he quotes the remark of Sir Orme Sargent[*] on Neville Chamberlain's repeated visits to Hitler at the time of Munich: 'He must be the only man to take a season ticket to Canossa.'[†]

I am most touched by the extraordinary charm and courtesy of Bobbety. Nothing is too much trouble and he carries his responsibilities with a lightness of touch that lesser men could well copy.

## 4 September 1964
John Egremont (as he now is) tells me that Bobbety Salisbury resigned from Macmillan's Cabinet in 1957 not in order to bring about Macmillan's downfall, but because he was definitely opposed to negotiating with Archbishop Makarios. At the same time he never expected that his resignation would be accepted. At the crucial interview Macmillan saw him in his sitting room upstairs at No. 10. After Bobbety had stated his case, Macmillan said he very much regretted this decision, but hoped that it would not affect their friendship. At this, Bobbety apparently went very white. He had expected immediate surrender by Macmillan.

John also describes to me how, when recalled to Downing Street to become a Private Secretary to Macmillan, he was waiting in the Private Secretaries' office. The door to the Cabinet Room was open, and the Cabinet was apparently discussing nuclear tests. Out of the Cabinet Room floated Bobbety's voice: 'I am all for letting these things off.'

## 9 September 1964
Anthony Benn tells me that at the forthcoming General Election it will be his seventh parliamentary election in fourteen years in the same constituency. The last six were November 1950, October 1951, May 1955, October 1959,

---

[*] Sir Orme ('Moley') Sargent (1884–1962), Permanent Under-Secretary of State for Foreign Affairs 1946–9.

[†] The Road to Canossa refers to the humiliating trek by Henry IV, Holy Roman Emperor, in 1077 to seek revocation of his excommunication by Pope Gregory VII. He was forced to humiliate himself on his knees for three days whilst a blizzard raged.

April 1961 and August 1963. The last two, of course, were after he had been disqualified from the Commons following his father's death and his becoming the 2nd Viscount Stansgate.

*Sir Alec Douglas-Home had an audience of the Queen on 15 September at Balmoral and sought a dissolution of Parliament on 25 September. The announcement of the date of the general election was made on 18 September, one calendar month before polling. The previous general election had been on 8 October 1959, but that date was not viable as the Queen was in Canada at the time. So 15 October was chosen, five years and one week since Harold Macmillan's victory in 1959. The Parliament was thus the longest in peacetime since the interval between elections had been reduced to five years in 1911. Some commentators mistakenly thought this to be unconstitutional, not realising that the electoral 'clock' starts on the day of the State Opening of the previous Parliament, which was 27 October 1959, not on the day of the previous general election. The customary State Opening of Parliament was not held in 1959, owing to the Queen's pregnancy, but the Parliament began with Lord Kilmuir, the Lord Chancellor, reading the Queen's Speech from the steps of the throne in the House of Lords.*

*The 1964 general election produced an unexpectedly narrow majority for Harold Wilson's Labour Party. With 44.1 per cent of the vote Labour won 317 seats; with 43.4 per cent of the vote the Conservatives won 304 seats; and with 11.2 per cent of the vote the Liberals won nine seats. The Labour majority was four seats, though, in effect, five seats as the Speaker of the House was the Conservative Sir Harry Hylton-Foster. It was clear that this Parliament would not last for five years, and indeed another election took place in March 1966 when Harold Wilson secured a majority of 97 seats, by which time Dr Horace King, Labour MP for Southampton Itchen, was Speaker.*

*October 1964 was the beginning of a new phase in Britain's post-war history. In his definitive study* The British General Election of 1964, *David Butler observed: 'The election of 1964 seemed less a confirmation of long-maturing trends than a break, a moment of change – a portent of greater changes to come.'\* For the first time in thirteen years the Labour Party was in office, if not in overwhelming power. Harold Wilson was only the third Labour Prime Minister, after Ramsay MacDonald and Clement Attlee. He was also one of only three members of the new government to have served in Attlee's 1945–51*

---

\* David Butler and Anthony King, *The British General Election of 1964* (Macmillan & Co., 1965), p. 300.

*Cabinet, the others being Patrick Gordon Walker and James Griffiths.* New figures emerged, such as Denis Healey and Roy Jenkins, who were to become dominating figures in political life.*

*Two men in the new government were key sources of information for Kenneth – his long-standing New College friend Anthony Benn, who became Postmaster General; and the polymath C.P. Snow, who became Parliamentary Secretary at the Ministry of Technology. After his lecture on 'The Two Cultures', Snow was a pivotal figure for Wilson in his drive to increase priorities for science in the white heat of his technological revolution. Indeed, within twenty-four hours of Wilson becoming Prime Minister, Snow was discussing these matters with Kenneth, as is shown in the first entry in his journal at this time.*

## 17 October 1964

Charles and Pamela Snow come round for a drink. They are of course pleased by the Labour victory and take the smallness of the majority calmly. Charles desperately wants the new Government to make him a life peer.[†] We deplore the shortage of intellect in the new Cabinet. Apart from Wilson himself, there is only Richard Crossman – who unexpectedly has been given the executive job of Housing – and Gerald Gardiner as Lord Chancellor.[‡] I am doubtful about the trade unionist Frank Cousins[§] as Minister of Technology, but Charles says he will be ably backed by Patrick Blackett.[¶] What Charles wants is to see more independent-minded men supporting Labour, i.e. men financially secure who can say exactly what they think without fear of the sack.

Charles interesting on the nationalisation of steel, a big issue at the election. He says it does not matter very much either way. English Electric have ceased to rely entirely on English steel and are buying it from Japan.

Much talk on his latest novel *Corridors of Power*. Charles and Pamela are both fascinated by the tiny points of detail I criticise, and I promise to embody these in a letter to him for a second edition of the novel. He tells me that he has gone to much more trouble than Maurice Edelman to disguise

---

* (1890–1975), Welsh Labour politician. Colonial Secretary 1950–51; Secretary of State for Wales 1964–6.

† His wish was fulfilled. He became Baron Snow of the City of Leicester.

‡ Baron Gardiner of Kittisford (1900–90), Labour politician. Lord Chancellor 1964–70.

§ (1904–86), General Secretary of the Transport and General Workers' Union 1956–69; Minister of Technology 1964–6.

¶ Baron Blackett of Chelsea OM (1897–1974), scientist. President of the Royal Society 1965–70.

the models of his characters. He does say what an immense amount of help he received from Maurice Macmillan in the details of the parliamentary scenes. Also from Harold Macmillan, who raised various technical points.[*]

## 9 November 1964

Morning train to York, rather delayed by fog, to see the new Dean, Alan Richardson.[†] A quiet, scholarly man. The most interesting piece of news he gives me is that there is now an arrangement by which the Minster Library can be used by York University. It is an important library of about 30,000 volumes, with a rich collection of medieval manuscripts. Also the best collection of Civil War material outside the British Museum. A problem which faces the Dean is how to make some sort of Christian impact on the million or so visitors to the Minster each year. On a summer's day alone there are often 5,000. He mentions that he reads the *Observer*, not because he likes it, but because it so often attacks Christianity and he must know the enemy.

## 17 November 1964

Noel Annan lunches with me at the Guards Club. He has just finished the life of J.F. Roxburgh, the headmaster of Stowe. But, he tells me, the main interest of the work will centre on the extraordinary career of the Revd Percy Ewart Warrington,[‡] who not only founded Stowe but a dozen other schools as well. Unfortunately, he burdened them all with enormous debts.

I ask Noel, who is, of course, on the Governing Body of Stowe, why they did not appoint Brian Rees as Headmaster last year. Apparently he made a mess of his interview, when he was almost entirely inarticulate. On the previous occasion, in 1958, that Stowe needed a Headmaster when Crichton-Miller was appointed, they made a big mistake in failing to appoint Oliver van Oss.

## 24 November 1964

Quintin Hailsham tells me: 'Had I said during the recent election campaign what I really thought would happen in the first thirty-five days of a Labour Government I should have been called crazy. As it is, I erred on the side of moderation.'

---

[*] In fact, Harold Macmillan redrafted so many sections that Snow in thanking him said that he was the first prime minister since Disraeli to have written a novel. D.R. Thorpe, *Supermac: The Life of Harold Macmillan*, p. 594.

[†] The Very Revd Alan Richardson (1905–75), Dean of York 1964–75.

[‡] (1889–1961), educationalist and evangelical C of E clergyman; he created the Allied Schools empire in the 1920s.

He has not yet appeared in court, but hopes for a long case soon concerning lots of money. 'Otherwise I shall need a begging bowl.'

On Harold Wilson he says: 'He is a dedicated man with something of William Pitt about him. One judges a member of the Opposition by whether one can do business with him in the Robing Room. The answer with Wilson is "Yes".'

George Wigg,* he says, 'is the man who will do anything dirty for his leader. He will assassinate a character whenever required.'

I ask Quintin what he would have done if the Tories had won the election. He replies: 'I should at once have put up the Bank Rate to 7 per cent, like Labour but for a different reason. Their victory has meant a great loss of confidence abroad & so the pound had to be strengthened. Our victory would have caused a great wave of optimism, which we should have had to curb by a 7 per cent Bank Rate.'

## 26 November 1964

At 5.30 p.m. to Claridge's for a talk with King Constantine of Greece.† The King looked more tired than when I last saw him in September. He tells me in fact he has lost six kilos in weight in the first few months of his reign – 'largely due to Makarios'. He finds it difficult to take exercise, but generally manages forty-five minutes of squash a day. The King tells me that he has about 500 documents a week to sign and also reads most of the foreign telegrams. He starts work early in the morning and tries to finish by 1 p.m. But too often he has to go on to 2.30 p.m. He also has a little more work to do later in the day.

His relations with the Prime Minister, Papandreou,‡ are excellent. 'The only trouble is that he gets tired very easily. But he gives me fatherly advice and I give him the advice of a young man – though he does not always take it.' He says that things will never be easy in Greece until the Cyprus problem has been solved. This really means the finding of a way in which the face of Turkey can be saved – for Turkey is naturally suspicious that Greece's interest in Cyprus is a form of territorial expansion.

The King wants the internal security of Greece tightened up. He feels that the Communists are still an enormous danger and he certainly does

---

* Baron Wigg (1900–83), Labour politician. MP for Dudley 1945–67; Paymaster General 1964–7.

† King Constantine II of Greece (b. 1940), last King of Greece 1964–73.

‡ Georgios Papandreou (1888–1968), Prime Minister of Greece 1944–5, 1963 and 1964–5.

not intend to visit Russia until the breach in NATO caused by the Cyprus problem has been healed. To do so would only encourage the Communists without bringing either him or his country any tangible result. Similarly, he would like to visit the United States, but wishes to wait until he could make it an occasion for thanking the Americans for all the help they have given in solving the Cyprus problem. His final word is to tell me that our own Queen very much wants to pay a State Visit to Greece, but that this will have to await the settlement of the Cyprus affair.

Before leaving I give the King two presents from the *Sunday Telegraph* – a pigskin cigarette case and a sugar bowl and spoon in the form of a coal-scuttle and shovel. He is absolutely delighted. Of the latter he says: 'I saw one of those at the silver vaults the other day, but it was too expensive.' I point out to him that it has the words 'Sunday Telegraph' engraved on it and that people will think he has been to tea with us and pinched our silver. This is just his sort of joke, and he gives tremendous roars of laughter.

Drink in Catherine Place with Maurice and Katie Macmillan. Story of Alexander,* soon after he had gone to Eton. When an older boy made an indecent proposal to him, he replied severely: 'What you need is a cold bath.'

## 29 November 1964

Wet, chilly day. At 5.30 to Cromwell Road for a drink with Charles and Pamela Snow. Both are very upset by the perpetual Press campaign of denigration which has now gone on for four years. Charles intends to consult Patrick Devlin for advice on whether to sue some of the offending papers. His little book on Lord Cherwell† some time ago was savagely criticised, but he now receives no praise when his critical view of the Prof. is proved right by recent revelations on German V1 and V2 weapons. He has also been attacked in reviews of *Corridors of Power* for being interested only in the successful. In fact, he is far more fascinated by the failures.

Charles likes his job as Under-Secretary to Frank Cousins at the new Ministry of Technology, though he finds the Ministry building itself, on Millbank, inconveniently inaccessible by public transport. But why should a rich man like Charles want to use public transport? He likes the Permanent Under-Secretary, Sir Maurice Dean,‡ 'who does his job

---

* Alexander Macmillan, 2nd Earl of Stockton (b. 1943), Conservative politician. Chairman, Macmillan & Co. 1986–2000.

† *Science and Government* (Harvard University Press, 1961).

‡ (1906–78), senior civil servant. Permanent Under-Secretary, Ministry of Technology 1964–6.

very loyally indeed in spite of being – like all senior civil servants – a Conservative'.

The House of Lords has made an instant appeal to Charles. Before he made his maiden speech he was given a lecture by Frank Pakenham on always being polite to the Opposition, particularly the stupid ones. 'But I find Reggie Dilhorne so offensive to harmless trade-union peers that I am going to ask for a dispensation.' Charles was so pleased the other day, when after a debate on Scottish development he was taken to the Carlton Club by Lord Cromartie.[*]

We discuss the future of his son, Philip, now twelve. If he gets a good place in the Eton election, he will go into College. Otherwise into an Oppidan House. I ask whether they have ever considered sending him to a state school. They reply that it would not be fair on the boy socially.

### 3 December 1964

Look in at a small party given by Toby O'Brien[†] at Brown's Hotel. I much enjoy some talk with M. Cartier.[‡] He tells me that during the German occupation of Paris they got rid of a tremendous amount of junk jewellery to officers of the German army. Cartier tells me that they have never made a Papal tiara, at which Anthony Allfrey[§] interjects: 'What, not even for the Bishop of Southwark?'

### 4 December 1964

Lunch with Peter Thorneycroft. Peter now has the time to paint again, and has done some very deft drawings. Peter says that he once flew up to Balmoral for a meeting of the Privy Council and during lunch talked to the Queen about pictures. She said that there was nobody nowadays who could draw as well as Landseer.[¶] Peter agreed but mentioned that John Ward came quite near.[**] About a week later John Ward was summoned to Balmoral and has been going up there regularly since to draw for the Royal Family.

---

[*] Roderick Mackenzie, 4th Earl of Cromartie (1904–89), won the MC in France with the Seaforth Highlanders, 1940; public servant in Scotland.
[†] Edward O'Brien (1909–79), journalist; sometime editor of the 'Peterborough' column.
[‡] Jean-Jacques Cartier (1920–2011) ran the London branch of Cartier 1945–74.
[§] (1930–2010), author.
[¶] Sir Edwin Landseer (1802–73), painter; Queen Victoria commissioned many pictures from him, including a portrait of Prince Albert.
[**] Artist and landscape painter (1917–2007); he was commissioned to paint a number of royal portraits and gave drawing lessons to Prince Charles.

## 16 December 1964

To the old Ministry of Defence in Storey's Gate to see David Muirhead,* head
of the Personnel Department of the Foreign Office, to discuss the impending amalgamation of the Foreign Office and the Commonwealth Relations
office. He is a large, amiable man, and much concerned that future recruits
to the service should not necessarily come almost entirely from Oxford and
Cambridge. Accordingly, members of his department, particularly youngish
men, go out to large universities once a year to collect suitable candidates.
At present there is little difficulty in finding quantity, but the quality is often
disappointing. On his desk Muirhead has a large bell with a wooden handle.
On it is an inscribed plate which reads: 'This bell was supplied to the Foreign
Office by the Ministry of Works, so that it can be rung to give notice to the
staff employed in the Foreign Office of the approach of enemy aircraft in the
Great War of 1914–1918.'

## 17 December 1964

At 12 noon to the Ministry of Aviation to see Roy Jenkins. He is very suave
and welcoming, and rings for sherry. I see a button marked 'Mess' and say to
him: 'I did not know you had a direct line to George Brown.' He replies: 'Alas
it is only to summon a messenger.'

We discuss the Concorde project and he agrees that the issue of whether
or not it should be cancelled was handled tactlessly. Nevertheless, he rightly
maintains that a review of the project was needed. As long ago as 19 July he
referred in an article in the *Observer* to 'Expensive status symbols.' On a personal level Roy has tried to heal the breach with the French by distributing
copies of his life of Asquith.

Lunch at the Beefsteak. Harold Macmillan is sitting a place away from
me. He appears very pale and withdrawn. Part of the reason for this may
be that he is living so much in the past while writing his memoirs. What I
find particularly odd is that from time to time he jumps up from the table,
picks up a newspaper, looks at it for a few moments, then returns to his place.
It could be that he is in physical pain. When he does talk, it is in the same
stage country-gentleman manner that I have come to expect. Thus when
somebody says how bad the telephone service has become nowadays, he
replies: 'Yes, I remember well the days when our local telephone exchange
was also an information bureau. I would telephone my wife from London
and the operator at Chelwood Gate would inform me that it was no use as

---

* Sir David Muirhead (1918–99), Ambassador to Peru 1967–70, to Portugal 1970–74 and to
Belgium 1974–8.

he had just seen Lady Dorothy going out hunting.'

Again, when somebody deplores the possible impending abolition of the public schools by the Labour Government, Macmillan launches into a long eulogy on them: 'The great advantage of the English education system is that one is always starting at the bottom and working one's way up over and over again – at one's private school, at one's public school and at one's university. So one is trained in discipline. People who have not enjoyed such a system take to drink.'

# 1965

*January 1965 began in sombre fashion with the death of T.S. Eliot on 4 January and Winston Churchill on 24 January. The state funeral for Churchill at St Paul's Cathedral, which received worldwide attention, was the first such since that for the Duke of Wellington in 1852.*

*In February Dr Beeching published the second phase of his review of the nation's railways,* Development of the Major Trunk Routes, *which detailed how 7,500 miles of track would be reduced to 3,000 miles. In March a Russian astronaut made the first space-walk, followed in June by the first American one. The Labour Education Secretary, Anthony Crosland, published his circular 10/65, requesting local education authorities to begin converting secondary schools to the comprehensive system. On 22 July Sir Alec Douglas-Home resigned as Conservative leader, and five days later Edward Heath succeeded him, the first Conservative leader to be elected to the post by fellow MPs.*

*In October the Moors murders were discovered. The following month the Abolition of the Death Penalty Bill suspended capital punishment, a change made permanent in 1969. On 11 November Ian Smith, the Prime Minister of Rhodesia, unilaterally declared independence from the United Kingdom. On 16 December the writer Somerset Maugham died at the age of ninety-one.*

## 1 January 1965

Start the New Year with lunch at the General Post Office, where Anthony Trollope once worked, with Anthony Wedgwood Benn, the new Postmaster General. It has a wonderfully Victorian aspect with lots of mahogany, model ships and mail coaches in glass cases, and office messengers in tightly buttoned scarlet frock coats. Benn's private office obviously find him more revolutionary than they like. One thing annoyed him intensely – a little spy hole between the secretaries' office and his own. So he screwed down the flap. They promptly unscrewed it. In one of the rooms is a framed proclamation of Charles II, dated 1660. It is entitled 'For Quieting the Postmaster General in the execution of his Office.' It was found at Longleat in 1942.

Anthony tells me an amusing story of how, when he was fighting his peerage case, he was asked to debate the Honours System on BBC with Sir George Bellew,* who was at that time Garter King of Arms. The producer told Bellew he was to open the discussion, but Bellew refused, saying quite seriously: 'Oh no, we must do things according to precedence and Stansgate is a Viscount.' Afterwards Anthony and Bellew had a private discussion on the subject. When Anthony pointed out how absurd it was for a young man like the Duke of Kent to have received the GCVO in 1960, Bellew replied: 'Oh well, I suppose you are right. But if one lives so near to the fountain of honour, one can hardly avoid being splashed.'

Anthony is determined to shock his civil servants. When his Private Secretary told him that as a minister he was entitled to a yearly haunch of venison from the Queen's herd at Windsor, he replied in an offhand way: 'Oh, give it to Oxfam.'

## 5 January 1965

Dine at home and listen to a recording of T.S. Eliot, who died yesterday, reading his *Ash Wednesday*. Very moving, especially the last few lines.

## 7 January 1965

I am preparing to go to Washington for President Johnson's Inauguration. Andrew Devonshire, who attended President Kennedy's Inauguration as a private guest, warns me that most of the ceremonies take place out of doors in bitter cold. So he advises me to have a flask of whisky or brandy with me. He also tells me a story about Cledwyn Hughes,† his successor as Minister of State at the CRO. He asked his Private Secretary what sort of weekend he was allowed to take. With great presence of mind, the Private Secretary replied: 'Oh, the Duke of Devonshire always used to take one from Friday to Tuesday.'

## 14 January 1965

Malcolm Sargent tells me how the committee of Pratt's were discussing arrangements for the Coronation in 1953. There was a great deal of talk about how tickets for the windows looking over St James's Street should be distributed to members. Andrew Devonshire, who of course owns Pratt's, in the chair, kept quite silent through half an hour of this, then said: 'I have always understood that they are my windows and I am letting my servants have them on Coronation Day. Now the next item of business . . .'

---

* The Hon. Sir George Bellew (1899–1993), Garter King of Arms 1950–61.
† Baron Cledwyn of Penrhos (1916–2001), Labour politician. Secretary of State for Wales 1966–8; Minister of Agriculture, Fisheries and Food 1968–70.

## 15 January 1965

I learn during the morning that Winston has had a stroke and is not at ninety expected to live. Evidently all the previous details of 'Operation Hope Not' are still valid. The Duke of Norfolk* is coming down from Scotland to supervise all the arrangements and a conference has been fixed for Monday 18 January at 11 a.m. One unknown is obviously the day of death, yet much depends on that. If Winston dies early on Monday or before, it will just be possible to lay on the funeral by the following Saturday – the best day of the week. Otherwise it would have to be held in the middle of the following week and cause much dislocation.

## 16 January 1965

Winston is still alive, but the probability is that he is in a coma. Having spent the early part of the morning packing for America, I am collected by a car at 11.15 a.m. and driven to London Airport.

Margot Fonteyn and Rudolf Nureyev† are also flying in my aircraft to Washington. Margot tells me that they are to dance before the President at his Inauguration Gala on Monday evening, but are flying back on Tuesday.

Just after 2 p.m. the captain broadcasts a bulletin about Winston. There has been no change in his condition. We land in Washington in a snowstorm. There are snow ploughs everywhere clearing the way from the airport.

## 19 January 1965

Astonishingly Winston is still alive, and there has been no further deterioration in his condition. At 11 a.m. to the British Embassy. The security guard who takes me up to the offices tells me he was in the Grenadiers and once used to guard Winston in Downing Street. 'How cantankerous he used to be,' he sighs.

An agreeable half-hour with David Harlech, who is retiring as Ambassador here in the second half of March. He tells me he has finally decided not to renounce his peerage. Had the Tories won the election, it is likely that he would have renounced it in order to take a post in Alec Home's Government – probably as Foreign Secretary. But to sit in the Commons day after day would have been for him a duty rather than a pleasure, and he is glad not to have had to take the plunge. It is not only that the Conservative

---

* Bernard Fitzalan-Howard, 16th Duke of Norfolk (1908–75), Earl Marshal 1917–75; as such the Duke organised the Coronations of George VI in 1937 and Elizabeth II in 1953, and the funeral of Sir Winston Churchill in 1965.

† A notable partnership for the Royal Ballet. Dame Margot Fonteyn (1919–91), celebrated ballerina; Rudolf Nureyev (1938–99), Soviet dancer who defected to the West in 1961.

Party, having indulged in eleven months of electioneering, lost the election in October and is unlikely to win the next one. Harlech also doubts whether his views would be entirely acceptable to the Conservatives at the present time. He believes that we should make every effort to get into the Common Market, particularly as the Commonwealth is no longer an effective body. Nor is he impressed by Conservative arguments that we should have our own Independent Nuclear Deterrent – though he thinks we must receive some appreciable advantage for abandoning it. The Tories, he adds, believe that we can continue to receive favourable terms from America out of regard for our old alliance: but the past is ceasing to be a factor, and we will come increasingly to be judged here by present performance.

If Winston dies, the Inauguration ceremonies will not be interrupted, but the President will almost certainly go to the funeral and Harlech may well go with him. Harlech tells me that the first time he ever saw Winston was in January 1936 when, as a boy in the Eton OTC, he lined part of the road between the road tower and St George's Chapel, Windsor, for the funeral of King George V. Winston came and talked to him in his Privy Councillor's uniform.

About 6.30 to the party given by Kay Graham.* A large house, with an awning in front and a marquee at the back. Excellent service of drinks and delicious food. Talk to Kenneth Galbraith† – tall, ungainly, untidy hair – about his book *The Great Crash*. He was annoyed to notice that it never appeared on sale at La Guardia Airport, New York. So one day he asked the girl at the bookstall why. With withering contempt, she replied: 'You don't think we should display a book with <u>that</u> title at an airport, do you?'

Adlai Stevenson, looking rather worn. I ask how United Nations goes. He replies: 'It's hell. But I am getting worse at my job, and don't now go to all the parties. The nations giving the parties get angry with me.'

## 20 January 1965
Winston still clings to life.

The day of the President's Inauguration. As I look out of my window I see that already there are police and other guards on the top of every roof. Walk along to the Capitol for the Inauguration ceremony itself. It is a memorable spectacle. Very good seat in the open air just in front of the Presidential Pavilion erected on the steps of the Capitol for the occasion. Above us towers

---

* Katherine Graham (1917–2001), American publisher, President of the *Washington Post*.
† John Kenneth Galbraith (1908–2006), influential economist. US Ambassador to India 1961–3; *The Great Crash* (Hamish Hamilton, 1954) is an economic history of the build-up to the Wall Street Crash of 1929.

the Capitol building itself, the colour of sugar icing and looking exactly as if erected by Metro-Goldwyn-Mayer for a billion-dollar production for life in the days of Nero. Everywhere stars and stripes are flying against an azure sky and the effect is curiously moving. Along the two terraces which flank either side of the pavilion, Senators and Congressmen are ranged like members of the Supreme Soviet Praesidium on top of Lenin's tomb in Red Square. They even have the same sort of ungainly hat because President Johnson has decreed that tall hats shall not be worn for his Inauguration. Among these Senators are Bobby and Edward Kennedy, both looking very young and very sad, with bowed heads. By contrast the President is lean and brown and immensely tough – not a man I should care to cross. The oath-taking ceremonies by the President are in themselves startlingly impressive, but the programme is interspersed by less relevant items, such as a selection by the Marine Band, songs by the Mormon Choir and Leontyne Price's rendering of 'America the Beautiful' – as if Dame Clara Butt were to sing 'Land of Hope and Glory' at the Coronation. The religious element of the Inauguration is emphasised by prayers by ministers of several denominations, including a melodious Rabbi and an unintelligible Archimandrite. The President's address is evangelical in tone, and deals almost entirely with domestic issues, which probably appeals to the heart of America more than the elegant European culture reflected in President Kennedy's address.

In the afternoon we watch the Inauguration parade. First comes the President and his wife* imprisoned in a glass bubble at the back of a large black car – the same one, in fact, in which President Kennedy was assassinated. Secret Service men stand on the side of the car, which is flanked by two open cars crammed with tense and hostile Secret Service men. These justifiable security precautions rob the drive of all spontaneity and isolate the President from the good cheer of the immense crowds along the route.

Vice-President Humphrey's car is less obviously guarded and he blows kisses to the enchanted teenagers who are shouting their heads off for him.†Then follows the main body of the parade, state by state. First comes a party

---

* Claudia Alta ('Lady Bird') Johnson (1912–2007), First Lady of the US 1963–9.
† There was no Vice-President of the United States between 22 Nov. 1963 and 20 Jan. 1965, when Hubert Humphrey (1911–78) took office until 1969. By the Presidential Succession Act of 18 July 1947, the next in line for the Presidency after the Vice-President was the Speaker of the House of Representatives. In 1963 this was John McCormack (1891–1980), who received appropriate Secret Service protection. The 29th Amendment to the American Constitution of 11 Feb. 1967 ensured that when there was a vacancy in the office of Vice-President, the President shall nominate a Vice-President who would take office on confirmation by a majority vote of both Houses of Congress. Although Humphrey was Johnson's number two, he was not formally Vice-President until 1965.

of flag bearers, then the Governor in his car, then a float depicting some aspect of his state, finally a band. There are the traditional drum majorettes, their well-exposed legs almost blue with the cold. Among the highlights of the procession, which takes several hours to pass, are a railway train emitting real steam; browned-off looking men wearing eighteenth-century wigs and military uniform; tiny cadets doing drill on the march; and a huge St Bernard dog belonging to the Chicago fire department.

In the evening I attend the Presidential Ball at the Washington Armory. It is a tremendous crush and the heat is stifling. The Presidential party makes an appearance for about half an hour and the President makes history by being the first ever actually to dance at his own Presidential Ball. This obviously terrifies the security guards, who form a close ring round the President and his party. For me, the best part of the evening is listening to Louis Armstrong playing the trumpet.

### 21 January 1965
Winston unchanged.

Still in Washington. By-election news from the UK. Patrick Gordon Walker has been beaten in the supposedly safe Labour seat of Leyton. He will surely have to resign now as Foreign Secretary. An immense blow to Labour at the end of Harold Wilson's much-vaunted 'Hundred Days'.*

### 22 January 1965
Winston is still alive. I see from the English papers that the business of the nation has practically come to a halt because of Winston's approaching death. Even the most trivial social and political engagements have been cancelled. Surely he would not have wished this until he was dead.

I also learn more details of Gordon Walker's defeat at Leyton. A Labour majority of 7,926 was turned into a Conservative one of 205. Later in the day I hear that Gordon Walker has resigned as Foreign Secretary and been succeeded by Michael Stewart.† Obviously personal factors play their part in this staggering defeat.

I hear that President Johnson is likely to attend Winston's funeral. When

---

* Patrick Gordon Walker did resign as Foreign Secretary. Despite losing his Smethwick seat in the 1964 general election, he was appointed Foreign Secretary, though not an MP. A supposedly safe seat was created for him by Harold Wilson by sending a reluctant Reginald Sorenson, MP for Leyton, to the House of Lords. The Conservatives won the seat on an 8.7 per cent swing by 205 votes.

† Baron Stewart of Fulham (1906–90), Labour politician. Foreign Secretary 1965–6 and 1968–70.

Winston first fell ill, Johnson's instinct was that it would not be necessary for him to fly to London. Now, sensing the national interest in Winston, only recently made an honorary American citizen, he is prepared to go. Eisenhower will also accompany him.

### 23 January 1965

At 7.30 I turn on the television in my hotel bedroom to hear the news. A grave-faced announcer appears and I expect him to tell us that Winston is dead. In fact, he is still alive – but President Johnson has evidently been taken to hospital in the night with a bad chest cold.

On to 2339 Massachusetts Avenue to see Felix Frankfurter.* Naturally he wants to talk about Winston. But he is also very interested in the resignation of Gordon Walker, though he does not feel it is any great loss. We discuss President Johnson, and Felix asks me how I enjoyed his Inaugural address. When I tell him that I feel it represented the true, homespun America When, he fervently agrees with me. 'Yes, it was the voice of Lyndon Baines Johnson himself, not that of a lot of smart-alec speech-writers. I have always liked Johnson better than Kennedy and supported him at Los Angeles.'

He is interested in news of British politicians. Surprisingly, he suggests that Harold Caccia would have been a good Foreign Secretary. Interestingly, he liked Lord Halifax very much, but does not think he caught the true atmosphere of the United States when at the Washington Embassy during the war. For Lord Chancellor he would have liked Hartley Shawcross, though he is fond of Gerald Gardiner too. This leads him on to talk about F.E. Smith, whom he thinks was a brilliant and underestimated Lord Chancellor, particularly in the opposition he put up to Lloyd George's appointment of old Lawrence† as Lord Chief Justice. I point out that whatever F.E. might have felt on this point he did not resign, to which Frankfurter replies cryptically: 'You are too young to know that resignation had by that time already become a lost art.'

Frankurter says that one of the most difficult things in public life is the ability to say no. On the subject of the Warren Commission to investigate President Kennedy's assassination, he says there is no doubt that its conclusions are sound. But such an unwieldy body should never have been appointed in the first place. Frankfurter's final words to me are memorable: 'When people try to tell me that Great Britain is no longer great, I reply that she is – and always will be – great in small things.'

---

* (1882–1965), American jurist and Justice of the US Supreme Court.
† Alfred Lawrence, 1st Baron Trevethin (1843–1936). Lord Chief Justice 1921–2.

## 24 January 1965

Winston died at eight o'clock this morning, British time, the seventieth anniversary of his father's death. Watch all the commemorative recollections of
his life on American television. I am very moved on listening to his speeches,
particularly over the outstanding quality of humanity. They also show the
film of the ceremony at the White House when President Kennedy conferred
American citizenship on him in his absence. The speech included the famous
sentence: 'He mobilised the English language and sent it into battle.' Like the
rest of the President's speech, it sounds contrived, and he reads it as if they
were not his own sentiments.

Plash through horrible slush and sleet to lunch with Nin Ryan. She finds
Washington very provincial compared to New York. There is the same small
social circle in which you know what everyone else is doing. 'In Washington
someone is always coming round unexpectedly to borrow one's ice-cream
freezer. In New York, one telephones to a firm which specialises in hiring
them out.'

Nin says that Angus Ogilvy* resisted considerable pressure from the Royal
Family, even from Prince Philip, to take a title. I should expect her to be well
informed on this, as her daughter is married to Angus Ogilvy's elder brother.

## 26 January 1965

I have a drink with Salvador Dalí,† at work in his apartment in the St Regis
Hotel, his pointed moustaches quivering like antennae. One brilliant touch
of surrealism was his empty television set, in which he houses his pet ocelot,
a beautiful leopard-like beast in a diamond collar which gazes out at me with
distaste. Recently an admirer of the artist turned up bearing a three-foot
iguana as an offering. Dalí was enchanted, one of the hotel porters less so:
'This place is getting to be like a pet store,' he snarled.

## 27 January 1965

Now in New York. While I am having breakfast I watch the television. It
includes some Telstar pictures of Winston's lying-in-state in Westminster
Hall.

I see that Maurice Macmillan has been adopted as Tory candidate for

---

* Sir Angus Ogilvy (1928–2004), businessman; husband of Princess Alexandra of Kent. Virginia Ryan married David Ogilvy, 13th Earl of Airlie, in 1952.
† (1904–89), Spanish surrealist painter. His painting *Christ of St John of the Cross* was bought
by Glasgow Corporation in 1952 from Dalí personally for what was considered the extravagant
sum of £8,200. The Corporation also bought the copyright, which has earned Glasgow Museums the original cost many times over.

Farnham, a safe seat. Nin Ryan gives me a copy of the *New York Review of Books*, in which Malcolm Muggeridge has a devastating article on the sickly adulation paid to President Kennedy in a recent succession of popular volumes.

Walk across to the United Nations, where I hear tributes to Winston in the General Assembly. They are all rather stilted but Hugh Caradon[*] is extraordinarily dignified and effective. One phrase he used is far removed from his radicalism: 'Sir Winston will be gathered to his noble ancestors in a country churchyard.'

I later meet Caradon. He greets me with much warmth and friendliness.

'I wonder why you have come to see me. You are only interested in scandal.'

'Not at all. I am interested in the workings of the machinery of government.'

'I think it is the same thing.'

He describes in some detail his position at the United Nations. He is the only non-Ambassador in the UN and he feels that this strengthens his position.

'It is embarrassing for an ordinary Ambassador to be too closely tied by instructions from his Government. Having taken a certain line when one Government is in power, he may then have to take quite a different line should the Government change. My position has also been strengthened here by the fact that I am widely known to have resigned as a Government servant over what I thought were the inadequacies of our policy in Africa. Thus the African nations now listen to me more readily and give me certain credit for my views.' In a few hours he is flying to London to attend Winston's funeral.

## 28 January 1965

Antony Acland[†] lunches with me. I have not seen him since he was a boy at Eton. After Christ Church he joined the Foreign Service and became Private Secretary to Selwyn Lloyd, and later to Alec Home. He has unbounded admiration for Home. Particularly for his powers of reading a document and then, with unerring instinct, underlining in red the sentence or two which really matter. Home also has the capacity to concentrate amid an incredible noise of beat music and children, which he has witnessed at Home's Hirsel in Scotland.

---

[*] Hugh Foot, Baron Caradon (1907–90), colonial administrator and diplomat. British Permanent Representative to the UN 1964–70.

[†] Sir Antony Acland KG (b. 1930), Permanent Under-Secretary for Foreign Affairs 1982–6; Ambassador to the US 1986–91; Provost of Eton 1991–2000.

He has much affection for Caradon. 'Yesterday, I went home thinking that I was working for a great man – in spite of the contradiction in some of his speeches.'

Tea with David Ogilvy in his office. A source of deep discontent to him is the small weight which is attached to the opinion of businessmen in England, which contrasts unfavourably with the deference paid to the world of business by the United States Government. Thus, not long ago, he found himself invited to the White House by President Johnson as a leader of business.

He likes President Johnson very much, though thinks him a rather vulgar fellow. After a recent White House dinner there was dancing and the President danced with almost everybody, and even leant over to slap a woman's behind. At the end of the evening David had arranged to go round to the house of Arthur Schlesinger, where some of the Kennedy old guard were assembled. They wanted to know every detail of the White House party. 'It was as if I had come straight from the court of Oliver Cromwell to give a report to the Jacobites in exile.'

There was one splendid story about L.B.J. at the time of his talks with Alec Home. He begged Home to try to stop the delivery of Leyland buses to Cuba, adding: 'Why not send them, with the bill, to the L.B.J. ranch?'

A personal story from David. When his *Confessions of an Advertising Man* was published in New York, he assigned the copyright as a twenty-first birthday present to his son, thinking it would bring him in 2,000 or 3,000 dollars. So far it has netted him over 50,000 dollars, and the sales continue to mount in eleven countries.

### 29 January 1965

Surprise and some anger that President Johnson, unable to attend Winston's funeral tomorrow because of a bad cold, has not nominated Vice-President Humphrey to represent him. Even the *New York Times* has a critical leading article.[*]

### 30 January 1965

At 7 a.m. watch the first TV pictures of Winston's funeral. These are not of particularly good quality, but they improve in the course of the morning as the actual recordings arrive by air. It is most impressive and moving, but I think we have all had enough of state funerals and national emotion to last

---

[*] A later theory that gained currency was that Johnson had not forgotten that Churchill did not attend President Roosevelt's funeral in 1945.

a very long time. Eisenhower's broadcast tribute is admirable. So too is that given by the Duke of Windsor. In talking about the Abdication he is both dignified and affectionate.

Evidently the Foreign Office was much concerned with the plans for getting Winston's body back to England should he die abroad. Jumping the gun somewhat, General de Gaulle determined that the French would more or less kidnap the body, were Winston to die in the South of France. He would have been taken by train to Paris, then to Dover in a French warship. When Winston was told about this he said he would be flown home by the RAF. So a bomber was kept perpetually earmarked for this duty. That presumably was how he came to be flown back so speedily by the RAF after breaking his leg in the South of France.

### 4 February 1965

Philip Ward,[*] now Brigade Major, Household Brigade, tells me of the secret plans for the funeral of the Duke of Windsor. If he dies abroad, as is likely, his body will be flown in an RAF plane to Benson, where it will be placed in a chapel. The Duchess will attend the funeral, but as she hates flying she will come from either France or the United States by sea. From Benson the coffin will be taken to St George's Chapel, Windsor. It will not lie in state, but at rest, and people will be able to file by it. By day it will be guarded by the Welsh Guards; at night by the nuns of Clewer, Windsor, who have this traditional right. After the funeral service in St George's Chapel the Duke will be buried at Frogmore. Presumably at some moment before the funeral there will have to be a reconciliation between the Duchess and the Royal Family, particularly the Queen Mother.

This afternoon Philip has a meeting with representatives of the Lord Chamberlain's Department and with the Royal undertakers to see if the weight of coffins at state funerals cannot in future be reduced. The bearer party of Grenadiers at Winston's funeral had to carry a coffin weighing a quarter of a ton and it nearly did for them. Martin Gilliat had told me how shocked he was by the appalling physical strain put on them – he worried throughout the service at how they would manage in carrying the coffin out of St Paul's. And Bill Deedes told me that one man dislocated his shoulder. Philip de Zulueta says that the Prime Minister hopes to make some award to the bearer party.

Lunch with Martin Gilliat at the Travellers'. He tells me he had an excellent

---

[*] Maj.-Gen. Sir Philip Ward (1924–2003), Welsh Guards officer. Lord Lieutenant of West Sussex 1985–6.

seat at Winston's funeral in St Paul's. He noticed how early members of our Royal Family lose their good looks and become Hanoverian, in contrast to young men like King Constantine of Greece. Harold Nicolson is lunching at another table, debonair in a pink shirt. I have a few words with him. Martin says to the head waiter: 'I believe Sir Harold often dines here with his valet.' 'Well, not quite, sir, it is with his companion.'

## 5 February 1965

Lunch with Jeremy Thorpe at the House of Commons. He says that at Winston's funeral, Eisenhower, during the singing of the Battle Hymn of the Republic, said to Alexander Gordon Lennox,[*] the Serjeant-at-Arms: 'I have arranged for this at mine too.'

Alan Barker telephones me from Cambridge. He says that the Fellows of Trinity were not consulted before having Rab Butler thrust on them as Master. He is certainly not thought to be in the distinguished tradition of the last three Masters – all of them OMs.

## 6 February 1965

To a party given by Anthony and Carol Wedgwood Benn in Holland Park Avenue. Rather a good cross-section of the Radical Establishment – Violet Bonham Carter, Kenneth Younger,[†] Kenneth Robinson,[‡] Arnold Wesker[§] and Tommy Balogh.[¶] I hear that he and Nicholas Kaldor[**] are now known in Whitehall as the Bulgarian Atrocities. Maurice Bowra says there are three sorts of conversation – monologue, dialogue and Balogh. Carol on Roy Jenkins: 'I am so sorry for him. He can never forget that he was a miner's son.' Amazing for one so polished and apparently self-possessed.

## 18 February 1965

Rab Butler, having been foisted on Trinity, tells me he wonders what sort of reception the Fellows will give their new Master. He is appalled by the size of the college – and there are no servants. The Master receives a very moderate salary, but good allowances. Rab says that had he not become Master, he

---

[*] (1911–87), Royal Naval officer. Serjeant-at-Arms of the House of Commons 1961–76; President of the Royal Naval Coll., Greenwich 1961–2.
[†] Sir Kenneth Younger (1908–76), Labour politician.
[‡] Sir Kenneth Robinson (1911–96), Labour politician. Minister of Health 1964–8.
[§] Sir Arnold Wesker (1932–2016), playwright.
[¶] Thomas Balogh (1905–85), economist; adviser to the Wilson government.
[**] Baron Kaldor (1908–86), special adviser to the Chancellor of the Exchequer 1964–8 and 1974–6.

would have been elected Chancellor of Cambridge. He characteristically continues: 'Now they want a member of the Royal Family. Mountbatten would be the nearest.'

### 23 February 1965
Mervyn Stockwood tells me that at one moment when at Lambeth Geoffrey Fisher nearly made Canon Collins his Chaplain. Had he done so, Collins would have become an Establishment figure, not an embittered man of the Left. Mervyn also admits that he once mistakenly confirmed a boy as a girl. 'I was misled by the hair.'

### 24 February 1965
To the House of Lords to see Rab Butler take his seat. He declaims the oath in sonorous tones. But not a single frontbench colleague from the Commons comes to see the ceremony – in spite of there being only Scottish questions there.

### 25 February 1965
Reggie Dilhorne, surveying the political situation in general, says that Harold Wilson does not possess the manner to inspire trust throughout the nation, and will never be able to make a universal appeal for effort and sacrifice in the way that Stanley Baldwin could. He believes Alec Home could do it, or even Quintin at a pinch.

### 3 March 1965
Maurice Macmillan tells me he is pleased to be the prospective candidate for Farnham. The Association is more enlightened in its attitude to the trade unions than are the bloody-minded Yorkshire wool-employers he had to deal with in Halifax.

### 7 March 1965
Read John le Carré's *A Murder of Quality*. It is a very thinly disguised book on Eton, where he taught for a while and was most unhappy. In fact, he has conceived a Gissing-like hatred for the place.* There are devastatingly cruel portraits of Oliver van Oss (the murderer) and of Hubert and Grizel Hartley.

### 17 March 1965
Lunch at the Beefsteak. John Egremont is, as always, in tremendous form,

---

* George Gissing (1857–1903), novelist known for his hatreds and antipathies.

particularly when talking about Harold Macmillan. He quotes a recent remark by Macmillan on Harold Wilson: 'He and his whiz-kid will do no more good than Jack Kennedy and his.'

We have a long talk about the ethics of Cabinet responsibility. I maintain that a Prime Minister has the right to sack one of his ministers, however unfairly, in order that the Government may continue, e.g. Stanley Baldwin and Sam Hoare in 1935. John agrees with me – as well he might in view of the seven Cabinet ministers whom Macmillan sacked in July 1962.

## 22 March 1965

Dine with Gladwyn and Cynthia Jebb.* Cynthia says that Sir Edward Grey†  used to issue this warning: 'Never trust a man who speaks good French or who wears a buttonhole.' And here is Malcolm Sargent inches away, wearing one.

## 24 March 1965

Lunch with Sir Edward Ford. He talks of the death of his pupil King Farouk‡ a few days ago. Edward says that Farouk failed his preparatory exams for entry to the Royal Military Academy, Woolwich, complaining that in Egypt he was always given the answers.

## 31 March 1965

Anthony Powell tells me that the other day he was surprised to be invited to a feast at Downing College, Cambridge. He understood that they were giving a series of dinners to distinguished guests outside the university. But his fellow guests seemed all to be metallurgists and he came to the conclusion that he had been invited only as a gesture of spite against F.R. Leavis.

## 1 April 1965

Dine with a few friends at Prunier. What makes the evening most entertaining is the presence of old Philip Swinton. I know of few men who can retell ancient political anecdotes with such a flavour of the times. One of his stories is about Edwin Montagu,§ who once asked to be excused before the end of a Cabinet meeting as he was going to the South of France for Easter. As he reached the door of the Cabinet Room Lloyd George looked

---

* Cynthia Jebb, Lady Gladwyn (1898–1990), political hostess.
† 1st Viscount Grey of Falloden (1862–1933), Liberal politician. Foreign Secretary 1905–16.
‡ King Farouk of Egypt (1920–65), penultimate King of Egypt 1936–52.
§ (1879–1924), Liberal politician. Secretary of State for India 1917–22.

up and said in honeyed tones: 'Happy Good Friday, Edwin.'

Philip has a fiery dislike of Sir William Hayter and says: 'Having filled the British Embassy in Moscow with homosexual spies, he is now determined to fill New College with tarts' – rather a strong comment on the proposal to have women undergraduates.

## 4 April 1965

George Weidenfeld gives a supper party in Eaton Square for General Moshe Dayan.* He is a lean, good-looking agreeable fellow who describes to me how he lost an eye in 1941 acting as a scout with British forces invading Syria, at that time held by the Vichy French. Last night he went to the play *The Right Honourable Gentleman* about the Charles Dilke scandal.† I ask him whether that sort of thing happens in Israel. 'Not yet,' he replies. 'These things take time.'

Raymond Bonham Carter‡ asks the General when he will be letting us have his version of the Suez Campaign and the diplomatic manoeuvres which preceded it. Dayan replies: 'There will be no book. I won't let you down.' Raymond: 'I assure you, General, there were two schools of thought in England about Suez.'

## 6 April 1965

Reggie Maudling was abroad when Rab Butler took his seat in the House of Lords with none of his former Commons colleagues present. I ask Reggie: 'Would you have been there if you were in England?' He replies: 'I was afraid you were going to ask me that.' Very astute answer.

## 21 April 1965

After an early dinner I go round to Cromwell Road for a drink with Charles and Pamela Snow. Charles is lying in bed with his eyes bandaged, like a huge stranded whale. He expects to have the operation on his eye next Tuesday, and is dreading the boredom of the post-operative period. As he does not like music, the wireless is of limited use to him. The doctors say the operation has a good chance of success. Even if it fails, the other eye is perfectly sound.

I ask Charles whether he has ever met Leavis, and whether he knows anything which could account for the savagery of Leavis' attack on him. 'I

---

* Moshe Dayan (1915–81), Israeli military leader and politician.
† Sir Charles Dilke, 2nd Bt (1843–1911), Liberal politician whose career was ended when he was cited in the divorce courts.
‡ Raymond Bonham Carter (1929–2004), leading banker.

hardly know him at all,' Charles says, and tells me what he once told me before that Leavis wanted to become a Fellow of Christ's and failed. 'This he may have attributed to me.' Charles says: 'There was also another occasion when I wrote to commiserate with him on something which had happened. This obviously damned me completely in his eyes.'

### 3 May 1965
Lunch with Christopher Soames at his flat in Tufton Street. He tells me that he is furious with Edward du Cann* for having publicly said that the Government announced a life peerage for Lady Churchill on Friday night in order to blunt the impact of their proposed Bill for the nationalisation of steel. This, Soames rightly thinks, was a mean and ungracious statement. He also tells me that Rab Butler was singularly ineffective in Cabinet: any strength of purpose he had came from his first wife.

'The Army has obviously been a link between me and my father-in-law. Our relationship has been as close as any can be between two men separated by so many years. I was never frightened of Winston. He liked and encouraged young men. He used to try things out on me – just the two of us sitting over the brandy until two o'clock in the morning. After Winston's stroke in 1953, my duties increased enormously. It was not just a question of finding pairs for him in the House of Commons. I woke him up in the morning and put him to bed at night.

'There are all too few independent-minded people in politics today. We have lost two of them in Alan Lennox-Boyd and Heathcoat-Amory. I like Edward Boyle, but he is not a leader of men.'

I ask Christopher if he would like to be leader of the party. 'If I had gone through what Alec has gone through,' he replies, 'you would not have seen me for dust.'

### 3 June 1965
Leslie Rowse gives a luncheon party at the Ritz. The best remark I hear is from Carola Oman[†] on Violet Bonham Carter's book on Winston: 'She is obviously in love with him, but then Winston always did like horses.'

### 24 June 1965
Harold Macmillan, as Chancellor of Oxford, gave an honorary degree to Harold Wilson. Apparently he included a word in his Latin greeting which

---

* (1924–2017), Conservative Party Chairman 1965–7.
† Lady Lenanton (1897–1978), writer.

could imply that the Prime Minister is clever in a very sharp sort of way.

Talk to Peter Carrington about the possible progress in the House of Lords of the Bill to abolish hanging. Several members of the Government, particularly Lord Gardiner, persuaded the Archbishop of Canterbury, Michael Ramsey, to promise that he would take charge of it. Now, on second thoughts, the Archbishop has rightly changed his mind. It would be an immense task for a man who is not a politician to grapple with all the amendments in Committee. It is also undesirable that he should give the impression that those who disagree with him are less good members of the Church of England.

Robert Menzies is having a very difficult time at the Prime Ministers' Conference. The African Prime Ministers heckle him constantly.

## 21 July 1965

Tom Driberg tells me that the most lavish purchasers of House of Commons Christmas cards are the MPs in marginal constituencies. 'When I moved from a marginal to a safe seat,' he says, 'I cut down my own Christmas card list from several hundred to twenty.'

## 27 July 1965

Spend the day at Goodwood. During the afternoon the loudspeaker at the course announces that Ted Heath has come top of the ballot for a new Tory leader. Maurice Macmillan says to me, 'It would have been better to have put it up on the board marked "Results from Other Meetings".'

## 28 July 1965

Give Selwyn Lloyd lunch at the Cavalry Club. He really is the best company in the world, with a dry humour unsuspected by most of those who only know him as a distant politician. He is amusing about his colleagues without being malicious. He tells me he is quite happy with Heath's election as leader of the party – though he would have been equally happy with Maudling. He has particularly happy memories of how unflappable and smiling Heath remained throughout the difficult days of Suez in 1956. But he much regrets that both the leading contestants had so obviously to go on show by being photographed either playing the piano or tending their hydrangeas. He tells me that Bill Anstruther-Gray* presided over the election of the new Conservative leader. He said of a newspaper article on his role: 'It made me look a bit of an ass – but then I am a bit of an ass.'

---

* William Anstruther-Gray, Baron Kilmany (1905–85), Scottish Conservative politician.

Selwyn also touches on his dismissal as Chancellor of the Exchequer by Macmillan in July 1962. After their final interview he was telephoned by one of the Prime Minister's secretaries to tell him that something had been forgotten. The Prime Minister wished him to accept the Companionship of Honour – and wanted an answer within half an hour as the list had to go to the Queen.

Selwyn did not really care one way or the other, but after consulting some friends he decided to accept. What he did not know was that the CH had also been offered to practically all the other sacked ministers. Had he known this, he would not have accepted. He thinks that Macmillan had not originally intended to sugar the pill of dismissal with any sort of honour for the departing ministers. But Harold Watkinson insisted on receiving something as otherwise it would affect his future prospects in the world of business. As it was clearly impossible to honour one minister without honouring them all, a hasty list of rewards had to be prepared.

Anthony Eden came to lunch with him the other day and is rather a sad figure. 'The trouble is that he thought he would die several years ago, so he made over most of his money. There is surely nothing more depressing than going on living under those circumstances.'

He is surprised to hear that Lord Casey has been appointed Governor General of Australia after so many turned it down. 'It will enable him though to fulfil a life-time ambition – accepting the resignation of Bob Menzies as Prime Minister.'

Mrs Pandit made an amusing remark to Selwyn the other day: 'What I like about England is that there is no colour discrimination. All our servants at the Indian High Commission in London were white.'

Selwyn is also entertaining about Pamela Berry. He says that, as he has begun to be asked there again, it is surely an indication that she thinks the Conservatives will soon be back in power. 'Why, it is only a month or two ago that I was pouring out drinks there for Tom Driberg.'

I also have a word with Maurice Macmillan later in the day. He is pleased about Heath's election as he considers he is one of the few men in the Government who will stand up to the Treasury officials. He also says that his father deserves much praise for having sacked an older generation of Conservative ministers in 1962, thus ensuring that before long the party would be led by a much younger man. I reply that this was certainly not Macmillan's intention at the time.

### 3 August 1965

Pass on my copy of Noel Annan's life of J.F. Roxburgh to Giles St Aubyn.

Giles makes a shrewd comment: that it was easy for Roxburgh to win popularity among the Stowe boys by lavish entertainment and presents; but he shirked the unpleasant problems of discipline. Giles also dwells mournfully on the predicament of a schoolmaster, which certainly affected Roxburgh: 'One gives the boys all the help & care possible for five years – then they go out of one's life.'

He also tells a story of Oliver van Oss visiting Stowe. In a deserted room there was a large nineteenth-century picture. It had two plaques. One said it had been presented by the mother of two Old Stoics. The other was the title: 'The Flight from Sodom.'

### 13 August 1965
Charles and Pamela Snow come round after dinner for a drink – a complete bottle of whisky to be more correct. It is amazing what a blimpish figure Charles is now becoming. He talks endlessly about the House of Lords and Eton, both of which he has now come to accept as pillars of his way of life. He tells me that the Labour Government have given much thought to how Eton can be abolished, but have decided that the necessary legal changes would be too complicated and too arduous, so it, and other public schools, will continue.

### 23 August 1965
Queen Frederica of Greece[*] tells me that apparently King George V had tried to persuade Field Marshal Smuts to become a British citizen so that he could succeed Lloyd George as Prime Minister after World War 1.

### 3 September 1965
John Russell[†] says that he once went to see Alec Home after he had become PM. Alec said to him: 'I wish I were back at the Foreign Office. All one's enemies there were on the other side!'

### 20 September 1965
Talk to Bill Williams at Rhodes House about the *DNB*. He admits that my task of writing the notice of Halifax's life will not be easy. In particular, it will be difficult to get across the fact that whereas Halifax was prepared to recognise social unpleasantness in the Nazi leaders, he was incapable of

---

[*] Queen Frederica of Hanover (1917–81), Queen Consort of the Hellenes as wife of King Paul of Greece.
[†] Sir John Russell (1914–84), Ambassador to Brazil 1966–9 and to Spain 1969–74.

recognising their wickedness. He makes one good remark about Birkenhead's* life of Halifax: 'As he could not publish his life of Rudyard Kipling because of family objections, he determined to use up all the purple passages in writing about Halifax's Viceroyalty.'†

## 3 October 1965

In Cambridge. At 11.30 I go to Trinity to see George Kitson Clark. First we talk about Rab's appointment as Master of the college. Kitson says there is some difficulty here as Rab does not yet know what needs to be done in Trinity, nor do the Fellows know what they wish him to do. For the moment Rab would do himself a great service by keeping his mouth shut.

I mention to Kitson that I am writing the notice on Halifax for the *DNB*, and how extraordinary it seems that a man who knew so little of foreign affairs should have been Foreign Secretary at so crucial a period in our history. Kitson agrees.

Walk across Trinity Great Court to have a drink with Rab in the Master's Lodge. The whole place is very disordered, with piles of books and furniture everywhere. Rab is very worried because he cannot offer me a drink. Although thousands of books have turned up and are more or less arranged on the shelves in his study there are no bottles among them, and this offends his sense of hospitality. He offers to send out for some, but I beg him not to bother. He is, in fact, rather proud of his library, and remarks: 'After all, I was a don originally.'

I ask him what are his plans for Trinity. He replies that his first task must be to get to know the college. There are 108 Fellows, and between 700 and 800 young men, not counting research students. Then there is the perennial problem of an appeal for funds. He does not intend to undertake any tutorial work.

Rab takes me on a tour of the Master's Lodge. The state rooms of the Lodge have their own pictures, including those of former Masters and some Royal portraits. There are also lots of signed photographs in the drawing room, including ones of the Queen, Prince Philip and Winston Churchill. In his own study, however, there is a photograph of Neville Chamberlain. I think it rather nice that Rab should still keep it on display.

Before I leave we have a word about Halifax as Foreign Secretary. Rab

---

* Frederick Smith, 2nd Earl of Birkenhead (1907–97), historian.
† This observation is correct. Certain descriptive passages are lifted verbatim from the text of the Kipling biography, which became clear when the earlier biography was eventually published.

thinks that Birkenhead has done a very good job in his biography and particularly stresses that Halifax was resolute both in the matter of the guarantee to Poland and in urging Neville Chamberlain to include Churchill in his government after Munich. When I point out to Rab that Halifax never followed up his initial suggestion, Rab replies: 'No, he was not a pusher.' That just about sums it all up.

At 3.30 I go to Churchill College, where Charles Snow has given me an introduction to George Steiner,* the English tutor. He is small, vivacious, entertaining and extraordinarily kind, inviting me to stay on for High Table. I ask him why I hear so much malicious talk against Churchill College. He gives me the following reasons:

1. The appeal for funds to found the college, with all its emotional undertones, coincided with a similar campaign which New Hall were making. Of course, everybody gave to Churchill and hardly anybody to New Hall. It was like the swamping of a rowing boat by an ocean liner. Some colleges have not forgiven Churchill for this. But would organisations such as ICI have given money so readily to New Hall as to Churchill? Steiner doubts it, and so do I.
2. Churchill has attracted some of the most distinguished younger men in the university, especially from Corpus, Peterhouse and Trinity. Thus the college has not escaped the charge of poaching.
3. There is naturally jealousy that Churchill is so rich, having raised over £3 million.
4. The college is very different from most others – co-educational, emphasis on research, and quotas of 70 per cent science and 30 per cent Arts embodied in the statutes.

The present Master of Churchill, Sir John Cockcroft OM,† holds his appointment until 1969. The post is in the gift of the Crown, a distinction it shares with Trinity, Cambridge, and Christ Church. Apparently, Winston did not trust the dons to make the best selection. Already there are vague manoeuvrings for the succession. Some would like to see Charles Snow as the next Master, though he has many enemies.

Churchill College has built a special fireproof room which at present is entirely empty. One day it will house eighteen tons of Winston's papers. They

---

* (b. 1929), American literary critic; Fellow of Churchill Coll.
† (1897–1967), winner of the Nobel Prize in Physics 1951. Founding Master of Churchill Coll. 1959–67.

are also acquiring the archives of Lord Woolton and in June Attlee gave them his War Cabinet papers. The papers of Ernest Bevin are expected to follow, and those of all other men who worked with Winston during the war will be very welcome.*

It is the first day of the new term and the undergraduates are wandering about looking at the modern architecture of the college with some awe. I dine with George Steiner on High Table – though in fact it is no higher than the rest of the hall, a huge brightly lit room. The food and wine are excellent. In the Common Room† after dinner we have much interesting talk. Steiner describes a party in New York on New Year's Eve at which Edmund Wilson‡ maintained that Oswald did not really assassinate President Kennedy but had been framed. Apparently, old Joe Kennedy, who had recovered sufficiently from his stroke to understand what had happened to J.F.K., gave his surviving sons unlimited funds to discover if in fact there had been an assassination plot. So they began a tremendous investigation, even including the remote hypothesis that L.B.J. had inspired the assassination. In spite of spending thousands of dollars and using the intelligence built up by Bobby Kennedy when Attorney-General, they found no evidence whatsoever.

I also hear that Hugh Trevor-Roper is desperate to become Provost of Oriel. This is the college to which he is now attached by virtue of his Regius Chair. He dines in Oriel, but then walks across to Christ Church for dessert and coffee, which is considered offensive by both colleges.

I ask Steiner what sort of impression Prince Philip made when he visited Churchill College. He replies: 'He was excellent with the kitchen staff, not too bad with the undergraduates, but appalling with the dons.'

## 22 October 1965

Talk to Anthony Wedgwood Benn. He tells me that in August 1954 Attlee and other members of the Labour Executive, on their way to Communist China, spent two days in Moscow. At a party given in his honour by Sir William Hayter, the Ambassador whispered to him: 'Which of the Russian leaders in particular would you like to meet?' Attlee replied: 'Frankly, none of them.'

---

* The Churchill College Archives Centre is the principal British equivalent of one of the great American Presidential libraries and now holds the papers of hundreds of politicians, including those of Winston Churchill and Margaret Thatcher.

† Combination Room in Cambridge. As an Oxonian K.R. obviously did not realise this.

‡ (1895–1972), American writer and literary critic. His famous 1934 essay 'The Ambiguity of Henry James' illuminated the hidden meanings of Henry James's *The Turn of the Screw*.

## 10 November 1965

Lunch at the House of Lords with Frank and Elizabeth Pakenham. I sit next
to Monty, who will be seventy-eight next week. But he looks at least twenty
years younger, very thin, alert and clear-eyed. But mentally he has solidified
into a permanent age of seventeen. He talks incessantly about himself. But he
is right to have a high opinion of himself – I sometimes think we might have
lost the whole Middle East without him. He certainly thinks so!

At present he is writing a history of warfare from 7000 BC to the present
day. He employs a research team in London which goes down to Hampshire
twice a month to give him the fruits of their scholarship. 'But the chapter
on generalship I am writing alone. And I am doing it all in my own hand –
good discipline, good discipline.' He adds: 'My memoirs have sold a million
copies.'

We have some talk about the last war and Monty cross-examines me on
my own inglorious record. 'What rank were you?' When I tell him I was a
subaltern, Monty replies: 'I was a Field Marshal. I don't suppose we ever met.
We were on different levels.'

I ask him whether he was always certain that he would one day rise to the
very top. He says: 'No, but I kept myself fit in case I should ever be needed.' I
ask him how his career might have gone if Gott had not been killed. Monty
evades my actual question and answers, astonishingly: 'If Gott had not been
killed we would have lost the Middle East.'*

He is rather touching in referring to his unpopularity among many people
when he first rose to fame. This, he explains, is because it was essential for
him to build himself up in the eyes of the Eighth Army, and this theatrical
approach inevitably annoyed people. When I ask him whether he minded
sacking people he replies: 'No, not at all, men's lives were at stake. Our generals during the last war had to be far more professionally minded than those
in World War I.'

I tell him that I see a certain amount of Bill Williams in connection with
the *Dictionary of National Biography*, and ask him about Bill's work as his
Chief of Intelligence. He replies: 'I first came across him as a major, and at
once made him my chief intelligence officer. His great virtue was that he
hadn't the constipated mind of a regular soldier. So he told me everything
I wanted to know and nothing that I did not want to know. I gave him

---

* Lt-Gen. William ('Strafer') Gott (1897–1942), senior British soldier. Gott was appointed to
take over the Eighth Army in Aug. 1942 after Churchill had sacked Auchinleck as C.-in-C. of
the Middle East. Gott was killed on 7 Aug. 1942 when his plane was shot down by two German
Messerschmitts. Montgomery was then appointed to command the Eighth Army.

everything. Made him a Brigadier and a CB. When I went to the War Office after the war as CIGS I asked him to become my Director of Military Intelligence with the rank of Major-General, but he refused.'

I find his excursions into autobiography very fascinating, but am astonished at his *enfant terrible* desire to shock. Thus when Elizabeth asks him about Wellington, Monty replies in a voice loud enough to carry all through the House of Lords dining room: 'Wellington should never have become Prime Minister. All politicians are liars.' And though he teases Frank Pakenham about the deviousness of all politicians, he also tells him that he approves of much of the present Labour Government's policy. He also proclaims that General de Gaulle is the greatest man alive in Europe today.

Notice the ostentatious bonhomie with which Monty greets Labour peers – as if he were an intellectual Socialist talking to a negro.

## 16 December 1965

Somerset Maugham died early this morning. He is not after all to be buried in the Cathedral precincts as such, but under the Maugham Library which he paid for at King's School, Canterbury. Lunching with him at his villa at Cap Ferrat was not the least of the delights of the French Riviera.

I have lunch with Maurice Macmillan, who has just been to the memorial service of his uncle Daniel in St Martin's. No address – 'He always used to say that he disapproved of them on three grounds. First, one couldn't hear them. Secondly, they never told the truth. Or thirdly, if they did tell the truth, it shouldn't have been told.'

## 29 December 1965

Read Christopher Hassall's[*] life of Rupert Brooke.[†] It is very long, but excellently done. Brooke wrote admirable letters, full of jolly jokes and unselfconscious humour. But it is almost physically painful to read of his tormented emotional life and his sad death – not in battle, as is often thought, but of septicaemia following a mosquito bite. The biography deals very clearly with his quality as a poet. His reputation exactly caught the historical spirit of 1914, but it is nevertheless true to say that he might have developed into a very great poet.

---

[*]  (1912–63), actor and author.
[†]  (1887–1915), the quintessential poet of World War I.

# 1966

*The Vietnam War continued and on 12 January President Johnson committed the United States to stay in South Vietnam until Communist aggression ended. On 3 February the Soviet Luna 9 achieved the first soft landing on the Moon. Harold Wilson called a general election for 31 March and secured a majority of 97 seats. On 2 April the Soviet Luna 10 became the first spacecraft to orbit the Moon. On 16 April Ian Smith, Rhodesian Prime Minister, broke off diplomatic relations with Britain. On 30 July England won the FIFA Football World Cup. On 8 September the Queen opened the Severn Bridge. On 21 October the Aberfan disaster in South Wales killed 116 children and twenty-eight adults when the slurry from a coal tip engulfed a primary school. On 30 November Barbados gained independence from Britain. In December talks between Harold Wilson and Ian Smith, held on HMS* Tiger *in the Mediterranean, failed to resolve the Rhodesian Crisis.*

### 26 January 1966

Letter from Lord Attlee in reply to my question whether the Labour Party would have been willing to serve under Lord Halifax as Prime Minister in May 1940. He replies that he does not know – they were merely asked whether they were prepared to serve under Neville Chamberlain (to which they said no) or, if not, under anybody else (to which they said yes). The letter is so erratically typed that I expect Attlee did it himself.

### 28 January 1966

Catch a train to Moor Park, as I am giving a talk to the boys of Merchant Taylors' on 'Politics and the Press'. Brian Rees, now in his element as Headmaster, tells me that the other day a prospective parent came to see him and admitted she could not decide between Merchant Taylors' and another school for her boy, adding: 'You see the other school has such a good Headmaster.' The talk goes very well and the boys are full of intelligent questions. I rather enjoy the day.

## 3 February 1966

At noon down to the Foreign Office to see Harry Walston.* He tells me a story about the late Lord Halifax. When Ambassador in Washington he heard one day that Lend-Lease was finally going through Congress, so he said to Charles Peake, who was then serving at the Embassy under him: 'We shall have a bottle of champagne to celebrate this. But we must tell the staff that it is Lady Halifax's birthday.'†

Dinner at the Dorchester with Anthony Grover.‡ He mentions that the other day a delegation of important shipbuilders went to see George Brown. Their leader put a case to him, at the end of which Brown simply said: 'You're a bloody fool.' The industrialist, very taken aback, replied: 'I may look a bloody fool, but I am not as big a one as you think.'

In fact, George Brown is dining at the Dorchester tonight. Although I have often heard stories of his drunken behaviour, I have never seen anything to match tonight's performance. He arrives rather drunk and goes round kissing all the women, even those he doesn't know. This particularly shocks the Mohammedan women, such as the wives of the Turkish Ambassador and of the Pakistan High Commission. At dinner he is at another table, but I hear him at one point turning to a guest and saying: 'Oh, do shut up, you are boring me.' I see Hartley Shawcross leaning across the table towards George Brown in obvious fury at one point during the meal. Fortunately, he leaves very soon afterwards, but not before he has done another round of kissing. It makes one feel dreadfully ashamed as half the guests at the function are foreigners.

## 6 February 1966

To All Souls to see Rohan Butler.§ He has carefully read through my draft of the *DNB* article on Lord Halifax and makes one or two valuable drafting points. He tells me the story of how Winston was once asked to write a Certificate of Regard for Pierre Flandin,¶ who was being tried for wartime collaboration with the Germans. Winston commented to Isaiah Berlin: 'What a difference there is between the way that we and the French do

---

* Henry Walston, Baron Walston (1912–91), farmer and Labour politician. Under-Secretary of State for Foreign Affairs 1964–7.
† Dorothy Halifax, Countess of Halifax (1885–1976), Vicereine of India 1926–31.
‡ Sir Anthony Grover (1907–81), Chairman, Lloyd's Register of Shipping 1963–73.
§ Dr Rohan Butler (1917–96), historian. Fellow of All Souls 1938–84.
¶ (1889–1958), French Prime Minister 1934–5; Minister for Foreign Affairs, Pétain Government 1940–41.

things. There is Flandin on trial for his life, and there is Halifax loaded with the honours of an Empire.'

At 4.30 go round to New College for tea with the Warden. William Hayter is very friendly and full of gossip. Apparently, Gladwyn has just been to lunch, talking endlessly about the Liberal Party – 'that stationary bandwagon on which he has jumped', Hayter says. He goes on to say that he thinks Gladwyn would have joined any party that promised him a job. After his retirement he expected to be made a minister at the Foreign Office by Macmillan. Winston always thought him unreliable and a Socialist, for he had served Dalton with immense fidelity. While Winston was in Opposition, he once sent David Eccles to tell Gladwyn that when the Conservatives came back to power, he could hope for no better post than Ecuador.

Dine with Hugh Trevor-Roper. We talk about appeasement and Hugh tells me of the appalling book[*] he thought was written by Martin Gilbert and Richard Gott, two young left-wingers. Gilbert has been taken up by Randolph Churchill, for whom he has acted as a researcher, and this has rather gone to his head. He treats Hugh, who after all is Regius Professor of History, with distant disdain.

I enjoy Hugh's company enormously, but he is one of the most egocentric people I have ever come across in my life. He boasts to me of his three great successes in getting people jobs:

1. He made Harold Macmillan Chancellor of Oxford.
2. He made Chenevix-Trench Head Master of Eton.
3. He was responsible for getting Oliver van Oss made Headmaster of Charterhouse, his alma mater.

Also, on the subject of appointments, he tells me that he lunched with a housemaster at Rugby the other day and heard that although Walter Hamilton would much like to become Master of Magdalene, he is unlikely to accept the post for fear of annoying all his staff at Rugby.[†]

## 17 February 1966

Philip de Zulueta tells me that the famous white fur hat worn by Harold Macmillan when he went to Moscow in 1959 was in fact acquired by him at the time he was giving support to Finland in their fight against Russia

---

[*] *The Appeasers* (Weidenfeld & Nicolson, 1963).
[†] Trevor-Roper's intelligence was inaccurate. Despite this, Walter Hamilton became Master of Magdalene in 1967.

more than twenty years ago. Of course, the Russians never realised this.

Go down to Blackheath to dine with John Grigg. After dinner I have a great deal of talk with Roger Bannister,* whom I know from siting on the same Save the Children Fund committee. He says that it now seems astonishing that the operation on King George VI for lung cancer in 1951 should have been carried out in Buckingham Palace and not in the operating theatre of the most up-to-date London hospital. He thinks that this treatment of Royalty as a class apart – even surgically – will never happen again.

Clement Price Thomas,† who performed the operation, realised in the middle of it that he would have to cut a certain nerve which might affect the King's voice. In order to cover himself against any future charge of negligence, he at once stopped the operation for a few minutes so that the physicians, who were waiting outside, could come in and see that the cutting of the nerve was surgically necessary and not a blunder on the part of Price Thomas.

### 18 February 1966

Lord Beaverbrook's narrative on the Abdication of King Edward VIII, discovered after his death by A.J.P. Taylor, had many errors. In fact, Lord Beaverbrook was so diffident about his talents as an historian that he insisted on publishing his books in relatively small editions, so that they would not be remaindered.

*The Times* showed much malice in handling the story of the Abdication. It published a small piece of journalism which seemed innocent on the surface, but which carried a wounding innuendo. Immediately under a statement by Mrs Simpson offering to withdraw from the whole situation, *The Times* printed this social item: 'Thelma Viscountess Furness arrived at Southampton in the liner *Queen Mary* yesterday from New York.' For Lady Furness‡ had been an intimate friend of the King's when he was Prince of Wales.

Beaverbrook thinks that the great mistake which the King made was to ask Baldwin for a morganatic marriage, a form of alliance unknown to law. Thus the Government would have had to initiate legislation and so made the King dependent on them. Instead, the King should have sat tight and

---

* Sir Roger Bannister (1929–2018), distinguished neurologist and Master of Pembroke Coll., Oxford 1985–93. In 1954 he was the first athlete to run the mile in under four minutes.
† Sir Clement Price Thomas (1893–1973), pioneering surgeon.
‡ (1905–76), mistress of Edward VIII.

possibly insisted on his right to appeal to the Dominion Governments personally, rather than allow Baldwin to put loaded questions to them.

Philip de Zulueta tells me that Harold Macmillan is very upset about the impending publication of Lord Moran's memoirs.* Apparently, they contain a great deal about Winston which he had picked up both as a doctor and a friend, but not as an author. Macmillan has written to Lord Thomson to try to persuade him not to serialise the book as it is, but in vain.

## 20 February 1966

Lunch with Bill De L'Isle at Penshurst. It is an enormous place. I find him sitting in the library completing the new guide he is writing for the opening of the tourist season at Easter. I notice how elegantly he writes, with every phrase counting. It is characteristic of him that he nowhere makes any mention of having been awarded the Victoria Cross and only reluctantly does he allow me to suggest a reference to this effect – on the grounds that it will interest visitors to the house.

Of Bobbety Salisbury, he says that it is Bobbety's own fault if he is now an unconsidered force in the House of Lords, as he never took any trouble to keep his friendships in repair. He also tells me that Lady Churchill was disgusted by Monty's refusal to fly back from Africa for Winston's funeral. When she received a Christmas card from Monty bearing a photograph of him standing by Winston's grave, she tore it up.

## 28 February 1966

The Prime Minister announces that he will go to the country at a General Election on 31 March. It looks like being a tremendously boring campaign, ending in a much-increased majority for Labour.

At three o'clock I go down to St Stephen's to see Jeremy Thorpe. He has a plan by which the Liberal Party should offer to form a coalition Government with the Labour Party – though not be absorbed by it. When he asks my opinion on this I feel that I must tell him, however brutal it sounds, that such a coalition would not work. If he wants political office – as he has every right to want – then he should cross the floor of the House and join the Labour Party, hoping to introduce Liberal principles into its politics. But a coalition between the two parties could be effective only as long as the Labour Party has a small majority and thus a pressing need for votes in the House of Commons. Supposing such a coalition took place and the government then increased its majority to sixty or seventy after an election, there would be

---

* Published as *Winston Churchill: The Struggle for Survival* by Constable in 1966.

absolutely no reason why the Socialists should listen to the Liberals for the abandonment of steel nationalisation and other such measures.[*]

### 3 March 1966

I attend an enormous lunch at Claridge's given by George Weidenfeld to launch his new world university library. I have some pleasant talk with Alan Bullock. He tells me it is quite true he was offered the Chairmanship of two Royal Commissions. They were those on Local Government and on the Public Schools. 'I turned them both down – though I should rather have liked to be Chairman of the Royal Commission on the Civil Service. But on the whole, I think that dons should either go into politics directly or write books. They should not attempt to exert political influence in a backstairs way.'

Jennie Lee[†] makes an appalling speech, entirely misjudging her audience of eggheads. It consists of an emotional appeal for a university which is truly international, drawing on all the best brains in the world, irrespective of country. I can hardly believe my ears and scribble a note to Alan Bullock who is on the other side of the table asking what on earth she thinks is the system at Oxford, Cambridge or at Harvard and Yale. Alan scribbles back: 'I don't suppose she has heard of them.'

### 6 March 1966

John Grigg tells me that when Queen Mary was at Badminton during the war, she came over to see old Lady Islington[‡] at her house. As was usual on such visits, she admired several objects which she wanted to be given as presents including a large vase bearing the Teck arms. But Lady Islington remained silent. Queen Mary, determined to secure at least one trophy, poured praise on a little table. Silence. So she had to continue her tour of the house without it. But at the front door, just as she was about to get in her car, Queen Mary turned to Lady Islington and said: 'I really must go back and say goodbye to that charming little table.' So Lady Islington led her back and Queen Mary said goodbye to it. Still Lady Islington refused to make a gesture of giving her it and Queen Mary departed in rather a huff. It must be the first time she had ever been outwitted in that way.

---

[*]  This was an accurate forecast of what happened to the Lib-Lab Pact of 1977–8.

[†]  Baroness Lee of Asheridge (1904–88), Labour politician; wife of Aneurin Bevan. Minister for the Arts 1964–70.

[‡]  Anne Dundas Dickson-Poynder, Lady Islington (1869–1958), mother-in-law of John Grigg.

## 7 March 1966

I have quite a lot of talk with Norman Collins,[*] who is in rather a huff with Ted Heath. Though it is well known that Norman used to advise Macmillan on all his television appearances, it was only the other day that Bobby Allan[†] asked him whether he would like to advise Heath too. But unlike Macmillan Heath cannot bear criticism and was very annoyed when Norman told him that there were not enough memorable phrases in his speeches.

## 8 March 1966

Lord Strang has sent me some interesting points on Lord Halifax's foreign policy for my *DNB* notice, and particularly stresses two points – that we began to make quite good headway in rearmament from 1937 onwards, and that we constantly overestimated the advances in rearmament made by the Germans at that time.

Go out to Putney by Underground to dine with Harry Hoff.[‡] He is a great friend of Derek Mitchell,[§] one of the Prime Minister's Private Secretaries. The other night, Mitchell put his head round the door of the Cabinet Room and said to Harold Wilson that he was just off to Covent Garden to hear *The Flying Dutchman*. The Prime Minister replied: 'Ah yes, the ship without a crew, what a pleasant prospect!'

A characteristic bit of gossip too about George Brown. Apparently, he has his senior civil servants into his room at the Department of Economic Affairs and criticises them individually in front of all the others.

## 10 March 1966

Martin Gilliat tells me that he met Hinchingbrooke, now Victor Montagu, at dinner the other night, and they had rather a brush. Hinch was saying that Prince Charles should have been sent to Eton, not to Gordonstoun, and much less to his present Australian school, Geelong Grammar School. Martin got annoyed with Hinch and told him to mind his own business.

In fact, Hinch comes to dine with me at the Beefsteak. He is in very low spirits indeed. He has applied to be a Conservative candidate for endless constituencies, but most of them do not even bother to reply. He has just been to a cocktail party given by the Rhodesians. There is no doubt that the

---

[*] (1907–82), television executive; author of the novel *London Belongs to Me* (Gollancz, 1945).
[†] Robert Allan, Baron Allan of Kilmahew (1914–79), PPS to the Prime Minister 1955–8; Parliamentary Under-Secretary at the Foreign Office 1959–60.
[‡] (1910–2002), novelist who wrote under the name of William Cooper.
[§] Sir Derek Mitchell (1922–2009), Treasury civil servant. Principal PS to Sir Alec Douglas-Home and Harold Wilson.

economic sanctions imposed by Great Britain are totally ineffective.

### 19 March 1966

Catch the 11.15 train to Oxford. Lunch with Alan Bullock at St Catherine's. He appears immensely grateful to me for my gift of the tree for the college and takes me to see it. It is bigger than I expected, about twenty-five feet high. We eat an excellent lunch in the very modern Common Room, then sit in the sun whilst Alan kindly reads through my *DNB* notice on Halifax. He likes it very much.

Alan tells me that he has just completed the second volume of his life of Ernest Bevin, dealing with the war years. He has gone very deeply into the history of administration during that period. This was a topic that Jack Wheeler-Bennett should have tackled when writing his life of John Waverley, but he shirked it. In the course of our conversation, Alan quoted a very good remark by Lloyd George. While returning from Versailles after the Peace Conference in 1919, the Prime Minister said: 'We do not quite appreciate the importance and the magnitude of the events in which we have been taking part.'

Alan then takes me on a tour of the new buildings. There is already a Barbara Hepworth in position and Henry Moore has promised two of his pieces to the college, one of which will stand near my tree.

### 26 March 1966

Leave for Eton at 1.30 to spend weekend with Giles St Aubyn. He is very worried about the result of next Thursday's General Election, though financially he is better equipped than most to survive it. What of course frightens him most is that the Socialists will sweep away his livelihood and main interest in life by abolishing the public schools.

### 31 March 1966

Polling day for the General Election, though I am ashamed to say I do not find time to vote. Pam and Michael Berry give their usual agreeable Election Night dinner party at the Savoy, followed by a general buffet. It is all very well done.

When the results start coming in it soon becomes clear that Labour are likely to have a majority of over 100. Eton, Oxford and Cambridge all go Labour. On the other hand Patrick Gordon Walker gets back at Leyton. Jeremy Thorpe also wins his seat, but with a majority reduced to just over 1,100. As the results come in there is some disagreeably gleeful cheering from Labour supporters, sitting down to champagne and bacon and eggs, without even greeting Pam or Michael.

## 5 April 1966

In the evening go round to St James's Court to talk to Selwyn Lloyd about Rhodesia. Not long ago he undertook an extensive tour there on behalf of the Conservative Party. The first point he makes is that no alternative Government to that of Ian Smith exists in Rhodesia. The Government is unpopular and powerless and white opinion is almost unanimously behind Smith. Secondly, economic sanctions are failing to work. Their impact has been cushioned by stocks and ingenuity in devising alternative ways of manufacturing forbidden imports. The main disadvantage of sanctions in Rhodesia has been a certain amount of unemployment. This will not affect Europeans, who can always get jobs in Johannesburg. There has been plenty of petrol everywhere and many people have accumulated big private stocks. Ian Smith has told Selwyn that the economy will decline until June, and should then pick up. What is astonishing is the optimism with which the British Government has used sanctions. Sanctions are a powerful thing towards a settlement though they will never cause surrender.

It is absurd to suppose that there is not a chance of an effective African Government in Rhodesia. The chiefs are not as useless as is generally supposed. I ask Selwyn whether Rhodesia would fight if we used force. He replied that they would fiercely resist any invasion by black troops, but not white. If we insist on marching in, most of the white Rhodesians will simply leave the country to stew in its own juice. So the only real solution must be unconditional talks on both sides, for neither side can win.

Selwyn does not think that his Conservative colleagues have handled the Rhodesian Crisis at all well. In September 1964 Alec Douglas-Home stated as one of his principles that 'any settlement should be acceptable to the people of Rhodesia as a whole'. But this is absurd, as it is unattainable. Humphrey Gibbs[*] is very unhappy as Governor and told Selwyn that he will resign if force is used.

All this talk with Selwyn reinforces me in my conviction that he is a far wiser man than most people are prepared to admit.

## 16 April 1966

In Rhodesia. I hear that in a six o'clock broadcast this morning, Ian Smith broke off all diplomatic relations with the United Kingdom. So Humphrey Gibbs's position becomes of particular interest. Fortunately, I have an appointment with him later this morning. So I take a cab up to Government House. No guards at gate, but still a notice, surmounted by a crown, pointing

---

[*] Sir Humphrey Gibbs (1902–90), Governor of Southern Rhodesia 1959–69.

to where visitors may sign the Governor's Book. Met by an ADC and after a brief wait in a pleasantly cool drawing room I am taken in to see Gibbs. His study is a pleasant, book-lined room. The Governor, tall and lean, looks a sick man. He rubs his eyes and forehead constantly, is rather deaf, and speaks in a tone of weary suffering.

I ask him some sympathetic questions about his own personal position to which he responds more readily than I expect. 'I should like to go, but will sit here as long as I think I can be of any use in a solution of the problem. I am a Rhodesian, and so want to see a solution agreeable to all concerned. I want to see independence on an agreed basis. Nothing but good could come out of exploratory talks without restrictions.'

When I ask him how he communicates with Downing Street, he replies: 'They have cut off my telephone, which is all right for me, but inconvenient for my staff. So I can have no direct talk with London – and certainly no conversation. We use James Bond stuff. So I exist on rumour.'

On the effect of economic sanctions he says: 'They are costing both Rhodesia and Britain a great deal, and our economy is running down. Instead of twenty-six or twenty-seven cars a day being produced by BMC,* there are now six. A lot of people are being paid to do nothing. On the unemployment brought about by sanctions he says: 'The African is hardest hit by sanctions. The English can always go down to the Republic of South Africa for a job.'

Gibbs says that he is now served by a small staff and they are able to carry on thanks to a privately subscribed fund to meet Government House expenses of about £1,000 a month. But he cannot go down to Bulawayo to see his farm in case the Smith regime attempts to seize Government House in his absence.

Government House is like a very quiet, well-run country house – there is even the Governor's private flag flying over the white-pillared portico. But it seems utterly remote from all political power.

By mid-afternoon Salisbury is as dead as a doornail: so many people go away for the weekend. But an attractive little city of arcaded shops and small skyscrapers. From looking in shop windows, I do not see much obvious effect of sanctions. There are all sorts of luxurious chocolates and marrons glacés. Bookshops seem to have more magazines than volumes. What delights me best is a whole window devoted to plastic gnomes and toadstools.

---

* The British Motor Corporation, formed in early 1952 to give effect to an agreed merger of the Morris and Austin businesses.

## 18 April 1966

On the way to the Ministry of Information, which is housed in a big block
of Government offices, I pass the Department of Industry and Commerce.
Over the entrance a notice has been put up saying 'Emergency Ward 10.'

I hear some interesting views on the political situation. The Rhodesian
Government is described as 'a bunch of hicks, entirely out of their class'. The
Governor is a Kipling-like character, who at present is exposed to terrible
pressures, but is standing up well. There is high praise for Selwyn Lloyd on
his recent tour: 'The only leading British statesman for years who has not put
someone's back up here.'

The British Government from the highest motives wants to secure a measure of advancement for the African; but they rarely appreciate the point of
view of the white Rhodesian.

## 19 April 1966

I am a guest of the Salisbury Rotary Club. Everyone talks of the hardening of the attitude towards Great Britain. Instead of the usual toast of 'The
Queen', the Chairman gave 'Rhodesia'. It is quite common for people to say
openly that they are ashamed of being British. Wilson's alleged threat to rule
Rhodesia directly from Whitehall, followed by a speedy advance towards
African majority rule, has caused particular fury, even among those with
liberal inclinations. There is nothing but scorn for the present regime,
though everyone has respect for the Governor and sympathy for the position
in which he finds himself.

## 21 April 1966

I notice that the *Rhodesia Herald* contains each day a selection of angry
letters from retired Group Captains and the like disowning their loyalty to
England – particularly in view of the Queen's having referred to the Smith
Government as an illegal regime in her Speeches from the Throne in both
Jamaica and Westminster.

At 10.30 I go along to see Roy Welensky[*] at the office he has in an old-
fashioned, colonial-style building, with a broad veranda. Find him sitting
happy and relaxed at a big oval desk. He tells me that during the present crisis
he has not been as passive as some people think – but he does not want to make
a public stand at a time when so many Rhodesians have entrenched themselves
in fixed positions. 'We need the services of an honest broker unconnected with

---

[*] Sir Roy Welensky (1907–91), Northern Rhodesian politician. Last Prime Minister of the
Federation of Rhodesia and Nyasaland 1956–63.

Great Britain and Rhodesia in order to find a common goal. The sort of person I have in mind is someone of the influence of Lyndon Johnson.' I suggest that Dean Acheson might be the best man. At this Welensky becomes most enthusiastic, bangs the table and says: 'Yes, what a good idea.'

I ask him what effect sanctions are having on the Rhodesian economy. He replies: 'We cannot be starved into submission. We grow plenty of food and get much of the power we need from Kariba. If all oil were cut off it would reduce the strength of our economy by about 30 per cent, but we would still limp along. In the long term, however, sanctions will have a crippling effect on our economy. The urgency of holding talks is twofold – the danger to Rhodesia and the danger to the British Prime Minister when he meets the other Commonwealth Prime Ministers at the conference in July. 'I oppose UDI, but I will do nothing to embarrass Smith and his Government in their efforts to settle the problems. It is Wilson who has made it impossible for any opponent of Smith to do anything helpful. For as long as Wilson retains his conditions of unconditional surrender, his policy is unacceptable even to moderates such as myself. I am an opponent of the present Government here, but I love my country. It is a hell of a position to be in.' He thinks that Smith is a weak man and has no doubts whatever about Wilson's stamina in the present fight.

I have much enjoyed my talk with Welensky, a warm and friendly man with a gleam of greatness about him.

## 22 April 1966

I visit Lord Malvern.* Now in his eighty-third year, he is very deaf, but has a mind as sharp as ever. He begins: 'Well, we are in a proper mess, aren't we?' He has a vast contempt for the Smith regime and indeed for white Rhodesian leadership in general. He tells me that in 1923, when there was a plebiscite to decide whether Rhodesia should be absorbed into the Union of South Africa, he voted for such an absorption because of the inferiority of white Rhodesians as politicians. But, the vote having gone the other way, he then spent more than thirty years trying to make Rhodesia work.

'We are living in what is virtually a police state. The only criticism of the Government that one hears is from the Opposition in Parliament. Smith is a very untruthful man and certainly made a bad impression in this respect on Lord Gardiner.'

---

* Godfrey Huggins, 1st Viscount Malvern (1883–1971), Rhodesian politician. Prime Minister of Southern Rhodesia 1933–53; Prime Minister of the Federation of Rhodesia and Nyasaland 1953–6.

I ask him what solution he sees. He replies: 'Sanctions are not having much effect at the moment, but when they begin to pinch, people will act against the present regime. What we really need is a new sort of Government under a Presidential figure, with safeguards for both black and white.'

About five o'clock in the afternoon, I see three petrol lorries arrive from South Africa. They are greeted by widespread cheers, blowing of horns and other signs of euphoria on the part of the people of Salisbury.

Drive up to a house in the suburbs for tea with Robert Birley. While investigating the affairs of the university here, he is keeping himself in complete seclusion, particularly from the Press. He has not even called on the Governor yet, in order that he may appear to be utterly impartial in his approach to the university problem.

He has both admiration and sympathy for Humphrey Gibbs. Last summer Birley was invited to give away prizes at the speech day of Peterhouse School. As the theme of his address he took divided loyalties and gave the usual talk on how it required much courage and fortitude when tempted to serve two masters. While in the middle of his speech, he happened to glance along the row of distinguished guests and there he saw Sir Humphrey Gibbs with a mask of doom on his face.

He gives me one astonishing statistic – that the 200,000 Europeans in Rhodesia, many of them young people, employ no fewer than 94,000 domestic servants. It is true that if the 94,000 were not employed as domestic servants they would have little other opportunity of earning their living. But what he objects to is the idea that they are incapable of doing anything else except domestic service. He adds that he himself has lectured in South Africa on the theme that a test of civilisation is how sparing a use it makes of domestic servants.

Birley has heard some very depressing evidence from African students on the way they are treated in Rhodesia. One young man told him that the most disagreeable experience of his life had been to spend a morning selling university rag magazines in the streets of Salisbury: the insults heaped on him by passing white women were indescribable.

This does not, of course, mean that he has any great faith in the African Nationalist leaders. 'Smith should have invited Harold Wilson to spend some days with the African leaders here. The Prime Minister would then have seen how impossible they were as an alternative Government – at least for the time being.' Birley stresses that it is to the credit of the Government that they have put down gang warfare in Rhodesian towns – 'there is hardly an African who does not prefer a strong police force. Although few Africans get to the university, those who do are paid for by the Government at the rate of about £300 a year. Such bursaries are not given by the Government of South Africa and the standard of university teaching in Rhodesia is higher than that in South Africa. The medical services for Africans, too, are impressive.'

### 24 April 1966

Take off for Livingstone, flying over the Victoria Falls on the way. A huge cloud of spray rises above them and from the ground is visible for miles around. At Livingstone Airport there are notices everywhere which read: 'Zambia, the Friendly Country.' But that does not prevent the customs officials from confiscating all Rhodesian newspapers that happen to be carried by tourists.

Drive out to the Victoria Falls. They are more than a mile wide, 350 feet deep, and 75 million gallons of water pass over them each minute. But as the Yorkshireman once observed at Niagara: 'There's nowt to stop it.' Standing on the banks of the Zambesi, I look down at the immense grandeur of the scene as the water falls into narrow basalt gorges surmounted by a rainbow. What adds to the dramatic effect is that the lethargic Zambesi suddenly shatters into ragged columns of immense force. Curzon, whose picturesque language I have sometimes thought exaggerated, said no more than the truth when he described the Zambia falls as 'the greatest river wonder in the world'.

### 25 April 1966

At ten o'clock I go up to Government House for a farewell talk with Sir Humphrey Gibbs. He is looking no happier than when I last saw him, and really seems to have little hope of an imminent solution. He repeats that no external force will persuade members of the Rhodesian Front to negotiate with the British Government: that initiative must come from dissidents within the party. But as unemployment increases, so, he believes, there will be a split within the party. He is certain that the economy of Rhodesia in general is running downhill. When eventually there is a negotiated independence, one of generous acts on the part of the United Kingdom must be to grant a substantial amount of money for education and development. I ask the Governor whether he will write his memoirs. He replies: 'No, I want to forget it all. I want to look forward not back, and I think it a pity that Welensky should have written his book.' He is, though, hungry for English gossip.

### 5 May 1966

Back in England after an illuminating Rhodesia visit. At the Beefsteak John Wyndham tells me that he has been asked by Macmillan & Co. to write his memoirs. He replied that he felt unable to do so as he had never kept a diary. At which Harold Macmillan promised to lend him his own diary. So now he is at work.*

Sitting next to John is an agreeable fellow called Philip Woodfield, one of the Prime Minister's Private Secretaries.† He has been working with Mountbatten on problems of immigration and describes how, on the passage to New Delhi, Mountbatten re-enacted the whole of his Viceroyalty for the benefit of his entourage.

### 10 May 1966

I have a long talk on the telephone with Edward Ford about the propriety of the Queen's having made a very political speech at a banquet in Brussels during her State Visit to Belgium. Edward maintains that the Queen has no latitude in such matters but must defer to the wishes of her Prime Minister. It would be, he says, more dangerous for the Queen to attempt to resist a policy of her Government than to incur the displeasure of its political opponents. After all, the Government pay her to carry out their policy – and pay her very well. And what could be a more useful instrument of foreign policy than a State Visit? I agree with him on the constitutional position, but maintain that she should be asked to make controversial political statements only on very rare occasions.

Dine in Chelsea with Frank and Elizabeth Longford. Much interesting political gossip from Frank. Harold Wilson apparently holds little hope that the present talks between the British Government and the Smith regime at a Civil Service level will lead to a permanent settlement of the conflict between Great Britain and Rhodesia. At first the PM thought that the initiative for the talks had come from Ian Smith. He now learns that it came from Sir Humphrey Gibbs, naturally anxious to bring about a settlement and so earn his release from an intolerable position of divided loyalties.

Reggie Dilhorne is very unhappy at having been sacked by Ted Heath as Deputy Leader of the Opposition in the House of Lords without even receiving a letter of gratitude for his past services. I have some sympathy with poor Reggie, but it is of course exactly what happened to Kilmuir when Reggie became Lord Chancellor – and again exactly what happened to Simonds in order to make Kilmuir Lord Chancellor.

---

* Published by Macmillan in 1969 as *Wyndham and Children First*.
† Sir Philip Woodfield (1923–2000), civil servant. PS to Harold Macmillan, Sir Alec Douglas-Home and Harold Wilson; Secretary to Commonwealth Immigration Commission under Lord Mountbatten.

## 11 May 1966

Lunch at the Turf Club with Peter Carrington. He tells me an amusing story of Harold Macmillan, who was one day expounding on the burden of making speeches: 'Not only has one to prepare the speech, but then one has to deliver and even act it. Why, at the Old Vic, I have seen Laurence Olivier absolutely exhausted at the end of *Othello* – and he has not written a word of it.'

## 12 May 1966

I write to Harold Wilson about my recent visit to Rhodesia to say that I think he has begun the present talks on Rhodesia rather too soon and that he should therefore spin them out as long as possible so that sanctions may bring the Smith regime to its senses.

Lunch with Martin Gilliat. Martin tells me that, without knowing very much about Rhodesia, he tends to support the Smith regime. So, of course, does the Queen Mother, influenced by Bobbety Salisbury. Astonishingly, nobody at the University College of Rhodesia has yet bothered to inform the Queen Mother, who is Chancellor, of the rows and disputes of the past few months. Martin asks me whether I will write an account of them for him to show to her, and I agree to do so.

Dine with Duncan Sandys. We talk about publication of Lord Moran's indiscreet diaries on Winston. Duncan himself describes an occasion when Winston was ill in bed with a high temperature in the Ministry of Defence headquarters in Storey's Gate. Duncan called to see him one afternoon, but could hardly get near Winston as the room was full of ministers, civil servants and generals. For an hour he watched Winston taking decisions of the highest importance. Later that night, Moran telephoned Duncan and said: 'I hope you won't go and see Winston again until he is better. You tired him out today.' No wonder Duncan disliked Moran.

I ask Duncan just how intimate Lord Moran was with Winston, particularly as in the diaries he makes Winston address him as Charles in almost every other sentence. Duncan replies: 'Well, after all, you call your butler Charles. Moran was not particularly intimate, but Winston always wanted to have chaps like Charles who would act as a captive audience.'

Duncan was astonished at the rapidity with which Winston recovered from his stroke in 1953. Just before Winston delivered his speech that autumn at the Conservative Party Conference at Margate, he said to Duncan: 'For once people are coming not to hear what I say, but to see whether I can.'

## 13 May 1966

G.M. Trevelyan* always advised people to read Kipling's *Puck of Pook's Hill* if they wanted to learn to write.

## 26 May 1966

Katie Macmillan rather exhausted by Lady Dorothy's death and funeral. When she died on Saturday just before leaving for a point-to-point, Harold was upstairs in bed. Poor Maurice had to break the news to him.

## 1 June 1966

Anthony Wedgwood Benn telephoned to ask if I am free for lunch today. Round to the GPO at 12.30 and he takes me to a pleasant new restaurant in the precinct surrounding St Paul's. When the Queen came to open the new Post Office Tower in Marylebone the other day, he suggested to her that some State Banquets might in future be held there. There is seating for 120 in the restaurant. The Queen could sit in the stationary part of the Tower, with her guests revolving about her. This would do away with protocol, as everyone would get a chance of exchanging remarks with the Queen every twenty minutes or so.

The other day he had some talk with Michael Adeane. They discussed the machinery by which the two main political parties chose their leader, and Michael Adeane said how relieved he was that the Conservatives had at last decided on a foolproof system of election. Anthony pointed out to him that the Queen's difficulties still might not be at an end. Let us suppose that Wilson was killed tomorrow. There would be a meeting of the Parliamentary Labour Party to elect a successor. But it could happen that they would choose somebody, e.g. Tom Driberg, who had a majority of votes among Labour MPs but was supported by very few members of the Cabinet. Several of these Cabinet members might thereupon refuse to serve under him and thus make it impossible for him to form a Government. The ball would therefore be back in the Queen's court. Poor Michael went away looking rather disturbed.†

## 1 July 1966

Read Lord Moran's *Churchill: The Struggle for Survival*. Its 800 pages have been my bedside reading for two or three weeks. Enthralling stuff, though

---

* George Macaulay Trevelyan (1876–1962), historian. Master of Trinity Coll., Cambridge 1940–51.

† A variant of this problem arose in 2015, when Jeremy Corbyn was elected Labour leader by the party membership against the wishes of the majority of Labour MPs.

obviously he should not have broken a doctor's confidence to publish it so soon after Winston's death and while Lady Churchill was still alive. I am also much irritated in the verbatim conversations he reproduces and the way in which he makes Winston and other great men address him as Charles several times on each page. Those who knew Winston well claim that he was not addicted to Christian names in this way. It makes the reader suspect the content as well as the style.

### 3 July 1966

I read the first volume of Harold Nicolson's diaries, edited by Nigel Nicolson and covering the years 1930 to 1939. It is a page-proof copy, and many small changes may yet be made in the text.

Curious how Harold felt the humiliation of being a gossip-writer for Beaverbrook's *Evening Standard*. But then the Press was treated with less respect in his day by politicians and other public men. He was paid £3,000, a very big salary for 1930.

Some endearing touches of Harold's silliness. When, after the Abdication, he goes to France to retrieve some notes left in an hotel by Mrs Simpson, he takes off his spectacles when examining them so that he shall not be able to read the exact words. What delicacy on the part of our twentieth-century Creevey.[*]

He thought *Some People* was so trivial that he was dissuaded with difficulty by Vita not to cancel publication when he saw the proofs.

I don't always trust his judgement. He will make an epigram, I suspect, for its own sake. Thus all the well-born wives of our diplomatists abroad have to look discontented in his eyes. How sad to read that he ceased to keep his diary in October 1964, having disappeared for good to the empty days of Sissinghurst.

### 9 July 1966

To Sissinghurst for the day. Before Harold appears for lunch, I have a long talk with Nigel about his father's diaries. He thanks me for the list of points I sent him after reading the first volume in page proof. He is having trouble with one or two people whose conversations Harold reproduced in the diary. Either they deny the accuracy of Harold's version or they threaten libel. Thus in volume two, which covers the war years, Bob Boothby is revealed as a bitter enemy of Churchill – presumably after the Czech gold affair. Bob now strongly denies that that was his attitude. Anthony Eden is also asking

---

[*] Thomas Creevey (1768–1838), politician and diarist much admired by K.R.

for omissions and is particularly annoyed at Harold's criticism of him for not having roused the country against Chamberlain after his resignation in 1938. The lawyers, too, are timid and have made Nigel take out a remark made by Baldwin to Harold after the Abdication – that the King had no religion. The implication that a man does not have a conscience is apparently worth £100,000 damages.

Nigel thinks that nobody has touched the worlds of politics and letters as closely as Harold. Chips Channon, it is true, kept a diary, but he was rather a stupid man. Harold's is very discreet and there is no mention of his sex life. What adds value to the diary is that the correspondence between Harold, Vita, Nigel and Ben* has all been preserved – which is just as well, as none of them said very much to each other when they met. After Harold's death, Nigel intends to write a book called *Portrait of a Marriage*, which will require a delicate touch, for Vita wrote her calm, sometimes stilted letters to Harold against a background of flaming passion in her own relationship with Virginia Woolf. Nigel says that when he got married, Harold told him: 'Don't worry about the physical side of marriage. It will not last beyond the first night.' Nigel adds: 'I never heard such nonsense in my life.'

The financial side of publishing the diary is astonishing. The serial rights of the entire thirty-four years were bought some years ago by the *Observer*, who had a three-year option on them. Several people read through the diary, but all agreed that in the mass it was almost unreadable. So they published one extract only. Then their option ran out and to renew it they offered only £250. So Nigel offered it to the *Sunday Times*, who snapped it up for £15,000.

## 11 July 1966

I talk to Oliver van Oss, who thinks that there are too many old men on the Governing Body of Eton. 'Bobbety Salisbury didn't want to attend the meeting of the Provost and Fellows which chose the new Head Master – because it meant missing a good day's shooting.'

## 13 July 1966

Queen's Garden Party at Buckingham Palace. Martin Gilliat asks me to come and talk to the Queen Mother. As always she greets me as if I were the one person she had been longing to see. I tell her that I have just been to see Harold Nicolson and she says: 'Ah, how sharp he used to be. He missed nothing, and he was such fun' – all this with a confiding gesture of the finger and a knowing look. And when I add that his diaries are to be published, she

---

* Ben Nicolson (1914–78), art historian.

replies: 'Well, I hope they will be discreet. We have too many lately that are not!'

At the back of the diplomatic enclosure I find Peter Carrington behind a rope barrier and ask if he is for sale. Peter tells me that Rab Butler has been writing his memoirs and claims that in 1955 it was touch and go whether Rab or Eden succeeded Winston as PM. When Peter mentioned this to Bobbety Salisbury, Bobbety replied: 'It sounds to be an interesting work of fiction.'

### 4 September 1966, letter to parents
I find it difficult to let a good story pass me by. I visited Gibraltar this week, hence my news story in today's *Sunday Telegraph* about Quintin Hogg's visit there. The paper is always grateful if I let them have that sort of news at a lean time of the year.

Gibraltar is an odd situation – a little bit of rocky land jutting out of Spain, with a population of only 20,000. Nor are they, as most people think, of Spanish descent. When we captured Gibraltar 250 years ago, the entire Spanish population left it, and the present inhabitants are mostly the descendants of Italians from Genoa and of Jews from Morocco whom we encouraged to emigrate there. Also, of course, a fair number of British officials and retired people, mainly Service officers. It is curious to find a little miniature London in the Mediterranean – red Post Office vans, policemen in helmets, eggs and chips in the cafés – and that rather strenuous sense of patriotism developed by those whose allegiance to the Crown has been acquired fairly recently. It must be infuriating for the Spanish to have these people on their doorstep, and to see a constant array of British warships in the bay. The celebrated apes are rather a disappointment – fat, lethargic, overfed beasts.

### 8 September 1966
Edward Ford tells story of how King George VI wanted to visit India before the war. P.J. Grigg, then a Finance Member of the Government of India, said the country couldn't afford it. So during the war, the King suggested he visit the British Army and pay a visit to India on the way back. Winston vetoed it on the grounds of danger. The King became furious and, trembling with rage, said: 'It was because I should have had the Burma Star & Winston wouldn't.' The King, of course, was always obsessed by the importance of medals and decorations.

### 9 October 1966, letter to parents
I managed a day at Brighton this week, talking to leading members of the Labour Party at their Conference. Anthony Wedgwood Benn gave me lunch

and the Longfords tea, so it was altogether a pleasant little excursion. I heard George Brown give his long lecture on foreign policy – for once he was sober in every sense – and had a few minutes' talk with the Prime Minister, who has the unenviable attribute of appearing furtive even when he is in fact telling the exact truth.

Frank Longford gave me an amusing account of his visit to Balmoral the day before. He told me that he saw his wife's life of Queen Victoria lying on the Queen's table. But she was silent about it and Frank felt too shy to ask her if she had enjoyed it. A lost moment of history! Frank has a high regard for the Queen, and says she misses nothing when ministers discuss their business with her. In twenty years' time she will be as formidable as Victoria herself.

### 15 October 1966, letter to parents

I am at the Tory Party Conference this week in Blackpool. On the second evening Pamela and Michael Berry gave a supper party at the Imperial Hotel. Everyone it seemed was there, including Alec Douglas-Home, Reggie Maudling, Ted Heath, etc. On the whole I thought Blackpool a very dreary place, without any of the character of Brighton or Scarborough. Even the illuminations are rather boring, except for tramcars ingeniously made into ships and trains with coloured lights.

The conference itself was a good workmanlike occasion, though without any spectacular oratory. Heath's speech was competent, but I was surprised at the very good Press he got the next day. It was revealing to notice how much more applause was given to Quintin Hogg and above all to Alec Douglas-Home.

### 5 November 1966

To Bradford for the installation of Harold Wilson as first Chancellor of the new university. The ceremony is held in St George's Hall. In order to get there I have to push through a crowd of young students who are demonstrating about Vietnam. The Prime Minister himself seems particularly unattractive today, with a horribly conceited and contrived address. At the end of the installation, I watch the Prime Minister try to reason with a huge mob of howling demonstrators, but the police very quickly bundle him into his car.

### 9 November 1966

At 9.45 to Claridge's to see the King of Greece. He looks far less worn and pasty than when I last saw him a year ago. The King is still immersing himself in foreign affairs. He has been to Rumania and is going to Persia in May. He cross-examines me about the British political scene. On

Mountbatten he says: 'What a machine that man is.' He says that in his opinion the worst mistake made by the Conservatives was in getting rid of Alec Douglas-Home.

### 13 November 1966

I give Hugh Trevor-Roper dinner at the Perch in Oxford. I tell Hugh that I am reviewing the Festschrift in honour of A.J.P. Taylor, edited by Martin Gilbert. Hugh hates Gilbert for being so pushing and for not treating him with the respect that is his due as Regius Professor of Modern History. It is now some years since Gilbert decided to produce the book. He asked Hugh to contribute an essay. Hugh demanded to know what was the occasion to justify such a volume. Gilbert replied: 'Taylor is so great a man that he does not need a special occasion.' So Hugh said he would not contribute unless there were a special occasion. When eventually the sixtieth birthday of Taylor fell this year, the book actually came to fruition. But Hugh was not asked to contribute.

After dinner we go on to the Senior Common Room at Christ Church, where we find that Tom Driberg is a guest. I am impressed with one point that Tom makes. He not only dislikes the annual Remembrance Day Service at the Cenotaph, but particularly objects to the presence of the Leader of the Opposition. 'Surely this is an occasion on which the Prime Minister should represent the whole nation?'

### 21 November 1966

Catch a train down to Kent to dine and sleep at Sissinghurst for Harold Nicolson's eightieth birthday. Lots of telegrams have arrived for Harold, but nothing from either the Queen or the Queen Mother. The best telegram is from Hugh Thomas and reads: 'Congratulations on reaching the age at which Verdi composed *Otello*.'

At about 7.45 p.m. Harold comes in, looking very smart in a blue suit and in better form than I have seen him at any time during the past two years. Then, with a large beaker of sherry in front of him, he receives his birthday presents. Ben and Nigel give him a drawing of Vita by William Rothenstein.[*] Harold is grateful: 'Vita was a beautiful woman.' We go in to dinner and eat pheasant and drink champagne.

Nigel asks Harold whether he has any regrets in his life.

'Well, I regret that Vita is dead – but I don't think I have any regrets for anything I could control.'

---

[*] Sir William Rothenstein (1872–1945), painter.

'What about leaving the Diplomatic Service?'

'No. It was really Vita who persuaded me to do so.'

'Joining Oswald Mosley?'

'Yes, I do rather regret that, but I suppose it was useful experience.'

Ben asks his father whether he now minds not having served in either war. Harold replies: 'Yes, I suppose I do rather, as I should like to have tested my courage.' At which Nigel justly interposes: 'Yes, but you were always being bombed in London during the last war and showed no fear.'

Harold goes off to bed about ten o'clock, having bidden us all an affectionate goodbye. I tell him what an old friend he is and we all agree to dine again on his ninetieth birthday.

After dinner we sit round a huge open fireplace. Nigel has just completed editing volume two of his father's diaries, and is now engaged on going through the original text for the third volume, covering the post-war years.

Nigel gives me a page-proof copy of the second volume to take back to London with me. He also asks whether I would like to read a volume of the original diaries in bed. But he says it would be better if I did not see any from 1954 onwards, when I first became a close friend of Harold. For he was capable of writing very sharply about his friends and it would be a pity to come across such a passage about one's self. So I take up the 1953 volume and cannot put it down till I get to 31 December – which I do at 2.30 a.m.

## 22 November 1966

Martin Charteris lunches with me at the Guards Club. I tell him how sad I am that neither the Queen nor the Queen Mother remembered Harold Nicolson's eightieth birthday by sending a telegram. Martin is seeing the Queen this afternoon, and will suggest that she sends a letter.

We discuss the future education of the Prince of Wales. Martin agrees with me that the Navy seems to leave its officers rather immature for life. He says: 'What Prince Charles really must learn is the importance of the intellect. For Gordonstoun certainly does not teach its boys that.'

## 23 November 1966

Dine with Norman Collins in St John's Wood. Norman tells me that the first job he ever had at the age of nineteen was as secretary to Lloyd George. In fact, he claims to have written the first two volumes of Lloyd George's War Memoirs. Norman would draft each chapter, and they would then discuss it at length and make alterations. If by any chance a document afterwards turned up which invalidated the theme of a chapter, Lloyd George would not rewrite it – he would merely tear up the document.

### 24 November 1966

Lunch with Anthony Wedgwood Benn in his office in the Millbank Tower, high up over London – much of which is today shrouded in heavy mist. He is loving his new job as Minister of Technology. I ask him why there are no pictures in his office (Charles Snow had Nolans) except an illuminated wall map, now out of date, of such things as atomic energy stations in the UK. Anthony says he has no use for pictures, but might put up some production charts or conversion charts to the metric and decimal systems. This depresses me. And I feel no lifting of the heart as he goes on to dwell on the glories of a universal system of measurement.

What really thrills him about technology is its revolutionary power. 'We are getting comprehensive schools not through political action, but because the technological age leaves us with no alternative. And that is only one aspect of the old world that is being swept away. I can foresee an alliance between the Labour Party and the managerial class that will make the Conservatives – with their dependence on financiers in the City of London – permanently out of date. The engineers are the really powerful men of today.'

I am full of affection for Anthony, but I fear his soulless rejection of all that is traditional in our national life.

### 28 November 1966

Read the proof copy of the second volume of Harold Nicolson's journals covering the years of the last war. They are full of good things, but Nigel has wisely left in enough to reveal the other side of Harold – his intolerance of Americans, Jews and the middle classes, as well as the way he would almost contrive a situation or an episode so that it made a good piece for his journal.

### 1 December 1966

Harold Wilson is flying off to Gibraltar for a meeting with Ian Smith on HMS *Tiger* – a melodramatic touch that recalls Winston rather than Harold Wilson.

### 4 December 1966

James Pope-Hennessy comes in for a drink before dinner. He was down at Sissinghurst the other day, but didn't enjoy it. He says that old age has brought out all Harold's worst qualities of selfishness. The trouble was that

Vita organised his life minutely for him and he now misses that more than Vita herself. Even his snobbery is more acute than ever before, which Nigel brings out in editing the diaries.

We talk about Vita and James describes an occasion when Nigel came to him at Balliol and said: 'What would you do if you suddenly realised at breakfast that your mother was in love with your aunt?' James replied: 'Keep it in the family.'

## 5 December 1966

Rather a tense day waiting to hear whether Ian Smith will accept the settlement of the Rhodesia problem proposed to him aboard HMS *Tiger* by Harold Wilson. In the late afternoon, news comes through that Smith has rejected it.

I go down to the House of Commons to hear Wilson make his statement on the Rhodesian talks. He is not unimpressive and I personally am inclined to accept the line he takes – that the agreement he reached with Smith of a constitutional settlement would be worthless without Smith's agreement to relinquish his illegal seizure of power. I am not sure what else he could have done to secure agreement with Smith. I do not believe for a moment that Smith would relinquish power even if the Royal Commission recommended it. Nor has he done anything at all to show that even in the most remote future he is prepared even to <u>share</u> power with the Africans in Rhodesia – much less to hand it over. It is an appallingly difficult and almost insoluble problem.

*In December 1966 Kenneth established a medical award at St Catherine's College, Oxford, in memory of his brother Toby. On Alan Bullock's advice it was agreed between them that the recipient should be a registered medical student at St Catherine's, who had passed the first BM; that he or she should have been placed in the First Class of one of the Honours Schools; and that the award should be made by a committee comprising the Master, the physiology and biochemistry tutors and the Chairman of the Examiners.*

## 8 December 1966

Lunch with Philip de Zulueta at the Ivy. He tells me that when Gladwyn was our Ambassador in Paris from 1954 to 1960, he used to correspond with Winston behind the back of Eden, who was Foreign Secretary. Then, when Eden became Prime Minister, he corresponded with him behind the back of Selwyn Lloyd, the then Foreign Secretary. This furtive behaviour so annoyed Eden and his other colleagues that Gladwyn was never appointed Permanent Head of the Foreign Office.

Hartley Shawcross gives a dinner at the Dorchester. Selwyn Lloyd is among the guests. Tonight the Commons debate Rhodesia and Selwyn Lloyd goes off to vote, returning about 10.30. Someone asks Selwyn whether Heath made a good speech. The answer might have fallen from the lips of Rab himself: 'It was as good a speech as it could have been under the circumstances. Of course, we gave him a standing ovation – because the other side gave Wilson one.'

# 1967

*The year began sadly with the death of Donald Campbell on Coniston Water, attempting to break his own water-speed record in* Bluebird. *On 27 January a fire in the US Apollo 1 space module killed three astronauts during a launch rehearsal. The* Forsyte Saga *ran from January to July on BBC2. Jeremy Thorpe became leader of the Liberal Party on 18 January. Harold Wilson announced on 2 May that the United Kingdom would apply for EEC Membership. On 19 May the USA bombed Hanoi. Colour television began in Britain on 1 July. The British liner* Queen Elizabeth 2 *was launched on Clydebank on 20 September. Sir Malcolm Sargent died on 3 October and Clement Attlee on 8 October. The spacecraft Surveyor 6 soft-landed on the Moon on 9 November and eight days later became the first man-made object to lift successfully off the Moon. At the same time the Saturn V rocket had its first successful test flight into Earth's orbit. The pound was devalued on 19 November from 2.80 dollars to 2.40 dollars. The Concorde aircraft was unveiled in Toulouse on 11 December.*

## 4 January 1967

Donald Campbell is killed while trying to break the world water-speed record on Coniston Water in *Bluebird*. The boat took off from the water and flipped over.

At 10.30 to the House of Commons to see Dr Horace King,* the Speaker. He has very kindly postponed his journey to Stockton, where he is going to attend the old boys' dinner of his school, in order to show me the important alterations that are being made to the library. As we walk through innumerable rooms where clerks, librarians and carpenters are at work, he greets them all with effusive courtesy.

The Speaker tells me how much he is missing the rough and tumble of political life and how hard he finds it to keep a guard on his tongue. When he visited Crete not long ago a Greek journalist asked him: 'Don't you think

---

* Baron Maybray-King (1901–86), Labour MP for Southampton Test 1950–55 and Southampton Itchen 1955–71; first Labour person to hold the office of Speaker 1965–71.

that the splendid economic policy of Harold Wilson should be applied to Greece?' But he saw that almost any answer would lead to trouble in both countries and wisely he kept his peace.

He insists on taking me up to his private rooms, which are above the state rooms, and there he gives me a signed photograph and also a signed copy of the Christmas carol he has written. He is particularly proud of the scroll of honorary degree given to him by the Queen Mother as Chancellor of London University, and of the freedom of Southampton, his constituency, contained in a box made in a carpentry shop of a local school.

I ask him what he has been reading over Christmas. He tells me it was Charlie Chaplin's autobiography, which he found disappointing. But he was moved by Chaplin's account of his boyhood in working-class London, south of the river – and here the Speaker gestures towards it from his windows overlooking the Thames.

### 15 January 1967
I start to read Randolph Churchill's life of Winston. Good material, including all Winston's early letters, but Randolph's commentary, though short and fitful, is obtrusive and facetious.

### 21 January 1967
About midday, leave for Strasbourg, to attend the new session of the Council of Europe. I fly to Basel. It is on the Franco-Swiss border. One walks out of one door into France and out of another into Switzerland. But what excites me most is to see a huge fox bounding across the airport as we come into land, or perhaps it is a wolf.

The British Mission in Strasbourg has sent a couple of cars to meet the Members of Parliament from England who are on the plane, including Douglas Dodds-Parker,[*] who kindly invites me to have a place in his car, and we drive in comfort to Strasbourg.

On the way we pass a local airport and see a parachutist dropping slowly from the sky. Douglas says: 'Is there no limit to the lengths to which Harold Wilson will go in his insatiable desire for publicity?' But Douglas is a fatiguing fellow to travel with. While sitting next to the Embassy driver, he never drew breath all the way from Basel to Strasbourg.

---

* Sir Douglas Dodds-Parker (1909–2006), wartime soldier and Conservative politician. MP for Banbury 1945–59; Parliamentary Under-Secretary of State for Foreign Affairs during the Suez Crisis; MP for Cheltenham 1964–74.

## 26 January 1967

Work quite hard drafting a lot of paragraphs about Strasbourg.

Later enjoy some talk with Norman Collins. He is very cool about Heath as leader of the Conservative Party, and would like to be consulted about his TV appearances and other public activities. 'I sat next to him the other day, and he talks well only if one asks him questions.' I tell him how gauche and stupidly rude Heath was about the *Sunday Telegraph* when I dined with him recently. Norman agrees and says that Macmillan would have handled a waspish journalist by saying: 'What a wonderful column I am told you write, such a pity I never have the time to read it.'

## 28 February 1967

At 5.30 I am interviewed at the BBC on how well or badly the Press has behaved in carrying rumours that Snowdon and Princess Margaret are having marital difficulties. These rumours have been in foreign papers for weeks – I saw them when I was in Paris last month. But on Sunday many of the tabloids printed them too. Last night Snowdon, on the way back from a four-week photographic trip to Japan without his wife, gave officials an official denial in New York. He should have said nothing. The programme I take part in is a recording. The compère ends: 'Well, that's all about Maggie Jones for today.'

## 11 March 1967

To Eton to stay with Giles St Aubyn. At 5.30 I have a talk with the Head Master, Chenevix-Trench, about the decision, taken in conjunction with Winchester, to abolish Latin as a compulsory subject for the scholarship exam to College. Without wishing to be too hard on him, I cannot avoid the feeling that he tries too hard to establish intimacy. I can see why the boys in a double-edged way call him 'Chummy Trench'. Thus he at once calls me Kenneth; and a few minutes later throws in a phrase, 'We don't want the Government to bugger us about' – presumably the language he thinks a man of the world should employ in talking to a journalist.

Yet he talks well on the problems facing the public schools, and in particular on the changing pattern of College at Eton. 'We have made the change in compulsory Latin not as a gesture of public relations to disarm outside criticism, but to make College a more intellectually adventurous place. I am tired of having only boys from schools such as Sunningdale, with its classical training that enables a boy to read a Greek play at twelve and a half. I want to see more cross-fertilisation.'

He is not an advocate of the intelligence test for the scholarship examination. 'We need to do much more research to discover what questions over the years, if correctly answered, give us eventually the sort of boy we want.' One candidate revealed himself as a passionate student of Trollope; and another the inventor of an ingenious clip-on tie.

On the subject of the Royal Commission on Public Schools, he says that only Dame Anne Godwin[*] has made up her mind: she is determined that Eton should become a V1-form college.

'I am prepared to consider all <u>educational</u> reforms, but not political interference.' I ask him what would, in practical terms, constitute political interference. He replies: 'If the Government ordered unwilling parents to send us unwilling boys.'

### 13 March 1967

A characteristic story of Monty. When his son David[†] was about to get married, he asked his father to take his fiancée to choose an engagement ring – but it was not to cost more than £120. Monty organised the occasion as if it had been the Battle of Alamein. The day before the official visit he went alone to the jewellers and asked to see all their engagement rings. Then he said: 'Put all those which cost less than £120 in this tray.' When he came with David's fiancée the next day he said to the jeweller: 'I want to see some engagement rings.' The selected tray was produced and Monty with a grandiloquent gesture declared: 'Take your pick.'

### 18 March 1967, letter to parents

Prince Eddie, the Duke of Kent, is to become the head of English Freemasonry. He will be proposed for election as Grand Master of the United Grand Lodge of England on 14 June. I forecast this as the eventual outcome in August 1964 in 'Albany'. Eddie's father was Grand Master from 1939 until his death in an air crash in Scotland while on active service.[‡]

I had a long talk with Rab Butler this week, very pleased at being asked to give the Romanes Lecture at Oxford in a few months' time.[§] He is taking 'Autobiography' as his subject, but does not quite know how to tackle the problem of the first volume of Macmillan's memoirs, *Winds of Change*. As Macmillan is Chancellor of Oxford, Rab thinks it would look pointedly rude

---

[*] (1897–1992), trade unionist. President of the TUC 1962–3.

[†] David Montgomery, 2nd Viscount Montgomery of El Alamein (b. 1928), politician and businessman.

[‡] K.R.'s father was a Freemason, but K.R. was not.

[§] The Romanes Lecture is an annual public lecture at Oxford. The first lecture was given in 1892 by William Gladstone.

if he did not refer to the book at all. On the other hand he thinks it a bad book. <u>How</u> he hates Macmillan – far more than any member of the Labour Party! He will probably get round it by praising the book for its description of the First War, and saying nothing of its political side.

I have made him tear up the first draft, which could have been written by any dim English don, and begin again, concentrating on his own experience as a politician. He has agreed and the result should be excellent. The title is to be 'The Difficult Art of Political Autobiography.' I like Rab, though I cannot admire him as a politician. He had not the guts to stand up to Harold Macmillan; had he done so he would have succeeded him as Prime Minister. He is, of course, a most valuable source of information about Cambridge affairs, and it was from him that I got the information about possible successors to Herbert Butterfield as Regius Professor of History.

### 21 April 1967

I hear on the 9 a.m. news that there has been a coup by the Greek army – supposedly supported by the King, although I should have thought him too sensible to take part in such an operation. All communications are cut off, and no planes flying in or out. Otherwise I should have been tempted to go. I desperately hope it will not end in tears, with Greece going Communist & the King living in Surrey.

### 6 May 1967

I manage to get to Greece to see King Constantine. I book out of my hotel and take a cab as if I am going to the airport. Instead I go to the offices opposite the Royal palace, where a car is waiting for me with a driver. I transfer my baggage and within seconds we are on the road to Tatoi, the summer palace of the Greek Royal Family, some twenty-seven km from Athens. On arrival I am shown into a little sitting room. Eventually the King's valet comes in and says that the King is ready to receive me. We pass through rather a lot of rooms – I notice the letters of Queen Victoria on a bookshelf – and are ushered into a medium-sized drawing room over-furnished with the usual array of Royal bric-à-brac. The valet withdraws.

The King is wearing a light-grey suit and as always has rather a smart shirt with cufflinks of diamonds and rubies forming the cross of St George. He welcomes me with much charm and warmth.

The King opens the serious part of our talk by inviting me to ask him anything I wish to know about the Colonels' coup, but of course on the understanding that I print nothing to suggest that I have seen him. I tell him about reaction in London. 'I am glad that some critical statements have been made in Great Britain,' he says. 'That puts those guys in the position of having to listen.'

He continues: 'They are absolutely courteous to me but it is a 100 per cent revolution and I have to walk a tightrope. The Athenians realise that I had nothing to do with the plot – I have made no public statement of support for the new regime. When it all began I told them privately, "You have the power, but you must not become too bossy." It took me two and a half hours to convince them to add civilian ministers to the Cabinet. If they should have executions, I shall lock myself up here. While touring the earthquake areas a few days ago I received tremendous cheers, and I turned to my aide and said, "You hear that? You cannot disappoint my people. After all the only reason the coup succeeded was that the units thought that I had signed the decrees."'

Again and again the King says, with dedicated determination, 'I am the only one who can bring the country back to democracy.' I ask him whether he feels isolated. 'Yes,' he replies, 'I've only got my own little brains!' I ask him whether he deliberately pulled a grim face when being photographed for the first time with the new ministers. He laughs and says, 'Yes.' At one point he says, 'Of course, there was corruption in previous Governments.'

He mentions that when he went down to Athens on the fateful morning he could hardly get into the palace, so closely grouped were the tanks encircling it. He adds that one day he will give me a lot more details of what actually happened, and says he hopes I shall be out again in the summer. 'You must tell us when you are coming.'

I presume to give him one final word of advice – that he should show himself to the people as much as possible throughout the country. He agrees, and repeats: 'I alone can bring the Government back to democratic rule.'

By now I have been with the King for just under an hour and I must leave if I am to catch my plane. So I take my leave and continue in the Royal car down to the airport.

### 14 May 1967, letter to parents

Staying at Eton. I have been busy for much of this week with the aftermath of my Greek visit. As I am still one of the very few people to have seen King Constantine and to have discussed with him aspects of the military coup, I felt I ought to tell the Foreign Office. So I lunched one day with Harry Hohler,* the Assistant Under-Secretary responsible for our relations with

---

* Henry Hohler (1911–2001), Ambassador to Switzerland 1967–70.

Greece. And I also had a talk with George Thomson,* and one of the most agreeable of all members of the present Government. They were both grateful for the information I gave them and asked my advice on what our policy should be towards the new regime. One particular problem is that the present Greek Ambassador in London, who has been here for some years, is being withdrawn by the regime. It is not, of course, diplomatic practice to ask for him to be left at his post, but our Government may be embarrassed if asked to receive a new representative of the regime, so we may exert discreet pressure in Athens for the withdrawal to be cancelled. It is all most delicate.

Princess Marina asked me to come for a drink on Sunday evening to hear my Greek news. She has heard nothing herself from the family and was most worried. So I was able to give her an up-to-date account. The only other two people present at her house in Kensington Palace were her sister Olga and her brother-in-law Prince Paul of Yugoslavia, both of whom I first met at Coppins many years ago. It was very ironical to be talking about the Greek situation to Prince Paul, for if he had shown anything like the guts of King Constantine when the Germans invaded Yugoslavia in 1941 the country might not have gone Communist. As it was, he was simply not up to being Regent, and Winston used afterwards to call him Prince Palsy. But he is a man of much charm with a profound knowledge of works of art. They have a house outside Florence which he asked me to come and see when next I am in Italy. Princess Marina was very welcoming and friendly, but she has suddenly started to show her years in a very marked way.

Another extra little job is that Rab Butler has sent me the first draft of his Romanes Lecture to be delivered at Oxford in a few weeks' time. His subject is 'The Difficult Art of Autobiography'. Unfortunately, he has so far produced a very poor paper indeed, so bad that it would damage his reputation to give it. I really will have to tell him so in discreet terms: what I will _not_ do is to rewrite it for him. I have quite enough work of my own at the moment. The trouble about his paper is that he has jotted down a number of random thoughts on autobiography, but without a theme or any attempt at that scholarship which is expected in such a lecture. I remember, for instance, how Herbert Samuel gave the Romanes on 'Creative Man', a most fascinating piece of philosophic learning.

As you can see, I came down to Eton for a restful weekend. Nothing much

---

* Baron Thomson of Monifeith (1921–2008), Labour politician. Secretary of State for Commonwealth Affairs 1967–8; Minister without Portfolio 1968–9; Chancellor of the Duchy of Lancaster 1969–70.

ever seems to happen here, although they all live under threat of extinction by the Public Schools Commission.

### 1 June 1967
Long talk with Selwyn Lloyd. Here are some of the points he made.

He behaved well to Anthony Nutting at the time of Suez. Spent hours trying to dissuade him from resigning, and even arranged with Oliver Lyttelton that Nutting could be moved sideways to another Ministry. 'Much Ado about Nutting,' he called it.

If one pursues feuds it wears one out and destroys one. So when I dined with Macmillan the other night I was all smiles.

The great Prime Ministers were Campbell-Bannerman, Stanley Baldwin and Anthony Eden. Eden was rude to one at night, but made amends in the morning. He has been talking to Attlee, who was very sharp and indiscreet about his colleagues.

Selwyn boasts that among his papers are (a) the last letter ever written by Curzon, in reply to the flowers which Selwyn Lloyd sent him from Cambridge in March 1925 on hearing of his illness. Curzon had been taken ill at Christ's College, just before giving a talk to the University Liberal Club that Selwyn had arranged. (b) The first telegram written by Field Marshal Montgomery from Normandy. Monty said of it to him: 'It is not entirely true, but it is what the people want.'

### 4 June 1967, letter to parents
I went to a most agreeable dinner party one evening this week, given by Norman Collins, the television pioneer. The guests included Selwyn Lloyd. The more I see of Selwyn the more I like him – a great sense of cheerful good humour and a refusal to be bitter at the shabby way in which Harold Macmillan, among others, treated him.

### 4 July 1967
By train to York to see Lord James, Vice-Chancellor of the university. He has his office in Heslington Hall, which has been charmingly restored. It looks out onto a sheet of ornamental water, and a large artificial lake has also been dug, both to drain the marshy site and to add to the beauty of the landscape gardening. Everywhere there are lots of trees; James tells me that by the time the development has been completed there will be more trees on the site than there were before.

Henry Moore has lent the university a large piece of sculpture. When he came to receive an honorary degree, he ran his fingers down a fine beech and said: 'Why do you want my work when you have trees like this?' It all seems profoundly peaceful, yet James tells me that within a quarter of a mile of where we are sitting, £4 million of building is in progress.

Money, he tells me, is scarce, as it is in most new universities. Nevertheless, the architects are keeping to the development plan published in 1962. The relationship between the university and its architects is virtually unique. They are seeking not to build monuments to themselves but are interpreting and clarifying academic ideas. 'They are so dedicated to this that they are wearing us all out with perpetual consultation.'

I ask him about the impression made at York by F.R. Leavis, the turbulent lecturer in English literature, who has been a visiting professor for the past two years. James replies: 'We originally asked him to come for one year, then asked him to remain for a second year. We are hoping that the association will continue even further. On Friday we are to make him an honorary doctor of the university – we do not give honorary degrees in specific subjects. That he should be given this after only two years among us is a mark of the great privilege we feel it has been for the university to have Leavis as a colleague. He has shown no prickliness at all. He cares very much for the young and has the habit of refusing to limit his seminars to an hour: he likes them to run on. The students who go to his lectures are not only those from the English School. One cannot ever hear him talk without his uttering at least one penetrating judgement. It is a splendid sight, too, to see him stride round the university site at 7.30 each morning. It will be interesting to see whether we can successfully combine the college system of Oxford and Cambridge with the faculty system of a red-brick university.'

Lord James tells me that in the middle of August he is going out to Witwatersrand University to deliver an endowed lecture on academic freedom. He says that his name was suggested by Robert Birley, whom he knew intimately when both were members of the Headmasters' Conference.

On his side table is an ornate plate bearing the face of Mr Gladstone who, he tells me, is one of his heroes. This leads us to talk about the nineteenth century and the art of letter-writing.

He says: 'I belong – but only just – to the generation that used to write letters in their own hand. If we still wrote all letters in our own hand, I am certain that a great deal of unnecessary paper would not be circulated.' And to emphasise his point he hands me the agenda for a weekend conference on social sciences. It is of foolscap size and about five inches deep.

## 5 July 1967

Lunch with Jeremy Thorpe at the House of Commons. He is rather disturbed by frequent newspaper reports about his relations with Harold Wilson. Political journalists profess to believe that the Prime Minister has made him a Privy Councillor and given him the same facilities in other ways as are offered to the leader of the Conservative Party merely in order to spite Ted Heath. I told Jeremy that, in so far as it is possible to peer into Wilson's mind, there is some substance in the allegations. I go on to suggest very forcibly to Jeremy – as I did immediately after Wilson had made him a Privy Councillor – that he should find an early opportunity for making a fierce political attack on the Prime Minister. Only in this way can he dispel the allusion that he is tied to Wilson by gratification.

In particular, I urge him to pitch into Wilson whenever the subject of the D-notice inquiry[*] is raised again in the House of Commons. Jeremy replies that he had previously decided to blame both Heath and Wilson impartially for their conduct in this matter – Wilson for not inspecting Radcliffe's report, and Heath for making too much capital out of it. I point out that the duty of the Leader of the Opposition is to oppose, and that Heath's shortcomings are infinitely less in this matter than those of the Prime Minister. Jeremy concludes by saying: 'Well, I will take your advice, but I don't suppose I will ever be able to get another Liberal life peerage.'

Throughout our conversation, it becomes obvious that Jeremy is rather wounded by the persistent hostile attitude which the Conservative Party has shown him since his election as leader, even the time they jeered at him across the floor: 'Where is the leader of the Liberal Party?', at which Jeremy became so annoyed that he determined to hit them below the belt. He shouted back: 'If it comes to that, why is your leader out of the House?'

## 20 July 1967, letter to parents

I had some talk with the Prime Minister after he had unveiled a memorial tablet to Walter Bagehot.[†] He made a very good speech indeed: he is much better at that sort of thing than when he is trying to score a political point. He is also, I think, getting used to receiving as well as giving hard knocks.

## 18 September 1967

When Dean Acheson was asked whether he had voted for Nixon in the 1960 Presidential fight with Kennedy, he replied: 'Yes, I voted for my party: but I held my nose.'

---

* In February Wilson had accused the *Daily Express* of breaching two defence notices advising the press against publishing material which might damage national security,
† (1826–77), economist and essayist; author of *The English Constitution* (1867).

## 14 October 1967

Go down to Eton to stay the weekend with Giles St Aubyn, arriving about teatime. This leads Giles to talk about Chenevix-Trench. Although Giles played an appreciable part in ensuring his election as Head Master some years ago, he is now thoroughly disillusioned with his choice. One drawback is that he is far too accessible to everybody. Here is an example. There are only a limited number of houses at Eton and thus only a limited number of housemasters. Some masters, therefore, will inevitably fail to get houses.

Trench makes his decisions and tells the masters concerned. Those who have not been fortunate enough to be promised houses thereupon go to him and complain. After much argument he gives in and says that they too can have houses; thus when eventually a house becomes vacant several people have been promised it. In other words, both with masters and with boys he wants to be all things to all men.

## 18 October 1967

Dine with Jeremy Thorpe in the restaurant of Marsham Court below his flat. Dick Crossman was also dining in the restaurant and afterwards joins us in Jeremy's flat. He says that he misses having a department to run: that of Lord President of the Council is minute. But as Leader of the House of Commons he has a sort of department, & one that enables him to see the Prime Minister at close quarters. He doesn't really care about Rhodesia, whereas Jeremy is rather obsessed by it. He compares George Brown at the Foreign Office to Ernest Bevin – both are vulnerable to the flattery of FO officials.

Crossman has an unfortunate arrogant manner. He describes how he scored off the Queen. There had to be a Privy Council to approve a new Constitution for the Seychelles & he asked if he & the requisite number of other Privy Councillors could fly up to Balmoral on a certain day. The reply came that the Queen had a private engagement that day which would mean her leaving Balmoral Castle at 10.30 a.m., & that she would prefer a day on which she could have Crossman & the other PCs to lunch. He said that if that was the obstacle, he & his colleagues would not mind lunching in the servants' hall. Hard luck on the servants. Eventually a suitable day <u>was</u> arranged.

## 26 October 1967

I run into Gladwyn. He tells me that he must be the only Englishman alive today who was at the Coronation of the Shah's father in 1927.* I reply: 'What

---

* Reza Shah (1878–1944), Shah of Iran 1925–41. His coronation was actually in 1926.

about Harold Nicolson?' Gladwyn callously says: 'I should have said the only Englishman who is *compos mentis*.' What a nasty fellow he is.

### 1 November 1967

Much speculation on the Crown appointment of the next Master of Churchill College. Jock Colville tells me that Winston and he decided on Crown appointments themselves to avoid squabbling among cathedral chapters and colleges.

Scandal reported in all the papers of how George Brown last night publicly & drunkenly insulted Roy Thomson, his host at a dinner at the Savoy for eminent US businessmen. Was there ever such a Foreign Secretary?

Work on my Curzon book, & finish a chapter on his religious life & its sublimation in imperialism.

### 7 November 1967

Luncheon party given by Raine Dartmouth[*] at her pretty house in Hill Street. Other guests included Lord Savile, who lives near Dewsbury, & is very musical: a nice, lively man; and Francis Watson, curator of the Wallace Collection.[†]

We talk a great deal about the Chips Channon diaries, and all agree how ghastly they are. I have read advance copies of the diaries, but the others have read the extracts we are publishing in the *Sunday Telegraph*. I hear that Paul Channon[‡] was asked the other night why he had allowed publication when Chips had said they were to be sealed for fifty years. Paul replied: 'Because I want people to know how nice a character my father had before he is forgotten.' Fantastic. The only nice trait that emerges from the diaries is his love of Paul.

### 8 November 1967

Selwyn Lloyd to lunch at the Guards Club. He appears in funereal black, having come from the memorial service for Lord Attlee.

He is not at all sorry to be released from the cares of office, but is working very hard on behalf of the Conservative Party, looking into its organisation,

---

[*] Later Raine, Countess of Spencer (1929–2016). Westminster City Councillor 1954–65; Board member, British Tourist Authority 1972–93.

[†] George Lumley-Savile (1919–2008), soldier in World War II, JP, borough of Dewsbury. Sir Francis Watson (1907–92), Keeper of the Wallace Collection 1938–63; Surveyor of the Queen's Works of Art 1963–72.

[‡] Baron Kelvedon (1925–2007), Conservative politician. MP for Southend 1959–97; Secretary of State for Trade and Industry 1986–7 and for Transport 1987–9.

especially in the North-West. 'I am the modern Lord Derby,' he says. He has addressed nearly 100 meetings already this year and is particularly anxious to raise funds for the Conservatives.

## 2 December 1967
A cruel story from Eton. Apparently 300 boys all came to Communion the other Sunday so that a great deal of wine and wafers had to be prepared; then, presumably to humiliate the Conduct, not one of them would go up for Communion – so the officiating clergy had to drink and eat the sacred elements themselves.

## 9 December 1967, letter to parents
Anthony Montague-Browne,* who used to be Winston's Private Secretary, told me a good Churchill story last week. Winston was once reproached for accepting so much hospitality from Philip Sassoon.† The old man replied: 'If one is going on a long journey, it is wise to have a restaurant car attached to one's train.'

## 10 December 1967
Rab Butler on telephone to consult me about his Romanes Lecture. He says he is disgusted by the Chips Channon diaries.

## 17 December 1967
Hans von Herwarth, former German Ambassador in London, now Ambassador in Rome, tells me that he spends much of his leisure improving his Italian. 'It is as important for a diplomat to speak Italian in Italy as it is for a foreign diplomat in Bonn to speak German. If one speaks their language, people are usefully indiscreet.'

From his conversation it is obvious that he loved London best of all his posts. There is a silver cigarette box on the table with the Royal Cipher. He tells me that he was given it when the Queen visited Germany on her State Visit. He had already been posted to Italy, but was specially recalled to help entertain her. He has a deep devotion to our Royal Family and tells me that on the occasions both of the death of George VI and of the Queen's Coronation, when H. was in the official German delegation, the Queen received

---

* Sir Anthony Montague Browne (1923–2013), diplomat. PS to Winston Churchill 1955–65. In 2016 it was disclosed that he was the biological father of the Archbishop of Canterbury, The Most Revd and Rt Hon. Justin Welby.
† Sir Philip Sassoon, 3rd Bt (1888–1939), Conservative politician and art collector.

more letters from Germany than from any other country outside the Commonwealth. He was most touched on the occasion of the Coronation in 1953 by the Queen's kindness. His little daughter, then aged ten, complained to him that it was a pity she had not been asked too, 'as it is a girl who is being crowned'. He mentioned this to Ivone Kirkpatrick, then British High Commissioner in Germany, as a joke. But an invitation duly arrived, together with a seat for her in the stand outside the Abbey.

When Adenauer came to England on an official visit he was asked to dine at Windsor, and H. interpreted. There was an affectionate relationship between H. and the Queen Mother. When he took Adenauer to tea at Clarence House he had to interpret so hard that he had no time either to eat or drink. So the Queen Mother, noticing this, popped a biscuit into his mouth with her own fingers.

### 27 December 1967

On the train I am delighted to see a kingfisher flying along a little stream outside Retford.

King Constantine would like to see me this week, so I make immediate arrangements for an air ticket to Rome and money.

A delightful letter from Lord Reith disclosing his unfulfilled ambition to become Viceroy of India. He mentions that he is to be Lord High Commissioner to the General Assembly of the Church of Scotland in 1968, the second year running.

At 7 p.m. I go along to Grosvenor House to see Helen Vlachos.* She tells me about the events in Greece in the past few months since the coup and her decision to close her newspaper *Kathimerini* rather than submit to censorship.

I tell her that I am going to Rome tomorrow, where the King is in exile, and she discusses what would be the best advice for me to give to Constantine. On the whole, she thinks that he ought to try very hard to get back to Greece, whatever the terms offered him by the regime. He could, after all, always fly there quite suddenly, give a Press conference on arrival and announce that the Colonels have accepted his terms. There are, she continues, two dangers in his remaining in Rome too long. The first is that after six months he will be forgotten in Athens, the second is that he may be tempted to become a playboy. In any case, however he returns to Athens, he will have the power to help those who are in prison. She does not know how much money, if any, the King managed to take abroad, but she has heard a rumour that he

---

* (1911–95), Greek journalist and leading opponent of the military junta.

sold part of the Tatoi estate, where I met him in secret after the coup, quite recently in order to raise money. We part on terms of much affection and promise to see each other after I return.

I read the second half of Harold Nicolson's third volume of diaries. There are two or three references to me, all most amiable. Two things impress me. First, the fantastic desire he had for a peerage and his corresponding depths of depression at not being offered it. Secondly, his immense powers of work – not only a steady stream of books, but also the weekly review in the *Observer*, the weekly 'marginal comment' in *The Spectator* and an assortment of other articles and broadcasts. Then, too, there was his diary every morning.

### 29 December 1967

I see the King at the Greek Embassy in Rome at 12 noon. When I arrive he comes in wearing a pair of flannel trousers and a sweater, looking very dazed and tired.

The military attaché of the Embassy comes in with a message for the King. It is a telegram from the regime in Athens demanding the return both of the Dakota aircraft which accompanied his own plane to Rome, and all those members of his staff who hold any military rank. The King is furious at this and tells me that he will return the members of his staff only if their rank and freedom from arrest is guaranteed.

He then outlines the course of negotiations since he arrived in Rome in the early hours of Thursday 14 December. The first thing he did was to telephone the Greek Embassy and ask whether he could have rooms for his family. The Ambassador replied that there was no room in the Embassy. The King thereupon said, 'I am coming all the same.' Since then the Ambassador and his wife have lived in their own rooms and have had the very minimum of contact with their Royal visitors.

The King realised that he ought to make his position clear to the world. So on the evening of Wednesday 20 December he made a public statement, declaring that he would not return to Greece until there was a timetable for the reinstitution of democracy.

After our talk I walk back through the Borghese Gardens and have a quick lunch. Soon after lunch the King telephones me with news he has just been told. The first is that all the ambassadors in Athens have declined to attend a New Year reception to be given by the Regent, Georgios Zoitakis.[*] The second is that the Regent has moved into an annexe of the palace.

---

[*] Maj.-Gen. Georgios Zoitakis (1910–96), Regent of Greece 1967–72, during the military regime.

At five o'clock I return to the Embassy to see Queen Frederika, who was driven in from the villa where she is now living. She looks older and more lined than I have ever seen her before. She begins: 'You always come to us when we are in trouble,' to which I reply, 'But you are never out of trouble.' She roars with laughter and cheers up immediately. She tells me that their hardest task at present is not to be bitter at what has taken place. What particularly horrifies Queen Frederika is the character of the men who are now controlling the affairs of Greece. At this moment the King comes in and asks me to come and see him again tomorrow at ten o'clock, and also to dine with the family tomorrow night.

## 30 December 1967

At 10 o'clock I go up again to the Greek Embassy. The King tells me the story of the counter-coup of 13 December. A few hours before it was due to begin, one of the officers in whom he had much trust told him that it would fail – 'Although I shall, of course, carry out your orders.' The officer presumably did carry out his orders, but sadly nothing has been heard of him since.

The King is very bitter against the army, the traditional support of the Greek monarchy, but which on this occasion has let him down badly. 'When I go back to Greece I shall have nothing to do with the army and these affairs. I shall concentrate on the people.'

At dinner in the evening, the King tells me the news that the Regent appointed by the regime has asked that his servants should be dressed in the royal livery. He also mentions that immediately after the coup, the regime began to make an inventory of all the possessions in the Royal palaces, including a photograph of each object. They did this so that they would not be accused of looting, but after working on the task for a couple of days, they gave it up in despair. It would have taken them years.

He shows me an article on himself from a Brussels paper. As he does not know French he asks me to give him the gist of it. He is much amused when I tell him that the article compares him to Don Quixote.

As the Ambassador and his wife are dining out tonight, we use the dining room. It is not particularly comfortable, as the five of us are spaced widely apart round an enormous table. There are lots of courses, all rather rich and good. Not for the first time I wonder how the Royals manage both to eat and to talk so much. I personally am left gasping. One reason is that they are always served first.

The entire family tell me of their deep disillusionment and bitterness at the behaviour of the two men whom they have trusted most in their lives. The first is Archbishop Ieronymos, who used to be their chaplain and is now the Archbishop of Athens. Even while the King was still on Greek soil, the Archbishop personally swore in the Regent at the request of the military bishop of Athens.* At least he could have delegated this distasteful task to another bishop. Secondly, there is their family doctor of forty years. He told the King that the present regime was one of the best governments that Greece had ever had.

On the other hand, he was touched by the agreeable remarks Harold Wilson made about him immediately after the coup and asks my advice on whether he should write to thank him. I say that it can do no harm and might do good.

## 31 December 1967

Up at seven o'clock and catch a plane to Madrid. Bleak Spanish landscape, like landing on the Moon. Met by Nicholas Gordon Lennox.

A sunny, cool day, with delicious air. Drive with Nicky to his house, a low rambling comfortable building a few miles out of Madrid. Notice an owl in a tree – a change from the universal magpie.

On the political situation, Nicky is bitter. Calls Franco Frankenstein and any official a Fascist. He says that living in Spain is the test of whether one is a liberal at heart or not.

The Press are bloody towards England, but sometimes have an engaging turn of phrase or euphemism. Thus, when the police clashed with students at the university, the papers described them as 'exchanging impressions'. There is not much imprisonment without trial or torture. But the people have had all the stuffing knocked out of them. They just talk and talk. The Spanish Foreign Office, on the other hand, are bloody-minded and unscrupulous and lack a sense of proportion. Similarly, Franco's New Year message hails the United Nations' vote on Gibraltar as one of the greatest blessings ever bestowed on Spain by Almighty God.

It is, says Nicky, a strongly aristocratic country. In the Ministry of Foreign Affairs alone there are eighteen Marquises, not counting those in Spanish Embassies abroad. At a party not long ago he heard two elegant ladies describing how a third slept with her chauffeur. 'And would you believe it, he has been in her employment for only three years.'

Spend a very agreeable New Year's Eve dining together. Nicky tells me

---

* Archbishop Ieronymos I of Athens (1905–88), Archbishop of Athens and All Greece 1967–73.

that he has certain social duties and had to look after the Duke and Duchess of Windsor during their recent visit. He liked them both and found her in particular to be kind and pleasant and polite.

# 1968

*The Vietnam War intensified throughout 1968, with several key battles. On 31 March President Johnson announced that he would not run for a further term as President of the United States in the November election. Martin Luther King was assassinated in Memphis on 4 April. President Johnson signed the Civil Rights Act on 11 April. On 20 April Enoch Powell made his 'Rivers of Blood' speech and was dismissed from the Shadow Cabinet by Edward Heath. Harold Nicolson died on 1 May. In May there were violent riots in Paris. Robert Kennedy was assassinated in Los Angeles on 5 June. Warsaw Pact troops ended the Prague Spring of political liberalisation in August. On 29 September a referendum in Greece gave more power to the military junta. The M1 motorway was completed in October. Richard Nixon won the US Presidential election on 5 November. On 26 November the Race Relations Act was passed in America. Over Christmas the Apollo 8 spacecraft became the first manned spacecraft to orbit the Moon.*

### 1 January 1968

Today, being New Year's Day, is a public holiday in Spain. We therefore get up early and Nicky Gordon Lennox drives me up a deserted road to the Escorial. A wonderful morning with champagne-cold air and strong sunshine. The Escorial looks huge and rather Russian from the outside. We go into the church and see the window from which Philip II[*] was able to look down and hear Mass being said. Drive on through some woods to the King's favourite seat, a superbly beautiful panorama.

On the way back we stop at the memorial to those who died in the Civil War, called Valle de los Caidos. Built in the style of Fascist architecture, it is like a vast underground cathedral. It looks better coming out than going in, but the incessant playing of canned music is irritating.

---

[*] King Philip II of Spain (1527–98), King of Spain 1556–98 and of Portugal 1581–98; known as Philip the Prudent. He was married to Mary I of England. Philip II is an important character in Verdi's opera *Don Carlos*.

Home in time for lunch with the family. Later in the afternoon we drive out to look at El Pardo, the little palace where Franco lives. On returning to the house I find a message asking me to call on Don Juan Carlos[*] at the Zarzuela Palace.

Received by a butler in a blue and gold livery, then taken into a room furnished in the Spanish style with lots of wood and royal souvenirs. It is dominated by a portrait of his grandfather Alfonso XIII painted by de Laszlo. We talk about the situation in Greece.

I give them a long account of everything that King Constantine told me in Rome. They have, of course, spoken to him on the telephone, but felt obliged to be guarded in their conversation. The Prince fears that the failure of the King's coup in December has damaged his own prospects of becoming King of Spain, although no doubt the memory of it will fade.

On the subject of his relations with Franco, he is very outspoken. So far, Franco has given him no sign that he intends to nominate him publicly as his successor as Head of State. The Prince tells me that of course there must be a public proclamation if he is ever to succeed, for nobody will take any notice merely of Franco's will once he is dead. From time to time, the Prince has attempted gently to remind Franco of this, but he invariably gets snubbed. He is disturbed at the lack of economic and political progress which Spain is making under Franco. He says, touching one end of the table: 'We should be here,' then touching the other end of the table, 'but we are only here.' The failure of King Constantine has also encouraged Franco to think that a policy of repression is best.

On Friday, Don Juan Carlos tells me, he will be thirty when, under the law of succession, he becomes eligible to be named the future Head of State. He then reads out to me the very complicated series of laws by which this could be done. I tell him I should like to make some notes on this, and reach for a book on which to rest a piece of paper. By chance, it turns out to be the official Red Book giving the Spanish Government's case on Gibraltar. The Prince roars with laughter and says: 'Don't use that. It will burn your knees!'

In the evening I dine with Nico and Mary Henderson.[†] Nico is the Minister at the Embassy in Madrid. He shows me today's *Daily Telegraph*, including the Honours List. Michael Berry has been made a life peer.

---

[*] (b. 1938), later King Juan Carlos I of Spain 1975–2014.

[†] Sir Nicholas Henderson (1919–2009), Ambassador to the Federal Republic of Germany 1972–5 and to France 1975–9; he was brought out of retirement by Margaret Thatcher to serve as Ambassador to the US 1979–82; m. 1951 Mary Cawadias (1919–2004), journalist and fashion promoter.

Nico is most amusing about Rab Butler, whose Private Secretary he used to be. Rab has two guiding themes in his life – never to get committed, and often to use indiscretion as a deliberate instrument. He also used to be very incompetent in managing his daily routine. One day, for instance, he looked at his programme and saw that there would be little time to change before dining out. So he arrived at the Foreign Office at 9 a.m. wearing a dinner jacket, and was very grubby by the end of the day. Nico also produces such a good remark on Alec Douglas-Home: 'He has taken to politics at sixty just as some people take suddenly to sex.'

### 3 January 1968

Back in London after my journeys, I talk to Oliver Chandos. He happens to mention superstitions, and tells me of the American lady who once enquired why her hostess had insisted that there should not be thirteen for dinner. The hostess replied that the tradition went back to the Last Supper. The American lady then said: 'But nobody died after the Last Supper?'

### 26 January 1968

I look up some Curzon references in the London Library.

Lord Reith on the telephone to arrange a date for tea together. He tells me he is having trouble with his newspaper cutting agency. Every time the Reith Lectures are mentioned in the Press, they send him a cutting. The price therefore mounts up hugely. He mentions that his TV appearances when being interviewed by Malcolm Muggeridge brought him 800 letters. He has answered them at the rate of about ten a day, sending off nearly 500 so far. 'I am still more than 250 astern of station.'

Talk to King Constantine of Greece on telephone to Rome about the recognition of the Greek military regime by the UK and USA this week, and forthcoming debate on Greece at the Council of Europe. He says he is bored and fed up with nothing to do.

### 7 February 1968

At 4 p.m. to Athenaeum for tea with Lord Reith. We sit on a leather sofa at the top of the stair beneath a huge dome. Endless men of distinction pass to and fro – Lord Adrian, Lord Caccia, Lord Radcliffe . . .

Reith is so pleased to have been asked to be Lord High Commissioner to the General Assembly of the Church of Scotland this year and asks me to suggest a theme for his address. As he is the Queen's personal representative he cannot be too controversial – otherwise he would be tempted to comment on the decline of the BBC since his day. I suggest what would in fact be a sermon, on the theme that acceptance of Christian doctrine does not imply a stultification of the intellect.

On the more worldly aspects of his duties at Holyrood, he mentions that this year he will have a Rolls-Royce: last year the Purse Bearer produced only an Austin Princess. I ask him whether he noticed that, as he did the *cercle* before dinner, quite a lot of the guests failed to pay him the compliment of a bow or a curtsey. He had noticed it, and with regret at this lack of respect to the Sovereign's representative. But agree on the difficulty of instructing guests how to behave; those who know would be particularly annoyed.

I suggest to him that in view of his early life as an engineer he should visit some Scottish engineering works. He is taken with the idea, and makes a note of it. He is particularly proud of having had the rare privilege as an apprentice of working in the iron foundry – and thus being a member of 'the black squad', as engineers were called in Glasgow.

He then asks me what he should do about his own diaries. The last volume was published in 1949, and I suggest another volume of selected passages. It should consist of plain extracts with a few editorial notes.

## 19 February 1968

Spend most of the day working on Curzon.

Dine with John Russell, who tells me that the Foreign Office is buzzing with a story of George Brown's behaviour when he was staying recently with Sir Ian Scott,[*] our Ambassador in Oslo. Just before a dinner party in the Embassy, Brown looked at the list of guests and asked why no Norwegian Labour leaders had been invited. The Ambassador replied that he had sent a message to the Foreign Office to ask Brown if there were any special guests whom he wished to be invited, but there had been no reply. Brown continued to be offensive, until at last Scott pointed out to him that every guest had certain duties of courtesy towards his hosts, at which Brown exploded: 'This is not your house, it's mine.'

We have some gossip about filling diplomatic appointments. Who will succeed Paul Gore-Booth[†] as Permanent Head of the FO early next year? It seems likely that it will go to Denis Greenhill.[‡]

---

[*] (1909–2002), Ambassador to Norway 1965–8.

[†] Sir Paul Gore-Booth, Baron Gore-Booth of Maltby (1909–84), Permanent Under-Secretary of State at the Foreign Office 1965–9; Head of the Diplomatic Service 1968–9.

[‡] Sir Denis Greenhill, Baron Greenhill of Harrow (1913–2000), Permanent Under-Secretary of State at the Foreign Office and Head of the Diplomatic Service 1969–73. Head of the Foreign Office 1969–73.

## 17 April 1968

Derek Hill* tells me how he painted Roger Scarbrough. He was assured he had been chosen because he was an 'informal' painter. Lord Scarbrough was asked whether this meant he would be painted in gardening clothes. Lord S. replied: 'Well, I shall want a <u>bit</u> of Garter ribbon showing.'

Derek is going to Broadlands to paint Mountbatten, but has refused to do him in uniform, only a sailor's jersey. Mountbatten's daughter Pamela told Derek: 'You will be lucky if he doesn't pin on a brooch at the last minute.'

After a heavy lunch we go to his studio where he works for more than two hours on a sketch of me, sitting on a chair with a book on my knees. Not at all a bad likeness, though a little younger than I am. But there is a strain of gloom in him. He is afraid that he is losing his powers of painting, and says he will have nothing left to live for when they are gone. I notice no deterioration whatsoever. He also complains that I am the only journalist who writes about him. But how <u>can</u> the critics do so except when he has an exhibition? Quite rightly, he has a horror of the social gossip columnists.

## 30 April 1968

Leslie Rowse telephones me. He begins quite calmly by inviting me to one of his luncheon parties at the Ritz in May. Then my chance remark about the recent award of the OM to Solly Zuckerman† sets him off on an almost hysterical tirade. 'They ought to have given <u>me</u> the OM in succession to G.M. Trevelyan. I have written the best biography of Shakespeare, and all my Elizabethan studies. I should turn down a knighthood or a CH.‡ Macmillan ought to have done something for me, but he is utterly cynical about Honours. They will have to be careful, or I shall become an American citizen. I am finished with this country,' etc. etc.

## 1 May 1968

The *Daily Telegraph* rings to tell me that Harold Nicolson has died. He was one of my dearest friends, but who could wish for his death to be further postponed. I have written the obituary for the *DT*.

Lunch with John Russell at White's. We run into Bob Boothby, who has lost a lot of weight & had to have a lot of beautiful new suits made. He says:

---

* (1916–2000), portrait painter. His subjects included the Prince of Wales, Lord Mountbatten, Anthony Eden, John Betjeman and Noël Coward.

† Sir Solly Zuckerman, Baron Zuckerman OM (1904–93), public servant; scientific adviser during World War II.

‡ K.R. was among those who lobbied for an honour for A.L. Rowse, who was awarded the CH in the 1997 New Year's Honours List, the year of his death.

'I addressed 2,000 Jews the other day about the foundation of the State of Israel. I don't know whether they liked my speech, but my suit was given a standing ovation.'

John is still rather upset that Soames has got the Paris Embassy. Incidentally, Paul Gore-Booth, Permanent Head of the FO, appears to have become increasingly eccentric in the past few days, dressing up as Sherlock Holmes & publicly fighting a lawyer representing Professor Moriarty on a Swiss precipice: all good clean English fun, but surely disturbing to the minds of our diplomatic allies?

Some talk of past events. Eden was a very difficult chief. Incidentally, John's signet ring & Russell arms were used to seal the 1941 agreement with Soviet Russia.

Catch Pullman train taking only one hour to Oxford, where the unlovely station is adorned with potted palms and red carpets for the Queen's visit. Taxi through blossoming Oxford to the site of the new Wolfson College to watch the Queen lay the foundation stone. Isaiah Berlin very gracious and stately, and Harold Macmillan, as Chancellor, giving his imitation of a very old man. Several friends and acquaintances – Hugh Trevor-Roper, Bill Deakin,[*] Jack Wheeler-Bennett (who liked my obituary of Harold Nicolson) and Gilbert Monckton[†] of the Wolfson Trust. How odd to see several dons, including Warden Hayter of New College, standing on chairs, as if they were at a Buckingham Palace Garden Party. Queen looks elegant in turquoise-blue, with enchanting complexion.

After the ceremony return to Oxford in order to talk *DNB* business. The text of the notice on King George VI has been sent to the Queen Mother, under the name of Bill Williams' assistant. If this name is attached to it, the *DNB* shrewdly feel the QM may feel at liberty to suggest drastic alterations. I give my Lord Halifax notice a final check.

## 11 May 1968

Visit Selwyn Lloyd at his home at Preston Crowmarsh, near Benson. A charming house and garden – rather Regency. Selwyn is addicted to his visitors' book, which I sign – lots of grand names – Anthony Eden, Alec Home, Ted Heath, Jack Profumo. Selwyn tells me that Prince Philip said to

---

* Sir William Deakin (1913–2005), historian; founding Warden of St Antony's Coll., Oxford 1950–68.
† Maj.-Gen. Gilbert Monckton, 2nd Viscount Monckton of Brenchley (1916–2006), soldier. Chief of Staff, British Army of the Rhine 1965.

him recently, 'What, are you still alive?' – later he apologised to Selwyn for his rudeness.

He is annoyed with me when I question Heath's competence as Tory leader. Selwyn himself is happy in the House of Commons. 'I still like the idea of power, which can only lie in the H of C. If Bobbety Salisbury were in the Commons, he would have a following of thirty MPs.' Later Selwyn says he would be a bit pushed to live as well as he does without parliamentary salary, so no peerage yet. He doesn't regret not being in the Shadow Cabinet – neither John Boyd-Carpenter nor Quintin Hogg could distinguish good points from bad.

He tells me the joke Oliver Chandos made when Bob Boothby got married: 'There was not a dry eye in Wellington Barracks last night.'

## 16 May 1968

Memorial service for Harold Nicolson at St James's, Piccadilly. Cecil Day-Lewis[*] reads beautifully, but the clergyman has an appallingly slow diction, & loses the rhythm of the prayers. Tommy Lascelles represents the Queen, holding his tall hat in front of him like a Victorian undertaker. The Duke of Wellington shown to a grand seat in the front, but insists on taking a humble seat at the side. I like that. Cyril Connolly[†] sits in front of me in a sad grey coat. Giles St Aubyn is there, but has to rush away to meet parents. Isaiah Berlin rather ebullient. John Sparrow gives an excellent address, saying that Harold 'touched life at many points'. One passage that it was brave of J.S. to include referred to H.N.'s impatience with those who, under the guise of perfectionism, are too lazy to undertake big tasks.

## 23 May 1968

At 3.30 go round to Claridge's to see King Constantine. I find him strolling about the Lobby, very relaxed and smiling. He takes me to his suite on the second floor. Much smaller than the large corner suite he previously had when reigning in Athens. There is a Special Branch man on duty outside the door. Inside, there are as many flowers as at a gangster's funeral. I say to him: 'I see that the Greek ship owners are re-insuring.' The King does not quite see the joke and replies rather shortly: 'They are not only from Greek ship owners.'

I ask the King whether he has seen the Greek Ambassador in London,

---

Verykios.* The King tells me that the Ambassador came to greet him at London Airport and was very polite, but that they are not likely to have any talks. The King then tells me an amusing story. Some weeks ago the Greek regime apparently ordered all its Embassies in Western Europe to hold a solemn *Te Deum* on the King's name day on Tuesday, but at the last moment they feared demonstrations, and so sent orders cancelling it. The King and Queen are staying here for about a week, seeing English plays and films and shopping. They will spend the weekend with Dickie Mountbatten in Broadlands.

### 6 June 1968

I hear from the Barkers in Cambridge that Bobby Kennedy died this morning, twenty-five hours after the shooting. I write a piece on Bobby Kennedy for the *DT*.

Alan tells me that the Mayor of Cambridge asked Prince Charles to lunch. Rab Butler said he should go. Prince Charles replied; 'Mum said I wasn't to do that sort of thing while at Cambridge.' But Rab insisted.

Afternoon train back to London. I hear that Randolph Churchill has also died today. Asked to write an obituary, but I refuse.

### 28 June 1968

Katie Macmillan tells me that Evelyn Emmet† came to see the Macmillans on political business at Birch Grove. As she entered the room, she fell down a step. But everyone was watching the Grand National on TV. Nobody looked up or took any notice or remarked on it, except for one person, glued to the TV, who said: 'Another one down.'

### 5 July 1968

To New College for the Gaudy. I meet Isaiah Berlin. He says he had difficulty in composing a speech for the Founder's Feast at Wolfson College. Then he remembered the story of the early 19th-century fellow of All Souls who went to France after the Peace of Amiens and met Napoleon. On his return he was asked what sort of man he had found him. He replied: 'One soon perceived that one was not talking to a University man.' An excellent story for a Gaudy – until Isaiah realised that he was sitting next to Isaac Wolfson.

Isaiah tells another Gaudy story of the Head of House who was determined

---

* Dr Panaghiotis Verykios (1910–90), Greek Ambassador to the UK 1967–9.
† Baroness Evelyn Emmet of Amberley (1899–1980), Conservative MP for East Grinstead 1955–65.

not to be too sentimental in referring to those killed in the Great War. So he said: 'We must remember all those who fell in battle' – then, looking at the list in his hand – 'a very mixed lot.'

## 11 July 1968

Dine Pratt's with Duncan Sandys. He talks of his early life as a diplomat. In the exam he came fourth out of fifty – there were only four places available that year so he got in. His mother said to him: 'Why are you bottom?'

He says how stupid it was of Quintin Hogg to claim in the House of Commons the other night that he had 'given up a great hereditary position' to enter H of C. In fact, he is only a 2nd Viscount. His father, Lord Hailsham, was very pompous. At a party at Buckingham Palace before the war, when Duncan was included only as a young member of the Diplomatic Corps, he saw Hailsham very embarrassed when old J.H. Thomas slapped him on the chest & announced to all & sundry: "Ogg & I likes a blow-out, don't we, 'Ogg?'

## 18 July 1968

Have a fifty-minute talk on the telephone with Lord Reith. He is obsessed by secrecy and several times asks me whether my secretary, or anybody else, is listening to our conversation.

The gist of our talk is the retirement of Sir Hugh Greene[*] and his appointment to be a member of the Board of Governors. Reith does not attempt to hide his loathing of Greene. 'He has undone everything at the BBC that I have ever stood for. Both morally and intellectually there has been a terrible decline since my day.'

I ask Reith whether he would like to have been appointed to the Board of Governors of the BBC when he himself ceased to be Director-General in 1938. He replies that he would have liked to join the Board, but it came to nothing. It is, after all, embarrassing to have an old Chief Executive to become senior to a new Chief Executive. So Reith withdrew his request to the Prime Minister, Neville Chamberlain, for a seat on the Board.

He tells me that Weidenfeld & Nicolson want to publish a volume of extracts from his diary. He would agree to this if they used a good editor, but says it makes him feel quite ill even to think of re-reading the millions of words he has written over the past years.

He asks me what sort of publishers are Cassells. I reply that they must be

---

[*]  Sir Hugh Carleton Greene (1910–87), Dir.-Gen., BBC 1960–69.

good as they published Winston Churchill. Reith replies: 'That is no recommendation to me.'

### 5 September 1968

Dine with Norman Collins. I meet Sir Arthur Bliss,* Master of the Queen's Music, for the first time. It is like shaking hands with Elgar. He talks of his grim experiences in the line during World War I. I ask him about his pattern of work. He says: 'I must work fixed hours. At 6 p.m. I have a double whisky, then do a little more work. If I meet a problem I have a long sleep on it, & it resolves itself.' He will shortly visit the USA again, & has accepted an invitation to write a piece of music for a football game there. He says: 'When people ask me if the Queen is interested in music, I reply: "She is interested in all things, but most of all in horses."'

### 18 September 1968

Give Oliver Chandos dinner at the Beefsteak. He tells me that when Winston saw his portrait by Graham Sutherland, he said: 'Wait until I paint <u>him</u>.'

Also Bobbety Salisbury's comment on the Archbishop of Canterbury, Michael Ramsey: 'He looks like an unmade bed.'

In Cabinet, Winston once cross-questioned Rab on a certain Government publication. Rab: 'Well, it is about 1,200 words long.' Winston: 'Yes, but what's it like?' Rab: 'Well, it cost threepence.' Winston, by now considerably annoyed: 'I didn't ask you what was its length or its cost, but what it was like.' Rab, by this time nettled: 'Well, Prime Minister, it is so simply written that I can't understand it.'

Oliver talks of the Other Club. When Winston died he thought it should be wound up. But is now pleased it goes so well. At one recent meeting, poor Harold Macmillan found himself between Rab and Lord Moran. So he lapsed into his masquerade of a very old man.

### 4 October 1968

Give Selwyn Lloyd lunch at the Guards Club. We are made a great fuss of, as I complained the other day that the grouse I had ordered was dry. Selwyn has still not got down to the task of writing his memoirs, and feels that he will not be able to do so without the help of a research assistant. This brings us to the subject of David Dilks,† and I tell him how shabbily he was treated

---

* (1891–1975), Master of the Queen's Music 1953 until his death.

† Prof. David Dilks (b. 1938), historian. Professor of International History at the University of Leeds 1970–91; Vice-Chancellor of Hull University 1991–9.

when researching for Harold Macmillan. Selwyn replies that he is not at all surprised. He recalls an occasion when he shared Chequers with Macmillan for a single weekend. He was astonished when a few weeks later Philip de Zulueta came to him in great embarrassment bearing a bill from Macmillan that represented Selwyn's share of the drink.

### 17 October 1968

Basil Spence* describes to me how, having designed Coventry Cathedral, he thought he might at a pinch get a promotion in the Order of the British Empire from OBE. Instead he got a letter from Michael Adeane asking him whether it would be agreeable to him to receive the Order of Merit. 'Agreeable!' he says. He tells me he has had a terrible time at Coventry with the Provost, Bill Williams,† who is very jealous of him.

### 12 November 1968

At S'Agaró in Spain, holiday resort Selwyn Lloyd recommended to me, I have some talk after dinner with Sean Connery, whom I like very much. He tells me how pleased he is that I have not attempted to ask him about his James Bond film role. Instead we talk largely about Scottish Nationalism. He comes from Fife and is particularly interested in the future of the Clyde shipyards. He has made a film on the subject, which he would like me to see one day.

### 14 November 1968

By car to Barcelona then take a plane to Madrid where Nicky Gordon Lennox meets me. He is very hard-worked at the moment. He tells me a story of a newly appointed British Ambassador to Venezuela who set off one day in Caracas to present his credentials at the Presidential Palace. He was faintly surprised to see that the streets were completely empty, and even more surprised to notice that planes were firing on the palace with tracer bullets. Finding his way blocked by a tank, he told his First Secretary to 'get it out of the way'. The First Secretary went up to the tank and knocked on the side. From within a muffled voice told him to go away as there was a revolution in progress. The Ambassador said: 'I have never heard such nonsense in my life. Doesn't he realise I have to present my credentials?'

I telephone Don Juan Carlos to arrange a meeting before I leave Madrid.

---

* Sir Basil Spence OM (1907–76), architect. Winner of competition to design the new Coventry Cathedral in 1951 and architect of the Hyde Park Barracks.
† The Very Revd H.C.N. (Bill) Williams (1914–90), Anglican priest. Provost of Coventry Cathedral 1958–81.

While I am on the telephone Nicky shouts to me: 'Be very polite to him. He may be King one day.' Later Nicky tells me that Don Juan Carlos invited the Italian and Canadian Ambassadors to dine with him a few weeks ago and told them that he would be prepared to accept the throne.

## 18 November 1968

In the morning I drive over to the Zarzuela Palace for a talk with Don Juan Carlos. We talk about his prospects in general and his relationship with Franco in particular. Not long ago, growing impatient at Franco's reluctance to nominate him as the future Head of State, he went to see Franco and said: 'Please tell me if you ever intend to make me King – or do you think that the Spanish people do not want a monarchy? At least give me some sort of answer.' Franco replied simply, 'Don't talk nonsense.'

His state of uncertainty, he says, could last indefinitely, for Franco is in very good health. We talk about the situation in Greece. The attitude of the Colonels towards King Constantine, Don Juan Carlos says, seems to be hardening. They recently sent out invitations to a reception to be given in Athens by the Greek Government, and the cards did not bear a crown. Again King Constantine wanted to send a wreath to the funeral of Papandreou. The regime replied that the King must not do so – as a wreath was being laid by the regime.

I tell the Prince that in my view King Constantine should not go back as long as the regime refuses to restore the basic rights of democracy. The Prince replies: 'That is exactly what happened with my father. When Franco came to power he said he would not go back as dictators did not last long. But of course Franco has gone on lasting and my father is still in exile.'

# 1969

*Richard Nixon was inaugurated as the thirty-seventh President of the United States on 20 January 1969. The first Concorde test flight took place in Toulouse on 2 March. Dwight D. Eisenhower died on 28 March. British troops were deployed to Northern Ireland on 20 April. The United Kingdom and Rhodesia severed diplomatic ties on 24 June. The Prince of Wales was invested with his title at Carnarvon Castle. First US troop withdrawals from Vietnam on 8 July. Neil Armstrong and Buzz Aldrin took mankind's first walk on the Moon on 20 July. General Franco appointed Prince Juan Carlos his successor in Spain on 22 July. The Prague Spring in Czechoslovakia was finally beaten on 21 August. Ho Chi Minh, former President of the Republic of Vietnam, died on 2 September. Hundreds of thousands of people demonstrated to end the war in Vietnam on 15 October. The abolition of the death penalty in the UK was made permanent by Parliament on 18 December.*

**15 March 1969**

Giles St Aubyn tells me that Princess Margaret has been talking to him about death. She said how awful Princess Marina's funeral was last August, especially when contrasted with the beauty of the memorial service in Westminster Abbey. She said she would not mind being buried at sea. 'Yes,' said Giles, 'wrapped up in Union Jack.' 'No, not in a Union Jack,' she replied. 'I have my own standard.'*

**26 March 1969**

To Buckingham Palace at 3.45 p.m. for a talk with Prince Philip about his recent visit to the game parks of Ethiopia. An ancient and very courteous page comes for me and takes me up the stairs and along a passage lined with marble busts to Prince Philip's room. It looks out on the garden, with walls

---

* Princess Margaret was cremated at Slough Crematorium on 15 Feb. 2002 after a funeral service at St George's Chapel, Windsor. Her ashes were laid next to her father's coffin in the King George VI Memorial Chapel off the North Nave Aisle.

entirely covered by bookcases. Here and there, instead of books, there are personal possessions such as model ships in glass cases and a set of papier-mâché figures, each about a foot high, of Churchill, Herbert Morrison, Nye Bevan, Geoffrey Fisher and Lord Kilmuir.

Prince Philip and I sit on two small sofas at right angles to each other. He has just had a meeting of his Gold Medal Awards Scheme. He wears a blue suit, trousers without turn-ups; very stoutly built, but beautifully polished black shoes; a white shirt; knitted tie and rather fancy blue socks. Through-out our talk he plays with a black squash ball.

In appearance he is younger than the photographs show. More hair, too, than one suspects. A very bright red nose, which is startling; I do not know whether it is sun, or a natural colour. He has an engaging habit of knitting his brow and almost squinting down his nose in a quizzical manner to emphasise a point. An agreeable light voice.

He begins by telling me that he was very unimpressed by what he saw of the Ethiopian organisation for preserving wildlife. But he wants to en-courage them to do better, not depress them with criticism. Although the Ethiopian Government has passed laws to control game parks and to restrict the slaughter of wildlife, they have not been implemented. There are, it is true, some excellent European game wardens. But their terms of service are uncertain, their powers limited and their morale low. 'There are more game wardens in HQ than in the field,' he adds.

'Of course, the country has terrible problems, far more serious than those of game preservation. The whole country is being turned into a dust bowl, and a great deal ought to be spent on health and education. But not much money is needed for game preservation – and it will come from abroad. The country is still as Evelyn Waugh wrote about it. The only good roads, bridges and buildings are those built by the Italians, and they are all beginning to crumble to pieces. This means that it is not as attractive as Kenya and Uganda from the point of view of tourism.'

'I suppose', I say, 'it is like trying to convert a pagan country to Christianity.'

'Yes,' he replies, 'except that the head witch-doctor is given the job of being the Archbishop.'

## 6 April 1969

In Egypt. Drive out to the pyramids for a performance of *son et lumière*. 'This', an Olivier-like voice declaims, 'is the most fabulous and celebrated place in the world.' It is certainly a picturesque spectacle with a superb use of colour against the starlit night. Surprisingly comfortable chairs. An occa-sional bat sweeps overhead, and once an irreverent dog trots across the stage of history. Driving back to Cairo when it is over, pass a regiment of artillery parked on the road.

## 7 April 1969

In the evening I have a drink with our recently appointed Ambassador to Egypt, Sir Richard Beaumont,* in his huge pale-blue palace by the Nile. Or rather it used to be the Nile, but a road has now been driven between the bottom of the Embassy garden and the river, which both spoils the prospect and adds to the noise. We sit under the portico, waited on by several white-clad servants who bring gin and tonic and hot little cheese pies in silver dishes.

Beaumont tells me that his task of furthering good relations with Egypt is made easier by an Egyptian readiness to forgive. Thus, Suez – to which, incidentally, Beaumont was strongly opposed – is referred to merely as 'the incidents of 1956'. But when he went to present his credentials to President Nasser the other day, he found it a disappointing occasion. He wished to talk about the course of Anglo-Egyptian relations, at which Nasser became studiously vague and said how one day he would like to retire to Assam, as it had such a good climate. 'As you can imagine,' the Ambassador adds, 'I did not go to see him in order to talk about the weather.'

He speaks warmly of de Gaulle. 'Whenever there is a Middle East Crisis, the General recalls his Ambassador here for consultations. But HMG say they cannot afford it. There is, however, much prestige to be gained from an airfare of a few hundred pounds.' He does not speak with any affection of George Brown, who, he claims, was liable to go off the rails through being too suspicious of the advice given him by his senior officials.

Ted Heath is coming here very shortly. Originally he was to have stayed at the Embassy, but a few days ago Nasser stepped in and asked that he should be a guest of the Egyptian Government.

As we part after an agreeable, friendly and amusing talk, I ask Beaumont whether he does not find it difficult while living in this splendid establishment to remember that he is not Lord Cromer.† 'Not on the present Diplomatic Service allowances,' he replies genially.

## 30 April 1969

News of Israeli commando raid on local power lines, bridges and dams on

---

* (1912–2009), Ambassador to Egypt 1969–73.
† Evelyn Baring, 1st Earl of Cromer (1841–1917), statesman and colonial administrator. Consul-General of Egypt 1883–1907.

the Upper Nile, Esma and Edfu included. From what I saw of them a fortnight ago, they were very sparsely guarded.

Lunch with Tom Monnington* at Burlington House. A very good lunch
indeed, particularly the wine. I sit next to David McFall, RA,† who did
the eight-foot-six-inch bronze figure of Winston Churchill that stands on
Woodford Green. While we are talking about pictures, he suddenly asks me
whether I saw the note in the *New Statesman* the other day speculating on
what had become of Graham Sutherland's portrait of Winston presented to
him by Parliament on his eightieth birthday. He adds: 'I think that I know
the story.' He then tells me that Lady Churchill came to see the model of the
Woodford Green statue which was then in his studio in Chelsea. Having
expected a very charming and gracious old lady, she was utterly horrified to
be faced by an hysterical old woman, red in the face and unable to contain
herself. She gazed at the statue and said to him: 'You have made Winston like
a roaring lion and he was as gentle as a dove. You have made a monstrosity.
But don't forget. Accidents can be arranged –as they have been in the past.'
The final touch of drama, McFall tells me, was that Lady Churchill clutched
so fearfully to her rope of pearls that they broke and scattered all over the
floor of the studio. So he and Lady Churchill's secretary had to scramble
about on their hands and knees looking for them. Later she attended the
unveiling ceremony, but spoke no word of commendation. McFall thinks
that any woman who could have uttered such words about his own statue
would be quite capable of destroying the Graham Sutherland portrait which
she hated so much.

McFall adds that Winston himself, whom he saw often at Chartwell, was
very modest about his own paintings, and almost apologised that someone
had hung a huge display of them round his own studio.

### 13 May 1969

Jock Colville tells me he is to write the biography of a man and offers me
twenty questions to guess it. I take seven before getting the right answer –
Field Marshal Lord Gort.‡

Maurice Macmillan thinks Dick Crossman both arrogant & a bully. He
once said to Maurice: 'I always knew your father would be a weak Prime
Minister. In Italy I once got into trouble & your father got me out of it. He

---

* Sir Thomas Monnington (1902–76), painter and war artist. President of the RA 1967–76.
† (1919–88), Scottish sculptor.
‡ FM John Vereker, Viscount Gort (1886–1946), Cdr of the British Expeditionary Force in
France 1939–40, when he was credited with saving the BEF in the evacuation from Dunkirk.

should have taken the opportunity of ridding himself of a dangerous political opponent.'

Maurice also complains that Hugh Trevor-Roper continues not to produce a big historical work. 'He has made so many enemies that he is reluctant
to expose himself. But, as his publishers, we suffer.'

### 16 May 1969

Talk to King Constantine. It is his name day on 21 May and I ask him
whether the regime will as usual declare it a public holiday in view of their
deteriorating relations with him. He replies: 'They will not risk <u>not</u> doing so.'

Oliver Chandos tells me that their family house used to be in Connaught
Place at the edge of Hyde Park, where my flat is. There was once some question of its being let to Harry Rosebery,* who turned it down on the grounds
that he did not want to live in the suburbs.

### 18 May 1969

I hear that Llewellyn Woodward† found that a great deal of All Souls port
had been ruined because central heating had been installed nearby, so he
sold it for a good sum to Balliol. Later he became a Fellow of Balliol – so he
had to drink it.

### 29 May 1969

Lunch at the Beefsteak. Paul Johnson tells me that he was talking to the
Prime Minister about me the other day. Harold Wilson said: 'He is the only
one to get his facts right.'

Paul also tells me two stories about Attlee. The first was when Paul was
interviewing him about a book which Attlee had just written. At the end of
the broadcast, Paul asked Attlee whether he would inscribe the book for him.
Attlee took it away into a corner and appeared to write for several minutes on
end, which Paul did not dare to open until later. He then saw that the inscription consisted of the single word: 'Attlee'. On the way back to the centre of
London from that broadcast, Paul offered to drop Attlee wherever he wished
to go. Attlee replied that he wanted to do some shopping at the Army and
Navy Stores, adding: 'Off to India tomorrow. Got to get kitted up.' It was still
the voice of Gallipoli.

---

* Harry Primrose, 6th Earl of Rosebery (1882–1974), Liberal politician. Secretary of State for
Scotland May–July 1945 in Churchill's Caretaker Government.
† Sir Llewellyn Woodward (1890–1971), historian. Fellow of All Souls 1919–44.

## 4 July 1969

As from 30 September, the Treasury are cancelling the concession by which a retiring Ambassador may bring back the remains of his cellar to England without paying duty on it. A bit of cheeseparing that has annoyed them all.

Jeremy Thorpe stayed with Lady Olwen Carey Evans* for the Investiture of the Prince of Wales this week. Two days before the ceremony, Lady Olwen decided that they should go over to Carnarvon and inspect the Castle. 'But how shall we get in with all those security checks?' asked Jeremy. 'That's quite easy,' she said, 'I have a key.' And she then produced the one, more than a foot long, which had been given to her father, Lloyd George, when he was Constable of the Castle at the last Investiture in 1911. It still fitted the lock.

## 5 July 1969

Lunch at the Beefsteak. Sit next to Michael Adeane. He tells me a little story that illuminates the difference in approaches to race problems that has taken place over the last twenty years. As a boy he once stayed in a house where, hanging in the loo, were photographs of the Eton and Harrow cricket elevens. It was an Etonian house and someone had coloured all the Harrovian faces black.

## 19 July 1969

Lord David Cecil, I hear, very much objected to Chips Channon's diaries, calling him a 'traitorous bugger'.

Christopher Soames was watching the Prince of Wales's Investiture on TV when a druid appeared. 'Look,' he said, 'it's Harold Macmillan pretending to be Lawrence of Arabia.'

Christopher Soames is taking enormous trouble over the British Press. He obviously wants to return to political life one day when he comes back from Paris and is keeping all his contacts in good order.

## 12 August 1969

Alun Chalfont† to lunch at the Guards Club. He has just been this week to Nottingham to address a Labour Party meeting, and has a huge lunch – beginning with pink gin, and ending with green Chartreuse – to get the taste of brown ale out of his mouth, he says.

His relations with Soames are not particularly agreeable. Soames thinks

---

* (1892–1990), the third child of David Lloyd George.

† Alun Gwynne Jones, Baron Chalfont (b. 1919), politician and historian.

he was responsible, as Minister of State at the Foreign Office, for declining
to allow the Prince of Wales to accept an invitation to the Soames's ball at
the British Embassy in Paris a few weeks ago. But the veto was imposed by
Michael Stewart, the Foreign Secretary. Stewart took that course both on
political and personal grounds. At heart he is a puritan. Alun illustrated this
trait in Stewart's character by describing a conversation the Foreign Secretary had with Julian Melchett.* Stewart said to him: 'I hear that you are going
to be paid £16,000 a year as Chairman of the National Steel Corporation. Is
this true?' Julian told him that it was true. 'But what on earth can you find to
spend all that money on?' Stewart asked him.

A.L. Rowse telephones me at 6.30 in a state of euphoria. 'I have', he says,
'just received a letter from the most powerful man in the world.' He goes on
to say that he sent an inscribed copy of his book on the Cornish in America
to President Nixon. And now Nixon has replied personally – not surprisingly
– with a letter of thanks. It includes the sentence 'History has always been
one of my chief interests.' Nixon has promised to read it during his vacation
in California, the same state in which A.L.R. wrote it, at the Huntington
Library. It gives A.L.R. some compensation for having been passed over for
the OM. 'I am properly appreciated in the States,' he says. And so on. Rather
sad.

### 17 August 1969

Chenevix-Trench is to leave Eton in 1970. I talk to Harold Macmillan about
the news. As a devoted son of Eton, Macmillan has decided views on the sort
of man to succeed Chenevix-Trench as Head Master. 'Preferably someone in
Holy Orders,' he told me, 'so that if he does not do very well he can always
be made a Bishop.'

### 29 October 1969

A very good review of my Curzon book in the *Irish Times*.†

I have lunch with the Persian Ambassador, Abbas Aram,‡ largely to discuss the speech he wants me to write for him to be given at the annual dinner
of the Iran Society next month. He is also very much exercised to know who
is likely to be the Foreign Secretary if the Conservatives return to power. I

---

* Julian Mond, 3rd Baron Melchett (1925–73), industrialist.
† K.R.'s *Superior Person: A Portrait of Curzon and his Circle in Late Victorian England* had
just been published by Weidenfeld & Nicolson. Noel Annan was one of many people who gave
the book a glowing review, describing it as 'a dazzling piece of work' in the *New York Review
of Books*.
‡ (1906–85), Iranian Ambassador to the UK Feb. 1967–Nov. 1969.

tell him that I think Alec Douglas-Home will take on the job. With rather a legalistic approach, he then asks me whether there is a precedent for an ex-Prime Minister accepting a lesser portfolio in a Cabinet. Yes, I tell him, Arthur Balfour was Foreign Secretary in Lloyd George's Government during World War I. He appears satisfied.

Dine with Oliver Chandos at St James's Club. He once asked Maynard Keynes[*] who was the greatest politician he had ever known. Keynes replied: 'Kingsley Wood, because he was the sort of man who could make even the French Revolution seem unromantic.'[†]

Oliver tells me that Arthur Balfour was his godfather. He didn't perform his duties very conscientiously, but he did give Oliver 100 volumes of Everyman's Classics.

The greatest Speaker of the House that Oliver ever knew was Edward FitzRoy.[‡] He liked Shakes Morrison very much, but he was a lazy man.

We agree that it was most embarrassing of Mervyn Stockwood to be so drunk at the Vintage Dinner the other night. Oliver says: 'What can one expect when he is only accustomed to a glass of Communion wine?'

### 30 October 1969

I meet Sir Michael Cary, Permanent Secretary to the Ministry of Works, at an evening party.[§] He is also the Fellow representing the assistant masters at Eton. I tell him that on Sunday I intend to include in 'Albany' a list of possible candidates to replace Chenevix-Trench as Head Master. He roars with laughter and asks me to tell him the names. When I do so, he laughs even more and tells me that I seem to have been very busy! He is particularly amused that I have got the name of R.M. Ogilvie, the Fellow and Senior Tutor of Balliol.[¶] 'Did you see him lunching with me in Brooks's yesterday?' he asks, with a twinkle. I assure him that I got his name from quite another source. I discreetly enquire from him what chance there is for Alan Barker of the Leys. He replies: 'There are formidable objections to him. Older beaks at Eton will not forgive him for having twice abandoned Eton for other jobs, in

---

[*] John Maynard Keynes, 1st Baron Keynes (1883–1946), economist; author of *The General Theory of Employment, Interest and Money* (Macmillan, 1936).

[†] Sir Kingsley Wood (1881–1943), Conservative politician. Chancellor of the Exchequer 1940–43.

[‡] (1869–1943), Speaker of the House of Commons from 1923 until his death.

[§] (1917–76), senior civil servant.

[¶] Prof. R.M. Ogilvie (1932–81). Senior Tutor of Balliol 1966–70; Headmaster of Tonbridge School 1970–75; Professor of Humanity, University of St Andrews 1975–81.

1953 and then in 1958, after a second spell teaching there. And the younger beaks think him rather a square.'

*Michael McCrum, formerly a Fellow of Corpus Christi College, Cambridge, and Headmaster of Tonbridge School since 1962, was appointed to succeed Chenevix-Trench as Head Master of Eton in 1970. R.M. Ogilvie then succeeded McCrum as Headmaster of Tonbridge School.*

## 4 November 1969

Lunch with David Gibson-Watt at Brooks's.*

David was once a temporary PPS to Macmillan, & much enjoyed the experience – particularly working with John Egremont. But David, who likes Jack Profumo very much, criticises the way that Macmillan handled the scandal. One day Macmillan said to David: 'If Jack had been a Duke sleeping with a tart, nobody would have worried.' David replied: 'Yes, Prime Minister, but if he had been a Duke he wouldn't have been in the House of Commons.' Macmillan walked angrily away.

Alan Barker on the telephone. He is resigned to not getting the Head Mastership of Eton, though he still retains a strand of hope. I don't tell him that I know that he has no chance.

## 11 November 1969

Through pouring rain at ten o'clock to see King Constantine at Claridge's. The King's apartment is a rather small sitting room filled with numerous vases of flowers sent by supporters, including a fabulous display of orchids. Ironically, the window is almost blocked by the huge Greek flag outside. The King looks very tired and tells me that although this is a private visit, he has had almost no time to himself.

He tells me that the political outlook remains drab but that there are three ways in which pressure may be put on the Greek Government in the near future – the Common Market, the Council of Europe and NATO. He tells me that it would do no good at all at present to make a public statement criticising the regime. Nevertheless, he lets me see the text of any New Year broadcast he intends to make to the Greek people in case I can improve either its substance or its construction.

The King tells me that he spent the weekend with Mountbatten at Broadlands. He was delighted with his own shooting – 'I could not miss.'

---

* David Gibson-Watt, Baron Gibson-Watt, MC and two bars (1918–2002), Conservative MP for Hereford 1956–74.

I ask him how he is spending his time in Italy. One pursuit is archaeology, and he talks enthusiastically of the discoveries made at Santorini, the Greek volcanic island, which I once visited. Apparently, the pumice stone has preserved objects such as pots in a wonderful original state, and shown the settlement to be contemporaneous with Knossos.

At 11.15 to the new Post Office headquarters by Waterloo Bridge, for a talk with John Stonehouse,[*] the first Minister of Telecommunications. He has a battery of the new telephone equipment on which one presses a sequence of buttons in order to ring a number.

He tells me that he is delighted to be relieved of the minute control he was required to exercise over the affairs of the Post Office. This has left him more time, not only for painting, but also for music and for reading political biography such as the new book on Baldwin.[†] But he still finds his constituency duties onerous, and would like to become less of a welfare officer.

I ask him what commemorative stamps have been planned for next year. He rings for a Private Secretary and asks for a certain file. When it arrives it turns out to be the carbon copy of a letter he has just sent to Michael Adeane, giving the Queen details of the stamps. I point out that the most popular stamp of all will surely be the one commemorating the 150th anniversary of Florence Nightingale,[‡] but that it is a 9d stamp. Should it not, I ask, be a 5d one? He is inclined to agree with me and says he will see what he can do.

## 12 November 1969

Charles Clore[§] has devoted the whole of a window at Selfridges to displaying my Curzon book. There is even a large paper streamer with my name on it!

Lunch with Roy Strong,[¶] Director of the National Portrait Gallery. He is very gloomy about the future of country houses and does not see how they can survive in private hands with taxation at its present rate. And if people have to leave them, who will keep them up? Even a system of curators appointed by the Government would be expensive, as well as robbing the houses of life.

Poor Roy is still having internal difficulties with his trustees, particularly

---

[*] (1925–88), junior Labour minister under Harold Wilson, most remembered for unsuccessfully trying to fake his own death in 1974.

[†] Keith Middlemass and John Barnes, *Baldwin: A Biography* (Weidenfeld & Nicolson, 1969).

[‡] Florence Nightingale OM (1820–1910), social reformer and founder of modern nursing. During the Crimean War she was known as 'The Lady with the Lamp'.

[§] Sir Charles Clore (1904–79), financier and philanthropist. Selfridges was one of his retail properties.

[¶] Sir Roy Strong (b. 1935), art historian and museum curator.

the Chairman, Lord Kenyon.* The other day Lord Kenyon looked at a newly decorated room and said: 'Why isn't it more like a country house?' Roy replied: 'Because the country-house style does not always go well in museums.' Kenyon: 'That shows the difference between your background and mine.'

## 26 November 1969

Invited with Dolf Bentinck† to a large dinner party in the rue de Lota in Paris to meet the Duke and Duchess of Windsor. The Windsors have already arrived, and there is no time before dinner for more than a brief introduction. I notice that most of the guests greet the Duchess of Windsor as if she were Royal. It seems only polite to do so.

After dinner the Duchess of Windsor sits in the main drawing room talking mostly to other women. The Duke, however, sits on a sofa in an alcove, and people are brought up to talk to him in the Royal fashion. When my turn comes, he keeps me talking for the rest of the evening. The first thing that strikes one is how tiny and shrunken he is, well below my own height. Standing, he leans heavily forward on a stick. But his head remains very handsome, in spite of a long upper lip, and he is dressed in an almost dandified fashion: his dinner jacket has vents at the back and he sports a red carnation. Throughout our talk he drinks quite a lot of whisky, rather fussily demanding of the butler that it should be mixed exactly as he likes it. He also smokes, or rather plays with, a large cigar. Apparently, the sight of one eye has gone, as he seems to have difficulty in applying a match to the tip whenever it goes out. He has a somewhat staccato voice, a little like Beaverbrook's, with a slight Canadian accent. 'Oh yerse, oh yerse,' he keeps saying. But what he really enjoys talking in is German. He is very proud of speaking it so fluently, and keeps interjecting, 'Jawohl, jawohl' in the course of our conversation.

The Duke tells me that people have been praising my book on Curzon to him, and he asks me all sorts of pertinent questions about it. He recalls that when he was at Oxford, the President of Magdalen, Sir Herbert Warren,‡ wrote a report on him which included the words: 'Bookish he will never be.' He did not really care for Oxford, he tells me, as he was abruptly removed from the Navy, where he had already settled down and made lots of friends. He also recalls that since drinking too much port at Oxford one night, he has never cared for the drink.

---

* Lloyd Tyrell-Kenyon, 5th Baron Kenyon (1917–93), university and museum administrator.
† Baron Adolph Bentinck (1905–70), Netherlands Ambassador to France 1963–70.
‡ (1853–1930), President of Magdalen Coll., Oxford 1885–1928.

When he mentions that he saw some of the Battle of Loos with the Guards in 1915, I mention that I, too, was a Welsh Guardsman. He tells me what an affection he still retains for the regiment. But says he is unlikely to come to any more dinners of the Prince of Wales's Company, as most of his contemporaries are now dead. But with his fantastic Royal memory he adds a few names of those he was with, including Douglas Greenacre.*

As he is very friendly and forthcoming in conversation, I gently lead him on to the subject of the Abdication, and he readily responds. On the refusal of the Government to make the Duchess of Windsor Her Royal Highness, the Duke says: 'I served my country well for seventeen years and all I got in return was a kick in the arse.' He pronounces it in the American way, 'ass'. And when I mention Archbishop Cosmo Gordon Lang, the Duke chuckles and says: 'Auld Lang Swine – that joke, I believe, comes from the Stock Exchange.† But he was a wicked man.' He adds that when Freddie Birkenhead was writing his recent life of Walter Monckton, he never consulted the Duke at all. The Duke is obviously rather wounded by this neglect.

He has one deep regret – that he never went to China. 'I could so easily have gone when I was on a visit to Japan. Now it is too late.'

I mention to him that I am seeing Sir Oswald Mosley tomorrow. He tells me that they are friends and dine with each other. 'He should have been Prime Minister, but it all went sour on him.'

The Duke tells me he is selling his house in the country because he can no longer garden in comfort, and that was its main pleasure for him. And then, not expecting to be taken seriously, he adds: 'And another reason is that I am broke.'

At this point the Duchess bustles up, looking quite remarkable for her years. She is smaller than I should have expected, but very trimmed and plucked and pressed, more like a woman of forty. She is dressed simply in pale blue, with no jewels except one huge sapphire round her neck. She has a harsh voice, but great vivacity and friendliness. She says to the Duke in slightly bullying tones: 'We must go, everyone is longing for you to go.' The

---

* Brig. Douglas Greenacre (1900–78), Welsh Guards 1918–47; equerry to the Prince of Wales 1924–6.

† Two days after the Abdication Lang made a critical broadcast about the King, condemning him for 'moving within a social circle whose standards and ways of life are alien to all the best instincts and traditions of his people'. The following lines, written by Gerald Bullett (1893–1958), man of letters, soon circulated:

My Lord Archbishop, what a scold you are!
And when your man is down, how bold you are!
Of Christian charity, how scant you are!
Auld Lang Swine, how full of cant you are!

Duke tells her about my Curzon book, and she tells me that she is a devoted 'Albany' reader. A few more pleasantries, and they depart very regally, with much bowing and scraping all the way to the door. Thirty-three years after his Abdication, he is still very much a King in manner, and nobody takes the slightest liberty with him.

## 27 November 1969

At three o' clock I call on Sir Oswald Mosley at No. 5, rue Villedo, off the rue Molière. It is a modest but charming little apartment in a small side street full of shops. He himself comes to the door, a tall well-preserved man dressed very formally in a black suit and tie. The two outstanding features of his appearance are rather staring eyes and teeth which slope slightly outwards, both top and bottom. He has immense charm and on this occasion is certainly exerting it.

I explain to him that several people have asked me whether I have consulted him about my book on his father-in-law, Lord Curzon. To those questions, I explain, I have replied no, for two reasons. First, because the scope of my book does not extend as far as Mosley's marriage in the 1920s. Secondly, that he has already given an illuminating picture of Curzon in his own recently published memoirs. Nevertheless, I add, I have felt that I ought to explain this to him personally in case people had tried to make mischief. He tells me that he quite agrees with all I say and that he is delighted by all he has heard of my book, although he has not yet read it. 'It is far better that his life should be written by someone outside the family, as there is so much tension within the Curzon family.'

We move on to politics, and Mosley tells me that he is now entirely out of the party political field, and will not stand as an MP at the next election. He lives in France on financial, practical and sentimental grounds. To avoid English taxation, he cannot spend more than three months in the year in England, but these he fully employs in seeing people. Paris is now his real home – 'Not the most powerful capital, but the most influential and attractive.' He believes that one day there will be a European Union – he is at pains to explain that the Union movement refers to the Union of Europe – and that when it comes, he may find a useful role in it. He formed his party, he tells me, 'soon after coming out of prison'.

I mention to him that the Duke of Windsor spoke to me last night about their friendship and said that Mosley ought to have been Prime Minister. Mosley replies: 'Yes, I used to see a lot of him as a young man when we both hunted. But, of course, I could no longer see him for political reasons once he had become King. Now we visit each other fairly often.' He adds: 'One of the reasons that I failed in politics was that I could not resist being rude to people, and naturally they resented it. That is one of the most serious mistakes I have ever made.'

We discuss the vanity of politicians and he tells me how many years ago he was once driving through France with Sir William Jowitt, who was looking pensive. Mosley asked him why. Jowitt turned his handsome profile and said: 'I was thinking that I should like to retire from the Bar for a couple of years and work in Hollywood.'

Mosley asks me what I intend to write next, and I tell him that I should rather like to do a book on the last generation of the Cecil family.* Mosley replies: 'Bob Cecil was the best of the lot, and if you write anything about him, you should certainly consult Philip Noel-Baker.'†

At the end of our lengthy talk, seated by one of those excellent French stoves, I reluctantly have to go. Mosley gives me an extraordinarily pleasant farewell and asks me to let him know when next I am coming to France, so that I can lunch with him at his house in the country.

## 2 December 1969

Lunch with Lord Salter in Chelsea. He shows me a letter which he had recently from Nigel Nicolson, which contains an interesting comparison between Harold Nicolson and the late Field Marshal Alexander, whose biography Nigel is now writing. Both men, Nigel writes, had ambitions, but also a certain melancholy and awareness of their own deficiencies.

Most of Salter's conversation consists of reminiscences about the fairly distant past. As he is now in his eighties, he wants to make certain that certain of his memories are recorded and presumably thinks that I am a suitable repository.

In spite of his reputation for statesmanship, Salter is rather melodramatic in the way he expresses himself. Thus at one point in our conversation he says: 'I have seen three British Prime Ministers go insane.' These he claims to be Ramsay MacDonald, Eden and Churchill. He noticed that MacDonald was making no sense at all when seeing him each morning during the London Economic Conference of 1933. Eden, he says, was virtually out of his mind during the Suez Crisis of 1956. He adds that Eden resigned as Prime Minister

---

* Published as *The Later Cecils* (Weidenfeld & Nicolson, 1975).

† Lord Robert Cecil, Viscount Cecil of Chelwood (1864–1958). Called to the Bar, Inner Temple 1887; Lord Privy Seal 1923–4; Chancellor of the Duchy of Lancaster 1924–7; President of the League of Nations Union 1923–45; Nobel Peace Prize 1937. Philip Noel-Baker, Baron Noel-Baker (1889–1982), Labour politician. Cabinet Minister under Attlee; the only man to have won an Olympic medal (1920) and the Nobel Peace Prize (1959).

in January 1957 on the express orders of Lord Brain,* who told him that it would be fatal to delay even by so much as a day. And Winston deteriorated sadly in mental alertness after the stroke of 1953.

We also discuss All Souls, and Salter says that the college began to decline in prestige immediately after the war when the candidates elected to Fellowships were of inferior calibre. He has tried to persuade John Sparrow, the Warden, that Fellowships should not be renewed automatically at the end of the seven years, but that those Fellows who had shown themselves to be lazy or immersed in subjects that were absolutely narrow should be denied a renewal. Sparrow replied that he had tried to do exactly what Salter wanted, but that all the young Fellows had ganged up on him.

He tells me that, all things considered, his relations with A.L. Rowse have not been too bad, although he has never been forgiven for failing to vote for Rowse as Warden of the college. I tell Salter that Rowse has frequently described him to me as the greatest public servant of our age, and this pleases Salter.

### 11 December 1969

Lunch with Jeremy and Caroline Thorpe[†] at their flat overlooking Westminster Cathedral. About fifty yards from their door a man comes up to me and says: 'Would you like to buy the universe?' I ask him how much it costs. He replies 'Only 7d.' I say: 'That's not a lot for the universe.' It then appears that the *Universe* is a Catholic newspaper, and he has a little pile of them in the shadow of the Cathedral.

Jeremy suggest that Callaghan's precipitate action in suddenly bringing forth the Bill to prolong the abolition of capital punishment is to thwart those backwoods peers – if they exist – who have previously asked for leave of absence from the House of Lords, but who might now be tempted to return to Westminster to vote in favour of hanging. For in order to take their seats again, they must give one month's notice.

Jeremy and Caroline were at the party for the Prince's twenty-first birthday at Buckingham Palace. It was not at all a stiff affair, and Noël Coward came in a brown dinner jacket. They show me the letter which the Prince sent to thank them for their present – very nicely phrased, in his own writing.

---

* Sir Walter Brain, 1st Baron Brain (1895–1966), neurologist.
† Caroline Allpass (1938–70), m. 1968 Jeremy Thorpe.

## 21 December 1969

Dine at Pratt's. Every single person round the table was in the Brigade of Guards. The talk is exclusively military. It is interesting how everybody now concedes that Monty was rather a fine General and cared not to lose lives: ten years ago – and much more twenty years ago – nobody in the Brigade had a good word for him.

# 1970

*In Cambridge on 13 February 1970 students rioted at the Garden House Hotel in protest against the Greek military junta. On 2 March Ian Smith declared Rhodesia a republic and broke all links with the British Crown. Eighteen-year-olds voted for the first time in the Bridgwater by-election on 13 March. Apollo 13 was launched to the Moon on 11 April and after a malfunction was safely returned to Earth. In the Vietnam War the Cambodian campaign was launched by the USA on 29 April. On 18 May Harold Wilson sought a disso-lution of Parliament from the Queen and announced a general election for 18 June. The Conservatives were unexpectedly returned to office under Edward Heath.*

## 5 January 1970

A very cold and beautiful morning, with the trees covered in frost. A large pile of letters. Baba Metcalfe writes to me about my book on Curzon. She has one interesting thing to say – that had her mother[*] lived, her father would not have become so difficult and embittered. There is also a kind letter from Wilfrid Blunt in which he describes my book as 'dazzling – a triumph'. Fi-nally, a long letter from the Duke of Windsor, in which he tells me that he always thought Kitchener's reputation to be 'somewhat phoney'.[†]

## 6 January 1970

Lunch with Nicky Gordon Lennox. He is returning to Spain later today. So far, he says, Don Juan Carlos has conducted himself well as the nominated successor to Franco as Head of State.

To my astonishment, I am sent a wonderfully generous review of my Curzon book in the *Sporting Life* of all publications!

---

[*] Mary Victoria Curzon, Baroness Curzon of Kedleston (1870–1906), Curzon's first wife.
[†] Herbert Kitchener, 1st Earl Kitchener (1850–1916), victor of the Battle of Omdurman 1898; War Secretary 1914–16; drowned en route to Russia on 5 June 1916 when HMS *Hampshire* struck a German mine in Scapa Flow.

## 14 January 1970

Lunch with Martin Gilliat and Charles Tryon.* We have much talk about
the television film last night of the Duke and Duchess of Windsor. I hear
that when Charles was appointed Keeper of the Privy Purse, he was warned
that the Duke of Windsor would keep coming to him in order to screw more
money out of the Royal Family – but that he was to harden his heart.

## 28 January 1970

Catch a morning train to Oxford. Lunch with Bill Williams at Balliol. I meet
Robert Ogilvie, the Classics tutor whom I wrote about as a fancied candidate
for the vacant Head Mastership of Eton. He bears no resentment whatever
and is amused when I tell him how Michael Cary suspected that I had seen
them lunching together in Brooks's not long before the Provost and Fellows
met to elect.

I have quite a lot of *DNB* talk with Bill, who tells me some of the problems
of editing. 'I often have to rewrite notices almost entirely,' he says, adding,
'The more distinguished the author, the more readily he accepts corrections.'

Wander round Blackwell's, where I see my Curzon book well displayed.
Run into Alan Taylor, whose lecture on Beaverbrook and Bonar Law I am to
listen to later this afternoon. He consults me on a point of taste. After Bonar
Law's death, apparently, a woman claimed that she had been his mistress and
had had a child by him. Beaverbrook, therefore, inveterately loyal to Bonar
Law, paid her £30 a week for many years to close her mouth. Alan tells me
that he will certainly include this in his forthcoming big biography of Beaverbrook, but is doubtful whether he should produce it this evening. I reply
that it might be better to reserve it for the finished work.

The lecture is very well attended, but unfortunately Taylor is too vain to
use a microphone and it is a constant strain to catch every word. At the end
of the lecture I talk to Isaiah Berlin, who invites me to come and see him
when I am next in Oxford to discuss the latest problems of Wolfson College.
He adds that he does not share my belief that so much of the credit for the
post-war revival of Covent Garden should go to David Webster.†

Give Hugh Trevor-Roper dinner. Hugh is rather unkind about Bill Williams, although by now one is used to the tone of elevated bitchiness in which
most dons talk about each other. Hugh says: 'As a well-connected wartime

---

* 2nd Baron Tryon of Durnford (1906–76), Keeper of the Privy Purse and Treasurer to the
Queen 1952–71.
† Sir David Webster (1903–71), Chief Executive of the Royal Opera House, Covent Garden
1945–70.

Brigadier, he expected to be offered all sorts of wonderful jobs when the war was over. But when no offers came, he lingered on in the Army, a source of embarrassment, much ridiculed.' This, I suspect, is mere jealousy on Hugh's part.

I ask Hugh when he is going to produce his large book, expected for many years, on the English Revolution. He replies: 'Never. I wrote 800 pages and then tore them up.' He will not elaborate on this dramatic statement, but merely insists vehemently that the job of a Regius Professor is to educate young men – even at the sacrifice of his own historical writing.

### 3 February 1970

Dame Rebecca West[*] has a splendid turn of phrase, thus she says of A.J.P. Taylor: 'He behaves exactly like Beaverbrook's widow.'[†] She also says that Lady Beaverbrook wanted to have her husband stuffed and kept prominently on view in a case, like Jeremy Bentham[‡] at University College, London, but that Alan Taylor persuaded her not to do so.

### 4 February 1970

Selwyn Lloyd and I agree to dine together at Pratt's, and in the course of the evening – in my flat, at the club and again in my flat after dinner – we have a great deal of talk.

He says that coming from a middle-middle-class background he has never ceased to be amazed at the apparent success he made of his life. He won scholarships both to Fettes and to Magdalene College, Cambridge, earned a good living at the Bar, became a Brigadier during the war, and has since been both Chancellor of the Exchequer and Foreign Secretary. There is another aspect of his life, in which, he says, he has been most fortunate. At the end of the war he had only £4,000, but has since become quite a rich man by his flair for successful investment on the Stock Exchange. But he says his expenses are very heavy, as at present he has four homes – a flat in St James's Court, the country house at Benson, a house in his Wirral constituency and yet another house which was recently left to him in somebody's will.

We discuss what office he might occupy when the Conservatives return to power. Having held so many important jobs, he has no great hankering after office. But he would like to be in a position to exercise power and influence,

---

[*] (1892–1983), author, journalist and literary critic.

[†] Marcia Christoforides, Lady Beaverbrook (1909–94), philanthropist and art collector.

[‡] (1748–1832), philosopher and social reformer, regarded as the founder of modern utilitarianism.

and this he could do from the back benches. There are, however, three possible jobs that he might be asked to undertake. The Lord Chancellorship lies between him and Quintin Hogg. As the office has nowadays become a Ministry of Justice demanding no outstanding judicial knowledge, he would stand no less of a chance than Quintin. The other day he lunched with the present Lord Chancellor, Gerald Gardiner, who showed him the paper describing the appallingly onerous duties of a present-day Lord Chancellor. It is, says Selwyn, a killer, and indeed he noticed during lunch that Gardiner could not pour out a drink for him without using both hands. In any case, Selwyn is not tempted to cut short his own life by becoming Lord Chancellor.

Another possibility is that he might be invited to stand as Speaker of the House of Commons, in which case he would almost certainly be elected. I ask him whether this would not be a very tedious job. He replies that a vigorous Speaker could carry out much reform of parliamentary procedure.

Or he might be asked to become Leader of the House of Commons again, combined with a sinecure such as Lord President of the Council. The disadvantage would be constant attendance in the Chamber of the Commons. He ends: 'I really do assure you that I am not seeking any sort of office and shall be quite happy to continue as I am.'

Some talk on the Greek situation. In informal conversations he heard the view that on no account should King Constantine make any political statement while in exile. He was also told by Averoff,* whom he had known well in the past as a fellow Foreign Secretary, that there may well be a move inside Greece against the Colonels – but it would be to the right and not, as is commonly said, to the left. In other words, the regime would become more, not less, Fascist.

### 6 February 1970

Noel Annan tells me that he intends to review my Curzon book in the *New York Review of Books*. He also adds: 'I though it a wonderful, entertaining, agreeable and knowledgeable book, and I shall say so.'

Lunch at the National Liberal Club with Sir Oswald Mosley, as charming in manner and as moderate in his views as when I saw him a few weeks ago in Paris. He is obviously determined to live down the charge of anti-Semitism. He says to me: 'The last time that I came to this club was to have tea with the editor of the *Jewish Chronicle*, a delightful fellow.' And later, talking about ministers he had known in the 1920s, he pays a special tribute to the first Lord Melchett, 'a very much under-rated figure'.

---

* Evangelos Averoff (1910–90), Greek Foreign Secretary 1956–63.

After lunch we sit round a green-baize table for coffee, and Mosley talks further for forty minutes. Here are some of his remarks:

'Hawtrey,[*] the Treasury civil servant, was as intellectually brilliant as Keynes in expounding economic theory.'

'The principal lesson of the 1920s is that successive Governments had no will to act.'

'What struck me most about Gandhi was that, like Hugh Cecil, he had a profound sense of humour.'

I ask Mosley what results there might have been in domestic and foreign policy had his father-in-law, Curzon, been chosen to succeed Bonar Law as Prime Minister in 1923 instead of Baldwin. Mosley replies: 'It would have been an interesting experiment. In the first place, we would eventually have gone into the war better armed than we were. Admittedly, Curzon gave the appearance of an old-fashioned, pompous Tory aristocrat, but in the days before television that mattered less than it would today. Again, Curzon knew little about economics, and I remember his showing ignorance of how the French franc had fluctuated. But he had the type of mind that could always speak from a brief, and I think he would have made a good Prime Minister.'

## 13 February 1970

Lunch at the Beefsteak with Ralph Richardson.[†] He talks about make-up, and tells me he feels quite naked if ever he acts without it. But he does not believe in elaborate make-up. 'Anything that takes more than thirty minutes to put on is practically always a failure.' In the old days, he says, when stage lighting was dim, a little red brick dust scraped from the wall was quite enough. It was put on with a hare's foot and rubbed off afterwards with a piece of raw mutton.

On the whole he likes a book at meals almost as much as a guest, and has had a little portable lectern made for his dining-room table. Before travelling by train, he says, close your eyes and pick a book at random from your shelves. Don't open it until you get into the train. 'It is amazing how exciting it can be to re-read a book, even if one had read it only recently.'

He much amused the Netherlands Ambassador recently by the vehemence with which he attacked proposals for our joining the Common Market. 'Did we really fight Waterloo in vain?'

---

[*] Sir Ralph Hawtrey (1879–1975), economist; friend of Keynes and a member of the Cambridge Apostles.

[†] Sir Ralph Richardson (1902–83), actor, noted for his Shakespearean roles, many in productions with Laurence Olivier and John Gielgud.

## 22 February 1970

In Cambridge. To Trinity for a drink with Rab and Mollie Butler. I only see Mollie* for a minute or two. She has conceived a profound dislike of the portrait of Rab done for Trinity, and turns the full force of her Mrs Proudie† eyes on me when I dissent.

Rab is looking rather old and tired, with a somewhat blotchy face. I feel sure that he is in need of some sort of medical treatment. At the moment, however, he is cock-a-hoop, having just come from chapel here. The chaplain delighted him by preaching for only twelve minutes. 'I could not resist saying "Hear, hear" at the end of it.'

He talks about the Prince of Wales, saying that he is really beginning to see too much of his parents. 'The Queen, although she does her job exceedingly well, never reads a book, and you know how tiresome Prince Philip is. The trouble about Charles is that adulation is going to his head. We've given him the best room in college, yet he hardly ever seems to be here. The week before last he spent three days in Strasbourg of all places, and last week he went to Wales for two days. Now he is going off to Australia and New Zealand. He seems to forget he has an exam to do soon, and at the present rate he will only just scrape through. He also spends a lot of time acting. I don't mind that at all. His whole life will have to be spent acting. One thing I must say for him, he has excellent manners, and never comes for a meal here without sending Mollie a nice letter afterwards.'

I ask Rab how wide the Prince's friendships are in social terms. He replies: 'He is very cautious indeed in choosing his friends. He thinks that most undergraduate opinions are far too drastic and insane. He has, however, made one friend out of his social class. He is an undergraduate called Jones,‡ who is President of the Student Union and who, as a Welshman, is rather in awe of the Prince. Originally Jones was very left-wing, but under the Prince's influence has gone over to the right. This has saved the college a great deal of friction. When a difficult problem arises in relations between the undergraduates and the college, I ask Charles to have Jones in for a drink – and the problem is solved. Charles has not only shown friendship towards him, but at the time of the Investiture he got him a job with a television company that

---

* Lady Butler of Saffron Walden (1907–2009), second wife of Rab Butler. Her hatred of Harold Macmillan was legendary. She once said to me: 'Mr Thorpe, when you realise that Mr Macmillan was an evil man, then you are well on your way to an understanding of post-war British politics.'

† The domineering wife of the Bishop of Barchester, one of Anthony Trollope's greatest characters.

‡ Hywel Jones (1948–99), economic consultant; partner, Hywel Jones and Associates.

brought him in £50 – a fortune for a young undergraduate.'

Before we go into Hall for High Table, Rab tells me how much he liked my book on Curzon. He adds: 'One of the troubles about my own autobiography is that my friends were far less brilliant than Curzon's – Michael Ramsey, Selwyn Lloyd and Geoffrey Lloyd.'

We make our way into Hall. Rab tells me he is very nervous in case he has to sit next to a woman on High Table. He is bitterly opposed to the majority of Fellows who have pushed through the proposal that members of High Table may bring in women as well as men guests. He does not mind so much if distinguished women scholars are brought – though even then he does not like them to drink port after dinner in the Senior Combination Room. Fortunately for Rab, there are only men dining tonight.

Rab tells me that Macmillan is coming for tea next week. 'Mollie hates him, but I take a more philosophical view. What I still can't understand is why, having received so much support from me in his economic and financial policies, he hated me to such an extent that he could not bear my succeeding him as Prime Minister in 1963. I suppose it all goes back to Munich. He thought that I was too much a part of the Establishment. For in spite of his own attachment to the Cavendish family, he felt alienated from the Establishment. And looking back to those days, he thinks that I lacked both courage and patriotism.'

On Alan Barker: 'As you know, just about the time that the Head Mastership of Eton fell vacant, Alan was also a candidate for the Headmastership of Westminster. As a governor of Westminster, I went up to a meeting at the school in order to press his candidature. But as soon as I arrived, the Dean showed me the letter he had received from Barker in which he said that above all he loved the Leys and Eton – and that he wished to serve one or the other. Accordingly, he wanted to withdraw his name as a candidate for Westminster. He thus missed an almost certain chance of being elected – and then had the disappointment of failing to get Eton.' A desperately sad story.

Rab said how pleased he was to see Jack Profumo at my party the other night. He thinks that the tragedy of his fall could have been averted had he been better advised. 'I should have told him that on no account must he mention his sex life from the benches of the House of Commons. Dilke, after all, never did so.'

There is a certain note of melancholy in Rab's conversation as the evening progresses. He still has a hankering for London life, and Mollie, he says, misses it even more than he does. 'We have both noticed that our London invitations are falling off.' He asks me whether, if Heath becomes Prime Minister and offers him an office such as Lord President of the Council, he ought to accept. I reply that it would be unsatisfying, having held so many of the great offices of state, to descend to what is virtually a sinecure. He says he is inclined to agree with me, and is happy to stay at Trinity, as so many members of his family live within an hour's drive from the university.

'David Eccles said to me the other day that we have both found ultimate happiness after politics – he at the British Museum, I at Trinity.'

Having said goodbye to Rab, I bump into Kitson Clark in the Great Court. He says: 'Of course, Rab is very fond of Trinity, but he is utterly out of his depth in the academic world.'

### 25 February 1970
In the evening I am invited to the private view at the National Portrait Gallery to see Annigoni's new picture of the Queen. It is rather a stark composition, with little warmth or humanity about it. As an exercise in symbolism that would not matter very much, but the quality of the painting seems to me rather poor, and particularly smudgy round the mouth.

While I am walking round with a glass of champagne in my hand, I run into Lord Salisbury, who astonishes me by saying: 'When are you coming to look at my archives at Hatfield?' I reply that I thought my proposal for writing a book about his father, his uncles and his aunts was in abeyance until David Cecil had decided the scope of his work on Hatfield. With a gesture of impatience, Bobbety replies that he doubts whether David will ever finish it. He adds that he hopes I will be able to write my book. His only doubt is whether there is enough material in the archives at Hatfield. I at once seize the opportunity and tell him that I will telephone to arrange a time when I can look at the archives. But I shall not feel secure until I am actually at work on them.

At about 6.30 the Queen herself arrives, dressed in orange and clutching a glass of tomato juice. She is beginning to look a little lined and grey-haired, but full of the vivacity and interest that Annigoni's portrait has missed. What a flutter people get into when the Queen is about.

### 28 February 1970
To All Souls to dine and spend the weekend with Leslie Rowse. I give him a medal from the French Mint of Louis XIV, as a little present in return for all the kindness and encouragement I have received from him over the years.

Dine in Hall next to Douglas Jay. He paints a very gloomy picture of our future economic life, but is himself much enjoying himself as a Director of Courtaulds. Isaiah Berlin makes one of his rare dining excursions to All Souls, and talks superbly throughout the evening. One story concerned the downfall of Ivan Maisky,* the wartime Russian Ambassador in London. In 1945 he was at the Potsdam Conference and happened to be alone in a room when Winston Churchill entered. Winston, as was his habit, launched into a long eulogy: 'Even while England stood alone, you were always one of her best friends . . .', etc. etc. In the middle of this encomium, Stalin entered the room and heard the last few sentences. Maisky was shortly afterwards dismissed and hardly ever heard of again.

I ask Isaiah about his plans for Wolfson College. He tells me he is rather worried as its income comes not only from Wolfson money, but also from an endowment of Ford shares – which have fallen by 30 per cent recently. This does not affect the income of the college, but precludes his asking for a further capital sum at present.

One of the things which I love about Isaiah is his endearing schoolboy greed. Throughout our entire conversation he is heaping sweet biscuits with jam and crunching them up.

### 1 March 1970, letter to his mother

It is rather nice to spend two weekends running in the ancient universities. Last week, I went to see Rab and Mollie Butler in Trinity College. We had a great deal of talk, and he told me that he was just a little worried about the Prince of Wales – for in spite of having to take an examination quite soon, the Prince is already carrying out several public engagements each week. 'I have written to the Queen about it,' Rab tells me, 'but she doesn't really understand how a university works.'

Rab is very portly and gracious as Master of the college. I think he still broods about not having become Prime Minister – and Mollie does not make things easier by constantly abusing Macmillan.

### 4 March 1970

In spite of a blizzard which blows all day, I catch a train to Hatfield from King's Cross. On arrival I have a long and difficult walk through deep snow up to the house, but soon thaw out in front of a huge log fire in the room of the archivist. We discuss the material that would be available to me if I decided to write my book on the children of the great Lord Salisbury. Altogether, there is a feast of material. I plod my way back through even deeper snow to Hatfield Station and am lucky enough to board a train quite soon. On arriving home I draft a careful letter to Lord Salisbury telling him that I should like to write the book, and hope (a) that I will not be treading on

---

* (1884–1975), Soviet diplomat; Ambassador to the UK 1932–43.

David's toes, and (b) that he will let me remove documents to work on in my flat.

## 5 March 1970

Have a long talk with Katie Macmillan at the Speaker's party in the lovely Pugin* rooms, rather badly redecorated. Katie is very enthusiastic about my proposed book on the Cecil family. She promises to help me in getting in touch with them all. She tells me a story she heard in Yorkshire. A man died and went to Heaven. He knocked on the pearly gates, and was utterly astonished when they were opened, not by St Peter, but by the Devil. The man bowed low and asked: 'Have I come to the wrong place?' The Devil replied: 'No, we have gone comprehensive.'

## 17 March 1970

I have a talk with Harry Batterbee.† When he was Private Secretary to Walter Long,‡ Balfour said of Long: 'He always reached the right decision by the wrong road.' Not long before Balfour died, Balfour visited him. Balfour said: 'Very soon I shall know the answer to all those problems which have perplexed me throughout my life.' I ask him if he has any memories of Bob Cecil. He tells me that he was once sent by Austen Chamberlain with a message for Cecil, and found him in his office reading *Punch*.

At one point in his career, Batterbee was employed as a secret go-between discussing tariff questions with de Valera. At the end of one afternoon's meeting in Dublin, Dev said to him: 'Tonight I am going to see *Juno and the Paycock*, and I wish you could come with me to see what wonderful actors we are. But I am afraid that if you were seen in the theatre tonight, you might be shot by the IRA.'

At the time of the Abdication in 1936, Batterbee was responsible for all those vital telegrams to the Dominions, asking whether they would be happy to have Mrs Simpson as their Queen.

## 25 March 1970

At 5.30 to the House of Lords to see Lord Salisbury, who has been given one

---

* Augustus Pugin (1812–52), architect in the Gothic revival style; his work culminated in the interior design of the Palace of Westminster.

† Sir Harry Batterbee (1880–1976), civil servant. PS to Walter Long at the Colonial Office 1916–19; Registrar of the Order of St Michael and St George.

‡ 1st Viscount Long (1854–1924), British Unionist politician. Colonial Secretary 1916–19; First Lord of the Admiralty 1919–21. Long and Chamberlain were deadlocked rivals for the leadership of the Conservative Party in 1911, when both stood down in favour of Bonar Law.

of the tiny rooms normally occupied by the Law Lords. Without my again raising the topic, he tells me that he has decided to allow me to take away bundles of his family papers from Hatfield so that I can work on them in London. But he adds, laughing, that the archivist is not at all pleased by this decision.

We then talk about the general lines of the book, and he surprises me by saying that Lady Gwendolen's* life of his grandfather is far too discreet. By this, he seems to imply that I need not worry about my own book mentioning family likes and dislikes, although I make a special point of telling him that should I come across anything in the family papers which he does not want published, I shall not only meet his wishes, but keep the information under the seal of the confessional.

Lord Salisbury talks a little about his family and says what a pity it was that Linky, who spent so much of his leisure hours in contemplation, committed practically nothing to paper.

In the evening I have a long talk with Edward Boyle at Pratt's, who tells me that he now feels he made a mistake in rejoining the Government under Macmillan so very shortly after resigning from the Eden Government in November 1956. It would have strengthened his moral position immeasurably had he remained out of office for longer. At the same time, had he not been tempted to serve under Macmillan at the Ministry of Education, his whole life would not have followed its present course at Leeds.

He tells me that once he is installed in Leeds, he hopes to offer an honorary degree to Anthony Eden, a most imaginative way of breaching their past differences. Edward says he would like me to come and dine with him and David Dilks, his new Professor of History, whom he is anxious to get to know better.

## 13 April 1970

Dine with Dean Acheson. On the subject of the investigation into J.F.K.'s assassination, Acheson says that he was consulted by L.B.J. a day or two after the President had been killed. Acheson told him that the investigating commission should not include any Federal officials or judges. Instead there should be a panel of senior State judges. But L.B.J preferred that Chief Justice Warren should preside over the commission.

---

* Lady Gwendolen Cecil (1860–1945), second child of the 3rd Marquess of Salisbury. Author of a four-volume uncompleted biography of her father. She and her sister, Lady Maud Cecil, Countess of Selborne (1858–1950), were known as the Salisbury Plains.

## 21 April 1970

A very pleasant cocktail party given by Nin Ryan at her flat overlooking Green Park. Lots of people talk to me about my Curzon book. Elisabeth Douglas-Home tells me that Alec is giving it as his contribution to the Adlai Stevenson Memorial Library now being established by the English-Speaking Union. Jack Wheeler-Bennett also says how much he liked it. He is sending a copy to Harold Macmillan to take with him on his Hellenic cruise. Jack makes me laugh very much when I happen to mention George Gissing, and he replies: 'I think that you and I must be the only two people in this room who have ever read anything by him.' They certainly look too well-heeled a crowd to immerse themselves in the life of a Grub Street hack.

## 22 April 1970

About 7.15 p.m., a chauffeur arrives at my flat with a letter. It is from Oliver Chandos, telling me that he is to become a Knight of the Garter tomorrow, on St George's Day. He wonders whether there have ever before been two living KGs belonging to the same family. In fact there have – the present Lord Salisbury and his father.

## 26 April 1970

In Israel with Charles Clore. I have some conversation at a dinner with Abba Eban. He enquires about the prospects of a General Election in England. He tells me he has been very unimpressed by Heath.

## 29 April 1970

Still in Israel. Visit the Israeli Museum, a wonderfully imaginative modern building surrounded by pleasant gardens. The prize exhibits of the museum are pieces of the Dead Sea Scrolls, shown to much advantage in a circular stone chamber. The rest of the museum is very rich in manuscripts.

From the museum I drive to the Knesset, the Parliament of Israel. The Chamber itself is a cool room, decorated in pale brown. There is a huge glass screen separating the public gallery from the seats of the Members, so that bombs cannot be thrown. Chagall has been called in to decorate the place extensively, and has provided mosaic floors and wall paintings.

On the way back to the hotel I see the following notice: 'Mount of Olives: donkey rides on Palm Sunday road.'

## 1 May 1970

At 9 a.m. to meet Ben Gurion by the service lift which gives him an unpublicised exit from the hotel. He is dressed in his habitual open-necked white shirt and accompanied by a detective. He is going along to the hot springs to be treated for rheumatism, and suggests that I accompany him. So we set off along the edge of the Sea of Galilee, walking at a fairly stiff pace.

He is anxious not to talk about the success or otherwise of the present Israeli Government, and tells me he is never consulted by them. But he talks quite freely about the past. Had Winston Churchill not been defeated in 1945, he says, the creation of the State of Israel would have been effected far more smoothly. As it was, 'Labour mismanaged it.'

I reluctantly say goodbye to him at the end of our talk and go back to the hotel, where our party is preparing to leave for the next stage of our tour. We drive up to the Golan Heights, which at that time were in Syrian hands and a grave threat to the life of Israelis living in this part of the world. Just how much of a threat can be seen when we inspect the captured Syrian positions. They are almost impregnable, consisting for the most part of very strong bunkers made of prefabricated concrete. Whatever else Israel may be prepared to concede during peace discussions she will never willingly relinquish the Golan Heights.

## 20 May 1970

Antonia Fraser tells me that she is about to write to Lord Hill,* Chairman of the Governors of the BBC, to complain about its treatment of her. Some time ago she was invited to take part in the programme called *With Great Pleasure*, in which various people read their favourite passages of verse and prose with a commentary. Among others who have done it recently is the Speaker of the House of Commons. Antonia recorded her programme on Tuesday in front of an invited audience at the BBC, and the programme was due to go out on 31 May. But the BBC now tells her that it must be postponed until after the election on 18 June, because she is married to a Tory MP.

Programmes by Enoch Powell and Michael Foot† have also been postponed – but that is understandable as they are themselves standing for Parliament. Antonia's point is that she was asked to take part in the programme not as an MP's wife, but as a writer. The attitude of the BBC, she claims, strikes at her livelihood as a professional writer. Where, moreover, will it end? Suppose there is another election quite soon, will she again be barred from the air? She will let me know what Lord Hill replies.

---

* Charles Hill, Baron Hill of Luton (1904–89), Conservative Cabinet Minister, doctor and television executive. Chairman, Independent Television Authority 1963–7; Chairman of the Governors of the BBC 1967–72.
† (1913–2010), politician and author. Leader of the Labour Party 1980–83.

## 2 June 1970

In Spain. At 9.45 to the Zarzuela Palace to see Don Juan Carlos. The Prince appears in the doorway and leads me into his study with a very warm embrace, clasping my forearm. He begins: 'How very nice to see a real friend.' I form a decided impression that he has matured enormously since I last saw him eighteen months ago. He is, unfortunately, more discreet than he was; at the same time he is far more shrewd and intelligent on what he says.

I ask him how his father has taken his nomination as the future Head of State. He replies: 'My father has not really accepted it in his own mind. Outwardly he must save face, so tells people that he hopes I shall succeed in my task. But I am sure that in his mind he really regrets the way it was done. I don't blame him for that. At the same time it could hardly have been done in another way. If I am to survive as King it will be as a national figure and not as leader of the monarchists.'

His relations with Franco, he tells me, are friendly but distant. Franco does not interfere in any way with his plans or engagements, and never either tells him to do something or to refrain from doing something.

I ask him whether he attends Cabinet meetings. He replies that he does not – nor has any wish to do so. 'If we had a Prime Minister, it would be all right for me to attend – but without a Prime Minister, I should be accused of trying to become an executive King.' The Prince tells me that he sees quite a lot of ministers, but has no special favourites. If he did, he adds, it would only cause trouble.

## 10 June 1970

Anthony Nutting tells me that two or three years ago, when he was about to publish his book criticising the Suez operation of 1956, much Conservative pressure was put on him to be uncontroversial. Even Macmillan asked if he could come and see him. The old man said to Tony: 'The Tory Party has not yet solved its problems. Ted Heath is certainly not the answer to them.' It dawned on Tony that Macmillan was suggesting that if he did not publish his book on Suez, he might one day lead the Tory Party. Tony simply replied: 'If they want me, they know my telephone number.' He also asked Macmillan what he himself intended to say about Suez in his own memoirs. Macmillan replied: 'I shall ignore it.'

Tony also tells me a story about Winston, who was once dining after the war with a party of young radical MPs, including Nutting. One of them said to him: 'I remember, Sir Winston, hearing you make a speech during the war that we should afterwards find ourselves in a classless society. What did you mean by that?' Winston, who had obviously forgotten ever making such a speech, replied: 'Oh, shaking hands with the hall porter on Christmas Eve and that sort of thing.'

*At the general election on 18 June, the Conservatives under Edward Heath won 330 seats, Labour under Wilson won 287 and the Liberals under Jeremy Thorpe 6. Kenneth was as surprised by this outcome as most commentators.*

### 20 June, letter to his mother

It was certainly a surprise result – and also a very welcome one. If the Labour Government had been returned this time, it would have been difficult ever to dislodge them. Practically nobody expected a Tory victory. Even as experienced a campaigner as Rab Butler told me on Election Day that he was afraid Labour would get back – though he thought with a small majority. There are some casualties over which I cannot shed many tears, Woodrow Wyatt,* for example.

*The swing from Government to Opposition – 4.7 per cent – was then the largest in a post-war election. Yet Heath was to face myriad problems and was only Prime Minister for just over three years and eight months, losing the February 1974 election. The first major blow came on 20 July when the Chancellor of the Exchequer, Iain Macleod, died unexpectedly. Troubles in Ulster were to be a backdrop throughout Heath's premiership. On 9 August police battled with riots in Notting Hill. On 28 September Gamal Abdel Nasser, second President of Egypt, died. President Nixon visited Edward Heath on 3 October at Chequers. On 9 November Charles de Gaulle, President of France, died. Michael Tippett's opera The Knot Garden premiered at Covent Garden on 2 December. The year's financial costs of the troubles in Northern Ireland were calculated at £5.5 million.*

### 30 June 1970

Cocktail party at the Portuguese Embassy. See Selwyn Lloyd, looking rather subdued. I tell him how sorry I am he is not in the Government. He makes loyal noises about Ted Heath.

I hear a story about Gladwyn. Sir Harold Beeley,† formerly our Ambassador in Cairo, went up to Gladwyn at a recent party and said: 'I don't know

---

* Baron Wyatt of Weeford (1918–97), Labour MP for Birmingham Aston 1945–55; reporter on the BBC's *Panorama* whilst out of Parliament; MP for Bosworth 1959–70; later a fervent supporter of Mrs Thatcher; Chairman, Horserace Totalisator Board 1976–97.
† (1909–2001), diplomat and Arabist. Ambassador to the United Arab Republic in Cairo 1961–4 and 1967–9.

whether you remember me. You once invited me to dine with you in New York.' Gladwyn replied: 'And did you come?'

## 2 July 1970

A very agreeable cocktail party given by Alec and Elizabeth Douglas-Home. They do not move to the official residence of the Foreign Secretary until next month. Apparently, the secretaries there have been in the habit of going on the roof on warm evenings and their stiletto heels have made holes in it. It is Alec's birthday, which adds to the jolliness of the evening.

I have a very friendly welcome from Willie Whitelaw,* the new Leader of the House, who tells me how much he enjoyed my piece in 'Albany' on the large number of former Brigade officers in the Government. He says I am to get in touch with him and insist on speaking to him personally when I need any help.

## 7 July 1970

Discuss Selwyn Lloyd's future with Jonathan Aitken,† his godson, over lunch at the Turf Club. Ultimately, Selwyn would like to be Speaker of the House of Commons, but for the moment is quite content to be a powerful backbencher.

*On 29 June Caroline Thorpe, wife of the Liberal leader Jeremy Thorpe, was killed in a car crash.*

## 14 July 1970

Jeremy Thorpe telephones me for the first time since the death of his wife. He says he is feeling very miserable, but mentions the tradition of suffering among Liberal Party leaders. He recalls that Asquith's first wife died, as did John Simon's,‡ Lloyd George lost a daughter, so did Clement Davis,§ and Jo Grimond's son committed suicide. Only Herbert Samuel jogged on without sorrow until in his nineties. The Archbishop of Canterbury is to take part in the memorial service to Caroline.

---

* William Whitelaw, 1st Viscount Whitelaw (1918–99), Conservative politician. Lord President of the Council 1970–72; Secretary of State for Northern Ireland 1972–3 and for Employment 1973–4; Conservative Party Chairman 1974–5; Home Secretary 1979–83; Lord President and Leader of the House of Lords 1983–8.
† (b. 1942), Conservative MP for South Thanet for twenty-four years. Chief Secretary to the Treasury 1994–5; war correspondent in Vietnam and Biafra; biographer of Richard Nixon, 1993.
‡ 1st Viscount Simon (1873–1954), leader of the National Liberals 1931–40. The first politician to serve in the three great offices of State: Home Secretary 1915–16 and 1935–7; Foreign Secretary 1931–5; Chancellor of the Exchequer 1937–40; he was also Lord Chancellor 1940–45.
§ (1884–1962), leader of the Liberal Party 1945–56.

I later talk to Lord Mountbatten about the Curzon–Kitchener conflict. I point out that in the long run Kitchener was wrong, since no single person could be both Commander-in-Chief of the Army in India as well as its representative on the Viceroy's Council. Mountbatten agrees with me, but says that Curzon's view – that there should be a comparatively junior general sitting on the Viceroy's Council – was equally wrong. The probable solution, he thinks, was to have a civilian military member of the Viceroy's Council. Mountbatten adds: 'If Curzon was as right as you say, why did the Government back Kitchener?' This is extraordinarily naïve of Mountbatten, and I reply: 'Because the Government was tottering to its doom, and did not dare incur widespread hostility by dismissing the leading national hero of the day. Curzon, on the other hand, was widely disliked and thus expendable.'

### 21 July 1970
Sudden news that Iain Macleod died last night at No. 11 Downing Street. A nasty problem for poor Ted Heath in finding a new Chancellor of the Exchequer.

### 5 August 1970
At 10.30 a.m. to see Dr W.R. Matthews,* who retired as Dean of St Paul's in 1967, and who is now in his ninetieth year, to talk about Lord William Cecil for my Cecil book.† Although his voice is rather thin and he is a little unsteady on his legs, his brain is astonishingly lively and his conversation amusing.

We have a great deal of talk about Lord William Cecil's days as Bishop of Exeter, especially his absent-mindedness. At a service in the private chapel at Exeter, he well remembers Lady Florence‡ suddenly interrupting her husband with a cry: 'No, no, Fish, not the Nunc Dimittis, the Magnificat.'

Again, he was notorious for his Christmas sermons when, describing the scene in the holy stable, he would always bring in a passage about manure. The choirboys always used to have a lottery on whether or not he would mention this.

At a diocesan conference a rather cheeky priest once made a long speech criticising the way in which the diocese was run. He ended: 'I hope, my Lord, you will not think that anything I have said applies to you personally.' The

---

* The Very Revd Walter Matthews, Dean of St Paul's 1934–67.

† Lord William ('Fish') Cecil (1863–1936), Bishop of Exeter 1916–36.

‡ Lady Florence Cecil (1865–1944).

Bishop started, as if he had just woken up, and said: 'I haven't heard a single word you have been saying.'

In more general talk, Matthews says: 'It is said to be a law of nature that there must always be friction between deans and bishops. I must confess that I was obviously never meant to be a dean as I have always got on so well with bishops. When I was first being considered for the Deanery of St Paul's, I was closely questioned both by the Archbishop of Canterbury and by the Prime Minister – not to ensure that I was a scholar, but that I was as unlike Dean Inge[*] as possible.'

## 6 August 1970

Through pouring rain to Haywards Heath by train, then a taxi to Birch Grove to lunch with Harold Macmillan. As I get out of the car at Birch Grove, I catch a glimpse of a red despatch box lying on a table inside. I am met and taken into a small sitting room, then given a glass of sherry. A minute or two later Macmillan himself appears, rather tottery on his feet and taking very short steps, but otherwise far brighter and more alert than he usually is in London. He wears an old grey suit heavily patched at the knees.

On a footstool is my *Superior Person*, which Macmillan praises in extravagant terms, saying over and over again: 'A wonderful book, a wonderful book.'

We go in to lunch, where there are two little Faber grandchildren and a nanny. H.M. asks one of them: 'And do you still have a Latin grace at Summer Fields?' and goes on to declaim it. The little boy eagerly confirms that his grandfather had got it right.[†] A lot of very good food – an omelette, escalope of veal, peach melba, cheese. Then we drink coffee on the terrace outside overlooking a lovely rose garden.

I talk about the scope of my Cecil book in general. H.M. is surprised that I have so many letters at my disposal from Hatfield. He never knew that the Cecils wrote to each other so much – although he says that he has quite a lot of long letters from Bobbety. He expresses much affection for him and tells me, with many chuckles, that Bobbety recently saw Makarios in Cyprus. 'I was very sorry when Bobbety resigned from my Government. But what could I do? Of course, I couldn't go on keeping Makarios in an aquarium like the Seychelles. I had to bring him back to negotiate. When Bobbety then came

---

[*] The Very Revd Dean Inge (1860–1954), Dean of St Paul's 1911–34; owing to his propensity for journalism it was said of him that from being a pillar of the Church he became a column in the *Standard*.

[†] This grandson was David Faber (b. 1961), historian. Conservative MP for Westbury 1992–2001; Headmaster of Summer Fields from 2010.

and said he must resign over it, I felt I had to accept his invitation. Winston later told me that in his Government Bobbety used to offer his resignation once a week, but it was never accepted.'

H.M. goes on to tell me what he knows about each member of the Cecil family who comes into my story. 'My family came to Birch Grove about 1902. The Cecils lived almost next door at Gale Cottage, so called because it was exposed to wind and rain. Bob Cecil was the most rigid Tory I have ever come across, with all the Tory prejudices such as anti-Semitism. He loved golf and would crouch down like a vulture when putting. When later he took up the cause of the League of Nations he was considered very odd indeed by his fellow Tories, who resented that he was so internationally minded. They thought it was all right for a man like Lansdowne to act like a traitor in 1917 by advocating a compromise peace – it was merely the Whig tradition. But it would never have done for a Hatfield Tory to behave like that.'

This leads H.M. to dwell on the extraordinary position of Lansdowne in the Conservative Party. Originally a Liberal minister, he parted company with Gladstone over Home Rule, for he was a prominent Irish landowner. But even when he became leader of the Conservative Party in the House of Lords, he never became a Tory at heart. One day Lansdowne was walking through London with the Duke of Devonshire and it began to pour with rain. The Duke suggested that they should seek shelter in the Carlton Club, then at the east end of Pall Mall, which they happened to be passing. Lansdowne indignantly refused to enter the Carlton and insisted on going on as far as Brooks's at the top of St James's Street, where his old Whig heart would be more at home.

On Linky, H.M. recalls how he suffered from pernicious anaemia, so that when staying in country houses nasty little saucers of raw liver used to be placed in front of him. Much was allowed him in his behaviour, largely because of his intellectual brilliance and wonderful oratory – in spite of a high nasal voice. Secondly, the gesture must precede the statement to which it is related. H.M. gets to his feet and demonstrates to me exactly what he means. He points out into the Sussex landscape and, keeping his arm extended, thunders: 'That is the man who betrayed his country.'

On the Cecils in general, he stresses their extraordinary family history. From the time of the first Queen Elizabeth to the year that Lord Salisbury became Prime Minister in 1885, they did nothing. They were like characters out of Proust. What caused their nineteenth-century flowering was an infusion of wealth and brains from two sources. First, from the Gascoyne heiress;[*] secondly from the Aldersons.[†] The Gascoynes probably had Jewish blood and this helped too. The most remarkable feature about them is how remote the Cecils remained from the people on whom the Conservatives depend – colonels and brewers and so on. The Cecils are unlike the silent Whigs, such as the Cavendishes, and talk endlessly. 'They did not care for The Souls and disapproved even of A.J. Balfour's attachments to them. They liked the Prince of Wales's[‡] flashy set even less. The Prince was never asked to Hatfield with his women and hangers-on, though he did propose himself to visit in 1909.

H.M. agrees that the Cecils have no particular regard for the Royal Family, in spite of the Prime Minister's reverence for Queen Victoria. This leads him to talk about the article written by John Grigg criticising the Queen in 1957. H.M., who was then Prime Minister, was a fellow member of Buck's Club, and several members, including Lord Sefton, wanted to expel him. But H.M. was rather experienced in these matters and warned Sefton that a member of a club could not legally be expelled simply because he had written an article – and that if the committee persisted, John could sue them. So the committee contented itself with merely reprimanding him.

H.M. next talks about A.J.B. and the biography of him written by Kenneth Young.[§] 'I believe that A.J.B. was impotent – or nearly so – and I cannot accept what Young says about his supposed affair with Mary Wemyss.[¶] Balfour was a great gentleman, and if he had had an affair with Mary Wemyss, he would never have promoted her husband. (I later look up biographical details of Wemyss, and find that he never held ministerial office, so presumably H.M. was thinking of someone else.)

We discuss why A.J.B. was such a failure as Prime Minister. H.M. suggests it was because he was essentially a philosopher, so out of touch with political party matters. I reply that there is something to be said for that view, but that essentially Balfour was a very lazy man. H.M. agrees and adds: 'He was good only when he was being led by Salisbury, just as Eden was good only when being led by Churchill. How A.J.B. would have dithered today over whether or not we should go into the Common Market.'

We talk about the Conservative leadership in general. 'Journalists – not

---

[*] Frances Gascoyne (1802–39), wife of the 2nd Marquess of Salisbury.

[†] Sir Edward Alderson (1787–1857), father-in-law of the 3rd Marquess of Salisbury.

[‡] Edward, Prince of Wales, later Edward VII (1841–1910).

[§] (1916–85), journalist and biographer. Editor of the *Yorkshire Post*; political and literary adviser to Beaverbrook newspapers.

[¶] Mary Charteris, Countess of Wemyss (1862–1937), wife of the 11th Earl of Wemyss, Conservative politician.

historians like you, of course – are always writing that Heath is the first leader of the Conservative Party to come from the people. What nonsense. Peel[*] came of merchant stock. Disraeli was hardly an aristocrat. Salisbury was really the first aristocrat.' Here I interpose: 'Derby?' H.M. says: 'Yes, Derby too.' He goes on: 'Balfour was half aristocrat, half Glasgow merchant. Bonar Law, Baldwin and Chamberlain all came from the merchant class. Winston was not really an aristocrat. On breeding he was half cad, half American adventurer.'

The Victorians delight H.M. as much as they delight me. He says that in country houses when he wants to relax, he loves reading obscure books of memoirs. One day he picked up a volume by one of the Lytteltons, in which there was a story about the 4th Lord Lyttelton[†] coming into his wife's room and saying that he had terrible news to give her about one of their eight sons. She wondered what it could be: theft, gambling debts or even running off with a housemaid? But it was none of those things. Lord Lyttelton said: 'He actually stepped back to play a half-volley.' H.M. adds: 'What trust in one's children that shows.'

By now it is nearly 3.30 and we have been talking hard for two and a half hours, either at lunch, sitting on the terrace, walking through the garden, or again sitting in the little summerhouse. So we move back towards the house. But before I leave he insists on showing me some of the pictures and sculptures in the house, most of them Victorian. An exception is a very beautiful head of Lady Dorothy recently completed by Oscar Nemon[‡] four years after her death. It is a wonderful likeness of her, particularly from a three-quarter view. It stands in the hall a few yards away from the one Nemon did of Macmillan himself many years before.

Then he takes me upstairs to see a series of portraits of celebrated Macmillan authors. He points to them one by one, sometimes with a comment – John Morley[§] ('like a butler'), Dickens ('what a sensual face'), Matthew Arnold ('how Jewish he looks'). There is also one of Lord Roberts.[¶] And a Sargent of Daniel Macmillan as a child. And a bust of H.M. himself as a child.

As I take my leave, I apologise for having kept him so long from working on his own book. He replies: 'No, you haven't. I can hardly do more than an hour a day.'

---

[*] Sir Robert Peel, 2nd Bt (1788–1850), Prime Minister 1834–5 and 1841–6.

[†] George Lyttelton, 4th Baron Lyttelton (1817–76), Conservative politician.

[‡] (1906–85), Croatian sculptor.

[§] 1st Viscount Morley of Blackburn (1838–1923), Liberal politician.

[¶] Frederick Roberts, 1st Earl Roberts (1832–1914), military commander.

## 12 August 1970

Give Cecil King* lunch. He claims that in one of the entries in his autobiography just after the war he prophesied that Harold Wilson would one day be Prime Minister. This leads us to talk about Harold Wilson's own memoirs. Apparently, he has asked for £250,000 for the complete rights. We agree that they surely cannot be worth as much as that unless Wilson does not intend to become Prime Minister again. If he does intend to become Prime Minister, he obviously cannot reveal the secrets and trivialities of Cabinet life during his last administration. Dick Crossman, King adds, is asking only £30,000 for his memoirs – but they are likely to be far more lively than those of Wilson. By contrast, King says, he has heard from Douglas Houghton, Chairman of the Parliamentary Party, that Transport House has already paid out £4,000 to impoverished MPs who lost their seats at the last election.

He tells me an extraordinary rumour he has heard – that Iain Macleod's death was caused not by a sudden and unexpected heart attack following his operation for appendicitis, but by cancer that was known to his doctors for several months. In the circumstances it seems extraordinary that he took office at all.

## 2 September 1970

With Juan Carlos and his family. We talk of the General Election that has brought Ted Heath to power. Most of the family were in England at the time to attend the Queen Mother's early seventieth birthday party at Windsor. It took place on the day the result became known. The King sat next to Heath there, who said to him: 'You know how it is when you've got your spinnaker up in a gale, and everyone says you're sinking. Well, I looked over the side and thought we were – but by that time we were over the finishing line.' The night before, Don Juan Carlos had been at the Mirabelle. 'As the results came in, there were cheers for the Conservatives and boos for Labour – and a perfect storm of applause when Enoch Powell got a big majority. It was very shameful. We have no colour bar in Spain.'

## 8 October 1970

To St Antony's College, Oxford, for the opening of a new hall by Hilda Besse,† widow of the man who founded the college in 1950 with a donation of one and a quarter million pounds. The hall itself is an elegant and spacious

---

* Cecil Harmsworth King (1901–87), Chairman, Daily Mirror Newspapers; Chairman, International Publishing Corporation 1963–8.
† (1904–81), widow of Sir Antonin Besse (1877–1951).

building, cleverly reflecting the medieval conception of a traditional college hall.

Harold Macmillan, who presides over the ceremony as Chancellor of the university, brings much distinction to his office. To begin with, he gives his imitation of a very old man limping in with the aid of a silver-topped stick. But his speech is delightfully done. He recalls how as an undergraduate – 'alas, nearly sixty years ago' – there was only a single graduate college in Oxford, All Souls. He ends his little speech with a splendid flourish of Latinity: 'Ego, auctoritate mea, et totius universitatis . . .'*

After the ceremony has been brought to an end with a genial speech from Raymond Carr, the Warden, glasses of champagne and little canapés are brought round. Macmillan, who never much enjoys meeting new people, notices my familiar face and asks me to come and sit by him. We talk for some time and he is in excellent form. He tells me that there are two profound differences between the Oxford of today and that of his own generation. 'In 1912, the great majority of undergraduates had been sent away to school at the age of eight or nine. They may have been unhappy for a term or two, but it did teach them to stand on their own feet. By contrast, most undergraduates today have been tied to their mothers' apron strings for the whole of their lives, never having been sent away to boarding school. So, for their first year at Oxford, they are somewhat out of their depth and often lonely and unhappy. This is why so many of them go about in droves. The other difference is that women played no part at all in our lives when I was an undergraduate. Even today, a boy of eighteen is much less grown up than a girl of eighteen. It was even more so in my day.'

Macmillan tells me that he has just received an affectionately inscribed copy of the new volume of de Gaulle's memoirs, which spurs him on to complete his own. He is now on the last volume. Twice I try to leave Macmillan, not because I don't enjoy his conversation, but because it means so much more to all the dons and their wives to have a word. Twice he keeps me talking, but at last Oliver Franks comes up to him and I depart.

## 9 October 1970

I have an amusing conversation with Dick Crossman about the limits to which journalists can publish political secrets. As the editor of the *New Statesman* he does not feel himself in any way inhibited from disclosing what went on in Cabinets of which he was a member – 'Churchill and Eden had no scruples about doing so.'

---

* 'I speak by my own authority, and that of the whole university.'

## 13 October 1970

I have some political talk with Peter Carrington, who is immensely confident about the fortunes of the Government. 'It really is time we stopped worrying about Africa and concentrated on British interests.' We recall the party at the Savoy on the night of the General Election. Although practically every Tory then thought that Labour would win, he is now the only senior minister to admit it. He tells me that the following evening, when victory was known, Heath asked him and Willie Whitelaw to come and see him at No. 10 at 7.45 p.m. Knowing that the talks would last a long time, Whitelaw telephoned the Private Secretaries at Downing Street and asked for some food to be provided for Peter and himself. When eventually they emerged from the lengthy meeting with the new Prime Minister, they found a jug of beer and two pork pies. Willie was furious and said: 'We must get rid of this lot.'

Living only five miles away from Chequers, Peter is frequently invited to lunch and dine there whenever the Prime Minister has official guests. The food is perfectly appalling and the wine provided by the Government Hospitality Department is correspondingly too lavish. Thus, the other day, when Heath entertained President Nyerere of Tanzania,[*] a man who obviously had little knowledge of wine, there were unlimited bottles of Château Latour 1945, a priceless vintage. Peter was so disgusted by the extravagance of it that he asked Heath to look into the matter.

Peter tells me that it was he who was responsible for the choice of Eccles as Minister for the Arts. Originally, it was to have been Paul Channon, who although a nice chap would be a bit of a lightweight in such a post. Dining one night with David and Sybil Eccles,[†] Peter asked Sybil whether she thought David might take the job if offered it. She replied that she thought he would probably like it – though it did not carry a seat in the Cabinet. Peter reported the conversation to Heath, hence the appointment of Eccles.

When I tell Peter how wonderfully lively I found Macmillan at Birch Grove when I lunched there recently, he tells me that he and Iona[‡] also had a delightful dinner there not long ago. Macmillan greeted them by asking: 'Do you know any tycoons? A tycoon came to see me today. He is called Val Duncan[§] and he runs a thing called Rio-Tinto. Do you know it? He seemed a most amiable fellow. But would you believe it, several hours after he had

---

[*] Julius Nyerere (1922–99), first President of Tanzania 1964–85.
[†] The Hon. Sybil, Viscountess Eccles (1904–77), author, dau. of Lord Dawson of Penn, Physician to the Royal Family.
[‡] Lady Carrington (1920–2009), World War II translator; garden designer.
[§] Sir Val Duncan (1913–75), Chairman and Chief Executive, Rio Tinto-Zinc Corporation 1964–75.

lunch with us, he sent his car back with a huge pot of caviar – and what's more, we are going to eat it tonight.'

Peter also describes a lunch he had a few years ago with Ava Waverley in Lord North Street. He was asked without Iona and the other guests were Field Marshal Alexander, Macmillan, Oliver Chandos and Richard Casey. It was Alex's birthday and everyone got rather merry and sentimental. At one stage H.M. said: 'Oh, that we could live our lives over again!' Alex replied: 'I am not so sure, Harold. Would we be so successful?'

## 27 November 1970

Lunch at the American Embassy given by Walter Annenberg,[*] in honour of Lady Bird Johnson, looking very smart in bright red. Billy Graham[†] is one of the guests. Mrs Johnson is shown round the wonderfully renovated Embassy and is impressed and rather awed by all she sees. While I am talking to her, Harold Caccia joins us and proceeds to cross-examine her in a courteous, but relentless, way about precisely when she knew that L.B.J. did not intend to stand again for the Presidency. It emerges that she really knew all the time and, contrary to some opinions, was never out of his confidence.

## 29 November 1970

Through pouring rain to Magdalene College, Cambridge, to see the Master, Walter Hamilton, and hear his recollections of Linky as Provost of Eton.

As Master in College, he sat next to Linky at lunch in Hall almost every day for seven years, so got to know his character intimately. There was a blend of formality and informality about him. In the daytime he never went out without a top hat, and at night he changed into breeches and silk stockings. But his conversation was extremely unconventional, often because he wished to shock the beaks. He had, or professed to have, an ingrained contempt for schoolmasters.

In particular, he liked teasing Henry Marten,[‡] the Vice-Provost, who was terrified of him. During the wartime air raids, a 'red warning' arrived one day during a chapel service. The Provost got to his feet and said: 'The service will be discontinued. The last to leave will be the Vice-Provost and myself.' Linky said all this well knowing that Marten was nervous of air raids.

Linky once said to Hamilton: 'I am sure that whenever Henry Marten recites the Apostles' Creed, he substitutes Eton College and the Old Etonian

---

[*] (1908–2002), US Ambassador to the UK 1969–74.
[†] (1918–2018), American Christian evangelist known for his large rallies.
[‡] Sir Henry Marten (1872–1948), Provost of Eton 1945–8; private tutor of Princess Elizabeth.

Association for the Catholic Church and the Communion of Saints.'

The remarks with which Linky would preface the reading of lessons in College Chapel became famous. One day, after saying that there were two comments he wished to make, he dealt with the first point, then said: 'The second I have forgotten, but it was not very important.'

Linky loved entertaining the boys to dinner, and never minded if they became rather drunk. It was all part of the war he waged against schoolmasters. The beaks themselves were not often asked to dine.

Hamilton recalls that when his mother died, he had a charming little note from Linky which said: 'When the dead have passed, they are at peace. It is dying that is horrible.' But he showed a harsher side to his Christianity when he wrote angry letters to Kenneth Wickham, who was about to marry a divorced woman.

After his retirement, he returned to Eton only once – to attend Henry Marten's funeral. As he left the service he turned to Hamilton and said: 'I cannot think why we had that lesson about the new Heaven and the new Earth. There is nothing that Marten would dislike more.'

Having completed our talk about Linky, we discussed some general matters. Hamilton tells me that the Duke of Norfolk was one of the wittiest speakers he ever heard at Eton. The Duke came down once to talk about the Coronation, and afterwards there were questions. 'Please, sir, did the peers carry sandwiches in their coronets?' The Duke replied: 'Probably, they are capable of anything.'

## 6 December 1970

Dine in Hall at All Souls. Sit next to Philip Larkin,[*] who has a visiting fellowship here, spent in preparing an Oxford book of twentieth-century poetry. Tall, dark, sardonic, most agreeable. He earns his living as Librarian at Hull University. Larkin asks me if I know Hull. I reply that I once passed through it on my way to Hornsea for tank gunnery during the war. 'Yes,' he says, 'whenever I ask anyone if they know Hull they always reply that they once went there during the war.'

## 12 December 1970

To Cockermouth to see Claude Elliott about Linky. The house is an isolated, rather rambling place, commanding a superb view of Buttermere.

After a cup of tea we began to talk about Linky. On the very first day of

---

[*] (1922–85), poet. Librarian of Hull University 1955–85; he declined the post of Poet Laureate, which he was offered after the death of Sir John Betjeman in 1984.

Linky's first half as Provost, he told Claude on the way out of chapel: 'I must warn you that I regard the Head Master as being far too powerful, and am determined to recover the powers which the Provost used to have before the Royal Commission of 1870.' Claude goes on to tell me about some of the rows he had with Linky.

1. 'He thought that I did not beat the boys enough, but that of course was my sphere of influence not his.

2. 'At the outbreak of the war he at first refused to allow me to build air-raid shelters for the boys. He told me it was the duty of Eton to educate boys, not to protect them – which was the duty of the Government. I replied that I could not educate them if they were dead. That, I think, was almost the only time I scored off him.

3. 'I complained to him that when he invited boys to dine with him, they would invariably return to their houses almost drunk. He snapped back at me that it was none of my business.

4. 'On the question of boys' Confirmation, Linky wished to invite whatever bishop he wanted. But the Bishop of Oxford insisted that only he, or his representative, could conduct Confirmations in his diocese. Linky was particularly annoyed that the Bishop of Lincoln, the Visitor, did not put up more of a fight against this, and used to refer to "that Quisling at Lincoln".

5. 'At the beginning of the war, there was a meeting at the Charterhouse in London of Chairmen of Governing Bodies and Headmasters of public schools, to discuss the admission of boys who had been educated at state schools. Archbishop Lang* was in the chair. On the way up to London, Linky, who hated the whole idea, told Claude: "I can deal with Lang. One only has to be rude to him and he will collapse." That is precisely what happened. This could be explained by Linky's belief that if one was ever to get what one wanted, one had to begin by being extremely rude and offensive. Another belief of Linky's was that all schoolmasters and bishops were stupid.'

## 15 December 1970

Edward Ford tells me that my Curzon book has fired one of his sons with a passion for history which he has never shown before. This gives me a great deal of pleasure.

---

* Cosmo Gordon Lang, 1st Baron Lang of Lambeth (1864–1945), Archbishop of Canterbury 1928–42.

## 17 December 1970

Talk to Selwyn Lloyd. He is very depressed as there are rumours that yet another candidate may be put up against him for the Speakership. Whether he gets it or not, the whole episode is likely to rankle in his memory.

## 19 December 1970

Martin Gilliat calls for me at 6.15 to drive me down to his house at Welwyn for the weekend. He has been acting as a steward at Ascot this afternoon, where he had to take the Queen, Princess Margaret and a covey of Royal children to see a race from one of the jumps. 'The trouble is,' he says, 'they never know when they have had enough. Having seen one race, they insisted on staying there for another. It was not easy to interest them in an open ditch for forty minutes. But I enjoyed hearing the Queen tell Princess Margaret, dressed in bright yellow, not to get too close to the fence in case she frightened the horses.'

## 20 December 1970

Martin drives me over to Hatfield. I find Bobbety writing letters at his desk, perched on the edge of a chair with his nose on the paper, exactly like a schoolboy. I give him a report of my researches up to date and tell him that my only fear at present is from the vast bulk of material available. He hopes that nothing will be dropped which could add to the portrait of his family. That, he believes, is more important than political material.

We are actually in the room which his grandfather used as his study when Prime Minister, and Bobbety is writing at the desk which contains slots into which the P.M. could put secret papers after reading them. These slots went down into locked drawers, of which the Private Secretaries had a key.

'One feature of my grandfather's life', he says, 'is that we tend to forget how little London had grown in his day. When my father was a child, he would ride by the side of his mother's carriage from Hatfield to London. It was utterly unspoiled until one got to Swiss Cottage.'

Bobbety also tells me that Linky had a vivid dislike of garden cities. He felt that as Adam and Eve had fallen in a garden, there could be no redemption of mankind through garden cities.

In the evening I hear that it is announced that John Boyd-Carpenter is not to allow his name to be put forward as a candidate for the Speakership of the House of Commons against Selwyn Lloyd. But there is still a lot of backbench grumbling at the lack of consultation that took place.

## 22 December 1970

Talk to Selwyn Lloyd. Although fairly certain that he will be elected Speaker of the Commons on 12 January, he is sick at heart about the subterranean campaign being waged by the disappointed candidate, John Boyd-Carpenter and his henchmen. One of the most active is Brandon Rhys-Williams,* who last Saturday called unexpectedly and uninvited to see Selwyn at St James's Court to try to persuade him to stand down in favour of Boyd-Carpenter.

Dine at Pratt's, where the Prime Minister comes in – his first visit to the club. Heath does not seem to fit too easily into Pratt's. When Andrew Devonshire greets him rather fulsomely, the PM says uncomfortably: 'I just came in for a bite of food.'

Later on Willie Whitelaw and Selwyn come in and dine. I have a private word with Willie afterwards. He confirms that Selwyn will certainly be elected Speaker, but deplores the dirty battle being waged by 'that goat Rhys-Williams'. He adds: 'If by chance Boyd-Carpenter had been the first choice, Selwyn would have vanished from the scene.'

I notice that most members of the club, including myself, have given £5 to the Christmas Fund for the staff. Harold Macmillan has given £2.

---

* Sir Brandon Rhys-Williams, 2nd Bt (1927–88), Conservative politician. MP for Kensington South 1968–74, then Kensington 1974–88. He was known for his lively sense of humour. Once, in the Smoking Room of the House of Commons, a fellow MP read out incredulously a story in the *Evening Standard* that a madam was offering at her establishment a three-course dinner, wine and a woman for £25. 'At that price', interjected Rhys-Williams, 'I don't think the wine will be up to much.'

# 1971

*The Troubles in Northern Ireland continued throughout the year. In America there were protests against the continuing Vietnam War. On 5 February Apollo 14, the third US manned Moon expedition, landed in the lunar highlands. On 15 February Britain adopted decimal currency. On 16 May the stage premiere of Benjamin Britten's television opera* Owen Wingrave *was performed at Covent Garden. On 24 June the EEC agreed the terms for Britain's proposed membership. On 30 July Apollo 15 landed on the Moon and the next day the astronauts took a six-and-a-half-hour electric car ride on the Moon. On 17 September the former Soviet leader Nikita Khrushchev died. On 24 September Britain expelled ninety Russian diplomats for spying. On 28 October the House of Commons voted in favour of joining the EEC by 356 to 244.*

### 7 January 1971

Dine with Selwyn Lloyd at the Turf Club. He is deeply depressed by the murmurs of opposition to his proposed election as Speaker next Tuesday. He recalls how, when Alec Douglas-Home first became Prime Minister in 1963, he was alone with Alec and Elizabeth in their Foreign Office flat in Carlton Gardens. Various ministers then telephoned Alec to tell him they would not serve under him. At which Elizabeth commented: 'This job is beginning to stink.' Selwyn continues: 'Well, that is exactly what I now feel about the Speakership.'

We discuss in some detail the finances of the job. As Speaker he receives £8,500 a year, of which the first £4,000 is tax-free. As he has a reasonable private income, he intends to spend a great deal on entertainment. He himself is able to lunch out, but never to dine out while Parliament is sitting. He also receives the use of a car from the official pool whenever he needs it.

As we both agree that he will in fact be elected Speaker on Tuesday, we give some thought to the various little speeches he will have to make, and I provide a good quotation for him – Speaker Lenthall's remark to Charles I when the King came to demand the arrest of the five Members: 'I have neither eyes to see nor tongue to speak in this House but as this House is pleased to direct me.'* I promise him though that I will not mention in my column Lord Rosebery's view of the Speakership: 'There is much exaggeration about the attainments requisite for a Speaker. All Speakers are highly successful, all Speakers are deeply regretted and are generally announced to be irreplaceable. But a Speaker is soon found, almost invariably, among the mediocrities of the House.'

An interesting reminiscence of Selwyn's days as Minister of State at the Foreign Office. He was handling the negotiations for the Bonn agreements that gave Germany her independence, and insisted that by fair means or foul we should release all war criminals in our charge, so that Anglo-German negotiations could get off to a good start. The only war criminals over which he had no control were those such as Rudolf Hess,† held jointly with the Russians in Spandau Jail.

### 9 January 1971

Catch the 12.30 train to Exeter, then catch a little local train that runs through a charming valley to Umberleigh, where Jeremy Thorpe meets me with the car. First we collect little Rupert from a village party, then look at the church where Jeremy hopes to erect a memorial window to Caroline. Unfortunately, there has been some local opposition to it from the parochial council, who at present are determined to retain the very ugly Victorian window – in spite of a similar one having been removed some time ago to make way for a private memorial.

Much political gossip. Jeremy tells me that it was his idea that Lloyd George's only surviving daughter, Olwen Carey Evans, should be made a Dame of the British Empire. He suggested it to George Thomas,‡ the then Secretary of State for Wales, who eventually replied that the award could not be made 'as she was a Lady already'. Such was his pathetic knowledge of styles and titles.

I am always amused by Jeremy's love of the ceremonial. At the time of the Prince of Wales's Investiture he borrowed a Privy Councillor's uniform, hoping that he would be able to wear it on the day. All depended on whether

---

* William Lenthall (1591–1662), appointed Lord Lenthall under the Protectorate, lawyer and Speaker of the House of Commons 1640–47, 1647–53, 1654–5 and 1659–60.

† (1894–1987), prominent Nazi politician who flew solo to Scotland in 1941 in an attempt to broker a peace with the Duke of Hamilton (1903–73), who was in the first flight over Mount Everest in 1933. Hess's plane crashed near Eaglesham and Hess was taken to Giffnock police station. After the Nuremberg trials he was imprisoned in Spandau Prison.

‡ 1st Viscount Tonypandy (1909–97), Labour politician. Speaker of the House of Commons 1976–83.

Ted Heath, not yet Prime Minister, would do so. Ted said no, so Jeremy too had to wear morning dress.

### 11 January 1971

Bishop Westall, Bishop of Crediton,* comes to lunch. He is an extraordinarily kind and jolly man, who has become a very close friend of Jeremy's since Caroline's death. He drives me back to Exeter in his car and we have a great deal of talk on the way. He tells me that his fine episcopal ring was given to him by John Betjeman. When he first received the present, it contained a tiny relic of St Vincent. But one day at lunch the ring fell on the floor, dislodging the little piece of mica which protected the relic, and the relic itself was instantly gobbled up by his dog. When people heard of this, they used to raise their hats to the dog in the street.

### 15 January 1971

Lunch with Julian Faber at his office in the City. Julian is full of good sardonic stories, particularly about his father-in-law, Harold Macmillan. I have never before heard Harold Macmillan's comment on having turned down the Garter: 'One cannot join every club one is asked to.' Julian adds that 'as one of nature's schoolmasters' Harold would very much like to have been Provost of Eton. He might have got it, but at the time Lady Dorothy was still alive. She had a passionate love for the garden at Birch Grove, and did not even accompany Harold to Chequers.

Julian talks about 'Harty-Tarty', the 8th Duke of Devonshire.† When King George V and Queen Mary came to stay at Chatsworth, the Duke was told by Clive Wigram‡ that the King would straight away like to present him with the GCVO. The Duke rather churlishly replied: 'I hope it won't interfere with my dressing for dinner.' In fact it did, and he came down to dinner ten minutes late, with the GCVO star upside down and all his fly buttons undone.

Julian has a particular dislike of Eton housemasters who cannot help becoming arrogant when parents are so cringing in their behaviour.

He tells me a story of Khrushchev's visit to Oxford in 1956. Among the colleges that they visited was Pembroke, where the Master§ apologised for

---

* Wilfrid Westall (1900–82), Anglican Suffragan Bishop of Crediton 1954–74.

† Spencer Cavendish Devonshire (1833–1908). Leader of the Liberal Party in the House of Commons 1875–80; Liberal Unionist Party 1886–1903; and of the Unionists in the House of Lords 1902–3.

‡ Clive Wigram, 1st Baron Wigram (1873–1960), PS to George V 1931–6.

§ Ronald McCallum (1898–1973), Master of Pembroke Coll., Oxford 1955–67. Dr Samuel Johnson (1709–1784) attended Pembroke Coll. 1728–9.

having so little of interest to show the Russians. 'But', he added, 'we do have Dr Johnson's teapot.' Khrushchev beamed: 'But of course we are so interested in seeing Dr Hewlett Johnson's teapot.'

### 17 January 1971, letter to his mother

I am glad Selwyn became Speaker after all, although his critics took a lot of the sugar off the prize. It was very nasty of them to propose poor Sir Geoffrey de Freitas,* without even consulting him. The case for having a secret ballot next time the Speakership is vacant has surely been accepted. Still, Selwyn is a tough nut and quite used to the ways of political life. Boyd-Carpenter didn't behave as well as was imagined. He withdrew as a candidate only after it became quite clear he would not win.

### 19 January 1971

Leo d'Erlanger[†] tells me the story of Lord Duveen,[‡] who once on his travels met a lady with whom he spent the night. The next day she asked him for his card. Fearing blackmail, Duveen gave her the card of his lawyer, which he happened to have in his pocket book. Some years later, the lawyer was astonished to have been left a legacy of some £½ million from someone he had never met!

### 20 January 1971

Talk to Jonathan Aitken to ask how his morale is keeping up during the Official Secrets trial at the Old Bailey.[§] He sounds cheerful, although he expects his legal expenses to total about £10,000 – more than one-third of his capital. But the National Union of Journalists and his grandmother are both contributing, and he hopes that Hartwell[¶] may make a contribution, however unwillingly. So far the attitude of Hartwell has been that Aitken

---

* (1913–82), Labour politician and diplomat. British High Commissioner to Ghana 1961–4. The Conservative MP Robin Maxwell-Hyslop (1931–2010) was a key figure at this time, not because he had objections to Selwyn Lloyd personally – he believed Lloyd in fact made an excellent Speaker – but because he did not think the Speakership should be settled at the whim of the government. See D.R. Thorpe, 'Sir Robert Maxwell-Hyslop', *DNB*.

† Baron Leo d'Erlanger (1898–1978), banker.

‡ Joseph Duveen, 1st Baron Duveen (1869–1939), influential art dealer.

§ In 1971 Aitken, a prospective parliamentary candidate, was accused under the Official Secrets Act of passing classified information to the *Sunday Telegraph* about the Biafran War in Nigeria. He was acquitted of all charges. Selwyn Lloyd, as Speaker, did appear as a witness for the defence.

¶ Michael Berry, Baron Hartwell (1911–2001), newspaper proprietor. Chairman and Editor of the *Daily Telegraph* 1954–87 and of the *Sunday Telegraph* from 1961.

landed an honest and unsuspecting *Sunday Telegraph* in a criminal case.

### 21 January 1971

Lunch with Jonathan Aitken at Diviani's restaurant, just outside the Old Bailey. Technically, he and his co-defendants should lunch in the cells below the court. But the judge has given them dispensation to lunch out as long as each is accompanied by his solicitor. We have a jolly table with Antonia Fraser. Jonathan tells me he is a little upset by Selwyn Lloyd, his godfather, who gave evidence of character on his behalf at the magistrates' court. But Selwyn now says that it would be a breach of privilege to call the Speaker to give evidence in the Old Bailey. My own view is that it would not in any way be a breach of privilege unless he received a subpoena against his will. But I expect he does not wish to be associated with the case, having so recently been elected to his high office.

In the evening I attend a party given at the Arts Council building in Piccadilly to mark the publication of a volume about lending rights and authors. Lord Goodman[*] makes a neat little speech in defence of an author's right to receive some reward every time his book is borrowed from a library. Also have some cheerful talk on publishing matters with Graham Greene[†] and Jock Murray.

### 30 January 1971

To Eastbourne on the train to stay with Hartley Shawcross at Friston. Very interesting talk at dinner with Laurence Olivier and his wife, Joan Plowright,[‡] a nice, tough, down-to-earth woman. She tells me how she and Larry love living in Brighton. When acting in London they catch the 11 p.m. *Brighton Belle* home each night, dining late on the train. Larry is soon to return to the stage after a longish interval of ill health, as Shylock. He will wear Victorian dress and appear as a sort of Rothschild with special teeth that make his upper lip curl back.

Olivier looks in good health and has an attractive, agreeable manner, though somewhat melodramatic. He tells me that his peerage, announced last June, has still not been gazetted. Garter King of Arms[§] refuses to allow him to call himself plain Lord Olivier as still some descendants of his uncle

---

[*] Arnold Goodman, Baron Goodman (1915–95), lawyer and political adviser.
[†] Graham C. Greene (1936–2016), publisher. MD of Jonathan Cape 1962–90; Chairman, British Museum 1996–2002.
[‡] Baroness Olivier (b. 1929), theatre and film actress.
[§] Sir Anthony Wagner (1908–95), Garter King of Arms 1961–78.

Lord Olivier* alive. He is, incidentally, astonished that I know all about Lord Olivier and his membership of the first Labour Government. But Larry is persisting, and has so far won the concession that he may have his way if all surviving descendants of his uncle give their formal consent. He will not bother to ask for supporters for his arms, but would like an imaginative crest including an Avon swan and the chain of Henry V and a player's crown. He still wishes to be known in the theatre as Sir Laurence, not Lord Olivier.

## 6 February 1971

Go with Edward Ford to lunch with Leo d'Erlanger. Freddie Birkenhead is also there. He is at present working on what may turn out to be rather a large book on Winston Churchill, his godfather – a more colourful supplement to the official documented biography now being produced by Martin Gilbert after Randolph Churchill's death. We all agree that Randolph's first two volumes, in spite of being largely written for him by a team of researchers, were very trashy – and that the reviewers, almost to a man, wildly overpraised the work.†

Return through Banbury and Edward takes me to look at St Mary's Church, a very fine classical building. In the evening I talk to Edward about the Suez operation in 1956. As in almost every other house in the country, it caused a split in the secretariat at Buckingham Palace. Edward and Martin Charteris were against it, Michael Adeane was for it. Their conflicting attitudes rather puzzled the Queen, who said: 'I have three Private Secretaries and all of them give me different advice.' Edward thinks it a pity that Prince Philip was out of the country at the time. With his instinctive mistrust of politicians, he might otherwise have stiffened the Queen to insist that Eden should not commit us to a dangerous military adventure against the wishes of both our American allies and other countries of the Commonwealth.

Some years after Suez Bobbety Salisbury, referring to proposals that we should bomb Rhodesia in order to bring the Smith regime to heel, publicly said that such a use of force would be justified only by (a) the defence of our country, and (b) treaty obligation. Edward thereupon wrote to him to ask him in which category Bobbety would put Suez.

---

* Sydney Olivier, 1st Baron Olivier (1859–1943), Secretary of State for India 1924.
† Lord Birkenhead's incomplete *Churchill 1876–1922* was published posthumously (Harrap, 1989). K.R. was similarly critical of the next six volumes of the official Churchill biography by Martin Gilbert.

## 26 February 1971

I tell Walter Annenberg how much I enjoyed meeting Billy Graham at the lunch at the American Embassy that he gave for Mrs Lady Bird Johnson. He tells me that at a recent dinner at the Embassy, Alec Douglas-Home, talking of international affairs, said to Billy Graham, 'I wonder why the Almighty in his wisdom put so much of the world oil in the Middle East?' Billy Graham replied: 'I'll ask him.'

## 6 March 1971

Go down to Eton to stay the weekend with Giles St Aubyn. I meet Michael Meredith,* the young beak who is School Librarian, and he shows me over the reconstructed school library, to be reopened by the Queen Mother to-morrow. It has been most elegantly done. All those gloomy desks have been removed, and in the centre is a huge mushroom that provides a well-lit reading space. I give him several volumes for the library and ask him to come to my flat one day to choose some more Etoniana and other works.

Although very pressed by final arrangements of the opening of the library by the Queen Mother, Meredith very kindly lets me take away the three bound volumes of the *Eton College Chronicle* that cover Linky's years as Provost. I work on them for the rest of the day. What astonishes me is that the issue of 28 September 1939, the first after the outbreak of the war, makes no single mention of anything to do with the war. The leading article is on the events of the summer half, and there is a letter on the effect of batting first on the outcome of the Harrow match at Lord's.

## 7 March 1971

Work in my room most of the morning, then to Election Chamber at 12.30 for the Provost's lunch in honour of the Queen Mother. Giles tells me that there is much resentment at Eton against the Provost in general, and against his handling of today's arrangements in particular. Apart from the Head Master and the Lower Master, the only beak to be asked to meet the Queen Mother is Michael Meredith. Apparently this is characteristic of Caccia's contempt towards the teaching staff – they are practically never invited to the Lodge, least of all on grand occasions. Today Caccia ought obviously to have given a cocktail party from 12 noon to 12.45 to meet the beaks; as it is, none of them will even have set eyes upon her.

The Queen Mother, dressed very engagingly in a mustard-coloured coat, is taken round the room by the Provost and has a bright smile and welcome

---

* (b. 1943), Eton Coll. Librarian for many years.

for everybody. Many of the other guests are old friends, including Peter Carrington and Bobbety Salisbury, who discusses further some of the people
whom I ought to go and see about Lady Gwendolen.

We have a most excellent lunch in Hall, preceded and followed by a Latin
grace – as if the Reformation had never taken place. The Queen Mother
enjoys herself hugely and stops to talk to the boys on the way out.

I am most amused to notice how many of the distinguished authors who
are present today sidle up to the library catalogue and pull out a drawer to
see whether their own books are in the library.

Martin Gilliat also has the time of his life greeting everybody and eventually departs in the wake of his employer, saying rather too loudly: 'Well, it
wasn't much of a lunch, so we must get back and have poached eggs for tea.'

There is a little cluster of boys waiting to see the Queen Mother off, but
they appear to be more interested in the car than in its owner.

### 19 March 1971

Alec Douglas-Home tells me how distressing and painful he finds it to be
shouted down by unmannerly and pointless interruptions in the House of
Commons, and thinks that this is a new unwelcome development in parliamentary life. I assure him that it has sometimes been worse – and that in 1910
Hugh Cecil shouted down the Prime Minister Asquith for a full half-hour.

### 6 April 1971

At 5.30 to the House of Commons, where I have a drink alone with Selwyn
Lloyd in his sumptuous Speaker's House. He himself opens the door to
me looking very elegant in knee-breeches. He tells me that he is surprised
how much work the job involves. He has to spend most of the morning on
administrative tasks and points to a large pile of files. Controlling debates,
particularly the storms of Question Time, is also exhausting.

Selwyn takes me on a tour of his private rooms looking out over the river;
downstairs he has another magnificent set of state apartments. The private
rooms are agreeable in a Pugin-like way, with heavy oak furniture. But
Speaker King redecorated the walls with the most hideous suburban paper.
Selwyn hopes to have it all replaced. All in all, he tells me, he is enjoying
himself. He obviously relishes the deference paid to him as Speaker, and
likes being asked to dine at Buckingham Palace again. At the end of much
excellent talk and whisky, we go down to his library where a man in a white
tie helps him on with his robe, then lifts a wig from a wig-stand and helps
him adjust it at a large looking-glass. I then take my leave while he makes his
stately way back to the Chamber.

## 7 April 1971

To the Foreign Office at 4 p.m. First, I have a few minutes with John Leahy,[*] Head of the News Department, who at one time was Selwyn Lloyd's Private Secretary. He recalls that when Selwyn had temporary charge of the Foreign Office as Minister of State, he had to endure a great deal of interference from Winston, especially about the verbosity of official minutes.

I am then taken to the Foreign Secretary's room, where I have a long talk alone with Alec Douglas-Home. As always, he gives one the impression that one is bestowing a huge favour by having come to see him. He maintains the same agreeable and relaxed manner throughout our entire talk.

First, we discuss what differences he finds between being Foreign Secretary now – including responsibility for the Commonwealth – and occupying the same position ten years ago. He does find the strain rather more, particularly the House of Commons. Ten years ago he was in the House of Lords. He also has to deal with a much greater bulk of paper nowadays. This he attributes to people dictating into machines rather than writing more concisely by hand. 'I have often reminded an Ambassador that if he wants to tell me the story of his life, he should make it a serial rather than a single huge volume!' He himself writes in longhand and rarely needs to correct it afterwards.

His morning begins at 6.45, when he works for one and a half to two hours. The difference in time between London and Washington means that he sometimes has to work very late at night. But he rarely goes through his boxes then. He mentions that whereas ten years ago Foreign Office telegrams used to come to him twice a day, there are now three deliveries.

With Peter Carrington in mind, I ask him whether it would still be possible today for a Foreign Secretary to sit in the Lords. He sees absolutely no obstacle to it, and thinks that the Opposition would soon come to accept it.

Discussing foreign journeys, he says: 'I think there is a lot to be said for directing foreign policy from a desk. It is less tiring. But, of course, one must travel a certain amount to attend meetings of security bodies, such as SEATO and NATO.' At the end of April he is going to Ankara for a CENTO[†] meeting.

We also talk about the progress being made on implementing the Val Duncan Report on the Diplomatic Service, 1969. The question of setting up an Estates Board to decide which Embassies should be bought and which

---

[*] Sir John Leahy (1928–2015), Ambassador to South Africa 1979–82; High Commissioner in Australia 1984–8.
[†] The Central Treaty Organization was formed in 1955 by Iran, Iraq, Pakistan, Turkey and the UK. It was dissolved in 1979.

rented is now being discussed. Alec agrees with me that in the past we ought to have bought more properties rather than leasing them. The present Government will not rebuild the Foreign Office, although he wishes to see the working conditions improved by interior structural alterations. The Duncan Committee wished us to reduce the size of the Diplomatic Service, and we have done so. Alec adds: 'I will never accept the recommendation of the Committee that the passport should become a limp document. It must always have a stiff cover.' As Alec shows me to the door of his room, I notice that all the newspapers are folded and unread, except for the *Daily Telegraph*, looking rather worn and open at the racing page.

### 1 May 1971

To Cambridge to attend the reopening by Rab Butler of the restored Wren Library at Trinity.\* Mollie has kindly asked me to a lunch party in the Lodge afterwards. Before we sit down I meet Lord Rothschild[†] and find him far more agreeable than I had been led to expect. He is not a man to bear fools gladly, but once one talks to him about the problems of Government and administration, he talks extraordinarily well. We discuss the Government 'Think Tank' over which he now presides. He is much impressed by Ted Heath, the only Prime Minister he has come across who really listens to what people tell him. He also mentions that he is an honorary member of Pratt's. But Rothschild says that so far he has been too frightened to enter the doors of the club. This leads us to some jolly jokes about C.P. Snow and how naïve he is to suppose that great decisions of State are always taken in clubs such as Pratt's and the Beefsteak.

### 6 May 1971

Some lively talk at a book launch at Brown's Hotel. As always, I enjoy talking to Alan Taylor. He says; 'The man who was really responsible for World War II was Edvard Beneš.[‡] In 1938 the Czechs should have gone to war with Germany. They would have beaten them.' He also tells me that his biography of Beaverbrook is approaching completion.

Mark Barrington-Ward[§] tells me a good Linky remark. Eager to

---

\* Designed by Christopher Wren (1632–1722) in 1676 and completed in 1695.

† Victor Rothschild, 3rd Baron Rothschild (1910–90), zoologist and public servant. Victor Rothschild was the subject of K.R.'s last biography in 2003, *Elusive Rothschild: The Life of Victor, Third Baron* (Weidenfeld & Nicolson). K.R. also wrote the notice of Rothschild's life for the *DNB*.

‡ (1884–1948), President of Czechoslovakia 1935–8 and 1939–48.

§ (b. 1927), Editor of the *Oxford Mail* 1961–79.

get back to the Provost's Lodge for breakfast, he shouted to the Conduct of Eton at the end of Holy Communion: 'Be quicker with the washing-up.'

Frank Longford says that Mountbatten congratulated him on becoming a Knight of the Garter with the words: 'What an <u>imaginative</u> appointment . . .'

## 25 May 1971

I am to fly to Japan to interview the Emperor Hirohito before he arrives on his State Visit here in October. John Pilcher, the Ambassador, has guaranteed the audience, which might be the only one given by the Emperor.[*] I shall not be able to quote him directly, but there are all sorts of ways by which one can tell precisely what one's subject has said.

## 28 May 1971

Talk to Angus Ogilvy about visiting the Emperor of Japan. He did so with Princess Alexandra a few years ago. He says that there were some odd features about it. Lunch was forty-five minutes late while all the protocol experts decided in exactly what order they should all go into the dining room. It was made clear to them that they should only address the Emperor in lower tones than he used. But as he happened to have a sore throat that day, Alexandra had to whisper and Angus merely mouthed.

## 2 June 1971

Lunch with George Weidenfeld. We discus Isaiah Berlin's OM, which George thinks is hardly deserved. He adds: 'One can divide all British Jews into two sorts – those who can do no right and those who can do no wrong. Isaiah belongs to the second category.'

## 18 June 1971

Waterloo Day – and of course the anniversary of the destruction of the Guards' Chapel twenty-seven years ago.

Lunch at Kensington Palace with Prince William of Gloucester to hear about Japan. William talks of the hidebound Japanese court officials who run the Emperor's life and are drawn from the higher ranks of the police. He tells me that what he says may differ from what John Pilcher will tell me: William knew a far younger generation than John, with less reverence for the established order. Thus William came to the conclusion that the Japanese

---

[*] Hirohito (1901–89), 124th Emperor of Japan 1926–89. Sir John Pilcher (1912–90), Ambassador to Austria 1965–7 and to Japan 1967–72.

may well be working secretly on the research for atomic weapons; John apparently doubts this.

The Emperor himself is very withdrawn and difficult of access. 'When one has been demoted from being a god, there is nothing much left.' No real attempt at public relations has been made. But the Emperor does like recalling his visits to London before the war. William suggests that I should ask him about pollution. The Japanese think that England still broods under Dickensian pea-soup fog, whereas it is in Tokyo that one finds it at its densest. And virtually the whole of the country looks like the East End of London. To avoid the dirtiness of the sea, the Emperor has had to move his summer residence. He still lives most of the time in rather a humble little house, but receives visitors in a huge new ugly palace nearby. William will kindly send me a rare copy of the Emperor's diary of his last visit to London.

### 29 June 1971
Party at the Italian Embassy. I have some talk with Ted Heath, very friendly. He tells me he will personally present the insignia of an honorary KBE to George Solti[*] at Covent Garden after his farewell performance as Music Director of *Tristan und Isolde*.[†] When I mention how pleased I am that he has similarly honoured Rudolf Bing, he proclaims: 'I am sometimes accused of being too generous to the Arts. But it is a reproach I can bear.'

### 7 July 1971
I ask Bobbety Salisbury point-blank why he resigned from Macmillan's Government in 1957 on what was apparently a trivial issue – whether or not Archbishop Makarios should be brought back from the Seychelles to Cyprus to take part in further discussions with the British Government. Bobbety replied: 'I opposed it both on personal grounds and as a matter of principle. I should have had to justify it to the House of Lords, and felt myself unable to do so. I also felt that it would encourage other rebels such as Kenyatta.[‡] Rather than that, I resigned.'

### 8 July 1971
Peter Carrington full of good stories about Harold Macmillan. Peter said to

---

[*] (1912–97), conductor. Music Director of the Royal Opera House 1961–71 and of the Chicago Symphony Orchestra 1969–91.

[†] This event took place on 3 July 1971 at Covent Garden, an occasion at which I was present. When Solti took British citizenship in 1972, his honorary KBE became a substantive knighthood and he was known as Sir Georg Solti.

[‡] Jomo Kenyatta (1891–1978), first President of Kenya 1964–78.

him the other day: 'I see you everywhere.' Macmillan replied: 'Yes, it's my season.' At Lord Portal's funeral the other day, old Lord Moran, whose diaries about his time as Churchill's doctor so scandalised the Churchill family, was put next to Lady Churchill. Macmillan, Peter says, observed this gaffe 'with scandalous delight'. And when Peter and Macmillan were the guests of Val Duncan on a picnic, Macmillan looked round and said: 'The classic cast for a detective story – the retired Prime Minister, the captain of industry and the Secretary of State for Defence.'

### 21 July 1971

Long talk with Bobbety Salisbury about the Cecil family. I begin by asking him why so many of his family have chosen politics as a career and whether he believes that there is a place in politics for the disinterested aristocrat. He replies that vocations are often hereditary, the influences and pressures under which one is brought up. 'We were all brought up in a political atmosphere, and went into politics from a sense of personal responsibility rather than from ambition. What have I to gain from going to the House of Lords every day at the age of seventy-seven? I feel I have a certain experience to offer, but little tangible to gain.'

His grandfather, the Prime Minister, Bobbety continues, did not worry much about political ideals; but he was a master of expediency. He used to say that at one time he had thought that bus drivers controlled the traffic. Later he came to the conclusion that their task was merely to avoid accidents. That was the lesson he applied to foreign affairs: one knew where one wanted to go, and one had to manoeuvre carefully to get there. Old Lord Salisbury was at heart a modest man, and listened to the views of others with much deference – even if he was not swayed by them. In Cabinet he would not infrequently say, after listening to his colleagues, 'Well, I am afraid I must be wrong.' He once translated the family motto 'Sero sed serio'* as 'Unpunctual but hungry'.

Another example of old Lord Salisbury's austerity. As an undergraduate at Christ Church he disliked the Bullingdon set. It was his mistrust of Christ Church that led him to send his own sons to Univ. Gladstone was loathed, and the family used to say that 'GOM' stood for God's Only Mistake.

### 24 July 1971

I hear that Maynard Keynes once said: 'A terrible thing has happened. Lydia,† my wife, has discovered the credit system.'

---

* 'Late but in earnest'.
† Lydia Lopokova, Baroness Keynes (1892–1981), Russian ballerina.

## 4 August 1971

My visit to Moscow. An Intourist guide with a car and a driver is waiting for me outside the hotel at 10 a.m. The guide is a thin, nervous, dark-haired girl who speaks good English. First, we drive round the Kremlin. It is extraordinarily attractive in the sunshine, a wonderful jumble of eighteenth-century palaces and little churches with striped or golden domes. There are already vast queues waiting to file through Lenin's black and gold granite tomb. We are to inspect it in detail this afternoon. Meanwhile we drive right round the city, with several of those terrible square sugar-cakes similar to the ones I first saw in Warsaw. They house various Ministries. Lots of monuments everywhere, including one to Chaliapin.[*] Then, in the same key as it were, to the nunnery that was the first scene of *Boris Godunov*. It has a dusty, unattractive garden. To the grandiose Moscow University where I am subjected to a torrent of statistics. A good view over the city.

At 12 noon to the British Embassy to call on Sir Duncan Wilson,[†] who is shortly leaving for England on his retirement from the Diplomatic Service. He is to become Master of Corpus Christi, Cambridge. He is a tall, bespectacled, donnish figure, with an irreverent turn of phrase and a ready laugh. We go out into the garden and sit on a wooden seat. He says one must assume that everyone is photographed in the garden and that all conversations are recorded, but he wonders whether the Russians really bother to accumulate and examine such a mass of reports.

Although the Embassy commands a fine view over the river towards the Kremlin and has some handsome rooms for entertaining, he dislikes it. It was once the house of a rich sugar merchant, so is utterly unsuitable for offices; and the study built on for the Ambassador into the garden is far too large. There is a possibility that we shall be given a different site by the Russians. But it will be a good one. Great Britain has the diplomatic numberplate prefix 01 – the sort of thing that still counts in Russia.

We move on to British political gossip. He expresses a profound scorn for Harold Wilson. When George [Brown] came to the Embassy his behaviour gave the Russians a great deal to talk about.

A characteristic remark of Rab Butler when someone spoke to him of Duncan Wilson's appointment to be Master of Corpus: 'Yes, but it is a very small college.'

Duncan Wilson is absorbingly interesting on Ted Heath. Every year he

---

[*] Feodor Chaliapin (1873–1938), Russian opera singer.
[†] (1911–83), Ambassador to the Soviet Union 1968–71; Master of Corpus Christi Coll., Cambridge 1971–80.

goes to stay with John Morrison, now Lord Margadale of Islay,[*] and has often found Heath there. 'He learns to shoot and fish, and will no doubt become very good at it. But he will never enjoy it.' The younger Morrison boy, Peter,[†] told me a story about Heath which I did not think reflected credit on him. Apparently, one evening they were once all playing Racing Demon at Islay. But Heath, never having had a childhood, did not know how to play. So he was taught, and then insisted on playing till all hours, keeping everyone up, until he won.

Lunch at the restaurant next door to the hotel. At 2.30 set out again with my Intourist guide, this time on foot to see some of the churches of the Kremlin. All are now museums, filled with splendid icons, altar pieces, vestments and other treasures.

In the evening I stroll out to Red Square in the warm twilight air, and by chance see the changing of the guard at Lenin's tomb. There are two men perpetually on guard outside the doors, which are slightly ajar. They are absolutely motionless, a very fine feat of discipline. The changeover is done at immense speed and the guards, when on the move, do the goose step. There are gasps and titters from the many Americans watching the spectacle.

## 6 August 1971

I fly on to Tokyo from Moscow. Very hot and damp. But John Pilcher is at the airport with an air-conditioned Rolls-Royce. The drive through the endless suburbs of Tokyo is slow and unlovely: an appalling vista of shanties and Coca-Cola signs.

Discuss with John the course my interview with Emperor Hirohito is likely to take on Friday. He warns me that the Emperor is a very nervous man, much afflicted by head-wagging and by an uneasy stomach. Neither he nor the court has any sense of public relations. He is particularly determined never to exceed his utterly non-political role as laid down by the Constitution. The idea of public engagement by the Japanese Royal Family is far removed from ours. Thus it was not he but the Crown Prince who actually declared open Expo 67. They accept few, and those they do carry out are paid for by the organisation concerned. This is characteristic of a mercenary streak that goes through Japanese life. John recently attended the cremation

---

[*]  1st Baron Margadale of Islay (1906–96), Conservative MP for Salisbury 1942–65; Chairman, 1922 Committee 1955–64.

[†]  Sir Peter Morrison (1944–95), Conservative MP for Chester 1974–92; Parliamentary PS to Margaret Thatcher July–Nov. 1990.

of a very rich man, and, like all the other mourners, was asked to contribute to the funeral expenses.

## 12 August 1971

The day before my audience with the Emperor, John Pilcher tells me a good story of how he went to see Lord Cobbold,* the Lord Chamberlain, about the Emperor's State Visit to London, mentioning to him among other matters that the Emperor hated very hot food. 'That's splendid,' Cobbold replied, 'the food at Buckingham Palace is always stone-cold.'

## 13 August 1971

At 2.45 I leave with John Pilcher in the Rolls for the Imperial Palace. We drive in through the main gates over a moat full of pink lotus flowers, past rather scruffy sentries in blue uniform. At the door of the Imperial Palace there is quite a large group of courtiers awaiting us. Characteristically, one of them is staring at his watch. We are received with many bows and conducted up huge flights of carpeted steps and along broad passages. Behind the courtiers hover footmen in dark blue. First, we are taken to an ante-room and given tea. One of the courtiers then explains exactly where we are to sit when received by the Emperor. After a few minutes we are on the move again. We come to some double doors guarded by more footmen. Then a little light begins to shine and a buzzer to sound. One of the footmen turns them off, then he and the other footmen simultaneously slide open the doors. A few yards inside the room stands the Emperor. We all bow and then sit down at the far end of the room. There are two rows, each of three armchairs, facing each other. The Emperor sits in the middle of one. Immediately opposite the Emperor sits John Pilcher and I sit on his right.

The entire palace is brand-new, but very hideous, lacking the sparse dignity of a traditional Japanese house. The Emperor wears a charcoal-grey single-breasted suit with a waistcoat and watch-chain, and blinks rather nervously through his rimless spectacles. The Emperor begins with a few words of welcome. The field is then open to me. He becomes very animated when I ask him about his visit to London as Crown Prince in 1921. He refers particularly to the kindness of King George V: 'He treated me like one of his own sons.' I ask him whether he recalls dining with Lord Curzon. He says that he remembers it well and was much touched by his friendliness. This gives me the cue to present him with a copy of *Superior Person*. The Emperor

---

* Cameron ('Kim') Cobbold, 1st Baron Cobbold (1904–87), banker. Lord Chamberlain 1963–71.

takes it with a bow. He then asks me whether, having written a large book on Curzon, I found that I liked him. I explained that there was a marked difference between Curzon's high spirits in youth and his depression caused by ill health in later years.

Remembering the Emperor's liking for the Prince of Wales, now the Duke of Windsor, I ask the Emperor whether he hopes to see the Duke during his few days in Paris. He replies that he certainly hopes to see him there at the Japanese Embassy, if it can be arranged. Moving on to more important events, I ask the Emperor whether he would consider his personal initiative in having ended the war in 1945 to have been the most momentous act of his life. He replies that I am perfectly right, and that he carried out his scheme to bring the war to an end in order to spare his people further suffering. 'It was not easy to do. Many of my people were against it.' In answer to my question whether there is any bitterness in Japan towards Great Britain twenty-six years after the war, he replies: 'No. We all want peace. But, of course, there may be a few people who still bear grudges.'

I then say to him: 'It must give Your Majesty much pleasure to see how Tokyo is once more flourishing. But may it not be that the technological revolution will rob your country of its traditional tranquillity and love of beauty?' Before replying, he gulps and gurgles and twitches, which is curious, as it does not seem to be a particularly difficult question. Eventually he replies: 'Technology can certainly lead to these things. But we must have industrialisation for the benefit of the people. We nevertheless hope that we can preserve our essential traditions.' Pursuing this point, I ask: 'As a scientist, do you consider that the good which scientists do can be separated from the bad for which they are no less responsible?' Rather shrewdly, he replies: 'Science itself is neither good nor bad, only the use to which it is put. We must hope that the good will triumph over the evil. In particular, I hope the problems of pollution can be solved.'

On the subject of his hobbies, he gives predictable answers – telling me that he devotes to marine biology and botany only such leisure as remains after he has performed his State duties. I ask whether he would be prepared to expose himself to a film similar to that made of our own Royal Family. He replies: 'If my people demand to know about some of my private life – and if it is not too exaggerated or exacting – then I must bow to the will of my people.' His final words to me are: 'Thank you for coming to see me. I hope that we may have an opportunity of meeting again in London.' We take our leave, bowing ourselves out. Although told that the audience would probably not last longer than fifteen minutes, it has, in fact, stretched to nearly fifty minutes. John and I are then, at the Emperor's request, taken on a tour of the new palace. It is not looking at its best, as much of it is under dust sheets, but we see most of the ceremonial rooms. Most of the windows look out on enchanting gardens.

## 15 August 1971, letter to his mother

I am staying at the British Embassy in Tokyo. On Friday I had my audience with Emperor Hirohito. I discovered that it is an almost unprecedented privilege for a journalist to be received by the Emperor, perhaps entirely unprecedented. Without the friendship and influence of John Pilcher, our Ambassador in Japan, I could never have managed it. The only drawback is that it was arranged only on condition that I do not quote the Emperor verbatim, much as in former days a Japanese Emperor could be measured for new clothes only from his reflection in a looking-glass. Direct quotes would be too great a break with tradition!

John Pilcher accompanied me to the huge new palace where the Emperor receives visitors, but does not live. He has a modest little house nearby in the palace grounds. The palace is very elegant outside, but rather too like an enormous suburban villa inside – bright carpets and 1930s silk armchairs. We were escorted by an army of courtiers and footmen to the audience chamber, where the Emperor was waiting – a slight, stooping, myopic figure in a dark-grey business suit and watch-chain (apparently the only one ever seen in Japan). We bowed, he bowed back, then shook hands, and sat down opposite each other. The interpreting was done (excellently, as far as I could gather) by a former Japanese Ambassador to Afghanistan. The Grand Chamberlain of the Court had told us before that our talk would last fifteen minutes. In fact, it went on for more than forty-five. The two most rewarding topics were the Emperor's first visit to England in 1921 and his personal initiative in ending the war in 1945, contrary to the wishes of many of his subjects. Of course, I could not ask him any questions on controversial topics such as Japanese war crimes or the extent to which the national religion of Shintoism treats him as divine. No man has fewer regrets for those pre-war days, when golden sand would be scattered and blinds drawn the whole way along his route. It is something to have begun one's reign as the Son of Heaven and to approach its end as a Fellow of the Royal Society.

I already knew that in 1921 he was entertained in London by Curzon, who was Foreign Secretary at the time, so I asked John Pilcher before I left England whether he thought the Emperor would care to accept a copy of my *Superior Person*. Pilcher replied that he had made enquiries at the Imperial Palace and that the Emperor (who doesn't usually accept presents) would be delighted. So I had a few copies sent out here by diplomatic bag, took one with me to my audience, and gave it to the Emperor. He looked pleased, and when the time came for us to take our leave he said he hoped we might meet again in London. I feel that I was fortunate in establishing some sort of friendly relationship with him. Apart from ambassadors, he practically never receives either foreigners or journalists: to be both presented formidable problems which I think I overcame. Historically it was astonishingly interesting.

### 19 August 1971

On the way back to Britain I stop over in Hong Kong and visit the Governor, Sir David Trench,* in Government House. The Governor is a largish, uncomplicated, rather tough man. It soon emerges that his personal interests run to golf rather than the Arts, but he has a passionate dedication to the colony which wins instant admiration. Of Murray MacLehose,† who succeeds him later this year, he says: 'Before he is really accepted here, he will have to prove himself to be a Hong Kong man, not an envoy of HMG in London. It may be difficult for him. Although he has served here before as Political Adviser, that is a post always held by a Foreign Office man.'

On relations between Hong Kong and Red China, Trench says: 'There is an element of brinkmanship in this. We don't provoke – even to the extent of censoring anything in films which might give offence to China – but we won't kow-tow. In the face of a stern stand on our part, the Chinese will back down. And on the whole they trust us. One result of this relationship is that there is no pressure here for constitutional reform. If we started to slide towards independence, the Chinese would never know who was in charge and our established relationship would be upset. Nor is there any reason to think that China would like to occupy Hong Kong. She gets foreign exchange and a propaganda base, and also realises the administrative difficulties there would be in taking us over. In any case, China is a Northern regime with a dislike of the South, and realises that Hong Kong's trade would vanish if she occupied us.'

When I ask whether there is much espionage, he replies: 'We pick up an odd agent or two and sometimes a man with some very unsafe explosives under the bed. And we take precautions.' Here he shows me that before we

---

* (1915–88) British Army officer and colonial governor. Twenty-fourth Governor of Hong Kong 1964–71

† Sir Murray MacLehose, Baron MacLehose of Beoch (1917–2000), politician and diplomat. Twenty-fifth Governor of Hong Kong 1971–82.

began our talk, he had unplugged his telephone, just on the chance that there was a bugging device inside it.

On Hong Kong's finances, he says: 'We are not rich, but prudent. We have no access to IMF borrowing right and must carry out all our works from savings. Nearly 40 per cent of our revenue comes from investment, not from taxes, e.g. from the rents of houses we have built. On only one point are we unable to defend ourselves: we cannot cope with trade restrictions imposed by other countries.'

His final topic is the attitude of Great Britain to Hong Kong. 'I am afraid that the English still regard HK as a music-hall joke and should like to see this changed.' He then accompanies me to the car, having given me an hour and a half of his time.

## 23 August 1971

In New Delhi on my way home. A tour which lasts all day. New Delhi is very handsome, with broad tree-lined avenues bearing such names as Hardinge and Irwin.[*] Not much motor traffic, but swarms of bicycles. Pass the President's House and notice how Lutyens' main dome sinks and rises again as one approaches it: the only unsuccessful feature of his vast complex.[†]

Then to the simple garden where Gandhi was cremated, called the Rajghat, and on to a similar place, the Shnata Vana, with nice rose beds, where Nehru was cremated.

## 24 August 1971

A whole day trip to see Agra, about 100 miles away. Agra itself is rather dusty. Over one shop I see the notice: 'By appointment to Queen Mary'. To the Red Fort with a wonderful view of the Taj Mahal appearing to float tranquilly by the side of the river, but how alarmingly near the pylons have been allowed to creep. Drive on to the Taj Mahal. It is breathtakingly beautiful at every distance and from every angle. Like all finely proportioned buildings, it seems at a distance to be smaller than it is. Every detail of it is enchanting, not least the flowers inlaid in the marble walls. If I had to find fault, it would be only in the lamp given by Curzon to hang above the tomb, a fussy fretted

---

[*] Referring to former Viceroys: Sir Charles Hardinge, 1st Baron Hardinge of Penshurt (1858–1944), Viceroy of India 1910–16; and Lord Irwin, later Lord Halifax (1881–1959), Viceroy 1926–31.

[†] Sir Herbert Baker (1862–1946), architect; designed the Secretariat Buildings at the foot of Raisina Hill, where Lutyens had designed Government House. As a result the gradient meant that only the dome of Government House was visible from below. The episode was known as Lutyens' Bakerloo.

object that hardly seems to justify all the research and money he spent on it.

## 25 August 1971

I am taken over the President's House, formerly the Viceregal Lodge. My guide has worked here for twenty-five years, and his father before him, going back to Irwin's time. At the top of the main stairs that leads up from the inner courtyard is a bust of Lutyens. There is a very impressive circular Durbar Room immediately below the huge dome. The statues of King George V and Queen Mary no longer face outwards towards the capital. They have been withdrawn inside the portico and now face the room from which one emerges.

There is a huge ballroom and a waiting room with chairs of gilt and red plush. The dining room is very long, dark and gloomy. It is still hung with viceregal portraits, including one of Hardinge, his hand on a plan of Delhi. The only exception to the stiffness of these portraits is Oswald Birley's[*] of Lord Willingdon,[†] wearing a grey frock coat and star; he looks back at ease in his study surrounded by red boxes.

The whole of the building is hung with a great number of very bad pictures, including Royal portraits copied by Indian artists. Even worse are some Indian pictures of ceremonial occasions such as Mountbatten handing over power.

Then into the enormous garden, in the Mogul style, with a network of little canals. There are endless beds of roses. There are also white peacocks in cages and some enchanting cranes doing their delicately floppy love dance. My guide plucks me a red and a mauve flower. He tells me that altogether the President's House employs 2,500 people, of whom 250 are gardeners. At the end of our tour I recall the remark by Clemenceau,[‡] 'This will be the finest ruin of them all.'

## 25 September 1971

News of the wholesale expulsion of about ninety Soviet spies from the Russian Embassy and other Soviet agencies in London.[§]

---

[*] Sir Oswald Birley (1880–1952), portrait painter.

[†] Maj. Freeman Freeman-Thomas, 1st Marquess of Willingdon (1866–1941), Liberal politician. Twenty-fourth Viceroy and Governor General of India 1931–6.

[‡] Georges Clemenceau (1841–1929), French politician. Prime Minister of France 1906–9 and 1917–20; one of the architects of the Treaty of Versailles at the Paris Peace Conference of 1919; nicknamed 'The Tiger'.

[§] The final number expelled by Sir Alec Douglas-Home was 105. See D.R. Thorpe, *Alec Douglas-Home* (Sinclair-Stevenson, 1996), pp. 415–18.

## 2 October 1971

Back from the office early to change into black tie. Prince Eddie comes round with his driver at 4 p.m. Then on to Covent Garden for the start of Wagner's *Gotterdämmerung* at 5. Eddie is not usually Royal on such occasions, but tonight the police have been warned and we drive to the Royal Box entrance the wrong way down a one-way street. What an odd place the Royal Box is – in one corner are some thrones and in another a card table and chairs, not to mention sundry sofas. Excellent supper between the acts, of smoked salmon and cold roast beef with white wine and claret. Edward Downes,* the conductor, keeps his eyes glued to the score throughout the evening and lacks the magic of Solti. But there is a fine upstanding Siegfried and a splendid Brünnhilde. Perhaps best of all is the Hagen.

In spite of the extraordinary heat for October, a very happy evening. Eddie drives me home. He has the Emperor of Japan three nights running next week.

## 3 October 1971

Dine with Oliver van Oss at Charterhouse to hear his recollections of Linky. He was an ardent preserver of trees and insisted that none should be cut down without his express permission. One day he went to see a dangerous-looking tree in Herbert Tatham's† garden. The gardener said to him: 'You should not stand there, my Lord, it is very dangerous.' Linky replied: 'So you think I am afraid to die?' He then began a long theological discussion with the gardener on death. He once said: 'There are two things which have done immense harm to the Church of England: bad preaching and good music.'

We discuss headmasterships, including his own failure to be appointed to Stowe in 1958. I ask him whether he was upset by this. He replies that the only thing he minded was to receive a very nice comforting letter from Noel Annan – who, he later discovered, had given the casting vote against him.

Oliver also said that beaks at Eton were often disconcerted by the generosity of parents of leaving boys. Once Richard Martineau‡ was brought a leaving present of a case of bottles of the finest vintage of Claret. Martineau said he was embarrassed to accept such a big present, so he took only two of them and asked the boy to return the other ten to his parents with his grateful thanks. The result of this diffidence was that the boy and

---

* Sir Edward Downes (1924–2009), operatic conductor. He and his wife died by assisted suicide at the Dignitas Clinic in Switzerland on 10 July 2009.

† (1861–1909), Eton schoolmaster 1886–1909. He fell to his death in the Alps at Chamonix.

‡ (1906–84), Eton schoolmaster 1928–66.

his friends promptly polished off the remaining bottles themselves before Lock-Up!

## 6 October 1971

Prince William of Gloucester lunches with me. He tells me that at the State Banquet for the Emperor of Japan at the Palace last night there was no departure from rigid protocol. He had no opportunity of speaking to any of the Japanese during dinner. Occasionally, he says, there are small round tables instead of one large horseshoe table: obviously, the Japanese visit was thought to be the epitome of formality.

William's impression of the Emperor is of a man older than his years who has to make a marked effort in public – and who is rather courageous to have undertaken a series of visits where he could hardly be welcome. William does not think that the visit will in any way bring the two peoples together: distance and language are enormous barriers. In any case, if Japan intends to swing away from the United States, she has only two courses before her – the unpalatable one of closer links with China, and the easier one of closer links with Europe.

## 8 October 1971

Dine with Rebecca West who at seventy-eight is deaf, but lively. She talks scathingly of some of her fellow writers. She thinks David Cecil is a light-weight, and calls E.M. Forster 'the regimental goat of King's'.

## 7 November 1971

To Trinity College to dine with Rab Butler at High Table. Talking about Bob-bety Salisbury, Rab says he very much admires his oratory. He also thinks that Harold Macmillan did not really want to lose his services in 1957, but felt obliged to accept his resignation to show how strong he was. This is con-trary to the other view I have heard, that Macmillan felt his Government would in any case last only a few months, so that it didn't matter whether or not Bobbety remained.

Rab is delighted with the reception given to his own memoirs, *The Art of the Possible*. He describes how at Grillion's the other night he found himself next to Harold Macmillan, who said to him: 'I am puzzled by your book, Rab. You see, I have written history. But you have written only an essay.' Rab thinks Macmillan behaved very badly in refusing his Garter. The Queen was very upset by it, and when Rab was offered the Garter, she told him that she hoped he would not refuse it.

## 15 December 1971

At a dinner in Albany I find myself next to John Gielgud* and Lord Wolfenden. Gielgud, like Ralph Richardson, is utterly without conceit. As I move across the room later to talk to someone else, I hear Gielgud greeting Wolfenden with the historic words: 'I cannot tell you how much I owe to you.'

## 21 December 1971

At 5.30 to the Speaker's House for a drink alone with Selwyn Lloyd. He is rightly proud of having improved the house enormously since I last saw it a few months ago. There are much nicer lamps and curtains, and he is gradually getting rid of the suburban wallpapers chosen by his predecessor. He also shows me a great deal of what he calls Royal loot – including a silver box and a signed photograph from the Emperor of Japan. Apparently, the Speaker is always on the list of recipients on occasions such as State Visits.

Selwyn also tells me that he is delighted by the proposal to increase his salary. The expenses are quite considerable – what he calls 'all this flummery', pointing to his frock coat and knee-breeches. He also says that he must wear a clean shirt every day – 'More than most people do here.' He misses dining out, but manages to lunch if it is not too far away.

He has just been presiding over a debate on the Royal finances, and tells me that he agrees with what Roy Jenkins has said – that the state should pay the Queen all necessary expenses, and take a generous view of them, but that she should lose her freedom from taxation.

## 22 December 1971

Jeremy Thorpe comes to dine with me. He tells me that at the State Banquet the other day at Buckingham Palace, Princess Margaret put out her tongue at him. When he raised his eyebrows in interrogation, she whined: 'You voted against our money.' He explained to her as calmly as he could that he had done nothing of the sort, but had merely suggested that for the Royal finances to be handled by a Department of State would protect the Queen from unfair charges of avarice and extravagance.

## 31 December 1971

Arnold Goodman asks me whether I would like to come round to his flat in Portland Place tonight, for an informal New Year's Party.

After supper there I have a long talk with George Wigg, who tells me that Harold Wilson will certainly not like his own forthcoming memoirs. He

---

* (1904–2000), actor and theatre director.

says of him: 'Harold prides himself on his memory, but all the things he remembers are trivial – how many inches from Marble Arch to Hyde Park Corner, and the like.'

Arnold Goodman tells me that when a new Poet Laureate had to be appointed when he was Chairman of the Arts Council, much pressure was put on Arnold to recommend John Betjeman. But he thought him unsuitable. So instead he recommended C. Day-Lewis. But he thinks John Masefield was the best Poet Laureate of all.[*]

We also have much talk on the Rhodesian Settlement which he recently negotiated with Ian Smith on behalf of Alec Douglas-Home. He is uneasy about Lord Pearce's Commission of Inquiry to sound out African opinion.[†] He regrets that the team will ask Africans merely to express a straight yes or no on whether they agree with the terms of the settlement. He would prefer that the answers should not be a straight yes or no, but yes or no, unless ... For what will happen if the Commission reports that African opinion is against the settlement? The British Government will have left itself no room for manoeuvre. And whatever may be the intentions of the Government, Tory MPs as a whole will not support the reimposition of sanctions.

Arnold was fascinated by his task. 'I was a private person involved in the tides of Government, yet compelled to assert my private personality. This demanded enormous tact.' He tells me he let it be known that he did not want any sort of honour for what he had done in Rhodesia. On his return, the question arose whether he should explain and defend the settlement during the House of Lords debate. It was decided that he should. The only precedent was Maynard Keynes on his return from negotiating our post-war loan from the United States.

We talk about honours. He tells me that J.B. Priestley[‡] desperately wants the Order of Merit. Goodman thinks he deserves it, and wrote to the Palace to recommend him. He received a polite reply, saying that 'any recommendation put forward by you as Chairman of the Arts Council must of course bear great weight'. But nothing has happened yet. He suspects that Priestley is considered too much of a middle-brow, although in fact he has written several works of great distinction, particularly plays.

---

[*] John Betjeman succeeded Day-Lewis as Poet Laureate in 1972. John Masefield OM (1878–1967), Poet Laureate 1930–67.

[†] Sir Edward Pearce, Baron Pearce (1901–90), judge.

[‡] Priestley was eventually awarded the Order of Merit in 1977.

# 1972

*On 9 January the National Union of Mineworkers held a strike ballot in which 58.8 per cent voted in favour. A seven-week strike then followed, including picketing of Saltley coke depot. On 20 January, unemployment exceeded one million for the first time since the 1930s. 'Bloody Sunday' in Northern Ireland on 30 January saw the deaths of fourteen when troops opened fire on demonstrators in Derry. The miners' strike led to a state of emergency being declared on 9 February. The Parliament of Northern Ireland was suspended and on 24 March Great Britain imposed direct rule over Northern Ireland. William Whitelaw became the first Northern Ireland Secretary on 26 March. On 20 April Apollo 16 landed on the Moon. On 18 May the Queen met her uncle the Duke of Windsor for the last time, in Paris. Ten days later the Duke died. The troubles in Northern Ireland intensified on 31 July. On 28 August Prince William of Gloucester was killed in an air crash near Wolverhampton. On 5 September eleven Israeli athletes were captured at the Munich Olympics and later killed. On 18 September thousands of Ugandan Asians arrived in Britain after being expelled by Idi Amin. John Betjeman was appointed Poet Laureate on 10 October. The final manned Moon landing was on 11 December with Apollo 17.*

## 20 January 1972

Telephone message from the Duke of Windsor's secretary in Paris inviting me to dine with the Duke and Duchess the weekend after next. So decide to combine it with two to three days in Paris. Later Christopher Soames asks me to lunch at the Embassy that day.

David Dilks comes to dine with me. He is working not only on a definitive biography of Neville Chamberlain, but also completing his account of British foreign policy between the wars. For the latter volume, I lend him a batch of unpublished Curzon papers that I copied but never used and he is most grateful. In return, he offers to tell me of any Cecil papers that he discovers, and says that there are some excellent letters in Gilbert Murray's[*] papers at the Bodleian. He is very happy as Professor of History at Leeds. Contrary to what is generally said, he finds the students 'polite, considerate and deferential'. And he has a harmonious relationship with Edward Boyle. I am to dine with him and Edward when I go up to Leeds in March.

### 25 January 1972

Group Captain Peter Townsend comes to see me in the office. Apparently, he is writing a book about the handing-over of power to India in 1947. He asks me about certain Indian archives and I am able to give him some information, suggesting that he could get the complete picture from Stanley Sutton[†] at the India Office Library.

Townsend is a man of immense charm, highly intelligent and without a trace of self-importance. He now lives in France and I notice that he constantly lards his sentences with French words and phrases. I promise to let him know if I come across any material that might help him. He says that he hopes to have access to certain papers in the Royal Archives, but that he will not go to Windsor personally, in order to avoid any possible embarrassment.

### 26 January 1972

Jeremy Thorpe tells me some amusing stories of his visit to Brussels for the signing by the Prime Minister of the Common Market Treaty. He returned in a plane with Heath, Macmillan, Alec Douglas-Home and George Brown. At one moment during the journey, as they were drinking round a table, Jeremy held up his hand, knowing that Harold Wilson had declined an invitation to the ceremony, and said: 'George would now like to propose a toast to absent friends.'

Another snatch of conversation which Jeremy tells me took place between Alec Douglas-Home and Harold Macmillan. Talking of his official residence at No. 1 Carlton Gardens, Alec said to Harold: 'It is a splendid house. Why do you not come and live next door in No. 2?' Harold replied: 'As a matter of fact, when my father-in-law sold Devonshire House, he bought No. 2 Carlton Gardens to store the furniture.'

### 27 January 1972

John Russell comes to the Guards Club for some talk about Spain. He tells

---

[*]  Gilbert Murray OM (1866–1957), classical scholar.
[†]  (1907–77), Librarian, India Office Library 1949–71; Director, India Office Library and Records 1971–2.

an amusing story of how, when a student mob was besieging the British Embassy in Madrid during the war, the Minister of the Interior* telephoned Sam Hoare, the Ambassador, to ask, 'Shall I send more police?' Sam replied, 'No, send fewer students.'

## 29 January 1972

Car at 7.45 to take me to London Airport for the flight to Paris. Lunch with Mary and Christopher Soames at the British Embassy. Since I was last there, it has been purged of all the dreadful modern pictures and sculptures from Patrick Reilly's† time. A warm welcome from both Christopher and Mary. Some nice pictures including the famous one of a room at Blenheim by Winston, and Jacques-Émile Blanche's painting of Edward VII taking the salute on Horse Guards Parade.

A very nice lunch in the small dining room. The centre of the table a mass of carnations. Footmen in bottle-green tail coats. We eat pâté with cucumber salad, pancakes containing slices of veal in a sauce, a Stilton cut into wedges like a fruit cake, and a sort of zabaglione, only more solid. Christopher calls it Bird's Custard, much to Mary's annoyance. He eats hugely, drinks a lot, then has a large brandy and a long cigar. It cannot really be good for him, and Mary whispers to me that sometimes she has a grilled steak specially done for him, instead of rich Embassy food.

Christopher has to fly to London this afternoon for a weekend conference at Ditchley. But before he goes, we have a word or two about current events. The whole Embassy is very busy preparing for the Queen's visit in May. It is quite a strain on the family, as they cannot abandon all entertainment in the intervening weeks. I ask what will become of the Windsors during the visit. Apparently, they will almost certainly go away in good time, in order to be out of the way. When I mention to Christopher that I am dining with them tonight, he asks how long it is since I last saw them. And when I say that it is about two years, he says that both are beginning to show their age very much – he physically and she by repeating herself a great deal. Mary adds that they are on very friendly terms with the Windsors and dine privately with each other about once a year. But they cannot really appear very much together in public, as Christopher, being the Queen's representative, must always take precedence.

I have some talk with Mary about her father, and quote to her his remark 'This war will be won by carnivores.' It is quite new to her and she is delighted, adding that it is one of the few Winstonisms that rings really true. Nothing annoys her more than stories about her father's alleged drunkenness. 'The whisky and soda I used to have to mix for him was so weak that if I gave it to you, you would ask for something stronger.' She emphasises how very much her father depended on Pug Ismay as a peacemaker, particularly among the Chiefs of Staff.

A splendid phrase of her father which is quite new to me. He would say: 'We must not do this pig-meal', meaning piece-meal. Mary tells me at length about the life she is writing of her mother. Apparently, she has long conversations with her mother, but never uses a tape-recorder. 'Her generation does not like talking into a machine. In any case, it is very hard to concentrate oneself on what is important if one knows that every word is being recorded.' She also has a batch of very interesting family letters and papers of her mother. Randolph was angry that Lady Churchill would not give them to him. But as Mary says, 'The alternatives were either that they should come to me or be burnt – there was never any question that they should be allowed to go to Randolph.' Mary's relations with Martin Gilbert have somewhat deteriorated, as she has insisted on having the first pick of her mother's letters to her father. For whereas the copyright of Winston's papers rests with the trustees, Lady Churchill is the owner of her own copyright.

All her papers and draft manuscripts are contained in a large red box that once belonged to Winston. On it are stamped in gold the words 'Secretary of State for the Colonies'. Her overflow papers are in a smaller red box that Christopher had as Secretary of State for War. Mary reads out a list of the wedding presents given to her mother and father in 1908. They include innumerable muff-chains, inkpots and a gold-topped walking stick from Edward VII, used by Winston for the rest of his life. This leads us to talk of Linky, who was of course best man, and there are shrieks of laughter when I tell them the story of Linky's crushing rebuke to Algernon Cecil, his cousin, a convert to Roman Catholicism:

'Algernon, why have you grown that absurd beard?'

'Our Lord grew a beard.'

'Our Lord was not a gentleman.'

•

In the evening I go on to dine with the Duke and Duchess of Windsor at their house in the Bois de Boulogne. Awaiting me at Hôtel de Crillon on my return from the Embassy is not only a reminder, but a small map, drawn by

hand. It takes about twenty minutes to get there, and would be very difficult
to find without such guidance.

There are two gendarmes at the gate and a butler on the steps. I sign the
visitors' book, and am then shown into the drawing room. It is like stepping
into a fairyland of fantastic luxury. Almost everything seems to be made of
gold or crystal. There are wonderful carpets, exquisite gilt furniture, little
tables covered with thickets of jewelled bric-à-brac. The only light comes
from candles, which cast their golden haze from chandeliers and sconces.
Beautifully arranged flowers. Two pictures dominate the room – one of the
Duke in Garter robes and another of Queen Mary. The Duke and Duchess
are sitting just inside the drawing room when I am announced. I am quite
staggered by the Duchess's appearance – the very slender figure of a schoolgirl and beautifully arranged auburn hair. She wears a very severe dark-blue
dress with a bare back, two huge diamonds on her left breast. A third large
diamond on one of her fingers that perhaps is a mistake, as it draws attention
to her large hands. The Duke very lame, but roars at me in his very strong
American accent: 'Why, Mr Albany himself.' He then personally takes me
round, introducing me to the other guests. But there is still a little knot of
them in a corner and he says: 'Oh, let's not bother about them.'

The Duke tells me he has been reading my book on Curzon, and much
enjoying it. 'He was a terrible man, a terrible man, but a good brain, a good
brain.' It is like hearing Monty with an American accent. He also recalls my
sending him those amusing letters to Curzon from Sir Charles Eliot,* our
Ambassador in Tokyo at the time of the Duke's official visit in 1922. He takes
me across to a large silver-framed photograph of the Emperor Hirohito,
given to him the other day. The Duke says: 'He came to see me. But he didn't
seem all there.'

While we are still drinking before dinner, I talk to the Spanish Ambassador to Paris, a small, wizened man called Don Pedro Cortina y Mauri.†
I draw his attention to a gold ashtray on the nearby table. It has let into it
a gold medal bearing the head of the Duke when King Edward VIII, and I
comment on how little the Duke has changed in appearance. At this moment
the Duchess joins us, and I repeat what I have said. She smiles wryly and
says: 'Yes, he is just the same – in profile.'

We move off to dine next door. The room is again lit entirely by candles.
There are two tables of eight or ten each, covered with gilt and silver objects,
painted porcelain candlesticks, delightful flowers and porcelain-handled

---

* (1862–1931), Ambassador to Japan 1919–26.
† (1908–93), Spanish Ambassador to Paris 1966–74.

cutlery that is rather heavy and difficult to manage. Endless butlers and footmen, all in white ties. Throughout the meal, the Duchess catches their eye from time to time so that they may receive swiftly whispered instructions, perhaps even rebukes. I sit at the Duchess's table with the Spanish Ambassador. The conversation is all very informal and there is a good rattle of talk across the table. The food is excellent. We begin with a rich sort of fish stew with rice and olives, and accompanied by several different sorts of bread. Then saddle of lamb, which characteristically has sprouted ten kidneys instead of the usual two. A lovely chocolate pudding, decorated with truffle chocolates. As it is being cleared away, the Duchess says to me: 'Now I am going to give you an English savoury. Most people have cheese, but I find it always sits here like a lump of lead' – and she smites her non-existent stomach. The savoury consists in fact of wafer-thin little pastry cups about two inches high, each filled with hot cheese soufflé. They are unbelievably delicious. The Duchess says: 'I always take two' – and she does. With all this splendid food, we drink hock, claret, champagne, then claret again with the savoury. I notice that the Duke is practically alone in taking a cigar when they are brought round the tables.

The Duchess tells me a story of how her husband one day wanted to telephone the office of a new lawyer whom he had acquired. He rang, and after enquiring who he was, the secretary said that her boss would ring back. But he did not do so, so the Duke tried again and was given the same answer. Still the call was not returned. So eventually, quite late in the day and by now furious, the Duke made a third telephone call and absolutely insisted on talking to the lawyer. The secretary replied: 'Do you really think I am going to believe that you are the Duke of Windsor with such an American accent?'

Among other topics of the Duchess are her insomnia, which at least drives her to read a great deal; whether or not social divisions are crumbling in France; and her five years in China – married to a naval officer who had gunboats. As soon as the meal is over, the Duchess leads out the ladies and we drift over to the Duke's table. But we have only been sitting there for two or three minutes when the Duchess reappears and beckons us all into the drawing room. The Duke obediently hobbles after her on his stick, and we all follow. At once, a man sits down at the piano and begins playing 'Smoke Gets in Your Eyes' and other antique melodies.

I am joined by the Duke. He says: 'Well, had enough to eat?' – as far as I can discern without a trace of irony. I seize the opportunity of asking him whether he is carefully keeping all his papers and whether he has yet appointed an official biographer. He says that he thinks he has lost very few papers indeed. As for an official biography, 'I really think I have written my own.'

But the Duke says he does possess a high admiration for Roger Fulford,[*] particularly his recent editing of Queen Victoria's letters.

I am amazed when, with many nudges, the Duke in conversation refers to 'You Know Who'. He means Harold Wilson. A little pug dog called Diamond comes and sits on my lap, then jumps onto a pretty little sofa until the Duchess shouts at it across the room to get down.

By now it is 12.15 and the party begins to break up. I notice that all the women say goodbye to the Duchess with a kiss and a curtsey. The Duke insists on coming out onto the doorstep, although the night is bitterly cold. Another guest kindly drives me back to the Crillon.

### 2 February 1972

Give lunch to George Wigg, the former Paymaster General, who has just written his memoirs. He tells me how Harold Wilson is trying to get passages removed from these forthcoming memoirs.

George tells me that after Gaitskell's death in 1963, Wilson was doubtful about the majority he would get in being elected leader of the Labour Party. Wigg told him that he would have a vote of at least 140, and said that he would bet him £1 on it. Wilson accepted the bet, and his vote was 144.[†] I ask George whether Wilson paid up. 'Yes, he paid, more than many, many colleagues on both sides of the House have done.'

This leads George to talk about his horses. He has not had very much luck recently. But he has a nice mare called Blue Iris. He says: 'Blue Iris is like me – moderate, honest and sound.'

### 18 February 1972

Lunch with Douglas Hurd at the Travellers' Club. He has had a rather arduous time with the Prime Minister, as the Government scraped home last night in the Common Market debate with a majority of only eight. Douglas and I agree that it is monstrously unfair of the Labour Party to blame Jeremy Thorpe and the Liberals for having voted with the Government. Nobody in their senses could expect the Liberals to abandon their long campaign in favour of the Common Market in order to exchange a Conservative for a Labour Government. Douglas agrees with me that undoubtedly Wilson feels Jeremy ought to be under an obligation to him, particularly for having

---

[*] Sir Roger Fulford (1902–83), writer; editor of the diaries of Charles Greville, and five volumes of the letters of Queen Victoria.
[†] In the first round of voting Wilson received 115 votes, George Brown 88 and James Callaghan 41. In the second round Wilson received 144 votes and George Brown 103.

treated him during Labour's years in office with the same seriousness as the Conservative Leader of the Opposition.

Douglas tries to recall similar occasions on which there have been very close votes in the House, and asks me whether the Reform Bill did not scrape home by one vote in 1831. I refer him to the magnificent account of it printed in Sir George Trevelyan's life of Macaulay,* and he says he will show it to Ted Heath.

I raise with Douglas the failure of Leslie Rowse ever to have appeared in the Honours List, and I ask whether it would be any use my writing direct to the Prime Minister. Douglas not only agrees that Rowse should have an honour, but says that if I send my letter to the Prime Minister directly to him, he will personally press the point.

## 24 February 1972

In the evening I give a little dinner party for the Kents and for Rab and Mollie Butler.

The Kents seem to have been having rather a gloomy time lately. Poor Katherine mangled her finger very badly when somebody shut a car door on it. Although the broken bone has healed, it is still black and very painful. They have also had a difficult time moving into part of York House, St James's Palace. The Ministry of Works have done everything very shoddily. In some instances it has been so badly done that workmen have had to come again to finish the job. Once the reconstruction is out of the way, it will be wonderfully peaceful. All Katherine ever hears at present is the Commander of the Ghurkha Guard at seven o' clock in the morning shouting: 'Dees-mees!'

I am astonished when Katherine tells me that they are going to leave Coppins quite soon. They simply cannot afford to keep it up. So, for the present they will live in York House and hope to find a smaller house somewhere in Norfolk.

We have some talk about Leeds University, where Katherine is Chancellor, and where, as it happens, she is going to give Rab an honorary degree in May. She whispers to me that I must write her speech for her on that occasion and I promise to do so. She passionately defends the students at Leeds who, she says, are very polite and agreeable, in spite of their scruffy appearance.

Katherine quotes a sad remark made to her the other day by a railway

---

* Sir George Otto Trevelyan, 2nd Bt OM (1838–1928), statesman and author. His life of Macaulay was published in 1876. The second reading of the Reform Bill on 22 Mar. 1831 was approved by only one vote. Thomas Babington Macaulay, 1st Baron Macaulay (1800–59), historian and Whig politician.

official talking about the abolition of Pullman trains: 'Oh well, we must say goodbye to those relics of better days.' We agree that the King's Cross to Yorkshire trains, although fast, are airless and unexciting.

Eddie is interested to hear about my visit to the Windsors, but speaks bitterly of the Duke. 'At the time of the Abdication, he treated even my father badly – and he was his greatest friend.' He also says that when Michael was learning Russian in Paris, he went to lunch with the Windsors one day, but found the place full of rich and disagreeable Americans.

Rab is in splendid heart. He professes to be on a diet, but I can see few signs of it in the course of the evening. He says: 'I was going to see the Prime Minister at 6.30 this evening before coming on to you. He needs all the help he can get. But he is under such pressure at the moment that I let him off.'

Nothing has pleased Rab more than the success of his memoirs, *The Art of the Possible*. His publishers have now suggested that he should bring out a volume of his collected papers and lectures, and Rab asks my advice. I urge him not to do so. It would have a very slender sale compared to the 30,000 of his memoirs. Mollie has now been asked to write her memoirs, and I tell her that she certainly must do so.*

On political matters, Rab thinks that Selwyn Lloyd is too old to continue very long as Speaker. He also believes that Selwyn's 'Foreign Office manner' is not suited to the Chair. 'Boyd-Carpenter would have been much better. He could have snapped their heads off when there was trouble.' Rab astonished me by saying that Bobbety Salisbury always wanted him to be Prime Minister. I have never heard that before and rather doubt it.

## 25 February 1972

Martin Gilliat dines with me. He tells me that the Queen Mother, although upset by Bobbety's death two days ago, characteristically shows no outward sign of sorrow. She always keeps her emotions bottled up; thus she made no mention at all either to Martin or to any other member of the Household at Clarence House about Prince Richard of Gloucester's recent engagement.†
The only change with age that Martin notices in her is an increasing reluctance to make up her mind about future plans. Sometimes Martin is frustrated by this, but later thinks: 'How much less fun life would be if she died tonight.'

I gather from Martin that Bobbety died late on Monday afternoon – so

---

* Published as *August and Rab: A Memoir* (Weidenfeld & Nicolson, 1987).
† Prince Richard of Gloucester (b. 1944) became engaged to Birgitte Eva Henriksen (b. 1946) in Feb. 1972 and married her on 8 July 1972.

it must have been at almost exactly the time that I was writing the opening words of my book on the Cecils. I read the passage to Martin and he thinks it admirable. He is also anxious to hear about my visit to the Windsors, and has the same regard for Proustian detail as I have.

## 28 February 1972

Catch the two o'clock train to Hatfield for Bobbety's funeral. On the platform at King's Cross I run into Frank and Elizabeth Longford, who ask me to share a carriage with them. As I have only a second-class ticket, and they have first-class tickets, they insist on coming into a second-class carriage with me. Frank is delighted when I say that I now recognise the true chivalry of a Knight of the Garter. He tells me he has been staying for a night or two in Dublin with Éamon de Valera, who, although about ninety, is still very alert.

At Hatfield Station there are cars to take us up to the church. See Anthony Eden looking very old indeed and leaning heavily on Clarissa's arm. I am greeted very warmly by David Cecil, who tells me he is about to write to me about my Cecil book. The entire family is there, including David Ormsby-Gore. Robert Salisbury* looks astonishingly like his great-grandfather, although of course without the beard. Quite a lot of other people I know are there, including Bill de L'Isle and Martin Gilliat. The service itself is rather rural and haphazard, which makes it all the more moving. Thus, the voluntary continues for about a minute into the singing of the first hymn. I do not stay for the last graveside rites, but walk down to the station straight after the service.

## 3 March 1972

At 11.15 to Speaker's House, Westminster, where I await Selwyn Lloyd. He emerges from the Chamber at 11.30 in a white tie and knee-breeches, does a quick change, and we are away in his car to the Wirral by 11.45. Once we are clear of London, we make very good progress, although it pours with rain and we drive through a perpetual heavy mist thrown up by other cars. After Birmingham we push on, in sudden sunshine, through nicer country. South of Chester we pass a signpost reading 'Saighton', which reminds me of George Wyndham.† Drive through Chester, where there has been some excellent modern reconstruction, and arrive at Hilbre House, West Kirby in time for tea.

---

* Robert Gascoyne-Cecil, 6th Marquess of Salisbury (1916–2003), Conservative politician.

† (1863–1913), Conservative politician and one of The Souls. Mistakenly believed to be the biological father of Anthony Eden. See D.R. Thorpe, *Eden: The Life and Times of Anthony Eden, First Earl of Avon, 1897–1977* (Chatto & Windus, 2003), pp. 18–20. Saighton Grange was the house of George Wyndham at one stage.

It looks out over the estuary of the River Dee, towards the Welsh mountains.

The house was left to Selwyn a few years ago by a woman called Mrs Macdona,* who died at the age of 104. She was the President of Selwyn's local Conservative Association and wanted the house to retain its links to Wirral Conservatism. Her father-in-law was the Revd J. Cumming Macdona,† Rector of Chedale, who later became Member of Parliament for Rotherhithe, after renouncing holy orders. He bred St Bernard dogs, setters and Arab thoroughbreds. By what a local paper once called his 'castellated mansion and wave-washed lawn' he built a tower to the memory of a dog. At the foot of the tower is an effigy of the dog in sandstone, with a long epitaph which reads: 'Underneath this tower lie the remains of Tell, the champion rough-coated Mount St Bernard dog of England and winner of the principal prizes in the kingdom, since his importation by his owner, the Revd J. Cumming Macdona in March 1866. *He was majestic in appearance, noble in character, affectionate in disposition and of undaunted courage.* Died 22 January 1871, aged seven years.' Selwyn says to me: 'It will do as my own epitaph.'

From the garden, full of snowdrops and primroses, we go back into the house. On a huge refectory table Selwyn has laid out some interesting documents of his own life, including summonses to the Privy Council and patents of his various appointments and decorations. We have a pleasant dinner. There are no other guests. Selwyn tells me that he has a very special way of making a dry martini: it consists in adding one drop of Angostura bitters for every four persons. 'What if you are drinking alone?' I ask. Selwyn replies: 'I drink enough for four.' Selwyn adds that the House of Commons is so physically tiring that he needs a certain amount of drink to keep him going. Thus, before lunch, he has a gin and tonic. With lunch itself he has a glass or two of wine, then a very small brandy, and in the evening he drinks whisky.

He hopes to remain Speaker for another three years or so, but has not yet decided whether he will take the peerage that is always offered to a retiring Speaker. He does not much care for titles, although he would certainly not refuse either the Garter or the OM. The great advantage of taking a peerage is that it would keep him 'in the club', i.e. he would see all his political friends regularly. If he does take a peerage, he would call himself Lord Hilbre.‡

---

* Egerton Macdona (1865–1969), President of the Wirral Conservative Association and a tireless worker for many Wirral charities.

† (1836–1907), Conservative MP for Rotherhithe 1892–1906.

‡ When Selwyn Lloyd was ennobled in 1976 he took the title Baron Selwyn-Lloyd. As there were other Lord Lloyds, and as the vogue for double-barrelled titles such as Gordon-Walker and George-Brown had been tolerated rather than approved, he had his name changed by deed poll to Selwyn-Lloyd.

Whatever drain the House makes on his physical strength, he does not suffer from mental strain, and only very rarely does he sleep badly. He manages to bring the temperature down whenever there is a sudden uproar, but he adds that there is no real protection against a group of Members determined to hold up proceedings by putting bogus points of order. He keeps a book containing the names of all Members of Parliament, when they last spoke, and for how long. Thus, if any Member complains that he has not been called enough, Selwyn can check at a glance whether or not the accusation is just. But characteristically Gerald Nabarro recently wrote an offensive letter to him complaining that he was not being called enough and adding: 'I sit because I signed a motion questioning one of your rulings?' Selwyn sent a stiff reply pointing out that Nabarro had been called on average twice a day – far more than most other Members. He ended his letter: 'Your concluding remark is resented, but it will not prejudice me against you.'

Selwyn attaches much importance to the opportunities which a Speaker has for entertaining. He himself is a comparatively rich man, so can do more than his predecessors. Every week he has a luncheon party to which he invites seven Members of Parliament – drawn from senior, middle and new Members. This is apparently much appreciated. On 23 March he is to give a big reception in the state rooms for about 400 people, including the Cabinet, the Shadow Cabinet, all heads of Diplomatic Missions in London and a small sprinkling of friends. There will be unlimited champagne, but not much to eat. He tells me that he is inviting me to the party.

We go on to have some talk about politics past and present. 'Although 98 per cent of Conservatives would disagree with me, I have always thought that George Brown is a far worse man than Harold Wilson.' 'At least', he adds, 'George has a warm heart.' Ted Heath, he adds, can be insensitive. Selwyn still remains the local MP and deals with a certain amount of non-political constituency business. Some time ago, a businessman asked Selwyn if he could manage to get hold of the Prime Minister to make a speech in Hoylake. So Selwyn wrote to the Prime Minister, adding that if he cared to come up to Cheshire, he could borrow Selwyn's house, where there was room for a Private Secretary and a detective. Heath wrote back a curt letter, saying that he was unable to speak, but making no reference at all to Selwyn's generous offer of hospitality. Almost the only other politician whom he criticises is David Kilmuir. He pulls out of his bookshelves – loaded incidentally with a wonderful collection of political memoirs – Kilmuir's autobiography, and reads me a long passage in which he is criticised. Selwyn took the strictures lightly and always tried to be nice to Kilmuir. But Kilmuir would turn away in shame whenever he saw Selwyn approaching. Selwyn generously attributes his behaviour to having suffered some sort of cerebral defect after his dismissal as Lord Chancellor by Harold Macmillan in 1962 in the Night of the Long Knives.

Talking of his years as Foreign Secretary, Selwyn says that by far the best Parliamentary Under-Secretary was Lord Inchyra.[*] Strang was also good, but rather tired. Kirkpatrick[†] was dictatorial, and Caccia was nice but not very clever. Of Gladwyn Jebb Selwyn speaks with affection, and found that he would always accept correction – a modest side to his nature that is unknown to most.

### 7 March 1972

To Covent Garden in the evening for Richard Strauss's *Ariadne auf Naxos* given by the Bavarian State Opera. I find the production fussy, but the music is splendid. Afterwards a very good supper party at the German Embassy. Have some talk with the Kents who are the guests of honour, and recall with Eddie how we went to Bayreuth as long ago as 1954. Katherine, who was sitting almost on top of the stage, says that the props were very unsatisfactory, including the sort of plastic cups that might have come from the Ministry of Works.

The German Ambassador asks me to sit at the same table as the Kents, but I tell him that there are all sorts of important people whom they ought to meet first. In fact, I have a delightful evening talking to Denis Healey and his wife, Edna.[‡] During his years as Secretary of State for Defence, Denis saw a great deal of Mountbatten, and produces a very characteristic story. Healey once had to give an enormous party, attended by about 800 guests. Towards the end, Edna complained to Mountbatten that her arm ached after all the handshaking. Mountbatten replied: 'That is nothing. My great-aunt, the Empress of Russia,[§] used to have a blister on the back of her hand each Easter where the peasants had kissed it.'

On political matters, Healey admits that he has made several mistakes in his career. One minor one was to have written a pamphlet in his youth suggesting that if we were in earnest about the Common Market, we should have only one sort of cheese. But he also says that he has done himself more

---

[*] Fredrick Hoyer Millar, 1st Baron Inchyra (1900–89), Permanent Under-Secretary at the Foreign Office 1957–62.

[†] Sir Ivone Kirkpatrick (1897–1964), Permanent Under-Secretary at the Foreign Office 1953–7.

[‡] Edna Healey, Baroness Healey (1918–2010), writer and lecturer.

[§] Alexandra Feodorovna, Alix of Hesse (1872–1918), Empress of Russia as the spouse of Nicholas II, the last ruler of the Russian Empire.

harm through arrogance. 'At least it is better than conceit.'

He has a high regard for Antony Head, who told him that after Suez he felt that the Army had been let down, so went to Macmillan and resigned. He happened to see on a piece of paper in front of Macmillan that the next name on the list of appointments was Duncan Sandys. He then realised – too late – that he had made a mistake in resigning, as Duncan succeeded him.

We also had some talk about the Brigade of Guards, and I tell him how proud I am that my own regiment could boast the two leading English philosophers of their day, Gilbert Ryle and Freddie Ayer.* He replies: 'That is no better than saying you could boast the two best cooks in England. Neither cooking nor philosophy is an English virtue.'

## 12 March 1972

At Eton with Giles St Aubyn. He takes me to have a drink with the Head Master, Michael McCrum, before lunch. As we leave, I hear a Dame saying goodbye to the HM: 'It is not that I have had too much to drink.'

I hear that Sir Kenneth Wheare is ceasing to be Rector of Exeter College two years early. The other Fellows have infuriated him by allowing undergraduates to keep women in their rooms overnight.

## 15 March 1972

Lunch at the Beefsteak with Harry d'Avigdor-Goldsmid. He tells me that the University of Texas bought Evelyn Waugh's library, and not long ago invited Cyril Connolly to go over and look at it. Predictably, Connolly insisted on seeing which of his books were in Waugh's library. He found them all, except *Palinurus* which, the librarian explained, was being repaired. He insisted on seeing it however, and to his mortification found that Waugh had annotated almost every margin with scathing comments on both text and author. 'What a wonderful story', Harry says, 'Henry James would have made of it.' Harry adds that almost the only advantage in being in the House of Commons is the unlimited writing paper of fine quality – the Socialists use a red crest, and the Tories a blue. The green is for non-party use.

## 21 March 1972

Catch the 1.10 train to Leeds. Edward Boyle sends his car and chauffeur to meet me at the station. David Dilks is lecturing on Chamberlain, Churchill and the fall of France. It is the first time I have ever heard David lecture, and I am agreeably impressed. As always, he is beautifully dressed, and has an

---

* Gilbert Ryle (1900–76); A.J. Ayer (1910–89).

exact command of modulation and gesture. Few other lecturers, I suspect, would have begun: 'My Lord and Vice-Chancellor'. The theme of David's lecture is the close, even affectionate, relationship between Churchill and Chamberlain from the outbreak of war in 1939 until Chamberlain's death in 1940. In retrospect, Chamberlain sometimes emerges as the wiser of the two. Thus, he wrote in 1939: 'France can never keep a secret for more than half an hour, nor a Government for more than six months.' By contrast, Churchill's Francophilia blinded him to France's defects. Thus, he said to General Alphonse Georges[*] in the summer of 1939: 'You are the masters.'

During the first months of the war, Churchill exhausted everybody by writing interminable letters to Chamberlain and to other members of the Cabinet, covering subjects which had already been exhausted in Cabinet. The reason was obvious: he was already writing the first volume of his war memoirs. By contrast, Chamberlain was brief and efficient in the conduct of his colleagues. To end the lecture, David shows us a newsreel of the signing of the Franco-German armistice at Compiègne in the summer of 1940. Unexpectedly, when the French delegation enters the old railway carriage, Hitler at once gets to his feet as a gesture of courtesy.

Afterwards Edward drives me up to his house. We have to thread our way through an enormous crowd of students waiting to attend a 'right to work' meeting. He says: 'Look, nobody is throwing stones at my car.' I reply: 'We have come to a pretty pass when a Vice-Chancellor has to draw my attention to his not being stoned by his students.'

Edward tells me that he would like to contribute to the *DNB*, especially the notice on Iain Macleod. I promise to pass on his request to Bill Williams.[†]

## 23 March 1972
Dine at the Beefsteak with John Sutro.[‡] He was staying with Randolph Churchill in Suffolk recently. A German girl was also staying there. Randolph Churchill got very drunk and abusive. John Sutro said to the girl: 'I am so sorry, it's awful for you.' The German girl replied: 'No worse than Hitler.'

## 24 March 1972
Edward Ford to lunch at Boulestin. He says that the Queen Mother was difficult as Queen. She insisted on being consulted by the King. This led to delay;

---

[*] (1875–1951), French C.-in-C. of the North-East Front 1939 and 1940.
[†] To no avail. The notice on Iain Macleod was written by Ian Gilmour.
[‡] (1908–85), film producer.

and what she told the King did not always conform to Tommy Lascelles'
advice.

## 27 March 1972

Catch the 11 a.m. train to Salisbury to lunch with David Cecil. David's house
in Cranborne is actually on the village street, but has a big garden at the back.
David tells me that almost his first introduction to political life took place at
Hatfield, when he was about seven. Winston Churchill was staying in the
house and began to orate on some subject. He went on and on, developing
his great theme. When he finished, David applauded and everybody roared
with laughter.

Winston was concerned with a later and more vital episode in his life. In
1938, when staying at Taplow, Ettie Desborough* asked him to read aloud
the opening chapters of his new book *The Young Melbourne*,† which had not
yet been published. He did so rather nervously, as his audience included not
only Winston, but also H.A.L. Fisher. When the reading was over, Fisher
invited David to come to New College as a don. So he took up residence there
in 1939.

David believes that Fisher is a greater historian than G.M. Trevelyan,
whom he calls 'Macaulay and water'. When I say that, after Boswell,‡ I think
that Macaulay's life of G.O. Trevelyan is the greatest in the English language,
David gives his own preference as Froude's life of Carlyle.§

## 9 April 1972

Talking to me about the House of Lords, Quintin Hailsham describes it as 'a
dustbin'. He much resents that it is full of fallen MPs who talk too much and
try to make the Upper House a carbon copy of the Commons. 'The purpose
of a House of Lords debate', he says, 'should be to rouse public opinion without attempting to sway important decisions of policy – rather like a leading
article in *The Times* or the *Telegraph*.'

## 14 April 1972

Sir Barnett Cocks,¶ Clerk of the House of Commons, lunches with me at

---

* Ethel Grenfell, Lady Desborough (1867–1952), hostess.
† William Lamb, 2nd Viscount Melbourne (1779–1848), Prime Minister 1834 and 1835–1841.
David Cecil's *The Young Melbourne* was published by Constable in 1939.
‡ James Boswell, 9th Laird of Auchinleck (1740–95), biographer of Samuel Johnson.
§ James Froude (1818–94), historian and biographer. His life of the Scottish philosopher and
social commentator Thomas Carlyle (1795–1881) was published between 1882 and 1884.
¶ (1907–89), Clerk of the House of Commons 1962–73.

Boulestin. He stresses two characteristics of his job. First, he is independent
of MPs, being appointed by the Crown on the recommendation of the PM.
Second, he is always prepared to put his experience and knowledge at the
disposal of any MP, including the Speaker.

Speaker Harry Hylton-Foster had a profound effect on the career of Jack
Profumo. After the notorious confrontation in a room of the Commons at
3 a.m. one morning when Profumo insisted to the Attorney-General and
others that he had never been to bed with Miss Keeler, Profumo's solicitor
drew up the statement which he later that day read to the House of Commons. Having no experience of parliamentary manners, the solicitor cast
it in defiant tone, with a threat to sue those who publicly challenged his
denial. Naturally, the Speaker received a copy before the House assembled.
Under normal practice, the Speaker should have shown it to the Clerk for
information and possibly advice. But Hylton-Foster apparently considered it
too confidential a matter. Had Cocks seen the draft, he would have advised
Profumo to take a much less drastic line, and to say to the House: 'If I have in
any way departed from the high standards which are expected of a Member,
then I throw myself on your mercy.' There is nothing that goes down better
with MPs than a penitent admission of frailty. Had Profumo been advised
to take a humble line, he would have kept both his seat and his ministerial
office. As it was, he lied defiantly and was ruined.

### 2 May 1972
Katie Macmillan is worried whether Maurice is doing well as Minister for
Employment, & I reassure her. She says that Maurice had a brisk exchange
with the railway union leaders the other day. They said to him: 'You talk to
us like a laird ordering us off your land.' He replied: 'You talk to me like the
Duke of Argyll* ordering my crofter ancestors to leave the Isle of Tiree.'

A Foreign Office official once sent Alec Douglas-Home a very boring
memorandum on some topic such as whaling rights, together with a covering note: 'The Secretary of State may care to read this.' Alec minuted: 'A
kindly thought, but an erroneous one.'

### 19 May 1972
Such a sad account of the Queen's visit to the Windsors yesterday afternoon
in the course of her State Visit to Paris. The Duke was apparently too unwell
even to come downstairs.

---

* George Campbell, 8th Duke of Argyll (1823–1900), cleared crofters from the Isle of Tiree.

**28 May 1972**

I hear that the Duke of Windsor died early this morning. I am sad, and recall with gratitude that I saw him just before his final illness; it must have been the last dinner party he and the Duchess ever gave.

**29 May 1972**

*The Times* reprints its famous leader on the Abdication, which is right, but adds a sanctimonious article on its supposed part in the event, which is not. It forgets it is only a newspaper and not an estate of the realm.

**31 May 1972**

Watch on TV as the body of the Duke of Windsor is flown into Benson RAF Station on its way to lying-in-state at Windsor and burial at Frogmore. Eddie makes a fine soldierly figure as he salutes the coffin of his uncle.

**8 June 1972**

Annual Welsh Guards dinner at the Dorchester. I hear that Johnny Henderson,[*] who used to board at Hartley's when at Eton, not long ago called to see Hubert and Grizel Hartley at Dorney. He found Grizel struggling to get her old and battered car to work, tried to start it himself, but failed. So he said he would go in to Windsor and find a good mechanic. He came back half an hour later with a brand-new car, which he presented to Grizel on the spot.

**18 June 1972**

Remember the Guards' Chapel, twenty-eight years ago today. As if to underline it, news of a dreadful air crash near Staines, with well over 100 killed.

**28 June 1972**

Mary Beaufort,[†] seeing that she had to sit next to Frank Longford, asked Lord Cobham[‡] what to talk to him about. He replied: 'Pornography.' She thought he had said photography, and they kept it up for two hours.

**16 July 1972**

Dine with Rab Butler on the High Table at Trinity. He tells me how tired he is after giving away degrees at Sheffield University, of which he is Chancellor.

---

[*] Maj. John Ronald Henderson (1920–2003), long-serving ADC to FM Montgomery. Lord Lieutenant of Berkshire 1989–95; amateur jockey and racehorse owner.

[†] Mary Somerset, Duchess of Beaufort (1897–1987), châtelaine of Badminton House.

[‡] Charles John Lyttelton, 10th Viscount Cobham (1909–97), ninth Governor General of New Zealand 1957–62.

'The Duchess of Kent works far too hard at it at Leeds,' he adds. 'She speaks to everybody at degree ceremonies, which I never do at Sheffield. I just bow.'

## 18 July 1972

The news comes in the afternoon of Reggie Maudling's resignation as Home Secretary. His business associations have not been dishonest or corrupt, but I think that financial greed has warped his judgement of people. It is all rather puzzling, as a former Chancellor of the Exchequer could surely have had his pick of reputable directorships.

At 6 p.m. to the Savoy for a drink with Noël Coward. Find him sitting rather mummified in an armchair wearing scarlet pyjamas. He is suffering, he tells me, from phlebitis. Rather a nice little oil painting of the Thames by Edward Seago, done from the suite in the Savoy which Noël used to occupy. But now he cannot bear the noise, and shudders as he recalls it: to me, his suite on the Strand side sounds far from quiet.

He is very sad for the Duchess of Windsor, whom he likes; but he never cared for the Duke. 'When he was Prince of Wales, I had to play the piano for him for hours on end while he learned the ukulele: it was a rough time. And the next day he would cut me in Asprey's.' Amusing on Winston's paintings of Morocco – 'magazine pictures: let us not think of them'.

## 1 August 1972

Dine with Frank Roberts.[*] Harold Lever[†] is a fellow guest, who amuses me very much before dinner when he telephones the House of Commons to find out the time of a division. He is so used to having his telephone calls made for him that he does not know the dialling code number for the Whitehall exchange. After dinner he talks brilliantly and at length. He says he deeply regrets that Labour did not lose the 1966 General Election, when they would have been spared the terrible difficulties of solving our balance of payments problem. Conversely, he wishes that Labour had won the 1970 General Election, when he himself would have been appointed the negotiator of our going into the Common Market and would have swung the Labour Party behind him. He also thinks that Labour might have done better than the Tories in opposing the Industrial Relations Bill.

Harold is obviously divided from many of his colleagues about strikes. He says: 'Men like Wedgwood Benn who support the strikers do not realise that

---

[*] Sir Frank Roberts (1907–98), Ambassador to the Soviet Union 1960–62 and to the Federal Republic of Germany 1963–9.

[†] Baron Lever of Manchester (1914–95), barrister and Labour politician.

those behind the strikers do not want to get only the Tories out: they want to get MPs of all parties out.' In particular, he cannot stand Wedgwood Benn, whom he thinks venomous and over-ambitious.

Finally, Harold talks about the *New Statesman*, of which he has just become a director. He thinks that Anthony Howard[*] is a very bright journalist, but is shocked by his lack of editorial wisdom and the malice he has shown towards both Harold Wilson and Roy Jenkins. Of previous editors, he admired Paul Johnson as a journalist, but not as an editor; and thought that Dick Crossman's tenure of the editorial chair was like that of a man trying to seduce an old flame whom he had pursued for twenty-five years.

### 28 August 1972
I hear that Prince William of Gloucester has been killed near Wolverhampton this afternoon while piloting his own plane in an air race. I am very sad: he sometimes had a bounderish side to him, but was a warm and stimulating friend. I last saw him a few weeks ago, the evening on which he had just delivered a speech to some provincial newspaper editors on which I had given him some help. I wonder whether Barnwell had been made over to him: in that case, there may be heavy death duties. In any case, will Prince Richard still want to become a farmer? What a horrible additional blow for the poor Duchess.

### 29 August 1972
The Court Circular states that 'The Queen has received with <u>regret</u> the news of the death of Prince William . . .' Surely it would not have been out of place to use the word <u>sorrow</u>.

It seems from all accounts that the crash was entirely William's own fault. He banked too steeply without having gained enough speed, and the plane stalled. Hardly a word in the papers about the co-pilot who was killed through William's error.

### 30 August 1972
Dine off a tandoori chicken and listen to *Parsifal*.

### 2 September 1972
Some political talk with Nigel Fisher.[†] Ted Heath is impervious to criticism.

---

[*] (1934–2010), journalist, broadcaster and writer. Editor of the *Listener* 1979–81 and of the *New Statesman* 1972–78; Obituaries Editor of *The Times* 1993–9; biographer of Rab Butler.
[†] Sir Nigel Fisher (1913–96), Conservative politician. MP for Hitchin 1950–55 and for Surbiton 1955–83; biographer of Iain Macleod 1973.

As a member of the Executive of the 1922 Committee, Nigel has been to see him several times as a member of a delegation. Nor has the PM any real political friends, only subordinates. When he came to power in 1970 he excluded all who had had more experience than himself, such as Duncan Sandys and John Boyd-Carpenter. There are now very few men who in Cabinet will dare to speak before the PM. It was the same in the Wilson Cabinet: only Callaghan, Jenkins, Brown and Healey. The lack of talent – or trust – at the top is illustrated by the double burden borne by both Carrington and Carr.* The second of these is almost always disastrous, for Carr is a slow reader, and always has to work till the early hours on his papers. Now, as both Home Secretary and Leader of the House, he must be finding it an intolerable strain.

Nigel is also amusing on the changing sartorial habits of the House of Commons. Twenty years ago almost every Tory MP and several on the Labour side wore a uniform of short black coat and striped trousers with dark ties. Now almost everybody wears a suit. And although Macmillan's wearing of the Old Etonian and Brigade ties encouraged others to do so, nobody wears such class emblems under Heath's rule.

Nigel talks at length on his relations with Duncan Sandys, who treated his civil servants abominably, and would not hesitate to humiliate them in front of other ministers. Nigel would say to him after his all-night committee meetings (a trick he must have learned from Winston, his father-in-law) that whereas he and Duncan could get home to their houses in Westminster, a few minutes away, the civil servants had nowhere to bathe and shave and change and rest. Duncan would merely reply: 'It's what they are paid for.'

Another cause of friction was the intense dislike of Duncan and Rab Butler for each other. Each would bully Burke Trend,† Secretary to the Cabinet, into giving his own version of events in the Cabinet minutes – and Duncan was the tougher.

## 5 September 1972

Read part of Nigel Fisher's forthcoming life of Iain Macleod. For someone who has never written before it is competent and in places highly interesting. Unfortunately, his publisher has made him cut it heavily, so that some of the autobiographical touches have had to go. Enoch Powell was the only one of

---

* Robert Carr, Baron Carr of Hadley (1916–2012), Conservative politician. Home Secretary 1972–4.
† Baron Trend (1914–87), civil servant. Cabinet Secretary 1963–73; Rector of Lincoln Coll., Oxford 1973–83.

Iain's political contemporaries who refused to help after repeated requests: he carries his strong views even into personal relationships, and both Nigel and Iain opposed his harsh approach to immigration. Eve Macleod* (to whom Nigel is making over all the proceeds of the book) has asked for all references to his numerous affairs with women to be deleted. One odd point. As a senior minister, he might have had all sorts of prestigious directorships when in Opposition. But he joined Lombard Banking, because they were the first to offer a car and chauffeur.

## 6 September 1972
Appalling announcement that all the Israeli hostages at the Munich Olympics have in fact been killed, as well as some of their Arab captors.

## 11 September 1972
Visit Noël Coward in his villa in the village of Les Avants near Montreux. He looks unwell and can hardly walk. He has had a lift put in the villa to carry him up and down stairs. His intonation is sometimes rather slurred and his memory occasionally at fault. But there is still a great deal of wit. Even with all the success that has come to him in recent years, Noël is still very bitter when he recalls what he suffered at the hands of critics. Ivor Brown,† in particular, he loathes. When *Private Lives* was first produced, Brown described it as a collection of stale aphorisms, and asked rhetorically who would remember it in fifteen years. When, at least fifteen years later, Noël met Brown and reminded him of his criticism, Brown replied sheepishly: 'I was young in those days.' Noël said to him: 'And I was five years younger.'

Throughout our entire conversation, he shows himself, like that other great talker, Max Beerbohm, to be an equally good listener, and again and again when he likes a story he exclaims: 'Oh, that is good; oh, that is wonderful!', almost writhing with delight. Only once or twice does his memory fail in a curious way, as when he cannot remember if Dorothy Macmillan or Malcolm Sargent are still alive.

## 1 October 1972
A glorious day. I go up to Primrose Hill to see Robert Wade-Gery on one of his Sunday walks on Hampstead Heath. We have a long talk about the economic possibilities facing the Government in trying to control inflation. Robert says that Heath, however tough he would like to be, dare not

---

* Evelyn Macleod, Baroness Macleod of Borve (1915–99), public servant.
† (1891–1974), drama critic.

antagonise the whole of the trade union movement by bringing in a measure curbing the payment of supplementary benefits to strikers: it would only weld together the militants and the moderates. In any case, such a measure could hardly be pushed through in the present Parliament. And a General Election would not strengthen his hand. Trade union militants are not impressed by parliamentary majorities. What Heath is trying to do is to isolate the militants from the moderates, without much apparent hope of success.

## 5 October 1972

To St Clement Danes Church for the memorial service to 'William, Prince of Gloucester', as the order of service calls him. The congregation is in a deeper shade of black than on most such occasions; but also a higher proportion of young faces. The sight of the Duchess of Gloucester wrings my heart – utterly ravaged, yet very upright and royal. Prince Richard and his wife came with Princess Alexandra. A most moving service without gloom or self-pity. The co-pilot, killed with William, is rightly included in the prayers.

## 14 October 1972

Watch the Prime Minister on television as he delivers the final speech to the Conservative Party Conference at Blackpool. It is terribly drab stuff, a cross between a talk from a headmaster and a sermon. The applause is comparatively tepid.

Staying with John and Guinevere Tilney* in Liverpool, a city I have hardly ever seen. Guinevere takes me to the Roman Catholic Cathedral, which from a distance looks like a gasometer. Inside it is rather like the chapel of Sussex University, on a much larger scale. Some of the abstract designs in the windows are rather unnerving, but there is one striking little chapel with pale-gold windows. It is a pity that all the woodwork has been varnished. From the modern part of the cathedral we descend to the crypt, built by Lutyens. It consists of three underground churches, side by side.

Then on to the Anglican Cathedral, the huge bulk of which dominates the Liverpool skyline. It is built of pink stone, which I do not find attractive. Inside it resembles a film set constructed for a Metro-Goldwyn-Mayer production entitled 'The Cathedral'. There are huge sloping staircases, soaring arches, quite good glass and heavily carved doors. The font is so contrived

---

* Sir John Tilney (1907–94), Conservative politician. MP for Liverpool Wavertree 1950–74. Dame Guinevere Tilney (1916–97), President, National Council of Women of Great Britain 1961–8.

as to be ludicrous. Astonishingly enough, they are still building on to the existing fabric.

## 18 October 1972

Jonathan Aitken tells me that the Prime Minister's speech on Saturday upset the television programme planners. It was expected to last exactly sixty minutes, but in fact took only forty-eight. The reason became apparent if one had managed to see his script. In various places there was the letter A, standing for applause. But the applause never came.

## 30 October 1972

Lunch with Hugh Trevor-Roper in the Senior Common Room at Oriel, the college to which his Regius Professorship is attached. I am much diverted by a group of leading dons who spend most of the meal discussing the puddings on the menu for next week. 'Why do we never have lemon sponge?' 'What a pity the chef does not put more treacle in his treacle tart.' 'Oh, for an apple pie.' Hugh seems to find it all quite normal.

By arrangement, I meet Isaiah Berlin at Oxford Station and we travel to London together. He tells me that the Wolfson Foundation is about to inject over £2 million into University College, Cambridge, which will then change its name to Wolfson College. Thus Isaac Wolfson will become the first Jew since Jesus Christ to have foundations at both Oxford and Cambridge named after him. I say: 'What about St John?' Isaiah, who has obviously been expecting the question, bursts out in triumph: 'The Oxford St John was the Baptist, the Cambridge St John the Evangelist.'

His own Wolfson College in Oxford is flourishing, although he will shortly have to present the trustees of the Wolfson Foundation with an enormous bill for increased building costs. Isaiah happens to mention that Wolfson has practically no prizes, so I tell him I will endow one. Having just begun to endow one at Sussex University, in addition to my one at St Catherine's, Oxford, I am spending a little more on education than I had intended. But my admiration and affection for Isaiah is boundless.

## 1 November 1972

There is a demonstration by cab drivers which blocks the entire centre of London so I am about half an hour late arriving at the Ritz to lunch with Oswald Mosley in a private suite. As luck would have it I run in the entrance hall into Isaiah Berlin and George Weidenfeld. Isaiah knows where I am going, because I told him on the telephone this morning, but like a loyal friend he keeps mum.

I find Mosley in a shabby but delightful suite that looks as if it has not been decorated – or dusted – since World War I. We have an hour and a half of sparkling talk, largely about the political past, but also about our going into Europe. He also tells me two stories about the Windsors. Although he was a fairly close friend of the Duke in the 1920s, he naturally saw little of him during his own Fascist phase. But during the Duke's brief reign, Emerald Cunard[*] asked him to come and meet the King. He was accompanied not only by Mrs Simpson, but also by Ernest Simpson.[†] That in no way inhibited the conversation. The Duke, with his love of talking about the past, exchanged steeple-chasing memories with Mosley until there came a sharp rap on the table from Mrs Simpson: 'Remember, sir,' she said, 'that Sir Oswald is a very serious person.'

The other story which Mosley tells is of a dinner party given by the Windsors after the war. Walter Monckton was also there, and the Duke turned to him and said: 'Come on, Walter, admit that it was the Jews who brought us into the war.' Monckton naturally refused to agree with the Duke, who then turned to Mosley and repeated the question. Mosley says to me: 'As I was interned for three and a half years for maintaining just that, I had had enough and declined to discuss the matter with the Duke.'

## 19 November 1972

At 8.30 to 10 Downing Street, for a party given by the Prime Minister in honour of the committees which have been organising the Fanfare for Europe celebrations. Two things strike me about the inside of the house: how enormous it is, and how mean is the staircase, lined with pictures of former Prime Ministers, which leads up to the state rooms. As one ascends, there seem to be Special Branch detectives standing rather obtrusively in all the doorways.[‡]

The Prime Minister greets every guest with the utmost geniality. To me he says: 'You will find it just like a Balliol concert, except that it is more comfortable.' In one of the large drawing rooms we are served with champagne. There is an agreeable collection of guests, including all the ambassadors of the Common Market countries in London. The atmosphere is euphoric and even David Eccles says good evening to me.

The pictures in all the rooms are superb. It is interesting how many of

---

[*] Maud Cunard (1872–1948), American-born society hostess.

[†] (1897–1958), American-born, naturalised British shipping executive; second husband of Wallis Simpson.

[‡] More recently, when guests ascend these stairs, Larry, the Downing Street cat, is in evidence clearly discomfited about his territory being invaded.

them contain a dog gazing fondly up at its master. I also notice a reflection of the Prime Minister's personal tastes – a table loaded with his sailing trophies.

After drinks, the Prime Minister personally shows us into the panelled dining room, where rows of litte gilt chairs have been laid out. There follows a glorious concert given by the Amadeus Quartet. The acoustics are wonderful and one seems to hear every single vibration with startling clarity. But I notice that both Charles and Pamela Snow allow their heads to loll in the most inelegant way during the music; and Eccles, all of whose aesthetic tastes are visual, looks as bored as any man I have ever seen.

As soon as the music ends, the Prime Minister makes a charming little speech. Without a trace of shyness or stiffness, he tells us that when he began negotiating for our entry into the Common Market about ten years ago, he and his staff would discuss during the silent watches of the night exactly how they would celebrate the end of their labours. 'We decided that we would have *Fidelio* in Vienna and *Rosenkavalier* in Munich. But we never thought we would have to wait ten years – or that at the end of that we would ourselves be the hosts to such great orchestras and companies in London.' He also draws a moral from the Schubert Quintet in C Major that we have just heard: 'There are long passages of suffering, ending on a note of joy.' It occurs to me what a marvellous impression Heath could make on the platform at occasions like the Conservative Party Conference if he tore up the scripts prepared for him and spoke like this from the heart.

### 22 November 1972

Julia Rees telephones in high delight to tell me that Brian is to be the new Headmaster of Charterhouse, in succession to Oliver van Oss. She herself spent part of her childhood there when her father Robert Birley was Headmaster, and remembers carrying the family hens from one house to another during the terrible winter of 1940. She also says that her father is Deputy Chairman of the Governors of Charterhouse. Far from being an advantage to Brian, it was a positive disadvantage.

### 23 November 1972

Alan Bullock, whom I have not seen for about a year, tells me that he is in a blazing fury with Margaret Thatcher, the present Secretary of State for Education. 'Why on earth should people vote Tory if they are to get a minister like that?' One expects Ted Short* to talk egalitarian rubbish, but not a Tory.

---

* Edward Short, Baron Glenamara (1912–2012), Labour politician. MP for Newcastle upon Tyne Central 1951–76; Secretary of State for Education and Science 1968–70.

She has a thoroughly suburban mind. Under her influence, the Government has come to believe that polytechnics are as educationally effective as universities, but cheaper. Neither is true.'

### 30 November 1972

Lunch with Princess Alice,[*] now in her ninetieth year. 'I am just a little tired. I have been shopping all the morning.' She asks for Dubonnet and tells me not to forget the lemon.

When she mentions the years that she and Alge[†] spent in Ottawa, I ask her whether Winston had been a good guest at Government House in Ottawa. She says: 'He was worse than you can possibly imagine. He hated talking intimately as you and I are talking, and would scarcely open his mouth unless he could hold the whole table. If he was bored, he would show it, taking a big glass of claret and plunging his nose into it. Then he would drink brandy and in fact get quite pickled. He also made a great fuss about special rooms for his maps. Roosevelt was a far better guest, but had some terrible Secret Service guards. I remember how they tried to prevent me from going from one room to another while the President was staying with us. They talked to me quite rudely and never took their feet off the table while doing so, and wherever they went, they left a litter of cigar ends.'

I lead her on to talking about Queen Victoria. The Queen was apparently not at all a glum person in private: that mournful face was put on only for the photographers. In the family circle, she would smile and talk a great deal. Except for the Queen, most of the Royal Family rather liked Mr Gladstone, and were fond of the slightly odd Mrs Gladstone.[‡] One night, Mrs Gladstone announced: 'I always take great care of my William. Whenever he arrives home from the House of Commons in the early hours of the morning, I always have some hot soup for him.' Queen Victoria asked her how she kept it hot. She replied: 'I fill a stone hot-water bottle with it and keep it in my bed.' And on another occasion, Mrs Gladstone electrified a dinner party at Windsor: 'It does William so much good to sleep between the Queen's sheets.' Princess Alice tells all these stories with immense vivacity.

### 3 December 1972

In the course of the weekend, I read E.M. Forster's posthumously published

---

[*] Princess Alice, Countess of Athlone (1883–1981), last surviving grandchild of Queen Victoria.

[†] Alexander Cambridge, 1st Earl of Athlone (1874–1957), sixteenth Governor General of Canada 1940–46.

[‡] Catherine Glynne (1812–1900), m. 1839 William Ewart Gladstone.

novel *Maurice*. Its theme is the astonishment and worry of a Cambridge undergraduate in finding himself attracted to same-sex love, and his bursts of
madness when his lover grows out of him. It begins well, but becomes rather
amorphous and wet. One unintentionally amusing note is that Maurice's
final lover is a gamekeeper. But Forster, in his introduction, disclaims any
intention of borrowing from D.H. Lawrence.[*]

## 5 December 1972

Hugh Trevor-Roper tells me that he is very anxious that Henry Chadwick,[†]
the present Dean of Christ Church, should be given one of the vacant bishoprics. He then reveals his real interest in the matter: he wants Chadwick out of
the way so that he himself may become the first lay Dean of Christ Church.
And he promises to send me a paper he has written showing that there is no
legal obstacle to a lay Dean.

## 6 December 1972

At seven o'clock to a cocktail party given by Evelyn Emmett. I have some
talk with the Prime Minister. I tell him how much we all enjoyed the recent
Fanfare for Europe musical party at No. 10. We discuss the impending
by-election, particularly at Uxbridge, which the Conservatives may find it
difficult to hold. Heath says that at this moment in the life of the last Labour
Government, they had already lost nine seats at by-elections, whereas his
own Government has lost one and gained one. Obviously, the sort of seat
that falls vacant is fortuitous. But perhaps it means that a Conservative Government can afford to be unpopular for longer than a Labour Government. I
ask him whether there is still any truth in the old doctrine that bad weather
deters more Labour than Conservative supporters from turning out to vote:
I should have thought that today they all had transport. The Prime Minister
thinks there might be something in it and, peering out of the window with
a sailor's eye, says: 'It seems to be drying up.' He adds with relish: 'But the
weather forecast for tomorrow is bad.'

We discuss whether or not the Government would be wise to bring in
legislation abolishing or amending the system by which strikers' families
receive supplementary benefits, thus putting the financial burden of strikes

---

[*] *Maurice* was written in 1913–14, but Forster (1879–1970) thought it unpublishable in his
lifetime. It was published in 1971.
[†] (1920–2008), academic and C of E priest. Dean of Christ Church 1969–79; Master of
Peterhouse, Cambridge 1987–93, the first person in four centuries to head a college at both
universities. Chadwick succeeded Hugh Trevor-Roper, who had been Master of Peterhouse
1980–87.

on the taxpayer rather than on the trade union. The Prime Minister asks my opinion and I reply that it would on balance be unwise to change the law at this stage, because (a) it would unite moderate and militant trade unionists, and (b) it would cling to the Prime Minister just as allegedly sending troops to Tonypandy stuck like a burr to Winston Churchill. The Prime Minister: 'Yes, I agree. The National Government ran into just such a difficulty over the Means Test.' I tell Heath that the only Prime Minister I can recall to mind who did not mind such vilification was Asquith, and I tell him the story of the heckler who shouted out: 'Why did you murder working men at Featherstone in 1892?' Asquith replied: 'It was not in 1892, but in 1893.'* The Prime Minister explodes with laughter and says: 'Ah, Balliol self-confidence.'

John Tweedsmuir[†] tells me that he has invented Tweedsmuir's law: whenever Russia wins at Henley, it is a good year for claret. Curiously enough, it has worked out very well.

### 7 December 1972
Do an evening's work at home, with one corner of my brain busy on the Uxbridge by-election. At about eight o' clock it begins to pour with rain, which is always considered to be in favour of the Conservatives. Turn on the wireless about 11.30 to hear the commentary on the result. All the BBC people appear to be left-wing and dismiss the Tory chances at Uxbridge with contempt. In fact the Conservative candidate romps home with a majority of 1,078, showing a shattering lack of confidence in Labour.

### 12 December 1972
Poor old Eugen Millington-Drake[‡] is dead, the only man who ever sent me a two-page telegram, asking me to become his Private Secretary.

### 14 December 1972
Lunch with Charles Johnston and his wife Natasha.[§] Harold Macmillan is

---

* The Featherstone Massacre on 7 Sept. 1893 happened when the Riot Act was read after an angry crowd gathered outside the Featherstone pit during a lockout. The South Staffordshire Regiment fired warning shots. Two people died of their injuries. As Home Secretary Asquith set up a parliamentary commission, which paid £100 compensation to the families of those killed, but said that the compensation did not imply any admission of responsibility.

† John Buchan, 2nd Baron Tweedsmuir (1911–96), colonial administrator.

‡ Sir Eugen Millington-Drake (1889–1972), diplomat. In 1939 he played a pivotal behind-the-scenes role in the Battle of the River Plate. Millington-Drake had been impressed by K.R.'s work for him at the British Council in Italy.

§ Princess Natasha Bagration, Lady Johnston (1914–84), Georgian noblewoman of the House of Mukhrani.

also a guest. The most interesting thing that Macmillan has to say is about Winston Churchill's last years as Prime Minister. 'It is often said that Churchill was gaga and had no grasp of the agenda at Cabinet meetings. In fact, the old man was very shrewd in his handling of such occasions. I remember one day when the Egyptian Treaty, of which Winston very much disapproved, was item number four on the agenda. He wanted to oppose it, yet not to have an open row in Cabinet with Eden. So he determined that the whole matter should be postponed. He therefore began wasting time until it was 12.45 and still the item on the Egyptian Treaty had not been reached.'

When Macmillan talks about the history of World War I he is obsessed by the supposed power of the Press, and says that the reason Lloyd George did not sack Haig at Passchendaele was that he feared the Press campaign that would be launched against him. I demur, and tell Macmillan that the over-riding reason was Lloyd George's fear, not so much of the Press as of the Tory Party, who formed a substantial part of the coalition. If Haig had been sacked, they would have voted against Lloyd George.

Macmillan tells the story of the old hall porter in White's who, when the whole club was awaiting news of the sinking of the *Bismarck*, suddenly appeared in the bar and announced: 'Gentlemen, the *Eisenhower* has been sunk.'

Macmillan very kindly offers to drive me down to Fleet Street after lunch as he is himself going to his office nearby. 'Of course, I prefer to travel by bus or Underground, but I recently had a fall and my family now insist that I have this hired car.' As we drive along the Mall in view of the Houses of Parliament, I ask him whether he ever feels a twinge of longing to be back. He says: 'No, aged actors should not hang about the green room. It is all right for junior ministers to go to the House of Lords when they retire. But if one has been the Queen's First Minister, one is expected to make speeches on all the big issues. How can I talk on Vietnam? I haven't seen the Foreign Office telegrams.' As I get out of the car, he puts his hand on my arm and, in trembling tones, says: 'Goodbye, dear boy.'

Although Macmillan talked a great deal during lunch, he did not entirely monopolise the conversation. Natasha Johnston told us a wonderful story. Apparently, Nixon, during his recent visit to Red China, said to Chou En-Lai:* 'I wonder what difference it would have made if Khrushchev and not Kennedy had been assassinated.' Chou

---

* (1898–1976), first Premier of the People's Republic of China 1949–76.

en-Lai replied: 'Well, Aristotle Onassis[*] would not have married Mrs Khrushchev.'[†]

## 21 December 1972

Walk through the park to Lancaster House for a meeting on conservation, presided over by Prince Philip. What an excellent Chairman he is, brisk and good-humoured.

I sit next to Edward Ford, who points to a pompous-looking man and says: 'Who is that Theudas?' I do not understand the reference, but he explains that it is a favourite remark of Tommy Lascelles. It comes from the Acts of the Apostles, chapter 5, verse 36: 'For before these days rose up Theudas, boasting himself to be somebody.'

---

[*] (1906–75), Greek shipping magnate, m. 1968 Jacqueline Kennedy.
[†] (1923–71) Nina Khrushcheva, third wife of Nikita Khrushchev.

# 1973

*On 1 January the United Kingdom, the Republic of Ireland and Denmark entered the European Economic Community. On 23 January President Nixon announced that an accord had been reached to end the Vietnam War. On 30 January two Watergate defendants were found guilty. On 26 March Noël Coward died. Value Added Tax came into effect in the UK on 1 April. On 22 May President Nixon confessed his role in the Watergate cover-up. The IRA detonated bombs in three places in the UK in September. On 26 September Concorde made its first non-stop crossing of the Atlantic in three hours and thirty-three minutes. On 29 September W.H. Auden died. On 8 October Edward Heath announced the Government's proposals for a counter-inflationary Price and Pay Code. On 12 November miners began an overtime ban. On 26 November Peter Walker, the Secretary for Trade and Industry, warned of possible petrol rationing as a result of the oil crisis in the Middle East. On 9 December the Sunningdale Agreement was signed in an attempt to establish a power-sharing Northern Ireland Executive. On 31 December the Three Day Week, announced on 17 December, came into force at midnight.*

### 3 January 1973

Change into a white tie and tails for the opening gala at Covent Garden of the Fanfare for Europe celebrations. Outside the Opera House there is an anti-Common Market mob, consisting mostly of members of the National Front. They have a gallows with an effigy of Heath hanging from it, rather disconcerting for him as he greets the Queen. But the police wisely decided not to risk a riot by clearing them away.

Inside the foyer are the small detachments of soldiers from the member countries of the European Community. They look very smart, especially the Danes, though I gather they are only Luxembourg traffic wardens. As the original idea for a gala was mine, I am rather pleased by the turnout. Garrett Drogheda is standing just inside the door and coyly unbuttons his overcoat so that I can see the Garter ribbon beneath. 'It is really a fake,' he explains, 'I have to button it on at the other end. It doesn't go the whole way round.'

The decorations in the Opera House itself are rather disappointing. Apparently £5,000 has been spent on flowers, but they are not easy to see against the gilt. In any case, there is such a splendid array of jewels and decorations that even gladioli would be put in the shade.

In the interval there is champagne and smoked salmon in the Crush Bar with the compliments of HM Government. I talk to Chips Maclean,* who like Alec Home is wearing his Order of the Thistle. The Queen herself looks splendid in silver, with her Garter ribbon and a huge tiara.

Laurence Olivier was a wonderful compère and dear old Sybil Thorndike stole the show at ninety, waving her stick cheerfully at the audience as she gave a flawless recitation from Robert Browning. There were some delightful extracts from Mozart, Donizetti, Verdi and Berlioz operas. The evening ends and we drive to Lancaster House for the supper party. The Prime Minister is an excellent host and greets every guest individually. Not many Socialists about!

While talking to Martin Charteris, I mention the heavy cost of the elaborate awnings put up outside Lancaster House as the Queen's car is too wide to go through the porte-cochère. I am astonished when he replies that it is the first he has heard of it, and that of course she could have come in some other car. It is an interesting example of how people toady to the Royal Family against what are in fact their wishes.

Run into Alan Bullock, who says: 'I thought you would be here. You like great occasions, being an Edwardian at heart.' There is a placement for the supper, which is extremely good – saddle of lamb and Cheval Blanc 1957. The Queen leaves about 12.30, and I stay on for another half-hour or so. When saying goodbye to the Prime Minister, we talk about the pictures at No. 10. He is quite agreeable, but once again I notice those suspicious little eyes peering out of a smiling face.

### 9 January 1973

To St Paul's Cathedral for a performance of Beethoven's *Missa Solemnis*. The inside of St Paul's is brilliantly illuminated, but the music is terribly distorted by the notorious echo. The Prime Minister is here again tonight and bares his teeth at me as he goes by. At the reception afterwards at Goldsmiths' Hall I have some talk with the Prime Minister. We discuss which Prime Ministers in history have ever been interested in music. He announces profoundly and without a hint of self-caricature: 'Well, I am the only Prime Minister ever to have conducted the London Symphony Orchestra.'

---

* As a baby he was described as 'a Chip off the old block' and 'Chips' stuck as a nickname.

## 30 January 1973

I hear that Claude Elliott feels he may have done me an injustice twenty-five years ago by not taking me onto the permanent staff at Eton. I think of him only with admiration and affection, and should be miserable if he imagined that I harboured any twinge of resentment or even of regret. The six months I spent at Eton as a temporary beak were among the happiest of my life. The stimulation of teaching lively minds, the easy cordiality of colleagues, the beauty of the place: all made a profound impression. But once I had left Eton, it did not take me long to realise what an unsatisfactory beak I should have made: too impatient of routine, too intolerant of authority, too restless to remain in that enchanted valley.

## 8 February 1973

I lunched with Asa Briggs at his official Vice-Chancellor's residence near Lewes with a few other guests. He had specially got hold of Harold Macmillan to come over to lunch, so it was a good occasion for talk. He wore an old-fashioned grey chalk-striped suit, a maroon waistcoat with a heavy gold watch-chain, a white shirt, Brigade tie and brown suede shoes. He carried a blackthorn stick which he relinquishes with reluctance in the dining room. Old Macmillan, as always when in the presence of a congenial audience, threw off his habitual mask of a very old man and held forth at length until well into the afternoon. He embarked on his favourite theme of oratory. 'It is extraordinary how radio and television changed the lives of politicians. Fifty years ago a Prime Minister needed to worry only about the Press – and very powerful it was, as there was no other way of communicating with the people. But today a politician can hardly survive without knowing the techniques of television.

'My maiden speech in the House of Commons was on economic affairs: it was exactly like a lecture at the London School of Economics. Later that day, I saw Lloyd George, who told me that what I said was excellent, but that I had no idea of delivering a speech. So I asked him for some advice. He replied that in any speech there had to be a complete variation in both pitch and pace. At that time Lloyd George was without a party, so if he wanted to make a speech, he had to attract an audience into the Chamber. He would therefore begin with provocative remarks and eventually, by the time the Chamber was filling up to hear the fun, he would launch into his main theme. If one comes to think of it, it was exactly like any other stage performance. You know, when one arrives at a play a few minutes late after dining at the Savoy, the curtain has gone up but nothing very much is happening except a telephone ringing and a butler answering it. The murder never takes place in the first five minutes.'

Someone asks Macmillan if he knows Heath well. He replies, almost as if he was referring to an upper servant: 'He was my Chief Whip.' Discussing the economic situation and the threats by the unions, he said: 'There may well be a revolution this year. We are approaching a situation similar to the General Strike of 1926. A revolution was only averted by Baldwin. Can Heath rise to the same heights? He is respected as much as Baldwin, but can he inspire affection? Both qualities are needed in a great peacetime Prime Minister. It did not matter that the means by which Baldwin inspired affection were bogus, so that in spite of his talk of pigs, he really hated the sight of those animals. What is happening now is the greatest political event since Peel's repeal of the Corn Laws. Of course, today there is no man who can play Disraeli to Heath's Peel.'

Macmillan also spoke of Enoch Powell, who he thinks is unbalanced. 'The House of Commons will tolerate rebellion on a particular issue: I was a rebel on economic affairs. But it does not like a man to attack his party on every issue as Powell does. When he was in my Cabinet, I gave orders that he should sit on the same side of the table as myself. I could not bear sitting opposite those mad eyes.'

### 15 February 1973

I hear that Anthony Blond,* the publisher, was a pupil of Isaiah Berlin at Oxford. The first time he went for a tutorial he knocked on successive doors, but found each of Isaiah's rooms empty. Eventually, he put his great shock of black hair round the door of the bedroom. Isaiah was fast asleep, but the greeting, 'I'm Blond' awoke him. Isaiah sat up in bed, said 'Palpably untrue, palpably untrue,' and went back to sleep again.

### 2 March 1973

To Oxford for the celebrations on the 150th anniversary of the Union. A champagne party opens the proceedings at seven o'clock. The dinner itself is too long and there are too many speeches. I sit next to Philip de Zulueta, which is always pleasant. He tells me an odd little story about his years as Private Secretary to Macmillan. One day an urgent matter suddenly cropped up, and Philip went upstairs to the little study in Admiralty House that has the view of St Paul's Cathedral. Harold Macmillan rather angrily shooed

---

* (1928–2008), publisher and author.

him away. Later that day, he apologised to Philip, explaining that he was reading Wilkie Collins' *The Woman in White*, and had just reached a very gripping moment.

## 12 March 1973

Leave for Leeds to hear Alan Lennox-Boyd lecture at the university on his experience as Colonial Secretary. Alan's lecture is discursive, but contains much amusing gossip. As Minister of State at the Colonial Office he served under Oliver Lyttelton, and was reluctant to accept promotion to be Minister of Transport. When he remonstrated, Winston said he could not keep two ministers whose height totalled twelve feet nine inches in the same department. Although loyal to Winston, Alan leaves his audience in no doubt that the old man disliked the Statute of Westminster* and accepted the replacement of the Empire by the Commonwealth with tepid enthusiasm. After the war, Alan tried to persuade him to visit every British territory overseas in order to thank them for their war effort. But Winston could not find the time; in any case, he was obsessed by the need for an Atlantic alliance. The Colonial Office, Alan says, lasted for exactly 100 years. During that time, there were no fewer than fifty Secretaries of State. As Joe Chamberlain, Leo Amery and himself totalled eighteen years, most of the others served for well under two years.

## 2 May 1973

The *Observer* is publishing extracts each week from Evelyn Waugh's diaries. They make very sad reading. They are almost entirely without literary merit, but reveal him as vilely selfish and snobbish. I doubt whether the diaries were ever written for eventual publication. I suspect they were simply notes which he made for future use in his novels. Even his crushing of Randolph Churchill gives one scant pleasure.

I attend the annual dinner of the Royal Academy at Burlington House. The Archbishop of York, Donald Coggan, tells me about the funeral of the Duke of Windsor, for which he stayed at Royal Lodge with the Queen Mother. In fact, he had been invited for that weekend weeks before the Duke died. He was deeply moved by the distress of the Queen Mother at the reproving remarks which people were making about her attitude towards the Windsors. This prompted him to send a letter to *The Times* praising all that the Queen Mother had done for the monarchy. He was doubtful how it would be

---

* In 1931 this established the legislative independence of the self-governing Dominions of the British Empire.

received, and only sent in the letter after consulting the Prince of Wales, who
gave his enthusiastic approval.

## 8 May 1973

Dine at Pratt's. Find myself next to Harold Macmillan. He talks of Beaverbrook with respect and affection, stressing his value in recharging Winston
Churchill's batteries at the end of a harassing day. On World War I he says:
'It wasn't all horror. We were all young and would go and get drunk in
Abbeville.' He then describes how he lay wounded all day in a shell-hole,
reading Aeschylus' *Prometheus Vinctus*. Someone on the other side of the
table leans across and asks: 'Did it help?' Macmillan replies: 'No.' As he talks
of his friends being killed, tears run down his face. He then embarks on a
passage about the need to avoid a confrontation between the Government
and the trade unions. 'We are all one people.'

About 11.30 he decides he ought to go, but can hardly stand. So I help
him to his feet and ask whether I can see him home. He replies that he is
staying at the Carlton Club nearby, and would be grateful for my arm. When
he pays his bill, he observes: 'What exorbitant charges His Grace makes.'* I
then help him up the stairs with much difficulty, and he leans heavily on me
as we make our way down St James's Street to the Carlton. Several people
turn round in the street to stare, as well they may. It is rather like an old
nineteenth-century caricature of Disraeli being helped home by Monty
Corry.†

## 12 May 1973

Harold Macmillan made a memorable remark to me today. 'Being Prime
Minister is a very lonely job. Friends do not like to bother one, and the only
people who see one are those who want something.'

## 10 June 1973

I have a great deal of gossip with Reay Geddes,‡ who is an accomplished
anecdotist. When Lloyd George had almost completed his war memoirs, he
invited Reay's father, Sir Eric Geddes,§ to read the draft. Having done so, Eric
Geddes told Lloyd George that he had given far too much credit to General

---

* Andrew Cavendish, 11th Duke of Devonshire, owned Pratt's Club.
† Montagu Corry, 1st Baron Rowton (1838–1903), Benjamin Disraeli's PS 1866–81.
‡ Sir Reay Geddes (1912–98), industrialist.
§ (1875–1937), businessman and Conservative politician, responsible for the 'Geddes Axe'
when Minister of Transport 1919–21.

Pershing[*] and the American army for our ultimate victory. Lloyd George simply replied: 'I have great hopes of my American sales.'

He also tells me that Harold Macmillan, when Prime Minister, was invited to address the Society of Motor Manufacturers. The somewhat pompous president talked at length of the role of the motor in a fruitful national life, including much detailed advice to the Government on road finance and taxation. Macmillan began his reply: 'I am grateful to your president for so much advice on political problems and economic problems and social problems. Perhaps, after all he has said, I may confine myself to talking about the Society of Motor Manufacturers.'

### 18 June 1973
Waterloo Day and also the anniversary of the destruction of the Guards' Chapel in 1944, where I might easily have lost my life.

### 28 June 1973
Evening party at the French Embassy. First, we drink champagne in the garden. As dusk falls, a troop of footmen walk round the garden lighting tiny lamps along all the paths. I have some talk with Denis Greenhill, who has just returned from more talks with Ian Smith's Government in Rhodesia. When I ask him how he managed to keep his mission secret from the Press he replies: 'We took no special precautions. We merely stayed at a multi-racial hotel in Salisbury – not the sort of place that journalists visit.'

### 30 June 1973
I hear that when de Gaulle came on his State Visit to England, he went down to Windsor and the Queen took him and Harold Macmillan round all the pictures in the Waterloo Chamber. At the end of the tour, de Gaulle said to the Queen: 'Alors, Madame, was it necessary to have all these messieurs to defeat Napoleon?'

### 12 July 1973
Lunch at the Ritz given by George Weidenfeld for Mrs Lyndon Baines Johnson. Mrs L.B.J. is not only an exceptionally nice woman, but also intelligent. Such is her interest in the present fuel crisis that she has flown up to Scotland to see the construction of a huge rig to be used in the search for North Sea gas and oil.

---

[*] Gen. John J. Pershing (1860–1948), Cdr of the American Expeditionary Force on the Western Front 1917–18.

## 18 July 1973

I sit next to Clemmie Churchill at a lunch party. Although approaching ninety, she still has that changeless beauty. But she is almost blind, very deaf and rather lame. Her mind, however, is exceptionally agile and she has a light, quick, youthful voice: I seem to recall reading that Queen Victoria had such a voice even in old age. By pitching my voice up and speaking fairly slowly, I think I penetrate her deafness. She is quite sharp in some of her judgements. She thinks Hatfield a very ugly house; Martin Gilbert's life of Winston 'far too big' and her grandson, Nicholas Soames,* far too fat. But she praises Ted Heath's taste at Chequers. Her own favourite colour for a room, she adds, is pale blue. Nowadays, she tells me, she hardly ever ventures out of London. Winston left her a cottage on the Chartwell estate, but the servants do not like moving from house to house, and she too finds it exhausting. So she spends nearly all her life being looked after in London.

## 5 August 1973

By chance, I hear Michael Tippett's oratorio *A Child of Our Time*. His music rarely gives me pleasure, but this is a most noble composition.

## 30 August 1973

At 11.30 to the Foreign Office to see Sir Thomas Brimelow. I have difficulty in entering the building, as the gates from Downing Street are closed and chained. So I walk down the steps to the Secretary of State's entrance and am taken up with much deference in the Curzonian lift. Brimelow is at present in his far from palatial office as Deputy Secretary of State. It has only one picture: a portrait of Lord Melbourne. Brimelow is delighted that I notice this.

Brimelow gives me the most interesting lecture on the principles of foreign policy. The first essential, he says, is peace; the second, conditions in which one can trade satisfactorily. 'One doesn't want warlike relations with one's enemies, but it certainly pays one better to look after one's alliances. One's friends come first.' He therefore thinks that Russia is far from being our principal concern in the field of foreign policy. In trade we sell more to Poland than we do to Russia and more to Sweden than to all the Communist countries combined. One great difficulty of Russia, he says, is that everything must be done in a bureaucratic way. 'There is no need to think that work is

---

* Sir Nicholas Soames (b. 1948), Conservative politician. MP for Crawley 1983–97 and for Mid Sussex from 1997.

well done only when done by Governments. It is done best by people who know best.'

Brimelow is a dedicated believer in delegating responsibility. Whenever he has to promote a member of the Diplomatic Service, he asks himself two questions. First, does this man expect responsibility? Secondly, does he show good judgement? He adds: 'The Service works best when responsibility is passed down as far as possible. To fail to delegate can do immense harm.'

He is dismayed by the amount of entertainment that takes up the time both of Foreign Office ministers and officials. The subject of sumptuous entertainment leads him to tell me a favourite Russian story about Leonid Brezhnev.* His old mother came to visit him, and he showed her first his splendid flat in Moscow, then his even more magnificent apartment in the Kremlin, then his luxurious dacha, and finally his palatial residence in the Crimea. His mother took it all in with delight, then said: 'Be careful, my son. If those Communists hear you have got all this, they will take it away from you.'

## 20 September 1973

Bill Deedes discusses whether Alec Douglas-Home is likely to go soon. Bill believes that the Prime Minister may well be planning almost as drastic a reconstruction of his Government as Macmillan carried out in July 1962. In that case, Alec could well depart. It may be significant that Willie Whitelaw has recently been staying with Alec in Scotland. Perhaps they had things other than shooting to discuss.

## 26 September 1973

Dine with Alan Urwick† at the Garrick. We have some talk about the Middle East. Alan tells me that there is still a monument to British influence in the public swimming baths in Baghdad. Even after the revolution, there remained a notice that read: 'Nannies sit here.'

## 28 October 1973

Dine with Rab Butler at Trinity. A little gleam of malice illuminates his conversation as he touches on Harold Macmillan. 'Of course, I am the first academic for 400 years to receive the Garter. The Queen, I believe, thought I had behaved well in October 1963. She said nothing at the time, then

---

* (1906–82), General Secretary of the Communist Party of the Soviet Union 1964–82.
† Sir Alan Urwick (1930–2016), Ambassador to Jordan 1979–84 and to Egypt 1985–7; High Commissioner to Canada 1987–9.

suddenly gave me the Garter by her own wish. Harold Macmillan refused it. He said he was only a crofter's descendant. I think he would like it now, but I doubt if he will get it.' As always, Rab monopolises me both at High Table and in the Combination Room.

### 13 November 1973
Jock Murray gives a party in Albemarle Street to mark the publication of a new book by Osbert Lancaster. As I arrive Jock warns me not to tease John Betjeman about the ghastly poem which he has just written for the Royal Wedding tomorrow of Princess Anne and Captain Mark Phillips.* Of course, I would not dream of doing so. But the moment I see John, he plunges into the topic himself and is obviously very upset at the news that a Member of Parliament has publicly demanded his dismissal as Poet Laureate.

### 20 November 1973
Katie Macmillan quotes a remark of the old Duke of Devonshire, Lady Dorothy Macmillan's father, out shooting one day: 'Here they come, low and weaving, like Tories.'

### 22 November 1973
Alan Bullock tells me how relieved he is to have given up the Vice-Chancellorship of Oxford just as the students are turning nasty again.

### 3 December 1973
I hear that when George Harewood was a prisoner of war at Colditz, the Germans, knowing that he was the King's nephew, asked him whether there was anything special which he would like. 'Yes,' Harewood replied, 'a woman.'

---

* Capt. Mark Phillips (b. 1948), equestrian Olympic gold medal winner; first husband of Princess Anne.

# 1974

*The industrial situation became worse in the opening weeks of 1974. In January Britain entered its first post-war recession. The Three-Day Week, introduced to conserve electricity during the miners' strike, ran from 1 January to 7 March. Eventually, after much disagreement among his senior advisers about whether to call a general election on the question of 'Who Governs Britain?', on 7 February Edward Heath named polling day as 28 February. Opinion polls on 14 February showed the Conservatives in the lead. On 27 February Enoch Powell announced his resignation from the Conservative Party in protest against Edward Heath's decision to take Britain into the EEC. The general election produced the first hung Parliament since 1929. After failing to convince the Liberal Party to form a coalition, Edward Heath announced his resignation as Prime Minister and Harold Wilson became Prime Minister on 4 March at the head of a minority government.*

*On 6 March the minority Labour Government settled the miners' pay claim. The Three-Day Week ended on 7 March. Direct rule over Northern Ireland was established on 29 March. Richard Nixon announced on 8 August that he would resign the Presidency of the United States following Watergate. The next day Vice-President Gerald Ford became the thirty-eighth US President. Harold Wilson confirmed the date of the year's second general election on 10 October. Opinion polls on 30 September showed Labour in the lead and well placed to gain an overall majority. However, the victory was only a narrow one. Edward Heath had now lost three out of the four general elections at which he had led the Conservatives and his leadership of the party was not expected to last long. His London home was bombed on 22 December in a suspected Provisional IRA attack. Inflation in the UK in 1974 soared to a thirty-four-year high of 17.2 per cent.*

## 10 January 1974

Weidenfeld and Nicolson are to publish a book about what Winston Churchill called 'My Most Secret Source', otherwise known as 'Enigma'.* Apparently, the Government captured a coding machine at the beginning of the war which enabled us to decipher a great deal of top German intelligence. I have a word with Jock Colville about it. He says that when he was Winston's Private Secretary during the war, he always understood that 'My Most Secret Source' was not called 'Enigma' but 'Boniface' and was a way of intercepting the code of the German air force. The results of such interception would arrive for Winston in a special yellow box, of which only he had the key.

## 15 January 1974

There are strong rumours of an imminent General Election. I cannot see what good it would do Ted Heath even if he came back with an increased majority. If the miners go on strike, all the Conservative MPs in the world will not help to get coal out of the ground.

## 16 January 1974

The economic situation is as gloomy as ever and I feel tired and seedy. As if all that were not enough, on turning on the wireless this morning, I get only Chopin's Funeral March.

## 24 January 1974

Dine with Nicky Gordon Lennox in Chelsea. When Nicky went to Moscow with Alec Home not long ago, there was the usual exchange of presents. Nicky's share of the loot was a handsome illustrated volume on Moscow, together with a little china samovar. I point out that it seems astonishingly heavy for its size and probably contains a concealed microphone. Nicky replies: 'It's odd you should say that. There is a standing instruction that any present received from the Russians which a member of the Diplomatic Service wants to keep in his room at the Foreign Office should first be carefully examined by our electronics people.'

## 25 January 1974

Read the awful news that James Pope-Hennessy has been found murdered in his London flat. I dined with him a few months ago after writing about his forthcoming biography of Noël Coward, but had not seen him for some years

---

* *The Ultra Secret* by F.W. Winterbotham (1897–1990), published in 1974, was the first extensive account in English of the Enigma-derived intelligence from Bletchley Park.

before that. I suspect there may be some appalling homosexual involvement behind the crime.[*]

### 5 February 1974

Lunch with Tony Royle, who is rather sad at having ceased to be Parliamentary Under-Secretary at the Foreign Office in the recent reshuffle, but relieved to be back in the City where he can make some money before old age overtakes him. At the Foreign Office he was very much the protégé of Alec Douglas-Home. He has the highest opinion of his abilities as Foreign Secretary, and declares that it is really Alec who has preserved the Anglo-American alliance in recent months by getting on very well with Henry Kissinger.[†] Heath and Kissinger absolutely loathe each other, and this could have had a disastrous effect on our foreign policy.

Tony is very disturbed about the strain under which Peter Rawlinson,[‡] the Attorney-General, now lives. As there are threats against his life from the IRA and various anarchist groups, he is perpetually surrounded by detectives. Even his little boy at school has to sleep with an emergency button under his pillow.

### 6 February 1974

Very depressing industrial news: a coal strike now looks almost inevitable, and could cripple the country for months.

### 8 February 1974

There is much excitement that Heath has now definitely called a General Election for 28 February. Discuss election prospects with Julian Amery. He says he is in favour of calling an election (although I do not really think he is), but that it will be immensely difficult to win. Tony Barber[§] is more optimistic about the election chances of the Conservatives. He also says how absurd it is that Members of Parliament, who for the first time are being paid between dissolution and the election itself, cannot go on using their offices in the Palace of Westminster.

---

[*] There was. He mixed with a rough crowd and was brutally killed by three young men, one of whom was his lover, on 25 Jan. 1974 in his flat.

[†] (b. 1923), American diplomat and political scientist.

[‡] Sir Peter Rawlinson, Baron Rawlinson of Ewell (1919–2006), barrister, Conservative politician and author. MP for Epsom 1955–78; Attorney-General 1970–74 and Attorney-General for Northern Ireland 1972–4.

[§] Anthony Barber, Baron Barber (1920–2005), Conservative politician. Chancellor of the Exchequer 1970–74.

Tom Brimelow is alarmed, not so much by Ted Heath's personal dislike of Kissinger, as by his antipathy to the United States altogether. This could be dangerous. Alec Douglas-Home and Peter Carrington, he adds, are above such petty likes and dislikes. I ask him whether he continues to draw comfort from the portrait of Melbourne which he acquired specially for his new room in the Foreign Office. He replies that his constant reading of Central Intelligence Reports puts him in mind of one of Melbourne's most memorable remarks: 'What all the wise men promised has not happened, and what all the damned fools said would happen has come to pass.'*

### 10 February 1974
Work for most of the day on Linky's papers at Eton, and find the familiar atmosphere stimulating. I happen to pass a window overlooking College Chapel just as it is getting dark. The John Piper windows lit from behind look absolutely dazzling.

### 15 February 1974
A strong rumour that Dr Donald Coggan may succeed Michael Ramsey as the next Archbishop of Canterbury. I rather doubt it myself, not so much because Coggan is already sixty-five, but because he is a fervent evangelical. He will never wear a cope and mitre unless specially requested. The other day Coggan preached at a local church in York. As he put on his mitre, a dead bat fell out.

### 23 February 1974
Watch Verdi's *Falstaff* on television. What a cruel opera it is.

### 24 February 1974
The Liberals seem to be doing remarkably well in all the pre-election opinion polls.

### 27 February 1974
After discussing election possibilities with Nicky Gordon Lennox, I place some bets with Ladbrokes:
> £100 at 14–1 that the Liberals will have 16 to 20 seats.
> £50 at 6–1 that the Liberals will have 21 to 25 seats.
> £25 at 30–31 that the Tories will have a majority of 61 to 66 seats.

---

* Melbourne was speaking of the Catholic Emancipation Act, 1829.

£25 at 35–1 that the Tories will have a majority of 67 to72 seats.[*]

The past few weeks I have re-read Harold Nicolson's diaries. I still feel much affection for him, but am increasingly irritated by his mannered phrase-making, his cringing social subservience to Vita, his dislike of Americans and Jews, and his manoeuvring for a peerage.

## 28 February 1974

General Election Day. A nice, crisp morning. Walk to the polling station to vote for Nick Scott,[†] the Tory. In the evening I walk down to Cowley Street where Michael Hartwell is giving an election party on a much-reduced scale. The results look fairly inconclusive. There is a swing to Labour, but hardly enough to give the party an overall majority. I am glad to see that Jeremy Thorpe gets back in Devon with an enormous personal majority. As the swing to Labour continues, Christopher Soames tells me how desperately upset he is at the prospect of a Government committed to renegotiating our role in the Common Market. George Weidenfeld, by contrast, obviously thinks that his turn has come once more: his eyes are alive with nervous ambition. Eddy Shackleton[‡] tells me that if Wilson does form a Government, he will not return to the Leadership of the House of Lords – or to any other post. He is too immersed in industry nowadays, and could not afford to interrupt his career. I notice Gerald Ellison,[§] the Bishop of London, among the guests. He looks like a very handsome stage prelate, hired out for the night.

## 1 March 1974

Very little sleep. There is an absolute deadlock between Labour and Conservatives. Jeremy Thorpe must be desperately unhappy at the Liberals having polled six million votes, but winning only 14 seats. Two seats more and I would have won about £1,300. The Queen is returning from Australia. I wonder whether she will be in any fit state, either physically or mentally, to take delicate decisions at once after a long flight.

## 2 March 1974

The final state of the parties is:

---

[*] K.R. lost his money on all these wagers.

[†] Sir Nicholas Scott (1933–2005), Conservative politician. MP for Paddington South 1966–74 and for Chelsea 1974–97.

[‡] Edward Shackleton, Baron Shackleton (1911–94), Labour politician. Leader of the House of Lords 1968–70.

[§] The Rt Revd Gerald Ellison (1910–92), Bishop of London 1973–81.

Conservative   296
Labour   301
Liberal   14
Scottish Nationalists   7
Plaid Cymru   2
Ind Lab.   1
Dem. Lab   1
United Ulster Unionists   10
SDLP   1
Protestant Unionists   1
The Speaker   1

The editor wants an article from me on the constitutional role of the Queen in choosing a new Prime Minister: also whether a Prime Minister who does not obtain a majority at a General Election should instantly resign or wait until he is defeated in the Commons. At the moment Heath seems to be taking the second course, hoping to secure the support of the Liberals.

### 3 March 1974

In a break from all the political uncertainty Norman Collins cheers me by telling me how C.P. Snow proposed J.B. Priestley's health on his seventy-fifth birthday: 'I dismiss all Jack's novels and most of his plays. But he will always be remembered for one play – *Journey's End*.'*

### 4 March 1974

Still no new Government. Heath remains Prime Minister but looks unlikely to win the support of either the Liberals or the Scottish and Welsh Nationalists.

On the news it is reported that Heath has finally given up hope of forming a coalition, and went to the Palace this evening to resign. So Wilson is the new Prime Minister.

### 5 March 1974

Cocktail party at the American Embassy. There is a good handful of recent Tory ministers at the party, now with time on their hands. Alec and Elizabeth Home both look immensely young and cheerful. Alec tells me that he will remain in the House of Commons for the present, but at the next election, which cannot be far off, he may be tempted to return to the House of Lords with a life peerage.

---

* The author of *Journey's End* was R.C. Sherriff.

I talk to Michael Wilford,* the Deputy Under-Secretary at the Foreign Office. The Office, he says, is not at all disappointed to have Jim Callaghan as the new Foreign Secretary.

Tom Brimelow is delighted that I referred the other day in 'Albany' to his love of quotations by Melbourne. He tells me another. When in 1834 Melbourne was initially reluctant to see the Monarch to accept the premiership, his secretary told him: 'Why damn it, such a position was never occupied by any Greek or Roman, and if it lasts only two months, it is well worthwhile to have been Prime Minister of England,' to which Melbourne replied: 'By God that's true. I'll go.'

## 6 March 1974

Garrett Drogheda asks me to the Royal Box at Covent Garden to hear *Rigoletto*. Other guests include Jock Colville. At the end of the scene in which Rigoletto is humiliated by the courtiers, Jock says to me: 'I think Verdi was very unfair to us courtiers.'

## 7 March 1974

It is announced in the evening paper that Nicky Gordon Lennox is being superseded as Head of the News Department at the Foreign Office. I telephone Nicky, who comes in later. He is slightly daunted at having been sacked in this way, although it has been made clear to him that no stigma whatsoever attaches to him. The new Foreign Secretary, Jim Callaghan, has made the change presumably because he does not trust a member of the Diplomatic Service. Robin Haydon† has similarly been removed as Chief Press Officer at No. 10. Earlier today, in fact, Robin gave Nicky an amusing account of how Wilson re-entered Downing Street. He marched in through the front door, followed by Marcia Williams,‡ followed by Gerald Kaufman,§ who in turn was followed by a lot of men in hairy tweed suits and red ties. Nicky expects to be given a job as head of a department in the Foreign Office, or perhaps abroad: there will be no demotion.¶ Nicky gives me some other news of Government appointments that have not yet been announced. Astonishingly,

---

* Sir Michael Wilford (1922–2006), Ambassador to Japan 1975–80.

† Sir Robin Haydon (1920–99), Chief Press Secretary, 10 Downing Street 1973–4; Ambassador to the Republic of Ireland 1976–80.

‡ Baroness Falkender (b. 1932), head of Harold Wilson's political office.

§ Sir Gerald Kaufman (1930–2017), long-standing Labour MP since 1970; Father of the House 2015–17.

¶ Lord Nicholas Gordon Lennox was made Head of the North America Dept. at the Foreign Office in 1974.

Tom Balogh* is to be included in the Government.

During his frequent tours with Alec Home, Nicky sometimes had to take part in discussions with Heath. The man still remains an enigma to him. He has absolutely no small talk and, having been given a piece of information, will digest it in silence for a very long time.

## 8 March 1974

The Government has settled with the miners on the most appallingly inflationary terms. I doubt whether their implications have yet been realised.

## 12 March 1974

Give Prince Eddie lunch at the Ritz. He has just come from the State Opening of Parliament, rather disturbed that it should have taken place without robes or any other pageantry.

I am interested in the warm, admiring terms in which he speaks of the Duchess of Windsor; he must be the only member of the Royal Family to do so. There will be a dreadful problem when she dies. She is to be buried beside her husband at Windsor. But what sort of funeral service will there be, and can all the family, including the Queen Mother, be persuaded to attend? I think they would really like to bury her without any ceremonial at all. Eddie adds how moved he was by the arrival of the Duke's coffin at RAF Benson.

After lunch, as we are walking along Piccadilly, we are stopped by two young people pushing a pram, who ask the way to Carnaby Street. Eddie, who of course is not recognised, directs them in his brisk military way. But how does he know?

## 14 March 1974

Dinner party at the French Embassy. The dining room has been sumptuously redecorated with dark-green walls and orange curtains.

Denis Greenhill says that nepotism in politics or in the Services or in the Foreign Office is nothing compared with nepotism in certain trade unions, such as printing and the docks. 'Think of the outcry if we chose recruits to the Diplomatic Service on such decidedly family principles.' He adds: 'When I was taken round *The Times* there were so many people round the first machine we were shown that I thought there had been an accident.'

---

* Thomas Balogh, Baron Balogh (1905–85), Minister of State, Dept. of Energy 1974–5; economic adviser to the Labour government 1978–9.

## 28 March 1974

Jeremy Thorpe comes for a drink. He looks and feels exhausted after the political manoeuvres of the past few weeks, with office in a coalition Government almost within his grasp. But as he explains, 'We could have joined a National Government of all three parties. But had we formed an alliance with the Tories alone, we would have been obliterated.' I nevertheless suspect that he personally would have been prepared to do a Ramsay MacDonald, as it were, by joining Heath, but that he was deterred by intense pressure against it from his rank and file. In some ways, he is his own worst enemy. He still cannot have a few moments of serious talk without breaking into an imitation of some public man: this leaves the impression that he is a lightweight.

## 2 April 1974

To Blenheim Palace for the opening of the Winston Churchill centenary exhibition by Mary Soames. A cold mist outside and picturesque flocks of sheep.

Mary does the ceremony with much charm and is presented with an ornate key to the front door, the boss of the handle in the shape of a ducal coronet. As the family walk round all the photographs, there are shrill cries of: 'Oh, Sunny,* come and look at yourself in 1940!'.

There is then a film of Churchill with a commentary by Dickie Mountbatten, but slurred as if he has had a stroke. Evidently it took eight hours in all to get the commentary right; by the end poor Mountbatten was exhausted.

On the 11 p.m. news I hear that President Pompidou has died.†

## 4 April 1974

Dine at the Persian Embassy to meet the Speaker of the Majles.‡ Peter Carrington is very depressed. 'Parties in defeat are very nasty,' he says. But I love his comment on the remark of the Young Conservative leader that the party ought not to be led by bloody aristocrats: 'First time we Smiths have ever been called that!'

Selwyn Lloyd tells me that when he went to Persia he was taken to see so many mosques that he is bent on revenge: he will take the Persian Speaker to see the Anglican and Roman Catholic Cathedrals in Liverpool.

---

* John Spencer-Churchill, 11th Duke of Marlborough (1926–2014); like his grandfather he was known as 'Sunny' Marlborough after his courtesy title of Earl of Sunderland.

† Georges Pompidou (1911–74). Prime Minister of France 1962–8; President of the French Republic 1969–74.

‡ The Iranian Consultative Assembly; an Arabic term meaning 'a place of sitting'.

## 10 April 1974

Jeremy and Marion Thorpe[*] to dine in my flat. Smoked sole, duck, bleu de Bresse cheese and Pol Roger 1964. What odd strains of vanity Jeremy reveals. He wants desperately to be a Bencher of his Inn, and when eventually he becomes a peer, it must be an Earldom, not just a life barony. Jeremy complains that Prince Philip was not at all agreeable to him at President Pompidou's funeral. I suspect that both Prince Philip and other members of the Royal Family would like Jeremy to be rather less obtrusive.

## 25 April 1974

In Monaco to see Prince Rainier. Walk up to the palace. It is like a toy fort, with sentries in elaborate uniforms. From his windows, high over the Mediterranean, Prince Rainier can survey all 500 acres of his domain. For its thirty-first hereditary ruler it remains both a cherished inheritance and an exciting business venture. It is not easy nowadays to see how he ever came to acquire the reputation of playboy, except by marrying the most beautiful film actress of her generation, Grace Kelly.

He does not believe in making too many public appearances: 'My grandfather used to tell me that if I showed myself in public too often, my presence would soon be neither appreciated nor even remarked.' He values his good relations with the Vatican; Monaco is an independent diocese: when a new archbishop is required, the Prince proposes three names, one of which is chosen by the Pope.

The widespread notion that most of Monaco's revenue (about £25 million last year) comes from the profits of the casino at Monte Carlo causes him perpetual annoyance. In fact, the Prince tells me, he has never seen a single spin of the roulette wheel in the casino. Monaco's Budget depends hardly at all on gambling. More than 80 per cent of it comes from VAT, state monopolies, including postage stamps, and industrial development. Fifty-three acres have been won from the sea in the past seven years. 'What other country', the Prince boasts, only half in jest, 'has in recent times extended her frontiers so far – or so peacefully?'

The most convincing testimony to Rainier's statecraft is that he remains an absolute Monarch. When I say that in England the doctrine of sovereignty had ceased to carry political weight after 1688, he politely asked whether we had not been rather careless to let it go. Yet by temperament he is the least autocratic or pretentious of rulers. Although prepared to wear a suitably

---

[*] Marion Stein (1926–2014), Austrian-born concert pianist; m. (1st) 1949–67 George Lascelles, 7th Earl of Harewood, (2nd) 1973 Jeremy Thorpe.

Ruritanian uniform on a very few ceremonial occasions each year, he has set his face against State Visits, either as host or guest. 'They have ceased to have the slightest value. They cause only expense, worry and fatigue.'

In his sense of proportion, he resembles another adroit representative of the *Ancien Regime*, the Abbé Sieyès,[*] who was once asked what he had done during the French Revolution, and replied: 'I survived.'

### 21 June 1974

To Cambridge to stay with Victor Rothschild. Other guests from the Think Tank are there. Much laughter at some of the schemes of the Think Tank. A man was sent to study what was reported to be an inspired system of parking meters in Zurich. But it was successful only because there is so little traffic in Zurich. And Victor has devised an intelligence test to be tried on Permanent Under-Secretaries to see if their brains work after a long flight.

Victor talks of Ted Heath, whose inability to communicate worries him. 'He gave me dinner at the Athenaeum the other night. I don't know which sort of Prime Minister one ought to prefer: a fitfully disagreeable Heath or a falsely friendly Wilson.' Ted was embarrassed when Victor once asked him to inscribe a photograph of himself. After a long time it came back: 'To Victor from Ted Heath.'

### 17 July 1974

Lunch with Peter Tapsell.[†] He is extremely enthusiastic for an all-party collation, primarily to solve the country's economic problems, but also, I suspect, because he has been denied office by Ted Heath. He has a firm dislike of Heath. During the time of the last Conservative Government, the *Sunday Express* ran a story predicting that Peter was shortly to receive office. A few days later, Peter was at the same party as Heath. Roaring with laughter, he said to Peter, 'You must not believe everything you read in the newspapers, you know.' Peter naturally thought that this meant Heath was about to bring him into the Government. But when a reshuffle took place a week or two later, Peter remained on the back benches. Peter quotes this as an example of Heath's insensitivity. Jeremy Thorpe once said to him: 'The reason Ted hates you is that you combine a patrician manner with radical views. I watch his neck muscles stiffen whenever you get up to speak in the House.'

---

[*] Emmanuel Joseph Sieyès (1748–1836), French RC clergyman and political theorist.
[†] (1930–2018), Conservative politician. MP for Nottingham West 1959–64, Horncastle 1966–83, East Lindsey 1983–97 and Louth and Horncastle 1997–2015.

## 20 July 1974

Prince Eddie is very worried about the economic and political outlook, believes that Heath cannot continue for long as leader, and would like to see him replaced by either Willie Whitelaw or Peter Walker.*

Talking of the gala at Covent Garden last Wednesday, Eddie says that not only were the speeches far too long, but that Garrett Drogheda made Prince Philip furious by mocking the Royal Family's indifference to opera. Apparently, the Prince told Garrett after his speech: 'Buggered if I ever come again.'

## 12 November 1974

To Oxford. Opening of Wolfson College in the afternoon by Harold Macmillan, as Chancellor of the university. Stand throughout several very long speeches. Macmillan is nice on Isaiah: 'If you happen to be in a mood of melancholy or frustration, who would you like best to come into your room? Isaiah Berlin!' Macmillan also calls Isaac Wolfson 'a great merchant prince'.

## 18 November 1974

To Leeds where I am staying at the university as Edward Boyle's guest. See David Dilks, then go with him to the Churchill Centenary Lecture given by A.J.P. Taylor. He speaks for an hour without a note, but absence of all quotation and illustration makes it unnecessary. He has some memorable remarks:

'In the long run, everything will be forgotten about Churchill except his leadership in World War II; yet this came after the age of retirement.'

'Had there not been a war in 1939, Churchill would not have stood again for the Commons in 1940.'

'India and the Abdication showed that he was spiritually in exile from modern Britain: a Jacobite.'

'He ran the war in a way no individual had done since his ancestor, the first Duke of Marlborough. His theme was: "All I wish is agreement with my wishes after reasonable discussion."'

What did Winston contribute to the war, Alan asked?

1.  He decided that the war should go on in 1940. The 'victory at all costs' speech was applauded by Labour but not by the Tories.
2.  Strategic bombing, which showed that we were at war, but did little

---

* Peter Walker, Baron Walker of Worcester (1932–2010), Conservative politician. Environment Secretary 1970–72; Trade and Industry Secretary 1972–4; Minister of Agriculture, Fisheries and Food 1979–83; Energy Secretary 1983–7; Welsh Secretary 1987–90.

damage until the last year; and it delayed the invasion of France.

3. Mediterranean campaign: there was nowhere else for us to fight. But 'the Italian campaign was a second and more grandiose Gallipoli'.
4. The combination of (2) and (3) mean that we lost Singapore.
5. Special relationship with the USA.

I sit next to Edward Boyle at the dinner he gives after the lecture. He once heard Sir Herbert Williams* say in the House of Commons that the only people who applied for National Assistance were those who had made a mess of their own affairs. Was it the last time such a sentiment was uttered at Westminster?

Edward also recalls that when he was given ministerial office for the first time, Winston was in a bad temper, preoccupied with replying to Oliver Lyttelton's letter of resignation. But that night in the Lobby, on the vote to abandon Suez as a base, Winston put his arm round him & said: 'I hope you are settling in.'

In Cabinet with Macmillan, the desire of Rutland to remain an independent county was discussed. Edward said that if she remained independent, she could not afford such services as therapists and drama consultants. This did not impress Macmillan: 'I don't know about that,' he said, 'what we want are more gamekeepers.'

## 24 November 1974

Took train to Cheddington, Bucks, where the Great Train Robbery took place. Eva Rosebery[†] meets me, looking very young and vigorous in trousers, and drives me in her Rolls to Mentmore. She has astonishing vitality for a woman of eighty-two. Mentmore was built by Sir Joseph Paxton for Baron Meyer de Rothschild, whose daughter was married to Lord Rosebery, the future PM in 1878.[‡]

Eva is furious over Kenneth Young's recently published life of Harry Rosebery,[§] which I read yesterday. It is a typical Beaverbrook-inspired

---

* 1st Bt (1884–1954), Conservative politician. MP for Croydon South 1932–45 and Croydon East 1951–3.
† Dame Eva Primrose, Countess of Rosebery (1892–1987), JP for Buckinghamshire.
‡ Sir Joseph Paxton (1803–65), architect and Liberal MP for Coventry 1854–65. As well as Mentmore, he also designed the Crystal Palace for the Great Exhibition of 1851. Baron Meyer Amschel de Rothschild (1818–74), businessman, MP for Hythe 1859–74. Hannah Primrose, Countess of Rosebery (1851–90), wife of the 5th Earl of Rosebery (1847–1929), Prime Minister 1894–5.
§ *Harry, Lord Rosebery* (Hodder & Stoughton, 1974).

production, written in a style of defensive jauntiness and unearthing every disobliging anecdote that has ever circulated. Apparently, Young saw Rosebery only twice: on both occasions Max Aitken* arranged it. He then wrote rather cheekily to Eva, saying that he had hardly mentioned her in his text, and could she tell him of anything of interest in her life. She replied that there had been nothing in her life that would interest <u>his</u> readers.

We spent a few minutes before lunch looking at some of the things in what had been the Prime Minister's study. There is a florid French bureau which Eva says has been valued at £200,000. There will be enormous death duties to pay after Harry's death in May, so much of the paintings and furniture may have to go, and eventually Mentmore itself.

## 19 December 1974

Colin Coote tells me a Winston Churchill story. When somebody once told Winston in old age that the only other survivor of the Battle of Omdurman had just died, leaving Winston alone in his glory, Winston replied: 'How civil of him.'

## 23 December 1974

Derek Hill tells me that when he asked Harold Acton† how he liked the portrait he had painted of him, Harold replied: 'I hate it, but it is very like me.'

---

* Sir Max Aitken (1910–85), President of Beaverbrook newspapers.
† Sir Harold Acton (1904–94), writer, scholar and aesthete.

# 1975

*On 24 January Donald Coggan was enthroned as the 101st Archbishop of Canterbury. Margaret Thatcher defeated Edward Heath in the Conservative Party leadership election on 11 February to become the party's first female leader. On 13 February Britain's coal miners accepted a 35 per cent pay rise offer from the Government. Unemployment exceeded one million in March 1975. Saigon fell to the North Vietnamese on 29 April. Proceedings in Parliament were broadcast on radio for the first time on 9 June. Unemployment reached 1.25 million on 21 August. Dougal Haston and Doug Scott became the first British people to climb Mount Everest on 24 September. Ronald Reagan announced his candidacy for the Republican nomination for US President on 20 November.*

## 10 January 1975

To Berlin to stay at the British Embassy with Nico and Mary Henderson. They have just arrived back from a five-hour lunch with Mikhail Yefremov,[*] Soviet Ambassador to East Germany, whose Embassy is the biggest in the world and where East Germany is run from. They show me a charmless typed menu of endless dim courses in bad English. Nico enjoyed teasing Yefremov about the growth of the Soviet navy and suggested that Russian ships should adopt the custom of the Royal Navy in distributing a tot of rum. Nico adds: 'I was going to quote Winston on our naval traditions of "rum, sodomy and the lash", but thought it might offend our prim, puritanical Russian hosts.' Nico was one of Ernest Bevin's Private Secretaries at the Potsdam Conference of 1945 and further enjoyed teasing the Soviet Ambassador on Stalin's profession of democracy and self-determination on that occasion, particularly over Poland. The Ambassador was embarrassed by this.

## 11 January 1975

We go to East Berlin today, via the Unter den Linden. Two stages of passing

---

[*] (1911–2000), Soviet Ambassador to East Germany 1971–5.

through Checkpoint Charlie. Police in fur hats and belted grey overcoats. One looks like a wistful Nureyev. We press our open passports against the glass of the car windows but do not get out. The immediate sight of East Berlin is rather more dismal than the West, though the difference is not startling. The stretches of the Berlin Wall are similar, with raked sand strips to reveal footprints. Some fine old churches, such as St Hedwig's Cathedral, heavy Hohenzollern government buildings, a radio tower superior in design to that of West Berlin; the vast mass of the Soviet Embassy, opera house, and wide, soulless streets like Warsaw, with little traffic. We enter the Pergamon Museum over a little footbridge. The Pergamon Altar, 180 BC, from Asia Minor is a large marble frieze. The gods are depicted as bestial giants.

## 12 January 1975

Peter Carrington has arrived at the Embassy. We are given an aerial tour of Berlin in an Army helicopter. My pilot is a very competent young man. We pass over the Brandenburg Gate; the Reichstag, handsome but battered; the Russian War Memorial; the site of Hitler's bunker; the radio station from where Lord Haw-Haw broadcast; and Spandau. As we approach this huge red-brick castle, my pilot says: 'Last time I flew over here I saw Rudolf Hess. By God, here he is.' And I gaze down on a tall man in a long black coat, with measured tread, his arms and legs not quite co-ordinated. He reminds me of Boris Karloff. Now aged eighty, Hess has been in Spandau for the past twenty-nine years, at a cost of well over £100,000 a year. He was pacing the spacious high-walled garden, originally laid out by Albert Speer.

Tall, gaunt and melancholy, he nevertheless moved with a firm tread for a man of his age. As we fly over, he looks up at 'that little tent of blue which prisoners call the sky'.

## 22 January 1975

Alec Home has this afternoon returned to the Upper House as a newly created life peer with the title Lord Home of the Hirsel. I ask him whether he notices any change since he was last a peer in 1963. 'Yes,' he says, 'it is very odd. In 1963 there were rarely more than eighty peers even for a quite important debate. This afternoon there was nothing much on the agenda, but there must have been about 300 peers present.' He simply did not realise that they had all come to see <u>him</u> take his seat again.

## 4 February 1975

An extraordinary result in the first round of the contest for a new Tory leader: Margaret Thatcher 130, Ted Heath 119 and Hugh Fraser 16. Ted at once resigns the leadership. Thatcher goes forward to the second round, when she will be challenged by Willie Whitelaw. He, I suspect, will be the ultimate winner.

### 9 February 1975

Met Rab Butler and discussed the political situation among other things. A note of malice pervades much of his talk. After telling me that he is trying to get Cambridge University to give Selwyn Lloyd an honorary degree, against left-wing opposition, he goes on: 'When I became Chancellor I thought he might do quite well as Financial Secretary to the Treasury, but when I telephoned to ask him, I found that Eden had already asked him to come to the Foreign Office as Minister of State. It was as Eden's cipher that he obtained rapid advancement. He ought to retire soon as Speaker. He has done well so far and ought to go before he gets worse.'

In the current contest for the Conservative leadership, Rab mildly inclines to Willie Whitelaw, 'though he does drink too much. But at least he is a Trinity man.' Rab adds that he now thinks he should have fought for the party leadership in1963 when Alec Home succeeded Harold Macmillan at No. 10.

In the Combination Room I notice that two huge Stilton cheeses now squat among the decanters and silver. 'Yes,' says Rab, 'you see the college now has every indulgence; it is more like a seraglio than a monastery.' A few minutes later over excellent Fonseca port 1960, Rab adds: 'Mollie thinks I drink too much port, but I <u>never</u> have it on Mondays.'

Jamie Fife* tells me that the Duke of Norfolk was playing cricket at Arundel with his butler as umpire. Obvious lbw and an appeal to the butler, who replied austerely: 'His Grace is not in.'

### 10 February 1975

At 5.30 to Palace of Westminster for a drink alone with Selwyn Lloyd at Speaker's House. He looks thinner, attributing it to having given up gin before lunch. But I suspect he is also finding the life increasingly arduous. He aims to give up the Speakership in February 1976, when he will have completed five years. But the sudden shifts of parliamentary life may upset his plan. He will then write a book about the Speakership.

With endearing frankness, he admits that he thought Ted Heath would win the first round of the leadership contest outright. After Ted's defeat, he thought Willie Whitelaw certain to beat Margaret Thatcher. Now he is not so sure.

---

* James Carnegie, 3rd Duke of Fife (1929–2015), Vice-President, British Olympic Association 1973–2000.

He is delighted at the prospect of an honorary degree from Cambridge (although I myself think it belated to the point of insult). He had the next set of rooms to Michael Ramsey, above the Pepys Library in Magdalene. It was Rab who, as President of the Union, called him for his maiden speech. Selwyn was also responsible for the Cambridge epigram: 'One never knows whether a Combination Room is a pantry or a vestry.'

## 11 February 1975

Margaret Thatcher wins the Tory leadership second ballot, so Selwyn Lloyd's instinct was right. The figures were: Margaret Thatcher 146 (53 per cent of the vote); Willie Whitelaw 79, Geoffrey Howe 19, James Prior 19 and John Peyton 11.[*] The others, initially staying loyal to Heath, came too late to the contest. Thatcher is rewarded for her boldness, when she could have lost everything. Interesting times ahead.

## 11 March 1975

I hear a story of George Weidenfeld, who was gazing hungrily at a girl. Somebody said to him: 'Well, George, why don't you ask her to dine?' He replied: 'I am waiting for her to come out in paperback.'

## 13 March 1975

At Wolfson College for Isaiah Berlin's retirement dinner. Michael Brock[†] does not hide from me his disappointment that he was passed over as Isaiah Berlin's successor as President of Wolfson College and that Harry Fisher[‡] got the position. All Oxford colleges are snobbish in this way, and prefer even marginally eminent outsiders to their own scholars. He would therefore like to find a Chair or other appointment away from Wolfson, but not one which could cause him financial loss. Meanwhile he is hoping to edit the letters of Asquith to Venetia Montagu.[§]

Derek Hill's portrait of Isaiah is on view. In a charming speech, Isaiah warmly commends it and the college. He envisages his retirement as a

---

[*] Geoffrey Howe, Baron Howe of Aberavon (1926–2015), Conservative politician. Chancellor of the Exchequer 1979–83; Foreign Secretary 1983–9. James Prior, Baron Prior of Brampton (1927–2016), Conservative politician. Served in the Cabinet under Heath and Thatcher. John Peyton, Baron Peyton of Yeovil (1919–2006), Cabinet minister in the Heath government.

[†] (1920–2014), Vice-President and Bursar, Wolfson Coll., Oxford 1967–76. Brock was Warden of Nuffield Coll., Oxford, 1978–88.

[‡] Sir Henry 'Harry' Fisher, lawyer. President of Wolfson Coll. 1975–85.

[§] Venetia Stanley Montagu (1887–1948), recipient of many letters from Asquith, mainly between 1910 and 1915. Michael Brock's edition of these letters was published by OUP in 1982.

dismal pilgrimage from college to college, clinging desperately to his dining rights in each: 'Monday, Corpus; Tuesday, All Souls; Wednesday, New College; Thursday, Wolfson. I shall be known as the-man-who-comes-in-on-Thursday, quite harmless, retiring behind a copy of *Country Life*.' In more serious vein he salutes his colleagues at Wolfson for their rationalism, their honour and their sense of the ridiculous.

After dinner there is a wonderful short entertainment when two junior members of the college sing Isaiah's entry in *Who's Who* to the music of the Papageno-Papagena duet from *The Magic Flute*.

Harry Fisher sits opposite me at dinner, and we have some entertaining talk. On his father, the Archbishop, Harry says that he admired his certainty in every problem of life, a quality which he does not possess himself.

Harry feels sorry for A.L. Rowse at having had to sever his long connection at All Souls. 'We could stand the Dark Lady at lunch, we could stand the Dark Lady at tea, we could stand the Dark Lady at dinner, but we could not stand the Dark Lady at breakfast!'[*] I am surprised, however, when he adds that John Sparrow is suspected of having wanted A.L.R. out of the college more than most other Fellows.

### 25 March 1975

Richard Thorpe, a beak at Charterhouse, comes to see me. He is writing a book on three men who failed to become Tory Prime Ministers – Curzon, Austen Chamberlain and Rab Butler. I am able to give him some help.[†]

See the film of *Death in Venice* in the evening. All rather treacly, and why is Aschenbach turned into a composer, instead of leaving him as a writer?[‡]

### 6 April 1975

Giles St Aubyn gives me the unedited typescript of the memoir of Prince William of Gloucester which he is slowly putting together.

Much of the Eton part will surely have to be revised. It is permeated by

---

[*] In his 1973 book *Shakespeare the Man* (Macmillan, 1973) A.L. Rowse claimed to have solved the identity of the Dark Lady of the Sonnets as Emilia Lanier, a subject on which he pronounced at length to those willing to listen, and to those who were not so inclined.

[†] This was my first meeting with K.R. and the beginning of a friendship of nearly forty years. *The Uncrowned Prime Ministers: A Study of Sir Austen Chamberlain, Lord Curzon and Lord Butler* was published by Darkhorse Publishing in 1980.

[‡] The change enabled Luchino Visconti (1906–76), the film's director, to draw parallels with the composer Gustav Mahler (1860–1911), and to use the Adagietto of Mahler's 5th Symphony as luxuriant background music. The film first appeared in 1971, when Benjamin Britten was composing his opera of *Death in Venice*, first performed in 1973. Britten was advised by his lawyers never to see the Visconti film so that he could not be accused of plagiarism.

sickly sycophancy, magnifying boyish traits into events of profound importance. The same air is in some of the contributions from Foreign Office people. The real root of the trouble is that William, more than most members of the Royal Family, wanted the best of both worlds: the maximum freedom of action, accompanied by the maximum use of his Royal blood. To quote a letter he wrote to a friend: 'shooting small birds and sleeping with bigger ones'.

William emerges as a considerable traveller, but his views on foreign countries and peoples may have to be toned down: he found the West Africans thoroughly incompetent and corrupt.

Discussing all this, Giles shows himself sympathetic in William's predicament of wanting the best of both worlds. Particularly when the Royal Family was trying to wean him from his Hungarian mistress, William would complain that he had not asked to be born into the Royal Family, unlike Prince Philip and his mother, who had chosen to become royal. William particularly resented the hostility of Prince Philip, whom he used to call the Hatchet Man. Apart from his own mother, the only member of the Royal Family who used to write to him with understanding was the Queen herself: a remarkable similarity to the sympathy from Queen Victoria in similar circumstances.

## 13 May 1975

Antony Acland, newly appointed to be our Ambassador to Luxembourg, tells me how easy Alec Home was to serve: he would read documents very quickly, marking with exact skill the sentences that really mattered. Antony also sees certain similarities between Alec and Jim Callaghan, not least a shared love of the soil.

## 3 June 1975

Talk to General John Hackett,* recently retired as Principal of King's College, London. He is aghast at the depths of intrigue in the SCR of our alma mater, New College, now that Warden Hayter's retirement approaches. It reminds him of the Fellows who passed a motion wishing their sick Master a speedy recovery – by thirteen votes to eleven, with two abstentions. The General also tells me of a meeting with Field Marshal Montgomery, recalling some past encounter. 'What rank were you at the time,' Monty asked, 'a full Colonel?' 'No,' Hackett replied, 'a Lieutenant-Colonel.' 'Ah,' Monty said, 'I

---

* Gen. Sir John ('Shan') Hackett (1910–97), soldier and university administrator. Principal of King's College, London 1968–75.

was quite junior myself then, I was only a full General.'

### 5 June 1975
Vote in the United Kingdom European Communities Referendum: to stay in
Europe. A referendum is an appalling constitutional innovation which I hope
will not be repeated. It has become a straight political issue in working-class
districts where there is hardly a voice to be heard in favour of the Common
Market. It will be a close thing: Arnold Goodman even thinks there will not
be a majority in favour of our remaining in Europe.[*]

Talking of unemployment, Harold Macmillan said privately that the sur-
plus steel and motor workers should be trained for new jobs – 'footmen, for
instance'.

### 6 June 1975
In Shrewsbury. Walk up through the old part of the town to look at the school.
Buy one or two pretty plates in an antique shop; then cross the Kingsland toll
bridge, paying a halfpenny. I suppose it must be almost the last thing that
can be bought for such a trifle. Walk past a house called Albany in Butler
Road – the best of all worlds – and up onto the school cricket field.

The setting is enchantingly beautiful. The main building of red brick is
perched high above a bend in the river. A pleasant study terrace bears a plaque
commemorating, in Latin, the Queen's visit to mark the 400th anniversary
of the school in 1952. The heavy scents of summer are almost suffocatingly
evocative of Repton more than thirty years ago. So too are the other sights
and sounds – fives courts; bells; an exhibition of bee-keeping and another of life under the Roman Empire; a notice saying that boys playing fives
must wear clean white shirts; flamboyant parents and mildly embarrassed
boys.

### 9 June 1975
Read the typescript of James Lees-Milne's *Ancestral Voices*, for possible
*Sunday Telegraph* serialisation. Having been invalided out of the Army quite
early in the war when in his early thirties, he worked for the National Trust.
These diaries are much occupied with visits to its properties and to estates
which were being considered for acquisition. He has a sharp eye for architecture and writes with feline cruelty about the seedy or eccentric owners of
country houses.

What makes the book entirely unsuitable for readers of the *ST* is his

---

[*] 67.23 per cent voted in favour of staying in the Common Market, 32.7 per cent against.

absorption in the sex lives of friends and acquaintances, mostly homosexual. It is a malicious chronicle of selfishness and intrigue, sparing nobody, including the late Duke of Kent. There is much about James Pope-Hennessy, toying with marriage, extraordinarily enough; Chips Channon and Harold Nicolson. I hardly think it could be printed anywhere without many excisions. He records much hateful gossip and spiteful comment, unredeemed by the political and social insights of the Harold Nicolson and Chips Channon diaries.

In between I hear the first public broadcast on radio of Prime Minister's Question Time in the Commons. Anthony Benn very polite and conciliatory; Wilson devious. In general not impressive; but then the Commons hardly ever is.

## 12 June 1975

Lunch given by George Weidenfeld for Leslie Rowse's new book on Oxford. I set next to Mrs T.S. Eliot,* handsome, well-preserved lady in a big feathered hat. She comes from Leeds and was Eliot's secretary. Much of her time is consumed by thesis writers from the universities of the world, which she accepts with good humour. She has a love of language which is endearing. Her husband was once struck by a chauffeur driving him from a railway station to a country house, where he was a guest, talking of his dog: 'He is a nice animal. But not what one might call a consequential dog.'

## 14 June 1975

12 noon train to Staplehurst, where Nigel Nicolson meets me and drives me to Sissinghurst. A glorious day of sunshine and breeze. We lunch simply in the garden.

Having handed over the notes made in the Royal Archives about George V by Harold Nicolson and lent to me some years ago, I am installed at a table under the mulberry tree to read through Harold's complete and unpublished diaries for the years he was writing his life of King George V between 1948 and 1952. They contain many interesting anecdotes told him by friends of the King and his courtiers. A good Lutyens story. For Queen Mary's Doll's House, he had one miniature pillow in the bedroom embroidered MG and the other GM. When Queen Mary asked him what they meant he replied that they meant 'May George?' and the other, 'George may'.

Nigel describes how as a young Grenadier he had to take one of Attlee's

---

* Valerie Eliot (1926–2012), second wife of T.S. Eliot and a major stock-holder in the publishing firm of Faber and Faber. Eliot's literary executor after his death in 1975.

daughters to a party at Buckingham Palace just after the war. Out of curiosity they wandered from the main room to the Prince Consort's room.* There they ran into King George VI, who was very cross and said: 'You have no business to be here.' Miss Attlee† was in floods of tears. Nigel told her not to worry, as the King would not have known who either of them was. 'Oh yes, he would,' she replied. 'I look so like Daddy.'

The garden looks enchanting in the evening sunlight, particularly after the paying visitors have departed. But I have so much to read that I do not dare break off for a moment. Reading the diaries shows me how skilful Nigel has been in separating his nuggets of gold from a considerable amount of dross.

### 17 June 1975

Alec Home has been reading an advance copy of my book *The Later Cecils* which I sent him. 'I suppose', he muses, 'that the Cecils were almost entirely destructive in their policies.' He is right. Like me, he regrets that Bobbety resigned on the issue of bringing back Makarios from exile in the Seychelles in order to negotiate on Cyprus. When I tell Alec of Bobbety's defence to me – that he would have had personally to defend the decision in the Lords, and that Makarios had British blood on his hands – Alec recalls the Queen's reply to him when he asked if she would object to meeting Idi Amin‡ of Uganda at a conference of Commonwealth Prime Ministers: 'It would not be the first time I have met murderers there.'

### 20 June 1975

Harold Wilson, piqued by his invariably bad Press, abolishes daily meetings between his Press Secretary at No. 10 and the parliamentary Lobby of political correspondents.

I have not been to Ascot on a single day in spite of receiving a Royal Enclosure voucher. I simply could not face the absurd and uncomfortable dressing-up with the country heading for apparently uncontrollable inflation.

### 23 June 1975

Michael St Aldwyn tells me that every peer who spoke in a foreign affairs debate a few days ago received a confidential memorandum from the Foreign

---

* Albert, Prince Consort, had several rooms at Buckingham Palace for his special use, including a writing room, a dressing room and a music room.
† Felicity Attlee (1925–2007), second dau. of Clement and Violet Attlee.
‡ (1928–2003), President of Uganda 1971–9.

Office begging him not to attack President Amin of Uganda, who is at present threatening to execute a British subject[*] for writing in an unpublished manuscript of a book that Amin was 'a village tyrant'. Even Alec Home was included.

## 12 September 1975

Thirty-first anniversary of the liberation of Brussels by the Welsh Guards.

## 17 September 1975

Hartley Shawcross is very critical of Asa Briggs for his permissive attitude towards the students. I reply that this is probably the only way to run a university nowadays without constant explosions. What astonishes me is how Asa manages to produce such a formidable output of work while 'dining himself away', as was said of Robert Browning.[†]

## 18 September 1975

To Scarborough for the last two days of the Liberal Party Conference. Warm welcome from Jeremy Thorpe and Marion. An unedifying demonstration by the Liberal Homosexual Group. Some of them embrace on the steps of the Spa Conference Hall, while a little ring of stout holidaymakers stands round exclaiming 'Eee!'.

Some pleasant talk with Douglas Hurd, who is doing a broadcast on the conference through Tory eyes. After dinner I am listening to Ian Waller,[‡] political correspondent of the *Sunday Telegraph*, when Jeremy and Marion suddenly pass by. Jeremy stops and launches into a furious attack on Ian for all the disobliging articles he has written over the years about the Liberals, particularly during annual conferences. It is a most embarrassing exhibition, especially as he adds that he has complained of Ian to Michael Hartwell. Ian remains calm, and afterwards tells me that it will not affect either way what he writes about this year's conference. Marion looks startled at Jeremy's outburst, and imperceptibly moves away.

---

[*] Denis Hills (1913–2004), author. His execution had been fixed for 23 June. Amin turned down a plea for clemency from the Queen, but after pressure from the Foreign Office agreed to a stay of execution if James Callaghan, the Foreign Secretary, visited Uganda to discuss the country's demands. On 9 July, when Callaghan was with Amin, Denis Hills was set free in his presence.

[†] (1812–89), poet and playwright. In a letter of 18 Jan. 1862 Browning acknowledged, 'I go out every night to dine in a cold-blooded way.'

[‡] (1926–2003), political journalist. He was at New Coll., Oxford at the same time as K.R.

## 21 September 1975

Read Lord Reith's diaries. It is extraordinary to find him almost literally suicidal with rage and frustration at being underemployed both during and after the war; and his hatred of Winston is nothing less than pathological. In all this one sees a touch of A.L. Rowse.

## 29 September 1975

Dine with Gerald Templer in Wilton Street. A gruesome account of a visit to Monty, who now never emerges from bed and is still utterly absorbed in himself. 'No, of course I don't look at the television. What could there be to interest me there?' His sole concern seems to be to live longer than Winston. Even his meals never vary from day to day, and have not done so for years. He does not even offer the Templers a cup of tea.

## 2 October 1975

Dine with Bob Boothby. He has aged since I last saw him, and has developed a curious habit of rapidly clicking his teeth together before speaking. He goes through several of his familiar hoops: how much he liked Lloyd George; how badly he was treated by Winston; how even at the end of his life Lloyd George could instantly dominate Winston – 'the relationship of master to servant'.

Bob also makes me laugh by recalling his heart attack of nearly twenty years ago, when I found him in Sister Agnes whispering instructions to his stockbroker on a forbidden telephone. He says: 'I also backed a series of winners at Goodwood from that bed, and so paid for the whole of my illness.'

## 10 October 1975

As a prelude to dining at Christ's with Charles Snow next Monday I skim through some pages of *The Masters*. See to my astonishment that Arthur Brown, the wise genial old healer of disputes, is in the novel five years younger than I am now.

Read Alec Home's memoirs *The Way the Wind Blows*. Since Sir Edward Grey ceased to be Foreign Secretary in 1916, no statesman has more consistently brought the flavour of the countryside to Westminster than Alec Home. An authentic love of the land permeates every page of this evocative, wonderfully good-natured autobiography.

## 14 October 1975

Cross-country train journey from Cambridge to Leeds, arriving in time for a lunch given by Edward Boyle for Harold Macmillan, who is opening a new wing of the university library. Later in the afternoon Harold Macmillan receives an honorary degree, preceded by an interminable procession of dons in their robes. In the evening Edward gives a small dinner for Harold at the Vice-Chancellor's Lodge. The party is completed by David Dilks and myself.

From the moment we sit down shortly before 8 to 12.45 the old man scarcely stops talking for a moment. Many of his stories are about Winston. During a gloomy meeting with the Chiefs of Staff one day in the war when things were not going well, Admiral Cunningham* said that there was no better co-operation between the Service chiefs and the politicians than in World War I. Winston replied: 'You take the most valiant sailor, the most courageous soldier, the most gallant air marshal, and what do you get out of them? The sum total of their fears.'

During his last declining years, Clemmie Churchill used to arrange for friends to come to lunch; Winston rarely talked, but liked to have people about him. Macmillan was at Hyde Park Gate one day when Mountbatten was also lunching. It so happened that Winston was in a bad temper because he could not hear any single conversation through the buzz of talk. Mountbatten nevertheless went on speaking to him. During the first course, Mountbatten talked of World War I; during the second course he talked of World War II; and during the third course he talked of the Royal Family. Absolutely no reaction from Winston. At last Mountbatten said he had to go. As he reached the top of the little staircase leading out of the dining room, Winston said: 'Who is that fellow? Should I know him?'

The last time Macmillan went to see Winston was not long before his death. Winston brooded in silence. 'How are you?' Macmillan asked. There was a long pause. 'I am waiting,' Churchill replied.

### 16 October 1975
To a huge evening party given by Macmillan & Co. at the Stationers' Hall in honour of Charles Snow's seventieth birthday. Harold Macmillan makes a graceful little speech, saluting Charles as the Trollope of the twentieth century, and praising the verisimilitude with which he depicts our society.

### 17 October 1975
Rab Butler writes characteristically to me: 'We saw the Leeds ceremony on television and thought Macmillan looked very old.'

---

* 1st Viscount Cunningham of Hyndhope (1883–1963). During World War II Cunningham led British naval forces to victory in various crucial battles, including Matapan; First Sea Lord 1943–6.

## 23 October 1975

Hugh Fraser has a hairbreadth escape from death when a bomb goes off under his car in Camden Hill Square this morning just as he was about to leave the house. But at that moment Jonathan Aitken of all people telephoned him, so he was spared. What a theme for a short story: to be saved from violent death by the former love of one's wife.

## 1 November 1975

Anthony Eden is very ill. Philip de Zulueta comes in for a drink to look at my memoir of Eden that will be published when he dies. He dissents from the abruptness with which I contrast his skilled, pacific record of negotiations with his sudden resort to force in 1956: there were, Philip says, reasonable grounds of policy for attempting to assert British power in the Middle East. Eden was already trying to achieve an internationalisation of Sinai. Behind the petulance lay a strategic plan. I think Philip is right & soften my text accordingly.

Philip is desperately worried about the economy. 'We must revert from being a dynamic economy to being a state economy.' The cost of the national debt and of state pensions terrifies him. Harold Macmillan, he says, sent Alfred Robens* to the Coal Board because he thought he would make a devastatingly successful leader of the Labour Party, if available as an MP.

## 3 November 1975

Some pleasant talk with the Foreign Secretary, Jim Callaghan. He seems to have become more urbane since I last saw him. He tells me that he still retains a portrait of Palmerston in his room at the Foreign Office – 'Who else?'. He does his papers each morning from seven to nine; insists that he shall never be given more than one box of papers to take home each night. He is now teetotal and further guards his energy by having a little nap after lunching in his room.

## 4 November 1975

Young Winston Churchill† tells me that neither he nor the family are particularly pleased with Martin Gilbert's volumes of his grandfather's

---

* Baron Robens of Woldingham (1910–99), trade unionist, Labour politician, industrialist. MP for Wansbeck 1945–50 and for Blyth 1950–60; Chairman, National Coal Board 1961–71;

† Winston Spencer Churchill (1940–2010), author, journalist, Conservative politician. MP for Stretford 1970–83 and Davyhulme 1983–97.

life. 'He has got too bogged down in detail, yet hopes to write the rest of his life from 1922 to 1965 in only two more volumes.'*

### 10 November 1975
How oddly Ted Heath continues to behave. He has tried to get an injunction to prevent publication in the *Sunday Times* of a story disclosing that, unknown to him, Slater Walker† made money for him by slightly shady means. The injunction was refused, as it was bound to be. Ted has merely succeeded in drawing more attention to his financial affairs.

### 20 November 1975
General Franco dies. The final torture inflicted on him by his doctors was to lower his body temperature appreciably in order to stop internal bleeding.

### 24 November 1975
Cocktail party given by Duncan Sandys. Ted Heath is as unendearing as ever and much stouter. It is curious to find him here at all. It was at Duncan's company, Lonrho, that he made his disobliging remark about 'the unacceptable face of capitalism'. When I ask him whether he would like me to write something in my column on his new book on sailing, he replies coldly: 'Don't bother. It has already sold 70,000 copies.'

### 25 November 1975
Prince Eddie tells me that the Duchess of Windsor is less dotty than many people think. 'She <u>hates</u> England, and is determined that none of the Duke's possessions – and least of all David's money – shall find a final home in England.' I suppose one can hardly blame her.

### 8 December 1975
Have some talk with Michael Adeane about my proposed book on King George V, now that *The Later Cecils* is published. He is quite enthusiastic, especially when I tell him that I do not think it will be necessary for me to seek access to the Royal Archives. He admits that the policy of admission is rather restricted, but adds that a clever historian can often find copies of the documents elsewhere.‡ Lambeth Palace is one

---

* In fact there were four more volumes to cover 1922–65.
† A British conglomerate, later bank, which specialised in corporate raids and got into financial difficulties in the 1970s.
‡ K.R. discovered that much restricted material on the Abdication was contained at the old India Office Library in letters written by successive Secretaries of State for India to the Viceroys.

source and I have found much in the India Office Library.

## 9 December 1975

William Rees-Mogg,[*] talking of Michael Foot's savagely authoritarian legislation in favour of the closed shop and other trade union practices says: 'He
is like Macbeth, beginning as a good regimental soldier, but ending covered
in blood.'

---

* Baron Rees-Mogg (1928–2012), Editor of *The Times* 1967–81.

# 1976

*The first commercial flight of Concorde took place on 21 January. Harold Wilson made the surprise announcement on 16 March that he was resigning as Prime Minister of the United Kingdom, to take effect on 5 April after the Labour Party had elected his successor as leader. Field Marshal Montgomery died on 24 March. James Callaghan became the new Prime Minister on 5 April. Jeremy Thorpe resigned as leader of the Liberal Party on 10 May. Harold Wilson's controversial Resignation Honours List on 27 May was dubbed the 'Lavender List', after the colour of the writing paper on which Lady Falkender was alleged to have written the original draft. June and July saw the heatwave reach its peak, contributing to the worst drought since the 1720s. On 7 July David Steel was elected as the new leader of the Liberal Party. Jimmy Carter won the Democratic Presidential nomination on 14 July. Gerald Ford won the Republican Presidential nomination on 19 August. Mao Zedong died on 9 September. Jimmy Carter won the United States Presidential election on 2 November. Benjamin Britten died on 4 December.*

## 7 January 1976

Selwyn Lloyd comes in for a drink. He will soon announce his retirement as Speaker, a sad moment after five years. But this evening he is in a state of euphoria, having completed the manuscript of his book *Mr Speaker, Sir*. It is partly historical, partly autobiographical, and his agent expects it to sell between 3,000 and 10,000 copies. He shows much concern about possible profits as the end of his Speakership will mean a steep drop both in income and emoluments in kind. He has also suffered a fall in the capital value of his investments, much on Slater Walker.

He will go to the House of Lords as Lord Selwyn-Lloyd, not as Lord Hilbre, as he once told me. One reminiscence of the war. When in East Anglia, armed with some American howitzers dated 1874, he was asked to tea by Lord

Ullswater,* the former Speaker of the Commons, who died in 1949 within a few days of his ninety-fourth birthday. Selwyn asked him whom he thought the greatest parliamentarian he had ever known. He replied: 'Asquith'.

Selwyn describes how, right at the end of the war, he was called from dinner one night because GHQ had received the news of Himmler's suicide and charged with identifying him. Selwyn gazed at the corpse and said: 'But that is not Himmler.' The guards replied: 'Oh yes, it is,' and a Corporal put his big Army boot under the head and lifted it up. *Rigor mortis* had not yet set in and all the double chins fell into place, so Selwyn realised it was in fact Himmler. Then the Corporal took his boot away and the head fell back with a dull thud on the floor, a sound that Selwyn said stayed with him for the rest of his life.

He has never quite forgiven Macmillan for sacking him in 1962. But he determined that to brood on it would poison his life, so he has always treated Macmillan with friendliness. He remained particularly grateful to the late Tim Bligh for having given him advance warning of his fate. So when Macmillan did send for Selwyn that evening, Selwyn was prepared for the encounter. Macmillan stuck to his guns – or to his knife – and complained that there were conspiracies against him. He was much put out when Selwyn refused to take a peerage. A few days later, when there was a vote of censure debate, Selwyn heaped coals of fire on Macmillan's head by sending a letter of warm support. Macmillan then asked Selwyn to lunch at the Turf Club. But Selwyn shrewdly refused to lunch there, where it would seem as if Macmillan had behaved well towards Selwyn. Instead he said he would meet him at Admiralty House. When they did meet, Macmillan was most apologetic about his sacking. On his time at the Treasury, Selwyn said: 'Neither of my two Treasury boys turned out as well as they should: Tony Barber and Edward Boyle.' He hopes to devote some of his new-found leisure to the Liverpool School of Tropical Medicine. Also to Methodist activities. 'One must stand up and be counted as a Christian.'

## 8 January 1976

Lunch with William Waldegrave. He says that Jeremy Thorpe came to lunch one day to meet Victor Rothschild, who, he hoped, would become as generous a subscriber to Liberal funds as old Dolly Rothschild.† But Jeremy gave so many imitations that Victor simply dismissed him as a comedian.

---

* James Lowther, 1st Viscount Ullswater (1855–1949), Conservative politician. MP for Penrith, 1886–1921; Speaker of the House of Commons 1905–21.
† Dorothy Rothschild (1895–1988), philanthropist.

An odd story about Jeremy Thorpe, hints of which have appeared in *Private Eye*: that after an emotional quarrel, he shot the dog of a particular friend in Devon. It sounds highly unlikely that Jeremy even knows how to use a gun, much less use it accurately.

On political matters, William Waldegrave thinks that Jeremy made the mistake of his life by not throwing in his lot with Ted Heath in February 1974. It would have given tremendous impetus to the Liberal vote, and far outweighed the charges of the radical Liberals that he was doing a Ramsay MacDonald on them.

## 10 January 1976
Patrick Gordon Walker tells me how shocked he is to hear that the present Labour Cabinet has slid into calling each other by their Christian names at Cabinet meetings, instead of by their official appointments.

## 17 January 1976
Read Anthony Powell's *Hearing Secret Harmonies*. The last of the twelve volumes of *A Dance to the Music of Time*. Tedious and improbable. Widmerpool is now an aged member of a hippy community. Powell shows contempt for the reader. Though the literary Establishment do not agree, C.P. Snow's eleven-volume *Strangers and Brothers* sequence is far superior.

## 21 January 1976
St Margaret's Westminster for the crowded memorial service for Jack Wheeler-Bennett. Much royal representation, and Princess Margaret attends in person. Macmillan reads the lesson and Pat Dean* delivers a workmanlike address. Rather too much music. Rab Butler, wearing a bowler hat literally green with age, tells me that Prince Philip has still not replied to Cambridge's enquiry on whether he would like to be the new Chancellor in succession to Lord Adrian.

## 27 January 1976
Dine with Edward Ford who talks in a most interesting way about King George VI. One of the regrets of his life was that he never went to India as the last Emperor. He would have liked a Durbar in 1938, and never forgave P.J. Grigg,† then Finance Member of the Viceroy's Council, for insisting that

---

* Sir Patrick Dean (1909–94), Ambassador to the US 1965–9.

† Sir Percy James Grigg (1890–1964), civil servant, later Conservative politician. Finance Member of the Government of India 1934–9; MP for Cardiff East 1942–5; War Secretary 1942–5.

India could not afford it. The King also had two grievances against Winston Churchill:

(a) That he was not allowed to sail with the fleet on D-Day.
(b) That he was not allowed to visit India during the war. 'And do you know why?' the King later told Edward. 'Because I would have had the Burma Star, and Winston wouldn't.'

### 29 January 1976

A terrible day for Jeremy Thorpe. First, the official report on the crash of London and County, of which he was a director, rebukes him for drawing £5,000 a year without really understanding the business. Secondly, a man of thirty-five called Norman Scott,[*] on a fraud charge in Devon, claimed in court that his downfall has been caused by a sexual relationship with Jeremy. I ask Jeremy if I can come in to see him at Orme Square and Jeremy gladly agrees.

Jeremy admits that he made an error of judgement about London and County, but makes three points in mitigation:

(a) He was reassured about the firm when he heard that several important firms, including Eagle Star, were investing pension funds in it.
(b) About eighteen months after joining the board he happened to lunch with Leslie O'Brien,[†] Governor of the Bank of England, and discussed the future of London and County. O'Brien told him there was no cause for him to resign.
(c) When finally his eyes were opened, he acted as swiftly as possible in consulting Arnold Goodman and insisting on a full board meeting with all the accountants present.

As for the Scott accusations, he says that he has not seen Scott for twelve years, and even before that there was no sexual relationship. But he did try to help him financially. When Scott spoke of bringing a gun to the House of Commons, Jeremy consulted the then Home Secretary, Reggie Maudling, who in turn asked Scotland Yard for a report on Scott. Although ostensibly confidential, this report revealed that Scott had a psychiatric history. There is shortly to be another case in a Devon magistrates' court. An airline pilot is accused of possessing a gun & endangering life. Apparently, he got into a rage with Scott, who had begun to blackmail him with a photograph of the pilot and a tart at a party. The pilot shot Scott's dog, then threatened to shoot

---

[*] Former stable lad (b. 1940).

[†] Leslie O'Brien, Baron O'Brien of Lothbury (1908–95), Governor of the Bank of England 1966–73.

Scott himself. There is a good chance that when his case has been tried, Scott
will be arrested for blackmail. On this last matter there is nothing I can do to
help Jeremy. He will just have to sit it out. As for the L&C crash, Goodman
has advised Jeremy to make no statement in his defence, for there is really
nothing to say.

Alun Chalfont has just finished his life of Field Marshal Montgomery. The
task has left him with a deep distaste for his subject, and the not entirely
successful moments, e.g. Arnhem and the pursuit after Alamein.

### 3 February 1976

Lunch Beefsteak. Nigel Nicolson brings me a box of the papers his father
used in writing his life of King George V, including the transcripts of letters
and memorabilia from the Royal Archives, some of them unpublished. Their
use by me will require Royal copyright permission. It is so very kind of Nigel.
He also says I can read his father's journals, which contain notes of conversations he had with politicians, etc. in the course of collecting material for
the life.

### 4 February 1976

Lunch with Selwyn Lloyd in Gray's Inn. I am the very first guest in his new
flat and am made most ceremoniously to sign the visitors' book. Selwyn is
still very moved by all the farewell ceremonies yesterday and the election of
George Thomas as the new Speaker.

We talk about Jeremy's troubles. Selwyn says it is certainly odd that he
should have taken the blackmailer Scott to his mother's house for the night;
but, of course, Jeremy is impulsively generous and kind. Selwyn also regrets
that Jeremy did not defy the radical element of his party and join Ted Heath
in a coalition Government in February 1974. It was the nearest, it seems,
that he will ever get to power. Spend an hour or so clearing up points about
Selwyn's book on the Speakership.

### 5 February 1976

Martin Charteris lunches with me at the Ritz. We have much talk and
laughter. He is wearing a very new, bright Green Jacket tie: apparently, the
regiment is mounting guard at the Palace, and this evening Martin is taking
the Queen to visit them.

He describes the macabre tea party he attended with the Queen during
her State Visit to Paris in 1972: much bright, polite conversation while the
Duke lay dying upstairs. All his papers are now safely in England, and most
of his possessions will follow.

## 3 March 1976

To the opera with Jeremy and Marion Thorpe. Jeremy is outwardly as ebullient as ever, but there is rather a despairing light in his eyes: I do not see how he can long remain as leader of the Liberals.

## 4 March 1976

I have some talk with Denis Healey. I find that he is a far more vehement supporter of private medicine than I am, and that he thinks his Government's present closed-shop legislation to be wicked beyond belief. He nevertheless adds: 'I think I can do more good by trying to oppose or palliate such measures in Cabinet than I could by resignation.'

## 15 March 1976

In Madrid to see King Juan Carlos. The palace itself has been much added to since I was last here six years ago. An ADC shows me into the King's room.

The King, in a greenish tweed suit, almost bounds across the room to greet me. 'I heard you were in Madrid, and of course I said at once that I wanted to see such an old friend.' He lights a tiny cigar, and we settle down to talk in armchairs.

He at once tells me that he is extremely perplexed about the way in which he should regard his new constitutional duties. 'I have tried to study the role which your Queen plays in England, but that does not really help: your own Constitution has been slowly evolving for hundreds of years. Now give me your advice as a friend. How do you think I should act?'

That of course is an impossible question, with political conditions in Spain still so fluid. But I do emphasise that the Queen has now been relieved of almost all political responsibilities, particularly those which could make her a controversial figure; and that such a monarchy should ultimately be possible in Spain. I add, however, that only he can judge the pace at which democracy should be extended.

'You will remember', he replies, 'how I used to compare Spain with a bottle of champagne. For forty years everything was kept in place by a strong cork. Well, the cork is out of the bottle now, but the wine is still fizzing. Still, I am pushing forward, and the situation remains fairly calm and stable.'

The King dwells at some length on the attitude of both Spanish and foreign newspapers to him. 'I would not mind if every Spanish newspaper were against me, as long as I have television on my side. There are about four and a half million sets in Spain, which means that about sixteen million people watch it. But I do not have Spanish television on my side. A few days ago, I was sitting watching the news. There was an item about the current strikes, followed by an item saying that I was skiing, followed <u>immediately</u> by more news about the strikes. It was obviously intended to show that I cared only about sport. It was not accidental, but carefully contrived. Now I know that we cannot interfere too much with the trade unions. But hearing that attack was like being struck in the face.'

On the foreign Press, he complains: 'They write about Spain as if Franco were still alive.' The other day he had a tumultuous reception in Barcelona that delighted him, particularly as he had told the chief of police that he did not want a display of force to protect him.

I explain that much of the apparent hostility of the foreign Press to post-Franco Spain springs from the apparent brutality of the police. And I ask whether the present Government cannot moderate this. The King replies that some of the Spanish demonstrators have been giving the Communist salute and shouting: 'Down with the King'. He continues: 'That is not a good thing at the beginning of a reign.' I feel sympathy for him in this, but suspect that he could exert pressure on the police without eroding public order.

While we are talking, the telephone rings, and the King has a conversation in Spanish lasting two or three minutes. When he has put down the receiver he says: 'That was the Prime Minister. He tells me that the Asturian miners are now all back at work, which is a relief.' I suggest that, like our own King George V at the time of the 1926 General Strike, he should attempt a gesture of conciliation in a speech on radio or TV: better to concede at a time when the miners are chastened than when they are militant. He appears impressed with the idea, and says he will consider it.

As I take my leave of the King after our talk, he says: 'I do hope you will write to me. Send the letter to my Private Secretary, with the one for me sealed up inside.'

## 23 March 1976

Still in Spain. Take the train to Estoril to see Don Juan, Count of Barcelona,* the father of King Juan Carlos of Spain.

Don Juan talks to me in his book-lined study upstairs, a tall bulky man with very throaty English. We talk of the political outlook in Spain. Instead of his son's metaphor of the opened champagne bottle, he prefers that of the pressure cooker. He is delighted with the personal qualities displayed by Juan Carlos, particularly patience, but disappointed with the slowness of the progress towards democracy: 'But what can one expect after forty years of

---

* Infante Juan, Count of Barcelona (1913–93), heir apparent to the defunct Spanish throne in 1933. In 1969 Franco passed over Don Juan in favour of his son, Juan Carlos.

Franco?' It is as the guarantor of democracy that he sees the role of his son, while also emphasising that he will make an excellent ambassador of Spain to the world. Don Juan certainly thinks that the Spanish monarchy has a far better chance of survival than that of Greece – 'a foreign dynasty'.

Don Juan asks me about the break-up of Princess Margaret's marriage, commenting grimly: 'She has never been of much help to her sister.' But he speaks warmly of Prince Eddie, who represented the Queen at the funeral of Queen Ena in 1969. I tell Don Juan something of Eddie's recently ended Army career, adding how humiliated and angry he was to be withdrawn from Ulster when serving with his regiment some years ago. Don Juan replies that he had a similar experience when serving in the Spanish navy before the war.

I mention my proposed book on King George V. Don Juan says: 'He was a very peppery man, but had standards of service and duty that are not usual nowadays. I was in England when he took Ramsay MacDonald by the scruff of the neck and made him form a coalition Government.' This leads us to talk of the present constitutional powers of the Queen, and say how few they are in spite of the considerable political experience which, after reigning for twenty-four years, she is able to put at the disposal of her ministers.

## 23 March 1976

An amusing account of Randolph Churchill in Moscow. Although he had come as a journalist, he was aggrieved that no special facilities were laid on for him at the British Embassy. At a party there one evening, his attention was drawn to the attractive view of the Kremlin across the river. 'The only good thing about it', Randolph replied, 'is that my brother-in-law* can at any moment blow it to pieces by pressing a button.'

## 24 March 1976

I am depressed to hear that Field Marshal Montgomery is dead.

## 26 March 1976

I begin to read James Pope-Hennessy's life of Queen Mary to see what I ought to quote from it. Perhaps a shade too elaborate in his description of places, but wonderfully constructed and written. It is curious how much he hated to be thought of as a 'Royal biographer', yet it is easily the best of his books.

---

* Averell Harriman (1891–1986), American Democratic politician, businessman and politician.

## 5 April 1976

Jim Callaghan elected to lead the Labour Party on the third ballot– and so to succeed Harold Wilson as Prime Minister by a far from commanding lead over Michael Foot, 176 votes to 137. A thought. Is Callaghan our first PM to have served in the Navy?

## 8 April 1976

I hear Callaghan's first Cabinet changes. He fires the venomous Barbara Castle[*] and the crooked Ted Short, but refuses to let Roy Jenkins have the Foreign Office, which goes to Tony Crosland.[†] Michael Foot becomes Lord President and Leader of the House; without a strong department such as Employment, he may lose some of his former power.

## 19 April 1976

Re-read James Pope-Hennessy's *Queen Mary*. I am lost in admiration at the exceptionally skilful construction of the book, the wonderful colour he brings to a somewhat drab character, and the quiet wit which lurks on every page. Sometimes it is as if I hear him talking at the Beefsteak, those sly little jokes ending in an explosion of laughter. Having re-read the book, I feel a sadness at his death far more acute than when I first read of his murder.

## 22 April 1976

George Weidenfeld gives a supper party for Alun Chalfont, to mark the publication of his book on Monty. It has received almost universally hostile reviews. This has made Alun very fierce and prickly.

## 9 May 1976

The storm about Jeremy Thorpe and his supposed homosexual involvement with a neurotic called Norman Scott continues to fill the papers. Jeremy has now released two of the letters he wrote to Scott fifteen years ago. He writes: 'Yours affectionately' and adds 'I miss you'. But from Jeremy that proves nothing.

The BBC begins a news bulletin: 'A Liberal MP has come out in support of Mr Jeremy Thorpe.' What a commentary on the failure of his colleagues to show him even the most elementary loyalty.

---

[*] (1910–2002), Labour politician. MP for Blackburn 1945–79; Cabinet Minister under Harold Wilson.

[†] Anthony Crosland (1918–77), Labour politician. MP for South Gloucestershire 1950–55 and for Great Grimsby 1959–77; Foreign Secretary 1976–7; author of *The Future of Socialism* (Jonathan Cape, 1956).

## 10 May 1976

About 4.15 the music programme of the BBC is interrupted for the announcement that Jeremy has resigned as leader of the Liberal Party. The newsreader
continues: 'And now we have an organ recital.' I blame the disloyalty of his
party, rather than the pursuit by the Press of Scott's allegations.

## 12 May 1976

Martin Charteris lunches with me. He tells me: 'I do a lot of carpentry on
the Queen's speeches – but then I can call on anybody in the country for
help and advice. Even then I sometimes have difficulty. I produce a draft
which both the Queen and I think excellent. But Prince Philip will insist on
rewriting it.'

The Queen takes her task with immense seriousness. When I tell Martin
of the letter from George V to Stanley Baldwin in 1935, telling the new PM
to have his Cabinet changes completed by the opening of the July meeting
at Newmarket, Martin says that the Queen would never allow a personal
preference to influence a State duty. Martin has seen volume two of the
Crossman diaries, and is both infuriated and sickened by his attitude to the
Queen.

The Duchess of Windsor, he tells me, is rather ill and could die at any
moment. 'I hope it will not be in Ascot week.' An official plane will bring her
body to England for a funeral service in St George's, Windsor, followed by
burial at Frogmore.

Jo Grimond asked to return to the leadership of the Liberal Party in succession to Jeremy.

## 17 May 1976

Austin Strutt comes to lunch at the flat to talk about my book on George
V. He was quite a junior official at the Home Office during that reign, but
picked up a great deal of Royal lore.

On the Abdication finances of Edward VIII, he says that the settlement
was as follows: George V had left each of his three youngest sons – York,
Gloucester and Kent – nearly £1 million (the Prince of Wales being well
provided for by the Duchy of Cornwall). So the Duke of York handed over
his share to Edward in return for Balmoral and Sandringham. Queen Mary
also used to give Edward up to £25,000 a year, which she could well afford:
she paid tax on only £8,000 of her £70,000 a year. Queen Alexandra had left
her jewels to the Prince of Wales, and these of course he kept, giving many of
them to his wife. Mountbatten has been concerning himself with persuading
her to leave them back to the Queen at her death. The famous Silver Jubilee

broadcast of King George V in 1935 was written by G.M. Trevelyan. George V resented the way in which Joynson-Hicks[*] was prepared to give away Royal patronage to boroughs. On later Royal topics Austin says that King George VI was a more rigid Tory than his father. In a certain murder case, Chuter Ede,[†] the Home Secretary, wanted to reprieve a man; the King wanted him to hang. Of course, the Home Secretary had his way.

Austin has recently been a member of a committee inquiring into masonic charities. They took their report to Prince Eddie, Grand Master of the United Grand Lodge of England, and were most impressed by his grasp of the essential points.

### 19 May 1976
Jeremy Thorpe now seems to have recovered his spirits and is more angry than crushed. Selwyn Lloyd has counselled him to lie low and to keep off the television for the time being.

### 20 May 1976
Hugh Trevor-Roper was asked recently what he thought of Elizabeth Longford as an historian. His reply was: 'Halfway down the slope to A.L. Rowse.'

### 2 June 1976
Talk to Ted Heath, who is extremely alarmed about the economic outlook. I suggest to him that he ought to make an important speech this week, congratulating the trade unions which had agreed to wage limitation, but also asking for a spirit of sacrifice throughout the country. 'You have a right to invoke Dunkirk,' I add, 'the Socialists have not.' He looks more thoughtful and receptive than I have ever known him before. Philip de Zulueta thinks that such a speech might do some good to the country and will certainly do much good to Ted.

### 3 June 1976
Arnold Goodman said to Jeremy Thorpe the other day: 'The only sort of trouble you have managed to avoid in recent months is being included in Harold Wilson's Resignation Honours List.'

Ted Heath tells me he has decided not to give a broadcast, but merely

---

* William ('Jix') Joynson-Hicks, 1st Viscount Brentford (1865–1932), solicitor and Conservative politician. Home Secretary 1924–9.
† James Chuter Ede, Baron Chuter-Ede (1882–1965), Labour politician. Home Secretary 1945–51.

to write an article in the *Sunday Express*. A fat lot of good that will do to save the economy of the country or the pound. He does, however, make one interesting remark to me: 'The three members who seemed to me to be best are Healey, Jenkins and Crosland, but Jenkins is going off to Europe.'

### 6 June 1976

Dine with Rab Butler at Trinity. He looks rather better than when I last saw him: thinner and without those bushy whiskers. He wears a scarlet gown for Whitsuntide. 'Of course,' he says, 'it isn't everyone who has a doctorate of the university. I got mine when I was Chancellor of the Exchequer.'

As always, I am embarrassed at how little Rab talks to his other neighbour, a rather arch don's wife, who tells him that she has been brought to dine to celebrate her husband's birthday. Rab arches his eyebrows.

In the Combination Room afterwards, Rab punishes the port. He talks of Peter Carrington: 'When he served under me at the Foreign Office, he and Harold Caccia did everything. I used to walk through the park – which was good for me – and did not need to arrive at the office until after 10.30. Peter has a difficult conflict to resolve: whether to become an industrialist or to try to be the next Conservative Foreign Secretary.'

The university is still waiting for Prince Philip to make up his mind on whether to accept the Chancellorship: he has had since November to do so.

### 9 June 1976

At 12 noon I go to see Mountbatten about King George V at his house in Knightsbridge. In a grey suit with a Royal Navy tie, he looks exceptionally lean and fit.

He begins by telling me how, at Fort Belvedere, on the day of the Abdication in 1936, the new King told him how unprepared he felt for his new role. Mountbatten's reply was to quote the words of his own father to the future George V on the death of the Duke of Clarence:[*] 'There is no more fitting preparation for a King than to have been trained in the Navy.'

The King showed much kindness to Mountbatten's father, Prince Louis of Battenberg,[†] who was shamefully forced to resign as First Sea Lord in 1914 because of his German origins – and in spite of having ensured the vital

---

[*] Prince Albert Clarence, Duke of Clarence and Avondale (1864–1892), eldest son of Albert Edward, Prince of Wales, later Edward VII.
[†] Prince Louis of Battenberg, 1st Marquess of Milford Haven (1854–1921), First Sea Lord 1912–14.

mobilisation of the fleet. But the King could not save him; nor would an almost broken Prince Louis have wished him to do so.

But soon after the war, the King did positively intervene to save Mountbatten's own career. It was the period of the Geddes Axe, and more than half the young officers in the swollen wartime Navy were to be prematurely retired. It was decided that those with private incomes should be the first to go: only then would merit be considered. 'I didn't have much money,' Mountbatten said, 'but enough to put me in the first category.' While he was in India with the Prince of Wales, his brother, George Milford Haven,[*] was summoned to see the King, who said that he hoped that Dickie would not mind too much being axed. George Milford Haven explained that if his brother had to leave the Navy, he would seek a job in the City – 'and that would cause some young stockbroker's clerk to be pushed out'. And he pleaded with the King to allow Dickie to remain – 'as he would make a better naval officer than a stockbroker's clerk'. The King kept his word and allowed Dickie to remain.

The King was the epitome of the bluff British sailor. Mountbatten says: 'I was never afraid of the King, and soon became used to his chaff.' This could sometimes be cruel. The King loved to hear his favourite stories repeated again and again. One of them was told to him by Mountbatten about his sister Louise, Crown Princess and later Queen of Sweden.[†] She was learning Swedish, but had not yet mastered it; so, on a visit to Uppsala Cathedral, the Archbishop spoke English to her – somewhat imperfectly. During a tour of its treasures he said, approaching a chest of drawers: 'With your permission, your Royal Highness, I will now open these trousers and reveal some even more precious treasures.'

Although Mountbatten found the King friendly, in spite of a certain gruffness, that was not the experience of the King's sons. Mountbatten once had a tremendous row with Prince George, Duke of Kent, who, without telling Mountbatten, had said to the King that he was going to stay with him; in fact, he was going off to see a girl. But the King found out, suspected Mountbatten of being a party to the deception, and was naturally very angry with both Mountbatten and his own son. When Mountbatten reproached George with having dragged him unfairly into a family row, George replied: 'I am sorry. But my father is so bloody to me that I might as well lie to him on the chance of getting away with it as tell him the truth.'

While on leave from HMS *Repulse* in 1921, Mountbatten saw off his father

---

[*] George Mountbatten, 2nd Marquess of Milford Haven (1892–1938), eldest son of Lord Louis Mountbatten.

[†] Louise Mountbatten (1889–1996), Queen of Sweden 1950–65.

to London at Inverness Station and went to stay at Dunrobin. There his fellow guests included the Prince of Wales, the Duke of York and Prince George. 'When, a few hours later, I heard the news of my father's sudden death, I was poleaxed. I broke down and wept. The Prince of Wales came to my room and said: "I envy your having a father you loved. If my father died, we should all be so relieved."'

We talk of the King's political attitudes. Mountbatten says: 'The Navy is not so aristocratic as the Army, and this was one of the advantages of the King's early naval upbringing.' When I ask whether George VI was as fair-minded towards Labour as his father had been, Mountbatten says: 'I think he was, although the court and the Queen Mother were not always so. I remember that when my son-in-law, John Brabourne,* called Mr Attlee "sir" while both were at Balmoral, a courtier rebuked him. This was reported to the King, who was very shocked at the courtier's behaviour.'

An example of Mountbatten's unexpected opinions. He describes how when HMS *Kelly* was sunk, the German planes machine-gunned the survivors in the water. 'There was an outcry at such barbarism, as it was called. Of course, we didn't like being machine-gunned. But war is war!'

## 12 June 1976

Kenneth Clark comes for a drink and to talk about King George V. He has a profound affection for the old King, even when recalling how he shook his stick at a Cézanne in the National Gallery. The King liked to observe people from his car, and even stop it to watch them. He regarded himself as the father of his subjects. One Easter, Kenneth heard him say: 'I know we need rain, but I hope it keeps fine for my people.'

At Windsor or at Buckingham Palace, the King liked to walk round saying: 'Everything here is of the best.' He and Queen Mary also played repeatedly a record entitled *The Departure of the Troop Ship*. It ended with a stirring rendering of the National Anthem, at which everybody, including the King and Queen, would rise to their feet.

Queen Mary liked little objects, but also had an eye for larger objects, saying 'I am caressing it with my eyes.' She was less mean than people said, and gave the Clarks several objects.

The accession of King Edward VIII was resented by some of King George V's courtiers. One day at Fort Belvedere, Kenneth pointed out to Edward VIII what poor china he was using, and suggested that he use some of the many superb services at Windsor. So they drove over together, and Edward

---

* John Knatchbull, 7th Baron Brabourne (1924–2005), television and film producer.

chose some china and silver from its immense store. The next day a courtier telephoned Kenneth and said: 'Do you know what that fellow has done? He has come over to Windsor by night and stolen some china and silver.'

## 13 June 1976

I have supper with William Rees-Mogg, who tells me that Rab Butler once said of Iain Macleod: 'He would have been a very much better man if he were not so deceitful.'

## 15 June 1976

Michael Adeane tells me that King George V did once shout at a footman at Windsor who had dropped a tea tray: 'That's right, smash the bloody castle.' I first heard it many years ago, but am glad to have it authenticated by such a source.

## 18 June 1976

Guards' Chapel Day, 1944.

Quintin Hailsham tells me how much he hates gambling. But when Archbishop Fisher said it was immoral to buy Premium Bonds, Quintin went out and bought the maximum permitted.

## 26 June 1976

I see Mary Beaufort* about Queen Mary. 'She often came to stay at Badminton House before the war, and it was decided that it would make a haven for her during the war. Queen Mary arrived with a huge staff. This was just as well, for most of our servants went off to the war. We did not do badly for food. Some of Queen Mary's time was spent in the muniment room. She paid to have a new floor put in.

'She also had an obsessive liking for cleaning old shrubberies. Her poor ladies, having laboured at this all day, were then expected to read aloud to her in the evening. The only person to refuse to help was Archbishop Lang. "I will <u>not</u> go into the wood to pick up sticks," he said – and he didn't. All sorts of people came to see her at Badminton, including Churchill and Smuts.

'Queen Mary thought the country awfully untidy. At Sandringham the paths were of asphalt, whereas here they were of real mud. She also hated ivy, and used to cut it off any wall she saw. But some of it was ornamental ivy. The villagers were proud of it and furious when Queen Mary cut it down. Unlike

---

* The Duchess of Beaufort hosted Queen Mary at Badminton House for most of World War II.

the King, who was particularly attached to a parrot, she was not an animal lover. When the parrot made messes on the dining-room table, he would guiltily cover them with a silver mustard pot. Once I was walking with him on the slopes of Windsor when he came on a dead bird, and his eyes filled with tears.'

She was never frightened of him. He had a loud, hoarse voice, though. He was always beautifully turned out. Perhaps it was the comparative sloppiness of his sons' dress which caused a gulf. One could see the boys stiffen when approaching their father's room. Once she saw the King look at the Prince of Wales and exclaim: 'Your trousers!'

Mary Beaufort also tells me that as a small child she was at Buckingham Palace on the morning of King Edward VII's Coronation in 1902. The King came into the nursery dressed in a gold tunic and said: 'Don't I look a funny old gentleman.' Mary's gloss on this: 'He was never funny, not old, and by no stretch of the imagination a gentleman.'

## 2 July 1976

A new volume of Churchill's official life by Martin Gilbert is coming out. The *Sunday Telegraph* has paid a lot of money for the serial rights, but Michael Hartwell thinks it is so dully written as to be unusable.

Jack Plumb* is a trustee of the Wolfson Prize for history, and he tells me that Martin Gilbert was put up for it, but dismissed as too uninspired.

## 3 July 1976

Spend morning reading some of Gilbert's new volume on Churchill, but Winston's bombast gives me indigestion. The book is only illuminating on Churchill's greed for money.

## 7 July 1976

Farewell lunch at the Savoy for the retiring *Daily Telegraph* Editor Brian Roberts, the sort of gruesome occasion I much dislike. But I enjoy sitting having Colin Coote on one side of me, Michael Kennedy† on the other. He tells me how he once met Oswald Mosley looking rather upset. 'I have just had a row with Cimmie, and I was so provoked that I told her the names of all the women I had slept with.' 'What, all of them?' Colin asked. 'Well, all except her sister and her stepmother.'

Michael Kennedy discusses Malcolm Sargent. He says that no conductor

---

* Sir John Harold Plumb (1911–2001), historian.

† (1926–2014), biographer and writer on classical music.

has ever been more loathed by orchestra players, and compares his social obsessions with those of Elgar.

## 8 July 1976

I have a drink with Alec and Elizabeth Home in their flat. We talk of Ted Heath, whose hatred of Margaret Thatcher does not diminish. Alec had to telephone Ted about something, but before he could get it out, Ted exploded: 'Have you seen what that bloody woman has been saying?'

Alec says of Quintin Hailsham: 'He should really have become Prime Minister in October 1963, but he made an unbelievable mess of the vital Conservative Party Conference in Blackpool.'

A professional backer of horses told Alec the other day: 'At the next election the Conservatives cannot win by less than 50 seats.' I doubt it.[*]

Some talk of King George V and Queen Mary. The King, Alec says, had all the birds driven to him when shooting, just as Tito[†] does today.

## 21 July 1976

Staying at Boughton House for a party given by Mollie Buccleuch.[‡] The Queen Mother is among the guests. She first of all talks to me about *The Later Cecils*. 'I very much enjoyed it. You see, I knew them all and you really got their flavour.' I then tell her that I am writing a book about King George V, at which she shows much interest, even enthusiasm.

'At Balmoral, the King used to let us go to his rooms in the evening to see him finishing dressing and winding up his watches – he had so many of them.

'The King was always sweet to me – but then I was never frightened of him. He simply could not bring himself to praise his children. The Duke of Gloucester once came to dine after being away for six months, but arrived a minute or two late. All that the King said to him was: "You're late, as usual."

'I agree with you that the King was very good with his Labour politicians, and that strengthened their patriotism. I was in Durham the other day and was very struck by the intense patriotism of the miners.

'Of course, there are very few people left who knew him. But if you came to lunch one day I am sure I could remember more.'

---

[*] The Conservatives' majority in May 1979 was 44.
[†] Josip Tito (1892–1980), first President of Yugoslavia 1953–80.
[‡] Mary Montagu Douglas Scott, Duchess of Buccleuch (1900–93), widow of the 8th Duke of Buccleuch.

### 27 July 1976
Martin Gilliat says to me: 'I hear you have a new collaborator for your book on King George V. You and the Queen Mother will write it together.'

### 28 July 1976
Lord Gage* talks to me at Goodwood about his memories as a Lord-in-Waiting to King George V. The King was not a clever man, but he was redeemed by his reverence for the job. By the end of his reign in particular, his visits to the East End were like the arrival of Father Christmas. There was a cheerful atmosphere, with everybody holding up little children and almost no security. At the opening of the Tate Gallery he called to Queen Mary: 'May, here's something to make you laugh.' It was a Cézanne.

### 17 August 1976
I hear that Canon Collins of St Paul's is writing his memoirs in two volumes. They could be titled *Bubble Reputation* and *Canon's Mouth*.

### 28 August 1976
Read Robert Rhodes James's *Victor Cazalet*. Too large a volume for a man who achieved so little and was so bland a diarist.† Nor does Rhodes James write at all enticingly.

### 7 September 1976
I visit Angela Lascelles‡ at Fort Belvedere, former home of King Edward VIII. Fort Belvedere bears an absurd resemblance to a child's fort. Its walls are of stone, inlaid with widely spaced thin lines of flints, culminating in an attractive toy tower. There is a wide semicircle of lawn, also a swimming pool, added by Edward when Prince of Wales.

Angela has decorated and furnished the rooms with much taste: this has not been easy, as there is hardly a right angle in the whole house. The sitting room used to be Edward's bedroom. The drawing room next door was where, at a table in front of the window, the Abdication instrument was signed. The dining room has mural paintings of Windsor and Harewood. There is a round, stained-glass window on the spiral staircase, bearing the Prince of Wales feathers.

---

* Henry Gage, 6th Viscount Gage (1895–1982), Lord-in-Waiting to George V 1931–6.
† (1896–1943), Conservative politician. MP for Chippenham 1924–43; killed in an air crash at Gibraltar.
‡ Angela Dowding (1919–2007), first wife of Gerald Lascelles, second son of Princess Mary, Countess of Harewood.

## 21 September 1976

To Kensington Palace at eleven to talk to Princess Alice about King George V and Queen Mary.

I found her crouched over her needlework by a window. Now ninety-three, she is a little more bent than when I last saw her, but no more deaf. In the course of a lively conversation lasting an hour and a half, she misses no more than three or four sentences. Beautifully dressed as always, and immensely alert.

She confesses that when she first knew the King she was shy of his 'loud voice, heavy chaff and old sailor talk'. On one occasion, the King roared at her: 'Good God, what a hat you've got!' She replied: 'I bought it because I was coming to luncheon with you,' and that silenced him. But, of course, when he shouted at his sons, they did not know how to respond. Sometimes she would daringly tell him that he was being too heavy-handed with them. He replied: 'You always take their part.' She responded: 'No, only when you are unfair to them.'

Princess Alice continues: 'The boys never wanted to come and stay at Balmoral. Why should they? They would only find people like Canon Dalton. If the King had asked a lot of nice young people, the Prince of Wales would never have gone off with Mrs Simpson.' Queen Mary, she says, had a clearer judgement than the King, but only occasionally would she dispute a point with him. 'In youth Queen Mary was amusing and vivacious, and would often be in fits of laughter. But as Queen she was so sedate. After the King's death her great worth came out once more. She blossomed!'

It is true that the King and Queen did not have a great deal of food; but the quality of it was superb. And although the King took the pledge during the Great War, he went on drinking cider, which he believed to be a non-alcoholic drink. After dinner during the Great War he would do his boxes, which he always found a burden. But he would enjoy reading aloud from them, particularly despatches from the front. I tell Princess Alice that I have heard that the King was a generous man. She replies sharply, but with a laugh: 'Well, he didn't shower money on me!'

I ask Princess Alice about some of the men around the King. Her replies are exceptionally sharp. Canon Dalton was a thorn in the flesh of every Dean and every other Canon. 'When he was preaching at Windsor, we used to say to each other: "Let us go and hear the Canon's roar."' Lord Stamfordham: 'Such a wise man. We all consulted him. He had beautiful handwriting, like Lord Kitchener's.'

The King, although undemonstrative, was deeply attached to Queen Mary. In his last years, he worried lest his death should leave her absolutely alone. So he would not allow the Athlones to accept either the Governor Generalship of Canada or the Viceroyalty of India. Canada came only several years after his death.

After all our talk, Princess Alice pours me a glass of sherry. 'What fun we have had,' she says. 'You have made me remember all sorts of interesting things.' Next to the sherry tray on her desk is a bust of the Prince Consort: extraordinary to think that he was her grandfather.

## 29 September 1976

The economic outlook is appalling, with the pound crashing daily. Meanwhile the Labour Party Conference at Blackpool veers sharply to the left, demonstrating every facet of greed, spite and ignorance.

## 3 October 1976

Michael Adeane comes to tea at four and stays until almost seven, having talked with absorbing interest about King George V and the office of the Private Secretary.

Duties of the Private Secretary

'Because you happen to be the equivalent of a Permanent Under-Secretary in terms of status, it is no good thinking that you are going to be a mandarin: you are more of a nannie. You will have to open the door or carry a small boy's mac. You must be a flunky. My grandfather was outstandingly good at this. He was a humble man, who used to say: "We are all servants here, although some are more important than others."'

Signed submissions to the Sovereign

'These were used far more when I joined the Royal Household than when I left. The submission is written on a piece of white printed paper divided vertically into two. On the left, the Private Secretary, "with humble duty", makes his submission to the Sovereign. The right-hand side of the paper is left blank for the Sovereign to write yes or no or add some comment. It may seem a laborious procedure, but it ensures that there is no ambiguity and that a record exists. Prince Philip had an intercom system installed, which saved time at the expense of preserving a record.'

Indian affairs

'These occupied a great deal of a Sovereign's time before the war: correspondence with Viceroys, ADC generals, visiting Maharajas.'

Relations with the Labour Party

'One reason King George V got on so well with Labour ministers was that he found them so much more agreeable than Lloyd George to deal with. All the senior Tories and Liberals commiserated with Stamfordham when the

Labour Party first came to office – and received a brush-off for their pains. It is possible that Clive Wigram did commit an error in 1931. He should have got Ramsay MacDonald as PM to <u>advise</u> the King to come south from Balmoral, instead of acting on his own.

'George VI allowed soft shirts to be worn at Sandringham after the war with a dinner jacket: stiff shirts were difficult to have laundered. But when Queen Mary was staying at Windsor, he asked for hard stand-up collars and soft shirts to be worn, as a mark of respect for her.'

<u>Canon Dalton</u>

'A remarkable intellect, but an aggressive personality. In reading the lesson, he would give Isaiah a piping voice and the Almighty a great nautical roar. When Dalton was once missed out during the collection, he roared at the Verger: "Bring it here, you damned fool."'

<u>Children</u>

'Prince George used to get into big scrapes, Prince Henry into small scrapes, the Prince of Wales into perpetual scrapes. Prince Albert did not get into scrapes, but suffered from handicaps of health.'

<u>Telephones</u>

'It was quite an occasion when George V spoke to Stamfordham by telephone. In those days all calls had to be made through an operator, so there was a reluctance to discuss secret matters. Today the telephone rings incessantly.'

<u>Elevated remoteness of the Sovereign</u>

'From above, the Sovereign sees everybody else as much of a muchness – a plain containing a few small peaks. But these peaks are not always high officers of State: much more likely to be a personal maid or the corn-cutter. People in the higher ranks of society cannot always appreciate this. So it is the humble people who often have a higher regard for the Royal Family.'

<u>Sovereign's choice of ministers</u>

'The preference of George VI for Ernest Bevin rather than Hugh Dalton at the Foreign Office in 1945 was no more than a suggestion from a well-informed source. No objection by a Sovereign to a proposed minister can ever be <u>sustained</u>.'

## 4 October 1976

Rab Butler, looking very stout and unwell, tells me that he had a guest to dine in Trinity last night. 'But it was a poor turnout. I was the only person there.' 'What, in the whole of Trinity you were the only person there?' I ask. 'Well, the only person of distinction.'

Give Peter Carrington lunch at Wheeler's. He tells me that Harold

Macmillan, on being asked about a visit recently from Mrs Thatcher when he was a patient in King Edward VII Hospital, replied 'The nurses enjoyed it.'

Peter knows that I have discovered the name of the new Provost of Eton, Martin Charteris. I have sat on it for a long time, and wish to spare him all embarrassment with the Queen, so I ask Peter when it may be best for me to write about it.

## 7 October 1976

To the Tory Conference at Brighton. Peter Carrington is putting the finishing touches to his speech on constitutional matters. He asks me whether he should include a joke in Latin – that the motto of the Labour Party is 'Semper in hock, semper ad hoc'. I advise against it: a lot of Tories no longer have even the simplest Latin phrases.

Poor Reggie Maudling has had a bad morning, openly derided for sloth by a speaker.

## 3 November 1976

Wake up about 5.30 and listen to some of the results of the US Presidential Election. It soon becomes clear that Jimmy Carter is likely to win. I hear that he has finally done so about eleven o'clock. So I win over £200.

Lunch at the Royal Garden Hotel organised by Norman Collins for Age Action Year. Macmillan gives his usual polished performance. He describes how as a child he thought the Albert Memorial the most beautiful thing he had ever seen. But the aesthetic wheel has returned to 1900 and there is hardly a laugh. Another observation of his childhood: 'One saw not a single ungloved hand, male or female.'

Dine in a private room at the Garrick to celebrate Selwyn Lloyd's book on the Speakership. The hosts are his publishers at Jonathan Cape, notably Graham Greene. Others there include Jack Profumo and Anthony Howard.[*] I notice one effect on him of his years as Speaker. When cornered in argument he raps on the table and says, 'Order, order'.

---

[*] When my biography of Selwyn Lloyd was published by Jonathan Cape in 1989, Graham Greene gave a dinner in the same private room with K.R., Jack Profumo and Anthony Howard again among the guests.

## 6 November 1976

To King's Lynn to stay with Solly and Joan Zuckerman[*] at Burnham Thorpe. Warm, comfortable, good talk. Anne Tennant[†] comes to dine. She is a lady-in-waiting to Princess Margaret. She says that Princess Margaret hardly reads at all, but does crosswords very quickly.

Solly says that when Maurice Bowra received his knighthood, John Sparrow wrote to him: 'Congratulations on your baronetcy. A mere knighthood would have been absurd.' Solly speaks with a touch of vinegar about Dickie Mountbatten. When, at Mountbatten's request, he once took part in a taped session of reminiscences, he seized the opportunity of asking Dickie: 'Why do all your contemporaries hate you?' He thinks him too oppressive a personality, particularly on the Prince of Wales. Also too fond of publicity. Nor has Mountbatten ever been the most loyal of friends. The Queen Mother hates him because he changed sides from the Duke of Windsor to King George VI too late for her to appreciate it, and he never exerted himself to get his friend Noël Coward made a Knight.

## 19 November 1976

Mrs Thatcher reshuffles her Shadow Cabinet and lesser Opposition offices. Reggie Maudling gets the boot as spokesman on foreign affairs, much protesting; the nice, but colourless, John Davies[‡] succeeds him. Astonishing that Tim Raison[§] should be sacked and the aggressive Nigel Lawson[¶] made a Whip. Peter Tapsell at last given a job, for foreign affairs.

Lunch Norman Collins, who tells me something interesting about Selwyn Lloyd: that in spite of his habitual modesty he <u>did</u> both hope and expect to become PM in succession to Macmillan. Apparently, Selwyn confessed this to Norman.

## 21 November 1976

Dine Jeremy and Marion Thorpe. Jeremy discusses his future. His finances are rather low with the loss of all his directorships, relinquished at the

---

[*] Lady Joan Rufus Isaacs (1918–2000), Zuckerman's wife.

[†] Lady Anne Tennant (b. 1932), one of Elizabeth II's maids of honour at the Coronation in 1953.

[‡] (1916–79), businessman and Conservative politician. MP for Knutsford 1970–78; Shadow Foreign Secretary 1976–8.

[§] Sir Timothy Raison (1929–2011), Conservative politician. MP for Aylesbury 1970–92; Shadow Environment Secretary 1975–6. He later served in Thatcher's government.

[¶] Baron Lawson of Blaby (b. 1932), journalist and Conservative politician. MP for Blaby 1974–92; Chancellor of the Exchequer 1983–9.

time of the London and County collapse, and the perks that went with the leadership of the Liberal Party. He thinks that a return to the Bar at his age would be laborious. So he hopes to land some fat TV contracts. He says, unrealistically in my view: 'The party will call me back in five years, though by then it will almost have ceased to exist. The only question will be whether I should accept the leadership or not.' This leads me to ask him what chance there really had been of a Tory–Liberal coalition after the General Election of February 1974, when he called on Heath at No. 10. I am astonished to hear that he kept no written records of his talk. But the topics they discussed were: industrial policy, electoral reform, with a Speaker's Conference; devolution; and of course seats for the Liberals in Government. There were two meetings.

Ben Britten is dying. He was born on 22 November 1913, St Cecilia's Day. May well die tomorrow. How appropriate to come in and to go out on St Cecilia's Day, the patroness of music.

### 24 November 1976

Dine with Toby Aldington.* It is not easy to realise that this small, ebullient man holds such an array of influential jobs, also an ex-minister, winner of the DSO, and Ted Heath's guru. He tells me that if Mrs Thatcher wins the next General Election Ted would serve in her Cabinet as long as Keith Joseph were not Chancellor of the Exchequer. Also an interesting bit of history that during those anxious days after the February 1974 election when Ted wondered whether he could continue as PM, Michael Adeane, the former Private Secretary to the Queen, came down to advise Ted at Toby's house in Kent.

### 26 November 1976

Lunch with Martin Charteris at White's, to discuss his impending appointment as Provost of Eton. It must remain utterly secret for several months, although I doubt if it will. He sees his role at Eton: (a) to entertain beaks, (b) to open its windows to the world, (c) to defend Eton in public, (d) and to stimulate some reforms.

Martin agrees with me that one of the best things that has happened to Eton in recent years is the near-disappearance of beating, especially of boys by boys. He tells me how his own tutor, Julian Lambart, once had the whole of the middle division of the house beaten because somebody had pinned a picture of an actress (fully clothed) to the noticeboard. Lambart reasoned that the library were too responsible and the lower boys too frightened to do

---

* Sir Toby Low, 1st Baron Aldington (1914–2000), Conservative politician. MP for Blackpool North 1945–62.

such a thing. It later emerged that it was a boy who had <u>not</u> suffered the mass punishment.

As Martin never went to a university, hence the change in the Eton statutes, he cannot wear a gown. So we must see that he receives an honorary doctorate. The name of a new Assistant Private Secretary to the Queen will be announced shortly, ostensibly to help with the Queen's Silver Jubilee arrangements. He is to be Robert Fellowes.[*] Dickie Mountbatten continues to buzz with self-importance. 'I have about three letters a week from him, usually on some topic such as how his decorations are to be arranged on the third cushion at his funeral.'

## 4 December 1976

Death of Benjamin Britten. I never found him at all agreeable on the two or three occasions when we met: once at Cliveden, where he berated me unnecessarily for some unimportant incorrect fact, and again in our Embassy in Mexico City. And I fear that most of his music causes me intense distress.

## 5 December 1976

Read the second volume of Dick Crossman's diary. An enthralling account of the political influences that distort policy, particularly an obsession with the Press.

## 6 December 1976

At the Leeds Art Gallery I hear that the previous Chairman of the Leeds Leisure and Arts Committee once said to Henry Moore: 'I am an undertaker. Have you ever done any monuments? I could put you in the way of some business.'

## 14 December 1976

Martin Charteris to lunch with me at the Ritz. It has now become an agreeable custom in our lives. We have much talk about the Queen, on whom I have to write a long article to mark the twenty-fifth anniversary of her accession.

1. The first function of the monarchy is to survive. This the Queen has ensured.
2. It has required luck. In every generation of the Royal Family there is a rotten apple; but they are not the ones who have reigned.
3. It is difficult to strike a balance between the myth or mystery of the

---

* Baron Fellowes (b. 1941), PS to the Queen 1990–99. He joined the Royal Household in 1977.

Monarch, which requires remoteness; and the popular acceptance, which requires public exposure. Perhaps the Queen does too many public engagements. If she appears too much in public we might as well have a president. What people really want (and often express in their dreams) is a romantic Royal world in which Princes marry Princesses and live happily ever after.

4. The Queen has scored a personal triumph by being immensely revered in middle age, easy enough in youth or old age.
5. The Commonwealth is becoming less important, but it is a civilised way of dissolving an Empire.
6. The Private Secretariat continues to be aristocratic, but the Queen wants people round her who speak her language. The next Private Secretary, Philip Moore,* is rather different: a civil servant by background and career.
7. Prince Philip has a role in making the monarchy less stuffy. The Queen does <u>not</u> allow him to interfere in matters of State.

## 29 December 1976

Read Lord Wolfenden's *Turning Points*. It is a dry and donnish autobiography, with only a few plums. Is he being ironic when he writes of 'the cream of Wakefield society' being at his wedding? The book makes me glad I did not go to Uppingham, where he was Headmaster, as I might have done.

---

* Baron Moore of Wolvercote (1921–2009), PS to the Queen 1977–86.

# 1977

*The United Kingdom held the Presidency of the Council of the European Union for the first time, January to June. On 3 January Roy Jenkins announced he was leaving the House of Commons to become the President of the European Commission. The former Prime Minister Anthony Eden died on 14 January. On 6 February Queen Elizabeth II reached the Silver Jubilee of her accession to the throne. Anthony Crosland, Foreign Secretary, died on 19 February after a stroke, aged fifty-eight. David Owen became Foreign Secretary on 22 February at the age of thirty-eight, the youngest since Anthony Eden in 1935. The Liberal leader David Steel made a pact with the Labour Government on 23 March. Silver Jubilee celebrations held in the UK 6–9 June. Former Liberal leader Jeremy Thorpe denied allegations of attempted murder and having a sexual relationship with Norman Scott. Death of Clementine Churchill, widow of Winston Churchill, on 12 December.*

## 9 January 1977

The sudden news that Anthony Eden has been taken ill in Florida and is being flown home to die in Wiltshire in an RAF plane put at his disposal by Callaghan.[*]

## 10 January 1977

Eden clings to life.

## 14 January 1977

Anthony Eden has died at his home in Alvediston. Posterity may well restore Anthony Eden's reputation to its early eminence. The tragedy of Suez and the broken years that followed can never eradicate the memory of a man who in

---

[*] Some churlish figures questioned the expense and the necessity of this gesture. But an RAF plane was about to bring home personnel from the Washington Embassy and Callaghan arranged a diversion to Miami. Callaghan was in absolutely no doubt that it was the correct thing – it was the least his country could do. Lord Callaghan to D.R. Thorpe, 29 Oct. 1992.

1938, with his resignation, put his country's honour before personal ambition; who served with unobtrusive wisdom as Foreign Secretary throughout World War II; and whose only failure was in the most exacting office of our national life.

## 15 January 1977

Dine with Selwyn Lloyd at his flat in Gray's Inn. He is rather annoyed at the critical tone of the obituaries on Eden. He stresses that Suez was not the work of Eden alone: he gave a reasoned case for military action and carried the Cabinet with him at the crucial meeting on 25 October.

Selwyn is now at work on a book about Suez and plans to follow it with an autobiography which he is tempted to call *A Middle-Class Lawyer from Liverpool*, a remark frequently made about him by Macmillan.* His resentment at being sacked in July 1962 lingers. 'If only I had kept more in touch with Harold, he would have kept me at the Treasury. I mistakenly thought I was safe.'

His inner uncertainty peeps through. He is hurt at not having been asked to the annual diplomatic party at Buckingham Palace in November. And he says he would like to have been made a Knight of the Garter – 'but I am not well born enough: if I had been a Labour man it would have been different'.

We talk of Jeremy Thorpe's future in politics, which looks bleak. Selwyn is indulgent towards homosexual behaviour, but with one qualification: he has what he calls a biblical hatred of sodomy.

As always, he is mildly worried about money. He has an inadequate pension as Speaker, yet is not allowed to accept directorships of public companies.

## 23 January 1977

In George V research I find the almost panic-stricken opposition of the King to the proposal of the Lloyd George Government that the Tsar should be given asylum in England after his arrest. Following the jubilation with which the Labour movement in England greeted the Russian Revolution, the King had cause to be worried at any identification between the British and Russian monarchies.

## 24 January 1977

Spend the day with Nigel Nicolson at Sissinghurst. As on my last visit in

---

* Selwyn Lloyd's *Suez 1956: A Personal Account* was published posthumously by Jonathan Cape in 1978. He never completed *A Middle-Class Lawyer from Liverpool,* though early drafts exist in his papers, which I was able to use when writing his biography.

the summer, I am too immersed in work to enjoy the garden. First, I look up specific points in Harold Nicolson's George V papers, particularly which letters he selected on the matter of the Tsar's being given asylum. I ask Nigel if I may take them all back to my flat; he readily agrees. Then I look at some of the early proofs of Harold Nicolson's life, annotated by Owen Morshead[*] and by George VI. Nigel also gives me the first half of his book on Mary Curzon to read in typescript. James Lees-Milne is writing the authorised life of Harold Nicolson, but Nigel thinks that Vita will be the figure of greater interest to posterity.

## 26 January 1977

In the India Office Library going through the letters of Lord Reading to George V. The Viceroy's style was impossibly turgid and verbose. In other collections I find a most indiscreet letter from Eric Mieville,[†] immediately after the Abdication, disclosing that Edward VIII's last act between giving his farewell broadcast at Windsor and leaving the country was to sit in his bedroom drinking whisky and soda, whilst having his toenails cut.

## 27 January 1977

On returning to the flat last night I received an urgent message to telephone Lord Goodman. He said that Henry Moore was handing over his collection of his own sculptures, together with the bulk of his future earnings, to a charitable trust; that Moore would like this news made public through a single journalist and had consulted Arnold; that Arnold had suggested me, and that if I liked the idea I was to go down to see Moore at Much Hadham. So I telephoned Moore and arranged to spend tomorrow, i.e. today, with him.

I am greeted with much warmth by Moore, small, vigorous, with more than a trace of a Northern accent. We do a tour of his thirty-acre estate: small comfortable studio where he works, fields dotted with Henry Moores. All the time a stimulating saga of autobiography, mingled with his craftsman's creed. Childhood in a small mining town in Yorkshire.

'After the war, I wanted to become a sculptor, but my father thought I would never earn a living that way. I nevertheless went to the Leeds School of Art on an Army grant, then to London. At that time there was only one

---

[*] Sir Owen Morshead (1893–1977), Royal Librarian 1926–58.
[†] Sir Eric Mieville (1896–1971), PS to the Viceroy of India 1931–6; Assistant PS to George VI 1937–45.

British sculptor with an international reputation – Epstein[*] – and he was really American.

'Up to the age of forty-two I had to depend on teaching for a living. When I did begin to earn from my work, in 1942, it was from drawings, not sculpture. Since then my income has been rising and rising beyond the bounds of worry.

'I am really the man responsible for open-air sculpture. It began with a few open-air sculptures in Battersea Park. Big sculptures must be seen against the sky: if Stonehenge were in a hollow, it would not arouse anything like as much interest. Of course open-air sculpture requires immense physical effort. Just think how tough Michaelangelo must have been.'

Back in the house, he gives me a striking photograph of him on a bicycle, which he inscribes for me. Until now I have been only a mild admirer of Moore's work; but an hour looking at his work in his company is immensely stimulating, particularly in his roomful of little drawings and models.

At dinner this evening I hear that at Trinity Rab gives overnight guests a bedtime copy of Alec Home's memoirs, saying: 'Would you like to read this book – it's all about fishing?'

## 28 January 1977

Lord Denning and two other appeal judges have decided that a private person may seek an order against a trade union which has threatened to commit an illegal act, if the Attorney-General fails to do so. A tremendous victory for the rule of law – and a corresponding blow at the encroachment of trade union power on the lives of us all.

## 2 February 1977

Talk to Malcolm MacDonald[†] about his father's dealings with George V.

He tells me: 'When my father became PM for the first time in 1924, there was considerable nervousness in the country at the prospect of a Labour Government. The Tory election slogan had been: "Labour is not fit to govern." The King therefore determined to dispel this apprehension by showing his own confidence in his new ministers, and gave a banquet in their honour.

'Again in 1931, the King kept the Labour Government in office for two days longer than the City thought fit in the growing economic crisis. My

---

[*] Epstein was born in the US. He moved to Europe in 1902 and became a British citizen in 1911.

[†] (1901–81), Labour politician and diplomat. MP for Bassetlaw 1929–35 and for Ross and Cromarty 1936–45; Secretary of State for Dominion Affairs 1935–8 and for the Colonies 1938–40; Minister of Health 1940–41; Governor General of Kenya 1963–4.

father telephoned from London to Lossiemouth to say that he was about to resign and would be home for a holiday. The next day all those plans were cancelled. The King had persuaded him to form a National Government.

'As a Cabinet Minister during the last months of the King's life, I remember only that one had to wear a frock coat to see the King; and that he would talk, talk, talk, expressing his views in an interesting and very forcible way.

'As long as King George V lived, I felt that Queen Mary was very much his No. 2. But she blossomed after his death. On leave from Canada during the war, I was asked to go down to see her at Badminton where she was living. She was out when I arrived, supervising the chopping of wood and helping to stack it. The Duke of Kent was also staying, just before he flew off to Iceland.

'When we were preparing to retire after an evening of talk, I told Queen Mary that as I had to leave for London by an early train, I would say goodbye there and then. But she insisted that she would breakfast with me the next morning at 6.30 – and did.

'I also look back on the visit for another reason. Only a few hours later I heard in London of the Duke of Kent's death: his plane had crashed in Scotland on the way to Iceland. And I thought how terrible I should have found it had I still been at Badminton when the news arrived.'

## 6 February 1977

Some thoughts on the day the Queen achieves twenty-five years on the throne: ministers still begin their letters to the Queen 'With humble duty'. Long may such customs continue. As the Church of England has yet to learn, the rewriting of a litany in modish language repels the faithful without attracting the agnostic. North and south of the Border, the Queen plays a more specific ecclesiastical role, whatever doctrinal differences separate the established Churches of England and of Scotland. One offers prayers for 'our most gracious Sovereign Lady Queen Elizabeth', the other expresses the same sentiment with more freedom of phrase.

The Queen and her courtiers naturally uphold the Christian concept of marriage, although in recent years the attitude of the court towards divorced persons has become less implacable. At the outset of the reign it was different. A Scottish nobleman who had been through the divorce courts pleaded against his exclusion from a Royal visit to Edinburgh. He had, an intermediary explained, been the innocent party. Lord Lyon King of Arms was unmoved. 'That may well allow him into the Kingdom of Heaven,' he pronounced, 'but it will not get him into the Palace of Holyrood House.'

Socially, too, the lists of those invited to Royal garden parties have become longer and more adventurous. Bishops, as top-hatted and gaitered as those drawn by George du Maurier* for *Punch*, queue nowadays behind bowler hats and pipes from the Welsh valleys; wives of air marshals jostle hospital matrons as the Queen progresses from Palace steps to the tea tent. Only a little has been lost by the abolition of presentation parties for debutantes. They were pretty occasions, yet seemed to condone the flourishing of wealth as a passport to Royal favour.

## 8 February 1977

I tease the amiable William Rees-Mogg by asking whether *The Times* is still a paper of record; and if so, why they did not pick up my story about the Henry Moore Foundation. He replied: 'Inefficiency, just inefficiency.'

## 11 February 1977

Alan Barker drives me down to Eton for lunch with Michael McCrum and his wife before Hubert Hartley's memorial service. Before lunch I have time to look at Harold Wilson's Garter banner in St George's Chapel, containing a great deal of nautical heraldry. There is a gap where Anthony Eden's banner hung until his recent death.

What an exceptionally nice couple the McCrums are, and how well they entertain in those handsome rooms. A huge congregation reflects the immense affection which Hubert and Grizel Hartley have always inspired. Fred Coleridge reads one lesson, Harold Caccia the other.

But some alarming news. All the beaks, and also Alan, know that Martin Charteris is to be the next Provost. I have a word with Harold Caccia about this, and tell him that to prevent inaccurate speculation an official announcement is overdue.

## 13 February 1977

Lunch with Alec and Elizabeth Home. Lady Elizabeth Basset† is also a guest. Alec is in sparkling spirits. He quotes Hensley Henson in the House of Lords on Archbishop Lang, 'like a little white terrier yapping at the heels of orthodoxy'.

On Edward Boyle he describes an occasion in Macmillan's Cabinet when the PM wanted some tedious task done, and minister after minister refused. When it came to Edward Boyle's turn, he said: 'Oh well, I suppose I could mug it up.'

---

* (1834–96), cartoonist for *Punch*.
† Lady Elizabeth Basset (1908–2000), Extra Woman of the Bedchamber to the Queen Mother 1953–81, then a Woman of the Bedchamber 1981–93.

Alec asked one of our ambassadors to Yugoslavia how good a shot Tito was. 'Not bad,' was the answer, 'but of course he always gets the best place.' Alec adds: 'Just like George V.'

Alec was asked to look at some proofs of Robert Lacey's* book on the Queen and spotted a wonderful howler about her stalking – that she took great care to get upwind of the stag. 'I think he must have meant downwind' is Alec's mild comment.

Elizabeth tells me that the other day Alec had to go to a service at the Grosvenor Chapel, but didn't know where it was. She explained, but still he found it difficult. At last she said: 'Well, it's near Purdeys.'† Then he knew.

At the end of lunch I walk up towards Hyde Park with Lady Elizabeth Basset. As Basil Spence's ugly Cavalry Barracks Tower comes in sight, she tells me that the Queen Mother once said to her as they drove past: 'Look the other way.'

## 21 February 1977

At 5.30 to 11 Downing Street for a drink with Edna Healey. In the hall there is a portrait of Gladstone by Millais. Upstairs to a pleasant sitting room looking out onto Horse Guards Parade, with the bell chiming the quarters. When we arranged our meeting, Tony Crosland was still alive and well. But since his stroke, and even more since his death on Saturday, there has been intense speculation on whether the PM will fulfil his promise of sending Denis Healey to the Foreign Office as soon as the economic situation allows; or whether Denis ought to remain at the Treasury to prepare the Budget and negotiate the next stage of wage restraint. About 7.30 Denis arrives at No. 11, looking very tired. He cannot tell me his future, as the Queen is on the Royal Yacht on her way to New Zealand, and the PM is awaiting her approval of the Cabinet changes; until she gives that, no public announcement can be made. Not until the 10 p.m. news at home do I hear that Denis is remaining Chancellor of the Exchequer and David Owen,‡ to everybody's surprise, becoming Foreign Secretary at the age of thirty-eight. In a sense it shows how comparatively unimportant is the role of British Foreign Secretary in 1977.

On life at No. 11, Edna says that the advantage is that Denis can come home for lunch. The disadvantage is that he lives almost over the shop, so

---

* Robert Lacey (b. 1944), historian; *Majesty: Elizabeth II and the House of Windsor* was published in 1977.

† James Purdey & Sons Ltd, Gun and Rifle Makers, is situated at 57–8 Audley Street, Mayfair. The Grosvenor Chapel is at 24 Audley Street.

‡ Baron Owen (b. 1938), politician and physician. Labour Foreign Secretary 1977–9; leader of the Social Democratic Party 1983–7.

gets no exercise, except at their weekend cottage in Sussex. Edna regrets, too, that No. 11 'has no back door'.

### 26 February 1977
Listen to Harold Wilson presenting a programme of records on the radio. It contains some delicious ironies. He does not like 'The Red Flag', but does like 'Forty Years On'. The school song not only of Harrow, but also of his own school. The cheeky chappie also emerges. On an official visit to Moscow Jim Callaghan asked him: 'How does it feel to sit in the seat of the Tsars?' Wilson replied: 'How does it feel to sit in the seat of Rasputin?'

### 19 March 1977
I hear from Alan Bullock that when Oliver Franks was asked recently whether a certain matter was confidential, he replied: 'It is secret in the Oxford sense – you may tell it to only one person at a time.'

### 17 April 1977
Johnnie Henderson, a former ADC to Monty, tells me he is furious about the Chalfont book, particularly the hint at homosexuality. He tells me a story about Bill Williams, besieged by war correspondents after Alamein. One of them asked him: 'Would you say the battle of El Alamein was the greatest thing since the crucifixion?', to which Bill Williams replied: 'Well, it only took four people to report that.'

### 5 May 1977
What I hear of the David Frost* interview with Richard Nixon is gruesome: an ex-President weeping crocodile tears for a great deal of money.

### 6 May 1977
To Clarence House at 12.15 to talk to the Queen Mother about King George V, followed by lunch. It is the fulfilment of a promise she made when we stayed at Boughton together last summer.

I am shown into the equerries' room, where the sergeant-footman brings me a copy of the *Sporting Life*. 'Sir Martin Gilliat thought you would like to see this,' he says. In a few minutes I am summoned through the large hall into the drawing room. Good French furniture and masses of tulips. The Queen Mother simply dressed in a flowered blue frock with hardly any jewellery. As always, that wonderful smiling welcome. By a coincidence

---

* Sir David Frost (1939–2013), journalist and television host.

it is the sixty-seventh anniversary of George V's accession.

I begin by asking about the King's discouraging attitude towards his children. The Queen Mother rather plays down this side of the King's character, emphasising that he was essentially a Victorian parent, weighed down by a sense of duty.

'Even the slightest departure from custom would annoy him. I remember a storm at breakfast once because the Prince of Wales was wearing hunting boots with pink tops.

'He was always angelically kind to me, but then I was never frightened of his gruff ways. He had an obsession about punctuality, and if ever he had to wait for somebody he would stamp about furiously.

'The King loved to be surrounded by his family. He was always delighted when we joined him in his dressing room about ten minutes before dinner. He would put a little scent on his handkerchief, and wind up all his watches.

'But Balmoral was not very lively for the younger ones. Only his old close friends came: Canon Dalton, the Archbishop of Canterbury and the like.

'He liked certain musical comedies and went several times to Drury Lane. But he disapproved of jazz – "horrible stuff", he would call it.

'One reason why he got on so well with his Labour ministers was his early life at sea – weevily biscuits and all that sort of thing. It made it easy for him to understand how other people lived.'

I add: 'His attitude towards the Labour Party was all the more remarkable in that he was a Conservative in all other things – perhaps I should say a conservative with a small "c".'

Queen Mother: 'I think that most of us are! Of course, the Labour ministers in those days were not the same as today – or even, between ourselves, as they were in the King's day, my King that is. They were not intellectuals.'

I mention how Lloyd George persuaded the King to become a teetotaller, but nobody followed his example. Queen Mother: 'Yes, just like sanctions against Rhodesia. We were the only people to enforce them. Everybody else poured stuff into the country.'

We have some talk about senior members of the King's household. 'Stamfordham was very firm,' the Queen Mother says, 'and the King leant on him.'

Queen Mother's summing up of King George V: 'He stood for duty and integrity. Those things are born in one. That is why it was so resented when the Prince of Wales took himself off.'

A few final words from the Queen Mother, with two contented corgis at her feet, after lunch, all exactly as it must have been in the reign of George V. She apologises for not having been able to think of more to tell me about King George V and asks me whether I have seen 'Aunt Alice Athlone'. When

I tell her that I have, she raises her eyes and throws up both hands in a gesture of delight. As I take my leave I hear her use the word 'spiffing'. Did ever a woman in her eighth decade enjoy life so much!

## 12 May 1977

Lunch with Alec and Elizabeth Home at the House of Lords. Alec thinks that Peter Jay's* appointment to Washington is bright and imaginative. I don't mind the nepotism, but I don't like appointing telly men to such posts.

Alec tells me a story of Christopher Soames at the Paris Embassy. A party of close friends lunching there arranged that they would all help themselves immoderately to the chocolate mousse – a particular favourite of Christopher's – so that it ran out just as it reached him. This all worked out exactly to plan, except that as the last spoonful was taken by his neighbour, a footman entered with a whole new one, just for Christopher.

Later in the day I talk with Martin Gilliat about the Queen Mother's generous style of living, which she continues in the face of all difficulties, particularly expense and scarce servants. She gives a lunch party about once every two weeks. Princess Margaret likes to propose herself to lunch quite often and then the Queen Mother feels she must have some amusing guests. But Princess Margaret often falls into long melancholy silences, which does not add to the success of a luncheon party. The Queen Mother herself is in fact a sparing eater. As long as she is alive, nobody, not even that restless reformer Prince Philip, attempts to curb her financial exuberance; but after her death, kitchen staff and footmen and cars will be pooled and made available to any Royal Household which has to carry out official entertainment. No longer will each household continue to maintain an elaborate establishment.

## 13 May 1977

The row over Peter Jay's appointment to Washington has now shifted from the nepotism and Jay's personal qualities to the smear campaign ('snobbish and stuffy') apparently launched in Lobby briefings by the Prime Minister's spokesman.

## 17 May 1977

I hear of the Eton reaction to the appointment of Martin Charteris as the new Provost. 'None at all. Hardly anybody here has ever heard of him.'

---

* (b. 1937), economist and diplomat. Ambassador to the US 1977–9.

How like Eton, surely the most insular of all communities.

Read David Marquand's biography of Ramsay MacDonald.[*] It is a magnificently conceived and executed book, with an impressive command of the vast material, fairness of judgement and narrative skill. Useful for George V too.

### 28 May 1977

To Cambridge for lunch at Christ's given by Jack Plumb to celebrate the publication of *Royal Heritage*, based on his series of television programmes. It is a handsome volume. Lots of guests, including Rab and Mollie Butler and George Weidenfeld. I sit next to Mollie Butler, as always the greatest fun. On my other side I have Mary Roxburghe,[†] whom I persuade to talk about her grandfather, Lord Rosebery. It is interesting to note that both she and Mollie Butler find Robert Rhodes James, now MP for Cambridge, odiously conceited. George Weidenfeld is obviously upset by the revelation that the committee of three Privy Councillors charged with examining Harold Wilson's controversial Resignation Honours List, in which George was awarded a life peerage, objected to certain names in it, but their objections were ignored by Wilson.

### 9 June 1977

I consult A.J.P. Taylor about the Bonar Law and Lloyd George papers: both collections are now available in the House of Lords. He offers to look at my King George V in typescript when completed. For a radical he takes a generous view of the King. In particular, he admires the King's awareness that the Zinoviev letter in 1924 might have been a fake;[‡] his suggestion to Lloyd George that more women ought to be employed in the 1914–1918 war effort, and his cordial relationship with George Lansbury.

### 18 June 1977

Waterloo Day and thirty-third anniversary of the bombing of the Guards' Chapel. I am still here!

---

[*] Prof. David Marquand (b. 1934), academic. Labour MP for Ashfield 1966–77; Principal of Mansfield Coll., Oxford 1996–2002.

[†] Mary Innes-Ker, Duchess of Roxburghe (1915–2014), patron of the Royal Ballet.

[‡] Grigori Zinoviev (1883–1936), Bolshevik revolutionary and Soviet Communist politician. The Zinoviev letter was published by the *Daily Mail* four days before the 1924 general election advocating seditious activities in Britain to hasten Communism. The letter is considered to have been a forgery to discredit Labour.

## 29 June 1977

Work in House of Lords Records Office on the Lloyd George papers. A rather cramped room overlooking Westminster Abbey. One of the librarians kindly lends me a catalogue of the correspondence between L.G. and Stamfordham, which I am able to have photographed in my office later in the day. This will save me an immense labour.

I meet David Frost at a cocktail party in the evening. He tells me that President Nixon apparently bore him no resentment for the stern, pitiless cross-examination to which David exposed him on television.

## 30 June 1977

At twelve to the House of Lords Records Office, where I work away on Lloyd George correspondence with Stamfordham. It must have been profoundly irritating for the PM, charged with the supreme direction of the Great War, to receive such a stream of irritating pinpricks from the Palace: occasionally on important points of principle, but more often about the trivia of custom, protocol, honours and appointments. I also find a few interesting letters in the Bonar Law papers.

## 7 July 1977

Michael St Aldwyn tells me that Harold Wilson was prepared to concur in the granting of an hereditary Earldom to Harold Macmillan after his retirement. His family, too, were agreeable to the plan. But Macmillan trotted out his old line that crofters should not be Earls. The Tories remain angry at this failure by Macmillan to establish a precedent for the creation of an hereditary peerage, even under a Labour Government. When somebody asked Macmillan whether he regretted not having gone to the House of Lords, he replied: 'No, it used to be like the Turf Club. Now it is like the RAC.'

Alec Home tells me that he is being pressed by Collins to write a second volume of memoirs or autobiographical essays.[*]

Dine at Pratt's with Anthony Montague Browne.[†] An enchanting story of Henry James, engaging a young man in conversation and relentlessly groping for the precise word. The young man said: 'Please don't worry – any old adjective will do for me.'

One or two Winston reminiscences. Winston allowed Anthony not to be on duty to receive Éamon de Valera, a man Anthony regarded as a murderer. Anthony never liked Rab and apparently this will colour his obit of him,

---

[*] Lord Home published *Letters to a Grandson* in 1983.
[†] Sir Anthony Montague Browne (1923–2013), PS to Winston Churchill 1952–65.

prepared for *The Times*. Bobbety Salisbury, on the other hand, he adored. As Winston's Private Secretary he once had an appointment to see Bobbety in his room in the House of Lords. He turned up but found no Bobbety, so waited. Two or three minutes later there was a pounding noise down the corridor: Bobbety running so that Anthony should not be kept waiting.

### 27 July 1977
Cocktail party at Selwyn Lloyd's flat in Gray's Inn. Almost the first man I run into is Reggie Maudling, exhausted but cock-a-hoop at his 'acquittal' by a vote of the Commons. There was much ill-feeling against Reggie before the vote. I must confess that I regard Reggie as lucky rather than heroic. He <u>was</u> deeply involved with Poulson.* Selwyn looks pinched and in need of a holiday.

### 28 July 1977
Tea with George Thomson in the House of Lords. It is pleasantly old-fashioned: we sit at a table with upright chairs. George Thomson tells me that he recently congratulated Morarji Desai[†] on becoming Prime Minister of India in his eighty-second year. Desai replied calmly: 'It is the will of God.' When George related this later to Jim Callaghan, the PM replied: 'I wish I could say the same. But all I can boast of are the votes of 176 Labour MPs.'

### 30 July 1977
Staying with Nicky Gordon Lennox. We are all enchanted at breakfast to see the photographs in the papers of Fred Mulley,[‡] Secretary of State for Defence, fast asleep as he sits next to the Queen at the RAF Jubilee display. It must be worth many thousands of votes for the Tories, particularly at a time when the Government is underpaying the Armed Forces.

A good story from Nicky Gordon Lennox about Reggie Maudling. He arrived one day at our Paris Embassy and asked if he could have a gin and tonic. 'You see,' he explained, 'although it is 11 a.m. here, it is really 12 noon in London.' So Reggie got his untimely drink. Only later did Nicky work out that the time in London was not 12 noon, but 10 a.m.

---

* John Poulson (1910–93), businessman convicted of fraud in 1974 and jailed. Maudling resigned as Home Secretary as he had been Chairman of one of Poulson's companies when in Opposition.
† (1896–1995), Prime Minister of India 1977–9.
‡ Baron Mulley of Manor Park (1918–95), Labour politician. Secretary of State for Defence 1976–9.

## 31 July 1977

Philip de Zulueta says that Harold Macmillan should not have been formally offered the Garter, thereby requiring him to refuse no less formally. If it had not been offered to Macmillan, it would have broken the custom by which Prime Ministers are more or less entitled to it. Thus Harold Wilson would not have had it (although the Queen was of course grateful to him for having pushed through the increase in the Civil List), nor necessarily any of his successors at No. 10.

Macmillan, Philip says, hates Healey most of all the Labour ministers: 'He is making us into a one-generation country.'

Philip consults me about the disposal of Harold Macmillan's papers. Macmillan thinks that they are too confidential in parts to go to the British Museum, the Bodleian or other such institutions. I reply that to keep them at Birch Grove would mean a stream of tiresome applications by student and scholars: better weed and give them to the Bodleian.*

## 12 October 1977

Deep in the latest three companion volumes, 1917–1922, of Martin Gilbert's life of Churchill.† I do not find Winston at all likeable.

## 13 October 1977

By train to Blackpool for the last twenty-four hours of the Tory Conference. Wonderfully warm and sunny weather. Almost the first person I see in the Conference Centre for a chat is Ted Heath. At the end of the afternoon session I walk back to the Imperial Hotel with Peter Carrington and Geoffrey Tucker. Peter tells me that he and several other frontbench Tories were nauseated by the much-heralded speech of a sixteen-year-old schoolboy called William Hague.‡ Peter said to Norman St John-Stevas: 'If he is as priggish and self-assured as that at sixteen, what will he be like in thirty

---

* K.R.'s advice was accepted. When I was researching my life of Alec Douglas-Home in the early 1990s I was the first person following the completion of Alistair Horne's official life of Macmillan in 1989 to be granted access to Macmillan's papers at Birch Grove. When I was researching my life of Macmillan in the early 2000s, his papers were by then at the Bodleian. Consulting them again, I noticed evidence of the weeding that had subsequently taken place.

† Eighteen companion volumes were published by the time of Sir Martin Gilbert's death in 2015, covering the events of Churchill's life up to 1943. Plans are in place for the publication of further volumes to cover the years 1943–65.

‡ Baron Hague of Richmond (b. 1961), leader of the Conservative Party 1997–2001; Foreign Secretary 2010–14.

years' time?' Norman replied: 'Like Michael Heseltine.'*

Geoffrey Tucker says that during a charity concert recently at Grosvenor House conducted by Ted Heath, the telephone rang in the middle of the *Siegfried Idyll*. Geoffrey whispered to his neighbour: 'It's Wagner ringing up to complain.'

## 14 October 1977
Hear Mrs Thatcher's closing speech of the conference: good rousing stuff, with several well-timed Macmillanesque jokes.

## 28 October 1977
The newspapers full of Jeremy Thorpe's news conference yesterday. Most admire his courage, but remain unconvinced about the exact relationship he had with the male model Norman Scott. The *Daily Telegraph* leader is cool, not to say sceptical. Answering questions yesterday after reading a prepared statement, he stumbled over an obstacle that should have been foreseen. One journalist asked him: 'Have you ever had a homosexual experience?' Before Jeremy could say a word, his solicitor intervened to declare it was an improper question which would not be answered. What could he have replied? It was obviously a mistake to submit to questions at all. It really does look as if his career in politics has effectively come to an end. I am very sad for him and Marion, but do not see how either he could have handled Scott's allegations or ultimately have survived the blow of the London and County bank collapse to his reputation.

## 29 October 1977
Staying with Giles St Aubyn. He has not thought highly of successive Eton Head Masters. He has now already acquired a deep loathing of Michael McCrum. He accuses him of wanting to destroy the traditional Eton: Tonbridge, McCrum's last school, is apparently his model. Giles even criticises him for sending an Eton newsletter to parents each half – 'as if they mattered!'.

## 1 November 1977
I talk to Dickie Mountbatten about the United World Colleges. I ask him what he proposes to do after handing over its Presidency to the Prince of

---

* Baron Heseltine of Thenford (b. 1933), Conservative politician. MP for Tavistock 1966–74 and for Henley 1974–2001; Cabinet Minister under Margaret Thatcher and John Major; Deputy Prime Minister 1995–7.

Wales. He replies: 'I'm going to try not to die.'

### 4 November 1977
I give Martin Gilliat dinner at Buck's. Martin hopes that the Queen Mother will ask Jeremy and Marion Thorpe to a meal to cheer them up, even though she finds Jeremy bumptious. But she is proving hard to pin down.

### 12 November 1977
Read volume two of the Crossman diaries with undiminished glee: he is as devastating on Anthony Benn as on Wilson.

### 16 November 1977
Give Peter Carrington lunch at Wheeler's. Wanting to have a working lunch with Ted Heath the other day, he asked him to come to the Ritz. 'I could not take him to White's, in case somebody kicked him down the steps.'*

Peter tells me that when he was First Lord of the Admiralty, Michael Adeane telephoned him one day and in a bleak voice said that the Queen wanted to see him at the Palace in half an hour. When he was shown into the Queen's room she did not ask him to sit down but pointed to a report in the *Daily Express* that the Royal Yacht *Britannia* was to be refitted at astronomical cost. Peter explained how the ship had been badly built in the first place, how extra equipment had to be taken aboard, and how any possibility of the vessel's breaking down in public had to be avoided. The Queen received all this without in any way melting. 'And who pays?' she asked. Peter, thinking he was at last on surer ground, replied with enthusiasm that of course it would be the Government, not the Queen. 'I see,' she said icily, 'you pay and I get the blame'. Peter was then shown out.

### 20 November 1977
I hear that when T.E. Lawrence wrote to Noël Coward, giving his regimental number, Noël replied: 'Dear 338171, May I call you 338?'

On the news some morning scenes as President Sadat of Egypt,† to the anger of the rest of the Arab world, addresses the Israeli Parliament. An immense act of courage.

---

* In 1951 Nye Bevan, who had recently said that the Tories 'were lower than vermin', was invited to lunch at White's where he was kicked down the steps by an irate member.
† Anwar Sadat (1918–81), President of Egypt 1970–81; assassinated 6 Oct 1981.

## 22 November 1977

Prince Henry was sitting next to an Arab potentate, I hear, on an official visit. After a long silence, the Duke of Gloucester eventually asked: 'Ever been to Tidworth?'

At the recent confirmation service at Eton the Bishop accused the boys of preferring to get into Pop rather than into the Kingdom of Heaven. They evidently looked at him as if he was mad – for who wouldn't?

Richard Strauss's *Salome* at Covent Garden this evening sung by Grace Bumbry.* She is as accomplished an actress as a singer and the audience seems overawed by the mounting horror of the plot. I find every moment of it enthralling. Is it possibly Strauss's greatest score?

## 26 November 1977

Dickie Mountbatten has been trying to persuade the Duchess of Windsor to return certain objects, particularly jewels that the Duke had inherited, and also to put her considerable fortune into a charitable trust. But the Duchess has never forgiven Dickie for supposedly deserting them both in favour of George VI and he got nothing out of her. The money will almost certainly go to her lawyers.

## 8 December 1977

Lunch with Ralph Richardson at the Beefsteak. He tells me how he learns a part in a play – writing it out, correcting his text by hand, re-learning, writing it out yet again – until he has it word-perfect. He also tells me that as a result of acting in so many films he has about twenty expensive but little-worn suits.

## 13 December 1977

Princess Margaret telephones me to say how much she would like to come to my party. She is so exactly like Jeremy Thorpe's imitation of her that I almost say: 'For heaven's sake, do stop clowning!' When I ask her if she would like to bring a lady-in-waiting, she replies: 'No fear!' She points out that the party is to be on Ash Wednesday. She continues: 'I really should not like to be a Catholic.' Extraordinarily friendly, with copious use of my Christian name.

## 14 December 1977

Lunch with Denis and Edna Healey at No. 11 Downing Street. The furnishing of No. 11 confirms my earlier impression: as if done up by Maples without

---

* (b. 1937), American opera singer.

too much attention to cost. Denis and Edna wonderfully warm and welcoming. Denis tells me of the strange cult among the visiting French Ministers on Monday for Disraeli. He also says that when one of them disparaged the Brontës, he replied: 'Why, Emily Brontë's *Wuthering Heights* is the greatest Russian novel ever written in English.'

### 15 December 1977

Solly Zuckerman talks of the Order of Merit service the other day. 'It disturbed me. I am now quite senior in the Order, and I could not help recalling that it is not uncommon to read of the deaths of its members.' Talking to Solly at the Palace luncheon which followed the service, Harold Macmillan said of Harold Wilson: 'I hope that <u>he</u> is not going to become a member of <u>our</u> Order.'

### 20 December 1977

This morning I received a card from Wilfrid Blunt to say that Grizel Hartley was in hospital in Windsor. I take a train to see her. She is in fact in good heart and shows no signs of a stroke. In her loud upper-class voice she tells me some good stories. At Hatherop Castle once she met a servant emerging from Williamstrip* with two terriers. 'Are they Jack Russells?' Grizel asked. 'No, they are Earl St Aldwyn's.' She also tells me of how a socially pretentious parent with a boy in their house said: 'Of course we hope that our daughter will marry a Moor.' To which Grizel retorted: 'What, like Desdemona?'

---

* A seventeenth-century mansion adjoining the land of Hatherop Castle and home of Michael Hicks Beach, 1st Earl St Aldwyn (1837–1916), Conservative politician. Chancellor of the Exchequer 1885–6 and 1895–1902.

# 1978

*A year of difficulties for Callaghan's government. On 13 February an opinion poll gave the Conservatives a lead of eleven points. Inflation was at 9.9 per cent on 17 February, a slight fall. The Conservative Party recruited the advertising agency Saatchi and Saatchi on 30 March. May Day became a Bank Holiday for the first time. Selwyn Lloyd died on 17 May. David Steel announced on 25 May that the Lib-Lab Pact would be dissolved at the end of the current parliamentary session, leaving the UK with a minority Labour government. Speculation mounted on 17 June that there would be a general election in the autumn as the Conservative lead in the polls declined. Pope Paul VI died on 6 August. Pope John Paul I was elected Pope on 26 August. On 7 September Callaghan announced that there would be no general election in 1978. On 17 September Anwar Sadat, Menachem Begin and Jimmy Carter signed the Camp David Accords at their peace summit. Pope John Paul I died on 28 September after thirty-three days as Pope. John Paul II was elected as Pope on 16 October and was inaugurated six days later, the third Pope of the Year. The latter part of the year became known as the Winter of Discontent, with serious consequences for Labour's chances of re-election in 1979.*

## 6 January 1978

Train to Exeter to stay with Jeremy and Marion Thorpe. Jeremy tells me that he has never had such a nightmare time as during the past few months – and the year ahead may be no better. He is being accused, either directly or by implication, of involvement in a murder plot against Norman Scott. Jeremy fears that although he will not be charged with personal involvement in the conspiracy, many will assume that he must have had some knowledge of it, even approval. There have been times, Jeremy tells me, when the sheer mental agony of not knowing what venomous rumour or accusation would next hit him has almost driven him to suicide.

## 7 January 1978

I have a walk with Marion, who tells me of her marriage to George Harewood.

When George first wanted to marry her, he asked his mother Princess Mary to break the news to Queen Mary and she promised to do so. But weeks passed without George having heard from his grandmother. So at last he decided to tell her himself. Queen Mary said: 'So that's what Mary has been trying to tell me for the past two months!'

### 11 January 1978
The late news announces that Lady Churchill destroyed Graham Sutherland's portrait of Winston not long after it was painted. I do not grieve.

### 12 January 1978
I hear the story of the Queen Mother watching on television the burial at sea of Edwina Mountbatten and saying: 'Of course dear Edwina always wanted to make a splash.'

Dine with Harold Lever. Talking of election prospects, Harold says that what he <u>doesn't</u> want is either a large Labour majority or a small Tory majority.

### 20 January 1978
Lunch at the Beefsteak with John Betjeman. He tells me that he would be delighted if I used his poem on the death of King George V as the conclusion of my biography.*

### 8 February 1978
Princess Margaret comes to my flat for a drink. We talk of learning languages. She says she does not know any German. 'You see my mother and father made the mistake of beginning my German lessons in 1939. As I determined during the war never to talk to a German again, I didn't get very far.' She talks also with some affection about her regiments. P.M. has to be at a theatre at 6.55, so see her down to her car. On the way down we talk of William Waldegrave.

'He could be the next Prime Minister but three if he manages to be ruthless enough,' I say.

'Is he politically too "wet"?' PM asks.

'No, too nice,' I reply.

---

* John Betjeman allowed K.R. to use the earliest version of the poem, in which the penultimate line read: 'At a red suburb ruled by Mrs Simpson' instead of 'At the new suburb stretched beyond the runway'.

### 18 February 1978

I hear *Desert Island Discs* – Mrs Thatcher chooses a lot of tripe and is utterly uninspiring. I wonder if Ted Heath is listening, grinding his teeth at her obvious ignorance of music.*

### 23 February 1978

Mollie Buccleuch tells me she was in the crowd watching the proclamation of the present Queen at St James's Palace in February 1952 when she was spotted from Marlborough House by Queen Mary and sent for. As she climbed the staircase, with Queen Mary standing at the top, Mollie wondered what on earth she could say to her. Queen Mary spoke first. Pointing to the grey stockings she had on, she said: 'I never know what to wear on such occasions.'

### 11 March 1978

As I know that Selwyn Lloyd is worried about his book on Suez, I telephone him after reading nearly half of it to say how good I think it is: a clear lawyer's presentation of the alternatives at every moment between Nasser's nationalisation of the Canal Company and our humiliating withdrawal from the Canal Zone four months later.

### 15 March 1978

Roger Sherfield tells me that when he was at our Washington Embassy, the Windsors asked if they could come and stay. Roger, of course, agreed. He then heard from an angry Foreign Office that although our Embassies were permitted to entertain the Windsors to meals, they should never be invited to stay.

### 18 March 1978

To Cambridge to lunch with Jack Plumb at Christ's. An entirely admirable meal in his dark dining room. He looks forward to even more spacious entertainment when he has taken possession of the Master's Lodge. His predecessor, Lord Todd,† has never once invited him to a meal there in the past fifteen years and has in recent weeks been heard to say that the college has made a bad choice for Master in Jack.

---

* *Desert Island Discs* was a favourite radio programme of K.R., though latterly supplanted in his affections by Michael Berkeley's *Private Passions*, where the music chosen is more the focus of attention. When I appeared as a guest on *Private Passions* in June 2012, Kenneth rang within minutes of the broadcast approving of my choices.

† Alexander Todd, Baron Todd of Trumpington (1907–97). Awarded the Nobel Prize in Chemistry 1957; Master of Christ's College 1963–78.

Some talk of the Royal Family. Jack thinks highly of the Prince of Wales, who is determined to model himself on his father, but who remains in awe of his mother. Jack recently asked him what he thought of the outlook for the monarchy. 'It would be better', the Prince replied, 'if we received some sort of support from right-wing intellectuals.'

### 21 March 1978
I see Lady Diana Cooper and I ask her about the Duchess of Windsor. 'She liked me, but I don't think that he did. She spent all her money on huge diamonds, which distressed the Duke: he didn't like to part with it.'

### 6 April 1978
The popular Press is once more in full cry after Princess Margaret, howling with supposed synthetic indignation at her affair with Roddy Llewellyn.* She has been indiscreet, but it does not lie either with the newspapers or with Labour MPs to issue the ultimatum: lead a more decorous life or give up your Civil List. It is particularly nauseating to read their rubbish dressed up as news, e.g. that the Prime Minister is to address the Queen on the subject. No constitutional issue is in the least involved.

### 12 April 1978
To the National Hospital, Queen Square, to see Selwyn Lloyd, who is very ill. I take him a bottle of Grouse whisky. As I walk in, he says: 'I cannot think why you want to visit a mental defective like me.' I reply: 'Well, how good to see that you are just as you've always been.' Shrieks of laughter from the nurse, in which Selwyn and I join. So we get off to a good start, and he produces well-iced champagne. What a dear old cactus he is. He is touched by the kindness of friends: a letter from Harold Macmillan, and one from Edward Heath with a hydrangea.

### 9 May 1978
I hear a story of Diana Cooper greeting a French General who came to our Paris Embassy in her day. He had only one arm, and Diana enquired sympathetically where he had lost the other. In Africa, he told her. 'Lions?' she asked.

---

* Sir Roderick Llewellyn, 5th Bt (b. 1947), gardening journalist, author and television presenter.

## 12 May 1978

Not long ago Alan Urwick asked Ted Heath whether he would like to return to the Foreign Office if the Conservatives win the next election. After a pause, Ted replied: 'My friends tell me that the only two times in my life that I have been really happy were at Balliol and in the Foreign Office.'

## 15 May 1978

I visit King Juan Carlos of Spain at the Zarzuela Palace. The park looks particularly romantic with fallow deer grazing. I say that I hear there may be a State Visit to London next year. King: 'Lillibet certainly said she would like one when we were in England a few months ago. But would it be possible without a settlement of Gibraltar?' He goes on to talk about the problem. 'I have tried to reduce tension by freeing the telephone service and in other ways. We want a solution in which all the people of Gibraltar will do well.'

We turn to the internal problems of Spain. I tell the King how I have watched his skilful influence on all parties. At this, he mimes a man walking a tightrope with arms outstretched, and laughs. I go on to tell him about King George V's trustful consideration towards the first Labour Government of 1924: he turned Labour from republicanism to monarchy. The King agrees emphatically that that is his role too.

In general, the King says, Spain is learning to stand on her own feet and does not go running to the Government for help in solving industrial or labour disputes, as happened in Franco's day. There is also an increasing sense of security in spite of the trouble in the North. The King adds: 'The Spaniards though don't like security nowadays. They think it is undemocratic.'

## 17 May 1978

Jack Profumo tells me that Selwyn Lloyd is dying. On coming out of hospital he went down to Benson. The radium treatment was soon given up as it did no good. Jack went over to see him, but found him in a sorry state, unable to recognise him. Now he has pneumonia which the doctors are deliberately not treating. He is unlikely to live to the weekend. Later I hear on the 10 p.m. news that he has died. I shall miss the dear old cactus.

## 23 May 1978

David Dilks dines with me at the Portman Hotel. He is a harsh critic of many of his fellow historians, particularly Martin Gilbert. He thinks, rightly in my view, that Martin has lost his nerve, and is frightened of expressing a judgement in the book. He merely chronicles Winston's activities, relying largely on Hansard and on letters, many of them trivial.

## 25 May 1978

Giles St Aubyn tells me he is having a great deal of trouble with Robin Mackworth-Young[*] in having his life of Edward VII passed by the Queen for publication.[†] He submitted the typescript to Windsor in December. Not only has the Queen not given her approval; but when Giles told Robin that Collins, his publishers, wanted to start printing in pages as opposed to galleys, Robin replied that they did so entirely on their own responsibility and that he could not rule out the Queen's wishing to have certain copyright passages deleted. It is astonishing that the Queen should personally assume the role of censor, and even odder that Robin should tell Giles that all figures of household expenditure must be omitted.

## 19 June 1978

Richard Wood tells me a New College story of how a history don once came to call on him to discuss his work. Richard could not get a word in until after forty minutes' continuous talk from the don. 'Yes, I see your point,' he finally managed to interpose. Don: 'You cannot see my point. I haven't reached it yet.'

## 26 June 1978

The Queen Mother tells me on General de Gaulle: 'When he went back to France at the end of the war, he said that the King and I were the only two people in England who had been nice to him.'

## 4 July 1978

Go to a party given by Paul Channon for the Prince of Wales. Almost as soon as I arrive I am taken up to the Prince. He is smaller than one expects. He tells me that he has read the chapter on Fish in my Cecil book. 'It made me laugh a great deal. The funniest story in it', he adds, 'is when the Bishop confirms a man with a very bald head. He laid his hands on it, and said, "I declare this stone well and truly laid."' It is indeed a good story, but it does not appear in my book – nor in David Cecil's. I keep this to myself.

The Prince asks me what I am writing now, and I reply 'a life of King George V'. 'Why?' he asks in the tones of his father. So I explain what a lot of material was either not used or deliberately neglected by Harold Nicolson's official life. He says: 'Have you seen my grandmother? She loved him.' I tell him what an exceptionally nice and human figure she makes of him. I also add

---

[*] Sir Robert Mackworth-Young (1920-2000), Royal Librarian 1958–85.

[†] *Edward VII, Prince and King* by Giles St Aubyn was published by Collins in 1979.

how successful King George was in turning the Labour movement away from republicanism. 'Yes,' he replies, 'every so often we have to begin this afresh.'

William Rees-Mogg is also at the party and asks me how best we can ensure the defeat of Labour at the forthcoming General Election, suggesting mischievously in an echo of Zinoviev in 1924, 'perhaps by a forged letter to him from John Vorster,* thanking him for making such brave efforts to supply arms to South Africa!'

### 5 July 1978

Selwyn Lloyd's memorial service in Westminster Abbey; lessons well read by Jack Profumo and Alec Home, both chosen by Selwyn, and a very Welsh address from the Speaker, George Thomas. But the chill of the building depresses me. The Queen is represented and James Callaghan is present, together with his two predecessors, Harold Wilson and Edward Heath but not Macmillan, who is in France. Afterwards I hear that when Selwyn was appointed Minister of State at the Foreign Office in 1951, Winston really meant to appoint Geoffrey Lloyd, but got muddled.

### 21 July 1978

Mollie Buccleuch tells me that Duff Cooper used to complain that he had been criticised unfairly for accompanying the King and Mrs Simpson on the cruise of the *Nahlin* in 1936. 'But we did not then know that the Simpson marriage was breaking up. Wallis used to send Ernest foreign stamps assid-uously from all the Mediterranean countries we visited.'

### 23 July 1978

Jeremy Thorpe has announced his intention of suing *Private Eye*. The maga-zine has been baiting him cruelly for years and may now have gone too far by insinuating that he faces arrest on a charge of conspiring to murder Norman Scott. He tells me that he is very low – 'Yesterday was a horrible day – with endless speculative newspaper stories.' I say to him that I have put aside a spare £2,000–£3,000 in the bank and that if he ever needs it in a hurry for legal or other purposes, he has only to lift the telephone.

### 28 July 1978

At the Goodwood Races with Charles March,† who tells me a story of the

---

* (1915–83), Prime Minister of South Africa 1966–78.
† Charles Gordon-Lennox, Earl of March and Kinrara (b. 1955), owner of the Goodwood Estate in Sussex.

woman who got into a lift at Church House, Westminster, at the same time as a bishop. 'What floor?' he politely asked. 'Six, please.' 'There <u>are</u> only five,' he replied. 'Six is headquarters.'

## 4 August 1978

Appalling news in the afternoon that Jeremy Thorpe <u>has</u> been charged with conspiracy to murder Norman Scott. He surely cannot have been expecting it. Only a few days ago Marion asked me whether I would like to stay with them this summer in Devon or Aldeburgh. I scribble him a line, offering him money or any other sort of help he might need. How *Private Eye* will gloat.

## 5 August 1978

Story of Martin Gilliat, accompanying the Queen Mother to an infant school in Slough. Martin bent down to talk to a little boy immersed in drawing – 'What a clever chap, oh how well you draw, an absolute genius in fact ...' and other patronising comments. The child suddenly shot up his arm and grabbed one of Martin's bushy eyebrows. 'Let go,' Martin exclaimed, 'you little bugger, let go.'

## 8 August 1978

I hear that the Duchess of Windsor <u>has</u> promised to leave Queen Alexandra's jewels back to the Queen – on condition that the Prince of Wales attends her funeral. Mountbatten arranged the deal.

## 25 August 1978

Bill Deedes lunches with me and tells me an extraordinary thing – that as long ago as 1963 Alec Douglas-Home was told by his security advisers that Jeremy Thorpe was a risk, because of his sexual habits. Alec in turn passed this on to Jo Grimond, the then leader of the Liberal Party.

## 30 August 1978

I hear that when Henry Douglas-Home went to prison for drunken driving, William Douglas-Home wrote advising him to take his dinner jacket, 'as you will surely be asked to dine with the Governor'.*

## 4 September 1978

To Orme Square to have a drink with Jeremy Thorpe. It is the first time I have

---

* The Hon. Henry Douglas-Home (1907–80). The Hon. William Douglas-Home (1912–92), playwright. Brothers of the Prime Minister, Sir Alec Douglas-Home.

seen him since his arrest. He is as elegantly watch-chained as ever, but thin and strained. He tells me that only in the last two weeks before his arrest did the Department of Public Prosecutions decide to include him in the conspiracy charges. He says he is innocent, and puts his faith in an English jury – particularly if the trial is held in Devon. Jeremy's own costs are likely to be about £40,000. He feels certain of raising quite a lot from the rich Zionists who admire his pro-Israel stand in politics. I suggest that it would do him no good if this were known. He adds that James Goldsmith* would also be willing to help him financially, as a fellow victim of *Private Eye*. I also say three more things to Jeremy in the course of the evening:

(a) I can always let him have £3,000 at short notice as a contribution towards his expenses.

(b) If ever he is tempted to commit suicide, he must telephone me. To this he replies that it <u>has</u> been on his mind. But he promises me that he <u>will</u> get in touch with me if the pressures on him become intolerable.

(c) To maintain a certain discretion in his public appearances and private conversations. This last point is indeed necessary. Jeremy tells me that he has already decided that Quintin Hailsham and George Thomas, the Speaker, shall be asked to give evidence in court as to his character. I tell Jeremy that his trial is not a social occasion and that he would not impress the court by producing an ex-Lord Chancellor and the Speaker: it could have just the opposite effect.

## 9 September 1978

Nigel Fisher talks to me about the book he is writing about Harold Macmillan.† The most sensitive episode is Dorothy's affair with Bob Boothby. It began in 1929 when Macmillan became interested in rating reform and put certain proposals to the Chancellor, Winston Churchill, who asked Bob, his PPS, to keep in touch with Macmillan. Bob thus became a frequent visitor to the Macmillan house. The affair lasted until 1944, after which Dorothy went out to join Harold for the first time at the Allied Headquarters in Caserta, where he was adviser to Harold Alexander‡ on all political issues.

Even while Nigel was at work collecting material for his biography, Bob wrote an article for the *Daily Mail* about the affair. Soon afterwards Nigel went to see Bob about some austere and political theme of Macmillan's life.

---

* Sir James Goldsmith (1933–97), financier and politician.

† Published as *Harold Macmillan: A Biography* (Weidenfeld & Nicolson, 1982).

‡ FM Sir Harold Alexander, 1st Earl Alexander of Tunis (1891–1969), Cdr of the 15th Army Group at the time.

But Bob would only talk of his affair with Dorothy, urging Nigel to put it all in his book. He said that Dorothy had in fact been a most tiresome and demanding mistress. Was there ever such a cad as Bob?

Nigel was in two minds whether to mention the affair in his book. But as it will not be published until after Harold's death, he decided to draft a passage on it. At Birch Grove recently Harold raised the subject with him, telling Nigel that he had offered Dorothy a divorce, which she had refused; and that the whole episode had been a terrible trial to him, causing a near nervous breakdown.

Bob's article, Macmillan added, had wounded him deeply. He said to Nigel: 'What do you suppose he received from the *Daily Mail* for the article? £1,000? I would have given him £10,000 not to write it – and it would not have been the first time I had given Bob money.'

Macmillan had always behaved magnanimously to Bob. He had made him a life peer, and when Bob wanted to be Rector of St Andrews University but found that Charles MacAndrew* had entered the lists as the official Conservative candidate, Macmillan advised Bob to resign the Conservative Whip, when he would win.

## 12 September 1978

News that the Queen Mother is to be Warden of the Cinque Ports: a most unexpected appointment. One could deny her nothing, but it seems rather a waste of Walmer Castle.

## 14 September 1978

Go up to Southport this evening in order to have a full day tomorrow at the Liberal Party Conference. The evening papers are full of Jeremy Thorpe's arrival at the conference this morning, utterly eclipsing the debates on policy and understandably arousing much bitter criticism.

He is attending a meeting of Liberal candidates in the hotel ballroom, with a bunch of photographers awaiting him outside the door. I manage to catch him as he flees up a back staircase to his suite. 'What are you doing?' I ask. He picks up a card and attempts to pin it on my coat, saying: 'Here is a special conference badge for you.' It reads: 'Please do not disturb.' And after all I have tried to do to help him.

---

* Sir Charles MacAndrew, 1st Baron (1888–1979), Scottish Unionist MP for Kilmarnock 1924–9, for Glasgow Partick 1931–5 and for Bute and Northern Ayrshire 1935–59; member of the Royal and Ancient Golf Club.

## 15 September 1978

Jeremy Thorpe, having made his ritual appearance at the conference and presumably thinking he has proved his point that a man on bail may continue to carry on in his chosen profession, returns to London. He leaves from a kitchen entrance, like Metternich* escaping from Vienna in a clothes basket. The attention of journalists and photographers was diverted by Jeremy's car being parked outside the main entrance of the hotel as if awaiting him. All rather absurd and not dignified.

## 8 October 1978

I hear from Gwyneth Jones,† who sings Brünnhilde in the present *Ring* cycle at Covent Garden. She confesses how frightened she is of the precipitous scenery on which she must perch: her feet have no firm base and she is literally shaken when Wotan moves about beneath her. How typical of modern trends in operatic production that a prima donna can be so unimaginatively neglected by the producer and designer.

## 9 October 1978

Dine Hartley Shawcross at Buck's. Much talk about the Thorpe case. He stresses the point that when he was Attorney-General, the DPP would authorise a man to be prosecuted only if there appeared to be a 70–80 per cent chance of conviction. Have the DPP now abandoned this policy, or is there some damning evidence against J.T. of which we as yet know nothing? 'The present bunch of advocates', says Hartley, 'are so feeble that I have a good mind to return to the Bar to defend Jeremy.'

## 10 October 1978

I read a new life of Edward Seago. It leaves me unconvinced that he was a great painter. He minded his lack of recognition – except by the public.

## 12 October 1978

To Brighton for just one day of the Tory Conference. Jolly lunch party with Spencer Le Marchant‡ in his hotel suite. The bath is full of champagne bottles. I jokingly tell him: 'If you give the working classes baths they keep coal in them; if you give Tory MPs baths they keep champagne in them.' Spencer explodes: 'You don't think I only have <u>one</u> bathroom here, do you?'

---

* Klemens von Metternich (1773–1859), Chancellor of Austria 1821–48.

† (b. 1936), dramatic soprano; DBE 1986.

‡ (1931–86), Conservative politician. MP for High Peak 1970–83.

## 21 October 1978

To Oxford for a weekend with Asa Briggs at Worcester College. We go to a performance of *Così Fan Tutte* at the New Theatre. Quite a good performance. With an admirable young conductor called Simon Rattle.[*] As always in England, too much slapstick.

## 29 October 1978

Supper with Jeremy and Marion Thorpe at Orme Square. Jeremy is hugely taken with the idea that Hartley Shawcross might be prepared to come back to the Bar to defend him. Marion: 'The return of Caruso![†] But would there be any false notes?' Jeremy talks of the case quite freely, but when I mention Jack Hayward's[‡] public demand to know what has become of the money he gave Jeremy for the Liberal Party, alleged by some to have been used to finance the murder plot against Norman Scott, Jeremy abruptly changes the subject.

## 13 November 1978

I have a talk with King Olav of Norway[§] at the Norwegian Embassy about George V. Olav knew the King well. As a child he was afraid of him, but later realised how much kinder the King was to other people's children than to his own, 'whom he treated as teenagers even when they were adults'. He would tease Olav for having gone to Oxford rather than Cambridge – 'which would be so much closer to Sandringham'. Particularly when out shooting with the King one had to be on one's toes. 'He hated dawdling.' Olav was impressed by his knowledge of the lie of the land and the exact place where the birds would most likely fly. Olav was always impressed by the attention which the King gave to the newspapers, so that he always seemed well informed. In later years he also read many books, particularly biographies.

The King, says Olav, was sometimes called 'the last of the Victorians'. But he had a shrewd knowledge of current politics, and although usually surrounded by Conservatives at Sandringham, he hated to hear his Labour ministers disparaged.

Olav talks of the King's diary, which always began with an account of the weather. 'It is the same in my own father's diary. It went back to their

---

[*] Sir Simon Rattle (b. 1955), Music Director of the City of Birmingham Symphony Orchestra 1980–98; first British conductor to be Principal Conductor of the Berlin Philharmonic Orchestra 2002–18; Music Director of the London Symphony Orchestra from 2017.
[†] Enrico Caruso (1873–1921), Italian operatic tenor.
[‡] Sir Jack Hayward (1923–2015), businessman, philanthropist and donor to the Liberal Party.
[§] (1903–1991), King of Norway 1957–91.

days of sail, when one's life depended on it.'

I ask Olav whether, as a constitutional Sovereign, he has followed the political crises of King George V's reign. He is well informed and expresses a strong antipathy to Asquith over the Parliament Bill; he also thinks that George V was wise to make Baldwin rather than Curzon PM in 1923. Under the Norwegian Constitution, Olav has little discretion and lacks the power to dissolve Parliament.

Olav is pleased when I tell him I have noticed that the medal ribbons he wears on his British admiral's uniform on State occasions here are arranged in British order: GCB, Jubilee and Coronation medals, etc. 'Yes, I did it specially. It is part of the game.'

## 19 November 1978

Harold Macmillan gave dinner to Philip and Marie-Lou de Zulueta recently at Buck's. They all ordered sweetbreads. H.M.: 'The sort of dish one used to give to the governess.'

## 20 November 1978

Jeremy Thorpe goes on trial at Minehead. Reporting restrictions are unexpectedly lifted, so we shall live with every detail for the next two weeks.

## 23 November 1978

I am deeply shocked to see in the report of the Thorpe case published this morning that in September the *Sunday Telegraph* paid £50,000 to Peter Bessell,* the ex-Liberal MP, for his story of the Thorpe case. It really is my blackest day as a journalist who has worked for twenty-six years for the *Sunday Telegraph*.

## 1 December 1978

Lunch given by Frank Longford at the Hyde Park Hotel for ex-President Nixon. An uncommonly excellent meal. Some talk with Denis Thatcher,† Mrs Thatcher's husband, an agreeable breezy man. Jonathan Aitken tells me that the Speaker, George Thomas, gave a party for Nixon last night in the state apartments of his house.

Nixon is received with much honour, with British and US flags standing

---

* (1921–85), Liberal MP for Bodmin 1964–70. Bessell's credibility as a witness against Thorpe at the trial was undermined when details of his financial arrangements with the *Sunday Telegraph* became known.

† Sir Denis Thatcher, 1st Bt (1915–2003), businessman.

stiffly behind him. He speaks well and dominates the room. He must be one of the few US politicians ever to admit the benevolence of British rule in pre-war India and the Colonies. Frank introduces me to Nixon and we have some talk about his visit to the Oxford Union yesterday.

## 5 December 1978

Bruce Chatwin* to dine. He has had a tremendous success with his travel book *In Patagonia*, which I would put in the Robert Byron class. It has sold exceptionally well in the United States, although not in England, where so few people buy any books at all.

## 6 December 1978

Read Freddie Birkenhead's long-suppressed life of Rudyard Kipling. It is not badly done, but the author's purple descriptive passages, some later included verbatim in his life of Halifax, on landscape and atmosphere are overwritten. He brings out all the nasty side of Kipling: bullying worship of force, anti-Semitism, vulgarity. Yet Kipling's constant ill health and a penance of a wife cannot have helped. What amazes me is that Robin Birkenhead† could wonder in the Preface why Kipling's daughter should have banned its earlier publication.

## 7 December 1978

The evidence against Jeremy Thorpe looks grave.

## 8 December 1978

Lunch Peter Carrington at the Turf Club. He is worried about the effect of Ted Heath's dislike of Mrs Thatcher on the General Election. 'Ted's one virtue is that he says what he thinks: not all what we want at a General Election.' Peter used to be close to him, but Ted now regards him as having gone over to the enemy.

When Mrs Thatcher does lead the Tories back to power, Peter would like to be Foreign Secretary, but on no account to lead the House of Lords.

He has read Birkenhead's life of Kipling, which he thinks diminishes the subject.

---

\* (1940–89), travel writer.

† 3rd Earl of Birkenhead, writer and historian. Mrs Elsie Bambridge, Kipling's daughter, commissioned the 2nd Earl of Birkenhead, under strict conditions that had led earlier possible authors to withdraw, to write the official biography. She withdrew permission for the eventual text to be published. After the death of Mrs Bambridge and Lord Birkenhead the book was finally published.

## 9 December 1978

Jeremy Thorpe tells me that he is in good shape and sleeping well. But he now has the task of raising up to £50,000 in costs. He says he will go to the Commons on Thursday to support the Government in its crucial vote of confidence. If there is an election before his trial, he cannot stand as a candidate. I do wish he would lie low a little.

# 1979

*1979 was a general election year. Margaret Thatcher became the United Kingdom's first female Prime Minister on 4 May.*

*On 10 January James Callaghan returned from an international summit in sunny Guadaloupe to a wintry Britain riven by strikes. At a Heathrow press conference he declared: 'I don't think other people in the world will share the view that there is mounting chaos.' The* Sun *newspaper headline the next day read: 'Crisis? What Crisis?' On 15 January rail workers began a twenty-four-hour strike. On 22 January tens of thousands of public workers went on strike. On 12 February over 1,000 schools closed owing to shortage of heating oil caused by the lorry drivers' strike. On 28 March Callaghan's government lost a motion of confidence by 311 to 310. The next day Callaghan announced that polling day would be on 3 May. On 30 March Airey Neave, Conservative Northern Ireland spokesman, was killed by an Irish National Liberation Army bomb in the House of Commons car park. On 4 May the Conservatives won the general election with a 43-seat majority after a post-war record swing of 5.2 per cent.*

### 3 January 1979

To Orme Square for supper with Jeremy and Marion Thorpe. Jeremy has already started rehearsing in his own mind – and even aloud – the smart answers he is going to give at his trial. We both tell him to be terse, restrained, factual and utterly unforensic when under cross-examination. He thinks the judge will stop the trial at the end of the prosecution case, so rotten is the evidence against him. I do hope he is right.

### 4 January 1979

News of the death of Frank Soskice. Hartley Shawcross says it is hardly worth dying until the strike-ridden *Times* reappears with its obituaries. Hartley also says he is not happy about Jeremy's chances of acquittal after reading the financial evidence of the committal proceedings. Isaiah Berlin tells me that Soskice taught him Latin for a short time at St Paul's.

## 9 January 1979

Dine with Rab and Mollie Butler at their flat in Whitehall Court. Mollie cooks a delicious dinner. Poor Rab, having now lost both political office and Trinity, is obviously bored with life. He is unusually generous in talking about Macmillan. 'I used to help him quite a lot you know, more than he would ever admit. He was fairly astute and very courageous.'

## 11 January 1979

Cast into gloom by the growing wave of strikes. As somebody said the other day, 'This is the year of the bloody-minded.'

## 14 January 1979

The industrial gloom over the country deepens, particularly the result of the lorry-drivers' strike; rail strikes impending, too.

## 17 January 1979

Robert Wade-Gery, on leave from Moscow, comes to drink champagne. He tells me that my *Later Cecils* book is studied at the English Faculty of Moscow University, presumably as an example of effete aristocratic life in England.

## 19 January 1979

Lunch with Anthony Montague Browne. Anthony talks to me about his old master, Churchill. He found Gladwyn Jebb's bombardment of letters from Paris a great bore, particularly as they often gave the PM unwanted advice on topics that were no concern of his. So Winston drafted a sharp letter to him. Anthony persuaded him not to send it. Instead the Permanent Under-Secretary at the Foreign Office was instructed to write a private letter to Gladwyn.

Anthony has a certain wary affection for Rab Butler. In May 1940 Rab could be heard saying: 'This is a grave hour for England. We are delivered into the hands of a drunken adventurer with all the worst characteristics of Charles James Fox.' A few weeks later he was comparing Winston to Chatham.

In old age Winston became dangerously extravagant. He would think nothing of flying first-class to the United States with a party of six. At Chartwell he decided to build a bridge by the lake at a cost of £4,000. When it was complete, he did not like it, so had it replaced. To replenish his funds Anthony negotiated the sale of the film rights of *My Early Life* for £100,000 down and 7½ per cent of the takings. Winston was so grateful that he wanted to give Anthony £25,000 of it. Of course, Anthony refused.

**23 January 1979**

Jeremy Thorpe telephones to ask my advice about the costs of his defence. These are likely now to amount to no less than £90,000. Of this sum he has raised about £30,000 from his rich Zionist friends. But they do not want him to apply for legal aid, even though it may be that he is eligible for it. On the face of it he looks to be a rich man; but he has no capital to speak of, and the house in Devon is mortgaged. The other two houses, Orme Square and Aldeburgh, are in trust for Marion as part of the Harewood divorce settlement. To apply for legal aid, Jeremy says, could create bad publicity. I disagree, telling him that if all is explained – and a man already so exposed has nothing to lose by it – he will attract public sympathy. I also say that there is no stigma in applying for legal aid, and that if his rich backers do not want him to do so, then they must make up the full sum out of their own pockets.

**27 January 1979**

William Waldegrave tells me that he recently received a letter from Rab, posted in Mull, in reply to an invitation. It bore two George VI stamps.

Norman Collins tells me Macmillan's latest remark about Rab: 'As a result of his years as Home Secretary there is a betting shop in every street and a call girl at the end of every telephone – and they call him a fuddy-duddy.'

**29 January 1979**

Dine with George Weidenfeld. Before dinner I have a few words with the suave Tony Quinton,* the new President of Trinity College. I can hardly believe my ears when I hear him say: 'I am wondering whether I should attend the memorial service after Jeremy Thorpe, a Trinity man, has blown his brains out.' It is really too callous for words.

**12 February 1979**

Alistair Horne† has been appointed to write the official life of Harold Macmillan. I do not envy him the task. What else is there to be said after six huge volumes of autobiography and several smaller works?

**15 February 1979**

I hear that Sir Alfred Munnings was once welcomed to speak at the Oxford

---

* Anthony Quinton, Baron Quinton (1925–2010), philosopher. President of Trinity Coll., Oxford 1978–87.
† Sir Alistair Horne (1925–2017), biographer and historian.

Union by the President, who described him as 'the only man who is both equestrian and pedestrian'.

### 16 February 1979

Martin Gilliat to dine. I had intended to take him to a restaurant, but the weather is so vile I give him dinner in the flat. He says the soup reminds him of his years in Colditz!

We discuss the Thorpe case. Martin says that the Royal Family was sorry for Marion during her marriage to Harewood. He tells me that the Queen Mother never knows how Jeremy is going to behave, and this makes her uneasy.

### 13 March 1979

Prince Eddie is still desperately worried about the state of the Army: badly underpaid and with a steady drain of middle-grade officers.

I tell him I would like to dedicate my biography of George V, his grandfather, to him and he is delighted.

Eddie asks me to come with him on Saturday to the Bach Choir performance of a modern work called *African Sanctus*.* When I pull a face, he says: 'Oh, come on, we will have a laugh!' So I agree.

### 28 March 1979

The day of the crucial vote of censure on the Government. The issue is undecided until the Commons division at 10 p.m., when the Government is defeated by a single vote. I hear Callaghan's speech on the wireless: vigorous rousing stuff. But votes, not oratory, count today. A General Election will follow.

I go to a huge gathering at South Audley Street after the vote. As I am talking to John Russell at the top of the stairs, Ted Heath arrives fresh from the Commons vote. I receive a vinegary smile. John Russell says: 'Good evening, Ted, and many, many congratulations.' The temperature drops twenty degrees and Ted does not reply. Any victory for Mrs Thatcher is undoubtedly a defeat for him. Jonathan Aitken tells me that a Northern Ireland MP made the long journey over for the debate – in order to abstain.

### 31 March 1979

Martin Charteris tells me that John Bratby† once came to paint the Queen

---

* (1972), the most famous choral work of the composer David Fanshawe (1942–2010).
† (1928–92), painter.

Mother at Clarence House. She said afterwards: 'He kept asking some odd questions – about the size of the dry martinis and the footman coming in to put coal on the fire. You know, I don't believe he had ever been in an ordinary house before.'

Talking of the Queen's recent visit to the Gulf States, Martin tells me that someone said that she must have been embarrassed at receiving such immensely valuable presents and giving so little in return. Martin: 'You don't know <u>her</u>!'

### 4 April 1979

I tell Prince Eddie that I am now embarking on King George V's relations with his children, and wondered what opinion he had formed in going through his father's correspondence with the King. He says that his father was the only one of the children who had the wits to manage the King and to turn his anger. The King was a dull letter-writer, so it is not easy to judge from the correspondence how much he loved his children. A typical letter would consist of some comments on the weather; a repetition of what his son had told him; and a bit at the end damning the Government of the day. But Eddie is certain that the King was not a cruel father, though he was an anxious one.

### 24 April 1979

To Clarence House at 2.30 for a talk with the Queen Mother about George V followed by lunch. She receives me in the morning room, all smiles. Two corgis accompany her: one friendly which licks my hand, the other unpredictable, which I am warned not to touch. We launch at once into our talk on King George V. 'It is not true to say that he inspired fear in his children; it was more a sense of awe. The upbringing of children in those days was very severe everywhere. When my husband went to Osborne as a naval cadet it was real torture.

'When the King was convalescing at Bognor he said to us one day that he thought David would never take over from him. We were astonished, and hardly understood what he meant.'

This leads us on to some talk about the Windsors.

'I am afraid that David never liked anything English, though he missed it all afterwards.'

I mention all the relics of his days as Prince of Wales and as King, which he liked to surround himself with at his house in the Bois, and how he liked to cross-examine me about what everybody in the regiment was doing, even remembering their initials. 'Oh yes,' the Queen Mother says, 'I remember that sort of thing.' On the Duchess of Windsor: 'I fear we must now think of her in the past. When I was last in Paris I tried to see her, but she was guarded by a dragon and I was told she saw nobody.'

I mention all the evidence I have found that the King felt both nervous and inadequate. She replies: 'I suppose that every Sovereign feels nervous and inadequate: the task is so overwhelming.'

When she speaks of the King's insistence on the correct clothes, even down to the last button, I say: 'What a lot of time seems to have been spent in changing one's clothes in those days. I have read that one even changed for tea at Sandringham.' Queen Elizabeth: 'Well, we still do change for tea at Sandringham!'

The King, she says, could not bear any of his possessions to be disturbed. Richard Molyneux,* who had his own ideas of taste, once rearranged all the objects in the green drawing room at Windsor. The moment the King entered the room he was furious, and ordered them all to be put back as they had been.

The Queen Mother loved her father-in-law's jokes. But they had an unfortunate consequence. 'As he told his stories, he would bang you on the arm. By the end of a visit it would be black and blue.'

Queen Mary, the Queen Mother says, was at heart adventurous, but was restrained by the King's conservatism. She defied him on only one thing. He hated her to wear long dangling earrings, as he thought they distorted her ears, but she continued to do so. After his death she blossomed out and was excited at being dressed by Norman Hartnell.†

The Queen Mother asks whether I would like to reproduce the Walter Sickert portrait of King George V‡ which hangs a few feet away.

Some talk of the Lord Wardenship of the Cinque Ports. The Queen Mother is to be installed in August, and is fascinated to hear from me that the King, as Prince of Wales, resigned the office because of the demands made on him by the mandarins of the Cinque Ports. The Queen Mother does not intend to live at Walmer Castle, but hopes to use it for luncheon parties.

By now it is about 1.30. We lunch at a round table in the small dining room. We have a hot creamy egg and cheese dish, chicken in a tomato sauce with mashed potatoes and courgettes; black cherries and an ice (I receive a surprised glance on declining the big silver jug of cream), and cheese. It is

---

* Sir Richard Molyneux (1873–1954), extra equerry to Queen Mary.
† Sir Norman Hartnell (1901–79), leading fashion designer, renowned for his work for the Royal Family.
‡ *King George V and his Racing Manager at the Grand National 1927* by Walter Sickert (1860–1942) appeared on the cover of K.R.'s biography of the King.

served by three men in livery. There is white wine and claret, the claret in an enchanting jug, shaped lke a bird, with the beak as its spout, ruby eyes and claw feet. The Queen Mother tells me she saw it in a catalogue. All the china is delightful, particularly the dessert plates.

During the second half of the meal I have a lot of talk with the Queen Mother, much of it on political matters She makes no attempt to conceal her strong Conservative sympathies. On Mrs Thatcher she is whimsical, particularly about the troubles she has with her voice, but her remarks stop just short of disparagement. She thinks that Ted Heath has behaved disgracefully in refusing ever to say a nice word about Mrs Thatcher. 'If only he had a wife to tell him how to do things in the right way.' On Ted, the Queen Mother adds: 'He never listens to what I am saying, I can see his eyes wandering. The only time I have ever seen him entirely at his ease was when conducting a children's concert.'

Last weekend the Queen Mother was at Badminton for the Horse Trials. 'The house was delightful. One felt that it was all still going on as it had for hundreds of years.' The only misfortune was that all the Sunday newspapers were put outside the back door, then stolen by somebody. So she missed my 'Albany' column note on Robert Cranborne,[*] who if elected for South Cranborne next week will be the seventh heir in succession to sit in the Commons. She asks me to send her the column.

After lunch, the Queen Mother opens up further. She is upset about the revolution in Persia which has removed the Shah and led to the slaughter of all his supporters. She will always be grateful, she adds, to have seen Persepolis and Shiraz before the Shah's regime collapsed. Then in more playful mood: 'What if such a thing were to happen here. Think of poor Mr Benn. And I suppose Dickie would be the first to be shot.'

On Suez she says: 'The Americans let us down. They usually do. It is the same in Ireland. We cannot abandon all those people in the North who are so loyal to us.'

On Winchester College: 'Such a pity that the boys are denied the most important thing of all: a room to themselves.'

When I say that I have never accepted Oswald Mosley's claim not to have encouraged either violence or anti-Semitism, she taps the table and agrees with considerable vehemence: 'He did, he did.'

---

[*] Robert Gascoyne-Cecil, 7th Marquess of Salisbury (b. 1946), Conservative politician. MP for South Dorset 1979–87; Leader of the House of Lords (under his courtesy title of Viscount Cranborne) 1994–7.

On Queen Wilhelmina of the Netherlands[*] in 1940: 'Do you know how much luggage she brought with her to England when she escaped from the Germans? Just this!' And she fishes under her chair and holds up a modest brown handbag.

What is the secret of this astonishing woman, who attracts more affection than any other living person in the kingdom? Who is on the verge of entering her eightieth year yet displays boundless reserves of energy? Who is utterly un-intellectual, yet captivates those who are with her with a phrase and a smile?

First, genuine warmth and gaiety of spirit. Second, an interest in all that goes on round her. Third, entire self-control: she is never taken unawares or embarrassed or in doubt. Fourth, I suspect, is a determination not to brood too much on the past, but rather to enjoy every present moment.

## 26 April 1979

Just as I am about to write a bread-and-butter letter to the Queen Mother for Tuesday's lunch, a thought strikes me. Is it not the anniversary of her wedding? I look it up. It is the precise date. So I have a bowl of African violets made up and in my letter quote the remark of King George V on her marriage to the Duke of York: 'The only gleam of sunshine in a black world.' Then I leave it at Clarence House.[†]

## 30 April 1979

In Canterbury Peter Pilkington[‡] tells me a good story about Canon Shirley. When somebody consulted him on marriage, Shirley expressed himself strongly against it. 'But you are married,' the proposed bridegroom protested. 'Ah yes,' Shirley replied, 'but with £40,000 to sugar the pill.'

## 3 May 1979

General Election Day. Up early and vote Conservative. A busy morning in the office. At 11 p.m. I go to the election-night party given by Michael and Pamela Hartwell in Cowley Street for *Telegraph* staff and politicians such as Rab Butler and Peter Carrington. It is rather a small affair this time, with plenty of space to watch TV or talk.

---

[*] (1880–1962), Queen of the Netherlands from 1890 until her abdication in 1948.

[†] Thereafter K.R. sent flowers to the Queen Mother every 26 Apr. to the end of her life and always received a handwritten letter of thanks.

[‡] Baron Pilkington of Oxenford (1933–2011), Headmaster of King's School, Canterbury 1975–86 and High Master of St Paul's School 1986–92.

Talk to Arnold Weinstock[*] about the campaign against nuclear reactors which has followed the leak of radioactive water from the Three Mile Island one in America in March. Arnold says 'Teddy Kennedy is leading the protest. But more people have died in the back of his car than from radiation leaks.'[†]

It soon becomes obvious that the Conservatives are going to have a majority of about 30–40: more than the opinion polls predicted.

## 4 May 1979

Turn on wireless at 7 a.m. after three or four hours' sleep. Poor Jeremy Thorpe badly defeated in North Devon; and on Tuesday he goes on trial. It was obviously a mistake for him to stand. Auberon Waugh[‡] gets seventy-nine votes for the Dog-Lovers' Party. William Waldegrave elected for Bristol West with a majority of 12,500.

There are now no fewer than five ex-PMs. Mrs Thatcher is our first woman Prime Minister with a comfortable majority in the Commons of 43.

---

[*] Baron Weinstock (1924–2002), businessman.

[†] The Chappaquiddick incident on 18 July 1969 resulted in the death of his automobile passenger Mary Jo Kopechne, after which Kennedy pleaded guilty to leaving the scene of an accident.

[‡] (1939–2001), journalist; elder son of Evelyn Waugh (1903–66).

# EPILOGUE

The election of a woman Prime Minister in May 1979 by any standards was an historic moment in Britain's history. Although Kenneth Rose admired Mrs Thatcher's achievement as an outsider in attaining the premiership, he did not always empathise with her legacy and was much exercised by the Falklands War of 1982.

The remaining thirty-five years of his life from 1979 were punctuated by events of unimagined drama, both at home and abroad, all of which he commented on with verve and frankness: the reforms in the Labour Party as it adjusted to new political realities; the convulsions surrounding the Royal Family, especially after the death of Princess Diana; the controversies over Britain's relationship with Europe, and the tensions of race relations at home. Several of his long-standing acquaintances departed the scene – figures such as Harold Macmillan and the Queen Mother – and there are many reflective and elegiac passages about the great and the good in a changing society. Many of the developments were alien to him and he became more censorious about the shifts in attitudes and what he saw as the cheapening of standards, in politics, the arts, architecture and in the world at large. What sustained him above all was friendship, for which he had such a spontaneous and generous gift, regarding it, as did Samuel Goldsmith, as 'a disinterested commerce between equals'. His journals from 1979 continue to reflect, with attention to significant detail, the unfolding panorama of the country's life and history, which never failed to stimulate his fascination with the quirks and idiosyncrasies of the national character. In recording such impressions, he continued to leave a unique account of his times, an historical overview of primary importance.

# INDEX

Phillips, Captain Mark 482, **482**
Pick, Frank 111, **111**
Pierre, Prince, Duke of Valentinois 492
Piggott, Lester **123**
Pilcher, Sir John 427, **427**, 431, 432, 434
Pilkington, Peter, Baron 578, **578**
Piper, John **49**, 85, **85**, 244, 486
Piper, Myfanwy (née Evans) 85, **85**
Pitt-Rivers, Michael **130**
Pius XII, Pope 133, 136
Plumb, Jack 527, **527**, 548, 558–9
Plunket, Patrick, 7th Baron 29, **29**
Pompidou, Georges 491, **491**, 492
Ponomaryova, Nona 90, **90**
Pope-Hennessy, James
    background **59**
    murdered 485, **485**
    and Nicolson 340
    private life 504
    Queen Mary biography 59, 146, 152, 520
    and Queen Mother 270, 275
Portal, Charles, 1st Viscount 117, **117**, 429
Poulson, John 550, **550**
Powell, Anthony 149, **149**, 274, **274**, 305, 514
Powell, Enoch 113, **113**, 400, 409, 476
Powers, Gary **162**
Prado y Ugarteche, Manuel 156, **156**
Premium Bonds 77, **77**
Price Thomas, Sir Clement 319, **319**
Priestley, J.B. 278, **278**, 441, **441**, 488
Prior, James, Baron 500, **500**
Profumo, John (Jack)
    Butler on 394
    and Hylton-Foster 458
    and Keeler 250, **250**, 252, 253, 380
    rumours about 275
    and Selwyn Lloyd **533**, 560, 562
Pryce-Jones, Alan 80, **80**
public schools xv
Pugin, Augustus 397, **397**

Quemoy dispute (1958) 136, **136**
Quennell, Sir Peter 69, **69**

Quickswood, Baron. *See* Cecil, Lord Hugh (Linky)
Quinton, Anthony, Baron 573

Radcliffe, Cyril, 1st Viscount 240, **240**
Raine, Countess of Spencer 353, **353**
Rainier, Prince 492–3
Raison, Sir Timothy (Tim) 534, **534**
Ramsden, James 105, **105**
Ramsey, Michael, Baron, Archbishop of Canterbury xiv, 81, **81**, 83, 87, 172, 211, 277, 308, 500
Rattle, Sir Simon 567, **567**
Rawicz, Sławomir 87, **87**
Rawlinson, Sir Peter, Baron 485, **485**
Rayne, Sir Edward 197, **197**
Read, Dick 130, **130**
Reading, Gerald, 2nd Marquess of 41, **41**, 74, 90–1, 115, 540
Reddish, Sir Halford 134, **134**, 162–3
Redmayne, Martin **250**
Rees, Brian **249**, 253, 276, 277, 286, 316, 467
Rees, Julia 467
Rees-Mogg, William, Baron 511, **511**, 543, 562
Reilly, Patrick 444, **444**
Reith, John, 1st Baron 79–80, 163, 250, 355, 362–3, 368–9, 507
Rhys-Williams, Sir Brandon 416, **416**
Richardson, Very Revd Alan, Dean of York 286, **286**
Richardson, Albert 46–7, **47**
Richardson, Sir Ralph 392, **392**, 554
Riddell, Sir John Buchanan 84, **84**
Ridley, Lady Anne 48, **48**
Ridley, Matthew, 4th Viscount xix, 48, **48**
Ridley, Nicholas, Baron 142, **142**
Rippon, Sir Geoffrey, Baron 231, **231**, 235
Rhodes James, Sir Robert 529, **529**, 548
Robens, Alfred, Baron 509, **509**
Roberti, Countess Carla **44**
Roberts, Andrew **161**
Roberts, Brian 171, **171**, 527
Roberts, Sir Frank 460, **460**